Government Printing Office

Annual Report of the Supervising Surgeon-General

of the Marine Hospital Service of the United States for the Fiscal Year 1888

Government Printing Office

Annual Report of the Supervising Surgeon-General
of the Marine Hospital Service of the United States for the Fiscal Year 1888

ISBN/EAN: 9783337021221

Printed in Europe, USA, Canada, Australia, Japan

Cover: Foto ©ninafisch / pixelio.de

More available books at **www.hansebooks.com**

OPERATIONS

OF THE

UNITED STATES MARINE-HOSPITAL SERVICE.

1888.

CONTENTS.

REPORT.

TREASURY DEPARTMENT,
OFFICE SUPERVISING SURGEON-GENERAL,
MARINE-HOSPITAL SERVICE,
Washington, D. C., October 24, 1888.

SIR: I have the honor to submit the following report of the operations of this service for the fiscal year ended June 30, 1888, being the eighty-ninth year of the service, and its fifteenth annual report:

RELIEF FURNISHED.

Patients relieved	48, 203
Treated in hospitals	14, 077
Treated in dispensaries	34, 126
Days' relief in hospital furnished	361, 709

This is the greatest number of patients furnished relief in any year since the organization of the service.

RECEIPTS AND EXPENDITURES, 1887-'88.

The receipts from all sources were $496,441.69, and the expenditures $528,844.66. This does not include the expenses for "repairs and preservation of marine hospitals, fuel, lights, and water, furniture and repairs of furniture," etc., which were paid for out of special appropriations.

The estimate for repairs and preservation of marine hospitals, for some reason, was not allowed, although it was based on the actual necessities, and $16,000 of the balance in the Treasury to the credit of the Marine-Hospital Service was expended for this purpose, which is accounted for in the $32,000 hereinafter named.

Summary.

Receipts, tonnage tax collected	$489. 381. 67
Receipts, repayments to the Marine-Hospital Service for care and treatment of foreign seamen, etc	7, 060. 02
Total available receipts	496, 441. 69
Expenditures	528, 844. 36
Total receipts	496, 441. 69
Amount expended from unexpended balance in Treasury	32, 404. 67

There have been expended from special appropriations:

From the appropriation for repairs and preservation of marine hospitals (by the Supervising Architect)	$29,470.03
Furniture and repairs of furniture	8,360.94
Fuel, lights, and water	37,415.88
Heating, hoisting, and ventilating apparatus	2,438.31
Making a total expenditure on these appropriations of	77,685.16

Preventing the spread of epidemic diseases from July 1, 1887, to June 30, 1888.

Consolidated account from July 1, 1887, to June 30, 1888, as per disbursements:	
Through George A. Bartlett, disbursing clerk, Treasury Department.	$56,996.49
Foreign inspectors (settlement through First Auditor)	525.00
Miscellaneous (settlement through First Auditor)	350.37
Stationery from Treasury Department (settlement through First Auditor)	61.82
Total	57,933.68
By stations from July 1, 1887, to June 30, 1888:	
Cape Charles, quarantine	10,486.14
Delaware Breakwater, quarantine	9,966.00
Egmont Key, Fla.* (including Tampa, Fla)	9,202.57
Foreign sanitary inspectors	525.00
Havana, Cuba, sanitary inspector, boatman and expenses	4,118.05
Key West, Fla.†	3,957.29
Miscellaneous	3,342.26
Sanitary inspectors (miscellaneous)	250.55
South Atlantic quarantine	6,778.68
Ship Island quarantine	9,245.32
Stationery from Treasury Department	61.82
	57,933.68

At the beginning of the year July 1, 1888, there was a balance remaining to the credit of the above-named fund of $159,260.04.

PURVEYING DIVISION.

The following is a summary of the supplies purchased for issue during the year:

Medical supplies	$11,668.41
Bedding and clothing	1,320.24
Instruments and appliances	2,699.24
Hospital stores	5,607.94
Medical books and medical journals	888.34
Miscellaneous articles of hospital supplies	6,791.21

Supplies have been furnished during the past year to 210 stations of the Marine-Hospital Service.

The vessels of the revenue-marine service and the several United States quarantine stations have also been supplied from the purveying division.

*This was a refuge camp established for refugees from Key West.

† Expended in aid of local board of health during epidemic of yellow fever.

Three hundred and seventy-four requisitions have been received and filled.

Chemical tests have been applied to all samples of inks and writing fluids received from the division of stationery, printing, and blanks; and comparative tests have also been applied to inks and fluids received from contractors marked "samples" and "delivery," and the result in each case reported to the department.

Laboratory and storage rooms.

Better facilities for laboratory work and more room for storage purposes have been recently secured by the removal of the Bureau from 1419–21 G street, N. W., to 1306–8 F street, N. W., the Department having leased the latter-named premises. The lease began July 1, 1888, but owing to the necessity of making repairs and alterations in the building, the store-room 1314 F street was occupied temporarily as a storage room and laboratory. The new location of the Bureau is a marked improvement over the old, but the necessity still remains for a building specially designed for the uses of the several divisions.

Laboratory of hygiene.

In August, 1887, a bacteriological laboratory was established at the port of New York. It is situated at present in one of the rooms of the main hospital building, which had formerly done service for a museum for the "Seaman's Fund and Retreat" Hospital. The different apparatus supplied was modeled after those used in the laboratory of Dr. Koch, of the Imperial German health board, and is supplied with Zeiss's latest improved microscope objectives and microphotographic apparatus.

Different animals are kept on hand for experimental purposes. Additions have been made from time to time, until a very complete plant of apparatus exists for analysis and bacteriological investigations.

In October, 1887, experimental studies were made from cases of Asiatic cholera occurring among the emigrant passengers on the steamship *Alesia*, followed later by the examination and diagnosis made upon cases occurring on the steam-ship *Britannia*, demonstrating the existence of Asiatic cholera, which was subsequently confirmed by other investigators.

An analysis of the waters of the New York Bay was made for the purpose of determining the power of sustaining the life of the cholera spirillum.

The comparative and confirmatory tests that were made use of in the experimental investigations of the efficiency of the Louisiana quarantine method were conducted within this laboratory.

At present special investigation is being done for the Louisiana board of health. Experimental studies are now being pursued on the supposed micro-organisms of yellow fever.

Owing to the fact that the scope of work of this character is constantly widening, its utility unquestionable, and its intimate association with matters pertaining to the successful administration of national quarantine and the dealing with public sanitation and hygiene, it is earnestly recommended that the laboratory be transferred to the national capital, where a proper building could be had for the complete equipment, and be placed under the supervision and control of the Department, where it can have the greatest range of usefulness to the service and as well to the general public.

The hygiene of the mercantile marine has been fairly good during the past year, and, with the new circular concerning foul ships, it will be possible to have a clean ocean-going fleet in a few years, as soon as the quarantine establishment shall have been completely furnished and in operation.

An investigation of the food of the seamen at some of the principal ports has been undertaken during the past year, and is elsewhere printed in this report.

THE QUARANTINE SERVICE.

The following are the laws and regulations at present relating to the quarantine service: It comprises section 4792 Revised Statutes, the national quarantine act of April 29, 1878, the act to perfect the quarantine service of the United States, approved August 1, 1888, the regulations of the Marine-Hospital Service, and the regulations of the State Department, the regulation for the government of officers of the Revenue-Marine Service, and a circular concerning the treatment of foul ships:

SECTION 4792 REVISED STATUTES OF THE UNITED STATES.

The quarantines and other restraints established by the health laws of any State, respecting any vessels arriving in, or bound to, any port or district thereof, shall be duly observed by the officers of the customs revenue of the United States, by the masters and crews of the several revenue-cutters, and by the military officers commanding in any fort or station upon the sea-coast; and all such officers of the United States shall faithfully aid in the execution of such quarantines and health laws, according to their respective powers and within their respective precincts, and as they shall be directed, from time to time, by the Secretary of the Treasury. But nothing in this title shall enable any State to collect a duty of tonnage or impost without the consent of Congress.

NATIONAL QUARANTINE ACT.

AN ACT to prevent the introduction of contagious or infectious diseases into the United States.

Be it enacted by the Senate and House of Representatives of the United States of America in Congress assembled, That no vessel or vehicle coming from any foreign port or country where any contagious or infectious disease may exist, and no vessel or vehicle conveying any person or persons, merchandise or animals, affected with any infectious or contagious disease, shall enter any port of the United States or pass the boundary line between the United States and any foreign country, contrary to the quarantine laws of any one of said United States, into or through the jurisdiction of which said vessel or vehicle may pass, or to which it is destined, or except in the manner and subject to the regulations to be prescribed as hereinafter provided.

SEC. 2. That whenever any infectious or contagious disease shall appear in any foreign port or country, and whenever any vessel shall leave any infected foreign port, or, having on board goods or passengers coming from any place or district infected with cholera or yellow fever, shall leave any foreign port, bound for any port in the United States, the consular officer or other representative of the United States at or nearest such foreign port shall immediately give information thereof to the Supervising Surgeon-General of the Marine-Hospital Service, and shall report to him the name, the date of departure, and the port of destination of such vessel; and shall also make the same report to the health officer of the port of destination in the United States, and the consular officers of the United States shall make weekly reports to him of the sanitary condition of the ports at which they are respectively stationed; and the said Surgeon-General of the Marine-Hospital Service shall, under the direction of the Secretary of the Treasury, be charged with the execution of the provisions of this act, and shall frame all needful rules and regulations for that purpose, which rules and regulations shall be subject to the approval of the President, but such rules and regulations shall not conflict with or impair any sanitary or quarantine laws or regulations of any State or municipal authorities now existing or which may hereafter be enacted.

SEC. 3. That it shall be the duty of the medical officers of the Marine-Hospital Service and of customs officers to aid in the enforcement of the national quarantine rules and regulations established under the preceding section; but no additional compensation shall be allowed said officers by reason of such services as they may be required to perform under this act, except actual and necessary traveling expenses.

SEC. 4. That the Surgeon-General of the Marine-Hospital Service shall, upon receipt of information of the departure of any vessel, goods, or passengers from infected places to any port in the United States, immediately notify the proper State or municipal and United States officer or officers at the threatened port of destination of the vessel, and shall prepare and transmit to the medical officers of the Marine-Hospital Service, to collectors of customs, and to the State and municipal health authorities of the United States weekly abstracts of the consular sanitary reports and other pertinent information received by him.

SEC. 5. That whenever, at any port of the United States, any State or municipal quarantine system may now or may hereafter exist, the officers or agents of such system shall, upon the application of the respective State or municipal authorities, be authorized and empowered to act as officers or agents of the national quarantine system, and shall be clothed with all the powers of United States officers for quarantine purposes, but shall receive no pay or emolument from the United States. At all other ports where, in the opinion of the Secretary of the Treasury, it shall be deemed necessary to establish quarantine, the medical officers or other agents of the Marine-Hospital Service shall perform such duties in the enforcement of the quarantine rules and regulations as may be assigned them by the Surgeon-General of that service under this act: *Provided*, That there shall be no interference in any manner with any quarantine laws or regulations as they now exist or may hereafter be adopted under State laws.

SEC. 6. That all acts or parts of acts inconsistent with this act be, and the same are hereby, repealed.

Approved, April 29, 1878.

[Extract from quarantine act of August 1, 1888.]

AN ACT to perfect the quarantine service of the United States.

Be it enacted by the Senate and House of Representatives of the United States of America in Congress assembled, That whenever any person shall trespass upon the grounds belonging to any quarantine reservation, or whenever any person, master, pilot, or owner of a vessel entering any port of the United States, shall so enter in violation of section one of the act entitled "An act to prevent the introduction of contagious or infectious diseases into the United States," approved April twenty-ninth, eighteen hundred and seventy-eight, or in violation of the quarantine regulations framed under said act, such person trespassing, or such master, pilot, or other person in command of a vessel shall, upon conviction thereof, pay a fine of not more than three hundred dollars, or be sentenced to imprisonment for a period of not more than thirty days, or shall be punished by both fine and imprisonment, at the discretion of the court. And it shall be the duty of the United States attorney in the district where the misdemeanor shall have been committed to take immediate cognizance of the offense, upon report made to him by any medical officer of the Marine-Hospital Service or by any officer of the customs service, or by any State officer acting under authority of section five of said act.

SEC. 2. That as soon after the passage of this act as practicable, the Secretary of the Treasury shall cause to be established, in addition to the quarantine established by the act approved March fifth, eighteen hundred and eighty-eight, quarantine stations, as follows: One at the mouth of the Delaware Bay; one near Cape Charles, at the entrance of the Chesapeake Bay; one on the Georgia coast; one at or near Key West; one in San Diego Harbor; one in San Francisco Harbor; and one at or near Port Townsend, at the entrance to Puget Sound; and the said quarantine stations when so established shall be conducted by the Marine-Hospital Service under regulations framed in accordance with the act of April twenty-ninth, eighteen hundred and seventy-eight.

SEC. 3. That there are appropriated for the purposes of this act the following sums, out of any money in the Treasury not otherwise appropriated, for the construction, equipment, and necessary expenses of maintaining the same for the fiscal year ending June thirtieth, eighteen hundred and eighty-nine:

For the Delaware Breakwater quarantine: Construction of disinfecting machinery, steam-tug, warehouse, officers' quarters, and expenses of maintenance for the fiscal year eighteen hundred and eighty-nine, seventy-five thousand dollars.

For the quarantine station near Cape Charles, Virginia: For the purchase of site, construction of wharf, repair of present hospital buildings and officers' quarters, disinfecting machinery, steam-tug, expenses of maintenance for the year eighteen hundred and eighty-nine, one hundred and twelve thousand dollars.

For the South Atlantic station (Sapelo Sound): Construction of disinfecting machinery, warehouse, wharf, small boats, and expenses of maintenance for the year eighteen hundred and eighty-nine, thirty-eight thousand five hundred dollars.

For the quarantine near Key West: Purchase of site, construction of disinfecting machinery, warehouse, small boats, steam-tug, hospital buildings and officers' quarters, expenses of maintenance for the year eighteen hundred and eighty-nine, eighty-eight thousand dollars.

For the Gulf quarantine (formerly Ship Island), provided for by the act of March fifth, eighteen hundred and eighty-eight, in addition to the amount appropriated by the act approved March fifth, eighteen hundred and eighty-eight: For the expenses for the year ending June thirtieth, eighteen hundred and eighty-nine, fifteen thousand dollars.

Quarantine station, San Diego Harbor, California: For the purchase of site and the construction of disinfecting machinery, warehouse, small boats, hospital buildings, officers' quarters, and for expenses of maintenance for eighteen hundred and eighty-nine, fifty-five thousand five hundred dollars.

For the quarantine station at San Francisco, California: Hospital buildings and officers' quarters, disinfecting machinery, warehouse and wharf, steam-tug, small boats, expenses for the fiscal year eighteen hundred and eighty-nine, one hundred and three thousand dollars.

For the quarantine station at Port Townsend: For the purchase of site, construction of disinfecting machinery, warehouse, small boats, hospital buildings and officers' quarters, for expenses of maintenance for the fiscal year eighteen hundred and eighty-nine, fifty-five thousand five hundred dollars.

Approved August 1, 1888.

[Extract from regulations of the Marine-Hospital Service. Approved by the President April 24, 1885.]

GOVERNMENT OF NATIONAL QUARANTINES.

322. At ports where quarantine may be established by the Secretary of the Treasury, every vessel, before being permitted to enter, shall present to the collector of customs satisfactory evidence either that said vessel had not, at any time during a period of thirty days immediately preceding its arrival, touched at or communicated with any foreign port where cholera, yellow fever, or small pox was known to exist in an epidemic form; that there had not been at any time during that period any case of contagious disease on board; and that said vessel does not convey any person or persons, merchandise, or animals affected with any infectious or contagious disease, or that the said vessel has been thoroughly cleaned and disinfected by the quarantine officer, and is free from infection at the time of entry. The certificate to that effect, of the medical officer of the Marine-Hospital Service, or other agent of the Treasury Department designated by the Secretary of the Treasury to act as quarantine officer for the United States at the port, shall be accepted by the collector of customs as satisfactory evidence, and the medical officer or agent referred to shall, before granting such certificate, satisfy himself that the matters and things therein stated are true.

323. Vessels coming from a foreign port or country where cholera, yellow fever, or small-pox is known to have existed in an epidemic form within thirty days preceding their arrival, and vessels or vehicles conveying any person or persons, merchandise, or animals affected with any contagious disease, or having had on board at any time during the thirty days preceding their arrival any case of contagious disease, shall not enter any port of the United States until such disinfection or other precautionary measures shall have been performed as prescribed by these regulations, and the certificate of the medical officer of the Marine-Hospital Service, or other designated agent of the Treasury Department, shall, in such cases, as in the case referred to in the preceding paragraph, be accepted by the collector of customs as satisfactory evidence of compliance with said regulations.

324. For the purposes of necessary disinfection of a vessel and its cargo and of the clothing and baggage of persons on board, the said vessel shall be required to repair to and cast anchor at such place as may be designated by the Secretary of the Treasury, at each port respectively, to be known as the United States quarantine station.

325. The disinfection and other precautionary measures referred to in paragraph 323 shall be carried out under the direction and supervision of the United States quarantine officer at each port respectively, and shall consist of, first, the isolation and treatment of the sick; second, the disinfection of all clothing and baggage liable to be infected; third, the removal of the cargo from the vessel to open lighters, and its thorough disinfection by chemical agents, by exposure to free currents of air, or by burning, as the case may require; and, fourth, the cleansing and fumigation of the vessel, or such other methods of disinfection as may from time to time be adopted by the Department.

[Extract from regulations prescribed for the information and government of the consular officers of the United States. Approved by the President and promulgated by the Secretary of State February 3, 1888.]

THE QUARANTINE SERVICE.

Section 2 of an act entitled "An act to prevent the introduction of contagious or infectious diseases into the United States," approved April 29, 1878, provides—

"That whenever any infectious or contagious disease shall appear in any foreign port or country, and whenever any vessel shall leave any infected foreign port, or, having on board goods or passengers coming from any place or district infected with cholera or yellow fever, shall leave any foreign port bound for any port in the United States, the consular officer, or other representative of the United States at or nearest such foreign port, shall immediately give information thereof to the Supervising Surgeon-General of the Marine-Hospital Service, and shall report to him the name, the date of departure, and the port of destination in the United States, and the consular officers of the United States shall make weekly reports to him of the sanitary condition of the ports at which they are respectively stationed."

The object of the foregoing section of the law is to secure timely advice of the outbreaks of cholera and yellow fever, and of the probable transportation of the poisons of these preventable diseases in vessels bound for the United States; and consular officers for the United States are directed to put themselves into communication with the health authorities of their respective stations, and from the information obtained from such authorities, or from other reliable sources where no regularly constituted health authorities exist, to prepare and transmit by the mails to the Department of State, for the information of the Surgeon-General of the Marine-Hospital Service, on forms prescribed by the Department, weekly reports of the appearance, progress, or termination of cholera, yellow fever, small-pox, plague, or typhus occurring in their respective localities, and are further instructed to include in said reports information in relation to the prevalence of other preventable diseases, as diphtheria, enteric and scarlet fevers, etc., the prevailing disease or diseases in port, if any, and, when practicable, the annual death-rate per one thousand of the population as shown by the official record of deaths for the week reported. Special interest should be taken in the healthiness of vessels, reporting those arriving from or departing to the United States in a bad sanitary condition; also reporting the facts of any serious sickness or unhealthiness of seamen in port, or of crews arriving from or departing to the United States.

In the event of the outbreak of Asiatic cholera, yellow fever, or Asiatic plague, or other contagious disease in epidemic form, the Department must immediately be advised by cable or telegraph of such outbreak, using such abbreviation as the Department may from time to time direct.

The following cipher and abbreviations should be used:

"Cholera"—meaning cholera has appeared.

"Yellow"—meaning yellow fever has appeared.

The name of a country—meaning that the disease has made its appearance at several places in the country named.

The name of a vessel—meaning that the vessel named has departed from the place whence the dispatch is sent, bound for a port in the United States.

"Poison"—meaning that the vessel referred to, though leaving a then healthy port, has on board passengers or goods (baggage) coming from a district infected with cholera or yellow fever.

When cholera or yellow fever has appeared at several places in a country, name the country only after the word "cholera" or "yellow," as the case may be; if it has appeared at the place only from which the dispatch is sent, do not repeat the name of that place in the body of the dispatch, but if at any other particular place, name it.

In a dispatch announcing the departure of a vessel to a port in the United States, the port of departure will be understood to be the place from which the dispatch is sent; hence the name of the port of departure need not be repeated. In the body of a dispatch the name of the vessel should be given first; second, the name of the country, when applicable; third, the day of departure, omitting the day of the month and of the year, as they will be understood without saying; fourth, the name of the port of destination (the importance of observing this order will appear obvious when it is understood that many vessels bear the names of ports in the United States); fifth, the name of the disease, "cholera" or "yellow," as the case may be, should be given, provided the Department has not been already advised of the outbreak of the disease. When advice has once been given of the appearance of cholera or yellow fever at a certain port, the name of the disease need not be repeated in dispatches announcing the subsequent departure of vessels from that port.

When the name of a vessel is given without stating whether it is a steamer or sailing vessel, it will be understood to be a steamer; if the vessel is a sailing vessel, its proper designation should be prefixed. The sender of the dispatch should sign his last name only.

The consul will give to every master of a vessel bound to a port in the Unted States a bill of health, on the form prescribed by the Department, giving full information of the number of persons on board such vessel at the time of sailing, and the sanitary condition of the vessel so far as known, and also the sanitary condition of the port of departure at the time. At such ports as may from time to time be designated by the Department, a physician will be employed or detailed to make the necessary inspection of the vessel, her passengers, crew, cargo, and ballast. In case the master of any vessel shall refuse to receive a bill of health, the fact shall be immediately reported to the Department by cable, if necessary.

When a vessel having received a bill of health touches at any other port while en route to the United States, the consul at such port shall *visa* the bill of health, and note thereon such changes as may have taken place since its original issue.

Monthly reports of the bills of health issued must be made to the Department on the regular forms.

Regulations for the government of officers of the revenue-marine service.

The Secretary of the Treasury issued the following circular, under date of June 4, 1888:

In order to assist local authorities in the maintenance of quarantine against the introduction of infectious diseases, as provided in section 4792 Revised Statutes, the act of April 29, 1878, and appropriation acts authorizing the President to maintain quarantine at points of danger, the President has determined to establish, by means of the vessels of the revenue marine, a national patrol of the coast of the United States, so far as it may be practicable under existing law and consistent with the performance of the other duties confided to that service.

You are accordingly directed to cruise, actively, with the revenue steamer under your command, upon the outer lines of your cruising grounds, and to exercise special vigilance in speaking all vessels arriving from foreign ports or from infected ports of the United States; directing your inquiries, first, as to the port from which the vessel sailed, and secondly, as to the health of those on board at the time of departure, during passage, and at the time of hailing; and should the information gained indicate a condition of contagion or infection in the vessel or crew, or that the vessel has left a port at which contagious or infectious diseases were prevailing, her master will be directed to proceed for examination to the outer quarantine station provided for her port of destination.

The following regulations will be observed, relative to the inspection of vessels:

If a vessel be found with sickness on board, or in a foul condition, she will be directed to proceed to the quarantine station hereinbefore indicated, and the revenue-marine officer will immediately notify the proper quarantine officer. In such case no person will be permitted to board the vessel until the medical officers in charge of the quarantine shall have given the usual permit.

Should the pilot or master of a vessel, when hailed, report cases of recent or present sickness on board, the revenue officer will not board, but will send her immediately to quarantine.

Quarantine officers will be recognized as follows, viz:

Medical officers or acting assistant surgeons of the Marine-Hospital Service in charge of Gulf, South Atlantic, Cape Charles, or Delaware Breakwater quarantines, or any officer of said service on duty at any port on the interior rivers, the Great Lakes, or Pacific coast, and all quarantine officers acting under proper State or local authority.

Special regulations to aid local quarantine authorities will be promulgated hereafter should occasion require.

CIRCULAR.—TREATMENT OF FOUL SHIPS.

TREASURY DEPARTMENT,
U. S. MARINE-HOSPITAL SERVICE,
Washington, D. C., October 5, 1888.

To medical officers of the Marine-Hospital Service, and others to whom it may concern:

In order to stimulate ship-masters to aid in securing a clean ocean-going fleet, the following regulation concerning the treatment of foul ships is hereby adopted, and will be observed at all national quarantine stations:

1. When a vessel arrives at any national quarantine station from an infected port, and requires disinfection, she will be subjected to ordinary disinfection, as provided in former regulations.

2. When any vessel shall arrive at a national quarantine station in such foul condition as to sender her dangerous from a sanitary point of view, and is found to require cleansing and disinfection, having at any former time within one year been subjected to ordinary disinfection, such vessel will be required to undergo extraordinary disinfection, which, in addition to the ordinary measures, will include holy-stoning, scraping, the taking out of rotten wood, a second disinfection, and interior repainting, all of which will be required before granting a certificate of free pratique.

JOHN B. HAMILTON,
Supervising Surgeon-General, M. H. S.

Approved:

HUGH S. THOMPSON,
Acting Secretary.
GROVER CLEVELAND.

An inspection of the foregoing will show that the arrangements for the maritime quarantine are very good indeed. They comprise the notification from abroad originally embodied in the law of April 29, 1878, as recommended by my predecessor, Dr. Woodworth, which includes the publication of the Weekly Abstract of Sanitary Reports, copies of which are not only furnished regularly to the officers named in the law, but upon request have been supplied to sanitarians throughout the country and several public libraries. They are of great use in the maintenance of the quarantine service.

As the island of Cuba is the principal source from which yellow fever is shipped to the United States, an inspector has been kept on duty at Havana during the year. The report of the inspector is as follows. It is worthy of careful study as showing the sanitary condition of vessels sailing into the port, and gives the key to the causes of the infection of some of these vessels and the exemption of others:

I have the honor to forward the following report of labors and experiences of the Sanitary Inspection Service at Havana, Cuba, during the year ending June 30, 1888:

In that period there were inspected 548 vessels of different classes and nationalities bound from this port to ports in the United States.

The information obtained in regard to their sanitary condition, and that of their crews, passengers, and freight, as well as that of the locality of their anchorage and the city and vicinity, was embodied in the United States consular bill of health which each respective vessel is expected to carry to the health officer at her port of destination. Weekly abstracts of such bills of health have been regularly sent to the office of the Supervising Surgeon-General, as also information by cable of the departure of dangerous vessels when the efficiency of the service seemed to require it.

The number, class, and nationality of the vessels are stated in the following table:

Nationality.	Steamers.	Barks.	Brigs.	Schooners.
American	274	54	25	58
British	23	7	2	3
Spanish	44	48	5	....
German	1	....	....	....
Norwegian	....	2	....	....
Swedish	....	1	....	....
Italian	....	1	....	....
Total	342	113	32	61

Total vessels of all classes 548.

Seventeen of the above vessels were found to have had yellow fever on board while here on that trip and 2 had small-pox.

The experience and observation of this sanitary inspective service has discovered, and can statistically demonstrate with sufficient accuracy for all practical purposes, that vessels do not become infected or invaded by yellow fever at all points and in all localities in this port in the same proportion. That while the following tables and statistics will prove that vessels at and near wharves on the Havana or city side of the harbor are (for reasons apparent to the true sanitarian) greatly exposed to invasion by yellow fever, those on the opposite or Casa Blanca and Regla sides are much less so, and those visiting only the open bay are so little that only under exceptional circumstances are they even infected at all.

The following table is formulated with reference to locality of vessels, numbers, and numbers infected, as also proportion during year ending June 30, 1888:

Vessels—	Number.	Infected.	Proportion.
Which were only in open bay	347	....	0 in 347
Which were at wharves on Havana side of harbor	151	15	1 in 10
At wharves on opposite side of harbor	50	2	1 in 25

The above table shows that out of 347 vessels, bound to ports in the United States, which entered the harbor of Havana during the year ending June 30, and remained in open bay, not going to or near the wharves, not 1 had yellow fever occur on board, while out of 151 which went to wharves on the Havana or city side of the harbor 15, or 1 vessel in 10, were known to have had yellow fever occur on board and of the 50 which went to the wharves on the opposite side of the harbor known as Casa Blanca and Regla, only 2 were infected, or 1 in 25.

This proportion of risk corresponds closely to the experience of the eight previous years of the same service which embraces the port history of 4,852 vessels bound from this place to the United States, and gives us a list of 218 infected vessels; and the table is as follows:

Vessels—	Number.	Infected.	Proportion.
Only in open bay	2,983	6	1 in 500
At wharves on Havana side of harbor	1,246	173	1 in 7
On opposite of harbor	623	39	1 in 16

By the above table it is seen that out of nearly 3,000 vessels which visited this port and left for United States ports during eight previous years and remained in the open bay while here, only 6 of them, or 1 in 500 had yellow fever occur on board, while of 1,246 that went to wharves on the Havana or city side of the harbor, 173 had yellow fever, or 1 in 7; and of the 623 that went to the Regla and Casa Blanca wharves on the opposite side of the harbor, 39 became infected, or 1 in 16.

It should be stated here that the 6 vessels which had yellow fever aboard in the open bay were found in close proximity to, and some surrounded by, vessels which had become infected at the wharves, and afterward had taken an anchorage in the open bay.

There is every reason to believe that many vessels at wharves become actually infected, particularly Spanish vessels, which do not reveal their dangerous condition by any sickness occurring on board as their entire crews have immunity from yellow fever by having had it. Others discharge all unacclimated persons on entering the port and ship new ones the moment they desire to leave.

It is found that the statements of the officers of the average sailing vessel are so unreliable that the sanitary history of the vessel must largely depend upon the vigilance and port experience of the inspector.

The statistical provings of infection of vessels in reference to locality in this harbor had for some time been preceded by casual observations that it must be so, for apparent sanitary reasons.

All wharves in the harbor of Havana are constructed on wooden piles driven close together.

Under those on the Havana side of the bay foul sewers of the city empty. The blood and liquid filthiness from all the slaughter-houses of the municipality must necessarily deposit more or less putrid organic material under them, as they are situated but a short distance above, and the little current there is passes under and toward them. Hospitals, in which yellow fever is to be found every month in the year, flank the wharves on the Havana side. Unfortunately some of them so front the bay that they receive but little benefit from the diffusive effect of the beneficent northeast trade wind.

All are given to understand that wharves are more or less dangerous, and particularly at some seasons of the year greatly so.

Some important lines, as those of Plant, Ward & Alexander, always keep their vessels in the open bay; and this, with their rigid cleanliness and disinfection of freight as soon as it comes aboard from the town and all departments, gives them that freedom from infection for which they are noted and render them safe to any port.

One of the labors of your inspector is to advise increased cleanliness of ships where it is needed, and the liberal use of disinfectants where experience indicates that they should be employed.

The sooner a vessel is disinfected after there is reason to fear she has received suspicious atmosphere and material in her departments the better, and the more effective it will be.

Some ports in the United States, with the view of keeping up travel throughout the whole year and at the same time have it done safely, have established certain regulations and restrictions which require, among other things, for immediate landing of passengers at their wharves, a health certificate, or certificate of acclimation, or protection or immunity from yellow fever, which certificate sets forth that the person was born and reared in tropical places where yellow fever is often found, or that he has had the disease, or that the individual has passed over five consecutive years in localities where yellow fever prevails in an endemic or epidemic form, and is therefore believed not liable to contract and convey the disease.

Acting under your instructions, and in the spirit of the service to render local boards of health in the United States all the service in my power, as well as to furnish all sanitary information possible, I have during the year ending June 30 issued as many as 8,000 health certificates.

In addition to this, and on account of small-pox becoming an active and devastating epidemic at Havana and many other places on the Island of Cuba, more than 4,000 persons en route to the United States have been gratuitously vaccinated by this inspection service.

A large proportion of that number were Cubans going to Florida, and many were entirely unprotected from small-pox either by former successful vaccination or by having had the disease.

While there is but little doubt that this inspection service has been an important factor in preventing small-pox from becoming an epidemic in Florida and other places, it is but just to say that this has been at the expense of an incalculable amount of a most difficult kind of work on the part of the sanitary inspector of the marine-hospital service at Havana.

I am, very respectfully, your obedient servant,

D. M. BURGESS,
Sanitary Inspector M. H. S.

HAVANA, ISLAND OF CUBA,
October 18, 1888.

SIR: In amplification of a short report which I made to you last month, and in explanation of the measures taken here to prevent the introduction of contagious and infectious diseases into the ports of the United States, particularly by some lines of steam-ships, I would say that on those of the Plant Line the following are rigorously observed:

(1) These steam-ships, especially during the quarantine or more dangerous season, enter the harbor of Havana only after sunrise and leave it before sunset, rarely being in this port more than seven hours.

In their movements of entering and leaving they are always to the windward of the city, while their anchorage is in the open bay, remote from other vessels and centers of population and in the direction of the prevailing northeast trade-wind.

(2) As far as practicable their crews are composed of acclimated persons who are prohibited from going ashore or visiting vessels in the harbor without a special permit from the sanitary inspector. They are individually examined every trip before the vessel leaves the harbor for the United States, and it is but just to say right here that not one of them has ever been found in the least sick of any contagious or infectious disease since the commencement of the line, now nearly three years.

(3) All bedding, etc., in the officers' and crew's apartments are, beside the necessary washing, taken out and aired once a week, when the ceilings, walls and floors, etc., are washed with fresh water and soap, and afterward sponged or wet down with the usual mercuric solution of 1 part to 1,000.

(4) State-rooms and apartments for passengers are washed and treated in the same way twice a week, or always after a trip here, and bedding, etc., cleaned and aired. All urinals are kept thoroughly clean and frequently washed in a solution of chloride of zinc or lime.

(5) All other apartments in the vessel are treated in a similar manner.

(6) The heavy carpets and woolens of winter use are removed from the vessel when quarantine begins.

(7) All water-closets are washed two or three times daily, and much oftener if necessary, employing at this time chloride of lime or chloride of zinc.

(8) Decks and some of the thicker and more exposed floors are holy-stoned frequently, chloride of lime being used during the process.

(9) The bilges and bilge spaces are cleaned and sponged out every week and treated twice a week alternately with solutions of bichloride of mercury and chloride of lime.

(10) The hold is also whitewashed weekly.

(11) The engine-room is kept clean and the bilge under the main engine is cleaned every two weeks and treated by disinfectants, while every two days salt water is run through the bilge-space and pumped out.

(12) Good ventilation is secured in all parts of the vessel (when fumigation is not being practiced), by the means made for that purpose in the construction of the vessel and by wind-sails.

(13) *No passenger* is permitted to take passage by these steamers who has not a health certificate from this office, which sets forth that he is acclimated to yellow fever, either by a previous attack of that disease or by a continuous residence of several years, five or more, in towns and cities subject to it in an epidemic form and has passed through at least one severe epidemic, or that he is a native of places frequently visited by it, and that practically there is no danger of his conveying the disease. It is of interest that, as a matter of fact, *no person* who has ever obtained such a certificate at this office has ever subsequently developed yellow fever on this or any other line.

The certificate further states that the individual is protected from small-pox either by a former attack of that disease or by successful vaccination and revaccination.

(13) Baggage of passengers for Tampa and points further on in the States must be from a locality which is regarded as healthy and from houses in which it is known that no yellow fever exists or it will not be received aboard. Said houses or hotels are visited by the inspector and the facts ascertained when they are not actually known before. Baggage has not infrequently for the above sanitary reasons been refused.

(14) When the baggage for the North is aboard, each article is separately sprayed over by the mercuric solution (1 part to 1,000) and the trunks and other receptacles for same are put in the close clean hold, where it all, with the small amount of freight for Tampa, is fumigated by the dioxide of sulphur, burning in the process 3 to 5 pounds of sulphur to the 1,000 cubic feet, as near as may be. When sulphur only is used for disinfecting baggage the articles are laid loosely around so that the gas can reach all parts of it.

The vessel leaves here with the Tampa baggage and freight being fumigated by the burning sulphur in the hold, and again between Key West and Tampa the process is repeated.

(15) No articles which can reasonably be suspected of being or becoming fomites for the conveyance of yellow fever are allowed to go aboard.

Very respectfully, your obedient servant,

D. M. BURGESS,
Sanitary Inspector M. H. S. at Havana.

With this effective system of inspection and with these quarantine safeguards it will be manifest that our coast will be guarded better than heretofore, and as soon as the quarantine hospitals shall have been fully equipped the sanitary defenses of the country will be practically complete, although it is probable that, as time goes on, the number of national quarantines will increase. It is apparent, however, that much time will necessarily elapse before they can be considered as completely equipped. A separate account of each station is subjoined.

Delaware Breakwater quarantine.

This station, as heretofore reported, has been maintained out of the contingent appropriation for the prevention of the spread of epidemic diseases and the maintenance of quarantine and maritime inspections at points of danger, but since July 1, 1888, the expenses of the station have been met from the special appropriation. A tug-boat has been chartered throughout the season. It is hoped to have the station fully equipped by the commencement of the summer. The War Department has been requested to make a formal transfer of the property, but in order to insure an absolute title an act of the Delaware legislature will be necessary.

Cape Charles quarantine.

As remarked in regard to the Delaware Breakwater station, this station has been maintained from the special appropriation since the 1st of July, 1888; prior to that time from the contingent appropriation for preventing the spread of epidemic diseases. The title to the land not being in the Government, legal proceedings have to be instituted to secure it. The offer of the receiver of the estate of the late Henry A. Wise to sell Fisherman's Island to the Government for $5,000 has been formally accepted, but a decree of court will be required to vest the title in the United States, as the heirs to the property are numerous. The building of the boats, and the establishment of disinfecting machinery, as provided for by the law, will be done under the superintendence of the revenue-marine service, which service has been requested to construct all vessels necessary for use at quarantine stations.

South Atlantic quarantine—Sapelo Sound, on Blackbeard Island.

This island being Government property, there is nothing to prevent the erection of the buildings contemplated by the statute. The station will be equipped as soon as possible.

Quarantine station at Key West.

The Board appointed by the Secretary of the Treasury to select a site for this station have reported that the only available key in the vicinity of Key West is that now occupied by Fort Jefferson, on Tortugas Island, 50 or 60 miles west from Key West. The War Department has been requested to formally transfer the island for quarantine purposes.

Gulf quarantine.

In accordance with a special act of Congress a new site has been selected for the Gulf quarantine. The Board having chosen the North Chandeleur Island, the Supervising Architect of the Treasury Department was requested to cause the buildings to be constructed, and I am informed that a contract has been made and the necessary buildings are being erected. The plans for the disinfection machinery and the scow for transfer-boat are being prepared by the superintendent of construction of the revenue-cutter service. It is impossible to fix the time when this work will be completed.

San Diego, Cal.

The board appointed to seclect a site for this station having completed that duty and selected a location for the quarantine station on a

Government reservation, the War Department was requested to make a formal transfer of the property for this purpose, but the Department declined to grant the transfer.

Quarantine Station at San Francisco.

The board appointed to select a site for this station consisted of the collector of customs of the port, the president of the State board of health of California,[1] and the surgeon of the Marine-Hospital Service on duty at that port.[2] The proceedings and report of a former board have been furnished them, but they have made no formal report; and request was recently received to have some surveys made in Raccoon Strait by the Coast Survey, and the Superintendent of the Coast Survey has directed the soundings to be made, as requested.

Port Townsend.

The board, consisting of the collector of customs, Captain Glover, United States Revenue Marine, and Passed Assistant Surgeon Glennan, of the Marine Hospital Service, recommend the establishment of the station at Squim Bay, Washington Harbor.

It fronts three-quarters of a mile on the Straits of Fuca; embraces lots 2, 3, and 4 of section 15, township 30, north of range 3, west of the Willamette meridian; contains 147.50 acres. It is embraced within a military reservation, has no improvements on it, a good anchorage, is convenient of access, is well supplied with fresh-water, is not on the direct line of general commerce, but is off to one side about 5 miles, and well sheltered from the prevailing winds.

The report of the board had scarcely been received when strong protests were filed against the selection of the site, and action has been held until local interests are further consulted in the matter.

EPIDEMIC OF YELLOW FEVER IN FLORIDA.

The yellow fever which appeared at Key West last year has lingered within the State, but appeared at a number of places, and is still prevailing at Jacksonville, the principal city of the State. An investigation into the origin of the epidemic is not only interesting but necessary to enable us to arrive at a conclusion. Mention was made in the report for last year (see report, 1887, page 13) of the extension of the disease from Key West to Tampa. It appears from reports on record in this office that the disease was brought to Key West in the effects of a person by the name of Bolio. The Bolio family were hotel keepers in Havana. They had kept a hotel in two or three different houses, in each of which persons had died of yellow fever, as certified by Sanitary Inspector Burgess. The last house kept by them in Havana was the Hotel Quinta Avenida (or "Fifth Avenue" Hotel). When this family removed to Key West they took bedding, pillows, mattresses, and different articles of furniture, but they did not take them at one trip, nor did they take them by regular line of steamers. The articles appear to have been shipped by the steamer *T. J. Cochran*, plying between Key

[1] Dr. R. Beverly Cole. [2] Surgeon H. W. Sawtelle.

West and Havana. The family went to and fro and brought back much household stuff as baggage. Key West at the time had no quarantine. The epidemic practically ceased at Key West before its recognition at Tampa, and it appears that the first case was a person by the name of C. M. Turk, a fruit dealer. It should be remembered that when the fever broke out at Key West the Hillsborough county board of health immediately quarantined against that port, that the Plant steam-ships transferred their freight by a lighter to the wharf at Key West, and during the epidemic at Tampa they laid 6 miles from the town, out in the bay. No communication was allowed between the crew of the ship and the town of Tampa, nor any person allowed to land except passengers coming through Tampa with proper health certificates. The steam-ship line established a hospital at the quarantine station at Ballast Point, in Tampa Bay, so as to be prepared for the appearance of occasional cases of fever, but there was but one suspicious case during the whole season, and that proved to be not yellow fever.

There was no regular quarantine at Tampa at this time, but the Hillsborough county board of health organized an inspection service, by direction of the president, Dr. John P. Wall. It appears that, so far as the introduction of the yellow fever into Tampa is concerned, the evidence shows that Charles M. Turk went in a boat to Key West by way of Punta Gorda, and, on his return from the infected port, was taken sick and died; that an Italian, Peep (or Pete), was taken sick at Ybor City. There is evidence to the fact that Turk and his clerk Pete were engaged in smuggling fruit into Tampa, as the steamer line would not bring such articles either from Havana or Key West; that the city of Tampa at the time was in an extremely bad sanitary condition, and that when fruit and infected articles were smuggled into the city the germs of the disease found ready lodgment and propagated the fever.

The fever soon extended from Tampa to Plant City and Manatee. It is not known at present how it reached Jacksonville. The statement at first made public that a man by the name of McCormick took the fever is incorrect, as I have been informed by Dr. George J. Potts, of Jacksonville, that he treated cases of yellow fever on Bay street as early as the 8th of June, and there is more than a suspicion that the fever prevailing in Jacksonville in February last was yellow fever.* Passed Assistant Surgeon John Guitéras, of this service, whose ability as an expert in the disease is well known, stated to me that he was sure that two of the cases reported by Dr. Daniel to the Florida Medical Association of this "mysterious" "society" fever were undoubted cases of yellow fever, as the clinical history would show. They show a record of a fever characterized by high temperature and a disproportionally slow pulse. It is probable that Fernandina, Gainesville, and Enterprise obtained their yellow fever by fomites from Jacksonville, and

* It is now believed that a man by the name of Lane had the fever in Tampa in October, 1887, and he came directly to Jacksonville. He was employed at Campbell's music store.

that the cases at Decatur, Ala., were due to the same cause. A refugee from Jacksonville, who left there before quarantine was made absolute as against Jacksonville, arrived in Decatur about the 21st of August* and lodged at the house of a Mr. Spencer. He at first denied to the authorities that he was from Jacksonville, but Jacksonville papers were found on him of a recent date, and he was directed to leave the city, but Mr. Spencer, at whose house he was lodged, was shortly afterward taken with the fever and soon died.

This office has no information at present as to the origin of the fever at Jackson, Miss., the statement promised by the accomplished secretary of the board of health, Dr. Wirt Johnston, not having reached me.

Shortly before the appearance of the fever at Key West I was requested by the presidents of the board of health, Monroe and Hillsborough Counties, to prepare a bill for submission to the Florida legislature to establish a State board of health, attention was given to their request and I prepared a bill, which was introduced into the Florida legislature, but although the epidemic was then in progress in Key West, motives of alleged economy are said to have prevented its passage in the legislature. The bill read as follows:

A BILL TO ESTABLISH A BOARD OF HEALTH.

Be it enacted by the legislature of the State of Florida:

That there is hereby established a State board of health, to consist of five members, to be appointed as hereinafter provided.

SEC. 2. The Governor shall within thirty days from the passage of this act nominate, and by and with the advice of the Senate appoint, five persons, who shall be learned in medicine and practitioners of not less than ten years' standing, to be members of the said board, and the members so appointed shall proceed to elect a president and a secretary. The term of office of the members of the said board shall be four years each unless sooner removed by the governor for cause: *Provided*, That the term of office of two of the members of the said board appointed at its first organization shall expire two years from the date of their original appointment. The regular meeting of the said board shall be quarterly, but the board may be convened in special session whenever in the opinion of the governor the public welfare shall require it. The salary of the members of the board shall be —— per diem while in session: *Provided*, That the secretary shall receive an annual salary of ———— dollars, and shall receive no additional or extra compensation. He shall be entitled to employ one clerk as statistician, who shall receive a salary of —— dollars per annum, and one clerk as writer, at a salary of —— dollars per annum.

SEC. 3. The said board of health shall meet at the seat of government of the State within sixty days from the passage of this act, and shall proceed to elect one of their members as president and one as secretary of the board, and the said board when organized shall have power to frame rules and regulations for the prevention of the introduction and spread of epidemic diseases and the management of quarantine inspection stations for the registration of vital statistics, for the prevention of charlatanry, and for the government of the board, which rules, when approved by the governor, shall be duly promulgated by the said board and observed by all officers of the State, and any willful violation of said rules and regulations shall, upon conviction thereof, before any court of this State, be deemed a misdemeanor and be punishable by fine not exceeding fifty dollars, or by imprisonment in a county jail not exceeding three months, at the discretion of the court. The said board of health shall make an

*At this time the Jacksonville authorities claimed that all cases were properly guarded and the city was not generally infected.

annual report to the legislature of its proceedings, including such abstracts of its reports and vital statistics as it may deem proper for the welfare of the people, and shall transmit within ten days after the meeting of the legislature an estimate of the appropriation necessary to be made for its support.

SEC. 4. There shall be established in each county a board of health of not less than three persons, two of whom shall be legally qualified practitioners of medicine and appointed by the county judge; and the county clerk, or person acting as such, shall be *ex officio* the clerk and executive officer of the county board, and he shall make such reports to the State board of health as the regulations of that body may prescribe, and he shall keep as a part of the county records a true account of all births, marriages, and deaths in such county; and it shall be the duty of each legally qualified physician or midwife to make a report, on forms to be furnished by the county clerk, within six days after each birth taking place in his or her practice in the county where such birth occurs; and it shall be the duty of each clergyman or magistrate solemnizing a marriage to make report thereof to the clerk of the county where the said marriage shall have been solemnized within six days from the date thereof; and it shall further be the duty of each legally qualified physician to make report, upon official forms, of the death of any patient under his charge, and of the cause of death of said patient, and it shall be the duty of each coroner or person, acting as such, and each superintendent of public jails, almshouse, or hospitals, or person acting as such, to make report to the said county clerk of any death occurring within any of the said institutions under their respective control; and any physician, midwife, clergyman, magistrate or other person herein named, failing to so report within the time specified shall, upon conviction thereof, be punishable by a fine not exceeding twenty-five dollars for each and every offense. The said county board of health shall have power to enforce the regulations of the State board of health made in pursuance of this act, and shall meet monthly at the county seat.

SEC. 5. All acts and parts of acts in conflict with this act are hereby repealed.

Had the legislature acted promptly on this bill there would have been proper authority to deal with municipalities. One of the principal sources of obstruction to the measures taken to prevent the spread of epidemics has been the lack of uniformity in the health regulations throughout Florida. Proper concert with the State health officers would have enabled the Government measures to have been taken more promptly and more efficiently, as in nearly every instance the Government has been obliged to wait until the disease had so far progressed as to make it a matter of great difficulty to arrest its spread, and in some cases it has been found impossible. With a bill such as is proposed for Florida, the secretary of the board, being its executive officer, could keep the State under constant surveillance, and would have authority to go into any town and examine into its condition, and this without providing for the delegation of any additional powers to the General Government. When the disease broke out in Tampa, and was so reported, the Governor of the State, October 14, 1887, requested aid (the fever having been in existence in Tampa, as already stated, since September), to the Hillsboro County board of health, of which Dr. John P. Wall was president. This board was authorized by this Bureau to procure disinfectants and such sanitary supplies as were necessary for the disinfection and fumigation of houses, and guards for the isolation of the sick. The disease continued, and Assistant Surgeon J. Y. Porter, U. S. Army, having volunteered his services, was placed in charge of a temporary hospital building which was established in Tampa, on the military reservation, a high and healthy location, and acclimated nurses were employed. Dr. Porter there remained until the alleged cessation of the epidemic. His services were deeply appreciated by the board of health and people of Tampa. Dr. Porter, on November 11, reported that yellow fever had appeared in Manatee. The air was quite cold by November 23, and was reduced to a freezing temperature. The nurses from Savannah and Key West were discharged, and the hospital was closed. On the 29th of November the Florida Protective Association raised the commercial quarantine against Tampa. The hospital was finally closed on the 5th of December, 1887. On the 13th of January Dr. Wall reported that rumors of the presence of yellow fever at Tampa were without foundation. In the meantime active disinfection and fumigation of the houses had been going on. Under date of January 16, Dr. King Wylly, president of the Florida Health Protective Association, stated that no yellow fever then existed in the State. Late in February I was informed that there were rumors of yellow fever in Plant City and Tampa, and some other places, and that the germs had probably remained through the winter undisturbed. Surgeon Murray, of this service, who was then about to change stations from Ship Island, was directed to proceed quietly along the west coast of Florida and inspect the towns therein. The result of his inspection, which was received in March, was sent to the governor of Florida, and Dr. Murray, as appears from his letter of March 17, made every effort to arouse the local authorities to a sense of the danger; and it should be remembered that at this time the Government had no authority to interfere in the State, as the governor had not requested it. Owing to the absence of a State health officer nothing was done except under the direction of the county boards of health. The following extract from the abstract of April 26 will give a correct account of the situation at this time:

U. S. MARINE-HOSPITAL SERVICE,
DISTRICT OF THE GULF,
Port of Key West, Fla., Surgeon's Office, February 10, 1888.

GENERAL: I have thought for some weeks that it might be proper for me to make you a personal report in regard to some rumors that cases of yellow fever are occurring upon the main-land. The information coming to me being mainly from local sources, and noticing that the report of Dr. Wylly in the Weekly Abstract of January 20 was rather uncertain, I have hesitated to do so, not wishing to appear as an alarmist.

It seems probable, however, that yellow fever is latent in Florida, and, with the approach of warm weather, danger may be apprehended from its spread northward. Cases of black-vomit are said to have occurred at Sanford, and a lady died a few days ago at Tampa with "acute Bright's disease," while a relative here asserts positively that it was yellow fever. A private letter from Dr. Caldwell states that there will be trouble "when the flowers bloom in the spring;" so that, taking it altogether, there seem to be some grounds for apprehension. The weather has not yet been sufficiently cold to kill out the disease, while some of the local physicians either do not know or do not care to recognize yellow fever when they see it, which adds to the danger of its vivification. Possibly a quiet inspection from Palatka to Manatee, in a month or so by a competent man, would serve to give you the exact condition of affairs in this section before the opening of the regular quarantine season; but I wish to report the current opinion in this quarter, rather than to make any recommendations.

With respect, very sincerely yours,

A. H. GLENNAN,
P. A. Surgeon, M. H. S.

Dr. JOHN B. HAMILTON,
Surgeon-General Marine-Hospital Service, Washington.

PLANT CITY, FLA., *March* 13, 1888.

GENERAL: There is yellow fever at this place, and evidently at other places in the State, of which due report will be made.

Suppressive measures are being instituted here. The death rate is low, and cases generally recover in a short time. The greatest desire is held by the health authorities to not have publicity given to the facts in the case, although rumors are spreading rapidly. No panic exists, and the only anxiety is in relation to the news reaching the general public. It is hoped that the press of Florida will not make prominent notice of the state of affairs.

Drs. J. P. Wall, King Wylly, F. H. Caldwell, J. Y. Porter, and others, advise that no public notice be given until a chance is given for complete checking of the fever here where it is most prevalent. In their view I join for many reasons, and trust that your office will consider this confidential.

The stress of duty and temporary loss of my valise prevent me from writing in detail and from penning a formal letter.

I hope to take the next steamer for Key West.

Frost this morning.

I am, very respectfully, your obedient servant,

R. D. MURRAY.

Surgeon-General JNO. B. HAMILTON,
U. S. Marine-Hospital Service, Washington, D. C.

U. S. MARINE-HOSPITAL SERVICE,
DISTRICT OF THE GULF,
Port of Key West, Fla., Surgeon's Office, March 17, 1888.

GENERAL: I have the honor to state that in obedience to M. H. S. letters Nos. 3079 and 3080 (G. W. S.) of February 16, 1888, I came to this port by way of Florida, and in my passage through the State visited De Funiak, Tallahassee, Jacksonville, St. Augustine, Palatka, Sanford, Apopka, Lakeland, Plant City, and Tampa. Having gained sufficient information, in order to lose no more time I did not visit Kissimmee, Bartow, Dade City, Micanopy, Gainesville, and Manatee, as I wished to. A full investigation would have consumed six weeks, which time I could not consider at my disposal.

That I sought for unfavorable facts and had no right to make my mission known, made it difficult to get prompt information. The rumors of doubtful fevers, and the frost and ninety-day theories compelled nearly all to be reticent, or, at least, unwilling talkers.

I could get no hint of yellow fever on the line of the railroads through the north end of the State. Some rumors were floating at Sanford of the disease having been at Pensacola during the autumn.

At Jacksonville a continued fever, affecting the highest circle of society *only*, has been prevalent for over two months, resulting in from 6 per cent. to 8 per cent. of deaths, which presents the general characteristics of enteric fever. This name is given by Doctor R. P. Daniel, who has treated most of the cases, and is concurred in by Doctors C. J. Kenworthy, J. D. Fernandez, and A. W. Knight. I fancy that Doctor N. Mitchell considers some of the cases more seriously, and know that Doctor J. C. L'Engle (not a practitioner) holds the idea of a yellow-fever wave overspreading the city.

Similar cases had lately occurred in St. Augustine and Mandarin. In spite of local prejudices and a few unproven charges which arouse suspicion, I think the fever at Jacksonville is enteric, but few doctors in South Florida will join in my opinion.

Dr. J. G. Ames claimed that Palatka had cases of yellow fever in the autumn, but was now free from all suspicion or risk of infection.

Doctors Caldwell and Wylly, at Sanford, insist that the town of Sanford had from 100 to 150 cases in the autumn with 6 deaths, and that mild cases are still occurring as late as my visit—the 6th and 7th—and later, one on the 13th. Georgetown and Mellonville, villages near Sanford, present suspicion. Doctor Herndon bitterly condemns the views of Doctors Wylly and Caldwell, while Doctor Montgomery unwillingly assents to it.

Apopka and the thickly-settled region around it seem to be free from all hints of past or recent fever.

No suspicion is thrown upon the Indian River country.

Lakeland, the junction of the South Florida and Florida Southern Railroads is prostrate in a business point of view from the presence of imported cases during last fall, but it was impossible for me to get any clue to recent cases from Doctors Perry, Derio, Marshall, Hart, Preston, and Vineyard.

At Plant City, junction of Florida Railway and Navigation Railroad with South Florida Railroad, 22 miles east of Tampa, cases have occurred since October 5—say, 120 cases and 9 deaths. The last death (the ninth) on March 11; the last case sickened the same day.

On March 8 Mr. Calhoun convalesced at Box Springs, Talbot County, Ga., from yellow fever engendered during one month's stay in Plant City, he having left for his home about February 27.

Tampa is declared free from fever by Drs. J. P. Wall and J. A. Jackson, but as there has been no radical system of cleansing in vogue, the place is by no means above doubt. The lady referred to by Doctor Glennan as dying of acute Bright's disease, *i. e*, the wife of Doctor Bruce, evidently died of yellow fever, about the 20th of January.

At the urgent request of Doctors Wall and Caldwell, I disembarked from the steamer at Tampa, on the night of the 12th, and returned to Plant City to supervise some sort of cleaning up of the town. Many acres of dead wood, brush, and rubbish were cleared off and burned; thorough fumigation of every house in the place was begun; lime and copperas were generally scattered about, and bichloriding of all houses and bedding where sickness had occurred was arranged for. Three days of hard work, and inhalation of sulphur and pine smoke gave me a bronchitis from which I still suffer. Micanopy, on the Florida Railway and Navigation Railroad north of Plant City, and Bartow south of Lakeland, are presumably danger points at present.

It is evident to me, painful as the idea is, that the lines of railroad from Tampa to Jacksonville are at various points infested by *fomites* which will, at the proper time, give all the trouble prophesied by Dr. Caldwell. The region south of the South Florida Railroad seems to be more secure, except Manatee, but is by no means safe.

I can not think the spasmodic and imperfect cleaning of towns will serve to obviate the recurrence of fever, for there is no power or panic to enforce, or even advise, a general and systematic riddance of all supposable *fomites*, retained air, and niduses. Two weeks' prompt work *now* would minify or avert the danger, but there is no common center of authority or confidence to advise sanitation or to subdue the bitterness of last season's quarantines, follies, and failures.

The governor will not, it is said, call a meeting of the legislature. The medical association will not meet till May. The helpless State Health Protective Association is exploded and bankrupt. I wished for privilege to visit more towns to beg for prompt action, but not caring to ask for it or to take it, will try by private letters to arouse the town authorities to work while some chance offers to avert a summer of terror and death.

I can not see any good to come from a publication of my opinions. Savannah is already warned, and all the chief cities are on the lookout.

Passed Assistant Surgeon Glennan is entitled to much credit for his forethought and courage in informing you of the expected and perhaps inevitable damage to the State.

I am, very respectfully, your obedient servant,

R. D. MURRAY,
Surgeon.

Surgeon-General JOHN B. HAMILTON,
U. S. M. H. S., Washington, D. C.

JACKSONVILLE, FLA., *April* 16, 1888.

SIR: Of course you have known of the existence of yellow fever at Plant City this winter; there have been cases throughout the winter, but it has been only until recently that there has been any alarm, and that occasioned, I presume, by the advent of warm weather. I can not say as to what may be the status of affairs there now, but sent the secretary of my board, Dr. Knight, down to-day, and shall be thoroughly posted by the latter part of the week. I am in somewhat of a quandary as to just what shall be done provided Dr. Knight reports a prevalence of the disease, as I have no doubt he will. I do not think it advisable, and shall not quarantine at present. The lesson of last year taught the many difficulties of quarantining at such a distance. It is my opinion that each infected locality should, by an effective cordon, be isolated. This the counties of Florida can not do; hence, if such a plan is to be adopted, some one with authority and the means for carrying out such requirements as may be deemed best—yourself—must take the matter in hand.

I will make a few general statements. Last fall yellow fever probably existed at many points along the lines of the South Florida Railroad and Florida Railway and Navigation Railroad, and may be developed at any of these points later in the season. The State, as you know, has no State board of health, hence every county acts for itself, thus inflicting upon the community quarantines which fail to meet the requirements for various reasons and destroys commerce. You are familiar with cases of this kind, and I wish your advice as to what should be done. I have made but few statements as to the conditions here, because I know you are already acquainted with them. Any suggestions you may make I shall be happy to receive. Our board represents the most powerful county in the State, and carries great weight. I am anxious that everything possible to avert a spread of the disease shall be done, and if you can suggest some plan our board will try to carry it into effect. I shall write Governor Perry to-night. Pardon this hastily written letter.

Respectfully,

NEAL MITCHELL, M. D.,
President Duval County Board of Health.

Surgeon-General HAMILTON.

Dr. A. W. Knight, of Jacksonville, who had been detailed by the Duval County board of health, reported as follows:

Florida.—Dr. A. W. Knight, in his report referred to in the last abstract, states that "on the 17th and 18th of April I was at Plant City, Fla. Two cases of yellow fever still remaining. One of these convalescent and out of danger. One case critical on 18th. No other cases there or at Lakeland, Seffner, Ybor City, or Tampa. Tampa and Ybor City unusually healthy. No cases at that date, either at Bartow or Micanopy. No excitement in any of the towns nearest Plant City. I visited these points per order of the board of health of Duval County."

The board of health of Hillsborough County adopted stringent precaution in regard to the steamers and claimed that they had stamped out the fever. They, however, failed to watch their smugglers.

Dr. Wall reported on the 23d of June, as follows:

The Plant steamers from Havana landed at Port Tampa for the first time on the 13th instant. * * * The disinfection is done on board of steamer for the present, as in previous years. I am, however, having a fumigation chamber and other disinfecting apparatus fixed up on the wharf at Port Tampa, which is about one mile from shore. The incomplete condition of the wharf prevented my having this done earlier, before the steamer began to make that the place of transfer. I think that before the 1st proximo everything will be in working order. As you know, it is the company's policy to prevent the steamers from becoming infected, and, although every pains will be taken here as to the disinfection of baggage, the rules and regulations of the company as to not allowing unacclimated persons to take passage will be still enforced as in the two previous years. I went out to Plant City yesterday, in company with Dr. Jerome Cochran, of Alabama. The place is healthy, and there had not been any case of fever there since week before last. I had the place thoroughly disinfected, burning all beds and mattresses in houses where sickness had been, and otherwise disinfecting houses and premices. I think the fever has been stamped out, though we will not allow people to return there before week after next, keeping up a vigilant observation and resorting to aeration as much as possible in the mean time.

This statement as to the active measures taken by the Hillsborough County board of health to stamp out the disease is corroborated by Dr. Jerome Cochran, of the State board of health of Alabama. (See Weekly Abstract No. 23, June 8, 1888.)

In July the Bureau was informed of the re-appearance of yellow fever in Plant City. The following is from the abstract of July 6:

Florida.—Yellow fever.—This Bureau is informed that about the middle of June yellow fever re-appeared at Plant City, and there was one death therefrom, June 22. Another case in the vicinity, 4½ miles from Plant City, died on the 26th. There have been several mild cases in the village, which contains less than 300 inhabitants, but for the present trains will not stop at Plant City, and it is understood that mails will be delivered at Cork post-office, 5 miles west of Plant City. In the mean time, by direction of the governor, the most active measures are being taken by the president of the county board of health, Dr. J. P. Wall. The board have promulgated the following regulation concerning the epidemic:

The Board of Health of Hillsborough County adopts and promulgates the following rules to prevent the spread of yellow fever at and from Plant City:

(1) Railroads passing through or into Plant City are prohibited from carrying passengers and baggage to or from Plant City, or from delivering or taking on freight, or transferring freight from the cars of one road to cars of another road at or near Plant City, except the delivery of the necessary supplies for the people living in the place. Said railroad companies are also prohibited from delivering or taking on the United States mail at Plant City.

(2) All employés of the railroads living at or near Plant City must be acclimated to yellow fever by a previous attack of the disease; and such employés should be enjoined to keep away from the sick, if any, and aloof from all places suspected of being infected with yellow-fever poison.

RULE 3. These rules are substituted for rule 2 of the rules adopted and promulgated April 24, 1888.

The president of the county board of health states that—

In explanation of the foregoing stringent rules, it is necessary to say that the board of health of Hillsborough County believes Plant City to be infected with the poison, or germs of yellow fever; and inasmuch as expensive efforts to disinfect the place and stamp out the disease have failed, it is due to the public safety and welfare of the State to isolate the place and have it shunned as an infected place until such time as the board of health may deem it safe for people to go there. It is deemed absolutely necessary to suspend all business and cut off all communication with Plant City to prevent the risk of a widespread epidemic of yellow fever this summer. It is true that there is not much sickness there, and happily the large majority of the residents in the place are acclimated by a previous attack of the disease, but by visiting the place or commingling much with the people who still reside in Plant City, there is unquestionably great risk of spreading the disease. The summer is here, and the time for temporizing measures has passed. It is probable that Plant City will remain infected for some time, if not for the whole season, and hence the necessity for these stringent measures. Everybody is especially cautioned from being deceived by assertions of the disease being anything else but what the board of health has honestly pronounced it, yellow fever.

On the 16th of July the presence of yellow fever in Tampa was again admitted, and on the 19th the governor of Florida made application for aid to the local authorities in suppressing the disease, and a house inspection of Tampa, Plant City, and Manatee was immediately commenced.* Surgeon Murray, of this service, was detailed to take charge of matters at Manatee, and instructions were given Dr. Wall to perform

* The following letter from Governor Perry explains why he did not convene the legislature in special session:

STATE OF FLORIDA, EXECUTIVE OFFICE,
Tallahassee, November 1, 1888.

JOHN B. HAMILTON,
Supervising Surgeon-General, M. H. S., Washington, D. C.:

SIR: I have the honor to acknowledge the receipt of your letter of the 25th ultimo, inclosing the draught of a bill for a State board of health. This draught of bill I will cheerfully turn over to my successor in office, who will enter upon the discharge of his duties early in January, some weeks before the convening of the legislature under the constitution of the State, unless an extra session is convened, which might not be improper in view of the fact that at the coming election a new legislature will be elected. For several sessions strenuous efforts were made to have enacted statute organizing such State board, but to no purpose. In 1885 the message which I sent in to the legislature strongly recommended a State board, but the legislature failed to provide for it. After the adjournment of the session the constitutional convention which was called in 1885 and adopted our new constitution provided in Article XV: "The legislature shall establish a State board of health and also county boards of health in all counties where it may be necessary."

The legislature, composed in part of the same members as the legislature of 1885, again convened in April, 1887. This body was cited to the constitutional mandate of Article XV, the attorney-general making a list of the legislation made necessary by the adoption of the new constitution, in which list, to which I called the attention of the legislature, the attorney-general says: "Under Article XV it is necessary that legislation be had on the subject of the public health."

The legislature in its session of sixty days was at work upon a bill or sundry bills to establish a State board of health, but could not agree and had defeated the measure when, near the close of the session news reached me of the breaking out of the fever in Key West. I at once sent my private secretary with the despatch to the legislature to urge reconsideration of its action and the necessary legislation to establish such board. The vote defeating the measure was reconsidered and again an effort made to pass it, which again failed. I have thus hurriedly detailed in part the efforts that were made to induce the old legislature to establish a State board. Can you wonder that that legislature was not reconvened in 1888 to effect an end which could thorough disinfection of dwellings and infected things in Tampa and Plant City. The inspection was completed on the 27th of July. The village of Manatee then contained about one hundred unacclimated persons. In August the fever was reported at Jacksonville, Fla. Passed Assistant-Surgeon Guitéras was directed to proceed to that port and report the facts. He found a patient by the name of McCormick with yellow fever in the Sand Hills Hospital, and the next day two more cases of yellow fever were reported. Two days later Passed Assistant-Surgeon Guitéras was directed to open an inspection station at Way Cross, Ga., and as soon as possible additional inspection stations were directed to be opened at Dupont, Ga., River Junction, Fla., and the order was given that all baggage passing through those stations from places in Florida should be fumigated before being allowed to come further north or west. The following account was given of the measures taken to prevent the spread of the disease, in the abstract for August 17:

PRECAUTIONS TAKEN TO PREVENT FURTHER SPREAD OF THE DISEASE.

Fumigation stations are now open at Chattahoochee, Fla., and Du Pont, Ga., in addition to that at Way Cross. These stations are not in immediate connection with the railway depots, but are some distance down the railroad towards Florida. The one at Chattahoochee is at River Junction, about 2 miles from Chattahoochee. This station is under the charge of Assistant Surgeon Geddings, of the Marine-Hospital Service. The one at Du Pont is at present under the general direction of Passed Assistant Surgeon Urquhart, whose headquarters are at Way Cross.

These fumigation stations are constructed from "box" cars, which are divided into two compartments by upright planking. In each compartment thus made wire-netting shelves are placed at regular intervals as thickly as practicable. When articles are to be fumigated they are loosely scattered on the shelves, and subjected to fumes of burning sulphur. Other cars similarly shelved have been provided for the Railway Mail Service, and clerks in that service open the mail-bags, puncture the letters and scatter them upon the wire shelves.

The cars, being movable, can be shifted from place to place, and the passage-way between the broad doors gives ample room for the shifting of baggage. Passengers coming North from an infected town must pass a short period of observation in the detention camp near Boulogne. From other towns in Florida they may pass the inspectors, but are not allowed to stop at any southern point by reason of local quarantine regulations.

The refuge camp near Boulogne is under command of Passed Assistant Surgeon Guitéras. Persons from Jacksonville and other infected points falling sick at this camp will be returned to Jacksonville by the first train. It has been supplied with tents and cooking-utensils, and the hardships of detention will be reduced as much as possible. Persons unable to bring rations will be furnished them while undergoing detention, but it is probable that only those able to buy tickets will avail themselves of the camp. Ten days at the camp will be required to enable one to pass the inspectors and come North. The inspectors have been provided with conductors' punches, and

---

not be accomplished in two whole sessions, one of which was held after the constitutional mandate upon the subject which I have cited?

There was great diversity of views upon the question of a State board in the old legislature—views which it seemed impossible to reconcile. I doubt not the new legislature will obey the constitutional requirement and establish a State board.

Thanking you for your interest in the matter and for the draught of bill you have kindly forwarded, I am,

Very respectfully, your obedient servant,

E. A. PERRY.

they punch and issue to each passenger a ticket showing to what points bound, where from, date, number of pieces of baggage, and the name of the inspector. The traveler must also sign his name to the ticket as a means of identification.

The situation in Florida is calming down, but the panic is still very great. Notwithstanding the death rate in Jacksonville is small, and that it has at no time been great either at Tampa, Manatee, or Plant City, yet the fears of the people in the adjoining towns are such as to lead them to establish rigid "shot-gun" quarantines in many places.

This panic, in many cases worse than the yellow fever itself, it is hoped to quell by furnishing a complete system of inspection under Government auspices. At the same time such internal measures of sanitation as seem to be necessary will be resorted to wherever the local forces are inadequate to properly perform the work. At Jacksonville the Duval County Board of Health are doing their utmost to stamp out the disease, and it is hoped that their efforts may be successful. It is too soon to speak with positiveness of the origin of the epidemic, but it is quite probable that the case of McCormick, imported from Plant City, was not the first case at Jacksonville. Rumors of yellow fever at Jacksonville had been prevalent for several weeks. It is now known definitely that the first cases in Tampa last fall were brought by a schooner engaged in smuggling.

At the same time a sanitary inspection of other towns in Florida was ordered, and as soon as it was definitely ascertained that the western portion of Florida was free from fever the inspection station was moved from Du Pont to Live Oak, and the one at River Junction removed. The one at Way Cross was placed in command of Surgeon Hutton and greatly enlarged by the construction of a large warehouse suitably fitted for sulphurous acid fumigation.

The following circular was issued under date of August 28:

CIRCULAR.

Regulations for the prevention of the spread of yellow fever from certain infected places in the State of Florida.

TREASURY DEPARMENT,
OFFICE SUPERVISING SURGEON-GENERAL,
U. S. MARINE-HOSPITAL SERVICE,
Washington, D. C., August 28, 1888.

In accordance with the act of April 29, 1878, and appropriation acts authorizing the maintenance of quarantine at points of danger, the following regulations are framed to assist in the work of preventing the spread of yellow fever, now prevailing as an epidemic in certain towns in the State of Florida:

1. A camp of refuge for persons from infected places in Florida is hereby established, to be under command of Passed Assistant Surgeon Guitéras, on the south bank of the St. Mary's River, near the crossing of the Savannah, Florida and Western Railroad, to be known as Camp Perry. Temporary quarantine stations are hereby established, under direction of Surgeon Hutton, Marine-Hospital Service, near Way Cross, Ga., and Live Oak, Fla. Those at Du Pont, Ga., and Chattahoochee River Junction are hereby discontinued.

2. At the stations aforesaid an inspection will be made of all persons, baggage, mail, and express arriving by rail from points south; and in case of arrival of any person, mail, baggage, or express matter capable of conveying infection, coming from an infected place or a place not known to be healthy, as shown by recent inspection reports, then such person shall either be returned to the original place of embarkation or to Camp Perry, at his or her option, and the baggage of such person shall be

held for fumigation, and fumigated under the direction of the officer in charge. Mail matter from infected places will be fumigated under the direction of the Railway Mail Service, under orders already issued by that service.

3. All persons arriving in Camp Perry will be under the orders of the commanding officer, and will not depart the camp without permission, until ten days shall have elapsed from the date of their departure from an infected place. A special daily train will run between Jacksonville and Camp Perry, for the purpose of conveying persons from Jacksonville and such other business as may be incident thereto, and at the expiration of the detention period such persons will be taken to Way Cross, and then allowed to proceed to their destination without further detention.

4. Railway agents, conductors, or other persons in charge of railway trains south of and including those of the Savannah, Florida and Western Railroad will not receive persons from infected places on board trains, except to the refuge camp as provided in paragraph 1 of this circular, and sleeping-cars will not be allowed to proceed south of Way Cross, Ga., until the cessation of the epidemic.

5. An additional refuge camp, under the same regulations as those governing Camp Perry, will be established in the mountains of North Carolina (the site hereafter to be determined) as soon as practicable.

JOHN B. HAMILTON,
Supervising Surgeon-General.

Approved:

C. S. FAIRCHILD,
Secretary of the Treasury.

The board of health of Duval County was aided by the authorization of the erection of certain cheap barrack huts, which were to be built near Jacksonville for negroes liable to propagate the fever, and it was provided that special excursion trains should run at intervals under guard to some point in the Tennessee, Georgia, or North Carolina mountains, whenever a sufficient number indicated their desire to go. Such persons on their destination were to be released under parole not to go to the seaboard or quarantine towns within ten days from the date of their departure from Jacksonville. The board of health of North Carolina were consulted prior to the allowing of any refugee train to leave, and the board of health of Tennessee had issued a circular under date of August 17, paragraph 2, which permitted refugees to go to the elevated plateaus and mountainous regions of Tennessee, or pass directly through the State. Many towns in Tennessee and North Carolina applied for the running of special trains to them, and asked for the sending of the refugees. One train containing forty-eight persons was sent to Atlanta, having previously asked the mayor of that city if he desired them to come, to which Mayor Cooper replied that while he did not solicit refugees from Jacksonville, they would not shut their doors against them. The Jacksonville people being desirous to go, and Atlanta being willing, as above indicated, the train was allowed to proceed. Surgeon Hutton was detailed to accompany the train and see that persons did not escape en route. Scarcely had they arrived in Atlanta when the board of health, with the approval of the mayor of the city, passed a resolution forbidding any further arrivals of trains. On receiving a notification from the secretary of the North Carolina board of health at Wilmington, Dr. Thomas F. Wood, that Hendersonville and other towns in North Carolina were anxious to receive refugees, a special train was provided at the expense of the Government to run to Hendersonville.*

The following is the report of Passed Assistant Surgeon Guitéras, who was detailed from Camp Perry to accompany this special train:

CAMP PERRY, FLA., *September* 16, 1888.

SIR: I have the honor to report as follows concerning the excursion train of refugees from Jacksonville and Camp Perry to Hendersonville, N. C.:

The train left Jacksonville on the morning of the 11th instant, and was joined by myself and the Camp Perry contingent at Folkston, Ga., making, in all, a total of 291 souls.

It was found that no keys had been furnished to lock the cars, and this evil it was found impossible to correct by applying to the railroad authorities, on account of the variety of cars furnished.

Unfortunately the trip was prolonged beyond the time anticipated, on account of several accidents on the road. These perhaps might have been provided for with greater promptitude by the railroad authorities had they fully recognized the gravity of the situation.

The evils resulting from this delay were twofold. First, the running short of rations. This was provided for to a great extent, sometimes by the generosity and in others by the cupidity of the towns along the road. Some parties at Atlanta and Macon generously furnished relishes, while others charged exorbitant prices. I must mention, however, the most conspicuous example of generosity. This was shown by the town of Easley, S. C., which provided, without any charges, and late in the night, the most abundant assortment of supplies.

The second and most important consequence of delay was the development of cases of yellow fever on the train. Only two cases developed in the first twenty-four hours, and three in the course of the second day. Of course it was to be expected that this would happen in an aggregation of people leaving Jacksonville; but it is very probable that the accumulation of people, clothes, and baggage for so long a time in hot cars, which could not be kept in a sanitary condition, created a secondary center of infection that will show itself in the development of cases after the arrival in Hendersonville.

The appearance of yellow fever among the refugees had a very unfavorable effect upon the *morale* of the party. They were truly panic-stricken. One car quarantined strictly against the other, and efforts to escape were frequently made, and, unfortunately, in a few instances, with success.

One lady was taken with labor-pains in the train, and, with the consent of a local physician, she was allowed to remain at White Sulphur Springs, near Gainesville, Ga.

A marked contrast was apparent between the two cars occupied by the refugees from Camp Perry and the rest of the train. Among the former no cases of yellow fever occurred, and the *morale* was excellent. The two cars were strictly quarantined against the rest. No complaint was heard, no fear expressed. In the other cars the spectacle was pitiful. The isolation of the sick in one car I discovered would have increased the excitement by bringing together and crowding still more people from the different cars who were suspicious of each other.

Great credit is due to that portion of the refugees who gave me their support throughout the journey. It was owing to their kind firmness that we had no decided breach of discipline.

---

* It has been claimed that the sending of this train violated the Augusta conference, but Hendersonville was not considered as a "populous city," as mentioned in that conference.

We arrived at Hendersonville on the 13th, at 2 o'clock a m. The hospitality of that generous people became at once apparent. They had been up all night preparing a building for the reception of the sick. Fires were built around the station, adding warmth and cheerfulness to the cordiality of the reception. With the assistance of Dr. Few, of Hendersonville, the patients were removed to the hospital. The refugees found accommodation at very reasonable rates.

On the morning of the arrival a sixth case of yellow fever developed. The comparatively large proportion of cases has caused much excitement, and it is probable that some of the refugees will break their parol.

It is apparent from the above facts that the experiment of excursions insisted upon by the people of Jacksonville is not a success. There is, of course, a possibility that Hendersonville may become a center of infection, but I do not expect this to happen. The large proportion of cases taken sick during the journey renders the measure one of questionable advantage to the people of Jacksonville, let alone the hardships of the journey.

The removal of a large portion of an infected population to high altitudes, where yellow fever spreads with difficulty, is a desirable object, and appears perfectly practicable if the health department of the nation was endowed with the same liberality as the Army and Navy. Such action would necessitate the existence of extensive permanent quarters in the mountainous regions, with a standing garrison of acclimated people; the fitting out of special trains exclusively under the control of the Government, and constructed specially for that purpose. These encampments and deposits of sanitary stores should be ever ready for action, in the same manner that the strategic points are maintained in readiness at great expense by military authorities. Provision should be made also for the constant training of a standing sanitary corps, by setting the machinery in motion during seasons when there are no epidemics, as is done in military and naval reviews and exercises.

I have the honor to submit the above report for your consideration.

Very respectfully, your obedient servant,

JOHN GUITÉRAS,
Passed Assistant Surgeon, M. H. S.

It subsequently appeared that some of these persons violated their parole and were found in various sea-board cities, and no further trains were sent, notwithstanding other towns in North Carolina asked for the sending of the refugees. At Hendersonville some cases of fever appeared among the refugees, but none among the citizens. On the 28th of September the Bureau was notified by the secretary of the North Carolina Board of Health that they had given their opinion to the governor that no more refugees from the yellow fever district should be received into the State of North Carolina unless placed in sanitary camps under guard.

On the 3d of September a conference was held at Augusta, Ga., an account of which appears in the Weekly Abstract of September 7, as follows:

CONFERENCE AT AUGUSTA, GA.

[Telegram.]

AUGUSTA, GA., *September* 3, 1888.

At the suggestion of Governor Gordon, Surgeon-General Hamilton had a conference here to-day with the health authorities of several cities in the State and with the State health officers of Tennessee and Alabama, Governor Gordon being present, as also Mayor Lester, Dr. Brunner, and General Manager Haines, from Savannah, Ga., and Mayor Dunn, of Brunswick. At the conference the following telegram was read, which was received by the Surgeon-General:

ATLANTA GA., *September* 3, 1888.

Surgeon-General J. B. HAMILTON (care Mayor, Augusta, Ga.):

I am instructed to wire following resolutions adopted at noon to-day:

Resolved, That the Board of Health of the City of Atlanta, his honor the mayor co-operating, cordially approves the plan of the Surgeon-General of the United States, requiring ten days' quarantine of all persons from infected or suspected districts in Florida conveniently near to infected points.

Resolved, That the wholesale removal of persons from infected districts to populous cities and the aggregation of infected individuals in any part of this country is regarded as hazardous in a sanitary point of view, and is unjust to any community upon whom such persons are forced, because of the probable necessity of maintaining many of them at the corporate expense.

JAMES M. BAIRD, *Secretary*.

After discussion of these resolutions, the following resolutions were adopted by the conference:

Resolved, That this convention cordially approves the plan of the Surgeon-General of United States Marine-Hospital Service requiring ten days' quarantine of all persons from infected or suspected places, together with fumigation and other disinfection of baggage, etc., from infected points.

Resolved, That the wholesale removal of persons from infected districts to populous cities and the aggregation of individuals from infected places in any city of this country is regarded as extremely hazardous to any such community; also, that the citizens of Jacksonville have no just cause for complaint against the quarantine regulations as at present operated, inasmuch as abundant provision has been and will be made by establishing healthful and cleanly camps for the inhabitants of Jacksonville, and provision made for maintenance of such citizens during detention in camp.

Resolved, That in the judgment of this convention, after the suspects shall have been detained in quarantine camp for ten days and their baggage shall have been fumigated under direction of United States Government, such persons should be permitted to go to any community willing to receive them.

An inspection of Camp Perry was made by the Surgeon-General on Tuesday.

Nashville, Tenn.—The president of the board of health telegraphed September 6: "Unless refugees have been in camp ten days, baggage disinfected, and each hold your certificate of health, they will not be admitted to State. The Augusta agreement is approved."

Atlanta, Ga.—September 7 the secretary of the board of health telegraphs: "Atlanta relies upon the Camp Perry quarantine and the decision at Atlanta conference."

The establishment of Camp Perry has proved entirely successful. This camp was first temporarily in charge of Passed Assistant Guitéras, but afterwards placed under command of Surgeon Hutton. The camp was open to refugees before it was fairly completed, and there was much complaint in consequence of the insufficient character of the accommodations. These complaints were intensified by the apparent desire of the Jacksonville people to break down the quarantine regulations, and public sentiment seemed to be forming in the same direction. I therefore issued the following card, which was widely published. Its effect was immediate and the tone of popular sentiment seemed to be changed:

To the public:

Certain criticism, mainly based on misinformation, concerning the present sanitary regulations have appeared in the daily press; and as these criticisms have a tendency to weaken the hands of the officers engaged in the prevention of the spread of yellow fever and to induce laxity in the maintenance of quarantine, and thereby greatly increase the danger to the whole country, I have thought it expedient to make a general statement of the condition of affairs.

The United States Government, acting through its Marine-Hospital Service, is engaged in helping the people of Florida, not in injuring them, and in particular the stricken city of Jacksonville has been treated with a kindly consideration suited to the calamity which has befallen it. They were permitted to go anywhere they desired so long as the disease was confined to circumscribed areas in the city; but when the city became generally infected, then the necessity of placing certain restrictions upon the movements of outgoing persons was apparent, and in restricting promiscuous travel from Jacksonville the Bureau is looking to the security of the country. The dreadful record of the ravages of yellow fever in the towns along the railroad lines leading out of New Orleans in 1878, where there were over 13,000 persons affected with yellow fever, of whom nearly 7,000 died, is too fresh in memory to risk its repetition long the Atlantic sea-board. The extension of the disease to Memphis in 1878, where nearly 3,000 persons died of the yellow fever, might have been prevented had there been any authority to restrict travel by proper quarantine. It may be a fearful alternative to compel persons from Jacksonville to remain within a camp of refuge for a period of ten days before being allowed to go at will, but that alternative is humane in comparison with the results which would follow the admission of the infection into all the sea-port and Southern cities, each of which, in a short time, would itself become a new center of infection.

The Government has not at any time established a strict cordon sanitaire about the city of Jacksonville, but has opened a camp of refuge in a high, healthy locality, and furnishes free rations to those detained. It has authorized, at a large expense, the building of two hundred pine cabins to shelter those poor people who are driven out of infected localities, and it is willing to provide for the further relief of Jacksonville by furnishing transportation by special excursion trains to any definite point that is safe and had opened its doors; but there are few places willing to receive large numbers of refugees. While it is probably true that the body of a healthy person does not carry the contagion, his clothes do carry it, and baggage packed in an infected house is dangerous in the extreme. Fumigation stations have been established at proper points, and all baggage will be fumigated which comes from the infected city. I do not think, therefore, there can be any reasonable ground of complaint.

But the complaints from Jacksonville were so numerous that there was danger of crippling the usefulness of the camp, and in obedience to the President's direction I proceeded to Camp Perry in order to reassure refugees and to give personal attention to the work of completing the camp. The huts previously contracted for arrived at the camp the day before my arrival and were soon placed in position, and the camp speedily put in good order; strict military discipline was maintained, and the guests of the Government provided with every comfort practicable.

The accompanying illustration gives the appearance of the camp better than a verbal description.

On my leaving the camp, complimentary resolutions were passed by the refugees, to which I replied in substance as follows.

This is given as part of the history of the time:

I am deeply touched by your sympathy and kindness. I am all the more sensible of this because of the unjust criticism directed against me in my official capacity and the attacks upon my private character. These commenced when I announced the presence of yellow fever in Florida last spring. As a matter of fact, the presence of fever in this State was reported by me to the governor nearly or quite two weeks before I made any public announcement of it. That the statement was true, the fact of the estabishment of this camp, and that we are here to-day in this pine wood, too well attests. But that is all past now, and let it be forgotten and forgiven.

CAMP PERRY.

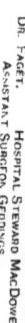

Dr. Posey.
Passed Assistant Surgeon Guitéras. Surgeon Hutton. Dr. Fagét. Hospital Steward MacDowell.
Assistant Surgeon Geddings.

Camp Perry Guards.

Yellow Fever Camp, one-half Mile from Camp Perry.

When I came here and hoisted our dear old flag over this camp, I, as the Government representative, felt that I wanted every man, woman, and child coming here to know that they were no longer poor, panic-stricken, fever-hunted refugees, but welcome guests of our common country. The warm, ruddy stripes of the banner which floats above us are emblematical of our country's love for its children, and each star in that azure field represents a State, every one of which must be protected when in distress, and suffered for, if need be. These sentiments I know actuate the officers of the service whom I leave in charge here.

I thank you, ladies and gentlemen, for your courtesy, and in saying farewell I assure you that you have made it a difficult word to speak.

It is proper to state that but two deaths have occurred in the fever hospital attached to the camp. The officers charged with this duty deserve especial mention here for the efficient manner in which they performed their delicate duty. Surgeon W. H. H. Hutton; Passed Assistant Surgeon John Guitéras; Assistant Surgeon H. D. Geddings, and Dr. C. Fagét, of New Orleans, all at Camp Perry; Passed Assistant Surgeon F. M. Urquhart, Way Cross and Live Oak inspection stations; Assistant Surgeon William Martin, U. S. Navy,* Dr. J. L. Posey, of New Orleans, Dr. J. F. Hartigan, of Washington, as sanitary inspectors; Assistant Surgeon G. M. Magruder, M. H. S., in charge of the inspection station at Way Cross, Ga.

At Jacksonville, Dr. Joseph Y. Porter, of the Army, having volunteered his services, was placed in charge of the Government relief measures at that place. At Fernandina Surgeon J. W. Ross, of the Navy, was given charge of Government relief measures at that place. These officers also deserve the special thanks of the Bureau, but Dr. Porter's duties have been especially trying at Jacksonville.

The Government was not called on to render special aid to the Duval County board of health and Jacksonville until their resources were practically exhausted and general appeals were made to the country for aid. The Bureau assumed charge of the municipal hospitals at Sand Hills and Saint Luke's and retained the officers and employés previously employed by the board of health, paid for the sanitary police, and purchased disinfectants and general sanitary supplies. The expenses at Jacksonville have been quite heavy. A fumigation station was also opened at Jacksonville and placed in charge of Dr. Julius Wise, of Memphis. Dr. Porter remains in Jacksonville at the date of this report in charge of the hospital and all Government relief measures in that city. At present, in consequence of the following request of the board of health of Jacksonville, refugees are prevented from returning to the city:

JACKSONVILLE, FLA., *October* 19, 1888.

Whereas the board of health recognizes as one of the gravest responsibilities which rests upon it at this time the urgency of protecting, in so far as ability will permit, those at a distance who are unacclimated, whether citizens of Jacksonville or others, from unwarrantably risking their lives by coming into this city or its surburbs before there are reasonabe grounds for believing that the danger of infection has passed.

* This efficient officer has lately taken charge of the Government relief measures at Gainesville.

Even thus early a disposition on the part of some of the absentees to return is manifesting itself, and as the fall advances and more confirmed weather occurs in the latitudes north of us, doubtless the pressure of business obligations or the longing for home, will constantly increase the number of those who will endeavor to deceive themselves in this regard.

The list of fever cases is being largely diminished and we have reason to hope that ere long the epidemic, in so far at least as the city proper is concerned, will be virtually at an end; but this will only be because the material for its further continuance will have been exhausted. The disease is now principally active in the suburban districts, even 4 or 5 miles from the city center, and new cases are likely to continue developing in these directions. Neither the houses nor atmosphere of Jacksonville are any less dangerous to the unacclimated than they were a month since, and we would earnestly warn all who are liable to contract yellow fever against coming here merely because they may see that there are no cases reported. Wait until the board of health notifies you that the epidemic is not only over, but that it is reasonably safe for absentees and strangers to come here again, and then return only under such directions as may be advised by the authorities. We would add that there does not appear to be any probable grounds upon which to base an expectation that this time, so earnestly desired by us all, will come earlier then the very last of November or the beginning of December.

In consideration of the great importance of this matter as it bears upon the preservation of the lives of our absent fellow-citizens, and likewise of an early and thorough re-establishment of Jacksonville's ordinary healthful reputation, this board respectfully suggests to the city authorities the enactment of such an ordinance as will most effectually aid in protecting the interests of all concerned in this direction: Therefore be it

Resolved, That until such time as the proper authorities shall officially declare it safe to remove such restriction no person who can not present satisfactory evidence to the authorities that he or she has had the yellow fever shall be permitted to enter any locality in Duval County where fever infection now exists, nor where such infection may develop, between the present time and the occurrence of frost; and this board of health requests Dr. Joseph Y. Porter, representing the Marine Hospital service of the United States, and who has signified the willingness of the Department to assume the duty and expense, to adopt such measures in conjunction with the civil authorities as will best prevent the return of the people to Jacksonville before it may be determined safe for this community as well as for the people returning.

There have been up to November 20, 4,643 cases of yellow fever in Jacksonville, and 403 deaths. The sanitary conditions of Jacksonville are not good. The sewers are inadequate to furnish drainage for the city, and the probabilities are that many infected articles in Jacksonville will escape disinfection. The city council has declined to enact a compulsory ordinance providing a penalty for persons concealing infected household effects, and the Bureau has not up to this time authorized payment for articles destroyed, except in cases of the poor. The accompanying copy of an official map of the city of Jacksonville and the report of the city engineer, hereto attached, will give a pretty clear idea of the inadequacy of the present system of sewerage:

OFFICE OF JACKSONVILLE AUXILIARY SANITARY ASSOCIATION,
16½ WEST BAY STREET,
Jacksonville, Fla., October, 1888.

DEAR SIR: By the request of the Auxiliary Sanitary Association, I herewith hand you a map of our sewerage system; the size of the sewers and the direction of the flow is indicated on the map; the elevation above mean high water is marked at each street intersection in feet and tenths; also a map of the city showing the city limits in 1879, on which I have plotted the sewers, and also a dotted red line showing approximately the settled portion of the city.

For description of the sewers I append extracts from my reports to the trustees of the sanitary improvement bonds, under whose administration the sanitary improvements of the city were made, the city having been bonded for $250,000 for sanitary purposes just after the yellow fever of 1877, said sum being spent in building water works, laying sewers, straightening and deepening Hogan's Creek, and filling up and draining low places, since which very little has been spent in sanitary work.

Yours, respectfully.

B. S. ELLIS,
City Engineer.

Dr. J. Y. PORTER,
U. S. Marine Hospital Service, City.

SEWERS OF JACKSONVILLE, FLORIDA.

[Extracts from reports of engineer.]

Work was commenced in November, 1879, and completed and accepted by the trustees on the 26th day of April, 1881.

"The sewers are constructed of vitrified terra-cotta pipe, made by the Potomac Terra-Cotta Company, varying in size from 8 to 24 inches, carefully laid to grade and alignment, and jointed with Portland cement.

The topography of the city made it necessary to build three principal sewers to discharge into the river. These run north and south, while all the laterals run east and west, connecting with the main sewers at the man-holes.

It was also necessary to build a special sewer to drain one depression between Market and Liberty streets and Forsyth and Monroe. The elevation of the surface of the ground, taking ordinary high water as datum, is 4½ feet on Bay street to 33 feet at the intersection of Market and Duval streets; the average height of the town above datum is about 16 feet. The area drained by the system of sewers just completed is about 270 acres, one-half of which is drained by the Pine street sewer, 24 inches, and its branches; one-fourth by Cedar street sewer, 15 inches, and its branches; and the balance by Catherine street sewer, 12 inches; and Market street, 12 inches.

The gradients of the sewers vary as follows: One foot in 300 on the 24-inch and 20-inch, 1 in 250 feet on some of the 15-inch, and 1 in 200 on some of the 12 and 15 inch, and on the laterals from 1 in 100 to 1 in 50. The average depth at which the sewers are laid is 7 feet; the extremes are 3 feet and 18 feet. Man-holes or lamp-holes were constructed at the intersection of each street, which makes them 285 feet apart on the main sewers and 385 feet on the laterals; the man-holes are built of hard brick laid in cement, 5 feet in diameter at the bottom, battered in to 20 inches at the top, and provided with cast-iron frames and ventilated covers.

The bottoms of the man-holes are of concrete, with water-ways through them 3 to 4 inches in depth, conforming to the inside perimeter of the pipe, so that when the flow is small nothing will lodge in them. Y-branches at an angle of 45 degrees to the direction of the flow were put in opposite each lot, for house connections. Catch-basins 2 by 4 in plan and 5 feet in depth, built in brick laid in cement, with a trap having a rise of 8 inches, the opening of which is located 3 feet from the bottom, so as to leave a large receptacle for sand that may be washed in from the streets, are located where the nature of the ground required it. These basins are provided with dressed bluestone covers 4 inches thick, with 20-inch man-holes cut in them, with a cast-iron cover.

The sewers on Pine and Cedar streets were laid in saturated sandy soil upon an insecure foundation, under protest from your engineer. But as the specifications for foundations were in general terms, the ground not having been thoroughly tested previous to the drawing up of the specifications, and the contractor being under guaranty for the stability of his work, the sewers were carefully examined on completion, and as a number of joints were found defective, it was decided not to accept the work until tested by the heavy rains. When the rains came on in the fall the 24 and 20 inch pipe on Pine street settled, opening the joints and allowing the sand to work into the sewer, enough to take the support from the sides of the pipe, and when the heavy storm of October came on it raised the line of saturation suddenly, causing the ground for a distance of four squares to settle down on the pipe, crushing some and fracturing nearly all the rest.

The contractor last winter took up the Pine street sewer from Forsyth to Ashley streets and put down a good plank foundation, on which the pipe was laid; after the joints had set it was concreted between the plank and pipe and upon the sides, so as to give a bearing of one-third the circumference.

The Cedar street sewer was also taken up from the river to Monroe street, and relaid on a good plank foundation, as were also most of the laterals that were in saturated ground, and I now consider them secure, so far as foundation can make them.

But as Pine street is the natural line of drainage for some hundred acres of land, 50 of which drain into the depression at the intersection of Pine and Church streets, and as the present system of sewers only received the water that finds its way over the surface to the catch-basins, the larger portion has to find its way to the river by percolating through the soil and will naturally follow the line of greatest depression and least resistance, which will be along the smooth sides of the Pine street sewer, thereby to some extent endangering its safety. This was the cause of the depressions which from time to time appeared along the line of the old brick sewer and caused For many months of the year the greater portion of about four squares of ground, at and near the intersection of Pine and Church streets, is saturated with water.

There should be a thorough system of porous tile drains put down at this point, which would lower the line of saturation some 3 or 4 feet, thereby making it more healthy, and at the same time protecting the main sewer from the danger to which it is now exposed.

There should be gutters laid where the catch-basins are in use, to keep the sand from washing into them, as it now requires considerable labor to keep them clean.

The whole system of sewers was tested before being received, by filling them with water from one manhole to another, and allowing it to stand long enough to insure their being tight; wherever leaks were found they were repaired by the contractor and the pipe again tested.

All the house connections made with the sewers thus far have been without a trap between the sewer and ventilating pipe, so as to insure good ventilation to the sewers; and, as evidence of how well it will work when more connections are made, there is now a strong indraught of air through the manhole covers in districts where there are several connections.

The ventilating pipes are of cast-iron, and are carried up to the highest point of the roof, and full size of the soil pipe. All connections with bath basins and closets are thoroughly trapped and ventilated; a grease trap is put in outside of the house, and the sink from the kitchen runs into it, and the down spouts of the house were practically discharged into a trapped gully. No sewers are laid under the house. I would recommend that an ordinance be passed embodying these points as a rule for making connections and plumbing. With well-ventilated sewers of small dimensions kept flushed, there will be no sewer gas to contend with.

Automatic flush-tanks should be put in at the head of all the main sewers and laterals, and the sewers extended to the deep water of the channel as soon as possible.

[Report of July 1, 1886.]

The sewers have been flushed and the catch-basins cleaned regularly during the year. A large amount of water has been used in flushing the sewers from the fire hydrants, and I must again urge the necessity and economy of putting in the flush-tanks at the heads of the sewers. The sewers would then be flushed automatically once or twice a day, which would keep them clean and save water and expense. The cost of cleaning and flushing for the year was $871.92.

In September, 1885, during the very excessive rains that fell that month, some 10¼ inches, the Clay-street sewer gave way between Bay and Forsyth streets. The mouth of the sewer had been obstructed for some time by the slabs, etc., put in by the Florida Railway and Navigation Company, which we had tried in vain to have removed. This obstruction caused the water to back up and start the joint, so that the sand ran into the sewer, forming cavities, and causing a heavy load of sand to fall in on the sewer and crush it. We at once dug down to the pipe and cleaned out the broken pipe and sand that had choked it, and opened up the sewer so as to let the water pass off and relieve the district flooded by the stoppage. The matter was at once reported by you to the city council, and funds asked for to repair the sewer and to put in iron pipes at the end where it passes under the railroad tracks. It was some time before this request was responded to, and the repairs were not completed until about the last of April. The sewer was found to have settled and a number of pipes broken between Bay and Forsyth streets, a distance of 250 feet, which was taken up and a good plank foundation put in, the pipes relaid and puddled around with clay. One hundred and eighty feet of 16-inch cast-iron pipe has been received to put in under the railroad tracks, and will be laid as soon as the tides will permit. The cost of the repairs and the iron pipe for the Clay-street sewer was $631.35.

The following extensions of sewers have been made: On Pine street, from Beaver to State, 560 feet of 10-inch pipe; on Cedar street, from Ashley to Union, 560 feet of 10-inch pipe; on Union, from Cedar to Pine, 1,648 feet of 8 inch pipe; on State street, from Pine to Laura, 490 feet of 8-inch pipe; on Beaver, west from Cedar, 240 feet of 8-inch pipe, making a total of 3,498 feet of sewer laid. Nine manholes were built on this line of sewer.

Some provision will have to be made for carrying off the storm waters from Bay and Forsyth streets before any more paving is done, as the present system of sewers was not designed to take the quantity that the paved street will contribute to them during heavy rains. To have done this would have made the sewers so large that it would have been impossible to have kept them clean in dry weather, and they would have become store-houses of filth.

I would therefore recommend the laying of storm-water sewers, from Forsyth street to the river direct, on Newnan, Ocean, Pine, Laura, and Hogan streets, and connecting the present catch-basins to these by large pipes beyond this point. The water can be carried to these sewers by the surface gutters.

I herewith submit, as directed, plans for sewering that portion of the city lying along the borders of Hogan's Creek too low to be reached by the present system of sewers, which have now been extended as far as possible, with the exception of a few short branches. The present system embraces all that portion of the city lying between Catherine street on the east and Clay street on the west, and between the river on the south and a line on the north beginning at the intersection of Clay and Beaver streets, east on Beaver to Cedar, north on Cedar to Union, thence east to Laura, north on Laura to State, east on State to Pine, thence south to Beaver, east on Beaver to Newnan, thence south to Ashley, thence east to Market, south on Market to Duval, east on Duval to Catherine. All of the city north of this line to the creek is to be provided for by the system now under consideration. This area, exclusive of the marsh along the borders of the creek, is equivalent to about twenty-seven city blocks, and the elevation above ordinary high water is from 1 to 25 feet. If the marshes were filled in and built upon there would be about as much more surface embraced in the drainage area. The probable amount of sewage to be disposed of will be as follows, viz: Twenty-seven blocks, averaging 18 houses to a block and 5 persons to a house, would give 27 by 18 by 5 equals 2,430 inhabitants. Allowing 30 gallons to each person, there would be 72,900 gallons of sewage to dispose of in twenty-four hours. The greater part of this has to be disposed of in twelve hours; therefore, the capacity of the sewer must be doubled to 145,800. Supposing the marshes to be built up, we would then require a capacity of 291,600 gallons, without taking in any roof water or drainage. The length of sewer required to drain this district will be about 8,428 feet, with a very slight fall, not more than 25 to the 1,000 feet. This will require a pipe about 12 inches in diameter. Having so little fall, this pipe will require flushing several times a day. This can be accomplished in two ways; one by building a dam across Hogan's Creek, raising the water 2 or 3 feet, which would give a large volume of water for flushing, but would be objectionable on account of flooding the swamp, which might be objected to by the owners; the other method, and probably the best, would be to sink an artesian well at the head of the sewer, put up a tank of, say, 20,000 gallons capacity, let the water from the well fill it, and have the tank discharged, automatically, two or three times a day by a siphon the size of the sewer, which would keep it clean. The lateral branches to this sewer will be comparatively short, and will be from 6 to 8 inches in diameter, and should have small flush-tanks at their heads. In estimating the cost of this sewer, the choice of line will make quite a difference. If it has to be laid along the existing streets (as shown by the dotted blue line on the map), the cost of laying will be double what it would be if we can get the right of way along the edge of the marsh, as shown by the solid blue line. The advantages of this latter line can be seen at a glance. It is shorter and more direct, avoiding the number of short bends that will have to be made if the streets are followed, and the amount of trenching will be lessened by half. Another point should be taken into consideration before deciding upon the size of the pipe; that is, the probable extension of the city limits, taking in the suburb of Hansontown, which is closely built up and will need sewering, and the best and cheapest way to do it will be to increase the size of the sewer now under consideration, as this is the natural line of drainage for that district. I would therefore recommend the laying of a 15-inch pipe in place of the 12-inch. The additional cost involved will only be the cost of the pipe, as the cost of trenching would be about the same with either sized pipe. I append estimates of cost by both lines; also, the additional cost of laying 15-inch pipe.

Estimated cost of out-fall sewer for the back part of the city

No. 1, by the street lines, distance 8,425 feet, average depth 10 feet:

8,428 feet of 12-inch pipe, at 38 cents	$3,201.50
Cost of trenching, back-filling, and laying	6,319.65
18 manholes	900.00
Total	10,421.15
Additional cost if 15-inch pipe is laid	1,179.50

No. 2, by the line of the marsh:

7,600 feet of 12-inch pipe	2,888.00
Cost of trenching, back-filling, and laying	3,800.00
18 manholes	900.00
Total	7,588.00
Additional cost of 15-inch pipe if laid	1,064.00
Cost of 4-inch artesian well	1,500.00
Automatic flush-tank, 20,000 gallons	300.00

Respectfully submitted.

R. N. Ellis,
City Engineer.

[Report of July 1, 1887.]

There has been no extension of the regular sewer system this year; they have been flushed regularly from the hydrants as usual and the catch-basins cleaned. The flush-tanks, which have been recommended for the heads of the sewers, from time to time, are still wanting. Manholes should be built on the Clay-street sewer and the catch-basins remodeled, as we now have much trouble keeping them free from street-wash

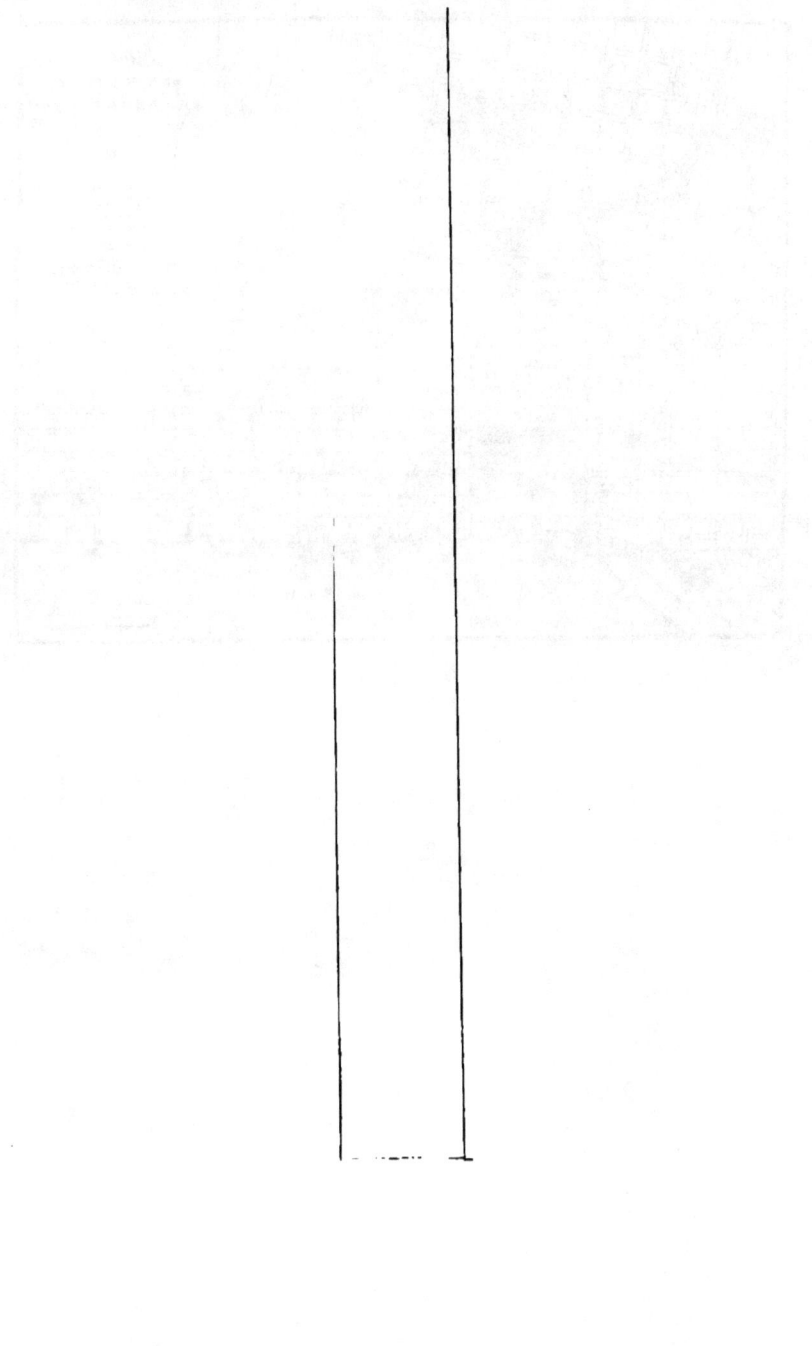

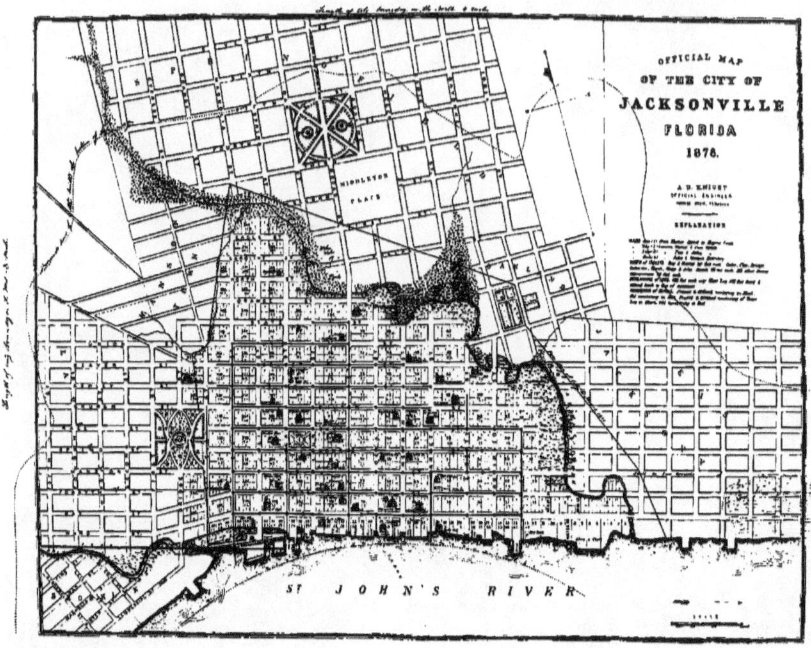
OFFICIAL MAP
OF THE CITY OF
JACKSONVILLE
FLORIDA
1878.
EXPLANATION
MIDDLETON
PLACE
ST JOHN'S RIVER

and sand, and when they get choked it is difficult to clean them. The iron pipe that was bought to extend the foot of Clay-street sewer under the Florida Railway and Navigation track has been laid, and the sewer is now in good order. The foot of the Market and Cedar street sewers are in bad condition, but cast-iron pipe, to replace the broken terra-cotta, is on hand and will be put in at once.

The Pine-street sewer should be extended to the channel along the bottom by a cast-iron pipe 24 inches in diameter at an early day, as more than half of the sewage of the city is delivered at this point, and it should be discharged into deep water where there is a strong current, which would take it away at once and not allow it to lay in the slackwater along the bulkhead, as it now does.

The other sewers should all be carried to the channel as soon as practicable. All the territory that can be drained into the present system has been reached with the exception of one block on Ashley and Church streets, between Market and Liberty streets, on which are located the grammar and high schools, and two blocks on Clay, between Church and Beaver streets, which can be reached by extending the Clay-street sewer. On one of these blocks is situated the Staunton public school. These sewers should be put in at once, to give the necessary facilities for the proper connection of the water-closets, so that the earth-closets now in use can be entirely abolished.

The city has had the storm sewers put in, recommended in my last report—a 15-inch pipe on Ocean street from Forsyth to the river, and two pipes, a 12-inch and 15-inch, on Pine street from Forsyth to the river. Three catch-basins have been built, which has relieved the paved streets of the floods caused by the rains. Two catch-basins are needed very badly at the head of Pine street to catch the water that now washes large quantities of sand into the creek. The out-fall sewer for the city, laying on the slope towards Hogan's Creek, recommended in my last report, should be put in at once, as this part of the city is now closely built up, and the only way to keep the water of the creek clean is to provide means of carrying off the sewage, and not allow it to find its way into the creek. The only safety for the health of all living on the borders of this creek is to keep its water clean. We have the example of a number of cities before us who allowed sewers and drains to empty into small streams until they became reeking cess-pools, which were only abolished after the city had been scourged by an epidemic, which cost ten times as much as the necessary sewers.

A large area is embraced within the new territory annexed to the city, and it will be necessary at once to make a comprehensive plan for draining and sewerage. There should be two or three large out-fall sewers, into which all the others should empty, placed so as to deliver the sewage at points as far removed from the center of the city as possible, and in deep water on the edge of the channel of the river; the lateral branches could then be built as required.

Respectfully submitted.

R. N. ELLIS,
City Engineer.

Incipient epidemics arrested.

Besides the places mentioned as having yellow fever, cases occurred at Callahan, Fla., Blackshear, Ga., and Uptonville, Ga. In each of these places the effective isolation of the sick and disinfection of premises of the sick, under direction of Surgeon Hutton, effectually stamped out the fever and prevented its spread.

THE OUTLOOK FOR THE FUTURE.

It was scarcely to be expected that the partisans of the *quasi moribund* National Board of Health would omit so favorable an opportunity to begin operations looking unto their restoration to the control of sanitary affairs, and with that end in view several organizations friendly to the board have passed resolutions criticizing the operations of this Bureau in Florida, and caused articles to be written setting forth that the crying need of the time is the re-instatement of the National Board of Health. The arguments have been best set forth by Dr. Bowditch, of Boston, in a communication under date of September 14, which has been reprinted as a circular and widely distributed. Dr. Bowditch begins with a statement that when the city of Memphis was stricken with a fearful epidemic of yellow fever the National Board of Health held the city surrounded by proper sanitary laws, and squelched the disease on the spot where it first showed itself in all its epidemic virulence.

The fact is that the great epidemic was in 1878. The Board of Health was not established until 1879, and the epidemic of which Dr. Bowditch speaks was the second epidemic in Memphis, and at a time when over one-half of the inhabitants were acclimated. It is probable, however, that they did good work. They certainly were not hampered by anybody, and they happened to have a resident member in Memphis. The argument is a good one to use, for this Bureau met with similar success in Brownsville in 1882, and in Pensacola in 1883.

It is stated in Dr. Bowditch's letter that the board was deprived of its funds under the "fatal influence of politics." That is not my understanding of the reason, which was that the board had mismanaged the funds intrusted to its care. This is clearly shown by the debates on the subject, and is now a matter of history. The letter is as follows:

YELLOW FEVER EPIDEMIC.—WHAT SHOULD BE DONE?—IMPERATIVE NEED OF A NATIONAL SANITARY BOARD.

To the editor of the Post:

SIR: Many years ago, when the city of Memphis was stricken with a fearful epidemic of yellow fever and the disease threatened all the States adjacent, if not the whole country, a national board of health, with full power and an ample supply of money from the United States Treasury, met the emergency vigorously and for the time being virtually held the city, and, surrounding it by proper sanitary laws, squelched the disease on the spot where it first showed itself in all its epidemic virulence. Having done this, Dr. J. S. Billings, the board's efficient agent, taught the people of Memphis how to purify themselves of the filth in which they had previously lived, all unconscious of the peril that springs from any unsanitary conditions, wherever existing.

To do all this the board needed and apparently possessed the full confidence of the nation at large, and could draw largely from funds voted by Congress.

It is greatly to be regretted that this harmonious co-operation between the board and Congress and the President was, under the fatal influences of politics, lost. The board, deprived of its funds, which were given into the hands of the United States Hospital Marine Corps, had, subsequently to its great work on the Mississippi, to resign its beneficent operations, and has been in obscurity since. Its members could not be dishonored, for they were honorable and able men. But they were virtually crushed, and all power was transferred to a body of men, most of them unknown as sanitarians. It was, as I think unwisely, argued that these gentlemen, surgeons of all the marine hospitals throughout the country, were a body fitted to cope with an outbreak of a terrible epidemic. To my mind such a proposition seemed wholly a mistaken one. How could a body, separated as the corps is into isolated positions throughout our immense domain, and with no special sanitary experience or tendencies, hope to equal in efficiency a body of experts in sanitary science, meeting in conclave at Washington, and, with eyes always open to such emergencies, able to act at once?

The bare statement of the difference between the two bodies must, I think, strike any unprejudiced mind of the real misfortune that befell the country when the change was made. And what made the matter seem worse to my mind was the rumor that the chief of the Marine Hospital Service had stated that he should not do anything in regard to malignant diseases appearing in any part of the country until he was officially informed by the executive of the State in which such disease existed that it was in an epidemic form, and therefore called for the national succor. To await for such appeal would inevitably always be too late for really efficient service.

A national sanitary board is established, or ought to be established, for the very purpose of preventing, if possible, the smallest sign of an epidemic. It would do this by summarily establishing sanitary rules of quarantine, by disinfection of the locality, and any other proper means. But what has been the fact in regard to this epidemic of yellow fever at Jacksonville? It has apparently been allowed to spread; or at least it has spread until it is seemingly beyond control. The recent sudden and melancholy death of Professor Proctor in New York is a ghastly warning to all of us. No one can foretell where the disease may hereafter show itself, for refugees from Florida may be in various parts of the country.

It becomes, therefore, the duty of every man and woman in the land to urge Congress to re-establish the National Board of Health, or at least to give us some national sanitary board, whose sole duty shall be to watch over the health of our people and to crush out immediately and with an unsparing hand even a spark of malignant disease as soon as it shows itself. Let no epidemics be allowed to go unchecked.

God grant that the National Board of Health have a new birth, and with greater powers, if need be, in the same manner as that by which our Massachusetts State board of health was regenerated after having fallen by the influence of political partisanship into hopeless imbecility and almost total disregard of sanitary work. As the Massachusetts board stands now vastly higher and has more power for good over our State than ever before, so let us hope for this nation. To gain this object the people must demand of Congress the establishment of some national sanitary authority with the fullest powers to act promptly and efficiently. Let us all take hold and help in this great cause. Every citizen should see to it that his Representative and Senators in Congress are appealed to on this grave matter. * * *

Meanwhile let us send ample help to our suffering fellow-citizens in Jacksonville. I see that our efficient mayor of Boston has established a bureau of relief at the City Hall. Let everybody send of his or her small or ample means, and thereby do a share towards the alleviation of the sufferings of the inhabitants of Jacksonville.

I remain yours, faithfully,

HENRY I. BOWDITCH.

BOSTON, *September* 14, 1888.

No bit of special pleading for a pet object could be more ingeniously constructed than this by the venerable Dr. Bowditch, but, unfortunately for the professor, the facts do not bear out the statements. In the first place, the officers of the Marine-Hospital Service pass a rigid examination in hygiene. They have charge of the maritime sanitary service, a duty for which their fitness is generally conceded. The National Board of Health never had a corps either of sanitarians or any other class. They hired men without examination to perform duty in certain localities when it was deemed expedient so to do. Does Dr. Bowditch pretend that the board had any peculiar ability to employ men? He states that the Marine-Hospital Corps has no special sanitary experience or tendencies.

The sanitary experience of the officers of this service compares very favorably with that of any of the alleged experts, and were such appointments a matter of examination as are required of the officers of the Marine-Hospital Service, the latter would have no cause to fear a competition of the sort. As a matter of fact, therefore, the officers in the Marine-Hospital Service acquire their positions after an examination in sanitary science. The National Board were not examined, no single member thereof has ever given sole attention to sanitary science, nor was any person in their employ employed by reason of having passed an examination, nor have the learned members of the board any occult wisdom. Sanitary science, so far as known, is embodied in the current literature. He further states, as a rumor, that the chief of the Marine Hospital Service had stated he should not do anything in regard to malignant diseases until informed by the executive of the State, etc., that the disease was epidemic. Dr. Bowditch need not to have stated this as a rumor. He might have stated it as a fact, for I have repeatedly announced, since the contingent fund was placed under the direction of this Bureau, that under that section of the law which forbade interference with local quarantines and local affairs, there would be no action taken in the boundaries of a State except at the request of the governor of that State. There is no law to warrant such action at this time, nor has there been in the past.

The National Board of Health never had such power as Dr. Bowditch seems to think; they never exercised any such power, and they could not have done so had they so desired. Their operations were conducted through the local boards of health in nearly every instance; either State or local board was called upon to become their almoner and executive arm. This course has this year been pursued in Florida, the result of which the good docter deprecates. The Hillsborough County board of health issued regulations concerning the management of their affairs. Dr. Wall, its president, is a man who had had years of experience and personal observation of yellow fever. In Jacksonville the Duval County board of health have had entire control of the matter until the exhaustion of their resources compelled them to ask the Government to perform the service. Any interference by this service in the operations of that board of health would have been resented, and this Bureau was not called on to exert any such interference. In no State in the Union would such interference be resented any more promptly than in the State of Massachusetts, as Dr. Bowditch can satisfy himself easily by causing the introduction of a bill turning over the quarantine of the city of Boston to the United States.

Furthermore, in my judgment, the boards of health of the several States have some duties to perform; among them the very essence of the local sanitary police is that it shall be under the control of the State board of health. When a State board of health shall require aid and assistance, then—and then only—should the Government interfere, until the laws are radically changed to put the whole work under one bureau or board, and even then no single board could be made large enough attend to all the municipal details without being unwieldy. The trouble in Florida has been all the time that there has been no State board of health. The severe lesson which that State has received, in my judgment, will be sufficient to cause the speedy establishment of a State board of health. In every State in the Union where there is a State board of health there has been little difficulty in thorough co-operation on the part of the State and national authorities whenever the occasion demanded, nor will there be in Florida when that State shall have created a State board of health. As to the regulation of interstate commerce so as to strip railroads of their power to convey disease from one State to another, there is no question of the duty of the Government in the premises, and the following bill has been prepared for the purpose of regulating that matter. Regulations framed under such a bill as this could be agreed on by the boards of health of the States affected, and enforced by the national authority.

[S. 3467. In the Senate of the United States, August 21, 1888. Mr. Harris introduced the following bill; which was read twice and referred to the Committee on Epidemic Diseases.]

A bill to prevent the introduction of contagious diseases from one State to another and for the punishment of certain offenses.

Be it enacted by the Senate and House of Representatives of the United States of America in Congress assembled, That when, in pursuance of the request of the governor of a State, the President shall, by order, direct the employment of any portion of the appropriation for the prevention of the spread of epidemic diseases within the boundaries of the said State, in the maintenance of quarantine at points of danger or otherwise, in his discretion, any officer, or person acting as an officer or agent of the United States, who shall knowingly and willfully violate any lawful order of his superior officers shall be deemed guilty of a misdemeanor, and when any such officer, or person acting as an officer or agent of the United States, shall so violate, disobey, willfully neglect to obey the order of a superior officer as to cause the extension of cholera, small-pox, yellow fever, plague, or other disease prevailing as an epidemic, such officer, or person acting as an officer or agent of the United States, shall be deemed guilty of a felony.

SEC. 2. That whenever any common carrier, through its officers, agents, or employees, shall violate any quarantine order or regulations made in accordance with the provisions of section one of this act, such officer, agent, or employee shall be deemed guilty of offense in the same degree as that defined in section one, and shall suffer the same penalty as that provided in section three of this act.

SEC. 3. That any person convicted of a misdemeanor under the provisions of this act shall forfeit and pay a fine of not less than three hundred dollars, and any person convicted of a felony shall forfeit and pay a fine of not less than three thousand dollars and suffer imprisonment at hard labor for a period of not less than one nor more than three years; and when any person in the service of the United States shall be convicted of a misdemeanor or of a felony under the provisions of this act he shall, in addition to the penalty aforesaid, be dismissed the service forthwith.

SEC. 4. That whenever it shall be made to appear to the satisfaction of the Secretary of the Treasury that any of the diseases specified in section one of this act exist in any State, and that there is danger of the spread of such disease by the usual channels of transportation to other States, he is authorized to adopt such rules and regulations as, in his judgment, may be necessary in order to prevent the spread thereof from one State to another, and to employ such inspectors and other persons as may be necessary for the purpose aforesaid, and any person who shall knowingly disobey or violate any order, rule, or regulation made by the Secretary of the Treasury pursuant to the authority herein conferred shall be deemed guilty of a misdemeanor, punishable by a fine of not less than five hundred dollars and by imprisonment for a period of not less than one year.

The lack of power to control municipal authorities, deprecated by Dr. Bowditch, is doubtless inherent in our system of government, but we have only to go to France to find that a board *Du Commité Consultatif d' hygiene publique de France* have reported a similar difficulty as late as the year 1887. The following extract from that report is inserted:

[Translation.]

The committee is not unaware, however, that in the propagation of imported epidemics and of those which originate on our own soil insalubrious conditions play an important part. It endeavors to realize the second term of the problem—the sanitation of our towns and country. Here the difficulties are great. Present legislation does not permit us to impose the most elementary measures of sanitation on a town or village. In spite of the efforts of the committee, Toulon and Marseilles are in very nearly the same state of insalubrity as in 1884, when they were ravaged during two successive years by cholera.

The New Hampshire State board of health subsequent to the quarantine in the year 1886, published a report criticising in an extremely harsh manner the operations of the service in the management of the Canadian quarantine. As usual, this criticism was directed for the purpose of rehabilitation of the National Board of Health. During the last winter, when a proposition to establish a bureau of health on a somewhat similar basis as the National Board of Health was broached, the New Hampshire board of health, or some person connected therewith, caused to be prepared a circular containing the whole or an extract from the report on this subject. A synopsis was also also issued in circular form and sent to various members of Congress. As there were many errors of statement in it, and its evident purpose was to misrepresent the facts, I referred it to Surgeon Austin, who had immediate charge of the measures against small-pox, for reply. His reply is printed herewith, from which it appears that not only was there scant co-operation on the part of the New Hampshire board of health, but its secretary seemed to try how not to co-operate with the Government service:

U. S. MARINE-HOSPITAL SERVICE,
DISTRICT OF THE GREAT LAKES,
Chicago, Ill., Surgeon's Office, June 25, 1888.

SIR: I have the honor to acknowledge the receipt of your letter of the 3d instant, transmitting the Annual Report of the State Board of Health of New Hampshire, and directing my attention to the numerous aspersive statements relative to the United States sanitary inspection service, organized on the Canadian frontier of

Vermont in the year 1885, for the prevention of the introduction of small-pox into the United States from Canada.

I must admit a degree of surprise when reading to-day for the first time so extensive a report upon the work performed by the United States sanitary inspectors, as for some reason I have not been favored with a copy until now. Of the forty or more pages devoted to the small-pox epidemic a large part can be credited with denunciation of the inspection service *in toto* with a special aim at its head, the Surgeon-General of the Marine-Hospital Service.

So severe and sweeping an arraignment of this service, for dereliction of duty, by the secretary of the board, who by an assumption of superior wisdom, discernment, and skill, which we are to infer were born of a wide experience in the management of railroad quarantines, warrants a reply.

First. I wish to invite your attention particularly to what appears to me to be the chief factor of criticism after a careful perusal of his report. I refer to certificates of inspection of passengers and baggage. On nearly every page of the report which refers to the inspection service, this is the substance of the complaint for which he denounces the service as being absolutely inefficient and its work *nil*. Other severe censures on the service are made which will be noticed, but let us examine first the evidence which he furnishes to prove the inspection service absolutely inefficient and worthless. On page 116 of his report, in a letter to Surgeon Austin, he requests, 'that some ticket system be at once adopted." On page 120 of the report, Dr. G. P. Conn, president of the board, in a letter to Surgeon Austin, says: "As your inspector did not give the passenger anything by which he could prove that he had been properly inspected, your work was *nil* so far as the public was concerned." Page 127 of report, in reported interview with Surgeon Austin, the secretary of the State board says: "First, that there was imperative necessity that Government inspectors should issue inspection tickets to all persons examined by them." Page 131, in a letter to Surgeon Austin, he states: "The report of George Cook, inspector for this board, for yesterday, October 20, shows that he inspected 111 passengers from Canada, who were supposed to have been examined by the inspector in your department, and of this number 4 had small-pox, 34 were in possession of physician's certificates, 10 had certificates issued by your inspector, and 44 had no certificate whatever. Passengers arrive in this State almost or quite daily over the Passumpsic Railroad via Sherbrook without any inspectors' or physicians' certificates. In some instances your inspectors do not give a certificate to those that they vaccinate. From these facts, which are daily demonstrated, it is evident that as yet a thorough reliance can not be placed in the protection which your service is supposed and is expected to give to the New England States against the introduction of small-pox from the infected districts in Canada.

Again, on page 142 by the secretary, the report is as follows: "The result of the thorough work done by Inspector Cook shows that not one-third of the passengers coming from Canada during the period of his inspection service possessed inspectors, tickets or showed any evidence of having been examined by an inspector. Moreover, it demonstrates the wisdom of not relying upon the Government service to protect New Hampshire interests."

I have cited only a few of the many paragraphs of like nature, but enough to show the kind of evidence adduced to prove that the United States inspection service was absolutely worthless and inefficient, and its work *nil*. By those who are familiar with railway quarantine service it is only necessary to point to this peculiar style of argument to convince them that it is worthless, unreliable, and in fact no argument whatever against the efficiency of the inspection service. But I propose to show conclusively to any honest minded intelligent person that his conclusions and declarations relative to the inspection service are false, misleading, and a calumny upon each sanitary inspector and medical officer connected with this service. Inspection of trains by the United States sanitary inspectors did not begin until the evening of

September 29, 1885, and not about September 25, as stated on page 112 of his report. Therefore it will be seen that inspections made by the New Hampshire board from September 25 to October 1, as stated by the secretary, could not "Have convinced us that no efficient work was being done or was likely to be done for some time." At Island Pond, Vt., the inspector did not receive his instructions or vaccine virus until October 4, which was entirely due to the delay of the mails, as the instructions to inspectors and vaccine virus was mailed to inspectors at Saint Albans, Rouse's Point, Richford, Newport, and Island Pond, from Burlington, the same date, September 29, 1885. Before the work of inspection of trains could be properly commenced it was necessary for me to visit the border towns where it was proposed to establish inspection stations to secure the services of reliable physicians to act as inspectors, and to arrange for a building or car to be used for the disinfection of baggage. Also to employ men to handle baggage to be opened, fumigated, and reshipped. This work could not all be performed in the five towns in various parts of the State in one day, but it was accomplished by night and day work, in a little less than four days. During this time regulations for the guidance of inspectors were prepared, and each inspector furnished with a copy. In point of time in the establishment of these stations it appears to me that this ought to satisfy any unprejudiced mind. Now, one word in regard to the selection of medical inspectors. Vermont had no State board of health to suggest the names of competent physicians, and the advice and recommendations relative to this was asked of Dr. A. P. Grinnell, dean of the faculty medical department, University of Vermont, Dr. Joseph Lindsley, health officer of Burlington, and Dr. Fassett, of Saint Albans, Vt., and appointments made accordingly. Two inspectors were appointed from Saint Albans, Vt., both reputable practitioners of medicine in that city; one formerly an Army surgeon who had had large experience in the management of small-pox cases in hospitals and in camp. Two inspectors were appointed from Richford, both reputable practitioners of that town; one whose experience in the management of small-pox epidemics is second to none in the State, and who is at present a member of the State board of health recently organized.

One inspector was appointed from Newport. He is a reputable practitioner in that town, engaged in a large practice. From Island Pond one inspector was at first appointed. He was a practitioner in good standing in that place. A second inspector was some weeks afterwards appointed from Maine to assist the inspector at Island Pond upon the recommendation of the Maine State board of health. One of the instructors in the medical department University of Vermont, was appointed from Burlington to act as inspector at Rouse's Point. The French language was fluently spoken by five of the above inspectors, which was considered valuable for this service. The physicians selected for this duty do not require any eulogy at my hands, their standing with the profession and the community is established, but I wish to say that I have no reason to doubt either their ability or integrity. They were competent, and it would have been difficult to obtain men better qualified for this work. The necessity of commencing the quarantine of the stations mentioned on the same date, and that the regulations for all should be uniform, is obvious. Had we commenced the inspection of trains at Saint Albans before we did at Newport or Rouse's Point it would simply have diverted travel from the first to the roads last mentioned, caused dissatisfaction and antagonism of the railroad companies, and given no protection whatever. Each inspector had been given verbal instructions relative to the method of inspection of trains and the fumigation of baggage; a request made of the railroad companies for co-operation; a car or room secured for the fumigation of baggage, or at one or two stations where the chief railroad officer could not be seen at this time, the inspector was instructed to obtain a car or room of the railroad company for this purpose; vaccine virus and a copy of the regulations furnished to the inspectors at the five stations mentioned. All of this accomplished on the evening of September 29, 1885. I find in the secretary's report, page 126, this statement: "The instructions to inspectors were explicit in ordering fumigation of baggage, but none of the inspectors received any instruction as to how the work was to be done, nor were they provided with any means for doing the same." Part of this statement only is true (instructions to inspectors were explicit in ordering the fumigation of baggage), the balance is false. When I made my first visit to the stations, before quarantine was commenced, the manner of fumigating baggage was explained to each inspector, and although it was impossible for me to remain at each station until a building was built, a room in the depot or a freight car was requested from the station agent, and the same I believe was granted at each station until buildings were built at the different stations. I do not deny that the advice of the secretary was asked by the United States inspector, and that it was given relative to the plan for a smoke-house, as all inspectors were requested to show especial attention and courtesy to the New Hampshire board of health, and to render them any information or assistance within their power. The plan was worthy the architect, and the inspector was most fortunate in securing advice of one having *le savoir faire* to design such a building. In the secretary's reported interview with me at White River Junction, page 127, the first statement "He succeeded in making an appointment with me at White River Junction" is true. I left my work on the frontier for a day and went to White River Junction to confer with the secretary at his request. That he represented to me that there was imperative necessity that the Government inspectors should issue inspection tickets to all persons examined by them is true, likewise his statements relative to revaccination and physicians' certificate, and fumigation of baggage. But that I admitted that all of these defects existed in our service is not true. I informed the secretary that all our inspectors were doing good work, and could be relied upon. I informed him that we were disinfecting all baggage coming from Montreal; that upon careful inquiry by the custom inspectors as well as the sanitary inspectors all baggage was considered infected or likely to be infected. At this time all Montreal baggage was not disinfected by our inspectors. I did not consider it necessary, and had issued no such instructions.

From the secretary's letter to United States Sanitary Inspector A. P. Hall, dated October 19, one week later, page 129, it will be seen the secretary did not consider it necessary to fumigate all Montreal baggage. He inquires, "To what extent is fumigation now carried out; is all baggage from Montreal except that of pleasure travelers and business men, who would not probably visit an infected district, fumigated at Saint Albans? It seems to me that among the laboring classes there is no way to make any distinction as regards fumigation."

I have to confess that this was not the method or rule which was adopted to determine whether baggage was infected. I went to Montreal for the express purpose to arrange some plan to aid the inspectors in ascertaining what baggage was liable to be infected. The health authorities of the provinces of Quebec and Ontario, having inspectors in the city of Montreal, were requested to furnish us with such information as they could relative to persons leaving the city for the United States. The United States consul consented to furnish certificates relative to baggage when possible. The United States custom inspector who had been on duty at the Bonaventure depot in Montreal for many years, and who is thoroughly acquainted in the city, was requested to inform himself relative to passengers and baggage bound for the United States and report on his customs manifest of baggage, or otherwise to the sanitary inspectors. Each United States customs inspector on the several roads leaving Montreal bound for the United States were also requested to obtain whatever knowledge they could relative to baggage and persons, and inform the sanitary inspectors. In their inspection of the contents of trunks and other baggage they would determine the character of baggage—whether the trunks contained articles of bedding or clothing which was not clean.

Information furnished our sanitary inspectors through these various channels was most valuable. A large quantity of baggage from the towns of the Provinces of Ontario and Quebec, bound for the United States, had to be rechecked at Montreal. An arrangement was made with the passenger agent at the Bonaventure depot, Montreal, to place a check upon such baggage, so that the sanitary inspectors would know where it came from. The method, although having some distinctive features from the one suggested by the secretary, was the one all adopted, and it furnished our inspectors reliable information in regard to a large part of the baggage requiring their judgment and decision as to the necessity for disinfection. In regard to physicians' certificates of vaccination presented by passengers, I have to state that it was made the subject of a paragraph in the first regulations, and each inspector was cautioned by me when I first visited the station not to receive such certificates unless they believed them to be reliable. Physicians' certificates, or certificates of persons signing as physicians, were refused by our inspectors every day, and on almost every train. Several physicians were prosecuted in Montreal for issuing false certificates to travelers, upon information furnished the provincial board by our inspectors. Many of the physicians of Montreal and of the Province of Quebec were personally known by our inspectors and their certificates were honored. Until November 1 the sanitary inspectors were authorized to exercise their judgment in regard to baggage that, from the various means provided, and from positive evidence which the passengers themselves might furnish, they were not absolutely certain was free from infection. The epidemic had reached such proportions in Montreal that it was considered unsafe to pass any baggage starting from Montreal, hence an order was issued to each inspector to fumigate all Montreal baggage coming to the United States. The fumigation of the baggage was done under the immediate supervision of the inspector. Men to handle the baggage, open, repack, and reship it, were employed at each station by the Government, and they were subject to the order of the sanitary inspectors.

Upon personal inspection of the several stations at different times I found the disinfection buildings full of baggage, trunks empty, clothing hung up or spread out upon lattice work, and the rooms dense with the fumes of sulphur. The secretary states, page 135 of his report, relative to my order to inspectors to fumigate all Montreal baggage, and cautioning inspectors against fraudulent certificates of vaccination, that the "order was significant by indirectly admitting that the inspection service was very far from being perfect even at this late date." The inference is entirely incorrect, and the secretary was in position to know this better than any one else. I had been absent from Vermont more than two weeks organizing inspection stations along the New York frontier. Upon my return to Burlington I found a letter from the secretary criticising our inspectors for not issuing certificates, and intimating that our inspectors passed without inspection passengers upon the presentation of fraudulent certificates, and that baggage was not disinfected as it should be. The order to inspectors was issued, upon the receipt of this letter, before I had visited the stations after my return from New York, and there was nothing whatever new in the order, except that relative to the fumigation of baggage. The secretary knew that this order was issued upon the receipt of his letter, and before I had inspected the stations, as a copy of the order was sent to him on the same date it was issued, with a letter of transmittal informing him of the fact. A copy of my letter is published in his report, page 134. The secretary reaches his highest point of criticism in his poetic description of a label pasted on baggage that had been disinfected. There were three letters which the secretary did not understand; hence he translates "Grand idiotic display." As I was not the author of the label I can claim no credit for it, but I will say that the man who originated it showed more wisdom than he who suggested the labeling baggage "fumigated." The latter label would be removed by the passenger who did not care to travel with baggage thus marked. Such a label upon trunks would excite the suspicion of the public and be very annoying to the traveler. The label used by our inspectors was made similar to an express time label, although distinctive, and the secretary was informed that when used it denoted baggage fumigated. That was all it meant, and the public were not alarmed or the traveler annoyed. Now, in regard to the inspection and vaccination of passengers on the trains, it will be observed that the regulation first issued to our inspectors relative to the vaccination of passengers, which was their orders and authority for this work, was clear and concise, leaving only such matter as was thought necessary to the professional judgment of the inspector. This was the regulation: "All persons bound for the United States, coming from Montreal or other places in Canada where small-pox prevails, must produce satisfactory evidence to the inspector that they are protected by a recent vaccination or submit to this operation before they are allowed to cross the boundary line. Inspectors will vaccinate all unprotected persons free of charge." That this work was properly, thoroughly, and conscientiously performed by each inspector I can testify from a personal knowledge obtained from frequent visits to the different stations and making the inspection of passengers on the trains coming from Montreal with the sanitary inspectors. Trains were stopped and passengers who would not submit to vaccination were put off in Canada by our inspectors. The highways crossing the frontier were watched for such persons and one man who had been put off the train and who was determined to come into the States without being vaccinated was arrested by one of our inspectors and locked up. He was given the alternative of being vaccinated or returning to Canada by train, when he chose the former and was released.

The only evidence which could be properly considered as such. submitted by the secretary in his report, relative to the inspection of passengers by our inspectors is that of George Cook, sanitary inspector for the New Hampshire board of health. It appears from the report, page 141, that Dr. Cook visited Saint Albans to see the work of inspection as performed by our inspectors. I will simply quote his report made to the New Hampshire board of health after a personal inspection. "On my return the same night I met one of the Government inspectors and had a chance to see the method used in inspecting passengers. Every one was examined and if not recently vaccinated as shown by personal examination of the arm they were vaccinated before they were allowed to enter the United States. I am sure the inspectors were very painstaking and careful that no guilty man should escape." Now we will turn to page 142 of the secretary's report, commencing on the fourth line will be found the following comment by the secretary, written after Dr. Cook had made his report. "The result of the thorough work done by Inspector Cook shows that not one-third of the passengers coming from Canada during the period of his inspection service possessed inspector's tickets, *or showed any evidence of having been examined by an inspector.*" Italics mine. What meaning did the secretary intend to convey to his readers by this last clause "or showed any evidence of having been examined by an inspector." Did he not wish it to be understood that he believed they had not been seen by a Government inspector. That was what I understood it to mean. From the context, page 141, it is evident that this is his meaning. He says, "A glance at the table rendered in the inspector's report show that the Government service in the inspection of passengers did not even approximate good work until about three months after the service was established." Doctor Cook, his own inspector of passengers, made after a personal examination about seven weeks after our inspection began, states conclusively that the work was well and thoroughly performed. But the furnishing passengers with a ticket and the labeling their traveling bags "fumigated" was the thing devoutly to be wished. In the mind of the secretary this is sanitary inspection of passengers; that there was a peculiar virtue in the ticket that would prevent the passenger from having small-pox conveying it to others. In other words, without tickets there was no sanitary inspection.

I will not criticise the secretary's ticket, which we finally adopted at his request, only to state that it had more letters upon it than our label, and that it was considered unnecessary by other State boards of health with which I had conferred. Four-fifths of the tickets furnished passengers were not seen by any health officer. Passengers frequently threw their inspection ticket away knowing that it would not be required at their destinations, as the trains were inspected in very few cities. I saw this done on several occasions when making inspection of trains with our inspectors. I had occasion to pass through New Hampshire several times during the time of the epidemic. I did not see any sanitary inspector or health officer to whom I could give a certificate of inspection. In a careful and conscientious review of this whole subject I know of but one just complaint which the secretary has any right to make against our service. In conference with the secretary at White River Junction, October 13, upon his request, I promised him that I would recommend that his inspection certificate be adopted by our service and furnished to passengers by our inspectors. The blanks were recommended, and a limited supply sent out by the Department, which was soon exhausted. The second day after my conference with the secretary I was ordered by telegraph to New York to organize the inspection stations there and did not get back to the Vermont stations for over two weeks; during a part of this time the inspectors had been without certificates, except those which they had had printed themselves and for which the Government re-imbursed them. I again made requisition for a quantity of these blanks, but there was a little delay in receiving them from the Department. When they arrived, each inspector was requested to give a certificate to each person inspected. There was no intentional slight of the secretary's request; *au contraire,* I was particularly anxious to please him, and had I not been called away just at this time, certificates would have been issued regularly to passengers who had been inspected. The delay was not great when the remedy was applied, and the matter was explained to the secretary. Another vulnerable point in the secretary's criticism is the employment of an inspector to report upon the efficiency of our service, the continuance and pay of said inspector to depend entirely upon his report His judgment may have been somewhat prejudiced by his interest. No task is so difficult as to please those who do not wish to be pleased. The secretary was opposed from the beginning to the United States Marine-Hospital Service establishing a quarantine on the frontier, and did all that was possible in his position to throw discredit upon the inspection service during the epidemic. Of the facts, I have abundant proof furnished me by men who are well known to the profession and whose integrity has never been questioned. Reports were given to the public by the New Hampshire board during the epidemic derogatory to our service. Press reports carping at the service were furnished from Concord, and letters were written censuring other State boards of health for requesting Government aid and co-operation of the Marine-Hospital Service. This was the spirit of co-operation we encountered from the New Hampshire board of health, and I believe was the animus of the secretary's report. From the statistics compiled from the several reports of sanitary inspectors at the five quarantine stations before mentioned, New York and Maine stations not included, which were published in the Annual Report of the Supervising Surgeon-General Marine-Hospital Service 1886, the evidence is conclusive that the sanitary inspection by the Government was not only not "worthless," but a great work which probably prevented the spread of small-pox to the United States: Seven thousand seven hundred and ninety-six passengers were vaccinated aboard trains; fifteen persons found aboard the trains bound for the United States suffering from small-pox were placed in quarantine or sent back to their place of departure; three thousand four hundred and ninety-four pieces of baggage were fumigated; and eleven passengers sent back who would not submit to vaccination. All medical men recognize the fact that any railroad quarantine consistant with free intercourse or non-detention of passengers, however perfect it may be in method or detail, can not give absolute immunity against the spread of small-pox. But what were the results that warranted such malevolent condemnation by the secretary.

The quarantine was a pronounced success, as very few cases of small-pox occurred in the United States after it was established. In the State of Maine not one case of small-pox occurred during the year. In New Hampshire no cases occurred after our quarantine was established. In the State of Vermont I heard of only one case after the quarantine was established. In Massachusetts there were but four cases more than occur every year in this State. A careful examination of reports of State and municipal boards of health in New York and New England, so far as I was able to obtain them at the time, revealed the fact that not one case of small-pox occurred in New York or in the New England States after the Government quarantine was established, that was reported to be due to infected baggage from Canada and coming to the United States by railroads. One case reported at Spa, N. Y., where there is a paper-mill, and where rags are received from all over the country, is an exception.

The success of the Government quarantine was admitted by other State boards of health and many municipal boards, and letters to that effect were written to me at that time that were forwarded to your office with other papers relative to the quarantine. Press or other copies of my letters to inspectors and to health boards were not made, and writing at this late date without any of the papers or records of the service, except the short report of the inspection service, which I made shortly after quarantine was raised, has made it necessary for me to omit much important evidence, and be extremely guarded in my statements to avoid errors and to make a fair and honest reply to the criticisms found in the report.

Very respectfully, your obedient servant,

H. W. AUSTIN,
Surgeon, U. S. M. H. S.

J. B. HAMILTON,
Surgeon-General M. H. S., Washington, D. C.

There is one fact connected with the proposition to re-establish the National Board of Health, or a "Bureau of Health," that is deserving of consideration, and that is the fact that for the proper administration of the maritime quarantine it is absolutely necessary that the reports from foreign countries and sanitary reports generally be received at the central office of administration of the quarantine, so that early action may be taken upon such information whenever it is of a character to require it, and there is no doubt that the quarantine system would be materially weakened by the taking away of the publication of the Abstract as at present issued, and it must be admitted that nobody is so well adapted for the proper conduct of the maritime quarantine as a body of active officers who have been engaged constantly in sanitary work for almost a decade, and thoroughly disciplined in the performance of their duties; any change just as the work has become systematized and the national quarantine laws perfected, would be disastrous to the best interests of the country.

MARINE HOSPITALS.

The several marine hospitals have been generally improved during the past year, and the number of patients, as will be seen by the report, is greater than in any previous year, there being an increase of more than 3,000 over the previous year.

Hospital at Baltimore, Md.

This is a new hospital, and only slight repairs have been required during the year. The approaches have been completed.

Hospital at Boston, Mass.

[Report of Surgeon Fairfax Irwin.]

The arches in the hall-ways of the first and second floors, which had become sprung and in danger of falling, were torn out and replaced. Tile floors were relaid on east and west verandas. All the chimneys were repointed and repaired. Tile relaid in bath-rooms on second and third floors. Foundations of outbuildings repaired. A new chimney on porter's lodge. The arches under verandas were pointed and white-washed. An unused iron fence with gates was moved from rear of hospital to front entrance and there erected in place of old wooden one. The entire roof main building was repaired and painted. Gutters and spouts repaired wherever needed; new tin roofs put on north, east, and west verandas. Eight new soap-stone laundry tubs with hot and cold water connections were put in. One new water-closet put in basement and one new one on first floor. General repairs to plumbing made wherever needed. The flagstaff was removed from top of building and a new one erected on grounds opposite center of south front. Entire new woodwork to veranda roofs north and east sides. Partitions of three small rooms southwest corner third floor were removed and made into one apartment for operation-room. Stormhouses were erected over all outside doors first floor. New floors on portion main hall second floor, entire main hall third floor, and three large wards were laid down with new stairway from kitchen to dining-room in south wing. The porter's lodge was reshingled. The stable floor was repaired; new sash-cords put in throughout building. The steward's dining-room was divided by lath and plaster partition to make an additional bedroom. Screen partitions were erected in bath rooms second and third floors, around bath tubs. The kitchen, operation-room, medical officer's and stewards' quarters were painted and calcimined where needed. A large amount of broken window-glass was reset. The heating apparatus received only temporary repairs during the year. A new boiler house is in course of construction which is expected to be ready for use before cold weather.

Hospital at Cairo, Ill.

The hospital buildings at this station are in good condition; repairs of a minor character have been made during the year.

Hospital at Chicago.

Four additional globe ventilators upon the roof over the wards, and eight Tuttle and Bailey registers put in to ventilate stair-ways leading to the wards. New wire screens have been put in all windows in the basement and first floor of the hospital, and in the windows of the second and third floor stories of the main building. There were four upper wards left unscreened, which work should be done at as early a date as possible to insure comfort to patients. A Hyatt filter that will deliver

37,440 gallons of water per hour, and filters all the lake water that is used in the hospital, is a valuable improvement. Considerable repairs have been made to the steam-heating apparatus. The boilers have been relined, horizontal supply and return pipes made new, all steam-valves in the building replaced with new ones, and the engine-house enlarged to accommodate a third boiler, and other minor repairs. The heating apparatus is now in good condition.

The steam laundry has been improved by the addition of one brass cylinder washing-machine, one mangle, and one shirt-ironer. The laundry is in good condition and quite complete. Minor repairs have been made to plumbing in the hospital, which is now in good condition. A new plank roadway from the front of the grounds to the engine-house has been constructed and a board walk laid from the main building to the barn. Minor repairs have been made to the electric bells, but further repairs are needed. Iron fire-escapes have been placed from the roof to the ground at each end of the building.

Four new iron hitching posts were erected and repairs made to the sewer. The buildings now are in excellent sanitary condition, and with the exception of inside painting are in good repair. All interior walls of central building should be painted. The grounds have not been improved since the building was built, and they are but sand hills. A new fence should be built and also a porter's lodge at the entrance gate. I understand that Congress has made an appropriation for this work.

Hospital at Cincinnati, Ohio.

New floors to front and rear porch of executive building and a new sky-light have been provided during the year, and the buildings are now in good condition.

Hospital at Detroit, Mich.

The improvements made in this building during the year included extensive repairs to verandas, repairs to furnace-room, new laundry tubs, repairs to plumbing, and painting and calcimining the interior of the building. The hospital accommodations at this station are inadequate for the requirements of the port, and the recommendation that an additional building be provided is respectfully renewed.

Hospital at Evansville, Ind.

An act of Congress establishing a marine hospital at Evansville has been passed, and a board was appointed by the Secretary of the Treasury to select the site. Final action has not been taken on the report of the board at this date.

Hospital at Key West.

Repairs of a minor character only have been made during the year. The hospital is in excellent condition.

Hospital at Louisville, Ky.

Repairs to plumbing and drainage pipes have been made, and hospital is now in fair condition.

Hospital at Memphis, Tenn.

The buildings at this station have been painted throughout and the plumbing and drainage pipes repaired, but the necessity still exists for the construction of a retaining-wall to prevent further erosions on the grounds, and the recommendation made in my annual report for last year is respectfully renewed.

Mobile, Ala.

Minor repairs only have been made. The hospital is in good condition.

Hospital at New Orleans, La.

[From report of Surgeon Goldsborough.]

Repairs to roof of surgeons' quarters, and galleries connecting ward. New sidewalks; grounds improved.

The water-tank was thoroughly cleaned, and raised 12 feet.

A Hyatt filter, capable of filtering 20,000 gallons of water, was purchased.

Fire-plug, with 1½ and 2½ inch hose connections.

An ambulance shed, 20 by 23 feet, was built adjoining the barn.

The water-closets in both white and colored wards repaired and put in good order.

Hospital at Portland, Me.

New storm doors, laundry tubs, and repairs of a minor character have been made. Repairs to roof and other improvements are still necessary.

Hospital at Port Townsend, W. T.

Repairs to medical officers' quarters, to patients' dining-room, a new picket fence, and a new wooden ventilator to the building have been provided, and the hospital is now in fair condition.

Hospital at Saint Louis, Mo.

[Report of Surgeon John Vansant.]

Roof of large old brick building repaired, under authority of Department letters, at cost of $24.90.

New roof on stable and other repairs thereto, done by contract, cost $120. Roof of large, old brick building more thoroughly repaired, under contract, cost $133. January 12, 1888.

Hospital at San Francisco, Cal.

[Report of Surgeon H. W. Sawtelle.]

One ward painted inside, including two ward floors and hall floor of executive building. Kitchen and dining-rooms painted inside, also eight rooms in quarters. Two halls and eight rooms kalsomined. Broken plastering in wards and kitchen repaired. New zinc flashing for veranda roof. New lattice for open spaces between veranda floors and ground. Roofs of engine-house, stable, and veranda reshingled and painted with mineral paint. Worn-out flooring in dining-room, hall, store-room, kitchen, and veranda repaired.

Repairs to heating apparatus.—Provision was made to furnish hot water for the wards. A water heater and iron-clad boiler, with a capacity of 60 and 80 gallons, connected and put up complete, was placed in a small room at the rear of each ward which affords an abundance of hot water. Hot and cold water was also provided for the operation room. A large porcelain bowl, set in a cedar closet with a marble top, was placed in position and necessary water connections made. One double sink for dish-washing constructed for pantry, and connections made for hot and cold water. The broken brick-work in the spaces around the ward heaters was replaced by encaustic tiling; the same for floors under ward urinals. Two Egyptian marble slabs were fitted to the walls around each ward urinal. Five terra-cotta chimneys, tops and caps, for kitchen and officers' quarters. Repairs to hood over kitchen range. Two cylinder stoves complete for assistant surgeon's quarters. In addition to the foregoing authorized work, many minor repairs were made by hospital attendants during the year.

Hospital at Vineyard Haven, Mass.

Repairs of a minor character only have been made during the year. The hospital is kept in good condition by the labor of the employés, but additional ground is necessary to make further improvements.

Hospital at Wilmington, N. C.

Repairs to plumbing, new water-closets, and new laundry tubs have been supplied; the basement of the building replastered and painted, and the stable and out-buildings painted. Further repairs are necessary, and the recommendation that a separate building be provided for officers' quarters, so as to allow greater ward capacity in the hospital proper, is respectfully renewed.

HOSPITALS NEEDED.

The necessity for the establishment of a marine hospital at New York is not less urgent now than in former years. As the reasons have been given in former reports, in detail, and reiterated, I can not at this time urge any additional reason to those heretofore stated, but it does seem singular that at this, the largest port in the country, it should have been found impossible to have a marine hospital established, while no such difficulty exists regarding the establishment of hospitals at ports of minor importance. A marine hospital at the port of Philadephia and one at Norfolk would be very advantageous to the service, and of great benefit to the sailors.

CONTRACTS FOR THE CARE OF SEAMEN.

The following contracts for the care of seamen entitled to relief from this service for the fiscal year ending June 30, 1889, were published for the information of accounting officers of the Treasury Department, disbursing agents, medical officers of the Marine Hospital Service, and customs officers. Charges are allowed only for actual time in hospital. The right is reserved by the Secretary of the Treasury to terminate any contract whenever the interests of the service require it. All relief must be furnished in accordance with the Revised Regulations approved 1885, and subsequent circulars.

Albany, N. Y.—The medical attendance to be furnished by an acting assistant surgeon; the Albany Hospital to furnish quarters, subsistence, nursing, and medicines, at $1 per day.

Alexandria, Va.—The medical attendance to be furnished by an acting assistant surgeon; Alexandria Infirmary to furnish quarters, subsistence, nursing, and medicines, at 90 cents per day.

Apalachicola, Fla.—Dr. J. D. Rush to furnish medical attendance and medicines, at $45 per month; Martha Campbell to furnish quarters, subsistence, and nursing, at $1 per day, and to provide for the burial of deceased patients, at $12.50 each.

Ashtabula, Ohio.—The medical attendance to be furnished by an acting assistant surgeon; Mrs. Henry Whelpley to furnish quarters, subsistence, and nursing, at $1 per day; contagious diseases, $1.50 per day. Patients requiring long-continued treatment will be furnished transportation to Cincinnati, Ohio; Sanders & Clover to provide for the burial of deceased patients, at $15 each.

Astoria, Oregon.—J. Frank Page, M. D., to furnish quarters, subsistence, nursing, medical attendance, and medicines at 95 cents per day; B. B. Franklin to provide for the burial of deceased patients, at $15 each.

Baltimore, Md.—Hospital patients to be cared for in the United States Marine Hospital; George Rinehart to provide for the burial of deceased patients, at $9.50 each.

Bangor, Me.—The medical attendance to be furnished by an acting assistant surgeon; Preble & Kanaley to furnish quarters, subsistence, and nursing, at $1 per day; Abel Hunt to provide for burial of deceased patients, at $10 each.

Barnstable, Mass, and subports.—Medical attendance and medicines to be furnished at Barnstable by Dr. G. W. Kelley, at $8 per month; at Chatham, by Dr. B. D. Gifford, at $12.50 per month; at Dennis, by Dr. H. S. Kelley, jr. at $45 per month; at Hyannis, by Dr. G. W. Kelley, at $38 per month; at Provincetown, by Dr. W. W. Gleason, at $12 per month; at Wellfleet, by Dr. William N. Stone, at $12.50 per month. Seamen applying for relief at Wood's Holl will be sent to the marine hospital at Vineyard Haven.

Bath, Me.—The medical attendance to be furnished by an acting assistant surgeon; William J. Howard to furnish quarters, subsistence, and nursing, at $1 per day; John M. Clark to provide for the burial of deceased patients, at $14 each. Cases requiring long-continued treatment will be furnished transportation to the United States Marine Hospital at Portland, Me.

Belfast, Me.—The medical attendance to be furnished by an acting assistant surgeon; John Dolloff to furnish quarters, subsistence, and nursing, at $1.25 per day.

Bismarck, Dak.—The medical attendance to be furnished by an acting assistant surgeon; quarters, subsistence, and nursing to be furnished by Sister Regina Otto, at 90 cents per day.

Boston, Mass.—Hospital patients to be cared for in the United States Marine Hospital at Chelsea, Mass.; burial of deceased patients at the hospital cemetery; burial of foreign patients, $10 each.

Bridgeport, Conn.—Quarters, subsistence, nursing, medical attendance, and medicines, to be furnished by the Bridgeport Hospital, at $1 per day; D. C. Peck, agent, to provide in like manner for small-pox patients, at $20 per week; John Cullinan to provide for the burial of deceased patients, at $15 each.

Brunswick, Ga.—The medical attendance to be furnished by an acting assistant surgeon; W. A. Holland to furnish quarters, subsistence, and nursing, at 80 cents per day; Moore & Valentino to provide for the burial of deceased patients, at $20 each.

Buffalo, N. Y.—The medical attendance to be furnished by a medical officer of the Marine Hospital Service; the Buffalo Hospital (Sisters of Charity) to furnish quarters, subsistence, nursing, and medicines, at 75 cents per day, and to provide for the burial of deceased patients, at $6 each.

Burlington, Iowa.—The St. Francis Hospital to furnish quarters, subsistence, medical attendance, nursing, and medicines, at 90 cents per day; P. F. Unterkircher & Sons to provide for the burial of deceased patients, at $15 each.

Burlington, Vt.—The Mary Fletcher Hospital to furnish quarters, subsistence, nursing, medical attendance, and medicines, at $1 per day.

Cairo, Ill.—Hospital patients to be cared for in the United States Marine Hospital; L. E. Falconer to provide for the burial of deceased patients, at $11.50 each.

Cedar Keys, Fla.—R. T. Walker, M. D., to furnish medical attendance and medicines, at $15 per month; John H. Sutton to furnish quarters, subsistence, and nursing, at $1.50 per day.

Charleston, S. C.—The medical attendance to be furnished by a medical officer of the Marine-Hospital Service; the city hospital to furnish quarters, subsistence, nursing, and medicines, at 90 cents per day; contagious cases, $1.50 per day; and to provide for the burial of deceased patients, at $10 each. Seamen requiring long-continued treatment will be furnished transportation to the United States Marine Hospital at Wilmington, N. C.; out-patients to be treated at the dispensary (Atlantic Wharf).

Chattanooga, Tenn.—The medical attendance to be furnished by an acting assistant surgeon; F. E. Tyler, chairman County Hospital, to furnish quarters, subsistence, nursing, and medicines, at 65 cents per day; contagious cases, $1.50 per day; Jerry Long to provide for the burial of deceased patients, at $10 each.

Chicago, Ill.—Hospital patients to be cared for in the United States Marine Hospital; J. A. Linn to provide for the burial of deceased patients, at $18 each.

Cincinnati, Ohio.—Hospital patients to be cared for in the United States Marine Hospital; dispensary at the hospital, southeast corner Third and Kilgour streets; J. J. Sullivan & Co. to provide for the burial of deceased patients, at $12 each.

Cleveland, Ohio.—The medical attendance to be furnished by an acting assistant surgeon; the "Cleveland City Hospital Association" to furnish quarters, subsistence, nursing, and medicines, in the United States Marine Hospital, under lease of September 21, 1875, at 64 cents per day. The hospital to be kept in repair by the association; J. V. McGorray to provide for the burial of deceased patients, at $12 each.

Corpus Christi, Tex.—The medical attendance to be furnished by an acting assistant surgeon; James E. Ellis to furnish quarters, subsistence, and nursing, at $1.40 per day.

Crisfield, Md.—The medical attendance to be furnished by an acting assistant surgeon; quarters, subsistence, and nursing to be furnished by A. D. Nelson, at 55 cents per day. Cases requiring long-continued treatment will be furnished transportation to Baltimore, Md.

Detroit, Mich.—Hospital patients to be cared for in the United States Marine Hospital; out-patients at the dispensary, room 16, Campau Building; E. H. Patterson to provide for the burial of deceased patients, at $8 each.

Dubuque, Iowa.—The medical attendance to be furnished by an acting assistant surgeon; St. Joseph's Mercy Hospital to furnish quarters, subsistence, nursing, and medicines, at $1 per day; M. M. Hoffmann to provide for the burial of deceased patients, at $14 each.

Duluth, Minn.—The medical attendance to be furnished by an acting assistant surgeon; St. Luke's Hospital to furnish quarters, subsistence, nursing, and medicines, at 92½ cents per day; Randall, Kendall & Co. to provide for the burial of deceased patients, at $16 each.

Eastport, Me.—Hospital relief to be furnished on the recommendation of the collector of customs.

East Saginaw, Mich.—The medical attendance to be furnished by an acting assistant surgeon; St. Mary's Hospital to furnish quarters, subsistence, nursing, and medicines, at $1 per day. Patients requiring long-continued treatment to be furnished transportation to the United States Marine Hospital, Detroit, Mich.

Edenton, N. C.—R. Dillard, jr., M. D., to furnish medical attendance and medicines, at $1.25 per visit; the collector of customs to provide for quarters, subsistence, and nursing, at $1 per day. Cases requiring long-continued treatment will be furnished transportation to the United States Marine Hospital at Wilmington, N. C.

Edgartown, Mass.—Hospital patients to be cared for in the United States Marine Hospital at Vineyard Haven.

Elizabeth City, N. C.—The medical attendance to be furnished by an acting assistant surgeon.

Ellsworth, Me.—The medical attendance to be furnished by an acting assistant surgeon. Emergency cases only will be furnished continuous hospital treatment; all other cases requiring hospital treatment will be furnished transportation to the United States Marine Hospital at Portland, Me.

Empire City, Oregon.—C. B. Golden, M. D., to furnish quarters, subsistence, nursing, medical attendance, and medicines, at $2.50 per day, and to provide for the burial of deceased patients, at $15 each.

Erie, Pa.—The medical attendance to be furnished by an acting assistant surgeon; Hamot Hospital Association to furnish quarters, subsistence, nursing, and medicines, at 71 cents per day; Riblet Bros. to provide for the burial of deceased patients, at $25 each. Cases requiring long-continued treatment will be furnished transportation to the United States Marine Hospital at Detroit, Mich.

Escanaba, Mich.—The medical attendance to be furnished by an acting assistant surgeon; Delta County Hospital to furnish quarters, subsistence, nursing, and medicines, at $1 per day; D. A. Oliver to provide for the burial of deceased patients, at $15 each.

Eureka, Cal.—The medical attendance to be furnished by an acting assistant surgeon; James Gill to furnish quarters, subsistence, nursing, and medicines, at 90 cents per day; contagious cases, $3 per day; and to provide for the burial of deceased patients, at $20 each.

Evansville, Ind.—The medical attendance to be furnished by a medical officer of the Marine-Hospital Service; the Evansville City Hospital Association to furnish quarters, subsistence, nursing, and medicines, at 75 cents per day; Joseph Schaefer to provide for the burial of deceased patients, at $10 each.

Fernandina, Fla.—The medical attendance to be furnished by an acting assistant surgeon; Mrs. S. Kruse to furnish quarters, subsistence, and nursing, at $1.10 per day; and to provide for the burial of deceased patients, at $18 each.

Fredericksburgh, Va.—The medical attendance to be furnished by an acting assistant surgeon; Mary G. Herndon to furnish quarters, subsistence, nursing, and medicines, at $1 per day.

Gallipolis, Ohio.—The medical attendance to be furnished by an acting assistant surgeon; Mrs. M. J. Thomasson to furnish quarters, subsistence, and nursing, at $1.50 per day; Hayward & Son to provide for the burial of deceased seamen, at $14 each.

Galveston, Tex.—The medical attendance to be furnished by a medical officer of the Marine-Hospital Service; Sister Augustine, superior, to furnish quarters, subsistence, nursing, and medicines, at $1 per day; contagious cases, $2 per day; and to provide for the burial of deceased patients, at $7 each. Cases requiring long-continued treatment will be furnished transportation to the United States Marine Hospital at New Orleans, at the discretion of the medical officer.

Georgetown, D. C.—The medical attendance to be furnished by a medical officer of the Marine-Hospital Service; out-patients to be treated at 1306 F street northwest, Washington; Providence Hospital, Washington, to furnish quarters, subsistence, nursing, and medicines, at 75 cents per day.

Georgetown, S. C.—The medical attendance to be furnished by an acting assistant surgeon; quarters, subsistence, and nursing to be furnished by M. S. Mustard and Susan Dennison, at $1.50 per day.

Grand Haven, Mich.—The medical attendance to be furnished by an acting assistant surgeon; Nancy Palmer to furnish quarters, subsistence, and nursing, at $1 per day.

Hartford, Conn.—The Hartford hospital to furnish quarters, subsistence, nursing, medical attendance, and medicines, at $1 per day; contagious cases, at $20 per week; G. W. Wooley & Son to provide for the burial of deceased patients, at $13 each.

Jacksonville, Fla.—The medical attendance to be furnished by an acting assistant surgeon; M. M. Gaines to furnish quarters, subsistence, and nursing, at $1 per day; contagious cases, at $2 per day; to provide for the burial of deceased patients, at $10 each.

Key West, Fla.—Hospital patients to be cared for in the United States Marine Hospital; Williams & Warren to provide for the burial of deceased patients, at $15 each.

La Crosse, Wis.—The medical attendance to be furnished by an acting assistant surgeon; St. Rosa de Viterbos Convent of the Franciscan Sisters to furnish quarters, subsistence, nursing, and medicines, at $1 per day; Walter Tillman to provide for the burial of deceased patients, at $15 each.

Little Rock, Ark.—The medical attendance to be furnished by an acting assistant surgeon; Mrs. M. Turkis to furnish quarters, subsistence, and nursing, at 66⅔ cents per day; F. Baer to provide for the burial of deceased patients, at $8 each; J. E. Gibson to furnish medicines, at 25 cents for each prescription.

Louisville, Ky.—Hospital patients to be cared for in the United States Marine Hospital; out-patients at the dispensary, 915 Jefferson street; David Ruhl to provide for the burial of deceased patients, at $7 each.

Ludington, Mich.—The medical attendance to be furnished by an acting assistant surgeon; William Peters to furnish quarters, subsistence, and nursing, at $1 per day.

Machias, Me.—The medical attendance to be furnished by an acting assistant surgeon; Amos Boynton to furnish quarters, subsistence, and nursing, at 71⅘ cents per day; L. H. Hanscom to provide for the burial of deceased patients, at $12 each.

Manistee, Mich.—The medical attendance to be furnished by an acting assistant surgeon; G. Gabrielsen to furnish quarters, subsistence, and nursing, at $1 per day.

Marquette, Mich.—The medical attendance to be furnished by an acting assistant surgeon; the Northwestern Hospital Company to furnish quarters, subsistence, and nursing, at $1 per day; contagious cases, at $4 per day; and to provide for the burial of deceased patients, at $15 each.

Memphis, Tenn.—Hospital patients to be cared for in the United States Marine Hospital; S. Farris & Co. to provide for the burial of deceased patients, at $13 each.

Milwaukee, Wis.—The medical attendance to be furnished by an acting assistant surgeon; out-patients to be treated at No. 159 Wisconsin street; St. Mary's Hospital to furnish quarters, subsistence, nursing, and medicines, at 80 cents per day; G. L. Thomas to provide for the burial of deceased patients, at $17 each; chronic hospital cases to be furnished transportation to the United States Marine Hospital at Chicago, Ill.

Mobile, Ala.—Hospital patients to be cared for in the United States Marine Hospital; Peter F. Alba to provide for the burial of deceased patients, at $12.50 each.

Nashville, Tenn.—The medical attendance to be furnished by an acting assistant surgeon; W. M. Vertrees, M. D., to furnish quarters, subsistence, nursing, and medicines, at 90 cents per day; contagious cases, $1.75 per day; and to provide for the burial of deceased patients, at $6 each.

New Bedford, Mass.—The medical attendance to be furnished by an acting assistant surgeon; seamen applying for hospital relief who are able to bear transportation will be sent to the United States Marine Hospital at Vineyard Haven.

New Berne, N. C.—The medical attendance to be furnished by an acting assistant surgeon; cases requiring long-continued treatment will be furnished transportation to the United States Marine Hospital at Wilmington, N. C.; Mrs. M. T. Whaley and daughter to furnish quarters, subsistence, and nursing, at 60 cents per day; Moses T. Bryan to provide for the burial of deceased patients, at $13 each.

New Haven, Conn.—The medical attendance to be furnished by an acting assistant surgeon; the New Haven General Hospital to furnish quarters, subsistence, nursing, and medicines, at $1 per day; contagious cases, $3 per day; and to provide for the burial of deceased patients, at $15 each.

New London, Conn.—The medical attendance to be furnished by an acting assistant surgeon; quarters, subsistence, and nursing to be furnished on the recommendation of the collector of customs, at a rate not exceeding 86 cents per day. Cases requiring long-continued treatment will be furnished transportation to the Marine Hospital at Stapleton, Staten Island, N. Y. Hammond & Caulkins to provide for the burial of deceased patients, at $12 each.

New Orleans, La.—Hospital patients to be cared for in the United States Marine Hospital; Thomas McMahon & Sons to provide for the burial of deceased patients, at $8 each.

Newport, Ark.—The medical attendance to be furnished by an acting assistant surgeon; Puss Watkins to furnish quarters, subsistence, and nursing, at $1.50 per day.

Newport, R. I.—The medical attendance to be furnished by an acting assistant surgeon; the Newport Hospital to furnish quarters, subsistence, nursing, and medicines at $1 per day; Michael Cottrell to provide for the burial of deceased patients, at $11.50 each. Cases requiring long-continued treatment will be furnished transportation to the Marine Hospital, Stapleton, Staten Island, N. Y.

New York, N. Y.—Hospital patients to be cared for in the Marine Hospital, Stapleton, Staten Island, N. Y.; out-patients to be treated at the dispensary, near the "New Barge Office, Battery;" G. F. Schaefer, of Staten Island, to provide for the burial of deceased patients, at $7.25 each.

Norfolk, Va.—The medical attendance to be furnished by a medical officer of the Marine-Hospital Service; Sister Isadore Kenney to furnish quarters, subsistence, nursing, and medicines, at $1 per day; J. E. Edwards to provide for the burial of deceased patients, at $10 each.

Ogdensburgh, N. Y.—The Ogdensburgh City Hospital to furnish quarters, subsistence, nursing, medical attendance, and medicines, at $1 per day; contagious cases, $2 per day; and to provide for the burial of deceased patients, at $15 each.

Oswego, N. Y.—The medical attendance to be furnished by an acting assistant surgeon; the Oswego Hospital to furnish quarters, subsistence, nursing, and medicines, at $1.25 per day.

Pensacola, Fla.—The medical attendance to be furnished by an acting assistant surgeon; R. W. Hargis to furnish quarters, subsistence, nursing, and medicines, at $1 per day; S. B. Hutchison to provide for the burial of deceased patients, at $15 each. Cases requiring long-continued treatment will be furnished transportation to the United States Marine Hospital at Mobile, Ala.

Philadelphia, Pa.—The medical attendance to be furnished by a medical officer of the Marine-Hospital Service; the German Hospital to furnish quarters, subsistence, nursing, and medicines, at 70 cents per day, and to provide for the burial of deceased white patients, at $10 each; colored patients, at $15 each. Transportation from the Marine-Hospital office to the hospital to be furnished by the hospital authorities when required. Care and treatment of contagious cases to be furnished by the Philadelphia Board of Health, at $1 per day; and to provide for the burial of such deceased patients, at $5 each.

Pittsburgh, Pa.—The medical attendance to be furnished by a medical officer of the Marine-Hospital Service; out-patients to be treated at No. 96 Wood street; the Mercy Hospital to furnish quarters, subsistence, nursing, and medicines, at 94 cents per day; J. J. Giltman to provide for the burial of deceased patients, at $13 each. Care and treatment of small-pox, yellow fever, or cholera cases to be furnished by the Pittsburgh Board of Health, at $2 per day.

Port Huron, Mich.—The medical attendance to be furnished by an acting assistant surgeon; "Hospital and Home" to furnish quarters, subsistence, nursing, and medicines, at $1 per day; contagious diseases at $2 per day. Patients requiring long-continued treatment will be furnished transportation to the United States Marine Hospital at Detroit: George Thompson to provide for the burial of deceased patients, at $12 each.

Portland, Me.—Hospital patients to be cared for in the United States Marine Hospital; Ilsley Bros. to provide for the burial of deceased patients, at $6.50 each.

Portland, Oregon.—The medical attendance to be furnished by a medical officer of the Marine-Hospital Service; St. Vincent's Hospital to furnish quarters, subsistence, nursing, and medicines, at 60 cents per day; and DeLin & Holman to provide for the burial of deceased patients, at $20 each. Out-patients to be treated at the dispensary, room 21, "Union Block," corner of First and Stark streets.

Portsmouth, N. H.—The medical attendance to be furnished by an acting assistant surgeon; Cottage Hospital to furnish quarters, subsistence, and nursing, at 75 cents per day.

Port Townsend, Wash.—Hospital patients to be cared for in the United States Marine Hospital; William Weir to provide for the burial of deceased patients, at $12 each.

Providence, R. I.—The Rhode Island Hospital to furnish quarters, subsistence, nursing, medical attendance, and medicines, at $1 per day, and to provide for the burial of deceased patients, at $12 each. Patients requiring long-continued treatment will be furnished transportation to the United States Marine Hospital at Chelsea (Port of Boston).

Richmond, Va.—The medical attendance to be furnished by an acting assistant surgeon; out-patients to be treated at the marine-hospital office, custom-house building; "Retreat for the Sick" Hospital to furnish quarters, subsistence, nursing, and medicines, at $1 per day.

Rome, Ga.—The medical attendance, to be furnished by an acting assistant surgeon; Mrs. Lou Echols to furnish quarters, subsistence, and nursing, at $1 per day.

Sag Harbor, N. Y.—Dr. George A. Sterling to furnish quarters, subsistence, nursing, medical attendance, and medicines, at $1.50 per day. Only such patients will be furnished hospital treatment at Sag Harbor as are unable to bear transportation to the marine hospital at Stapleton, Staten Island, N. Y.

Saint Louis, Mo.—Hospital patients to be cared for in the United States Marine Hospital; Jacob Michel to provide for the burial of deceased patients, at $10.50 each.

Saint Paul, Minn.—The medical attendance to be furnished by an acting assistant surgeon; St. Joseph's Hospital to furnish quarters, subsistence, nursing, and medicines, at $1 per day; contagious diseases, except small-pox, $2 per day; and to provide for the burial of deceased patients, at $10 each.

Salem, Mass.—The Salem Hospital to furnish quarters, subsistence, nursing, medical attendance, and medicines, at $2.50 per day, to patients unable to bear transportation to the United States Marine Hospital at Chelsea (Port of Boston); and to provide for the burial of deceased patients, at $15 each.

San Diego, Cal.—Dr. W. A. Winder to furnish quarters, subsistence, nursing, medical attendance, and medicines, at $1.30 per day; contagious cases, $3 per day; and to provide for the burial of deceased patients, at $15 each.

Sandusky, Ohio.—The medical attendance to be furnished by an acting assistant surgeon; the Good Samaritan Hospital to furnish quarters, subsistence, and nursing, at $1 per day; Deck & Andres to provide for the burial of deceased patients, at $10 each.

San Francisco, Cal.—Hospital patients to be cared for in the United States Marine Hospital; burial of deceased patients at the hospital cemetery; burial of foreign seamen, $10 each; out-patients to be treated at the Marine Hospital office, rooms 1-3, Appraiser's building.

Sault Ste. Marie, Mich.—The medical attendance to be furnished by an acting assistant surgeon; James and Mary Jane Walker to furnish quarters, subsistence, and nursing, at $1.25 per day; N. V. Gabriel to provide for the burial of deceased patients, at $15 each.

Savannah, Ga.—The medical attendance to be furnished by a medical officer of the Marine-Hospital Service; the St. Joseph's Infirmary to furnish quarters, subsistence, nursing, and medicines, at $1 per day. Patients requiring long-continued treatment will be furnished transportation to the United States Marine Hospital at Wilmington, N. C.; John H. Fox to provide for the burial of deceased patients, at $7.50 each.

Seattle, Wash.—The medical attendance to be furnished by an acting assistant surgeon; Grace Hospital to furnish quarters, subsistence, nursing, and medicines, at 90 cents per day; O. C. Shorey & Co. to provide for the burial of deceased patients, at $15.45 each.

Shreveport, La.—The medical attendance to be furnished by an acting assistant surgeon; out-patients to be treated at the Marine-Hospital office; T. J. & J. W. Allen to furnish quarters, subsistence, nursing, and medicines, at $1.50 per day; W. W. Waring to provide for the burial of deceased patients, at $14 each.

Sitka, Alaska.—The medical attendance to be furnished by an acting assistant surgeon.

Tacoma, Wash.—"Fannie C. Paddock Memorial Hospital" to furnish quarters, subsistence, nursing, medical attendance, and medicines, at $1 per day; for contagious diseases, at $1.50 per day; and to provide for the burial of deceased patients, at $15 each.

Tappahannock, Va.—Dr. W. G. Jeffries to furnish quarters, subsistence, nursing, medical attendance, and medicines at Tappahannock, Dr. W. J. Newbill, at Carter's Creek, and Dr. W. S. Christian, at Urbana, at $1.50 per day.

Toledo, Ohio.—The medical attendance to be furnished by an acting assistant surgeon; St. Vincent Hospital to furnish quarters, subsistence, nursing, and medicines, at 80 cents per day; contagious cases, $2 per day; and to provide for the burial of deceased patients, at $15 each.

Tuckerton, N. J.—The medical attendance to be furnished by an acting assistant surgeon; Elizabeth Jones to furnish quarters, subsistence, and nursing, at $1 per day.

Vicksburg, Miss.—The medical attendance to be furnished by an acting assistant surgeon; the Vicksburg City Hospital to furnish quarters, subsistence, nursing, and medicines, at $1 per day; contagious cases, at $3 per day.

Vineyard Haven, Mass.—Hospital patients to be cared for in the United States Marine Hospital; M. C. Vincent to provide for the burial of deceased patients, at $14 each.

Waldoborough and Rockland, Me.—At Rockland the medical attendance to be furnished by an acting assistant surgeon; and Mary H. Raulett to furnish quarters, subsistence, and nursing, at $1 per day. Cases requiring long-continued treatment to be furnished transportation to the United States Marine Hospital, at Portland, Me.

Wheeling, W. Va.—The medical attendance to be furnished by an acting assistant surgeon; the Wheeling Hospital to furnish quarters, subsistence, nursing, and medicines, at $1 per day.

Wilmington, Cal.—R. W. Hill, M. D., to furnish quarters, subsistence, nursing, medical attendance, and medicines, at $1.37½ per day; contagious cases, at $4 per day; and to provide for the burial of deceased patients at $13 each.

Wilmington, N. C.—Hospital patients to be cared for in the United States Marine Hospital; J. W. Woolvin to provide for the burial of deceased patients, at $16 each.

Wiscasset, Me., and sub-ports.—Emergency cases only will be furnished continuous hospital treatment; all other cases requiring hospital treatment will be furnished transportation to the United States Marine Hospital at Portland, Me.

NOTE.—At all ports not otherwise specified, the dispensary is located at the custom-house or marine hospital. The rate at ports not specifically provided for by this circular will, in each special case, be fixed by the Department, upon the recommendation of the proper officer, in accordance with the regulations of 1885.

The rate of charge for seamen from vessels of the Navy and Coast Survey, admitted to hospital under the provisions of paragraph 215, revised regulations, and for foreign seamen admitted under the act of March 3, 1875, is hereby fixed at the uniform rate of $1 per diem at ports where there are marine hospitals, and at contract rates at other ports.

MEDICAL CORPS.

Appointments and Promotions.

During the year there have been appointed five assistant surgeons; one passed assistant surgeon has been promoted to be a surgeon, and five assistant surgeons have been promoted to be passed assistant surgeons.

Resignations.

Two passed assistant surgeons and one assistant surgeon have resigned since the last annual report.

Legislation.

Both houses of Congress have passed the bill providing for the enactment into the statutes of the present regulation governing appointments into this service, but owing to a verbal amendment in one House, there was a disagreeing vote, and the bill is now in conference committee. It is expected to be speedily reported back and finally disposed of.

An additional officer is needed in this office, in order to have the work properly divided.

I have again to commend the efficient and satisfactory work of the clerks in this office, and to report that, notwithstanding the fact that the exigencies of the service during the past summer have caused on many occasions, the performance of extra hours of labor, not only has there been no complaint of the hardship, but an enthusiasm in the work as unusual as it is commendable.

I am, sir, very respectfully, your obedient servant,

JOHN B. HAMILTON,
Supervising Surgeon-General, Marine-Hospital Service.

Hon. C. S. FAIRCHILD,
Secretary of the Treasury.

Table of Relief Districts.

1.—North Atlantic District.

Bangor, Me.; Barnstable, Mass.; Bath, Me.; Belfast, Me.; Boston, Mass.; Bristol, R. I.; Burlington, Vt.; Castine, Me.; Eastport, Me.; Edgartown, Mass.; Ellsworth, Me.; Fall River, Mass.; Gloucester, Mass.; Hyannis, Mass.; Kennebunk, Me.; Machias, Me.; Marblehead, Mass.; Nantucket, Mass.; New Bedford, Mass.; Newburyport, Mass.; Newport, R. I.; Plattsburgh, N. Y.; Plymouth, Mass.; Portland, Me.; Portsmouth, N. H.; Providence, R. I.; Rockland, Me.; Saco, Me.; Salem, Mass.; Vineyard Haven, Mass.; Waldoborough, Me.; Wiscasset, Me.; and York, Me.; together with all subordinate ports.

2.—Middle Atlantic District.

Albany, N. Y.; Bridgeport, Conn.; Bridgeton, N. J.; Greenport, N. Y.; Lamberton, N. J.; Lewes, Del.; Middletown, Conn.; Newark, N. J.; New Haven, Conn.; New London, Conn.; New York, N. Y.; Patchogue, N. Y.; Perth Amboy, N. J.; Philadelphia, Pa.; Sag Harbor, N. Y.; Somers Point, N. J.; Stonington, Conn.; Troy, N. Y.; Tuckerton, N. J.; and Wilmington, Del.; together with all subordinate ports.

3.—South Atlantic District.

Alexandria, Va.; Annapolis, Md.; Baltimore, Md.; Beaufort, N. C.; Beaufort, S. C.; Brunswick, Ga.; Charleston, S. C.; Chincoteague, Va.; Crisfield, Md.; Eastville, Va.; Edenton, N. C.; Elizabeth City, N. C.; Fernandina, Fla.; Fredericksburgh, Va.; Georgetown, D. C.; Georgetown, S. C.; Jacksonville, Fla.; New Berne, N. C.; Norfolk, Va.; Petersburgh, Va.; Richmond, Va.; Saint Augustine, Fla.; Savannah, Ga.; Tappahannock, Va.; Wilmington, N. C.; and Yorktown, Va.; together with all subordinate ports.

4.—District of the Gulf.

Apalachicola, Fla.; Brashear, La.; Brownsville, Tex.; Cedar Keys, Fla.; Corpus Christi, Tex.; El Paso, Tex.; Galveston, Tex.; Indianola, Tex.; Key West, Fla.; Mobile, Ala.; New Orleans, La.; Pascagoula, Miss.; Pensacola, Fla.; Rome, Ga.; Shreveport, La.; and Tampa, Fla.; together with all subordinate ports.

5.—District of the Ohio.

Chattanooga, Tenn.; Cincinnati, Ohio; Evansville, Ind.; Gallipolis, Ohio; Louisville, Ky.; Nashville, Tenn.; Paducah, Ky.; Parkersburgh, W. Va.; Pittsburgh, Pa.; and Wheeling, W. Va.; together with all subordinate ports.

6.—District of the Mississippi.

Bismarck, Dak.; Burlington, Iowa; Cairo, Ill.; Dubuque, Iowa; Galena, Ill.; La Crosse, Wis.; Little Rock, Ark.; Memphis, Tenn.; Natchez, Miss.; Newpoit, Ark.; Omaha, Nebr.; Pembina, Dak.; Saint Louis, Mo.; Saint Paul, Minn.; and Vicksburg, Miss.; together with all subordinate ports.

7.—District of the Great Lakes.

Ashtabula, Ohio; Buffalo, N. Y.; Cape Vincent, N. Y.; Chicago, Ill.; Cleveland, Ohio; Detroit, Mich.; Duluth, Minn.; Dunkirk, N. Y.; Erie, Pa.; Escanaba, Mich.; East Saginaw, Mich.; Grand Haven, Mich.; Green Bay, Wis.; Kenosha, Wis.; L'Anse, Mich.; Manistee, Mich.; Manitowoc, Wis.; Marquette, Mich.; Milwaukee, Wis.; Muskegon, Mich.; Ogdensburgh, N. Y.; Oswego, N. Y.; Racine, Wis.; Rochester, N. Y.; Saint Joseph, Mich.; Sandusky, Ohio; Sault Ste. Marie, Mich.; Sheboygan, Wis.; and Toledo, Ohio; together with all subordinate ports.

8.—District of the Pacific.

Astoria, Oreg.; Empire City, Oreg.; Eureka, Cal.; Portland, Oreg.; Port Townsend, Wash.; San Diego, Cal.; San Francisco, Cal.; Sitka, Alaska; Wilmington, Cal.; and Yaquina, Oreg.; together with all subordinate ports.

All relief stations where the service is under the charge of a medical officer of the Marine-Hospital Service are known as relief stations of Class 1. Relief stations where specific arrangements have been made for the care and treatment of sick or disabled seamen at rates fixed by the Treasury Department, but where collectors of customs, on account of the absence of a medical officer of the Service, are authorized and required to issue permits and to supervise the relief furnished, are known as relief stations of Class 2. All other ports where there are officers of the customs revenue, but where, on account of the infrequency of applications for relief, the absence of any hospital, or from other causes, sick or disabled seamen are cared for only in cases of emergency, are known as relief stations of Class 3.

THE NATURAL HISTORY

OF

EPIDEMICS OF YELLOW FEVER.

SOME OBSERVATIONS ON THE NATURAL HISTORY OF EPIDEMICS OF YELLOW FEVER, BASED ON A STUDY OF THE MORTALITY STATISTICS OF THE CITY OF KEY WEST; ALSO A PLEA IN FAVOR OF A CONTINUED INVESTIGATION OF THIS DISEASE BY THE GOVERNMENT OF THE UNITED STATES.

By JOHN GUITÉRAS, M. D.
Passed Assistant Surgeon U. S. Marine-Hospital Service.

The mortality statistics upon which this paper is based have been compiled by myself from death certificates found in the cemetery of Key West. They cover the period from 1875 to 1887, both inclusive, and excepting the year 1876, of which no records could be found. I have also once introduced the records for 1873 and 1874, because, though incomplete, their deficiencies could not affect the results. The records for the other years (1875–1887) are sufficiently complete. Since 1880 the health-officer of the city has kept a register of death certificates. The records since October, 1880, are, therefore, absolutely complete. A comparison with previous years shows that the figures obtained for these earlier years from the certificates alone are sufficiently complete. In fact I can find no evidence of any loss of death certificates, though these documents had been kept with little care.

It is the first time that these data have been classified and made use of. Their importance from a medical point of view is greatly in excess of the political or commercial importance of the place, for the following reasons:

I. Key West is a tropical city, built on a coral reef washed by the waters of the Gulf Stream. Its climate is distinct from all others in the Union. The products of the soil are tropical. A portion of the inhabitants are Anglo-Saxons, another portion belong to the Latin race (Spanish creoles), and the remainder are negroes.

II. Key West is not a malarious locality.

III. Epidemics of yellow fever have occurred frequently in Key West. This port is more exposed than any other in the Union to become a focus of endemicity of yellow fever if this has not already happened.

The second of these propositions requires very careful consideration. All students of yellow fever will recognize the importance of this fact. In the very beginning of the history of yellow fever we find the shadow of the malarial diseases as a source of difficulties and confusion. The time is passed when it was necessary to prove that yellow fever and malaria are two distinct diseases, but we still have to contend against the imperfection of our means of diagnosis, and against preconceived notions, negligence, ignorance, and even against dishonesty and political intrigue to separate what is yellow fever from what is malaria.

I have never seen a single case of undoubted malarial infection originating on the island of Key West. In all malarial regions there occur cases of obscure fevers that, without positive evidence, are classified as malarial. In the majority of such cases the diagnosis is probably correct. Corresponding, however, to this group we have another and larger one of frank intermittents. Let us examine, for instance, the annual rate per 100 of sickness in the Army of the United States during the civil war.

TABLE I.—*Ratio of cases of malaria to mean strength.*

Typho-malarial fever	6.37
Remittent fever	22.67
Congestive intermittent	1.85
Intermittent fevers	99.31

In Key West the intermittent fevers are not to be found except in strangers from the main-land or from Cuba. All the malaria we find on the island presents itself in questionable shape. If we grant that these doubtful cases, mostly children, are cases of malaria, where, I ask, is the corresponding majority of intermittent fevers?

The following table will give further support to my opinion:

TABLE II.—*Number of deaths from malarial diseases in Key West.*

Year.	Presence of yellow fever.	Age.				Race.				Unknown as to—		Total deaths from malaria.	Total deaths from all causes.
		Natives.		Strangers.		Natives.		Strangers.					
		Children.	Adults.	Children.	Adults.	White.	Colored.	White.	Colored.	Race.	Nativity.		
1873	Yes	2	0	0	2	1	0	1	0	2	0	4	130
1874	Yes	3	1	4	1	1	1	3	0	4	0	9	218
1875	Yes	7	0	5	12	6	1	14	2	1	0	24	295
1877	No	0	0	0	1	0	0	1	0	0	0	1	232
1878	Yes	3	0	2	7	3	0	9	0	0	0	12	242
1879	No	2	0	0	1	2	0	0	1	0	1	4	184
1880	Yes	5	0	6	4	5	0	9	1	0	0	15	236
1881	Yes	4	0	0	2	3	1	2	0	0	0	6	200
1882	No	2	0	0	0	2	0	0	0	0	0	2	205
1883	No	0	1	0	2	1	0	2	0	0	0	3	226
1884	No	3	0	0	3	3	0	3	0	0	0	6	353
1885	No	5	1	0	1	4	0	0	1	1	0	7	330
1886	No	4	0	0	2	4	0	2	0	0	0	6	439
1887	Yes	14	0	5	5	14	0	7	3	0	0	24	622
		54	3	22	43	49	3	53	8	8	1	123	4,020

The above figures furnish results that are diametrically opposed to what we know to be true concerning malaria. It follows, therefore, that a majority of the deaths ascribed to malaria must have been due to other causes.

Those who maintain that Key West is a malarious locality will be surprised, I am sure, to find that the number of deaths from this cause is smaller than they had anticipated. Let us compare these figures, such as they are, with those I have obtained for other places. We have for Key West a total of 4,020 deaths for the years 1873–'87, exclusive of 1876. Of these 123 were due to malaria, or 3.05 per cent.

TABLE III.—*Number of deaths from malaria to every one hundred deaths from all causes.*

For Key West in no-fever years	1.46
For Charleston[1] from 1881 to 1886	2.34
For the United States, census of 1880	2.67
For Key West in all years recorded	3.05
For Key West in yellow-fever years	4.60
For New Orleans, census of 1880	4.47
For Grand Group IV[2] census of 1880	6.58
For the State of Florida, census of 1880	9.52

It is easy to show that the percentage of 3.05, given in the above Table III, is much in excess of the actual proportion.

I am not the first to point out how vitiated the statistics of malaria are apt to be in yellow-fever countries. Chaillé[3] and Sternberg[4] have expressed themselves decidedly on this subject. But it is doubtful if the present record has ever been equaled. Let us examine, for instance, the relative mortality of white and colored from this cause. In page xxxvi, vol. xii, of the census for 1880, we find the following statement: "In those regions (of the United States) where the distinctions of white and colored are made the proportion of deaths from these causes (malarial fevers) is decidedly greater in the colored than in the whites." The most remarkable deviation from this rule is found in the South Atlantic States or Grand Group III. It will be seen in the following table, however, that this deviation from the normal, in the case of our Key West statistics, far exceeds that of Grand Group III, and, in fact, anything within the bounds of possibility.

TABLE IV.—*Showing the number of deaths from malarial fevers, in several regions, for every one hundred deaths from all causes, contrasting the white and the colored.*

	Whites.	Colored.
For the United States (1880)	3.0	4.8
South Atlantic coast region (1880)	8.2	5.0
Gulf coast region (including Key West, 1880)	7.2	6.8
State of Florida (including Key West, 1880)	5.3	4.1
Key West (1873–1887)	2.5	0.2
Key West (1880)	5.5	0.39

The negro, I believe, enjoys some immunity toward the malarial fevers, but never to such extent as represented for Key West in the above table. In fact the mortality from malarial fevers is often higher in the colored than the whites, because the former are more exposed. Yellow fever is the only disease that could produce so marked a difference in favor of the negro.

The following table shows that this difference can not be accounted for by the fact of a small colored population:

TABLE V.—*Showing the ratio per cent. of colored to white population, together with the ratio of deaths from malaria.*

Percentage of colored to white population in the State of Florida (1880)	88.9
Percentage of colored to white mortality from malaria in Florida (1880)	78.1
Percentage of colored to white population in Key West (1880)	46.3
Percentage of colored to white mortality from malaria in Key West (1880)	7.1
Percentage of colored to white mortality from malaria in Key West (1873–'87)	10.7

[1] This is the correct estimate for Charleston, though a lower estimate has been erroneously given.

[2] Grand Group IV or Gulf coast region. This region includes the entire State of Florida, and the coast counties of Alabama, Mississippi, Louisiana, and Texas. See Tenth Census of the United States, 1880, vol. xii, Mortality and Vital Statistics, by John S. Billings, surgeon, U. S. Army. All the data used in this paper for comparison with Key West have been obtained from the same invaluable compilation.

[3] Report on yellow fever in Havana and Cuba, by Stanford E. Chaillé, A. M., M. D., Report of the National Board of Health, 1880.

[4] Malaria and Malarial Diseases, by George M. Sternberg.

If our attention is directed to the element of age in Table II we shall find further proof that these deaths are attributable to other causes than malarial fever.

TABLE VI.—*Showing a disproportionate excess of the infantile mortality from malaria in Key West.*

[The table gives the number of deaths from malaria for adults and children ten years old and under in one hundred deaths from all causes.]

	Adults.	Children.
For the United States (1880)	1.56	1.11
For Grand Group 4 (1880)	3.26	3.05
For New Orleans (1880)	2.83	1.64
For Grand Group 3 (1880)	2.50	3.22
For the State of Florida (1880)	4.17	5.34
For Key West (all the years recorded)	1.14	1.89
For Key West (1880)	1.69	4.66
For Key West (in yellow-fever years)	2.00	3.54
For Key West (in no-fever years)	0.63	0.80

I may add, to quote again from the census report, that "in the United States the mean age at death of those reported as dying from this cause (malarial fevers) during the census year was twenty-four years.

Finally, the most conclusive proof of the vitiation of the statistics for malaria is to be found in a consideration of the nativity and ages recorded in Table II. Here we have a locality reporting 122 deaths from malaria in fourteen years, and of these 122 only 3 were adult natives, 54 were native children, and 65 were strangers, both adults and children.

It appears to me that we are forced to reject the diagnosis of malaria in the majority of these cases. I have no doubt that not one case of malaria has originated for many years on the island of Key West. A few have died there of malarial poisoning, but these were infected in Cuba or on the mainland of Florida, or they were sailors with chagres fever from Central America. It is a well-known fact that the inhabitants of the mainland of Florida come to Key West to get rid of malarial infection contracted on the continent.

Now, if these cases are not malarial fever, what are they? Every fact that disproves their malarial origin suggests with equal weight the probability that they are cases of yellow fever. This is a grave matter. Here we have a large number of children dying of a disease that is far more likely to be yellow fever than any other disease, and the fact is not recognized. If we remember the small mortality of yellow fever amongst children it is appalling to consider the number of cases that such mortality represents.

It is true that many authorities maintain that the children of yellow-fever countries are exempt from the disease; that the creoles do not have yellow fever. This opinion, more or less qualified, is found to prevail throughout the yellow-fever countries, and the great majority of writers on the disease believe, at least, that children are less susceptible than adults.

Dr. Daniel Blair[1] and Dr. Stanford E. Chaillé[2] are amongst the few who have explicitely maintained, and the latter has proven, that creole children are amenable to the yellow fever. Dr. Blair states that "infancy was one of the most favoring causes of the action of the yellow-fever poison. The constitution of the new-born or young white creole was highly susceptible." Dr. Chaillé has brought the weight of statistical figures to show that the natives of New Orleans are liable to the disease,

[1] Blair's Report on yellow fever in British Guiana, London, 1852 and 1856.

[2] Report on yellow fever in Havana and Cuba, Report of the National Board of Health, 1880.

and that their supposed immunity is merely the protection conferred by a previous attack. See Tables XIII and XIV of the report.

These opinions are far from being generally accepted. The majority of creole physicians in the Antilles still hold to the theory of a special immunity enjoyed by children who are born in yellow-fever centers. Others will concede that the creoles may have yellow fever, and the discussion between these two parties reduces itself to the question: Is it possible for the natives to have yellow fever? The arguments in this discussion will be found to consist of the presentation of exceptional cases, generally fatal, with black vomit and other characteristic features of yellow fever occurring in natives, or the cases occurring in the inhabitants of the interior when they come to the sea shore, are brought forward. Some maintain that these are cases of yellow fever, others that they are unusual forms of malaria. The question, it will be seen, is made one of exceptions.

Dr. Blair, openly and decidedly, the French physicians like Rufz de Lavison, Cornillac, Lota, and Béranger-Feraud, and also Finlay of Havana, more reservedly, and often very obscurely, have pointed to the possibility, not of an exceptional infection of children and inhabitants of the interior, but of a general susceptibility of the natives to the disease. It is often difficult to understand the meaning of these authors, and contradictory passages are found in their excellent works. An idea may be formed of the confusion existing in this chapter of nosology if we compare it with the agitation that is going on in the border lines of typhoid fever. In both cases the result has been the creation of a neutral ground under the name of a distinct disease. This is the fièvre inflammatoire of French physicians.[1]

My statistics enable me to prove for Key West what Dr. Chaillé has done for New Orleans. The absence of malaria and of a large floating population of adult strangers in Key West justify, I believe, more decided conclusions than were reached by the New Orleans physician.

Before taking up a detailed consideration of the statistical data I deem it important to remind the reader of the very decided immunity towards yellow fever that is enjoyed by the colored race. If they prove nothing else, my tables certainly prove this. Though it must be acknowledged that this immunity is not absolute, yet it is sufficiently marked to make the colored mortality a sort of test by which the presence of yellow fever may be detected. There is nothing in human pathology that is comparable to this immunity. It reduces the comparative mortality of the negro in Key West to a very low figure in contrast with other cities of the Union.

For a clear understanding of the tables and charts that are to follow it is advisable to present here a general explanation of them.

I have divided the years of which I have a record into two groups, namely, the yellow-fever years and no-fever years. In all my observations one year of one group is always contrasted with one of the other group. They are arranged in the following order:

Yellow-fever years.	No-fever years.	Yellow-fever years.	No-fever years.
1875	1877	1881	1883
1878	1877	1881	1884
1880	1879	1887	1885
1881	1882	1887	1886

[1] See Appendix.

I have divided the year into quarters after the manner of Borious, which I consider the one best adapted to medical purposes.

First quarter.—December, January, and February.

Second quarter.—March, April, and May.

Third quarter.—June, July, and August.

Fourth quarter.—September, October, and November.

In some of the charts and tables I have introduced the four quarters of the year, in others I introduce only those quarters in which cases of yellow fever occurred, contrasting them with the same quarters in the no-fever years. When the yellow fever covers more than one quarter an average is taken of the two or three quarters. In the year 1875, for instance, the cases of yellow fever occurred in the second and third quarters. An average of the death rate of these two quarters will be compared with the average of the same quarters in 1877.

TABLE VIII.—*Showing the influence of yellow fever upon the death rate of the two races, by comparing the death rate of whites in every 1,000 of white population and the death rate of the colored in every 1,000 of colored population.*

Yellow-fever years.	White.	Colored.	No-fever years.	White.	Colored.
1875	15.68	8.74	1877	9.52	7.04
1878	6.94	7.13	1877	7.52	7.24
1880	9.91	3.83	1879	3.16	1.36
1881	7.88	5.66	1882	4.09	4.55
1881	7.88	5.66	1883	4.50	6.68
1881	7.88	5.66	1884	6.05	8.03
1887	10.85	9.86	1885	5.51	7.04
1887	10.85	9.86	1886	8.28	7.84
Average for the quarter	9.73	7.05	Average for the quarter	6.07	6.22
Average annual death rate*	38.92	28.20	Average annual death rate*	24 28	24.88

* This is not the actual annual death rate, but such as would correspond to the quarters selected—the yellow-fever quarters.

The different susceptibility of the two races can be shown at a glance in the following chart:

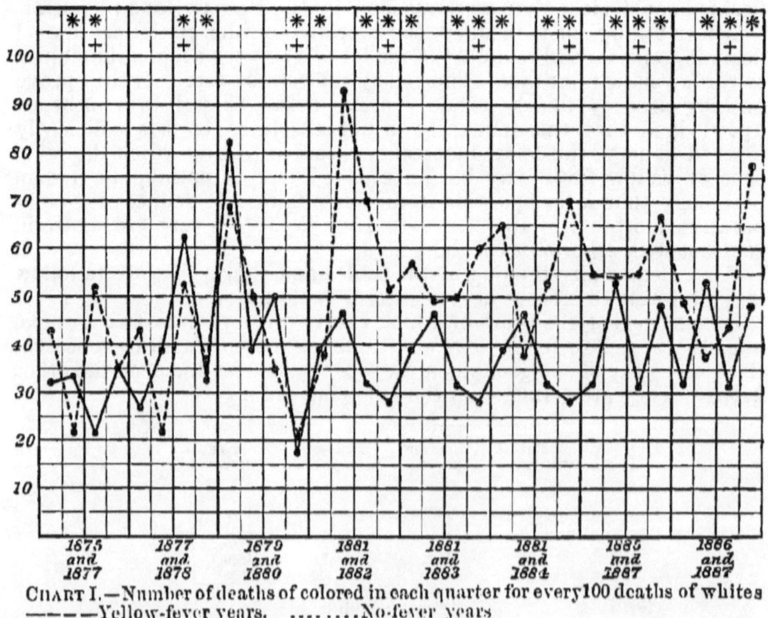

CHART I.—Number of deaths of colored in each quarter for every 100 deaths of whites

– – – –Yellow-fever years. . . . . . . .No-fever years

* Quarters in which cases of yellow fever occurred.

‡ Quarter in which the greatest number of cases of yellow fever are reported.

It should be observed that this excess of the white mortality during fever years takes place in spite of the exodus of the white population during the sickly summers. This, however, is not as great as elsewhere, because yellow fever causes no panic among the natives.

It will be seen in the above chart that, with the exception of 1878, the quarter of highest yellow fever mortality gives always the lowest proportion of colored mortality.

In 1878 there was an epidemic of whooping-cough. This disease appears to exert upon the mortality of the two races an action opposite to that of yellow fever. Whooping-cough prevailed also in 1884.

I propose now to show that the mortality of children of the two races is affected by yellow fever in the same manner with the total and the adult mortality, thus proving that yellow fever must have been at work amongst the white children, though it does not appear on the face of the records. The difference in the number of deaths of white and colored children in the two series of years is very striking. I ask, what else can it be that so shapes the death-rate curve of these children so strangely in accordance with the known operations of yellow fever?

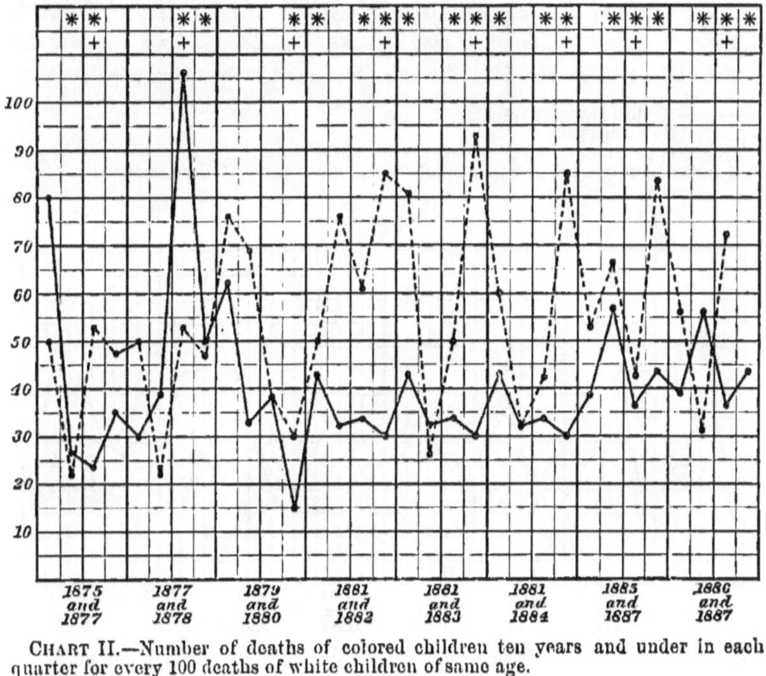

CHART II.—Number of deaths of colored children ten years and under in each quarter for every 100 deaths of white children of same age.

————Yellow-fever years.

........No-fever years.

* Quarters in which cases of yellow fever occurred.

‡ Quarter in which the greatest number of cases of yellow fever occurred.

However striking the above charts may be, the only reliable method of contrasting the two series of years should consist in a comparison of the death-rates per 1,000 of the living population in each quarter of the year. This has been done in the following charts, for adults, for children five years old and under, and for children one year old and under.

The rate is indicated in the following charts by the whole number and one decimal.

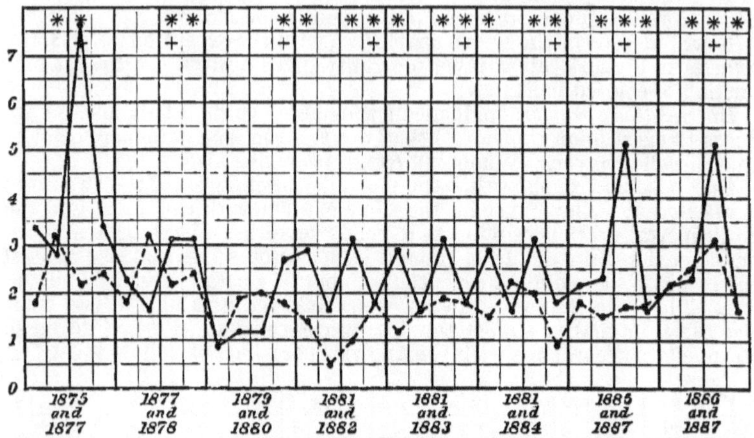

CHART III.—Number of deaths of white adults per 1,000 of living population fo each quarter.
——— Yellow-fever years.
........No-fever years.
* Quarters in which cases of yellow fever occurred.
⁑ Quarter in which the greatest number of cases of yellow fever occurred.

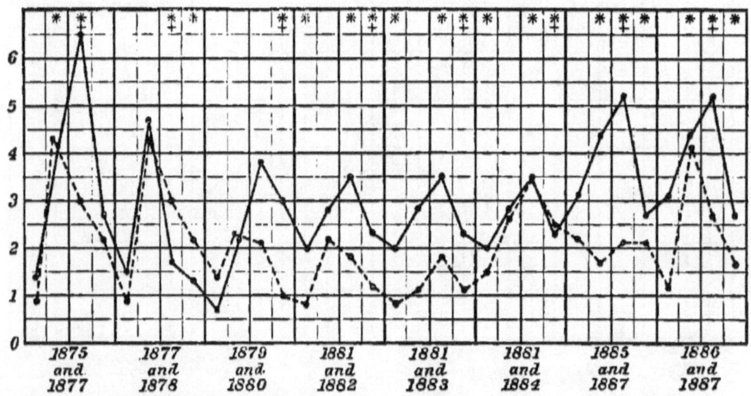

CHART IV.—Number of deaths of white children five years of age and under per 1,000 of living population.
——— Yellow-fever years.
.... No-fever years.
* Quarters in which cases of yellow fever occurred.
⁑ Quarter in which the greatest number of cases of yellow fever occurred.

CHART V.—Number of deaths of white children one year old and under per 1,000 of living population.

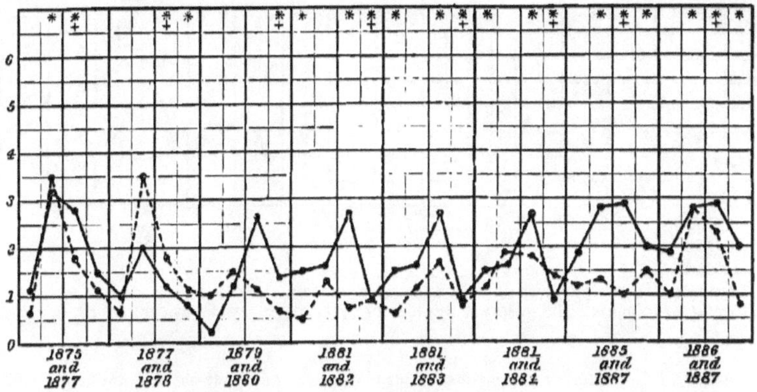

——— Yellow-fever years. .... No-fever years.
* Quarters in which cases of yellow fever occurred.
‡ Quarter in which the greatest number of cases of yellow fever occurred.

CHART VI.—Number of deaths of colored adults per 1,000 of living population.

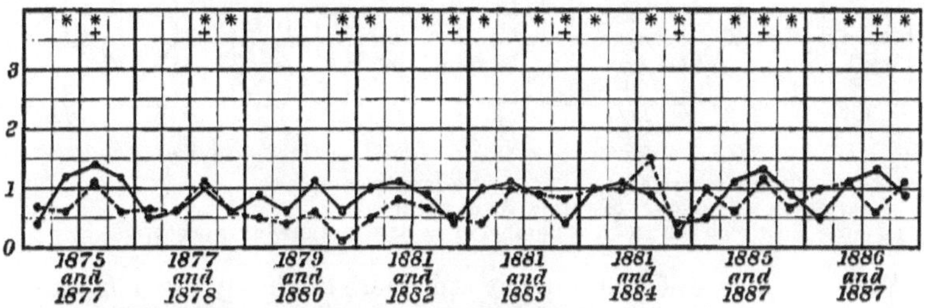

——— Yellow-fever years. .... No fever years.
* Quarters in which cases of yellow fever occurred.
‡ Quarter in which the greatest number of cases of yellow fever occurred.

CHART VII.—Number of deaths of colored children five years and under per 1,000 of living population.

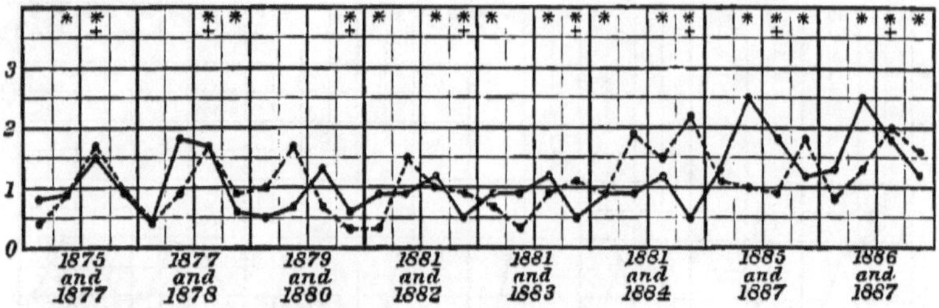

——— Yellow-fever years. .... No fever years.
* Quarters in which cases of yellow fever occurred.
‡ Quarter in which the greatest number of cases of yellow fever occurred.

CHART VIII.—Number of deaths of colored children one year old and under per 1,000 of living population.

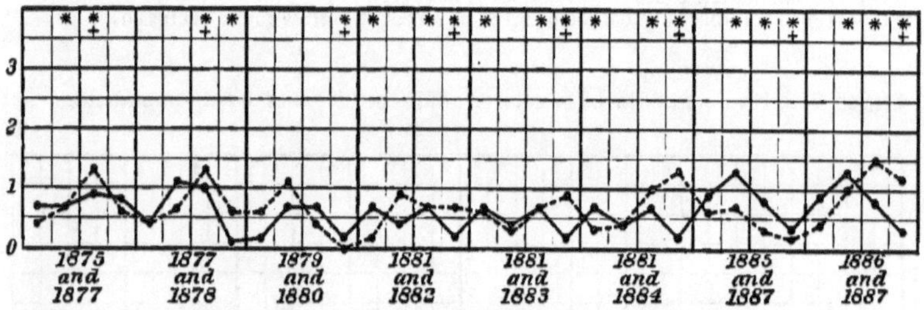

——— Yellow-fever years. .... No-fever years.
* Quarters in which cases of yellow fever occurred.
‡ Quarter in which the greatest number of cases of yellow fever occurred.

With the object of pointing out still more distinctly the influence of yellow fever on the mortality of adults and children in the two series of years, the following charts have been constructed. Instead of comparing the four quarters of the year, I have selected those quarters only in which cases of yellow fever occurred, and I have obtained the average of their death rate for each yellow-fever year. I have contrasted this with the average of the same quarters for the no-fever years. It will be seen that the closer we come to the vortex of the yellow-fever storm the greater is the influence of the disease upon the mortality of white children:

CHART IX.—Death rate per 1,000 for quarters in which cases of yellow fever occurred.

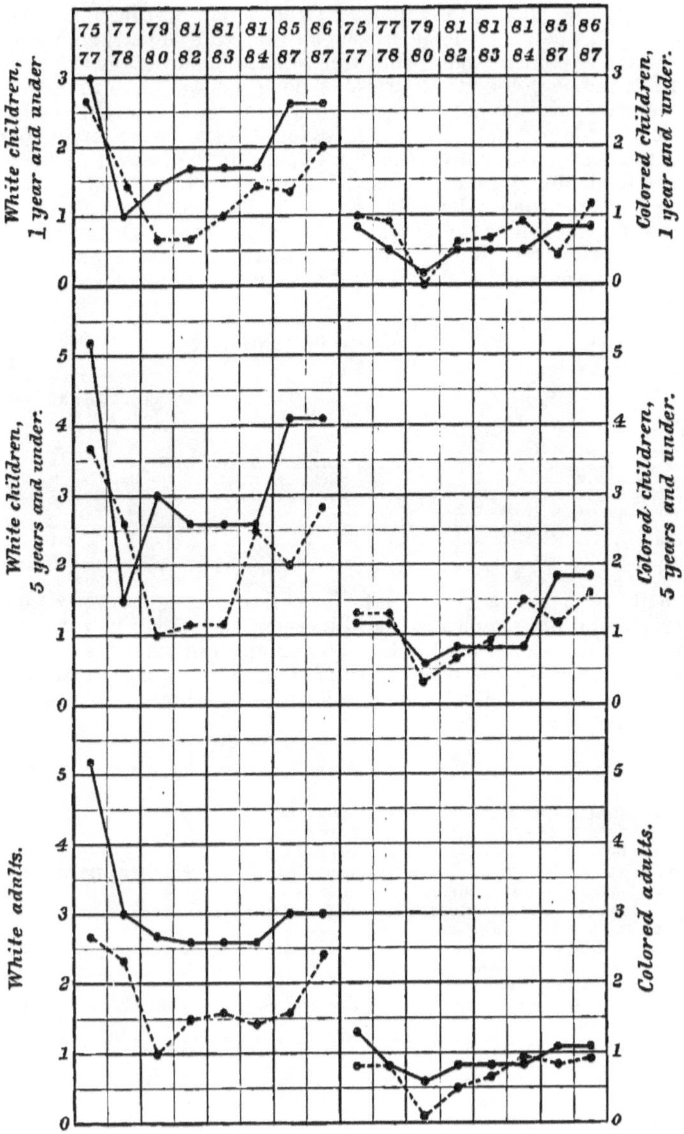

We find, then, that a marked increase of the mortality of white children corresponds with the prevalence of yellow fever. The only disease that seems capable of counteracting the influence of yellow fever is whooping-cough, through its lethal action upon the negro. There were epidemics of whooping-cough in 1878 and 1884. But it is surprising to me that these perturbations are not more marked and more frequent, for we are dealing, it must be remembered, with mortality statistics, and yellow fever is comparatively mild in the young. How all pervading, how wide-spread, must be the action of this poison upon infantile life when its effects are so constant and so marked upon the mortality. Is it any wonder that this infant population grows to adult lifein full possession of that precious boon for the inhabitants of the American tropics—immunity against yellow fever? My statistics show how dearly this population pays for its lease of life in the torrid zone.

The next step in our investigation should be to discover under what head is to be found this increased infantile mortality that belongs to fever years; for the reader will be surprised to learn that it certainly does not appear under the diagnosis of yellow fever. Out of a total of 134 deaths reported from yellow fever in the five years, only 33 were children ten years old and under. These deaths are distributed in the following manner:

TABLE IX.—*Deaths from yellow fever.*

Year.	Children.	Adults.	Total.
1875	6	28	34
1878	1	10	11
1880	11	6	17
1881	2	6	8
1887	13	51	64
Total	33	101	134

The above yields an annual rate for children of only .63 per 1,000 of living population, a number, it will be seen, very far from sufficient to account for the increased death rate of children in yellow-fever years.

Before taking up the consideration of certain special causes of the mortality, I shall dwell a moment upon the distribution of the deaths from yellow fever:

TABLE X.—*Distribution of the deaths from yellow fever.*

The greatest mortality from yellow fever occurred:
  Three times in the third quarter of the year.
  Twice in the fourth quarter of the year.
In the five yellow-fever years the greatest mortality of white children (under five years of age), from all causes occurred:
  Four times in the third quarter.
  Once in the second quarter.
The greatest mortality of colored children, from all causes, occurred:
  Three times in the third quarter.
  Twice in the second quarter.
In the same years the total mortality was most frequently at its height in the third quarter.
In the seven no-fever years, the highest mortality of white adults and of white children, occurred four times in the second quarter.
In the same years the colored children had their highest mortality:
  Three times in the fourth quarter.
  Twice in the second quarter.
  Twice in the third quarter.
The yellow fever, it will be seen, appears to bring about a change in the quarter of highest mortality for the white children, which is the second quarter for no-fever years, and the third quarter for fever years, the latter being also the yellow-fever quarter.

In Table XIII, I shall introduce special causes of death. These are represented under the heads of several groups: Group A, Group B, etc. These special causes have been selected with the object of determining under what heads is to be discovered the excess of deaths encountered in yellow-fever years, especially among children. The diseases classified under the heads of Group A, Group B, etc., are such as I considered suspicious, or likely to be confounded with yellow fever. The great majority of the cases here introduced were children. I proceed to describe the several groups:

Group A.—Consists of acute cerebro-spinal lesions, and represents the following reported causes of death: "Anæmia of brain" (in children); "Inflammation of brain" (children); "Cerebritis" (children); "Brain fever" (children); "Congestion of brain;"[1] "Congestion of the spinal cord;" "Cerebral apoplexy" (in a child under one year old); "Encephalitis with pneumonia;" "Cerebral meningitis;" "Meningo-encephalia;" "Meningitis;" "Acute meningitis;" "Arachnitis;" "Cerebro spinal meningitis;" "Cerebro-spinal fever;" "Acute spinal meningitis."

Group B.—Consists of cases of acute tuberculosis of the nervous system in children.

The result of a comparison of the mortality from these diseases in the two series of years confirms my suspicions, as will be seen in the table; but I must confess that I expected a more decided contrast. I had suspected that I would find here the majority of the deaths to account for the excess in yellow-fever years. My reason for this is, that we can not converse long with physicians in the tropics without being struck by their references to idiopathic meningitis of childhood as a matter of frequent occurrence. This opinion of physicians in the tropics is not based, it will be found, on a careful investigation of the disease. The investigation, if there has been any, is conspicuous for the absence of *post mortem* examination. I ventured once in Key West to diagnosticate acute meningitis, but the *post mortem* demonstrated that I was in error. I had to acknowledge to myself that I did not know what was the cause of death. The case, of course, appears now in Group A.

I have examined the mortuary tables of the city of Havana, compiled by Dr. Ambrosio Gonzalez del Valle.[2] I find in them a most extraordinary record of the disease under consideration.

TABLE XI.—*Deaths from "meningitis" in the city of Havana, per 1,000 of living population.*

Year.	Per cent.	Year.	Per cent.
1872	1.02	1876	1.09
1873	1.34	1877	1.16
1874	1.54	1878	1.49
1875	1.26		

Nothing comparable to this can be found in the mortality statistics of the United States, as illustrated in the census report for 1880.

[1] Even when not stated the majority of such cases are children. Occasionally the case of an adult may be introduced. For instance, if I find in the death certificate, that a young man from the Northern States is reported to have died of congestion of the brain, I call the case suspicious, as every one should do who is familiar with the ingenuity exercised at times to find names for cases of yellow fever.

[2] The student of tropical pathology can not mention this name without paying a tribute of admiration to this noble Cuban. His statistical labors were performed under the most adverse circumstances. Had these been different he certainly would have ranked with the most distinguished sanitarians.

TABLE XII.—*Deaths from cerebro-spinal fever and meningitis per 1,000 of living population, in the localities named (Census of 1880).*

Locality.	Per cent.	Locality.	Per cent.
The United States	0.20	Baltimore	0.53
State of Florida	0.15	Philadelphia	0.30
Indianapolis	0.27	Charleston	0.12
Louisville	0.50	New York	0.45
New Orleans	0.41	Average of seven years in Havana	1.27

Group C—Other nervous affections.—This includes the following diagnoses: "Convulsions" (children), "spasms," "eclampsia" (children), "angina pectoris" (in an infant), "congestion," "dentition." This group does not give results in accordance with my suspicions. I had expected to find here a portion of the excess of mortality of yellow-fever years. The reason for the failure may be found in the fact that under the head of spasms and convulsions are included a large number of cases of infantile trismus. This disease is not influenced by the prevalence of yellow fever.

Group D—Acute gastro-intestinal affections.—This was introduced as the most frequent cause of death among children. I wished to find out whether this class of diseases had not been drawn upon in an emergency. The diagnoses included under this head are: "Cholera infantum," "gastritis," "acute gastro-enteritis," "cholera morbus," "gastro-enteritis," "dyspepsia," "colic," "bilious dysentery," "worms" (under this head there is one case of an adult stranger who died during an epidemic of yellow fever), "hepatitis," "jaundice," "biliary colic," "acute yellow atrophy of the liver" (a case known to be of yellow fever).

I may mention here that the Key West statistics do not corroborate the opinion, of French physicians particularly, that there is an epidemic antagonism between dysentery and yellow fever. It is true that the former disease is not common in Key West.

Group E—Miscellaneous.—This includes "acute Bright's disease" (children), "nephritis" (children), "mercurial salivation" (one case known to have been of yellow fever), "typhoid peritonitis from orchitis," "passive hemorrhage from an alteration of the blood," pulmonary apoplexy, fulminating" (a child), "unknown."

Group F—Malarial affections.—In this group I do not include all cases diagnosed as malarial fever. I have excluded a few adult natives and adult Cubans who could not be called suspicious cases. The group is made up mostly of children.

The discrepancy between fever and no fever years is more marked in this group than in any other. There is an enormous preponderance of the malarial fevers in yellow-fever years. And yet in studying the history of epidemics of this disease we find that, if we except those localities in which yellow fever in a native is called by another name (pernicious fever, bilious remittent, etc.), the effect of an epidemic of yellow fever is rather to lessen than to increase the mortality from malarial fevers.[1] The following diagnoses are included in group F: "malignant fever," "putrid fever," "bilious pleurisy," "malarial pleurisy," "febris perniciosa cerebralis," "pernicious fever," "remittent fever," "malig-

[1] La Roche, Vol. 2, p. 281.—Exceptions to this rule are pointed out for a special purpose in page 277. It is probable, as he observes, that when a severe epidemic of yellow fever prevails, the material for the malarial infection is reduced to a minimum. This may not be noticeable in small epidemics.

nant remittent fever," "bilous remittent fever" "malarial bilious fever," "congestive bilious fever," "febris gastrica biliosa," "biliosa maligna," "congestive fever," "malarial fever," "intermittent fever," "melanuric bilious fever."

Group G—Other fevers.—"Ataxic fever," "adynamic fever," "thermic fever," "rötheln," "febris typhoides," "typhoid fever," epidemic continued fever," "acute rheumatism of chest and bowels while doing well from yellow fever," "cerebral typhoid fever," "typho-malarial fever," "typhus fever," "irritation fever," "gastric fever," "febris intestinalis," "gastro-enteric fever."

The following table presents all these data in a convenient form. Each year is represented by the average of the mortality per 1,000 of living population, for the quarters in which cases of yellow fever are reported. These are found on the left-hand column; on the right side are found the averages for the same quarters in no-fever years.

In this table will be seen at once the several facts showing the profound and widespread influence of yellow fever upon all classes of the white population. These features I need not repeat here, but I wish to call attention to some that I have not previously mentioned.

(1) The characteristic features of the fever years, including the effects upon the special cases of death, will be found to be well developed even though some of these years could scarcely be called epidemic, the number of deaths from yellow fever reported being very small.

(2) The features in question are specially accentuated in those years in which the number of deaths from yellow fever is greatest.

(3) The same features become again specially accentuated if a table, similar to Table XIII, is constructed with the single quarters in which the greatest number of cases of yellow fever occurred. A general average obtained from such a table is introduced in the lower line of Table XIII marked with parenthesis.([2])

TABLE XIII.—*Number of deaths per 1,000 of living population*

Quarters.	Total mortality.				White adults.				Colored adults.			
	Yellow-fever years.		No-fever years.		Yellow-fever years.		No-fever years.		Yellow-fever years.		No-fever years.	
	Years.	Average death rate.	Years.	Average death rate.	Years.	Average death rate.	Years.	Average death rate.	Years.	Average death rate.	Years.	Average death rate.
Second and third	1875	13.48	1877	8.92	1875	5.24	1877	2.72	1875	1.34	1877	0.86
Third and fourth	1878	7.00	1877	7.49	1878	3.01	1877	2.35	1878	0.86	1877	0.86
Fourth	1880	7.98	1879	2.59	1880	2.73	1879	1.08	1880	0.60	1879	0.10
First, third, and fourth	1881	7.19	1882	4.26	1881	2.63	1882	1.52	1881	0.81	1882	0.58
Do	1881	7.19	1883	4.78	1881	2.63	1883	1.69	1881	0.81	1883	0.74
Do	1881	7.19	1884	6.67	1881	2.63	1884	1.48	1881	0.81	1884	0.94
Second, third, and fourth	1887	10.55	1885	6.05	1887	3.07	1885	1.67	1887	1.15	1885	0.88
Do	1887	10.55	1886	7.97	1887	3.07	1886	2.44	1887	1.15	1886	0.93
Corresponding annual rate[1]	.....	35.56	....	24.36	.....	12.50	.....	7.47	.....	3.76	.....	2.94
One quarter[2]	.....	39.09	.....	25.21	.....	14.67	.....	7.54	.....	3.61	.....	2.85

Quarters.	Group A.—Meningitis, etc.				Group B.—Tubercular.				Group C.—Other nervous affections.			
Second and third	1875	0.49	1877	0.61	1875	......	1877	0.06	1875	0.28	1877	0.18
Third and fourth	1878	0.34	1877	0.49	1878	......	1877	0.06	1878	0.28	1877	0.06
Fourth	1880	0.40	1879	......	1880	....	1879	.....	1880	0.50	1879	0.21
First, third, and fourth	1881	0.31	1882	0.14	1881	0.06	1882	.....	1881	0.40	1882	0.23
Do	1881	0.31	1883	0.27	1881	0.06	1883	0.02	1881	0.40	1883	0.24
Do	1881	0.31	1884	0.12	1881	0.06	1884	0.02	1881	0.40	1884	0.76
Second, third, and fourth	1887	0.50	1885	0.45	1887	0.16	1885	0.02	1887	0.31	1885	0.07
Do	1887	0.50	1886	0.37	1887	0.16	1886	.....	1887	0.31	1886	0.28
Corresponding annual rate[1]	.....	1.58	.....	1.22	......	0.25	.....	0.09	.....	1.44	.....	1.01
One quarter[2]	.....	1.68	.....	0.96	......	0.38	.....	.....	....	1.31	.....	1.09

[1] The annual death rate per 1,000 corresponding to the above mortality of selected quarters.

[2] The annual death rate per 1,000 corresponding to the quarterly mortality, not of the several fever quarters, but of the one quarter of each year in which the greatest number of deaths from yellow fever are reported.

for quarters in which cases of yellow fever are reported.

Yellow-fever years.		No-fever years.		Yellow-fever years.		No-fever years.		Yellow-fever years.		No-fever years.		Yellow-fever years.		No-fever years.	
Years.	Average death rate.	Years.	Average death rate.	Years.	Average death rate.	Years.	Average death rate.	Years.	Average death rate.	Years.	Average death rate.	Years.	Average death rate.	Years.	Average death rate.
White children, five years and under.				Colored children, five years and under.				White children, one year and under.				Colored children, one year and under.			
1875	5.25	1877	3.71	1875	1.27	1877	1.35	1875	3.04	1877	2.72	1875	0.84	1877	1.05
1878	1.55	1877	2.66	1878	1.21	1877	1.35	1878	1.04	1877	1.48	1878	0.57	1877	0.98
1880	3.03	1879	1.08	1880	0.60	1879	0.32	1880	1.41	1879	0.75	1880	0.20	1879	......
1881	2.67	1882	1.26	1881	0.87	1882	0.79	1881	1.72	1882	0.76	1881	0.59	1882	0.61
1881	2.67	1883	1.28	1881	0.87	1883	0.96	1881	1.72	1883	1.06	1881	0.59	1883	0.76
1881	2.67	1884	2.56	1881	0.87	1884	1.56	1881	1.72	1884	1.49	1881	0.59	1884	0.92
1887	4.16	1885	2.03	1887	1.83	1885	1.29	1887	2.63	1885	1.31	1887	0.85	1885	0.47
1887	4.10	1886	2.86	1887	1.86	1886	1.67	1887	2.63	1886	2.03	1887	0.85	1886	1.27
......	13.08	......	8.72	......	4.70	......	4.64	......	7.95	......	5.80	......	2.54	......	3.03
......	14.46	......	8.58	......	4.60	......	5.56	......	7.11	......	5.56	......	2.41	......	3.84
Group D.—Diarrheal diseases.				Group E.—Miscellaneous.				Group F.—Malarial affections.				Group G.—Other fevers.			
1875	1.02	1877	0.98	1875	......	1877	......	1875	1.05	1877	0.12	1875	0.78	1877	0.21
1878	0 28	1877	1.24	1878	......	1877	0.06	1878	0.31	1877	0.06	1878	0.28	1877	0.21
1880	......	1879	0.10	1880	......	1879	......	1880	1.31	1879	......	1880	0.10	1879	......
1881	0.55	1882	0.17	1881	0.03	1882	0.05	1881	0.18	1882	......	1881	0.12	1882	0.02
1881	0.55	1883	0.54	1881	0.03	1883	......	1881	0.18	1883	0.08	1881	0.12	1883	0.02
1881	0.55	1884	0.36	1881	0.03	1884	......	1881	0.18	1884	0.12	1881	0.12	1884	0.07
1887	0.60	1885	0.38	1887	0.08	1885	0.02	1887	0.45	1885	0.14	1887	0.16	1885	0.09
1887	0.60	1886	0.24	1887	0.08	1886	0.02	1887	0.45	1886	0.04	1887	0.16	1886	0 17
......	2.32	......	2.10	......	0.12	......	0.07	......	2.15	......	0.28	......	0.92	......	0.42
......	2.49	......	1.92	......	1.25	......	0.10	......	3.04	......	0.43	......	1.25	......	0.71

The epidemic of 1887 deserves some special consideration. Thanks to the energy of the president of the board of health of Monroe County, Dr. J. Y. Porter, U. S. Army, we can obtain some information concerning the number, age, etc., of those attacked. The State of Florida can never repay the services of this able officer. Overcoming the most inconceivable obstacles, in the midst of onerous duties, generously discharged at the sacrifice of his own health, in the care of the sick, he contrived to create a public hospital, to enlist the assistance of the National Government, and to keep at the same time as careful a record of the epidemic as was practicable.

In these records, kindly furnished me by Dr. Porter, I have discovered a very interesting fact, as shown in the following table:

TABLE XIV.—*Showing the ages and nativity of those attacked with yellow fever during the epidemic of 1887 in Key West.*

Age.	Natives.	Strangers.
Less than 1 year old	2	....
1 year	4	....
2 years	10	3
3 years	13	....
4 years	13	3
5 years	15	1
6 years	3	....
7 years	....	....
8 years	....	1
9 years	6	3
10 years	7	1
11 years	1	1
12 years	4	4
13 years	....	....
14 years	1	3
15 years	....	2
Above 15 years	....	113
15 to 20 years	2	....
20 to 25 years	1	....
To al	82	136

The total number of cases reported was 283. Dr. Porter was unable to obtain the ages of 65. The majority of these were native children. The most striking fact observable in this table is the absence of any cases of the ages, respectively, of seven and eight years amongst the native children. I find, however, one death recorded of a child seven years of age, and there may have been others amongst those of unknown age; but the number was certainly very small. It is, therefore, of importance to look back and into the history of these children that were so singularly exempt during the epidemic of 1887. We find that they are children who were in their first and second year during the epidemic of 1880—a year in which many children were affected, as may be seen by the death rate. It follows, in my opinion, that the immunity of these children in 1887 was due to a previous attack in 1880. In fact, the protection conferred by this epidemic of 1880 was already apparent during the following fever year of 1881, in which we find the infantile mortality comparatively small for a fever year. The year 1887 was the first epidemic year since 1881.

I witnessed these two epidemics of 1881 and 1887. I suspected what was going on amongst the children in 1881. My opinion was confirmed in 1887. The number of children affected during the latter epidemic was extraordinary. I believe that the reports received by Dr. Porter are far from representing the truth. The mortality statistics prove this. I know, furthermore, that several physicians denied that the children could have yellow fever, and their cases were not reported to the health authorities.

A thorough acquaintance with this epidemic confirmed me in the generally received opinion that the disease is comparatively mild amongst children. How great must be the number of cases represented by the increased mortality that appears under the heads of meningeal inflammations, malarial fevers, etc. A clinical description of the disease in childhood will form the subject of a separate communication. Suffice it to say here that many cases were perfectly characteristic of the disease. But it must be confessed that in others the attack is so mild that a positive diagnosis is not possible with our present means.

The facts presented in this communication, and the application of the laws governing other infectious diseases, warrant, in my opinion, conclusions that are opposed to generally received opinions. These conclusions, I believe, have a greater significance than has been given to them by my predecessors in this field, who have pointed out facts similar to those presented in this report. The natural history of epidemics of yellow fever becomes clear if we see the true significance of these facts.

From them I conclude that the prevalence of yellow fever amongst the children of yellow-fever countries must not be considered as a matter of exception, but, on the contrary, that in early life there is a special and constant predisposition to the disease; that it is a disease essentially of white creole children. Amongst them is to be found its natural habitat. Their infection is not a matter of accident. The accidents, the abnormities in the natural history of the disease, are really the migrations to foreign soil and the immigration of the foreign element in the native soil. The new comers, newly born or newly arrived, are the victims. For the natives this is a process of evolution, and they stand it better; for the foreigners it is a revolution, awful and menacing at the entrance to the loveliest gardens of the earth.

The endemicity of the disease depends essentially upon the infantile native population. By endemicity I mean that the disease may recur, after an interval, in the same place, without the necessity of importation from another locality. The question of the spontaneous origin of diseases should not be allowed to obscure this subject. As I understand it, the spontaneous origin implies one of two things: We must either admit the possibility of spontaneous generation, which is, so far as we know, absurd; or else we must define the point at which and the circumstances under which a certain species of micro-organism becomes pathogenic. Pregnant though these subjects may be with the solution of most important problems, their field appears as yet to be circumscribed to the laboratory. In defining the source of endemicity we should confine ourselves, as probably nearer the truth, to the consideration of those elements that maintain the vitality of the micro-organism and the susceptibility of the population.

In the present case of yellow fever these conditions are maintained, in the natural course of events, in the habitations of the natives. The facts point to the following as the natural history of the disease.

I wish to introduce this subject by reminding the reader of the well-known fact that, as a rule, the infection of yellow fever disappears readily from circumscribed spots; that, for instance, the history of the U. S. S. *Plymouth* is exceptional; that houses unquestionably infected during a season frequently cease to be so without any special measures having been taken for their disinfection. But if it is true that the germ of yellow fever is easily destroyed by means unknown to us, it is also true that at times, for reasons also unknown, in certain spots it retains its vitality for longer periods of time. Hence the Memphis epidemic of 1879 and the outbreak of the *Plymouth*.

Admitting this, let us see what is the course of events in some regions of the yellow-fever zone. Let us start at the end of an epidemic in one of the lesser Antilles, or one of thé second-class ports of Cuba, or in Key West, all places that belong to the same category from an epidemiological point of view. What would be the consequence if a few houses remained infected at the end of an epidemic? Not necessarily an epidemic on the following year. The child born during the epidemic and who escaped the disease may be the only susceptible person brought within the influence of the poison during the following winter or summer, because he continues to live in the same house. The social relations between the native families may bring to that house one or more similarly susceptible children. This one child or few children sicken. The disease is not diagnosed as yellow fever. If the cases are very few, and fewer or none the deaths, no attention is paid to the matter. The year is called a healthy year. The existence of yellow fever is not recognized. No stranger has been attacked. And why not? Because, in the first place, the immigration of foreigners is considerably checked on the year following an epidemic of yellow fever; and, in the second place (a point that has been overlooked), the stranger, the foreigner, is not a frequenter of the homes of the natives. In many of these countries there is an avoidance of intimacy between the foreign element and the natives. I do not mean to imply that this is always the case, but it is sufficiently so to account for the exemption of that element that is supposed to be the only test of the presence of yellow fever. Under these circumstances, it will be asked, why do we not meet with exceptional cases of recognized yellow fever? The answer to this is that we do meet with them. They are the cases, known in all these localities, of sporadic yellow fever.

In Key West in the year 1884 there was no yellow fever apparent in town. I was residing in the city at the time but did not then hold the same views that I do now, or I might have been able to point to an occasional and unexplainable attack of fever amongst the children. In the month of August an officer of a United States ship, who came ashore, as well as others, on several occasions, was attacked with yellow fever. He was treated for a few days on board ship and subsequently by myself at the marine hospital. The vessel immediately sailed for the North. No other cases occurred on board or in town.

There is also the history of the wife of a collector of customs in Key West. She had resided for many years on the island and was supposed to be acclimated, as they call it. She was taken sick and died of yellow fever during the cold season, at a time when there was no suspicion of the existence of the disease. But I need not multiply the histories of sporadic cases of yellow fever.

The above description does not apply to all post-epidemic years. It is not difficult to account for the variations from that type. Either because a greater number of children escaped during the epidemic, or because a larger number of foci of infection remained, or because some of these happened to be in more frequented places, the result is that a greater activity of the disease will be apparent, though still perhaps unrecognized. In such years the French authors will note the existence, amongst the natives of the *mauvaises fièvres*, or the *fièvre inflammatoire;* the Cubans will report the presence of some cases of *fiebres malas*, or *perniciosas*, the English will speak of a rather sickly season amongst the children, and will report cases of ardent fever, or bilious remittent. The history of the season is completed with one or more sporadic cases of yellow fever.

In the course of a varying number of years this situation must have either one or the other of the following terminations:

(1) The disease will exhaust itself; it will disappear entirely from a locality where it has had a self-supporting existence, if I may so express myself, for several years. This termination, I claim, must be very rare in the majority of the ports of Tropical America that are subject to yellow fever. And yet we find that in many of these ports several series of years of exemption are pointed out. I believe that it would not be difficult to prove that this exemption is only apparent, and that, for many of the years at least, the status is merely one of restriction of the endemic to its natural habitat, such as I have described above. When, however, the disease has entirely disappeared, we may say that the endemicity in that locality has ceased; it requires fresh importation for its re-establishment.

What little we know of the aborigines in those latitudes of America would lead us to think that such was with them the usual termination of these epidemics, as it is with our own epidemics of small-pox, whooping cough, measles, etc. These savages were at least acquainted with and practiced the best means towards procuring such results. I refer to their custom of changing their residences every eight years. It should also be remembered that they were less exposed to the accident of importation on account of the restriction of means of communication between different sections.

(2) The other termination is the usual one at present, namely, the development of another epidemic. This is the result of a natural evolution or of an accident. The first takes place through the gradual accumulation of susceptible natives born since the last epidemic, and of susceptible foreigners; the second is the result of importation.

The last epidemic of Key West was brought about by the operation of both causes. I believe that yellow fever is at present endemic in Key West. That isolated, sporadic, unrecognized cases occurred every year since 1881. I recognize now that I had myself some of these to treat amongst the children. Besides these we had, to my knowledge, the case of the officer of the *Galena* in 1884, and the case of a Scotchman who died under suspicious circumstances in October of 1882.

Let not the reader demur at the possibility of thus keeping in a state of activity isolated foci of infection. It is simply the consequence of an utter disregard of all sanitary measures. Has not small-pox become an endemic disease in the city of Havana? Has not cholera threatened to implant itself upon the same soil? And does not the history of the *Plymouth* prove the possibility of maintaining such isolated foci of infection?

To return to Key West. The year 1887 found a large susceptible population of domestic origin and of foreign importation. The winter quarter, December, 1886, and January and February, 1887, showed already a remarkable increase of the death rate of white children under five years of age, in excess of any previous year for that quarter. Not so the adults. These showed no perturbation at this time. Therefore we hear nothing of yellow fever.

Now during this same winter the family of Mr. Bolio brought over from Havana the furniture belonging to a hotel kept by them in that city. This furniture was stored in a house situated in the center of the commercial portion of the city.

The Havanese are certainly not afraid of yellow fever, and hotel-keepers are no exception to this rule. When the United States yellow-fever commission visited Havana in 1878 there was a war amongst the first-class hotels as to which would secure the prize, namely, the commission, with its laboratory and no scarcity of infected material. It was not necessary, therefore, to obtain, as it was done, certificates to show that cases of yellow fever had been treated in the hotel of Mr. B.

The first cases of recognized yellow fever occurred in the house immediately adjoining that of Mr. B., and very soon after the death of this gentleman. Not that he had yellow fever, for he had lived many years in Havana, but the mattress on which he died, and which was part of the furniture brought from Havana, was exposed in the yard, and it is natural to suppose that there was some further upturning of the house and furniture. The first cases of yellow fever immediately followed in the adjoining Baker restaurant, and from hence the further ramifications of the epidemic. These ramifications can be followed for a short distance, but they soon become lost in a general outbreak of the disease.

This account of the natural history of epidemics of yellow fever would be incomplete if I did not take cognizance of two other elements in the causation of epidemic outbreaks. One is the possibility that a focus of infection may be for a time entirely inoperative, because it is inaccessible. The cleaning out of a house, the opening of some old drain may be the means of bringing into action the germ of the disease.* The length of time that the poison may lay dormant in this manner has not been determined; but the further removed such outbreaks are from the last epidemic, the greater should be our suspicions that the cause of the outbreak may be looked for elsewhere. I am not convinced that such periods of absolute latency have ever extended much over one year.

The other agency that I have not yet discussed is much more important than the above. I refer to the epidemic wave. By this I do not mean the transmission of the poison from place to place by some aerial wave. I mean that in certain years some meteorological or other unknown conditions prevailing over more or less extent of territory, are favorable to the maintenance and diffusion of the foci of infection. This theory is by no means strained. It certainly explains many of the facts in the history of yellow fever, and has been very generally accepted. These favorable conditions to the development of yellow fever have always received careful attention. They have been discussed as essential causes of the disease or as requisites for its spontaneous development, but their true position in the etiology of infectious diseases is, I believe, the one assigned to them in the above passage.

Of these several influences I propose to discuss only one, and it is the prevalence of winds. The importance of this has been advocated by very high authority, and the recorded facts prove it to be true, at least in some localities in the West Indies. (Compare especially the reports of French physicians.) Here the suspected winds are from the southwest. I do not think that it is necessary to suppose that these winds have any direct action in stimulating the growth of the special

* This sentence, written by Dr. Guitéras and filed here some months before the outbreak of the Jacksonville epidemic, has lately received a singular confirmation of its truth in the outbreak of the yellow fever at Jackson, Miss., this summer of 1888, where the tearing down of an old depot, with its adjacent latrine, was the cause of the reappearance of the disease. There had been no yellow fever in Jackson since 1878.—J. B. H.

micro-organisms. The oppressive feeling engendered in those regions by the southwesterly winds finds, in my opinion, a sufficient explanation in the construction of the houses. From the palace to the hovel everything is built with an aim to get the full benefit of the prevailing easterly winds. The blessed trade-winds penetrate through every one of the large openings in tropical houses, and sweep through them, ventilating the inmost recesses. The houses seem to breathe from the eastward, and turn their backs to the westward. The winds from the latter quarter remove the natural means of disinfection of these dwellings.

It is very probable that other unknown causes are operative in favoring the activity of the foci of infection.

The centers of population that are subject to yellow fever can be divided into three classes: (1) Centers of annual epidemics; (2) centers of periodic epidemics; (3) centers of accidental epidemics. In the latter the disease is not endemic. There are, however, no permanent lines of demarkation, nor can there be in any classification suggested. The second class is the original type of the yellow-fever country, such as it existed, in my opinion, before the discovery and colonization of America. (See p. 42.)

To this category belong some of the second-class ports of Cuba, such as Baracoa, the French islands of Martinique and Guadalupe, and probably all the lesser Antilles, together with many ports along the tropical Atlantic in America and Africa. Here belongs also the city of Key West. It is very probable that the cities of Charleston and New Orleans have belonged to this category during the present century, but they do not now. The description I have given above of the natural history of yellow-fever epidemics applies especially to centers of this class. Here the conditions are favorable for the maintenance from year to year of isolated foci of infection. The number of these may diminish and become circumscribed to the infantile native population, or they may increase, producing another outbreak of the disease. In the first instance we may have an absolute disappearance of the disease, but much more frequently only a period of apparent exemption. During these periods it does not appear necessary to restrict the commercial intercourse with these ports, provided we are satisfied that they uphold an honest administration of health matters, and that prompt information will be given of any change in the situation. Otherwise these ports are to be considered as suspicious.

If the second class is the representative of the original yellow-fever country, we find that the first and third classes are the outgrowth of the foundation of permanent cities, and the establishment of commercial intercourse along the shores of the tropical Atlantic.

It will suffice to mention some examples of the third class. Such are New York, Philadelphia, Cadiz, etc., and, at present, I believe, also all the Southern ports of the United States except Key West. A rigid prevention of the introduction of infected material will keep them free from the disease.

To the first class belong the cities of Havana, Matanzas, Santiago de Cuba on the island of Cuba, and Vera Cruz in Mexico. Of these I can speak positively. There are other ports that belong to the same category, including some that our present information would lead us to classify in the second class. But these matters have to be determined by personal inspection, or absolutely reliable information. In weighing the latter we should know the nativity, the business relations, and the medical opinions of the person that furnishes it.

In July of 1883 I visited Vera Cruz under orders of the surgeon-general of the Marine Hospital Service, and found evidence that yellow fever was annually epidemic in that city, and had been so for many years, though a report had been made to the contrary not long before. In a report[1] presented on that occasion I called attention to a distinctive feature of the epidemics in localities belonging to this group, and it is that the number of cases of yellow fever regularly increase with the advent of summer. For instance, the annual epidemic of 1883 in Vera Cruz developed in the following manner:

The number of deaths from yellow fever were:

January	5
February	3
March	7
April	16
May	90
June	261
July up to the 18th	144

This is, of course, evidence of the origin of the disease from numerous local foci. When the disease is imported it generally commences later in the season, often in August or September.

In the cities of the first class it is found that there is a comparative preponderance of the foreign adult population, which occupies the commercial portions of the city and receives yearly additions. The result is that the disease does not depend for its maintenance upon the presence of growing generations of susceptible children. The foreigners and the natives keep up effectually their several foci of infection, and will continue to do so until a war of thorough sanitation is carried into both places of fastness of the disease. By so doing we may hope to convert these centers into centers of the second class.

The question arises whether the supposed immunity of the creoles that I have combated in this paper may not be a phenomenon restricted to these cities of the first class, where, it is said, children become accustomed from the moment of their birth to the influence of the yellow-fever poison. Beside the very cogent argument advanced by Dr. Chaillé, to the effect that there is no known poison, whether infective or otherwise, to which human beings become accustomed by taking it in the largest doses during early childhood, I would add the following:

(1) Many children are born in these centers of the first class during periods or seasons which exactly correspond to the years of restriction of the endemic in the centers of the second class. I refer to all the children that are born in the former centers during the winter months.

(2) That some of the children affected in Key West were born in Havana. They had left that city before having had yellow fever.

(3) That, judging from what I have seen and heard of infantile pathology in these localities, I have no doubt that the records of the mortality, if properly made, would teach the same lesson that is found in my Key West tables. We have for Havana the mortuary tables already mentioned of Dr. del Valle. But they give neither the age or the nativity under the heading of the several causes of death. We are unable, therefore, to eliminate the disturbing element of the movement of troops and other foreigners. A high death rate from yellow fever would lead us to expect a corresponding effect upon the children, when the truth may be that the force of the epidemic has shown itself among large bodies of troops that have been moved with the usual reckless-

[1] Annual report of the surgeon-general of the United States Marine Hospital Service for 1883.

ness into the city. The adult population in Havana is vastly out of proportion to the infantile, and the excess is made up of foreigners. These are mostly Spanish males, young, vigorous fortune seekers. During the first years of their stay on the island of Cuba they are very generally excluded from the society of the natives, where alone they could find white women to marry. The result is that a large proportion of their earlier progeny, if they have any, belongs to the colored race, the mortality of which, as I have shown, is not sensibly affected by yellow fever.

The fact is, in my opinion, though I have no statistical data to support it, that in the cities of the first class we should be able to trace the operations of the separate centers of infection, the native and the foreign. The former following the course of a center of the second class, the latter of the first class. Hence it is that we hear, periodically, certain years in which the *fiebres malas*, *fiebres perniciosas*, etc., are very prevalent. In such years even an exceptional case of a native is reported as yellow fever.

It will be acknowledged that our means of combating this disease, whether as hygienists or therapeutists, are very unsatisfactory. And they must so remain as long as we have no knowledge of the essential cause whose operations have been partially studied in this paper. It is a matter of very serious importance and should receive for its solution very liberal aid from the Government of the United States. The disease may strike at any time upon the shores with a deadlier hand than foreign foe. Patriotism grows exultant over political platforms wherein are mentioned the means of defense against an armed invasion, but not a voice is raised for the public health. And yet that flag for which millions are voted to uphold its honor with gunpowder will be found flying at half-mast over the vessel that brings pestilence to our shores. Costly public buildings are erected, expeditions are sent to the north pole, but the Government has been slow in making appropriation for the establishment of necessary quarantine stations, and has never yet made any sustained effort towards investigating this or any other disease.

I shall conclude this report by indicating several plans that have appeared to me to be the most apt to reach the desired end.

No method of investigation of this disease can be successful if it is not systematic and continued. Nothing, for instance, can be more painful than to read the numerous obstacles encountered by Surgeon G. M. Sternberg in a hurried trip made to Brazil and Mexico to investigate, under provisions of a bill of Congress, the claims of Freire and Carmona. It is not in this manner that the patient and self-sacrificing labors devoted to this end for many years by this distinguished scientist are to be utilized.

The best and most thorough plan, in my opinion, is to fit out a vessel with all the appliances of etiological research, to cruise in the Gulf of Mexico and the Caribbean Sea. By this means we could secure a reliable history of the disease at different ports, and a thorough and continued investigation of bacteriological problems, with the advantages of a selection of the site, and independence of action, whilst, at the same time, the Government and the health authorities throughout the country would be kept informed as to the sanitary condition of ports in commercial intercourse with the United States.

Other plans that suggest themselves are, the establishment in connection with the office of the United States sanitary inspector of a well-equipped bacteriological laboratory in the city of Havana, or at one of the quarantine stations of the United States in southern waters. The latter seems to be the most practicable method under the existing provisions of the Government for the care of the public health. An objection to this plan may be found in the probable scarcity of material for research. But this may be obviated if one of the quarantine stations is located within easy access of the city of Havana.

I append below the original tables constructed from the data of the death certificates. Others, more experienced than myself in handling statistical data, might have presented the subject more clearly and more tersely. I hope, however, that all errors have been avoided.

In regard to the facts that I have adduced, and the opinions that I have ventured to advance, I may be permitted to say, in conclusion, that I have given my attention to this subject for many years, and that, being myself a Cuban, my acquaintance with some of the countries and people of which I speak may be considered thorough.

[Yellow-fever year, 1875; no-fever year, 1877.]

Quarter.	Total number of deaths.	Adults.		Children five years and under.			One year and under.		Children ten years and under.			Yellow fever.			Group.						
		White.	Colored.	White.	Colored.	Unknown.	White.	Colored.	White.	Colored.	Unknown.	Children.	Adults.	Total.	A.	B.	C.	D.	E.	F.	G.
1875.																					
First	46	24	3	10	6	....	8	5	10	8	....	...	..	...	1	..	3	1	...	5	..
Second	66	20	9	28	7	...	23	5	29	8	....	...	2	2	5	...	2	8	...	5	...
Third	124	54	10	46	11	....	20	7	48	12	....	6	26	32	2	...	2	15	...	10	11
Fourth	61	24	9	19	7	....	11	5	20	7	....	....	....	..	1	...	2	4	...	4	3
Total	297	122	31	103	33	....	62	22	107	35	....	6	28	34	9	...	9	28	...	24	14
1877.																					
First	35	15	6	8	4	2	6	4	8	4	2	...	...	..	2	..	...	2	...	...	1
Second	76	26	5	35	8	1	29	6	35	8	1	...	..	..	7	1	2	7	..	1	1
Third	68	18	9	25	14	1	15	11	26	14	1	...	...	...	3	...	1	9	...	1	3
Fourth	53	20	5	18	8	....	9	5	19	9	..	...	...	...	5	1	...	3	1	...	1
Total	232	79	25	88	34	4	59	26	88	35	4	...	...	...	17	2	3	21	1	2	6

NOTE.—Population in 1875, 7,043; in 1877, 8,067.

[Yellow-fever year, 1878; no-fever year, 1877.]

Quarter.	Total number of deaths.	Adults: White.	Adults: Colored.	Children five years and under: White.	Colored.	Unknown.	One year and under: White.	Colored.	Children ten years and under: White.	Colored.	Unknown.	Yellow fever: Children.	Adults.	Total.	A.	B.	C.	D.	E.	F.	G.
1878.																					
First	42	20	5	13	4	....	9	4	13	4	....	...	...	...	3	...	...	2	2	1	...
Second	79	14	6	41	16	1	23	10	42	16	1	...	...	...	2	...	13	7	...	1	2
Third	68	26	9	15	15	....	11	9	16	17	....	...	6	6	4	...	5	4	...	3	3
Fourth	53	26	6	12	6	....	7	1	14	7	....	1	4	5	2	...	...	1	...	6	2
Total	242	86	26	81	41	1	50	24	85	44	1	1	10	11	11	...	18	14	2	11	7
1877.																					
First	35	15	6	8	4	2	6	4	8	4	2	...	...	...	2	...	...	2	...	..	1
Second	76	26	5	35	8	1	29	6	35	8	1	...	...	...	7	1	2	7	...	1	1
Third	68	18	9	25	14	1	15	11	26	14	1	...	...	...	3	...	1	9	...	1	3
Fourth	53	20	5	18	8	....	9	5	19	9	....	...	...	...	5	1	...	3	1	...	1
Total	232	79	25	88	34	4	59	26	88	35	4	...	..	...	17	2	3	21	1	2	6

NOTE.—Population in 1878, 8,631; in 1877, 8,067.

[Yellow-fever year, 1880; no-fever year, 1879.]

Quarter.	Total number of deaths.	Adults.		Children five years and under.			One year and under.		Children ten years and under.			Yellow fever.			Group.						
		White.	Colored.	White.	Colored.	Unknown.	White.	Colored.	White.	Colored.	Unknown.	Children.	Adults.	Total.	A.	B.	C.	D.	E.	F.	G.
1880.																					
First	31	9	9	7	5	....	2	2	8	5	....	....	..	...	1	...	...	1	2	...	2
Second	49	12	6	21	7	3	12	7	21	7	5	...	...	...	1	...	8	4	...	...	1
Third	77	12	11	38	13	....	26	7	30	15	....	....	....	...	9	...	3	12	..	1	2
Fourth	79	27	6	30	6	....	14	2	40	6	....	11	6	17	4	...	5	...	...	13	1
Total	236	60	32	96	31	3	54	18	108	33	5	11	6	17	15	...	16	17	2	14	6
1879.																					
First	40	9	5	13	10	....	10	6	14	11	....	....	....	....	3	...	2	4	...	1	...
Second	64	18	4	22	16	....	14	11	24	17	....	....	....	....	3	...	1	8	1	...	1
Third	54	19	6	20	7	....	11	4	21	8	....	....	....	....	2	...	1	1	...	2	5
Fourth	24	10	1	10	3	....	7	....	10	3	....	....	....	....	....	...	2	1	...	...	...
Total	162	56	16	65	30	....	42	21	69	39	....	....	....	....	8	...	6	14	1	3	6

NOTE.—Population in 1880, 9,889; in 1879, 9,240.

[Yellow-fever year, 1881; no-fever year, 1882.]

Quarter.	Total number of deaths.	Adults.		Children five years and under.			One year and under.		Children ten years and under.			Yellow fever.			Group.						
		White.	Colored.	White.	Colored.	Unknown.	White.	Colored.	White.	Colored.	Unknown.	Children.	Adults.	Total.	A.	B.	C.	D.	E.	F.	G.
1881.																					
First	76	31	11	22	10	....	16	8	23	10	....	1	1	2	1	...	6	7	...	2	1
Second	70	17	12	30	10	..	17	5	31	10	....	...	...	...	2	...	5	8	...	...	2
Third	94	33	10	38	13	....	29	8	38	13	....	...	1	1	5	1	5	6	...	2	2
Fourth	59	20	5	25	6	...	10	3	26	8	....	1	4	5	4	1	2	5	1	2	1
Total	299	101	38	115	30	....	72	24	118	41	....	2	6	8	12	2	18	26	1	6	6
1882.																					
First	37	19	6	8	4	....	6	3	8	4	....	....	....	....	....	...	2	1	...	...	1
Second	60	6	10	25	17	....	15	11	25	19	....	..	....	....	1	...	8	8	1	1	2
Third	55	12	8	21	12	....	9	9	21	13	....	....	....	....	2	...	5	4	1	...	...
Fourth	53	21	6	14	11	....	11	9	14	12	....	....	....	....	3	...	1	1	1	...	...
Total	205	58	30	68	44	....	41	32	68	48	....	....	....	....	6	...	16	14	3	1	3

NOTE.—Population in 1881, 10,585; in 1882, 11,328.

[Yellow-fever year, 1881; no-fever year, 1883.]

Quarter.	Total number of deaths.	Adults.		Children five years and under.			One year and under.		Children ten years and under.			Yellow fever.			Group.						
		White.	Colored.	White.	Colored.	Unknown.	White.	Colored.	White.	Colored.	Unknown.	Children.	Adults.	Total.	A.	B.	C.	D.	E.	F.	G.
1881.																					
First	76	31	11	22	10	....	16	8	23	10	....	1	1	2	1	...	6	7	...	2	1
Second	70	17	12	30	10	....	17	5	31	10	....	...	...	...	2	...	5	8	...	...	2
Third	94	33	10	38	13	....	29	8	38	13	....	...	1	1	5	1	5	6	...	2	2
Fourth	59	20	5	25	6	....	10	3	26	8	....	1	4	5	4	1	2	5	1	2	1
Total	299	101	38	115	39	...	72	24	118	41	....	2	6	8	12	2	18	26	1	6	6
1883.																					
First	41	15	6	10	9	...	8	8	11	9	....	....	....	..	3	...	2	3	...	1	...
Second	52	20	13	15	4	....	14	4	15	4	....	....	....	....	2	...	1	5	...	...	5
Third	72	24	12	23	12	....	21	9	24	12	....	....	....	....	5	1	2	14	...	1	...
Fourth	61	23	9	14	14	....	10	11	15	14	....	....	....	....	2	...	5	3	...	1	1
Total	226	82	40	62	39	....	53	32	65	30	....	....	....	....	12	1	10	25	...	3	6

NOTE.—Population in 1881, 10,585; in 1883, 12,124.

[Yellow-fever year, 1881; no-fever year, 1884.]

Quarter.	Total number of deaths.	Adults.		Children five years and under.			One year and under.		Children ten years and under.			Yellow fever.			Group.						
		White.	Colored.	White.	Colored.	Unknown.	White.	Colored.	White.	Colored.	Unknown.	Children.	Adults.	Total.	A.	B.	C.	D.	E.	F.	G.
1881.																					
First	76	31	11	22	10	....	16	8	23	10	....	1	1	2	1	...	6	7	...	2	1
Second	70	17	12	30	10	....	17	5	31	10	....	...	...	...	2	...	5	8	...	...	2
Third	94	33	10	38	13	....	29	8	38	13	....	...	1	1	5	1	5	6	...	2	2
Fourth	59	20	5	25	6	....	10	3	26	8	....	1	4	5	4	1	2	5	1	2	1
Total	299	101	38	115	39	....	72	24	118	41	....	2	6	8	12	2	18	26	1	6	6
1884.																					
First	66	20	14	20	12	....	15	5	20	12	...	..	...	...	...	..	7	3	...	...	1
Second	93	31	14	34	11	3	25	6	34	11	3	...	...	...	7	2	8	6	...	...	3
Third	114	26	20	46	20	....	24	13	48	20	...	...	...	...	3	1	12	14	...	4	2
Fourth	80	12	8	34	29	....	19	18	35	30	...	...	...	...	2	...	11	5	...	1	...
Total	353	89	51	134	72	3	83	42	137	73	3	...	...	...	12	3	38	28	...	5	6

NOTE.—Population in 1881, 10,585; in 1884, 12,976.

[Yellow-fever year, 1887; no-fever year, 1885.]

1887.																					
First	118	36	8	50	21	....	31	15	53	21	....	...	...	...	7	1	2	6	2	2	1
Second	171	38	18	71	40	1	46	21	73	41	1	...	4	4	11	1	5	15	...	1	4
Third	223	82	22	84	29	....	47	14	87	32	....	12	47	59	9	4	6	8	2	20	2
Fourth	110	27	15	44	20	....	33	6	47	21	...	1	...	1	4	3	4	6	2	1	2
Total	622	183	63	249	110	1	157	56	260	115	1	13	51	64	31	9	17	35	6	24	9
1885.																					
First	87	25	14	31	16	....	17	9	31	17	....	...	...	...	3	...	7	2	...	1	...
Second	71	22	9	24	15	....	19	11	24	16	....	...	...	...	9	1	1	2	...	...	1
Third	87	24	17	30	13	....	15	5	32	14	....	...	...	...	3	..	2	8	1	5	3
Fourth	94	24	11	31	26	2	21	4	31	26	2	..	...	...	7	...	...	6	...	1	...
Total	339	95	51	116	70	2	72	20	118	73	2	...	...	...	22	1	10	18	1	7	4

NOTE.—Population in 1887, 15,906; in 1885, 13,877.

[Yellow-fever year, 1887; no-fever year, 1886.]

1887.																					
First	118	36	8	50	21	...	31	15	53	21	....	...	...	..	7	1	2	6	2	2	1
Second	171	38	18	71	40	1	46	21	73	41	1	...	4	4	11	1	5	15	...	1	4
Third	223	82	22	84	20	....	47	14	87	32	...	12	47	59	9	4	6	8	2	20	2
Fourth	110	27	15	44	20	....	33	6	47	21	....	1	...	1	4	3	4	6	2	1	2
Total	622	183	63	249	110	1	157	56	260	115	1	13	51	64	31	9	17	35	6	24	9
1886.																					
First	82	34	15	19	12	....	16	6	21	12	....	...	...	...	2	2	3	...	...	1	...
Second	136	38	17	61	20	....	43	16	61	20	....	...	...	..	8	...	8	7	...	...	...
Third	132	47	10	41	31	....	35	23	43	31	....	...	...	...	6	...	4	4	1	2	6
Fourth	89	24	15	26	24	....	13	18	26	24	....	...	...	...	3	...	1	...	...	...	2
Total	439	143	57	148	87	....	107	63	151	87	....	...	...	...	19	2	16	11	1	3	8

NOTE.—Population in 1887, 15,906; in 1886, 14,863.

I have ventured, in the course of this paper, to criticise the opinions of fellow-practitioners concerning the diagnosis of certain cases. On one or two occasions I have referred to willful deception. This is, unfortunately, too true. Such occurrences, however, are met with among physicians who combine politics with pathology, or we may grant an attenuating circumstance in the panic and excitement of the first announcement of the presence of yellow fever.

It is very satisfactory, on the other hand, to notice everywhere an honest endeavor to ascertain the truth. In this spirit my observations have been written, and they concern my own former opinions, as well as the opinions of others.

The authors that I have quoted may have been wiser than I have been in not pushing their conclusions as far as I have ventured to do. It is interesting, however, to observe how far they go in this direction in some passages of their work, and then to find others that are contradictory or show an unwillingness to accept all the consequences of an acknowledged truth. It appears to me that the position of these authors is well described in a passage of Mr. Darwin, referring to another subject. He says: "Nothing is easier than to admit in words the truth of the universal struggle for life, or more difficult—at least I have found it so—than constantly to bear this conclusion in mind."

M. Bérenger-Féraud, after having pushed the matter almost to a satisfactory conclusion, to the effect that the "fièvre inflammatoire" (to which, he admits, the natives are subject) is the yellow fever, asks most unexpectedly: "But if we push the subject to the extreme, can we admit that they are in all cases identically the same disease? I firmly believe that this would be a great mistake." (Page 368, vol. 1, Maladies des Européens aux Antilles.)

Again, we are surprised to find, in page 499, the following statement: "I know of no case of yellow fever in a child less than five years of age, whether native or foreigner," and in page 495: "As to the question of immunity of the creoles, it must be observed, that, other things being equal, this immunity is far greater amongst the inhabitants of the cities of the littoral where yellow fever prevails."

In the modest and invaluable work of M. Rufz de Lavison (Chronologie des maladies de la Ville de Saint Pierre, Martinique) we find the most decided expression of opinion on the subject that we are discussing, in the shape of a question, to which no answer is given. And if we seek for an answer in his own opinions, as expressed throughout the rest of the book, I am afraid we should have to answer no. The question is found in page 63: "May we not consider the children born since the last epidemic as being in the same conditions with the non-acclimated, and may we not look upon yellow fever as one of those diseases that occur but once in the same individual, and against which the best protection is a previous attack?" We look in vain throughout his work for any evidence of this first attack among the children. Considerable space is devoted to the consideration of what are called "les fièvres graves du pays." These are said to be very prevalent among the creoles in yellow fever years; but at the same time our author resents (page 67) an attempt made by Chervin to show that in his (Lavison's) opinion these "fièvres graves du pays" and yellow fever are one and the same thing. On the other hand, in pages 45 and 53, speaking of the use of quinine, it is apparent that he is not satisfied with the opinion that these fevers are malarial.

Dr. Carlos Finlay, of Havana, an indefatigable student of the yellow fever, in his Apuntes sobre la Historia primitiva de la Fiebre Amarilla, 1884, contributes also interesting matter to this discussion. We find, in the first place, that he expressly assents to the views of Bérenger-Féraud. In so much as Dr. Finlay excludes the discussion of creole immunity, to that extent are his views clearer than those of the French author. But when this subject is touched upon we find him to state (page 5): "The day might arrive in which even the inhabitants of the locality would become amenable to the yellow fever, almost on an equal with foreigners;" and again (page 15), "the indigenes were not endowed with that immunity which characterizes the inhabitants of localities habitually visited by this pestilence." And (page 28), "the yellow fever amongst the aborigines was perpetuated along the sea shore by means of the communications with the highlands, from whence the subjects came that were apt to reproduce in its full strength the primitive morbific agent."

In the opinion of Dr. Finlay we have a true and a bastard form of yellow fever—*fiebre amarilla vera* and *fiebre amarilla frustra*, the latter being a result of the attenuation of the virus. But there is no distinct statement of the operations of this bastard form upon the mass of the population. The bastard form, our author tells us, is the fièvre inflammatoire of the French. In a second memoir on the history of yellow fever he says: "The fièvre inflammatoire or bastard yellow fever still prevails in those islands (the lesser Antilles) during the intervals between epidemic periods of true yellow fever."

M. Cornillac (Recherches Chronologiques et Historiques sur l'Origine et la Propagation de la fièvre jaune, etc., 1886) states very positively, page 266: "*Les indigènes qui habitent le littoral où règne ordinairement la fièvre jaune, arrivés à l'âge adulte, sont seuls indemnes de cette affection*, ils subissent un acclimatement relatif qui les rend alors inhabiles à la contracter." This acclimatization is brought about either by successive gradual attacks or by one definite attack, either of which occur, ordinarily, in childhood, after the age of two years." He quotes Leroy de Méricourt to the effect that this operation is similar to that of vaccination with respect to small-pox. He further gives support to his opinion by citing the interrogation of M. Lavison, above quoted.

But M. Cornillac presents no proof of his assertion, and does not, in my opinion, bear it in mind in the course of his valuable contribution. We find, for instance, in page 103: "If the Antilles are *par excellence* the country for childhood and old age, on account of the temperature, they certainly are not favorable to adult life. We are born and we die there, but we do not live unless we are endowed with a special organization." At page 125, to show that the natives of Martinique and Guadeloupe may have yellow fever, he cites exceptional cases of natives coming from the interior to the sea shore in 1852 and 1853. Speaking of the early historians (page 250) he says: "They describe the hemorrhages, the black vomit, and they establish, above all, that redoubtable preference that the disease shows towards the newly arrived Europeans." Finally, we note in page 149: "We do not believe that the scourge that ravages to-day the islands and continent of America was endemic to the aborigines of the greater Antilles who inhabited the littoral of the sea, from whence they derived their sustenance, and who, consequently, must have enjoyed the immunity of all those who are born and live in the yellow-fever zone."

I would finally refer the reader to a very important communication by Dr. A. Lota (Archives de Médicine Navale, Tome 14me, 1870, p. 315.)

This paper contains the report of several cases showing the similarity of the fevers of creole children with mild cases of yellow fever. This author leaves no doubt in the mind of the reader as to his opinion. He says: "The fevers that affect creole children during epidemics of yellow fever, are more or less accentuated forms of the same disease; and the immunity of creole adults, who have resided during childhood in their native countries, is not the result of ethnical or climatic influences, but merely the preservation obtained by a previous attack of the disease."

I give now two examples of what is the received opinion concerning the influence of age upon yellow fever. "Rare in childhood and old age, yellow fever attacks principally the adolescents and the adults." Traité de Fièvres Bilieuses et Typhiques des Pays Chauds. A. Corre, 1883. This much esteemed contemporary believes that the natives suffer a process of mithridatic infection.

The recent work of Dr. Fernand Roux (Traité Pratique des Maladies des Pays Chauds) states: "Children and the aged show but little predisposition to be attacked by yellow fever."

I conclude these few quotations with one from Greensville Dowell (Yellow Fever and Malarial Diseases, 1876). "Every person is liable to have it who has not had the disease; either old or young, thick or thin, creole or foreigner, black or white, and all seem to have it alike." A very broad assertion, in support of which I do not find that he presents any proof.

INVESTIGATION

INTO THE

FOOD SUPPLY OF SEAMEN.

PHILADELPHIA, SAN FRANCISCO, AND NEW ORLEANS.

REPORT ON THE FOOD OF SEAMEN COMING INTO THE PORT OF PHILADELPHIA, PA.

By Preston H. Bailhache, Surgeon M. H. S.

VESSELS OF THE UNITED STATES.

Evidence obtained from seamen and others:

Andrew Johnson, seaman on board brig *Harry Smith*, from Bangor, Me., to Italian ports on the Mediterranean and return; three months on the vessel. Provisioned in Bangor, Me., for the round trip. Crew received, salt meats, all they wanted; canned meats twice a week; potatoes, onions, beans, canned tomatoes, rice, soft bread daily; common bread for breakfast; salt fish once a week. Always two vegetables, with meat, for dinner; hash and potatoes for breakfast, with coffee; water, all they wanted. He says that United States vessels furnish the best and most abundant food of any nation, and do not confine themselves to the allowance table. (See inclosure marked C.)

Jens Carl Jensen, seaman on bark *E. D. Peters*, from Boston to Boca Bune, with lumber; ninety-two days out, and eighty days on return trip, in ballast. Provisioned in Boston for round trip: salt beef, pork, and fish, ham, canned meats, potatoes, rice, beans, turnips, canned tomatoes, preserved butter, condensed milk, dried apples, dried prunes, eggs preserved in lime and water, grog in bad weather or when all hands are called, soft bread every day, and corn-bread for breakfast. Canned meats were issued twice a week, onions in hash daily, butter Sunday, also ham and eggs, coffee 4 and 8 a. m., and tea or coffee 6 p. m.; all the water they want. Says United States vessels furnish most liberal allowance and best food; British come next, and then the German.

Ole A. Hendrickson, bark *Fluorine;* eleven months on board; sailed from Philadelphia with cargo of coal for St. Thomas, thence in ballast to Mexico, thence with cargo of mahogany and cedar to London, thence in ballast to Greenland, thence with cargo of ores back to Philadelphia. Obtained stores for round trip at this port, consisting in salt beef, pork, and fish, hams, flour, corn-meal, canned meats, potatoes, beans, onions, rice, and other vegetables. Soup generally for dinner, with meat and two kinds of vegetables, coffee daily, soft bread, very little hard bread unless the flour ran short, but plenty hard bread on hand for emergency. The smaller stores replenished if they ran short at the various ports touched. (Abundant provisions stored in Greenland for emergency.) Water, abundant supply and generally good, taken at various ports as needed. United States vessels furnish best and most abundant food.

Note.—Physical examination of seamen of this vessel is made each year at the marine-hospital office, Philadelphia, Pa.—P. H. B.

Thomas McDonald, ship *Nancy Pendleton;* on board one hundred and fifty-one days; sailed from San Francisco to Limerick, Ireland, with grain; thence to New York in ballast; thence to Yokohama with oil; thence to San Francisco with coal obtained in northern British possessions. Stores principally obtained in New York for round trip; small stores taken in at various ports as needed: Salt meats and salt fish, canned meats, soft bread, potatoes, rice, beans, pease, onions, etc. Two kinds of vegetables at dinner, and no stint as to meat and bread or water; coffee, tea, sugar, and molasses also furnished.

John Boyd, bark *Alaska* from New York to African ports and return, nine months' voyage. Vessel provisioned at New York for round trip. Similar statement to that of other seamen on American vessels. Canned meats used mostly in making soups. Lime juice not much used nowadays, as canned meats render it unnecessary. It is issued once a week on long voyages.

A mass of statements similar to above obtained from seamen, which would only be a repetition to produce here. Found only one "complainer" among those questioned, and he was an old chronic.

GREAT BRITAIN.

Seamen on vessels of Great Britain state that supplies are obtained at English ports, except American flour, salt beef, and pork, which are preferred; also American canned food. The supply is governed by the allowance table and is usually sufficient. Many vessels obtain their supplies on this side. No Government inspection is required.

Nova Scotia vessel, ship *Grande*, from Cardiff to Hong-Kong and Hong-Kong to New York: one and one-half pounds salt beef, no pork or fish, and no canned meats; hard bread and spoiled soft bread; had potatoes for eight days after leaving port; after that other small vegetables sparsely; pea soup and rice soup alternated daily; obtained fresh beef at Hong-Kong, but it was not good; four or five of the crew sick and full of boils; two going to hospital. Lime-juice plentiful.

NOTE.—This master was reported to consul on return to New York, but upon trial no action was taken against him.

One seaman stated that English vessels furnished very salt meat on long voyages, which was usually "freshened" by hanging it behind the vessel in crates. All food weighed and measured. Hard bread principally furnished on long voyages; "sea pie," made of flour, potatoes, small pieces beef and other scraps of meat, a frequent "bill of fare" for dinner. Vessels built and manned at Prince Edward Island are said to furnish very poor food, mostly salt fish, though "jerked beef" is furnished when in Cuban ports. This article is said to be used extensively by "sugar and molasses" vessels while waiting for the crop to come in. It is brought to Cuba from Texas by small schooners and piled up on the wharves in great abundance. It is sold to any vessel that will take it and is cheap, but not very palatable. Fresh meat in Cuba is also cheap, but very poor.

NOTE.—Attention is invited to the letter of the British consul and the allowance table. (See inclosure marked "B.")

DANISH VESSELS.

Vessels of Denmark are supplied with salt pork, salt beef, rye and hard bread, potatoes, onions, and small vegetables; also 1 pound butter per week and coffee daily. The salt pork and beef is said to be splendid, even better than American, which is next best.

See allowance table, inclosure marked "F," which is strictly adhered to, and all complaints investigated by the Government. The health of the crew is especially looked after and no excuse accepted if the medical supplies are not provided.

PRUSSIAN VESSELS.

Seamen state that food is abundant, but not so palatable as on United States and English vessels. Breakfast, barley bread and coffee; 1 pound butter per week. Dinner, 1 pound beef or pork, potatoes, cabbage, onions or rice, sour krout, bean or pea soup; fish Wednesday. Supper, hard bread, butter, and tea.

NOTE.—See bill of fare (inclosure marked "D") furnished by the German consul, C. H. Myer, who stated to me that "rations are subject to regulations of each port."

ITALIAN VESSELS.

J. K. J., on board schooner *Gelda*. No meats furnished. Supplies obtained in Italian ports and consist mainly in macaroni, rice, and oil. Breakfast, coffee and hard bread; dinner, macaroni or rice, with fried oil and onions poured over it; supper, hard bread and dumplings boiled in oil. Once a day eggs are furnished from chickens on board, and pancakes three times a week. Macaroni is furnished four times a week and rice three times a week.

Similar statements are made by other seamen on Italian vessels.

NOTE.—Attention is invited to the letter of Baron Squitti, Italian consul, in which he states that the "amount of provisions must not be less than that fixed for the Royal navy," and giving a copy of the "allowance," in which it will be seen meat is included, notwithstanding the statement of seamen to the contrary. (Inclosure marked "E.")

FRENCH VESSELS.

T. F. seaman on bark *Raunpra*, of Bordeaux, loaded with grain from San Francisco to Falmouth, one hundred and twenty-nine days out; obtained supplies at French ports; mostly fed on salt pork and potatoes, fresh bread three times a week and hard bread the balance of the time; onions occasionally, but no lime-juice; grog every morning and claret at dinner and supper; for extra work got extra grog; a condenser attached to galley stove furnished plenty of water.

NORWEGIAN VESSELS.

Salt meat and hard bread are furnished *ad lib*, but no soft bread. "Duff" once a week at dinner; salt fish twice a week; potatoes and rice occasionally. As a general thing the rations are of poor quality and not great variety.

GERMANY.

NOTE.—See "bill of fare" furnished by C. H. Myer, German consul, inclosure marked "G." Seamen's statements agree in the main with the allowance provided by the Government. There appears to be a great deal of discretion allowed, however, both to the masters of vessels and their agents, but the supplies are usually abundant and give satisfaction.

Very respectfully,

PRESTON H. BAILHACHE,
Surgeon United States Marine-Hospital Service.

Allowance schedule.

Vessels.	Food furnished.	Obtained	Remarks.
United States.	1 pound bread, 1½ pounds beef (or 1¼ pounds pork), ½ pound flour, ⅛ pint peas, ⅛ ounce tea, ½ ounce coffee, 2 ounces sugar, 3 quarts water, 1 ounce coffee, cocoa, chocolate, may be substituted for ⅛ ounce tea; molasses for sugar; vegetables may be substituted for each other; water ad. lib.	At home port, for round trip. Small stores as needed at ports touched.	Soft bread is now furnished, also canned meats, and a great variety of vegetables. Sleeping accommodations are usually poor—no water-closets. No inspection of food, water, or medicine-chest is had.
Great Britain.	1 pound bread, 1½ pounds beef (or 1¼ pounds pork), ½ pound flour, ⅛ pint peas, ⅛ ounce tea, ½ ounce coffee, 2 ounces molasses, 3 quarts water. Equivalents furnished at master's option.	.... do......	The bread allowed is hard bread; very little soft bread furnished. Fresh meat, or tinned meats; fresh vegetables, or preserved or compressed vegetables, may be substituted for each other. Inspection of food only on passenger steamers.
Germany	1 pound bread, 1 pound beef (or ¾ pound salt pork, or ½ pound smoked pork, or salt, dried or fresh fish in sufficient quantities), 1 pound butter per week (or lard or olive oil), 1½ gallons water, potatoes, beans, peas, barley, oatmeal, flour or other vegetables in sufficient quantities; $\frac{7}{16}$ pounds coffee per week, $\frac{1}{16}$-pound tea per week, and pepper, salt, molasses according to want. Equivalents at option of master.	..... do......	Hard bread referred to. All rations may be reduced by master if he deem it advisable on account of scarcity, etc. No inspection of food, water, or medicine-chest.
Prussia	7 pounds hard bread per week, 1 pound butter per week or 2 pounds molasses per week, 1 pound coffee per month, 3 ounces tea per month, 1 pound fresh meat three times per week when in port, ½ pound pork or ¾ pound codfish 4 times a week; vegetables in moderate quantities, and brandy or whisky if master desires.	..... do	Soft bread is not furnished; canned meats not furnished; no inspection of food, water, or medicine-chest.
Italy..........	1⅛ pounds white biscuit or 1½ pounds fresh bread daily, 1½ ounces cheese, 10 ounces fresh meat, 2 ounces rice, 1½ ounces legumen, 4 ounces macaroni, or peas, or beans, ¾ ounce coffee, ⅝ ounce sugar, 1½ ounces red wine, salt, pepper, etc. Sunday, macaroni and ragout; Monday, rice and bean soup; Tuesday, macaroni and meat; Wednesday, rice and bean soup; Thursday, macaroni and meat; Friday, macaroni; Saturday, rice, bean soup, and boiled meat.	..... do	Salt meat while sailing instead of fresh meat. Engineers are given an extra quantity of wine or brandy. All persons on sailing vessels are entitled to 1 pound of wood.
Denmark	7 pounds bread per week, 1½ pounds bacon for 2 days, 3 pounds beef for 3 days, 1 pound stock or dried fish for 2 days, 1 pound of butter per week, barley, peas, sugar, coffee, tea, and beer in sufficient quantities, the latter 1 "pot" (equal to 1 quart per day); vegetables may be substituted one for the other.	..... do......	Hard rye biscuits or wheat biscuits. Fresh meat with greens twice a week, or preserved meat while at sea once a week, and ½ pot soup. Health of crew carefully looked after and medicine-chest inspected once a year.
France	1 pound fresh bread 3 times a week, hard bread balance of time, 1½ pounds beef or 1¼ salt pork, potatoes and other vegetables, tea and coffee in sufficient quantities; wines twice a day, and grog if weather stormy.	..... do......	French vessels are supplied with a greater variety of fancy provisions and nicknacks, which are given out as master directs.
Norway	1 pound hard bread or biscuit, 1½ salt meats, but not of best quality, salt fish twice a week; potatoes and rice, or barley once or twice a week. Cooking poor.	Purchased at ports where cheapest.	No soft bread furnished; 1 pound of butter is expected to last a month, and is issued monthly, so that seamen have it to take care of.

Allowance schedule—Continued.

Vessels.	Food furnished.	Obtained.	Remarks.
Sweden.......	About same as Norwegian vessels..	Purchased at ports where cheapest.	Same. No inspection is made and but little interest is taken by the masters of vessels of Sweden and Norway, or by the Government in the manning of their vessels, the exodus of the young men of those countries being already too great to need such encouragement as well-supplied ships.
Austria.......	......do	..... do......	Do.
South America	......	......	Little or no commerce among the vessels of South America and Philadelphia; mostly carried on by British steamers, which put in at Baltimore and New York.

The following is a copy of a circular letter addressed to the various consulates in this city:

SIR: I have the honor to respectfully request the following information, if not inconsistent with your rules: (1) A schedule of the food furnished seamen on board merchant vessels coming into this port, showing kind of food, quality, and amount allowed each seaman, also amount of water allowed daily. (2) Do seamen of steam and sailing vessels receive the same kind and quantity of food and water? (3) At what places are food and water obtained before leaving home ports? (4) Have you a printed blank agreement between masters and seamen governing the quantity of food, etc., allowed, and if so, will you please send me a copy of the same.

Very respectfully,

PRESTON H. BAILHACHE,
Surgeon, U. S. M. H. S.

BRAZILIAN VICE CONSULATE,
Philadelphia, February 21, 1888.

MY DEAR SIR: I am entirely unable to give you the information asked for in yours of 16th instant.

There is nothing in this consulate bearing on the matter. When Brazilian vessels are in this port the matter of the subsistence of the crew is left entirely to the purser, whose purchases are controlled by the commandant and are entirely unknown to the consulate.

I remain, very respectfully,

JOHN MASON, JR.,
Vice-Consul.

PRESTON H. BAILHACHE,
Surgeon, U. S. M. H. S.

CONSULADO DE ESPAÑA EN FILADELFIA,
Philadelphia, February 27, 1888.

SIR: There is no law in Spain relating to food and cloth furnished to seamen on board merchant vessels. This a matter left entirely to the interested parties, but they must make especial contracts, in every particular case stating the conditions agreed upon. And so that these may have the necessary legal force, they are copied in a book kept by the masters for the purpose, and this book must be presented to the captain of the ports in Spain and to the consuls in foreign countries, so that they may *visé* the agreements made by the contracting parties, being the only duty of the consuls to see that food and clothing are adapted to the climates to which the vessels are bound to. Consequently, I am unable to furnish you the requested printed blank.

Respectfully, yours,

JOSÉ CONGOSTO,
Consul for Spain.

The SURGEON, U. S. MARINE HOSPITAL SERVICE, *Philadelphia.*

JOHN WANAMAKER,
Philadelphia, February 18, 1888.

DEAR SIR: Yours of the 16th is duly at hand. In reference to the questions about food and water, full information may be obtained from the United States consul at San Domingo, Hon. H. C. C. Astwood.

With great respect, yours, truly,

THOS. B. WANAMAKER.

PRESTON H. BAILHACHE,
Surgeon, U. S. Marine Hospital Service.
[Dictated.]

ANNUAL OF THE UNIVERSAL MEDICAL SCIENCES—EDITORIAL DEPARTMENT,
1632 *Chestnut Street, Philadelphia, February* 18, 1888.

DEAR DOCTOR: Your favor of February 16, addressed to me as consul, has just come to hand.

I will send you full particulars when the next Red Star steamer arrives, the crew list of those vessels bearing the necessary information.

Yours, very truly,

CHAS. E. A. SAJOUS.

CONSUL FOR NICARAGUA,
Philadelphia, February 18, 1888.

DEAR SIR: Nicaragua is improving, but I have to report that she has no vessels that come to the United States.

Yours

HENRY C. POTTER,
Consul of Nicaragua.

Dr. PRESTON H. BAILHACHE,
Surgeon, U. S. Marine-Hospital Service.

CONSULATES OF CHILI, ARGENTINE REPUBLIC, AND ECUADOR,
532 *Walnut street, February* 18, 1888.

SIR: Your favor of the 16th is received this morning. In reply I am sorry to say that I have no information whatever from either of the above Governments from which I can give you answer to the questions propounded.

Very respectfully, yours,

EDW. SHIPPEN,
Consul.

PRESTON H. BAELHACHE,
Surgeon, U. S. M. H. S.

[Frederick Ferdinand Myhlertz, His Danish Majesty's vice-consul, office Twenty-second and Market streets, residence 730 North Twentieth street.—United States of America, royal Danish vice-consulate.]

PHILADELPHAI, *February* 20, 1888.

DEAR SIR: Yours of the 16th instant just received. I inclose to you the printed regulations which you want. I have only this one copy, and have to ask you to return it to me when you are done with it, and oblige,

Yours, truly,

FRED. F. MYHLERTZ.

Dr. PRESTON H. BAILHACHE,
Surgeon, U. S. M. H. S., Philadelphia.

Regulations for the maintenance of the crew and the supply of medicine on board Danish merchant vessels.

With reference to the law of February 23, 1866, concerning discipline on board merchant vessels, misconduct and crimes committed by mariners, as will as hiring agreements, etc., section 41, the following regulations shall hereby be fixed regarding the maintenance of the crew and the supply of medicine on board Danish merchant vessels:

I. Of the maintenance of the crew in general, the weekly fare or allowance for one man shall consist of:

Bread, hard rye biscuits or wheat biscuits	7 pounds.*
Bacon, raw, salted for two days	1.50 quint.
Meat, raw, salted for three days	3
Stockfish or dried fish for two days	1
Butter	1
Barley-groats, for boiled groats or soup	⅓ ottingkar.†
Peas	⅜ ottingkar.
Brown sugar, for tea and coffee	75 quint.
Coffee	25 quint.
Tea	4 quint.
Beer	7 pots.‡

A proper quantity of mustard, salt, vinegar, sugar, or sirup, as well as prunes or dried fruit for barley soup shall be distributed. Potatoes, mash of dried potates, sour-kraut, horse-radish, or dried or preserved vegetables shall be distributed by way of refreshment at least twice a week, both in harbor and in the open sea.

Fresh meat with greens shall be granted to the crew at least twice a week when the vessel is in port, and the allowance thereof is 1 pound of meat for each meal. When the vessel is in the open sea the crew is entitled to the same quantity of fresh meat once a week at least, or, in default thereof to preserved meat, the allowance of which is respectively 50 quint meat without bones and 50 quint strong soup, which is to be diluted with water, so as to make half pot of soup for each man. When fresh meat has been distributed, the meal of salt meat, bacon, or stockfish fixed for the day is to be withheld. On board fishing vessels, where fresh fish is usually to be had, the weekly meal of fresh meat, regulated for the crew when the ship is keeping the sea, can be left out.

All provisions of a vessel shall, at the beginning of a voyage, be fresh, wholesome, and well conserved, and the ship shall be copiously supplied therewith, according to the destination of the voyage, lest any scarcity might arise. At the distribution of allowances the climate on the spot where the vessel is must be taken into due consideration.

From the above regulations the following exceptions can be made:

Bread.—Instead of 7 pounds wheat biscuits a week there can be given 7 pounds hard black biscuits (navy bread), or 10½ pounds soft rye bread, or 7 pounds soft wheat bread.

Stockfish.—If fish is not to be had, instead thereof an allowance of fresh meat, salt meat, or bacon can be granted.

Butter.—In case of the butter being used up, and if no other butter can be procured, there can, instead of the same, be distributed 50 quint olive oil, with necessary vinegar, or 2 pounds sugar, or 2 pounds bacon, as the circumstances and the climate might require.

Barley-groats.—In default of these the same allowance of rice can be given.

Peas.—In default thereof the same allowance of barns can be granted.

Beer.—On short voyages or on voyages in northern climates, where the beer can keep for a long time, a sufficient quantity thereof shall always be in store for the crew on board merchant vessels, in as far as unforeseen circumstances or very long voyages might not render it impossible. When the beer is consumed, and the ship sojourns in places where wine is to be had, for instance in France, Portugal, Spain, and anywhere in the Mediterranean, each man is to have one-fourth pot of wine a day instead of beer. In the open sea, or in places where wine is not a common beverage, there shall, instead of 1 pot beer, either be granted an allowance of brandy and water ("grog"), consisting of one-tenth pot French brandy or rum, with 3 quaint of sugar and due water, or one-sixteenth pot of corn brandy, as circumstances might require; the latter allowance is only to be had at dinner.

Corn brandy shall, beside the case just mentioned, only be distributed when the captain might think fit to do so, for instance during rough weather and fatiguing work, or in hard climates, both cold and warm.

Drinking water.—Vessels bound on long voyage shall be provided with tanks, on short voyages and in cold climates wooden water-casks may be used, but in this case

*A Danish pound (lb.) is subdivided in 100 "quint," and is somewhat exceeding the English pound, as to make 0.907 Danish pound like 1 English pound (avoirdupois).

†One ottingkar Danish (ottkr) is c. 0.061 bushel English measure.

‡One pot Danish is somewhat less than an English quart, as to make 1.2 pot Danish like ˙ quart English measure.

the inside of these casks must either be carbonized or the water must be purified and filtered before it is made use of.

If any article, on account of an unusually long voyage, should be scarce, the crew is entitled to a compensation of another kind for that day, for instance, bacon instead of meat, grits instead of peas, or *vice versa*, with which the crew then must be satisfied.

II. How the health of the crew is to be cared for, and what supply of medicine there shall be on board?

It is the duty of the captain, as far as it lies in his power, to take care of the crew being kept hale, and he must not by an unnecessary over-exertion or by want or deficiency expose them to losing their health. He shall, therefore, at the beginning of the voyage, be mindful that the crew are provided with the necessary clothes according to the length and destination of the voyage as well as with good bedding, that they are kept to order and cleanliness, that their bed clothes shall often be aired, and that they never lie down in wet clothes, and so on.

With regard to anything connected with the regimen on board, the captain shall, morever, make himself acquainted with, and follow such directions as are given about this matter in the "Medical Book for Mariners," by C. W. Horneman, physician of the navy, published in Copenhagen in 1861.

Any vessel that is bound for a foreign port shall, at the beginning of her voyage, be provided with the necessary aliments for a proper sick diet, that any one who, on account of sickness is unable to do his duty, may be put on sick diet. In many cases the sick will be healed merely by a proper diet, which must always be attended to, except in slight cases, particularly external ones. The ship must, for the purpose of being able to procure sick diet, which, according to circumstances, shall be "fever diet," "half diet" or "nutritive diet," as prescribed in the above-mentioned book, p. 142, 143, besides the provisions generally appointed be supplied with a proper quantity of groats, rice, sago, or wheat grits, saloop and light caret or white wines.

The medicine chest of a vessel bound on a longer voyage, shall be supplied with medicine both for internal and external use, bandages, etc., according to the length of the voyage and the number of the crew in which respect the directions given in the above-mentioned "Medical Book," p. 143–150, are to be observed.

Vessels bound for the Baltic, Sweden, and Norway, as well as for the North Sea or the channel (consequently not beyond the channel or west of the Orkneys) shall be supplied with the following common medicine and apparatus, to be used in cases of bodily injuries:

a. Medicine for internal use, calculated for a crew consisting of 4 *to* 6 *men:* Elder-flowers, $\frac{1}{8}$ ℔* (flores sambuci concisi, ℥ii). Chamomile flowers, $\frac{1}{8}$ ℔ (flores chamomillæ vulgaris concisi, ℥ii). Licorice, $\frac{3}{16}$ ℔ (succus glycyrrhizæ, ℥iii). Camphor essence, $\frac{1}{16}$ ℔* (spiritus sulphurico-æthereus camphoratus, ℥i). Hoffman's drops, $\frac{1}{16}$ ℔ (spiritus sulphurico-æthereus, ℥i). Soothing pectoral essence, $\frac{1}{16}$ ℔ (tinctura opii benzoica, ℥i). Bitter rhubarb tinctura, $\frac{1}{16}$ ℔ (tinctura rhei amara, ℥i). Castor oil, $\frac{1}{4}$ ℔* (oleum ricini, ℥iv). Epsom salt, $\frac{1}{4}$ ℔* (magnesia sulphurica, ℥iv). Tartaric acid, pestled, $\frac{1}{16}$ ℔ (acidum tartaricum pulveratum, ℥i). Bitter tea, $\frac{3}{16}$ ℔ (thea amara, ℥iii). Linseed tea, $\frac{3}{16}$ ℔ (semina lini contusa, ℥iii). Copaiba balsam, $\frac{1}{8}$ ℔ (balsamum copaivæ, ℥ii).

b. Medicine for external use: Arnica flowers, $\frac{1}{8}$ ℔ (flores arnicæ concisi, ℥ii). Camphor, $\frac{1}{16}$ ℔ (camphora raffinata, ℥i). Soap spirit, $\frac{1}{8}$ ℔ (spiritus saponatus, ℥ii). Sal ammoniæ spirit, $\frac{1}{8}$ ℔* (liquor ammonii caustici, ℥ii). Alum-powder, $\frac{1}{16}$ ℔* (alumen crudum pulveratum, ℥i). Chloride of lime, $\frac{1}{2}$ ℔ (calcaria chlorata, ℥viii). Blistering plaster, $\frac{1}{8}$ sheet (emplastrum cantharidum perpetuum supra alutam extensum). Gum plaster, $\frac{1}{16}$ ℔* (emplastrum gummosum, ℥i. Sticking plaster, 1 ell † (emplastrum adhæsivum album supra linteum extensum). English plaster, sticking taffeta, a piece of 8 square inches (emplastrum adhæsivum anglicum). Healing salve, $\frac{1}{8}$ ℔* (ceratum simplex, ℥ii). Tar salve, $\frac{1}{8}$ ℔ (unguentum piceum, ℥ii). Chancre-oil (virid æris, ʒss, olei vaparum cocti, ℥ss.). Eye water $\frac{1}{32}$ ℔ (aqua ophthalmic amercurialis, ℥ss).

c. The medicine-chest ought, moreover, to contain: Old linen, $\frac{1}{2}$ sheet. English lint, $\frac{1}{32}$ ℔* (linteum carptum anglicum, ℥ss). Two bandages of linen or cotton cloth of a length of 6 and 8 ells.† Touch-wood, without saltpeter, $\frac{1}{32}$ ℔ (agaricus chirurgorum, ℥ss. Washing-sponges, 2 pieces, small. Field-tourniquet No. 1. Paste-board for splints, $\frac{1}{2}$ sheet.

The medicine is to be delivered from the apothecary's shop where packed, distinctly labeled and furnished with numbers in accordance with the above-mentioned "Medical Book." If some single article of the medicine shall be consumed during the voyage, it is incumbent on the captain to procure a new medicine of the same kind, wherever, for that purpose, an occasion might offer. The medicine-chest ought

*By a pound (℔) is meant the common commercial weight: 1 lb=℥xvi.

†1.5 ell Danish is c. 1 yard English.

to be inspected at least once a year, and such medicine as might possibly be damaged is to be renewed.

Vessels bound for ports in the Kingdom (except, however, the Faroe Islands, Iceland, Greenland, or the West Indies) need only be supplied with such sorts of the above-mentioned medicine and apparatus as are furnished with the subjoined mark (+).

III. *General dispositions.*—The royal mandates of 19th November, 1827, and 22d April, 1828, concerning allowances of crews on board merchant vessels are hereby repealed.

Bill of fare of Bremen vessels.

The ration for each seaman is—

a. Meat—Per day either 500 grams (1 ℔) beef, or 375 grams (¾ ℔) salt pork, or 250 grams (½ ℔) smoked pork (bacon) or salt; dried or fresh fish in sufficient quantities. These meals are furnished generally as follows: Beef four times a week, pork (bacon) twice a week. Fish once a week, or in place of this beef or pork in the foregoing proportions.

b. Bread—Up to 500 grams (1 ℔) per day.

c. Butter—500 grams (1 ℔) per week; however, on trips lasting over six months, in places where butter is not well obtainable, it can be replaced by lard or olive oil, in which case 500 grams (1 ℔) lard, or one-half bottle or 312 grams (⅝ ℔) olive oil are given for 500 grams (1 ℔) butter. But when both of the said articles are not obtainable, one-half ration more of meat or bacon according to position *a* of the foregoing schedule are given.

d. Water—Up to 6 liters (1½ gallons) per day.

e. Vegetables—Dried peas, potatoes, beans, barley, oat-meal, flour, or other vegetables in sufficient quantities.

f. Coffee—156 grams ($\frac{5}{16}$ ℔) per week.

g. Tea—31 grams ($\frac{1}{16}$ ℔) per week.

h. Vinegar—Salt and spices, molasses, all according to wants. Always provided, however, that the captain, in case of need can reduce the rations as he may deem advisable and replace or exchange them for some other article. In ports where fresh meats can be obtained the crew shall receive such at least once a week instead of salt or smoked meats.

NOTE.—The above handed to me by C. H. Myer, German consul.—P. H. B.

Bill of fare of Prussian vessels (Dantzig).

Seven pounds hard bread (biscuit), 1 pound butter, or 2 pounds molasses per week.
One pound coffee per month.
Three ounces tea per month.
One pound fresh meat three times a week when in port, if obtainable.
One-half pound pork, or three-fourths pound codfish, four times a week.
Vegetables in moderate quantities.
Brandy (whisky, etc.), if the captain should deem it advisable.
NOTE.—The above handed to me by C. H. Myer, German consul P. H. B.

PHILADELPHIA, *February* 21, 1888.

DEAR SIR: In reply to your favor of the 16th instant, I am sorry not to be able to give you full information on the subject of the same.

As a rule the amount of provisions to be furnished to the seamen on board of Italian vessels is agreed upon between the parties and fixed by contract. If there is no contract then the amount of provisions must not be less than that fixed for sailors of the Royal navy, a copy of the list of allowance of which you will find here inclosed. There is no difference between seamen of steam and sailing vessels. No mention is made of water.

Yours, very truly,

BARON SQUITTI,
Italian Consul.

PRESTON H. BAILHACHE, Esq.,
Surgeon U. S. Marine Hospital Service, Philadelphia, Pa.

Allowance of victuals to sailors of the Royal navy.

Quality of victuals.	Daily ration: Monday, Wednesday, Saturday.	Tuesday, Thursday, Sunday.	Friday.
White biscuit or ......grams..	550	550	550
Fresh bread ......do....	750	750	750
Cheese * ......do....	50	50	100
Fresh meat † ......do....	300	300	....
Rice ......do....	80	....	....
Legumen ......do....	50	....	140
Macaroni (peas or beans or lentils) ......do....	....	120	120
Coffee ......do....	20	20	20
Sugar ......do ..	25	25	25
Red wine ......centiliters..	46	46	46
Salt ......grams ..	12	12	12
Olive oil ......do....	....	....	30
Pepper ......do ..	....	....	.25
Vinegar ......centiliters..	....	....	3

* On Thursday and Sunday there will be given Holland cheese, and in all the other days Italian cheese. To the persons employed at the engines will be given an extra 23 centiliters of wine and 8 centiliters of brandy. On sailing vessels every person on board is entitled to 500 grams of wood.

† During navigation the portion of salt meat instead of fresh meat will be 290 grams, and that of preserved meat of 133 grams, and the same quantity of broth.

NOTE.—Sunday: Macaroni with ragout. Monday: Rice and bean soup with vegetables and boiled meat. Tuesday: Macaroni and seasoned meat. Wednesday: Rice and bean soup and boiled meat Thursday: Macaroni and stewed meat. Friday: Macaroni soup. Saturday: Rice and bean soup and boiled meat.

BRITISH CONSULATE,
Philadelphia, February 23, 1888.

SIR: In reply to your letter of the 16th instant, with reference to the schedule of food furnished the crews of British vessels, I have to inform you:

(1) That a schedule of food furnished seamen in accordance with the requirements of the merchant shipping act, 1854, is herewith inclosed, showing the nature and amount allowed to each seaman, including water. The quality, as a rule, is good, especially on board steamers, as their voyages are necessarily of a shorter duration, rendering better facilities for fresh supplies. On board sailing-ships on deep-water voyages the food is probably not so good on the whole, being more or less of a greater amount of salt meats and hard bread, subjecting the men to greater risks of getting scurvy, although the law requiring a plentiful supply and use of anti-scorbutics on voyages to warm climates is *stringent.*

(2) The same scale of provisions applies alike to steam and sail. On board the former, however, the practice is to supply a greater amount of fresh bread.

(3) Food and water are obtained at the port where the voyage begins, and all necessary further supplies are taken on board at other ports at the master's option. The water is taken from wells on shore or public water-works.

It may be stated that for some years past complaints as to the quality of food supplied have been *rare,* and when they do arise are rigidly inquired into by the superintendents of the mercantile marine officers at home ports and by Her Majesty's consular officers at foreign ports.

I am, sir, your obedient servant,

ROBT. CHAS. CHIPPERDON,
H. B. M.'s Consul.

PRESTON H. BAILHACHE, Esq., M. D.,
Surgeon U. S. Marine Hospital Service, Philadelphia.

[Office copy (to be forwarded to the registrar-general of seamen). Original executed in twenty pages.—*** Any erasure, interlineation, or alteration in this agreement will be void unless attested by some superintendent of a mercantile marine office, officer of customs, consul, or vice-consul, to be made with the consent of the persons interested.]

B.—Agreement and Account of Crew—Foreign-Going Ship.

[The term "foreign-going" ship means every ship employed in trading or going between some place or places in the United Kingdom and some place or places situate beyond the coasts of the United Kingdom, the islands of Guernsey, Jersey, Sark, Alderney, and Man, and the continent of Europe between the River Elbe and Brest inclusive.]

Name of ship.	Official number.	Port of registry.	Port number and date of register.	Registered tonnage. Gross.	Registered tonnage. Net.	Nominal horse-power of engine (if any).
(Steamers and sailing vessels.)						

Registered managing owner. Name.	Registered managing owner. Address (state number of house, street, and town).	Number of seamen for whom accommodation is certified (30 and 31 Vict. c. 124.)	Distance in feet and inches between center of the disc, showing the maximum load line in salt water and upper edge of lines, indicating the position of the ship's decks above that center. First deck above it. Feet.	First deck above it. Inches.	Second deck above it. Feet.	Second deck above it. Inches.

Scale of provisions to be allowed and served out to the crew during the voyage, in addition to the daily issue of lime and lemon juice and sugar or other antiscorbutics in any case required by 30th and 31st Vict., c. 124, s. 4.

	Bread.	Beef.	Pork.	Tinned meats.	Soup and bouilli.	Preserved potatoes.	Compressed or preserved vegetables.	Flour.	Peas.	Rice.	Tea.	Coffee.	Sugar.	Molasses.	Water.
	Lb.	*Lb.*	*Lb.*	*Lb.*	*Pint.*	*Lb.*	*Lb.*	*Lb.*	*Pint.*	*Lb.*	*Oz.*	*Oz.*	*Oz.*	*Oz.*	*Qts.*
Sunday	1	1½	....	....	.....	.....	....	½	.....	....	⅛	½	....	2	3
Monday	1	....	1¼	....	.....	.....	....	....	⅓	....			Daily.		
Tuesday	1	1½	..	....	.....	.....	....	....	.....	..	....	..	....	....	....
Wednesday	1	....	1¼	....	.....	.....	....	½	.....	..	....	....	..	....	....
Thursday	1	1½		..	.....	.....	....	....	⅓	..	..	....	..	....	....
Friday	1	....	1¼	....	.....	.....	....	....	....	....	..	....	....	....	....
Saturday	1	1½	...	...	.....	.....	....	½	⅓	....	....	....	...	....	....

NOTE.—In any case an equal quantity of fresh meat or fresh vegetables may, at the option of the master, be served out in lieu of the salted or tinned meats or preserved or compressed vegetables named in the above scale.

Substitutes.—Equivalent at master's option.

The several persons whose names are hereto subscribed, and whose descriptions are contained on the other side or sides, and of whom —— are engaged as sailors, hereby agree to serve on board the said ship, in the several capacities expressed against their respective names, on a voyage from[1]

And the crew agree to conduct themselves in an orderly, faithful, honest, and sober manner, and to be at all times diligent in their respective duties, and to be obedient to the lawful commands of the said master, or of any person who shall lawfully succeed him, and of their superior officers, in everything

[1] Here the voyage is to be described, and the places named at which the ship is to touch, or if that can not be done the general nature and probable length of the voyage is to be stated.

relating to the said ship and the stores and cargo thereof, whether on board, in boats, or on shore; in consideration of which services to be duly performed, the said master hereby agrees to pay to the said crew as wages the sums against their names respectively expressed, and to supply them with provisions according to the above scale. And it is hereby agreed that any embezzlement or willful or negligent destruction of any part of the ship's cargo or stores shall be made good to the owner out of the wages of the person guilty of the same. And if any person enters himself as qualified for a duty which he proves incompetent to perform, his wages shall be reduced in proportion to his incompetency. And it is also agreed that the regulations authorized by the board of trade, which are printed herein and numbered[1]
are adopted by the parties hereto, and shall be considered as embodied in this agreement. And it is also agreed that if any member of the crew considers himself to be aggrieved by any breach of the agreement or otherwise, he shall represent the same to the master or officer in charge of the ship in a quiet and orderly manner, who shall thereupon take such steps as the case may require. And it is also agreed that[2]

The authority of the owner or agent for the allotments mentioned within is in my possession.[3]

——— ———,
Superintendent, Officer of Customs, or Consular Officer.

In witness whereof the said parties have inscribed their names on the other side or sides hereof on the days against their respective signatures mentioned.
Signed by ——— ———, master, on the ——— day of ——— 188—.

Port at which voyage commenced.	I hereby certify the above to be a true copy of the agreement entered into by the persons whose signatures or marks are herein subscribed, and that the entries contained in this office copy are the same in every respect as those contained in the original agreement entered into before me. ——— ———, *Superintendent.*

N. B.—This form must not be unstitched. No leaves may be taken out of it, and none may be added or substituted. Care should be taken at the time of engagement that a sufficiently large form is used. If more men are engaged during the voyage than the number for whom signatures are provided in this form an additional form Eng. 1 should be obtained and used.

Name of ship, ——— ———.

Reference number.	Signatures of crew.	Particulars of engagement.													Address of master and crew.
		Year of birth.	Town or county where born.	If in the reserve, number of commission or R. V. 2.	Ship in which he last served, and year of discharge therefrom.		Date and place of signing this agreement.		In what capacity engaged, and if master, mate, or engineer, number of certificate.	Time at which he is to be on board.	Amount of wages per week, calendar month, share, or voyage.	Advance agreed to.	Amount of weekly or monthly allotment.	Signature or initials of superintendent, consul, or officer of customs.	
					Year.	State name and official number of port she belonged to.	Date.	Place.							
	1	2	3	4	5	6	7	8	9	10	11	12	13	14	15
1 2	Master to sign first.								Master.						
3															
4															
5															
6															

[1] Here are to be inserted the numbers of any of the regulations for preserving discipline issued by the board of trade and printed on the last page hereof, which the parties agree to adopt.
[2] Here any other stipulations may be inserted to which the parties agree, and which are not contrary to law.
[3] This is to be signed if such an authority has been produced, and to be scored across in ink if it has not.

B.

Account of apprentices on board (if any).

Christian and surnames of the apprentices at full length.	Year of birth.	Registry of indenture.	
		Date of—	Port of—
1	2	3	4

Regulations for maintaining discipline, sanctioned by the Board of Trade in pursuance of the merchant shipping act, S. 149.

These regulations are distinct from and in addition to those contained in the act, and are sanctioned but not universally required by law. All or any of them may be adopted by agreement between a master and his crew, and thereupon the offenses specified in such of them as are so adopted will be legally punishable by the appropriate fines or punishments.

These regulations are all numbered, and the numbers of such of them as are adopted must be inserted in the space left for that purpose in the agreement, page 1, and the following copy of these regulations must be made to correspond with the agreement by erasing such of the regulations as are not adopted. If the agreement is made before the superintendent of a mercantile marine office, his signature or initials must be placed opposite such of the regulations as are adopted.

For the purpose of legally enforcing any of the following penalties, the same steps must be adopted as in the case of other offenses punishable under the act—that is to say, a statement of the offense must, immediately after its commission, be entered in the official log-book by the direction of the master, and must at the same time be attested to be true by the signatures of the master and mate, or one of the crew; and a copy of such entry must be furnished or the same must be read over to the offender before the ship reaches any port or departs from the port at which she is, and an entry that the same has been so furnished or read over, and of the reply, if any, of the offender, must be made and signed in the same manner as the entry of the offense. These entries must, upon discharge of the offender, be shown to the superintendent of a mercantile marine office before whom the offender is discharged; and if he is satisfied that the offense is proved, and that the entries have been properly made, the fine must be deducted from the offender's wages, and paid over to the superintendent.

If, in consequence of subsequent good conduct, the master thinks fit to remit or reduce any fine upon any member of his crew which has been entered in the official log, and signifies the same to the superintendent, the fine shall be remitted or reduced accordingly. If wages are contracted for the voyage or by share, the amount of the fines is to be ascertained in the manner in which the amount of forfeiture is ascertained in similar cases under section 252.

No.	Offense.	Amount of fine or punishment.	Signature of superintendent.
1	Striking or assaulting any person on board or belonging to the ship (if not otherwise prosecuted)	Five shillings.	
2	Bringing or having on board spirituous liquors	Five shillings.	
3 {	Drunkenness, first offense	Five shillings.	
	Drunkenness, second and for each subsequent offense	Ten shillings.	
4	Taking on board and keeping possession of any fire-arms, knuckle-duster, loaded cane, slung-shot, sword stick, bowie-knife, dagger, or any other offensive weapon or offensive instrument without the concurrence of the master, for every day during which a seaman retains such weapon or instrument	Five shillings.	

SHIPPING ARTICLES.

Notice is hereby given that section 4510 of the U. S. Revised Statutes makes it obligatory on the part of the master of a merchant vessel of the United States to cause a legible copy of the agreement (omitting signatures) to be placed or pasted up in such part of the ship as to be accessible to the crew, under a penalty not exceeding one hundred dollars.

Notice is also given that section 10 of the act of June 26, 1884, prohibits the payment of advance wages to seamen shipping in ports of the United States, and that section 11 of the same law requires that vessels shall be provided with slop-chests. These two sections, being of special importance to seamen, are annexed in full.

C. B. Morton,
Commissioner of Navigation.

Advance wages.

Sec. 10. That it shall be, and is hereby, made unlawful in any case to pay any seaman wages before leaving the port at which such seaman may be engaged in advance of the time when he has actually earned the same, or to pay such advance wages to any other person, or to pay any person, other than an officer authorized by act of Congress to collect fees for such service, any remuneration for the shipment of seamen. Any person paying such advance wages or such remuneration shall be deemed guilty of a misdemeanor, and, upon conviction, shall be punished by a fine not less than four times the amount of the wages so advanced or remuneration so paid, and may be also imprisoned for a period not exceeding six months, at the discretion of the court. The payment of such advance wages or remuneration shall in no case, except as herein provided, absolve the vessel, or the master or owner thereof, from full payment of wages after the same shall have been actually earned, and shall be no defense to a libel, suit, or action for the recovery of such wages: *Provided*, That this section shall not apply to whaling-vessels: *And provided further*, That it shall be lawful for any seaman to stipulate in his shipping agreement for an allotment of any portion of the wages which he may earn to his wife, mother, or other relative, but to no other person or corporation. And any person who shall falsely claim such relationship to any seaman in order to obtain wages so allotted shall, for every such offense, be punishable by a fine of not exceeding five hundred dollars, or imprisonment not exceeding six months, at the discretion of the court. This section shall apply as well to foreign vessels as to vessels of the United States; and any foreign vessel the master, owner, consignee, or agent of which has violated this section or induced or connived at its violation, shall be refused a clearance from any port of the United States.—*Act June 26, 1884.*

SEC. 3. That section 10 of the act entitled "An act to remove certain burdens on the American merchant marine and encourage the American foreign carrying trade, and for other purposes," approved June twenty-sixth, eighteen hundred and eighty-four, be amended by striking out the words "That it shall be lawful for any seaman to stipulate in his shipping agreement for an allotment of any portion of the wages which he may earn to his wife, mother, or other relative, but to no other person or corporation," and inserting in lieu thereof the following: "That it shall be lawful for any seaman to stipulate in his shipping agreement for an allotment of all or any portion of the wages which he may earn to his wife, mother, or other relative, or to an original creditor in liquidation of any just debt for board or clothing which he may have contracted prior to engagement, not exceeding ten dollars per month for each month of the time usually required for the voyage for which the seaman has shipped, under such regulations as the Secretary of the Treasury may prescribe, but no allotment to any other person or corporation shall be lawful." And said section ten is further amended by striking out all of the last paragraph after the words "vessels of the United States," and inserting in lieu of such words stricken out the following: "And any master, owner, consignee, or agent of any foreign vessel who has violated this section shall be liable to the same penalty that the master, owner, or agent of a vessel of the United States would be for a similar violation."—*Act June 19, 1886.*

Vessels of United States must have slop-chest, etc.

SEC. 11. That every vessel mentioned in section forty-five hundred and sixty-nine of the Revised Statutes shall also be provided with a slop-chest, which shall contain a complement of clothing for the intended voyage for each seaman employed, including boots or shoes, hats or caps, under clothing and outer clothing, oiled clothing, and everything necessary for the wear of a seaman; also a full supply of tobacco and blankets. Any of the contents of the slop-chest shall be sold, from time to time, to any or every seaman applying therefor, for his own use, at a profit not exceeding ten per centum of the reasonable wholesale value of the same at the port at which the voyage commenced. And if any such vessel is not provided, before sailing, as herein required, the owner shall be liable to a penalty of not more than five hundred dollars. The provisions of this section shall not apply to vessels plying between the United States and the Dominion of Canada, Newfoundland, the Bermuda Islands, the Bahama Islands, the West Indies, Mexico, and Central America.—*Act June 26, 1884.*

SEC. 13. That section eleven of "an act to remove certain burdens on the American merchant marine and encourage the American foreign carrying trade, and for other purposes," approved June twenty-sixth, eighteen hundred and eighty-four, shall not be construed to apply to vessels engaged in the whaling or fishing business.—*Act June 19, 1886.*

UNITED STATES OF AMERICA.

Articles of agreement between master and seamen in the merchant service of the United States.

[Required by act of Congress, Title LIII, Revised Statutes of the United States.]

U. S. SHIPPING COMMISSIONER FOR THE PORT OF ——— ———, 18——.

It is agreed between the master and seamen, or mariners, of the ——— ——— of which ——— ——— is at present master, or whoever shall go for master, now bound from the port of (1) ——— ——— to and such other ports and places in any part of the world as the master may direct, and back to a final port of discharge in the United States, for a term of time not exceeding ——— calendar months. (2)

Going on shore in foreign ports is prohibited, except by permission of the master.

No dangerous weapons (3) or grog allowed, and none to be brought on board by the crew.

[1] Here the voyage is to be described, and the places named at which the ship is to touch, or, if that can not be done, the general nature and probable length of the voyage is to be stated, and the port or country at which the voyage is to terminate.

[2] If these words are not necessary they must be stricken out.

[3] Section 4608, Revised Statutes, prohibits the wearing of sheath-knives on shipboard, and the master informs the crew of this law.

Scale of provisions to be allowed and served out to the crew during the voyage in addition to the daily issue of lime and lemon juice and sugar, and other antiscorbutics in any case required by law.

	Bread, lb.	Beef, lb.	Pork, lb.	Flour, lb.	Peas, pint.	Tea, oz.	Coffee, oz.	Sugar, oz.	Water, qts.
Sunday	1	1½	....	½	....	⅛	½	2	3
Monday	1	....	1¼	....	⅓	⅛	½	2	3
Tuesday	1	1½	....	½	....	⅛	½	2	3
Wednesday	1	......	1¼	....	⅓	⅛	½	2	3
Thursday	1	1½	....	½	....	⅛	½	2	3
Friday	1	....	1¼	....	⅓	⅛	½	2	3
Saturday	1	1½	......	....	......	⅛	½	2	3

Substitutes.—One ounce of coffee or cocoa or chocolate may be substituted for one-quarter ounce of tea; molasses for sugar, the quantity to be one-half more; one pound of potatoes or yams; one-half pound flour or rice; one-third pint of peas or one-quarter pint of barley may be substituted for each other.

When fresh meat is issued, the proportion to be two pounds per man, per day, in lieu of salt meat.

Flour, rice, and peas, beef and pork, may be substituted for each other, and for potatoes onions may be substituted.

And the said crew agree to conduct themselves in an orderly, faithful, honest, and sober manner, and to be at all times diligent in their respective duties, and to be obedient to the lawful commands of the said master, or of any person who shall lawfully succeed him, and of their superior officers, in everything relating to the vessel, and the stores and cargo thereof, whether on board, in boats, or on shore, and in consideration of which service to be duly performed the said master hereby agrees to pay to the said crew, as wages, the sums against their names respectively expressed, and to supply them with provisions according to the annexed scale. And it is hereby agreed that any embezzlement or willful or negligent destruction of any part of the vessel's cargo or stores shall be made good to the owner out of the wages of the person guilty of the same: *And if any person enters himself as qualified for a duty which he proves himself incompetent to perform his wages shall be reduced in proportion to his incompetency.* And it is also agreed that if any member of the crew considers himself to be aggreived by any breach of the agreement or otherwise, he shall represent the same to the master or officer in charge of the ship in a quiet and orderly manner, who shall thereupon take such steps as the case may require.

It is also agreed that[1]

The authority of the owner or agent for the allotments mentioned within is in my possession.

——— ———,

Shipping Commissioner or Consular Officer.

This is to be signed if such an authority has been produced, and to be scored across in ink if it has not.

In witness whereof the said parties have subscribed their names on the other side or sides hereof on the days against their respective signatures mentioned.

Signed by ——— ———, master, on the ——— day of ———, 188—.

Date of commencement of voyage.	Port at which voyage commenced.	These columns to be filled up at the end of the voyage.			
		Date of termination of voyage.	Port at which voyage terminated.	Date of delivery of lists to shipping commissioner.	I hereby declare to the truth of the entries in this agreement and account of crew, etc. ——— ———, *Master.*

N. B.—This form must not be unstitched. No leaves may be taken out of it, and none may be added or substituted. Care should be taken at the time of engagement that a sufficiently large form is used. If more men are engaged during the voyage than the number for whom signatures are provided in this form, an additional form should be obtained and used.

Any erasure, interlineation, or alteration in this agreement will be void, unless attested by a shipping commissioner, consul, vice-consul or commercial agent, to be made with the consent of the persons interested.

[1]Here any other stipulations may be inserted to which the parties agree and which are not contrary to law.

Signature of seaman.	Birthplace.	Age.	Height. Feet.	Height. Inches.	Description. Complexion.	Description. Hair.	Wages per month.	Wages per run.	Amount of monthly allotment.	Time of service. M.	Time of service. D.

Whole amount wages.	Wages due.	Place and time of entry.	Time at which to be on board.	In what capacity.	Shipping commissioner's signature or initials.	Allotment payable to—	Conduct and qualification.

Certificates or indorsements made by shipping commissioners and consuls.

REPORT RELATIVE TO FOOD ISSUED TO SEAMEN ON MERCHANT VESSELS ARRIVING AT SAN FRANCISCO, INCLUDING STATEMENTS OF SEAMEN RELATIVE THERETO. REPORT OF SCURVY TREATED DURING THE SEVENTEEN YEARS ENDED JUNE 30, 1888.

By Surgeon HENRY W. SAWTELLE, *U. S. Marine Hospital Service.*

It is a well known physiological fact that proper aliment furnishes the elements requisite to compensate for the constant waste of the tissues and fluids of the body, and that by the process of digestion and assimilation living organisms are maintained in a state of healthy nutrition. The staple alimentary principles required embrace four classes of solid constituents; namely, albuminous matter, fats, carbo-hydrates, and salines in varying proportions, in conjunction with pure air and water. Hence, considering the functional lesions that may supervene either from an excess or deficiency of these elementary principles, the value of a diet table constructed and enforced in conformity with the requirements of the economy can hardly be overestimated.

Within the past few years ship dietaries have been made the subject of special attention with a view of protecting sailors from those diseases of a preventable nature the outgrowth of improper food, and as a result some reformatory measures based upon wise legislation have been instituted for the accomplishment of the end desired. Under the shipping act of 1884 the Government has adopted a scale of provisions to be allowed and served in certain specified quantities to the crews by masters of all merchant vessels of the United States engaged in the foreign trade, or those trading between the Atlantic and Pacific coasts. This law compels the insertion of the scale in the articles of agreement for each cruise, and the issue of lime or lemon juice or other antiscorbutics is made compulsory. The ration provided for by this scale contains, it is believed, the elements of a complete food in abundance, assuming that the articles are of good quality and served as contemplated. The object of this report being to determine as to the observance of the regulations at sea, the scope of the inquiry was limited mainly to an inspection of incoming vessels, principally those from long voyages, including such data as could be obtained from seamen in hospital lately on deep-water ships. Quite a number of vessels were visited hailing from New York, Liverpool, Australia, Sandwich Islands, etc., consisting of American and British bottoms. During the visits on board it was impracticable to secure documentary evidence as to the actual amount of food issued to the men on the voyage, but the schedule was invariably found embodied in the ship's papers, the stores on board were excellent, and this, taken in connection with the further fact that there was no sickness among the crews worthy of mention, notwithstanding the severe weather that many of them had encountered during the voyage, forced the conclusion that the men had been generally well cared for. The accompanying quite detailed statements of a number of seamen in hospital, representing seventeen ships (ten American and seven foreign), may be taken as illustrative cases, and will perhaps indicate pretty closely as to how far the law is carried out aboard many ships respecting the supply of food. Though it was impossible to obtain the exact amounts issued in all cases, the different lists show that oftentimes a more elaborate and varied diet is provided than that found in the regular scale. In several instances some of the provisions were reported by the men as deficient in quantity and inferior in quality. Six American and two foreign vessels failed to serve lime or lemon juice, but the most of them used instead vinegar or other antiscorbutics. The United States Shipping Commissioner for this port advises me that no complaints relative to food have ever been filed at his office. I also learned from the British, French, German, and Swedish and Norwegian consuls that but comparatively few complaints had been received by them during the past few years. But notwithstanding this favorable testimony from such reliable sources, it is believed that the food or lime-juice regulation is strictly observed on but few, if any, merchant vessels arriving here; and the only rational explanation for the apparent contradictions is, that the facts relating to the treatment of sailors are to a great degree concealed, probably in the majority of cases, by a lawless and inhuman horde of vagabonds that swarm around vessels before they drop anchor even, and who take charge of the sailors as if they were animals, drug and debauch them in low boarding-houses, and in case they offer any remonstrance the punishment is cruel treatment on the spot. It is generally understood also that these outrages are frequently committed with the knowledge if not the consent of the officers of the ship. This view is confirmed by seamen and others interested in maritime affairs. It is also asserted that in many instances the question of diet is agreed upon between the master and crew after the ship sails from port, without regard to the scale inserted in the articles of agreement, the men in most cases accepting the ration offered and provided at the discretion of the commander in place of the governmental allowance. It is quite evident from the foregoing that, to guard against an inferior quality and quantity of supplies, an inspection of the stores should invariably be made before any deep-water ship is allowed to clear. Moreover, if it was understood that surveys would always be held at the port of destination on any portion of the provisions, and investigations made regarding the issue of food and lime-juice whenever proper cause is shown therefor, and penalties inflicted should the charges be proved, it would undoubtedly secure a more strict compliance with the laws promulgated for the guidance of mariners and increase the efficiency of sailors correspondingly.

Among the dietetic diseases treated at this hospital, scurvy forms the most interesting and instructive part; and this report would be incomplete without mentioning the subject here. This is a disease of malnutrition, and without dwelling upon the ætiology, pathology, treatment or history of the malady, it is sufficient to say that all authorities agree that it is caused, for the most part, by long continued privation of certain nutritive principles contained in fresh vegetable food. Among the contributing or additional causes may be noted in general terms various disabilities contracted prior to shipment; extremes of heat and cold; the habit of many eating sea bread soaked in "slush," or grease; long continued service at sea; overwork; damp and filthy quarters; individual uncleanliness, etc. It was known to the Father of Medicine, and has prevailed more or less extensively from time immemorial. One of the most notable epidemics on land broke out during the potato famine in Ireland in 1847, and in the early months of the Crimean war the French lost more men from scurvy than from bullets. During the last war in this country, 1861–'64, out of 807,000 cases there were 47,000 of scurvy with a death rate of 16 per cent. On account of shipwreck and other disasters incident to navigation, it has always been a special foe to seamen, owing to the impossibility of procuring frequent supplies of fresh food and water; but under ordinary circumstances in modern times, with steam largely utilized in place of sail, there is but little excuse for the appearance of such a scourge. Indeed, it has been said, justly, that when "a sailor dies of scurvy, some one must be as responsible as if the fatal event were due to poisoning."* The record of the disease at this hospital is therefore of special value in this connection. During the past seventeen years 9,951 sick and disabled seamen were admitted, including both American and foreign sailors, and out of this number 391 suffered from scurvy and 12 died. The subjoined table compiled in chronological order gives the number of cases treated each year, together with the nationality of the vessels from whence they were admitted, viz:

Years.	American vessels.	British vessels.	German vessels.	French vessels.	Italian vessels.	Russian vessels.	Japanese vessels.	Norwegian vessels.	Belgium vessels.	Total.	Remarks.
1872	18	5	....	13	......	....	.....	....	5	41	
1873*a*	32	......	.....	......	......	......	......	......	......	32	1 death, American.
1874*a*	29	......	.....	......	......	......	......	......	......	29	1 death, American.
1875*a*	12	......	......	......	......	.....	......	....	......	12	
1876	28	43	5	....	1	......	......	....	......	77	2 deaths, 1 Italian, 1 British.
1877	15	9	.....	......	......	......	......	....	......	24	1 death, American.
1878	12	3	.....	......	......	.....	4	....	.....	19	1 death, British.
1879	13	2	.....	......	....	......	......	......	......	15	
1880	8	1	.....	.....	......	......	.....	....	......	9	
1881	23	4	7	.....	......	.....	.....	.....	......	34	3 deaths, 2 Americans, 1 German.
1882	5	18	8	.....	......	1	.....	.....	......	32	1 death, British.
1883	7	5	2	.....	......	......	....	......	......	14	
1884	13	1	......	......	......	......	......	......	......	14	2 deaths, Americans.
1885	7	4	......	.....	7	......	......	.....	......	18	
1886	6	2	......	......	......	....	......	1	......	9	
1887	3	1	2	......	......	......	......	......	......	6	
1888	4	2	......	......	......	......	....	......	......	6	
Total	235	100	24	13	8	1	4	1	5	391	

a Foreign seamen not treated at Marine Hospital during the years 1873, 1874, and 1875.

From the above statistics it will be observed that scurvy has diminished very largely at this port within the period covered by the table, both from American and foreign vessels, while the total number of patients admitted for treatment has gradually increasd. Similar results have been obtained in foreign countries, more especially in the British mercantile marine. In the American Navy, as well as on European war vessels, it is practically extinct, and this immunity from the disease has been brought about by intelligent attention to the health and comfort of the men, by a more rigid observance of sanitary rules, the regulation of diet, and the issue of anti-scorbutics under the authority of law. Thus, with the decrease of scurvy among American seamen, it is shown pretty conclusively that the Congressional enactment of 1884 has been

*Dr. Thomas Hawkes Tanner.

in the main effectual in providing for the physical necessities of our sailors better than formerly, and more in accord with an advanced civilization.

Statement of seamen, giving schedule of food furnished them on vessels arriving at the port of San Francisco.

Name of vessel and voyage.	Scale of food issued during voyage.	Whence obtained.	Quality.	No. sick.
American ship *Arabia*; voyage from Liverpool, England, to San Francisco; one hundred and thirty-four days out.	Fresh bread, two times per week.	Liverpool, England.	Good	2
	Hard-tack, three times a day.	do	do	
	Salt beef, once a day	do	do	
	Salt pork, once a week	do	do	
REMARKS.—One sick with bubo; one, disease unknown. Exact quantity of food not stated. Statement of one member of the crew.	Fresh corned beef, 4 times during voyage.	do	do	
	Salt cod, one time during voyage.	do	do	
	Fresh pork, three times during voyage.	do	do	
	Sugar, coffee, tea, potatoes, vinegar, water, daily.	do	do	
	Lime juice, ½ pint per month	do	do	
American whaling bark *Ohio*; voyage from Honolulu, Sandwich Islands, to Arctic Ocean, thence to San Francisco; two hundred and forty days out.	Bread and hard-tack, salt beef and salt pork, coffee and tea, potatoes, vinegar and water, daily.	Honolulu	do	2
	Bean soup, three times per week.	do	do	
REMARKS.—Disease of sick unknown. Exact quantity of food not stated. No lime juice issued. Statement of one member of the crew.	Cracker hash, every morning.	do	do	
	Pea soup, occasionally	do	do	
	Barley soup, occasionally	do	do	
American schooner *Edward E. Webster*; voyage from Gloucester, Mass., to San Francisco; one hundred and ninety days out.	Hard-tack	Gloucester, Mass	do	12
	Flour	do	do	
	Salt beef	do	do	
	Salt pork	do	do	
	Salt fish	do	do	
REMARKS.—One died; nature of disease unknown, probably scurvy. Entire crew sick, but only two unable to do duty. Flour musty after ninety days out. Put into Montevideo for repairs and purchased 15 bushels of potatoes and 80 pounds fresh pork; thirty days without coffee or tea; one hundred days without vinegar; ninety days without lime juice; seven days without plenty of water. Captain and men ate together. No regular issue of food. Statement of two members of the crew.	Potatoes	do	do	
	Turnips	do	do	
	Apples, fresh	do	do	
	Rice	do	do	
	Beets	do	do	
	Vegetables for soup	do	Poor	
	Oleomargarine	do	Good	
	Sugar	do	do	
	Coffee	do	do	
	Tea	do	do	
	Vinegar	do	do	
	Lime juice	do	do	
	Water	do	do	
	Raisins	do	do	
	Condensed milk	do	do	
	Blue berries	do	do	
	Cornstarch	do	do	
American bark *General Fairchild*; voyage from Philadelphia, Pa., to San Francisco; one hundred and fifty-two days out.	Fresh bread, sugar, coffee, tea, potatoes, vinegar, lime juice, and water, daily.	Philadelphia	do	None.
	Salt beef, salt pork and fresh canned beef, twice per week.	do	do	
REMARKS.—Exact quantity of food not stated. Statement of one member of the crew.	Salt cod or salmon, once a week.	do	do	
	Apples, stewed, and peaches, stewed, twice a week.	do	do	
	Dried vegetable soup, once a week.	do	do	
	Fruit pie, twice a week	do	do	
	Rice, once a week	do	do	
American steam-ship *Alemeda*; voyage from Australia to San Francisco; twenty-five days out.	Fresh bread, fresh beef, butter, marmalade, sugar, coffee, tea, potatoes, and water, daily.	Australia and Honolulu.	do	None.
REMARKS.—Exact quantity of food not stated. No lime juice. Statement of one member of the crew.	Fresh mutton, occasionally	do	do	
	Fresh fish, Fridays	do	do	
	Poultry, twice a week	do	do	
	Rice, once a week	do	do	
	Pies, cakes, and pudding, occasionally.	do	do	

Statement of seamen, giving schedule of food furnished them on vessels, etc.—Continued.

Name of vessel and voyage.	Scale of food issued during voyage.	Whence obtained.	Quality.	No. sick.
American ship *Spartan*; voyage from Hong-Kong, China, to San Francisco; sixty-four days out.	Fresh bread daily	Not known	Not good.	None.
	Salt beef daily	do	Tainted	
	Coffee, tea, water, daily	do	Good	
REMARKS.—No fresh beef, hard-tack, lime juice, or vinegar during the voyage. Exact ration not stated. Statement of one member of the crew.	Salt pork, three times a week.	do	Tainted.	
	Pea soup and bean soup, occasionally.	do	Good	
	Yams, daily for thirty-four days.	do	do	
	Potatoes, daily for thirty days.	do	do	
American ship *Snow and Burgiss*; voyage from New York to San Francisco; one hundred and ninety-four days out.	Fresh bread daily	New York	do	4
	Oatmeal or corn-meal mush, daily.	do	do	
	Vinegar, daily	do	do	
REMARKS.—Two cases scurvy, 1 of intermittent fever, 1 stricture urethra. No potatoes except for the two first days of sailing. Exact quantity of food not stated. No lime juice during voyage. No fresh vegetables or fresh meats during voyage. Three members of the crew certify to this statement.	Hard-tack for hash, salt beef, salt pork, and corned beef, twice a week.	do	do	
	Rice soup, Wednesdays and Saturdays.	do	do	
	Beans, baked, Tuesdays	do	do	
	Bean soup, Fridays	do	do	
	Apples, dried, twice a week.	do	do	
	Pea soup, twice a week	do	do	
	Water, three quarts daily, one hundred and forty-nine days; last forty-five days good drinking water, but poor water for cooking.	do	do	
American ship *Manuel Llaguno*; voyage from New York to San Francisco; one hundred and twenty days out.	Fresh bread, hard-tack, oatmeal, and corn-meal mush, vinegar, and water, daily.	New York	do	3
	Salt beef, three times a week.	do	do	
REMARKS.—One case of scurvy and fracture of rib; one fracture of arm. No butter or marmalade during voyage. Exact quantity of food not stated. Potatoes every morning for two and one-half months; none after that. No fresh vegetables. Statement of one member of crew.	Salt pork, three times a week.	do	do	
	Fresh canned-beef soup, twice a week.	do	do	
	Beans, baked, once a week	do	do	
	Pea soup occasionally	do	do	
	Rice, occasionally	do	do	
	Apples, dried, occasionally	do	do	
	Lime juice, Mondays	do	do	
American whaling bark *Reindeer*; voyage from Honolulu to Arctic Ocean, thence to San Francisco; two hundred and forty days out.	Fresh bread, cracker hash, hard tack, salt beef, salt pork, coffee, tea, potatoes, vinegar and water, daily.	Honolulu	do	
REMARKS.—Some of the men were sick for a day or two. One man wounded by explosion of bomb lance. Exact quantity of food not stated. No lime juice issued. Two members of the crew certify to this statement.	Bean soup, pea soup, and barley soup, occasionally.	do	do	
American steam-ship *New York*; voyage from Yokohama and Hong-Kong to San Francisco; sixty-nine days out.	Fresh bread, fresh beef, fresh mutton, fresh pork, tea, coffee, sugar, butter, and water, daily.	Yokohama and Hong-Kong.	do	1
REMARKS.—One passenger died, nature of disease unknown. Fresh beef, fresh pork, and bananas were obtained at Honolula. Exact quantity of food not stated. No lime juice issued. Two members of the crew certify to this statement.	Poultry, twice a week	do	do	
	Fresh fish, Fridays	do	do	
	Eggs, and oranges, twice per week.	do	do	
Norwegian bark *Europa*; voyage from Bergin, Norway, to San Francisco; two hundred and forty days out.	Hard tack, tea and coffee, potatoes and water, daily.	Cardiff, Wales	do	2
	Salt beef, 1½ pounds, twice per week.	do	do	
	Salt pork, ¾ pound, twice per week.	do	do	

Statement of seamen, giving schedule of food furnished them on vessels, etc.—Continued.

Name of vessel and voyage.	Scale of food issued during voyage.	Whence obtained.	Quality.	No. sick.
Norwegian bark *Europa*—Continued.	Fresh dried fish, twice per week.	Cardiff, Wales	Good	
REMARKS.—Nature of disease unknown. No lime juice or vinegar during the voyage. Exact ration not stated. Statement of one member of crew.	Fresh canned beef, once per week.	do	do	
	Pea soup and bean soup, twice per week.	do	do	
	Butter, 1 pound per week	do	do	
British ship *Dumerdale*; voyage from Cardiff, Wales, to San Francisco; one hundred and fifty-nine days out.	Hard tack, coffee and tea, lime juice, water and sugar, water, daily.	do	do	3
REMARKS.—One case dysentery; two nature of disease unknown. Potatoes four times first week of voyage. Statement of one member of the crew.	Salt beef, 1¼ pounds, twice per week.	do	do	
	Salt pork, ¾ pound, three times per week.	do	do	
	Fresh canned beef, 1 pound, once per week.	do	do	
	Flour, ½ pound, three times per week.	do	do	
	Sugar, 14 ounces per week	do	do	
	Pea soup, three times per week.	do	do	
	Butter, 8 ounces per week	do	do	
	Rice, once a week	do	do	
British ship *Micronesia*; voyage from Liverpool, England, to San Francisco; two hundred and forty days out.	Flour, ½ pound, three times per week.	Liverpool, England.	do	None
REMARKS.—Statement of one member of crew.	Hard tack, coffee and tea, lime juice, water and sugar, ½ pint, water, 3 quarts, daily.	do	do	
	Salt beef, 1½ pounds, three times per week.	do	do	
	Salt pork, 1¼ pounds, three times per week.	do	do	
	Pea soup, three times per week.	do	do	
	Butter, ½ pound per week	do	do	
	Marmalade, 1 pound per week.	do	do	
	Sugar, 1 pound per week	do	do	
	Potatoes, once a week	do	do	
German ship *Undine*; voyage from Antwerp, Belgium, to San Francisco; one hundred and ninety-four days out.	Hard tack, butter, potatoes, water, coffee, and tea, daily.	Bremen	do	None
REMARKS.—No sugar, lime juice, or vinegar issued during the voyage. Exact quantity of food not stated. Statement of one member of crew.	Flour, salt beef, salt pork, cabbage (pickled), beans, and pea soup, twice per week.	do	do	
	Barley soup, once a week	do	do	
	Cucumber pickles, three times a week.	do	do	
British bark *Staffordshire*; voyage from Hull, England, to San Francisco; one hundred and ninety-two days out.	Coffee and tea, daily	Hull, England	do	3
REMARKS.—Two cases scurvy; one disease unknown. Not enough water. Poor potatoes served for four or five days after sailing. Two members of the crew certify to this statement.	Water, daily	do	Poor	
	Flour, 1½ lbs., three times per week.	do	Good	
	Salt beef, 1 lb., three times per week.	do	do	
	Salt pork, ⅔ lb., three times per week.	do	do	
	Fresh canned beef, ½ lb., four times during voyage.	do	do	
	Pea soup, three times per we k.	do	do	
	Butter, ½ lb. per week	do	do	
	Marmalade, ⅓ lb. per week	do	do	
	Sugar, 12 ounces per week	do	do	
	Rice, once per week	do	do	
	Lime juice, water and sugar, ½ pint daily.	do	do	
British ship *Orrissa*; New Castle, New South Wales, to San Francisco. Statement of one member of crew.	Same as the above, with the exception of beef four times per week. No fresh beef or rice during voyage.	New Castle, New South Wales.	Good	None
Britith ship *James Livesey*; Hamburg, Germany, to San Francisco. REMARKS.—Disease unknown. Two members of crew certify to this statement.	Same as the above, with the exception of beans, navy, once per week.	Hamburg, Germany.	do	1

REPORT ON THE FOOD OF SEAMEN ON VESSELS SAILING OUT OF NEW ORLEANS.

By Surgeon Chas. B. Goldsborough.

Food of seamen, as seen on vessels arriving and departing from New Orleans, La., embracing facts as to its character, sources from whence obtained, and quantities issued during voyages.

A few general statements in regard to the trade of New Orleans may be of interest before entering more minutely into the subject of this paper.

During the fiscal year ended June 30, 1888, the entries were as follows:

Nationality.	Sailing.	Steam.	Seamen.	Nationality.	Sailing.	Steam.	Seamen.
American	80	304	11,616	Spanish	24	46	2,168
English	78	379	10,553	Mexican	10	....	96
French	1	15	661	Belgium	3	2	131
German	21	11	635	Portugal	2	....	28
Austrian	7	......	105	Honduras	2	....	19
Italian	27	21	849	Russian	2	....	23
Norwegian	5	....	86				
Swedish	2	....	28	Total	204	798	26,996

The clearances for the same period were:

Nationality.	Sailing.	Steam.	Seamen.	Nationality.	Sailing.	Steam.	Seamen.
American	53	323	10,473	Mexican	10	.....	97
English	81	365	11,194	Belgium	1	3	107
French	1	15	653	Portugal	2	....	28
German	23	10	683	Honduras	2	......	18
Austrian	8	......	106	Russia	3	....	36
Italian	26	21	846	Costa Rica	1	....	10
Norwegian	7	1	127				
Swedish	1	....	12	Total	241	765	26,522
Spanish	22	47	2,132				

Trade between New Orleans and Mexico and Central America is extensive, and there are now several lines of steam-ships so engaged, such as the Oteri Pioneer Line; the New Orleans and Columbia Steam-ship Company; the New Orleans and Balize Royal Mail Steam-ship Line; the Costa Rica and Honduras Steam-ship Line; the Morgan Line, whose steam-ships run to Brazos Santiago, Nicaragua, Vera Cruz, Cuban ports, and Florida.

Between New Orleans and Liverpool there are several lines of steamships doing a large business, such as the Harrison Line, the West India and Pacific Steam-ship Company, and the Liverpool, Brazil and River Platte Line.

Between New Orleans and New York the Cromwell Line and the Morgan Line have several large vessels running.

The vessels engaged in trade with ports south of New Orleans carry lumber grain, etc., and on their return trip they bring tropical fruits, coffee, etc.

Vessels going from New Orleans to Liverpool are loaded with cotton and grain.

The United States shipping articles, which are always signed by masters and crews of vessels, contain what is known as "a scale of provisions," and this scale describes the amount and kind of food which the master of the vessel is obliged by law to furnish each seaman while at sea. When in port this scale is not followed except perhaps as to the amounts, as it is then customary to provide fresh meat and green vegetables, instead of salt meats and canned articles. The following is the scale required by the United States shipping articles:

Scale of provisions.

Days.	Bread.	Beef.	Pork.	Flour.	Peas.	Tea.	Coffee.	Sugar.	Water.
	Pounds.	*Pounds.*	*Pounds.*	*Pounds.*	*Pints.*	*Ounces.*	*Ounces.*	*Ounces.*	*Quarts.*
Sunday	1	1½	....	½	....	⅛	½	2	3
Monday	1	....	1¼	....	⅓	⅛	½	2	3
Tuesday	1	1½	....	½	....	⅛	½	2	3
Wednesday	1	....	1¼	....	⅓	⅛	½	2	3
Thursday	1	1½	....	½	....	⅛	½	2	3
Friday	1	....	1¼	....	⅓	⅛	½	2	3
Saturday	1	1½	....	½	....	⅛	½	2	3

One ounce of coffee or cocoa or chocolate may be substituted for one-quarter ounce of tea; molasses for sugar, the quantity to be one-half more. One pound of potatoes or yams; one-half pound of flour or rice; one-third pint of peas or one-quarter pint of barley may be substituted for each other. When fresh meat is issued the proportion to be two pounds per man per day in lieu of salt meat. Onions may be used instead of potatoes. The scale is in addition to the daily allowance of lime and lemon juice and sugar or other antiscorbutics required by law.

The "agreement and account of crew," which foreign-going ships sailing under the British flag are obliged by law to follow, contains also a scale of provisions to be allowed and served out to the crew during the voyage. This scale is exactly the same as the one already given, and in fact the United States scale was taken from the British one.

The "agreement" (British) also has the following statement:

Besides this (*i. e.*, the scale) all vessels bound south of the thirty-fifth degree of north latitude must carry lime or lemon juice and sugar. The master may serve out in lieu of salted meats and preserved vegetables, fresh meat and fresh vegetables in like quantities.

Sweden, France, and several other nations have scales of provisions, but they are all very similar in character.

Norway and Italy have not adopted any special diet, so far as I can learn.

. These scales seem to be used only as guides to the master, though each sailor can, however, if he demands it, oblige the master to weigh out to him his daily allowance of food. It is seldom the case that such measures are resorted to, and the usual custom seems to be, to assemble the crew soon after leaving port, and the question is put, "whether they, the crew, wish their food measured out to each one in accordance with the scale required by law, or whether they will trust to the master to feed them." Almost invariably the latter plan is adopted, and I have been informed by the United States shipping commissioner, that so far as United States vessels are concerned, he has not heard any complaints from sailors arriving in New Orleans. It is considered very poor policy on the part of a master "to feed badly," for a reputation of this kind once established against him renders it a difficult task for him to obtain a crew. The United States vessels have the reputation of giving the best food, and of being the most liberal in their allowances. The British vessels follow the scale more closely, probably because they make longer voyages, and because the sailors often try to desert upon reaching an American port (after having shipped for the round trip), or to plead, as an excuse for violating the contract, that they were not fed properly. If the sailor can prove that the captain gave him less than the law allows, the consul has the power to release him from the vessel, and to make the master re-imburse him at the rate of 3 shillings per day. The Norwegian and Swedish vessels feed their sailors well, considering the quantities allowed, but their food generally is of an inferior grade, when compared with that given on English, French, and American vessels.

Italian vessels are said to give as little as possible, and that little is of the poorest quality in the market.

All American steam-ships and sailing vessels, coming into or sailing from New Orleans. and owned by persons living in the city, purchase their entire supplies there, and the articles of subsistence are of the best quality obtainable and of the character used in an ordinary first-class hotel. The lines of steam-ships running between New York and New Orleans are owned chiefly in New York, and they buy all their salt meats and groceries in the latter city. Fresh meats and fresh vegetables are procured at both cities in quantities sufficient to last for the trip from one port to the other.

British vessels engaged in what is known as "direct trade" with Great Britain and the British colonies, of which about two hundred annually enter and clear from New Orleans, purchase all their provisions in England. This does not seem to be due to the fact that provisions are any cheaper or better in England, but it is largely on account of some one of the owners (being either a ship-chandler or else interested in some special grocer) insisting upon the purchases being made from him. British vessels engaged in "indirect trade," of which about three hundred enter and clear from New Orleans annually, purchase about 10 per cent. of their supplies in New Orleans, and the rest in England. British vessels engaged in trade between New Orleans and Central America purchase all their supplies in New Orleans. There are very few of these vessels, and the usual voyage is from the home port in England to South or Central America, thence to New Orleans, where they change cargoes, and then sail direct to their home port.

When in port fresh meats and fresh vegetables are given to the crew, and these articles have to be bought in the open market; but the purchase of salt meat, etc., is only made in the case of some special kind being exhausted, and then only what will be sufficient to last on the voyage home is taken.

French, German, and Spanish shipping is about on the same ratio as the English. Comparatively few of these vessels come to New Orleans, and they all procure their subsistence stores at their home ports, and it is only when some special articles are exhausted that they replenish their stock.

Norwegian and Swedish vessels purchase largely in New Orleans of certain classes of provisions, such as bread, peas, beef, and butter, but canned goods and fancy groceries, such as many American vessels furnish, they either purchase elsewhere or do not give them to the crew.

Italian vessels buy freely in New Orleans, but, as previously stated, the articles are of a poor grade. Many of the vessels coming into New

Orleans are only "ocean tramps" seeking cargoes, and these have no regular place for laying in supplies, but they simply replenish their stock with quantities sufficient to carry them to another port. I found it rather difficult to obtain information in regard to food from masters of vessels, but from careful inquiries made of the United States shipping commissioner, of the various consuls residing in New Orleans, of such seamen as had intelligence sufficient to give reliable data, I arrived at the above conclusions, and through the kindness of Messrs. Woodward, Wight & Co. I was enabled to examine carefully the class of goods bought by many vessels, and I could therefore judge satisfactorily, not only as to the quality, but also as to the quantity purchased for a voyage. Of the actual quantity allowed each man and of the methods of distribution, etc., while at sea I have been able to form only a rough estimate.

The following lists of supplies purchased by vessels will give some idea of the quantities allowed.

The American ship *Lydia Skofield*, 1,264 tons, with four officers and fourteen men, bound for Havre, France, estimated length of voyage about three months, bought the following list of articles of subsistence:

Irish potatoes	barrels	9	Molasses	gallons	50
Sweet potatoes	pounds	80	Lard	pounds	40
Salt beef	barrels	10	Tea (crew)	do	10
Flour	do	10	Coffee (crew)	do	100
Salt pork	do	2	Tea (cabin)	do	5
Ham	pounds	95	Dried apples	do	10
Codfish	do	100	Butter	do	20
Mackerel	do	300	Vinegar	gallons	3
Common brown sugar	barrel	1	Raisins	pounds	10
Granulated sugar	pounds	75	Nutmegs	do	1

The American ship *Cora*, bound for Havre, France, with four officers and fourteen men, length of voyage about three months, laid in articles as follows:

American pressed beef	barrels	4	Rio coffee, best quality	pounds	70
Resalted beef	do	6	Rio coffee (crew)	do	25
Rump pork	do	4	Oolong tea, best quality	do	20
Ham	pounds	54	Tea (crew)	do	25
Flour	barrels	10	Granulated sugar	barrel	½
Lard	pounds	55	Green peas	do	½
Rice	do	100	Tapioca	pounds	25
Corn meal	barrel	½	Dried apples	do	25
White beans	do	½	Condensed milk (Daisy)	cans	30
Codfish	pounds	100	Vinegar	gallons	5
Navy bread	barrels	2	Pickles	pounds	20
Molasses	do	1	Table salt	do	12
Butter	pounds	57	Common brown sugar	barrels	2
Mackerel, No. 1	kit	1	Raisins	pounds	10
Buckwheat	pounds	10	Buckwheat	do	10
Crackers	do	34			

The American schooner *Lillian Hyatt*, 116 tons, with two officers and five men, bound for Mexican ports, voyage about twenty days, made purchases as follows:

Flour	pounds	100	Canned peas	pounds	18
Onions	do	56	Codfish	do	10
Pork	do	30	Green peas	do	10
Potatoes	barrels	3	Oatmeal	do	10
Ham	pounds	30	Canned tomatoes	do	24
Sugar	do	50	Pie plant	do	24
Lard	do	20	White beans	do	25
Tea	do	4	Rice	do	5
Coffee	do	15	Dried apples	do	15
Butter	do	40	Pickles	do	10
Condensed milk	cans	6			

As a matter of comparison, the following list of supplies purchased by a Norwegian vessel is submitted.

The Norwegian bark *Orient*, bound for St. Petersburg, Russia, length of voyage about fifty days, with three officers and sixteen men:

Salt beef	barrels..	6	Pork	barrels..	4
Navy bread	pounds..	150	Flour	do....	5
Green peas	do....	20	Molasses	do....	1
Dried apples	do....	20	Potatoes	do....	6
Granulated C sugar	do....	200	Codfish	pounds..	35
Ham	do....	96	Canned corn	do....	36

I could cite many more, but they are so similar in character to the above that they would be of little value.

Judging from a number of diet lists given me by masters and stewards of vessels, and indorsed by many of the most intelligent class of seamen that I have interrogated, I have drawn up the following scale of provisions as representing the most liberal allowance furnished. It will be noticed that it exceeds in quantity and variety any scale established by law.

Scale of provisions.

Days.	Bread.	Salt beef.	Salt pork.	Salt fish.	Potatoes.	Onions.	Flour.	Beans or peas.	Tea.	Coffee.
	lb.	*lbs.*	*lbs.*	*lbs.*	*lbs.*	*lbs.*	*lbs.*	*pints.*	*oz.*	*oz.*
Sunday	1	1½	......	......	*2	......	†1	......	¼	1
Monday	1	......	1½	......	......	1	......	½	¼	1
Tuesday	1	1½	....	....	*2	......	†1	......	¼	1
Wednesday	1	....	1½	......	......	1	......	½	¼	1
Thursday	1	1½	....	....	*2	......	†1	......	¼	1
Friday	1	......	......	2	......	1	......	½	¼	1
Saturday	1	1½	......	......	*2	......	†1	......	¼	1

Days.	Sugar.	Dried fruit.	Molasses.	Salt.	Pepper.	Vinegar or pickles.	Water.	Extras. Butter.	Extras. Milk.	Extras. Ice.
	oz.	*oz.*	*oz.*	*dram.*	*dram.*	*oz.*	*qts.*	*oz.*	*oz.*	*lbs.*
Sunday	3	1	1	¼	⅛	1	3	1½	6	2
Monday	3	......	1	¼	⅛	1	3	1½	6	2
Tuesday	3	1	1	¼	⅛	1	3	1½	6	2
Wednesday	3	....	1	¼	⅛	1	3	1½	6	2
Thursday	3	1	1	¼	⅛	1	3	1½	6	2
Friday	3	......	1	¼	⅛	1	3	1½	6	2
Saturday	3	......	1	¼	⅛	1	3	1½	6	2

* Or 3 ounces tomatoes. † Or ¼ pound rice.

Butter, milk, and ice are seldom furnished, unless the crew subscribe for the payment, except on steam-ships and vessels making very short voyages.

AVERAGE DAILY SCALE OF MEALS.

Breakfast: Coffee, 1½ pints. Sugar, 1½ ounces. Bread, one-half pound. Butter three-fourths ounce. Beef, one-half pound; or pork, one-half pound; or meat stew, one-half pound. Potatoes, three-fourths pound; or onions, one-half pound. Salt, one-eighth dram. Pepper, one-eighth dram. Water, 1 quart.

Dinner: Soup, 1½ pints. Meat, vegetables, etc. Beef, 1 pound; or pork, 1 pound; or fish, 2 pounds. Potatoes, 1½ pounds; or tomatoes, 3 ounces; or onions, 1 pound. Beans, one-half pint; or peas, one-half pint. Dried fruit, 1 ounce; or pudding, 4 ounces (duff). Salt, one-eighth dram. Pepper, one-eighth dram. Vinegar, 1 ounce; or pickles, 1 ounce.

Supper: Tea, 1½ pints. Bread, one-half pound. Sugar, 1½ ounces. Rice, one-fourth pound; or mush, one-half pint. Molasses, 1 ounce. Butter, three-fourths ounce. About twice weekly, meat stew, one-half pound.

In regard to quality, so far as I could examine, the meats were of the best brands in the market, and they are in fact the cheaper, as they are more easily preserved. The coffee and tea served to the crew are of the poorest grades in the country, the coffee costing about 7 cents per pound and the tea about 20 cents. The officers generally use a much finer grade of these articles.

The great conveniences now existing for preserving food, even on comparatively long voyages, enable those who prefer fresh meats and vegetables to keep themselves provided with them, and in certain seasons they are cheaper. The old plan of giving nothing but salt meat, hard-tack, etc., is gradually disappearing, and those who have to provide the subsistence stores for the crew realize that they get better men and more work from them when they are well fed.

Anti-scorbutics, though always carried on vessels, are seldom used except in cases of very long voyages; and as steam seems to be superseding all other methods of navigation and thereby shortening the time required to make a voyage the necessity for such articles is diminishing in proportion.

The character of the cooking and the methods of serving the food vary greatly, and this affects chiefly the soups, tea, coffee, and the so-called desserts, like "duff."

Different nations have recognized the idiosyncrasies of their countrymen, the English feeding in greater quantities of meats, etc., while the Italians prefer their soups, oils, and macaroni.

The above are about all of the facts that I have been able to collect in regard to the food of seamen coming into the port of New Orleans, but I would add in conclusion that as the majority of the vessels make short voyages and touch port frequently, they are therefore better able to procure good food and of greater variety than those arriving and departing from other cities.

NEW ORLEANS, LA., *July* 7, 1888.

REPORT OF SURGICAL OPERATIONS.

REPORT OF SURGICAL OPERATIONS.

FISCAL YEAR 1888.

Operations.	No. of cases.	Remarks.
Total number of operations	**603**	
REMOVAL OF TUMORS	24	
For sebaceous cysts	8	Excision.
For cyst of face	1	Do.
For cyst of neck	1	Do.
For cyst of testicle	1	Do.
For cyst of hand	1	Do.
For cyst of abdominal wall	1	Do.
For cystic goitre	1	Incision to relieve larynx.
For lipoma	3	Excision; 1 of back.
For lipoma of eyelid	3	Excision.
For lipoma of thigh	1	Excision; still under treatment.
For angeioma (mixed)	1	Do.
For papilloma	3	Excision, 1; strangulation, 2.
For epulis	1	Ligation of tumor and application of thermo-cautery to pedicle.
For epithelioma	3	Excision.
REMOVAL OF FOREIGN BODIES	12	
For gunshot wound of chest	1	Ball removed: unsuccessful.
For gunshot wound of neck and abdomen.	1	Ball removed.
For gunshot wound of shoulder and thigh.	1	Do.
For gunshot wound of fore-arm	2	Fragments of ball removed.
For gunshot wound of leg	2	Ball removed, 1; buckshot extracted, 1.
For gunshot wound of ear	1	Ball removed from external meatus.
For gunshot wound of axilla	1	Ball removed.
For splinter in hand	2	Incision (1, steel, 3 centimeters long).
For foreign body in rectum	1	Removal by forceps.
OPENING OF ABSCESSES	27	
Opening of abcess of frontal sinus	1	Recovery.
For abscess of liver	7	Aspiration, 2; incision and drainage, 3; died, 2.
For abscess of axilla	3	Incision.
For abscess of arm	1	Do.
For abscess of hand	2	Do.
For abscess of abdominal walls	1	Do.
For abscess, psoas	1	Incision; still under treatment.
For abscess of gluteal region	1	Incision.
For abscess of thigh	1	Incision; still under treatment.
For abscess of head of tibia	1	Incision; portion of knife-blade removed.
For abscess of scrotum	1	Incision.
For abscess of subperitoneal tissue	2	Incision and drainage; 1, pyæmia at time of operation.
For abscess of peritoneum	1	Incision.
For abscess, ischio-rectal	5	Incision; division of sphincter and curetting.
OPERATIONS ON THE NERVES	1	
For neuralgia	1	Excision of 2.5 centimeters of median nerve, just above wrist.
OPERATIONS ON THE EYE AND APPENDAGES	14	
For entropion	4	Excision; one V-shaped incision and sutures.
For strabismus	1	Tenotomy.
For dacrocystitis	1	Canaliculi slit and duct probed.
For pterygium	2	Excision.
For occlusion of iris	1	Iridectomy; failure.
For cataract	2	Linear extraction.
For staphyloma	1	Paracentesis corneæ.
For shrunken eyeball	2	Excision.
OPERATIONS ON THE EAR	3	
For occlusion of meatus	3	Division of meatus.

Operations.	No. of cases.	Remarks.
OPERATIONS ON THE HEAD	1	
For fracture of skull	1	Trephined; dura mater incised; recovered.
OPERATIONS ON THE FACE AND MOUTH	11	
For removal of tonsils	4	Hypertrophy.
For elongation of uvula	2	Excision.
For cleft of soft palate	1	Staphylorraphy.
For stricture of nasal duct	1	Dilatation.
For nasal polypus	3	Torsion.
OPERATIONS ON THE ARTERIES	3	
For wound of radial artery	1	Ligation.
For aneurism of ulnar artery (traumatic)	1	Do.
For aneurism of popliteal artery	1	Compression; improved.
OPERATIONS ON THE VEINS	2	
For varicose veins of both legs	1	Ligation.
For varix of leg	1	Ligation; subcutaneous, catgut.
OPERATIONS ON THE RESPIRATORY ORGANS	22	
For pleuritis	11	Aspiration; paracentesis, 1; 1 died.
For empyema	7	Pleurotomy, 1; concussion and drainage, 1; aspiration, 4; still under observation, 1; 2 died.
For hydrothorax	1	Still under treatment.
For hæmathorax from fractured ribs	1	Aspiration.
For œdema of larynx	1	Laryngotomy; unsuccessful.
For wound of thyroid cartilage	1	Suture.
OPERATIONS ON THE HEART	1	
For pericarditis	1	Aspiration; died.
OPERATIONS ON THE DIGESTIVE ORGANS	73	
For hernia, inguinal, strangulated	2	2 died; 1 peritonitis at time of operation.
For hernia, inguinal, radical cure	2	Strangulated, 1.
For hernia, inguinal, radical cure	1	Heaton's operation; unsuccessful.
For hernia, right oblique, radical cure.	9	Recovered; one still under treatment.
For hernia, left oblique, radical cure	2	Recovered.
For fissure of anus	1	Forcible dilatation of sphincter.
For stricture of rectum	1	Forcible dilatation.
For fistula in ano	14	Incision; 1 still under observation.
For fistula in ano and stricture of rectum.	1	
For ascites	10	7 died.
For hæmorrhoids	21	11 ligature; 10 injection of carbolic acid.
OPERATIONS ON THE ABDOMEN	4	
Exploratory	1	Laparotomy; successful.
For gunshot wound	1	Laparotomy; unsuccessful.
For obstruction of bowels, carcinoma of omentum and peritoneum.	1	Exploratory laparotomy, wound healed by primary union; death from progress of disease.
For intestinal fistula	1	Laparotomy; died.
OPERATIONS ON THE LYMPHATIC ORGANS	23	
For fistula of groin	1	Incision and cautery.
For sinus of groin	1	Incision.
For suppuration of inguinal glands	14	Scraping.
For inflammation of inguinal glands	4	Removal of glands.
For inflammation of glands of neck and chin.	1	Excision.
For hypertrophy of inguinal glands	2	Do.
OPERATIONS ON THE URINARY ORGANS	155	
For stricture of the urethra	150	
a. Gradual dilatation	54	2 still in hospital.
b. Forcible dilatation	35	1 died; 2 still in hospital.
c. Internal urethrotomy	52	1 died; 1 failure.
d. External urethrotomy	5	
f. Perineal section	1	
g. Slitting meatus	3	
For urinary fistula	4	1 perineal urethrotomy and incision of fistula; 1 incision; 1 urethroplasty; 1 external urethrotomy.
For retention of urine	1	Aspiration of bladder.
OPERATIONS ON THE GENERATIVE ORGANS.	101	
For paraphimosis	4	Incision of stricture and manipulation; 1 adhesion of foreskin.
For phimosis	66	Circumcision 58; slit prepuce 8.
For gangrene of prepuce	1	
For hydrocele	21	Radical cure; 1 sac opened and packed with carbolized tape; 1 tapped; 1 excision of sac; 1 aspirated.

Operations.	No. of cases.	Remarks
OPERATIONS ON THE GENERATIVE ORGANS—Continued.		
For hydrocele of the cord	1	Aspiration.
For condylomata of perineum	1	Excision.
For condylomata of penis	1	Do.
For epithelioma of penis	1	Amputation.
For primary syphilitic disease of pen is	2	Circumcision.
For sarcoma of testicle	1	Castration.
For medullary cancer of testicle	1	Castration (both testicles).
For tuberculosis of testicle	1	Castration.
OPERATIONS ON THE ORGANS OF LOCOMOTION	68	
On bones	35	
For gunshot, fracture of humerus	1	Twelve small fragments removed.
For caries of superior maxilla and abscess of antrum.	1	Antrum opened above and below.
For necrosis of inferior maxilla	3	Dead bone removed.
For necrosis of clavicle	1	Do.
For osteitis of ulna	1	Drilling of bone.
For necrosis of metacarpus	1	Removal of bone.
For necrosis of femur	2	Removal of dead bone.
For necrosis of tibia	6	Do.
For necrosis of metatarsal	2	Do.
For necrosis of ribs	2	1 removal of dead bone; 1 resection of portion of rib.
For caries of first metatarsal	2	
For contused wound of foot	1	Excision of second metatarsal.
For (hallux valgus) osteitis deformans.	2	Resection of head of first metatarsal.
For caries of tibia	3	Removal of dead bone.
For caries of femur	1	Removal of carious bone, still under treatment.
For ununited fracture of tibia	2	1 ends united and leg in plaster; 1 ends united by iron.
For ununited fracture, both bones	2	Ends wired; still in hospital.
For compound comminuted fracture of femur.	1	Excision of condyles and 3 inches of shaft.
For compound comminuted fracture of leg, both bones.	1	Removal of fragments of bones.
On joints	33	
Reduction of dislocation:		
Shoulder	3	Manipulation; successful.
Ankle	1	Do.
For ankylosis of jaw	1	Formation of false joint; successful.
For old dislocation and ankylosis elbow-joint.	1	Excision of joint.
For compound fracture of femur	1	Resection of $1\frac{1}{2}$ inches of shaft; patient had leaped from third-story window of hospital, died twenty-six hours afterwards from internal injuries (suicide).
For acute synovitis knee joint	2	Aspiration.
For chronic synovitis of knee-joint	10	Do.
For contusion of knee-joint	1	Do.
For ankylosis of knee-joint	1	Adhesions broken up.
For suppuration of knee-joint	3	1 aspirated and washed out; 1 incision and drainage; 1 died.
For rupture of quadriceps extensor femoris.	1	Aspiration.
For contractions of tendons	2	Tenotomy.
AMPUTATIONS	53	
Fingers, for ankylosis	2	
Fingers, for whitlow	2	
Fingers, for frost-bite	2	
Fingers, for wound	13	
Fingers, for fracture	2	
Fingers, for necrosis	8	
Fingers, for caries	3	
Fingers, for osteitis	1	
Fingers, for gangrene	1	
Arm, for compound comminuted fracture of humerus.	1	
Forearm, for caries	1	Lower third, circular.
Thigh, for neuralgia of stump	1	Superior third, circular.
Thigh, for compound comminuted fracture.	2	1, middle third, recovered; 1, lower third, died.
Thigh, for tuberculous disease of knee-joint.	1	Lower third, died
Leg, for compound comminuted fracture.	1	Superior third, circular
Toes, for frost-bite	4	
Toes, for ankylosis	1	
Toes, for necrosis	1	

Operations.	No. of cases.	Remarks.
AMPUTATIONS—Continued.		
Toes, for osteitis	1	
Toes, for fracture	1	
Toes, for wound	2	
Feet, for frost-bite	1	Hey's and Symes's.
Foot, for caries	1	Chopart's.
OPERATIONS ON THE SKIN	5	
Carbuncle	1	Incision.
Ingrown nail	1	Removal.
Webbed fingers	1	Incision; unsuccessful.
Ulcer of skin	2	Sponge grafting.

STATISTICS

UNITED STATES MARINE-HOSPITAL SERVICE.

STATISTICS UNITED STATES MARINE-HOSPITAL SERVICE.

TABLE I.—*Comparative table of number treated*—1867 *to* 1888.

The following tabular statement illustrates the results of the reorganization of the Marine-Hospital Service in 1871:

Operations of the Marine-Hospital Service from July 1, 1867, *to June* 30, 1888.

Fiscal years.	Number of places at which relief is authorized.	Number of sick and disabled seamen furnished relief.
Prior to reorganization:		
1868	64	11,535
1869	64	11,356
1870	74	10,560
After reorganization:		
1871	72	14,256
1872	81	13,156
1873	91	13,529
1874	91	14,364
1875	94	15,009
1876	94	16,808
1877	100	15,175
1878	210	18,223
1879	210	20,922
1880	210	24,860
1881	....	32,613
1882	....	36,184
1883	....	40,195
1884	....	44,761
1885	....	41,714
1886	....	43,822
1887	....	45,314
1888	....	48,203

TABLE II.—*Exhibit of operations of the service during the year ended June 30, 1888.*

Ports.	Total number of seamen treated.	Patients in hospital July 1, 1887.	Admitted during the year.	Total number treated in hospital.	Discharged.	Died.	Remaining in hospital June 30, 1888.	Number of days relief in hospital.	Number of seamen furnished office relief.	Number of times office relief was furnished.	Number of persons examined physically, including pilots.	Amount expended.	Tonnage-tax collected.
Total	48,203	769	13,308	14,077	12,728	468	881	361,709	34,126	52,811	3,044	$461,201.16	$489,371.67
Albany, N. Y	3	2	1	3	1	1	1	508			50	477.24	
Alexandria, Va	96		2	2	2			46	94	151		309.10	111.54
Apalachicola, Fla	73	4	44	48	46	1	1	969	25	30		1,461.60	348.18
Ashtabula, Ohio	187		1	1	1			18	186	511		258.85	
Astoria, Oregon	71	4	32	36	33	1	2	1,167	35	40		1,293.10	836.43
Baltimore, Md	1,789	23	389	412	367	17	28	12,762	1,377	1,761	111	13,006.91	24,042.61
Bangor, Me	88	2	25	27	25	1	1	442	61	361	8	1,369.46	94.80
Barnstable, Mass	222								222	1,686		1,707.26	135.03
Bath, Me	67		19	19	17	2		458	48	136	21	989.46	74.97
Beaufort, N. C	12								12	17		45.55	3.15
Beaufort, S. C													779.97
Belfast, Me	35	1	4	5	5			159	30	217		673.70	158.13
Bismarck, Dak	21	1	7	8	8			280	13	64		560.10	
Boston, Mass	2,040	52	842	894	787	28	79	26,210	1,146	1,430	213	22,843.60	44,106.41
Brashear, La	4								4	4		21.00	3.00
Bridgeport, Conn	5		5	5	5			115				112.00	85.38
Bridgeton, N. J													109.38
Brownsville, Tex												129.30	12.64
Brunswick, Ga	86		15	15	14	1		274	71	72		460.69	4,129.62
Buffalo, N. Y	1,304	19	279	298	271	9	18	7,753	1,006	1,203	136	8,271.62	17.97
Burlington, Iowa	10	1	9	10	9	1		188				173.68	
Burlington, Vt	1		1	1		1		23				23.00	470.83
Cairo, Ill	1,129	18	358	376	342	16	18	7,833	753	910	4	10,568.53	
Cape Vincent, N. Y	1		1	1	1			60				60.00	2.88
Castine, Me	7								7	17		16.00	37.80
Cedar Keys, Fla	84	2	10	12	12			159	72	153		463.50	8.86
Charleston, S. C	1,168	10	190	200	171	7	22	5,059	968	1,447	29	7,416.07	3,176.61
Chattanooga, Tenn	45								45	88	5	313.29	
Chicago, Ill	4,734	30	787	817	734	23	60	23,760	3,917	5,185	92	28,906.19	89.91
Cincinnati, Ohio	1,700	19	366	385	352	11	22	7,809	1,315	2,050	12	11,792.74	
Cleveland, Ohio	1,179	16	275	291	273	7	11	5,991	888	1,237	81	4,724.78	222.18
Corpus Christi, Tex	23	1	10	11	10	1		221	12	18	6	581.34	2.19
Crisfield, Md	28		8	8	8			27	20	20		293.10	

Detroit, Mich	2,407	27	516	543	478	15	50	15,977	1,864	2,525	75	17,856.85	107.73
Dubuque, Iowa	105	11	69	80	76		4	1,318	25	34	10	1,821.92	
Duluth, Minn	147	2	21	23	19		4	299	124	148	24	600.17	46.56
Eastport, Me	64		4	4	4			96	60	398		488.00	832.44
East Saginaw, Mich	63	2	23	25	25			494	58	98	9	833.96	
Edenton, N. C	47		3	3	3			19	44	57		135.15	
Edgartown, Mass												7.50	287.46
Elizabeth City, N. C	76								76	109	120	300.00	
Ellsworth, Me	96		10	10	9		1	264	26	759	14	1,166.00	29.01
El Paso, Tex													25.36
Empire City, Oregon	31	2	9	11	10		1	270	20	146		1,124.20	
Erie, Pa	90	3	37	40	35	2	3	937	50	155		924.21	
Escanaba, Mich	93	4	18	22	19	1	2	542	71	132		921.95	
Eureka, Cal	72	3	51	54	51	1	2	990	18	20	11	1,276.95	218.22
Evansville, Ind	648	9	176	185	175	3	7	3,402	463	657	18	4,749.97	
Fall River, Mass	1		1	1	1			23				12.19	62.70
Fernandina, Fla	125	2	39	41	41			690	84	117		1,299.65	548.58
Fredericksburgh, Va												200.00	
Gallipolis, Ohio	370	1	95	96	88		8	1,926	274	552	7	3,858.11	
Galveston, Tex	563	23	208	231	209	8	14	6,245	332	421	69	9,026.44	5,246.86
Georgetown, D. C	206	1	62	63	57	2	4	1,278	143	218	3	963.29	95.34
Georgetown, S. C	116		18	18	16	1	1	268	98	188		714.29	219.39
Gloucester, Mass	30		3	3	3			157	27	92		458.25	1,459.20
Government Hospital for the Insane	19	13	6	19	2	1	16	5,881				3,780.64	
Grand Haven, Mich	52	2	13	15	12	1	2	442	37	51	80	875.77	
Hartford, Conn	20		11	11	10	1		265	9	84		368.00	21.81
Jacksonville, Fla	141	4	104	108	98	2	8	2,723	33	56		2,822.90	106.77
Key West, Fla	890	7	112	119	112	2	5	3,208	771	1,046	11	6,413.72	743.94
La Crosse, Wis	82	5	60	65	60		5	1,208	17	56	5	1,711.25	
Little Rock, Ark	19		3	3	3			46	16	31	2	279.54	
Louisville, Ky	962	10	235	245	231	5	9	5,961	717	987	10	9,923.51	
Ludington, Mich	32		1	1		1		1	31	40		197.80	
Machias, Me	107	2	37	39	38		1	932	68	109		1,074.05	56.82
Manistee, Mich	36		2	2	2			43	34	64	17	266.90	
Marblehead, Mass													92.79
Marquette, Mich	66	4	27	31	28	2	1	674	35	42		1,100.00	
Memphis, Tenn	1,603	3	395	398	360	28	10	5,915	1,205	1,707	12	11,651.93	
Milwaukee, Wis	704	14	289	303	278	4	21	7,312	401	536	104	7,861.26	
Mobile, Ala	1,006	27	454	481	442	11	28	11,044	525	629	40	9,998.44	3,048.51
Nashville, Tenn	25		14	14	14			444	11	18	6	700.69	
Newark, N. J													282.42
New Bedford, Mass	47								47	92	28	273.26	290.73
New Berne, N. C	400	2	65	67	61		6	1,648	333	461	26	1,901.47	18.09
Newburyport, Mass													77.04
New Haven, Conn	62	1	46	47	44	1	2	1,342	15	22	23	1,753.23	410.97
New London, Conn	105	3	36	39	37	2		1,028	66	71		1,325.42	99.54
New Orleans, La	2,121	21	592	613	549	22	42	13,677	1,508	2,217	55	18,707.25	33,419.52
Newport, Ark	21		7	7	7			104	14	24		335.90	
Newport, R. I	48	1	22	23	21		2	436	25	28	54	771.30	199.11
Newport News, Va	1								1	1		3.20	2,271.24
New York, N. Y	3,237	82	1,079	1,161	1,018	62	61	32,404	2,076	3,114	458	48,040.75	204,918.30
Norfolk, Va	1,568	18	490	508	470	12	26	12,028	1,060	1,350	101	16,918.29	2,559.57

TABLE II.—*Exhibit of operations of the service during the year ended June 30, 1888*—Continued.

Ports.	Total number of seamen treated.	Patients in hospital July 1, 1887.	Admitted during the year.	Total number treated in hospital.	Discharged.	Died.	Remaining in hospital June 30, 1888.	Number of days' relief in hospital.	Number of seamen furnished office relief.	Number of times office relief was furnished.	Number of persons examined physically, including pilots.	Amount expended.	Tonnage-tax collected.
Ogdensburgh, N. Y	58	1	1	2	2			25	56	112		$225.90	$132.72
Oswego, N. Y	58		11	11	9	2		346	47	86	38	730.15	1,192.20
Pensacola, Fla	113	4	91	95	92	1	2	2,626	18	31	19	3,319.90	14,371.47
Perth Amboy, N. J													1,853.11
Petersburgh, Va	6								6	8		13.30	
Philadelphia, Pa	1,684	37	475	512	457	18	37	12,329	1,172	1,467	172	13,689.75	53,643.93
Pittsburgh, Pa	1,421	14	338	352	334	7	11	8,030	1,069	1,389	28	10,591.35	
Plattsburgh, N. Y													2,029.23
Plymouth, Mass	1								1	1	30	146.80	24.36
Port Huron, Mich	210		15	15	13	1	1	426	195	843		645.50	17.97
Portland, Me	819	15	230	245	223	7	15	7,666	574	746	44	10,010.80	3,862.71
Portland, Oregon	405	7	92	99	91	4	4	2,014	306	421	41	3,800.85	1,613.22
Port Lavaca, Tex	1		1	1	1			56				137.30	
Portsmouth, N. H	36	2	14	16	14		2	351	20	21	14	561.25	181.68
Port Townsend, Wash	682	21	308	329	305	9	15	8,501	353	552	12	8,312.09	3,621.33
Providence, R. I	171	5	107	112	104	3	5	2,820	59	60		2,965.65	590.79
Richmond, Va	124	2	56	58	49	2	7	1,116	66	73		1,592.09	387.33
Rochester, N. Y													10.83
Rome, Ga	78		6	6	6			157	72	85		452.50	
Sag Harbor, N. Y	27		4	4	3	1		184	23	298		685.21	8.64
Saint Augustine, Fla													7.17
Saint Louis, Mo	1,173	28	298	316	277	19	20	10,115	857	1,231	27	12,564.19	
Saint Mary's, Ga													120.00
Saint Paul, Minn	37	7	30	37	31	1	5	970				1,283.79	
Salem, Mass	14		5	5	5			91	9	9		235.50	504.45
San Diego, Cal	116	4	70	74	72	1	1	2,414	42	121		4,993.30	7,131.85
Sandusky, Ohio	71	1	23	24	21		3	748	47	87		973.14	
San Francisco, Cal	2,281	48	726	774	667	47	60	25,774	1,507	418	127	22,736.52	41,328.16
Sault Ste. Marie, Mich	153	3	35	38	36	2		686	115	720	17	1,218.99	
Savannah, Ga	957	14	356	370	349	5	16	7,042	587	721	36	9,604.54	7,432.48
Seattle, Wash. T	168		29	29	22	4	3	620	139	253	21	1,423.96	
Shieldsborough, Miss												2,274.38	3,233.25
Shreveport, La	108	1	75	76	70	1	5	989	32	73		833.71	
Sitka, Alaska	14		4	4	4			42	10	14		78.00	168.11
Somers Point, N. J	6								6	78		6.00	

Stonington, Conn	2								2	2			28.18
Tacoma, Wash	20	2	18	20	19		1	365				1,877.80	
Tampa, Fla	1								1	1			
Tappahannock, Va	243	3	95	98	96	1	1	1,128	145	192		1,538.20	
Toledo, Ohio	100	4	40	44	41	2	1	1,509	56	76	6	579.38	11.70
Tuckerton, N. J	18								18	29	146	2,316.00	
Vicksburg, Miss	150		99	99	96	2	1	1,716	51	190		6,005.22	
Vineyard Haven, Mass	202	5	93	98	85	2	11	2,217	104	120		1,370.96	
Waldoborough and Rockland, Me	182	1	53	54	53	1		831	128	378	12	587.30	754.11
Wheeling, W. Va	22	1	13	14	13		1	339	8	10	14		
Wilmington, Cal	137	13	107	120	107	2	11	4,245	17	17		5,993.50	4,454.10
Wilmington, Del	9		8	8	7		1	130	1	1		143.00	24.57
Wilmington, N. C	783	12	120	132	120	3	9	4,309	651	987	44	7,325.03	2,793.15
Wiscasset, Me	17		1	1	1			50	16	35		210.18	82.29
Cape Charles, Quarantine Station												(*)	
Delaware Breakwater Quarantine Station	135		71	71	67	2	2	1,008	64	88	36		
Sapelo Quarantine Station	4		2	2	2			58	2	18			
Ship Island Quarantine Station	230		55	55	54		1	1,372	175	279			

* Expenditures for quarantine given elsewhere.

TABLE III.—*Summary of physical examinations of seamen made by medical officers of the United States Marine-Hospital Service, year ended June 30, 1888.*

Summary of examinations and causes of rejection.	Pilots.	Revenue marine.	Merchant marine.	Life-Saving Service.	Total.
Summary of examinations:					
Total number examined	1,841	93	91	1,019	3,044
Number passed	1,788	86	82	979	2,935
Number rejected	53	7	9	40	109
Causes of rejection:					
Color-blind	52	1	2	8	63
Malarial fever	......	......	2	......	2
Malarial cachexia	......	2	......	......	2
Secondary syphilis	......	......	......	2	2
Tubercle of lungs	......	......	1	......	1
Myopia	1	1	......	......	2
Deafness	......	......	......	1	1
Heart disease	......	2	......	13	15
Excessive growth of fat around the heart	......	......	......	1	1
Bronchitis, acute	......	......	1	......	1
Pleurisy	......	......	1	......	1
Hernia	......	......	......	5	5
Inflammation of glands of groin	......	......	......	1	1
Incontinence of urine	......	1	......	......	1
Stricture of urethra	......	......	1	......	1
Varicocele	......	......	......	5	5
Ankylosis	......	......	......	1	1
Undetermined	......	......	1	2	3
Fracture of leg	......	......	......	1	1

TABLE IV.—*Statement, by districts, of the number of patients treated during the year ended June 30, 1888.*

Districts.	Total cases.	Patients in hospital July 1, 1887.	Admitted during the year.	Total number treated in hospital.	Discharged.	Died.	Patients in hospital June 30, 1888.	Number of days hospital relief furnished.	Number of seamen furnished office relief.
Grand total	**48,203**	**769**	**13,308**	**14,077**	**12,728**	**468**	**881**	**361,709**	**34,126**
North Atlantic	4,295	86	1,471	1,577	1,395	45	117	43,226	2,738
Middle Atlantic	5,178	125	1,665	1,790	1,582	86	122	48,305	3,388
South Atlantic	7,991	104	2,018	2,122	1,924	54	144	56,298	5,869
The Gulf	5,065	90	1,603	1,693	1,549	47	97	39,351	3,372
The Ohio	5,193	54	1,237	1,291	1,207	26	58	27,911	3,902
The Mississippi	4,350	74	1,325	1,399	1,269	67	63	29,702	2,951
The Great Lakes	11,765	132	2,415	2,547	2,298	72	177	68,016	9,218
The Pacific	3,997	104	1,446	1,550	1,381	69	100	46,432	2,447
The Quarantine Stations	369	....	128	128	123	2	3	2,438	241

TABLE V.—*Ratio of patients treated in hospital in each district.*

Districts.	Per cent. of total number of patients.	Districts.	Per cent. of total number of patients.
North Atlantic	8.91	The Mississippi	9.02
Middle Atlantic	10.74	The Great Lakes	24.41
South Atlantic	16.58	The Pacific	8.29
The Gulf	10.51	The Quarantine Stations	.77
The Ohio	10.71		

TABLE VI.—*Average duration of treatment in hospital in each district.*

Districts.	Average number of days.	Districts.	Average number of days.
North Atlantic	27.76	The Mississippi	21.23
Middle Atlantic	26.99	The Great Lakes	26.72
South Atlantic	26.53	The Pacific	29.96
The Gulf	23.24	The Quarantine Stations	19.01
The Ohio	21.62		

TABLE VII.—*Tabular statement, by districts, of diseases and injuries treated during the year ended June 30, 1888.*

DISEASES.	NUMBER OF CASES.								
	Remaining under treatment from previous year.	Admitted during the year.	Discharged. Recovered.	Discharged. Improved.	Discharged. Not improved.	Died.	Remaining under treatment at the close of the year.	Number furnished office relief.	Total treated in hospital and dispensary.
Grand Total of all Cases	**769**	**13,308**	**8,744**	**3,733**	**251**	**168**	**881**	**34,126**	**48,203**
GENERAL DISEASES	376	6,161	4,025	1,800	105	218	389	15,392	21,929
LOCAL DISEASES	282	5,313	3,294	1,577	129	228	367	16,268	21,863
POISONS		42	34	7		1		55	97
INJURIES	111	1,792	1,391	349	17	21	125	2,411	4,314

NORTH ATLANTIC.

DISEASES.	Remaining under treatment from previous year.	Admitted during the year.	Recovered.	Improved.	Not improved.	Died.	Remaining under treatment at the close of the year.	Number furnished office relief.	Total treated in hospital and dispensary.
TOTAL CASES	**86**	**1471**	**942**	**415**	**38**	**45**	**117**	**2738**	**4295**
General Diseases	**48**	**603**	**391**	**180**	**12**	**21**	**47**	**1145**	**1796**
Small-pox		3	1			2		1	4
Cow-pox		1	1					2	3
Measles		1	1					4	5
Scarlet fever		3	3						3
Mumps								2	2
Diphtheria		1		1					1
Simple continued fever		7	6	1				7	14
Febricula		1	1					5	6
Enteric fever	2	28	24	2		2	2	34	64
Typho-malarial fever		5	4	1					5
Cholera, sporadic								4	4
Epidemic diarrhœa		1	1					1	2
Dysentery	1	18	16	1		1	1	19	38
Malarial intermittent fever	3	81	71	10			3	122	206
Malarial remittent fever	2	64	59	2		3	2	39	105
Malarial cachexia		12	5	5		1	1	33	45
Erysipelas, simple		3	2		1			5	8
Syphilis:									
Primary	6	48	27	23			4	71	125
Secondary	7	86	21	61	1		10	139	232
Gonorrhœa	3	61	57	5			2	265	329
Scurvy		2	2					1	3
Alcoholism		5	4		1			4	9
Fissure of palate		1	1						1
Debility		4	3		1			44	4[illegible]
Old age								1	1
Rheumatic fever	4	24	18	5			5	19	47
Rheumatism	6	74	49	25	3		3	261	341
Gout								3	3
Osteo-arthritis		3	1	1			1	2	5
Fibroma		1		1					1
Lipoma								3	3
Adenoma		1	1						1
Dermoid cyst		1	1						1
Warts								4	4
Condyloma		1	1					3	4

TABLE VII.—*Tabular statement, by districts, of diseases and injuries, etc.*—Continued.

NORTH ATLANTIC.

Diseases.	Number of cases.								
	Remaining under treatment from previous year.	Admitted during the year.	Discharged.			Died.	Remaining under treatment at the close of the year.	Number furnished office relief.	Total treated in hospital and dispensary.
			Recovered.	Improved.	Not improved.				
General Diseases.									
Lymphoma								1	1
Sarcoma		1	1						1
Carcinoma	1	1		1		1		4	6
Epithelioma	1	5	4		1	1		3	9
Scirrhus		2				2		1	3
Tubercle of lung	12	45	1	31	4	8	13	31	88
Acute miliary tuberculosis		1		1				1	2
Scrofula								1	1
Anæmia		6	4	2				5	11
Glycosuria		1		1					1
Local Diseases	28	672	396	200	24	23	57	1392	2092
DISEASES OF THE NERVOUS SYSTEM	4	60	20	25	3	6	10	103	467
Congestion of the brain								1	1
Hæmorrhage, cerebral		2		2					2
Inflammation of cerebral membranes								1	1
Neuritis		2		2				1	3
Sclerosis		1				1			1
Progressive muscular atrophy		4		1		1	2		4
Locomotor ataxy	1	3		2			2		4
Apoplexy		2		2					2
Hemiplegia	1	6	1	3			3	1	8
Local paralysis		2	1	1				4	6
Spasm of muscle								1	1
Paralysis agitans								1	1
Neuralgia	1	14	5	9		1		39	54
Facial								14	14
Sciatica	1	9	8	1			1	11	21
Vertigo		1	1					3	4
Megrim		1	1					1	2
Epilepsy		2		1		1		7	9
Hypochondriasis		4	1		2		1	4	8
Insanity								1	1
Mania		3		1	1	1		1	4
Dementia		3	1			1	1		3
General paralysis of the insane								12	12
Toxic insanity		1	1						1
DISEASES OF THE EYE		11	5	6				34	45
Conjunctivitis, catarrhal		7	4	3				16	23
Pterygium								1	1
Ulcer of cornea								1	1
Opacity of cornea								2	2
Iritis		1	1					2	3
Choroiditis								1	1
Retinitis		1		1				1	2
Cataract, lenticular		1		1					1
Myopia								1	1
Astigmatism								1	1
Night-blindness								2	2
Day-blindness								1	1
Amblyopia								3	3
Blepharitis		1		1				1	2
Stye								1	1
DISEASES OF THE EAR	1	4	1	3	1			15	20
Abscess of the external meatus								1	1
Sebaceous cyst		1			1				1
Accumulation of wax								5	5
Inflammation of the middle ear	1	2	1	2				8	11
Deafness		1		1				1	2
DISEASES OF THE NOSE		1		1				31	32
Epistaxis								3	3

TABLE VII.—*Tabular statement, by districts, of diseases and injuries, etc.*—Continued.

NORTH ATLANTIC.

Diseases.	Number of Cases.								
	Remaining under treatment from previous year.	Admitted during the year.	Discharged.			Died.	Remaining under treatment at the close of the year.	Number furnished office relief.	Total treated in hospital and dispensary.
			Recovered.	Improved.	Not improved.				
Local Diseases.									
DISEASES OF THE NOSE—Continued.									
Inflammation								1	1
Nasal catarrh								25	25
Ulceration								1	1
Ozæna								1	1
Necrosis of nasal bone		1		1					1
DISEASES OF THE CIRCULATORY SYSTEM	3	59	5	39	2	9	7	48	110
Hydropericardium		1		1					1
Pericarditis	1	1	1			1		1	3
Endocarditis		4	2	1			1		4
Valvular disease:									
Aortic	1	11		8		2	2	4	16
Mitral	1	22		16		4	3	16	39
Hypertrophy of heart		4		2	1	1		7	11
Inflammation of heart		2		2					2
Degeneration of heart, fatty		1		1				1	2
Dilatation of heart		2		2				6	8
Palpitation and irregular action of heart		2	1				1	3	5
Aneurism of arteries		5		3	1	1		1	6
Varix		4	1	3				9	13
DISEASES OF THE RESPIRATORY SYSTEM	8	97	65	28	2	3	7	211	319
Laryngitis:									
Acute		1	1					29	30
Chronic								11	11
Catarrhal								19	19
Narrowing of larynx								2	2
Aphonia								2	2
Bronchitis:									
Acute	1	27	23	3	1	1		55	83
Chronic		2	1	1				13	15
Catarrhal		1		1				37	38
Spasmodic asthma		2		1		1		10	12
Passive congestion of lung								3	3
Hæmoptysis		1	1					1	2
Pneumonia	4	22	21	4		1		10	36
Cirrhosis of lung		1					1		1
Pneumonic phthisis:									
Acute	2	4	2	3	1				6
Chronic	1	15		13			3	4	20
Pleurisy:									
Acute		18	13	2			3	17	35
Chronic		3	3					1	4
DISEASES OF THE DIGESTIVE SYSTEM	1	131	60	35	7	2	8	417	549
Stomatitis		1	1					2	3
Caries of dentine and cementum		1		1				12	13
Abscess of dental periosteum		1	1					1	2
Toothache								8	8
Inflammation of the tongue		1	1						1
Ulcer of the tongue								1	1
Hypertrophy of tonsils		2	1		1				2
Elongated uvula								2	2
Sore throat		3	3					15	18
Quinsy		2	1	1				2	4
Follicular tonsillitis		7	6	1				12	19
Ulceration of fauces		3	3					3	6
Sloughing sore throat		1			1			1	2
Salivation		1	1					1	2
Follicular inflammation of the pharynx		4		3			1	38	42
Post-pharyngeal abscess		1	1						1
Ulceration of pharynx		1	1					2	3
Inflammation of the stomach		6	1	4		1		23	29
Ulceration of the stomach		1		1					1
Dyspepsia		15	8	3	2		2	113	128

TABLE VII.—*Tabular statement, by districts, of diseases and injuries, etc.*—Continued.

NORTH ATLANTIC.

Diseases.	Number of Cases.								
	Remaining under treatment from previous year.	Admitted during the year.	Discharged.			Died.	Remaining under treatment at the close of the year.	Number furnished office relief.	Total treated in hospital and dispensary.
			Recovered.	Improved.	Not improved.				
Local Diseases.									
DISEASES OF THE DIGESTIVE SYSTEM—Cont'd.									
Gastrodynia								3	3
Pyrosis		1	1					4	5
Vomiting								1	1
Enteritis		3	1	2				3	6
Typhlitis		3	2	1				3	6
Colitis		1			1				1
Obstruction of the intestines		1	1						1
Hernia		5		5				30	35
Tænia solium		1	1						1
Ascaris lumbricoides								1	1
Diarrhea	1	42	30	9	1		8	65	108
Constipation		3	2	1				22	25
Colic								6	6
Abscess of the rectum		1	1						1
Abscess of the anus								3	3
Ulceration of the rectum								1	1
Piles:									
Internal								11	11
External		3	2	1				10	13
Fistula in ano		5	4				1	1	6
Pruritus ani								1	1
Hypertrophy of the liver								1	1
Congestion of the liver		2	2					3	5
Hepatitis								3	3
Perihepatitis								1	1
Cirrhosis of liver		3		2	1			1	4
Abscess of liver		1	1						1
Jaundice		2	2					6	8
Inflammation of hepatic ducts and gall-bladder		1	1						1
Biliary colic								1	1
Peritonitis		1				1			1
Omental hernia		1					1		1
DISEASES OF THE LYMPHATIC SYSTEM		58	42	11			5	33	91
Induration and enlargement spleen from ague								1	1
Hypertrophy of lymph-glands		5	4	1				7	12
Suppuration of lymph-vessels								1	1
Inflammation of lymph-glands		14	9	4			1	19	31
Suppuration of lymph-glands		39	29	6			4	5	44
DISEASES OF THE THYROID BODY		1					1		1
Goitre		1					1		1
DISEASES OF THE URINARY SYSTEM		29	14	11	1	2	1	54	83
Acute nephritis		3	1	1	1			5	8
Bright's disease		8	1	5		2		1	9
Pyelitis		1	1						1
Nephralgia								1	1
Diabetes insipidus		2		2				4	6
Hæmaturia		1	1					1	2
Lithuria								2	2
Inflammation of bladder:									
Acute		11	7	3			1	13	24
Subacute								3	3
Chronic		3	3					14	17
Suppurative								1	1
Irritability of bladder								2	2
Retention of urine								2	2
Incontinence of urine								5	5
DISEASES OF THE GENERATIVE SYSTEM	3	72	57	10	1		7	170	245
Urethritis								12	12
Gleet		3	2	1				27	30

TABLE VII.—*Tabular statement, by districts, of diseases and injuries, etc.*—Continued.

NORTH ATLANTIC.

Diseases.	Number of cases.								
	Remaining under treatment from previous year.	Admitted during the year.	Discharged.			Died.	Remaining under treatment at the close of the year.	Number furnished office relief.	Total treated in hospital and dispensary.
			Recovered.	Improved.	Not improved.				
Local Diseases.									
DISEASES OF THE GENERATIVE SYSTEM—Continued.									
Stricture of urethra, organic	1	22	18	2			3	21	44
Urinary fistula		3	2				1		3
Hypertrophy of prostate gland								1	1
Acute inflammation of prostate gland								2	2
Chronic inflammation . prostate gland								1	1
Œdema of the penis								1	1
Inflammation of glans penis		1		1				9	10
Ulcer of penis		12	10	1			1	51	63
Phimosis		4	4					1	5
Paraphimosis								3	3
Chordee								1	1
Varicocele								4	4
Hæmatocele of tunica vaginalis								2	2
Hydrocele of tunica vaginalis	1	6	5	2				13	20
Atrophy of testicle		1			1			1	2
Orchitis:									
Acute		10	6	3			1	6	16
Chronic		3	2				1	4	7
Epididymitis	1	6	7					4	11
Protrusion of tubuli		1	1						1
Spermatorrhœa								6	6
DISEASES OF THE ORGANS OF LOCOMOTION	4	38	22	16			4	21	63
Ostitis	1	2		2			1		3
Periostitis	2	4	3	2			1	4	10
Caries		1	1						1
Necrosis		8	3	4			1		8
Ununited fracture, or false joint								1	1
Dropsy of joints		1	1						1
Synovitis:									
Acute		3	2	1				5	8
Chronic		1	1						1
Ankylosis		5	4	1					5
Loose cartilage		1		1				2	3
Dislocation of articular cartilage		1	1						1
Angular curvature of spine		2	1	1					2
Lateral curvature of spine		1	1					1	2
Anterior curvature of spine	1			1					1
Abscess of muscles		1	1						1
Inflammation of tendons		1					1	2	3
Contraction of tendons								1	1
Inflamed bursa		4	3	1				2	6
Bursal abscess		1		1					1
Thecal abscess								2	2
Bunion		1		1					1
Bursal tumor								1	1
DISEASES OF THE CONNECTIVE TISSUE		31	21	3	1	1	5	37	68
Œdema		2	1	1				4	6
Inflammation		2	1		1			5	7
Abscess		27	19	2		1	5	28	55
DISEASES OF THE SKIN	4	80	64	12	6		2	215	299
Erythema								5	5
Urticaria		1	1					7	8
Eczema	2	4	4	2				20	35
Impetigo								1	1
Lichen								5	5
Psoriasis	1	2	2	1				10	13
Herpes		2	1				1	12	14
Zona								3	3
Pemphigus		1	1					1	2
Acne								2	2
Steatorrhœa								1	1
Frostbite		18	18					16	34

TABLE VII.—*Tabular statement, by districts, of diseases and injuries, etc.*—Continued.

NORTH ATLANTIC.

Diseases.	Number of Cases.								
	Remaining under treatment from previous year.	Admitted during the year.	Discharged.			Died.	Remaining under treatment at the close of the year.	Number furnished office relief.	Total treated in hospital and dispensary.
			Recovered.	Improved.	Not improved.				
Local Diseases.									
DISEASES OF THE SKIN—Continued.									
Ulcer	1	18	16	2	1			33	52
Boil		10	7	2			1	36	46
Carbuncle		1	1					2	3
Gangrene		1	1						1
Whitlow		12	8	4				19	31
Cheloid		1		1					1
Wen		1	1					2	3
Pruritus								2	2
Ringworm								11	11
Itch		3	3					9	12
Phthiriasis								3	3
Malingerer		3			3			5	8
Undetermined		2			2			1	3
Poisons		10	7	3				10	20
Lead		2		2				1	3
Alcohol		7	7					4	11
Tobacco		1		1				2	3
Ivy								3	3
POISONED WOUNDS		4	4					1	5
Venomous animals		4	4					1	5
Injuries	10	182	144	32	2	1	13	186	378
GENERAL INJURIES		21	11	8			2	5	26
Burns and scalds		9	5	3			1	1	10
Effects of cold								2	2
Sunstroke		2	1	1				1	3
Multiple injury		7	4	2			1		7
Exhaustion		3	1	2				1	4
LOCAL INJURIES	10	161	133	24	2	1	11	181	252
Strain of muscles								8	8
Rupture of muscles								1	1
Rupture of tendon		1		1					1
Foreign body in subcutaneous tissue								1	1
Contusion of scalp		1	1					1	2
Scalp wound:									
Bone not exposed								10	10
Bone exposed		6	5				1	1	7
Contusion of skull								1	1
Fracture of the base of the skull		1	1						1
Concussion of brain								3	3
Compression of brain								1	1
Contusion of face		1	1					1	2
Wound of face		1		1				3	4
Fracture of facial bones		1	1						1
Rupture of sclerotic		1		1					1
Contusion of the eye		4	4					1	5
Foreign body in cornea or conjunctiva		1	1					1	2
Wound of eyelid		2	2					1	3
Wound of pinna								1	1
Wound of neck								1	1
Foreign body in the pharynx								1	1
Contusion of the chest		9	6	2	1			7	16
Fracture of the ribs		7	6	1					7
Contusion of back	1	3	3	1				5	9
Sprain of back		8	8					10	18
Wound of back		1	1						1
Wound of spine		1	1						1
Concussion of cord								1	1
Contusion of abdomen	1	1	1	1				1	3
Contusion of pelvis								1	1

Table VII.—*Tabular statement, by districts, of diseases and injuries, etc.*—Continued.

NORTH ATLANTIC.

Diseases.	Number of Cases.								
	Remaining under treatment from previous year.	Admitted during the year.	Discharged.			Died.	Remaining under treatment at the close of the year.	Number furnished office relief.	Total treated in hospital and dispensary.
			Recovered.	Improved.	Not improved.				
Injuries.									
Local Injuries—Continued.									
Wound of organs of generation								1	1
Rupture of urethra		1	1						1
Contusion of testicle								2	2
Contusion of upper extremities	2	8	9	1				24	34
Sprain of the shoulder		2	1	1				3	5
Sprain of the elbow		1	1					1	2
Sprain of the wrist		1					1	6	7
Wound of the upper extremities	1	25	22	3			1	28	54
Separation of epiphyses	1			1					1
Fracture of the clavicle		1		1				1	2
Fracture of the humerus		1		1					1
Fracture of the radius		3	1	2					3
Fracture of the ulna		2	2						2
Fracture of both bones of forearm	1	2	2				1	3	6
Fracture of carpus, metacarpus, and phalanges		4	3	1				2	6
Dislocation of the clavicle								1	1
Dislocation of the humerus		2	2					2	4
Dislocation of the ulna		2	1		1				2
Dislocation of the radius and ulna		1	1					1	2
Dislocation of the carpus		1	1						1
Dislocation of the phalanges of thumb								2	2
Contusion of the lower extremities		19	15	1			3	23	42
Sprain of the knee		1	1					1	2
Sprain of the ankle		9	9					4	13
Sprain of the foot		1	1						1
Wound of the lower extremities		6	4	1			1	4	10
Wound of joint, lower extremities		1		1					1
Fracture of femur	1	3	3				1		4
Fracture of cervix femoris	1		1						1
Fracture of patella	1	2	3					1	4
Fracture of leg, both bones		4	2			1	1	2	6
Fracture of tibia alone		2	1				1	3	5
Fracture of fibula alone		4	3	1				2	6
Fracture of tarsus		1	1					2	3
Dislocation of the femur at the hip		1		1					1
Amputations								4	4
Amputation of arm								1	1
Amputation of hand								1	1
Amputation of fingers								1	1
Removal of the eye by operation								1	1

MIDDLE ATLANTIC.

Diseases.	Remaining under treatment from previous year.	Admitted during the year.	Recovered.	Improved.	Not improved.	Died.	Remaining under treatment at the close of the year.	Number furnished office relief.	Total treated in hospital and dispensary.
Total Cases	125	1665	1025	493	64	86	122	3888	5178
General Diseases	52	773	471	237	23	40	54	1498	2323
Small-pox		4	4						4
Cow-pox								1	1
Chicken-pox								1	1
Measles		5	5					1	6
Mumps		2	2					3	5
Diphtheria								1	1
Cerebro-spinal fever	1						1		1
Simple continued fever								2	2
Enteric fever	1	39	28	2		4	6	6	46
Typo-malarial fever		3	3						3
Yellow fever		1			1				1
Epidemic diarrhea								1	1
Dysentery	2	16	16			1	1	15	33

TABLE VII.—*Tabular statement, by districts, of diseases and injuries, etc.*—Continued.

MIDDLE ATLANTIC.

DISEASES.	NUMBER OF CASES.								
	Remaining under treatment from previous year.	Admitted during the year.	Discharged.			Died.	Remaining under treatment at the close of the year.	Number furnished office relief.	Total treated in hospital and dispensary.
			Recovered.	Improved.	Not improved.				
General Diseases.									
Malarial intermittent fever	9	203	183	18	1	1	9	337	549
Malarial remittent fever		55	47	1	5	2		41	96
Malarial cachexia		5	3	2				32	37
Beri-beri		1	1						1
Erysipelas:									
Simple	1	12	12			1		6	19
Phlegomonous		1				1			1
Pyæmia		1	1						1
Septicæmia								1	1
Syphilis:									
Primary	3	52	9	41		1	4	81	136
Secondary	3	77	15	50	5		1	244	324
Gonorrhœa	2	62	39	19	1		5	342	406
Effects of heat		1	1						1
Scurvy		2	1	1					2
Alcoholism		11	6	4			1	11	22
Delirium tremens		1	1						1
Malformation of iris								1	1
Debility		15	5	6	1	2	1	73	88
Rheumatic fever	5	54	37	17		2	3	133	192
Rheumatism	9	87	48	37	3		8	112	208
Osteo-arthritis								2	2
Fibroma								1	1
Lipoma								1	1
Myoma		1			1				1
Warts								1	1
Condyloma								9	9
Granulation tumors		1					1		1
Sarcoma		1		1					1
Carcinoma	1	1	1			1			2
Epithelioma		1	1					3	4
Colloid	1		1						1
Tubercle of lung and other organs	13	56		29	5	22	13	26	95
Acute miliary tuberculosis		1				1			1
Scrofula	1		1					3	4
Anæmia								6	6
Diabetes mellitus		1				1		1	2
Local Diseases	63	703	415	215	35	40	61	1669	2435
DISEASES OF THE NERVOUS SYSTEM	11	42	12	20	4	3	14	90	143
Congestion of pia mater								2	2
Hæmorrhage, inter-meningeal								1	1
Inflammation:									
Of cerebral membranes		2				1	1		2
Of spinal cord and its membranes								1	1
Neuritis		1					1		1
Sclerosis								1	1
Locomotor ataxy	3	2	1	1	1		2		5
Apoplexy		1	1						1
Paralysis		2		1	1				2
Hemiplegia	3	5		3	1	1	3	1	9
Paraplegia	3	2		1	1		3	4	9
Local paralysis	1	4	1	4				7	12
Lead palsy		1		1					1
Anæsthesia								3	3
Eclampsia		1		1					1
Spasm of muscle								1	1
Wry-neck		1	1						1
Aphasia		1					1		1
Neuralgia		5	3	2				39	44
Facial		1	1					11	12
Sciatica		10	3	5			2	11	21
Vertigo		1	1					1	2
Megrim		1		1				1	2
Epilepsy								1	1

TABLE VII.—*Tabular statement, by districts, of diseases and injuries, etc.*—Continued.

MIDDLE ATLANTIC.

Diseases.	Number of Cases.								
	Remaining under treatment from previous year.	Admitted during the year.	Discharged.			Died.	Remaining under treatment at the close of the year.	Number furnished office relief.	Total treated in hospital and dispensary.
			Recovered.	Improved.	Not improved.				
Local Diseases.									
DISEASES OF THE NERVOUS SYSTEM—Cont'd.									
Chorea		1				1			1
Hypochondriasis								2	2
Melancholia								3	3
Dementia	1						1		1
DISEASES OF THE EYE	1	18	9	4	2		4	40	59
Conjunctivitis:									
Catarrhal		7	3	1			3	21	28
Granular		1					1	2	3
Pterygium								2	2
Keratitis	1	3	3	1				1	5
Opacity of cornea		1			1				1
Inflammation of the sclerotic		1		1					1
Iritis								1	1
Neuro-retinitis		2	1	1				2	4
Detachment of retina		1			1			1	2
Retinitis								1	1
Cataract, lenticular								1	1
Hypermetropia								1	1
Asthenopia								1	1
Night-blindness								2	2
Stricture of nasal duct								1	1
Epiphora								1	1
Hæmatoma		1	1						1
Blepharitis		1	1					1	2
Ptosis								1	1
DISEASES OF THE EAR	1	6	1	4	1		1	19	26
Inflammation of the external meatus:									
Acute								2	2
Chronic								3	3
Abscess of external meatus		1	1						1
Accumulation of wax								3	3
Inflammation of the middle ear	1	3		3			1	9	13
Obstruction of Eustachian tube								1	1
Perforation of membrana tympani								1	1
Deafness		2		1	1				2
DISEASES OF THE NOSE		3	2	1				25	28
Epistaxis		1	1					2	3
Inflammation								2	2
Nasal catarrh		1		1				16	17
Abscess		1	1						1
Ulceration								2	2
Ozæna								3	3
DISEASES OF THE CIRCULATORY SYSTEM	3	30	2	14	5	8	4	46	79
Endocarditis		1	1						1
Valvular disease:									
Aortic	1	3		2		1	1		4
Mitral	1	13		6	3	2	3	7	21
Hypertrophy of heart		1				1			1
Dilatation of heart		1				1		1	2
Angina pectoris		1		1				7	8
Syncope								1	1
Palpitation and irregular action of heart		4	1	3				23	27
Aneurism of arteries		3			1	2		1	4
Obstruction of arteries		2		1		1			2
Varix	1	1		1	1			6	8
DISEASES OF THE RESPIRATORY SYSTEM	9	105	55	33	7	14	5	296	410
Hay-asthma								1	1
Laryngitis, acute		3	2	1				1	4

TABLE VII.—*Tabular statement, by districts, of diseases and injuries, etc.*—Continued.

MIDDLE ATLANTIC.

Diseases.	Number of cases.								
	Remaining under treatment from previous year.	Admitted during the year.	Discharged.			Died.	Remaining under treatment at the close of the year.	Number furnished office relief.	Total treated in hospital and dispensary.
			Recovered.	Improved.	Not improved.				
Local Diseases.									
DISEASES OF THE RESPIRATORY SYSTEM—Continued.									
Bronchitis:									
Acute	2	37	23	12	2	2		183	222
Chronic	3	10	1	8	2		2	21	34
Catarrhal		4	4					35	39
Spasmodic asthma		1	1					25	26
Hæmoptysis		1	1					4	5
Pneumonia	1	15	10	1		5			16
Pneumonic phthisis:									
Acute		10		7		3		3	13
Chronic		4			1	2	1	1	5
Pleurisy:									
Acute	2	15	13	1	1		2	18	35
Chronic		3		3				4	7
Empyema	1	2			1	2			3
DISEASES OF THE DIGESTIVE SYSTEM	7	126	84	24	5	11	9	470	603
Fissure of the lips								1	1
Stomatitis								4	4
Ulcerative stomatitis								1	1
Caries of dentine and cementum								9	9
Necrosis of dentine and cementum								2	2
Abscess of dental periosteum								1	1
Inflammation of gums and alveoli		1	1					1	2
Ulceration of gums and alveoli								4	4
Caries of the alveoli		1	1					1	2
Necrosis of alveoli		1	1						1
Toothache								1	1
Ulcer of the tongue								1	1
Elongated uvula								1	1
Sore throat		3	3					19	22
Quinsy		2	2					2	4
Follicular tonsilitis		6	6					13	19
Ulceration of fauces		1				1		4	5
Abscess of salivary glands		1		1					1
Salivation		1		1					1
Follicular inflammation of the pharynx		4	3	1				10	14
Hæmorrhage of the stomach								1	1
Inflammation of the stomach		18	10	5		2	1	53	71
Dyspepsia	1	2	2	1				47	50
Gastrodynia								1	1
Catarrhal inflammation of the intestines		12	9	2	1			16	28
Obstruction of the intestines	1		1					1	2
Hernia		6	3	1	2			105	111
Bothriocephalus latus		1	1					1	2
Tænia solium		3	3					3	6
Ascaris lumbricoides								2	2
Oxyuris vermicularis								1	1
Diarrhœa	2	22	19	2		2	1	60	93
Constipation		4	2	1		1		33	37
Colic		1	1					2	3
Abscess of the rectum	1			1				1	2
Piles:									
Internal		3	3					10	13
External		10	6	3			1	10	20
Prolapsus of the rectum		1					1		1
Fistula in ano		2	1	1				2	4
Hypertrophy of the liver	1					1			1
Congestion of the liver								21	21
Hepatitis		5	2			2	1	3	8
Cirrhosis of liver		3			1	1	1	1	4
Abscess of liver		3	1		1		1		3
Jaundice		5	3	2				9	14
Inflammation of hepatic ducts and gall-bladder	1	2	1	1		1		2	5
Gallstones								1	1

TABLE VII.—*Tabular statement, by districts, of diseases and injuries, etc.*—Continued.

MIDDLE ATLANTIC.

Diseases.	Number of cases.								
	Remaining under treatment from previous year.	Admitted during the year.	Discharged.			Died.	Remaining under treatment at the close of the year.	Number furnished office relief.	Total treated in hospital and dispensary.
			Recovered.	Improved.	Not improved.				
Local Diseases.									
DISEASES OF THE DIGESTIVE SYSTEM—Cont'd.									
Ascites		2		1			1		2
Peritonitis		1					1		1
Omental hernia								1	1
DISEASES OF THE LYMPHATIC SYSTEM	5	52	30	23	1	1	2	81	141
Hypertrophy of lymph-glands		1		1				3	4
Inflammation of lymph-glands	3	31	20	14				62	96
Suppuration of lymph-glands	1	20	10	8	1		2	19	40
Lymphadenoma	1					1			1
DISEASES OF THE URINARY SYSTEM	8	30	4	28	2	3	5	59	101
Congestion of the kidney		1		1				3	4
Acute nephritis	1	11	1	11				2	14
Bright's disease	2	19		12	2	3	4	5	26
Nephralgia								4	4
Chyluria								1	1
Hæmaturia		2		2				5	7
Lithuria								1	1
Inflammation of the bladder:									
Acute		2	1	1				14	16
Subacute								3	3
Chronic		3	1	1			1	5	8
Calculus of bladder								1	1
Irritability of bladder								12	12
Incontinence of urine		1	1					3	4
DISEASES OF THE GENERATIVE SYSTEM	11	87	61	24	5		8	213	311
Urethritis		3	2	1				5	8
Gleet		1			1			35	36
Ulcer of the urethra								1	1
Stricture of the urethra:									
Organic	3	24	20	4	2		1	16	43
Traumatic		1					1		1
Spasmodic	1			1				4	5
Urinary fistula	1			1					1
Recto-urethral fistula		2	1	1					2
Acute inflammation of prostate gland	1	1	2						2
Chronic inflammation of prostate gland								10	10
Œdema of the penis		1	1					2	3
Inflammation of glans penis								7	7
Ulcer of penis	3	23	13	10			3	70	66
Phimosis		5	3	1	1			1	6
Paraphimosis	1	1		1			1		2
Abscess of scrotum								1	1
Gangrene of the scrotum		1	1						1
Hydrocele of spermatic cord								1	1
Inflammation of spermatic cord								1	1
Varicocele								6	6
Hydrocele of tunica vaginalis		7	4	2			1	8	15
Orchitis:									
Acute		10	9				1	18	28
Chronic		3	1	2				9	12
Epididymitis	1	2	3					7	10
Abscess of testicle		1	1						1
Spermatorrhœa		1			1			8	9
Impotence								3	3
DISEASES OF THE ORGANS OF LOCOMOTION	3	26	13	10	2		4	34	63
Ostitis		2	2						2
Periostitis		3		2			1	4	7
Caries	1	4	2	2	1				5
Necrosis		3	3					1	4
Dropsy of joints								3	3
Synovitis:									
Acute		4	3				1	4	8
Chronic	1	2	1	1	1			13	16

TABLE VII.—*Tabular statement, by districts, of diseases and injuries, etc.*—Continued.

MIDDLE ATLANTIC.

Diseases.	Number of cases.								
	Remaining under treatment from previous year.	Admitted during the year.	Discharged.			Died.	Remaining under treatment at the close of the year.	Number furnished office relief.	Total treated in hospital and dispensary.
			Recovered.	Improved.	Not improved.				
Local Diseases.									
DISEASE OF THE ORGANS OF LOCOMOTION—Continued.									
Ankylosis	....	1	.....	1	.....	...	.....	2	3
Loose cartilage	.....	1	.....	1	.....	...	.....	....	1
Relaxation of ligaments	.....	.....	.....	.....	.....	...	.....	1	1
Angular curvature of spine	1	....	....	1	.....	...	.....	.....	1
Anterior curvature of spine	....	1	.....	.....	.....	...	1	....	1
Atrophy of muscles	....	2	.....	1	.....	...	1	1	3
Abscess of muscles	....	1	.....	1	.....	...	.....	....	1
Inflammation of tendons	....	1	1	.....	.....	...	.....	1	2
Inflamed bursa	....	1	1	.....	.....	...	.....	3	4
Bursal tumor	.....	....	.....	.....	....	...	.....	1	1
DISEASES OF THE CONNECTIVE TISSUE	4	47	39	10	.....	...	2	53	104
Œdema	....	3	.....	3	.....	...	.....	3	6
Inflammation	2	15	14	2	.....	...	1	13	30
Abscess	2	20	25	5	.....	...	1	37	68
DISEASES OF THE SKIN	5	122	103	20	1	..	3	240	367
Erythema	.....	2	1	1	.....	...	.....	2	4
Urticaria	.....	.....	.....	.....	.....	...	.....	1	1
Eczema	....	6	5	1	.....	...	.....	17	23
Impetigo	.....	1	1	....	.....	...	.....	.....	1
Rupia	.....	1	1	....	.....	...	.....	2	3
Prurigo	.....	.....	.....	.....	.....	...	.....	1	1
Lichen	.....	.....	....	.....	.....	...	.....	2	2
Psoriasis	.....	.....	....	.....	.....	...	.....	2	2
Herpes	.....	2	2	.....	.....	...	.....	6	8
Zona	....	2	.....	1	.....	...	1	5	7
Acne	.....	.....	.....	.....	.....	...	.....	1	1
Sycosis	.....	.....	....	.....	.....	...	.....	2	2
Chloasma	....	.....	....	.....	.....	...	.....	1	1
Alopecia	.....	.....	.....	.....	....	..	.. ..	1	1
Chilblain	.....	.....	.....	.....	.....	...	.....	2	2
Frostbite	2	24	22	3	.....	..	1	21	47
Ulcer	3	63	55	10	.....	...	1	70	142
Cicatrices	.....	.....	.....	.....	.....	...	.....	1	1
Boil	.....	9	9	.....	.....	...	....	44	53
Carbuncle	.....	1	1	....	.....	..	....	7	8
Whitlow	....	5	4	1	.....	..	.....	8	13
Onychia	.....	.....	.....	.....	.....	...	.....	2	2
Corn	.....	.....	....	.....	.....	...	.....	1	1
Lupus	.....	1	....	1	.....	...	.....	1	2
Wen	.....	1	1	.....	.....	...	.....	5	6
Pruritus	....	.....	.....	.....	.....	...	.....	1	1
Itch	.....	1	.....	1	....	...	.....	24	25
Phthiriasis	....	.....	.....	.....	.....	...	.....	1	1
Effects of irritants	....	1	1	.....	.....	...	.....	.....	1
Malingerer	....	2	....	1	1	...	.....	1	3
Undetermined	.....	.....	.. ..	.....	.....	...	.....	2	2
Poisons	.....	.....	.. ..	.....	.....	...	.....	3	3
Alochol	.....	.....	....	.....	.....	...	.....	2	2
Tobacco	.. ..	.....	.....	.....	.....	...	.....	1	1
Injuries	10	187	138	41	6	6	6	215	412
GENERAL INJURIES	3	13	12	2	.....	2	.....	9	25
Burns and scalds	2	13	11	2	.....	2	.....	8	23
Multiple injury	1	.....	1	.....	.....	..	.....	1	2
LOCAL INJURIES	7	174	126	39	6	4	6	206	387
Compression of nerves	....	1	.....	1	.....	...	.....	1	2
Strain of muscles	.....	.....	....	.....	.....	..	.....	1	1
Foreign body in subcutaneous tissue	....	....	.....	.....	.....	...	.....	2	2
Contusion of scalp	....	1	....	1	....	...	.....	2	3

TABLE VII.—*Tabular statement, by districts, of diseases and injuries, etc.*—Continued.

MIDDLE ATLANTIC.

Diseases.	Number of Cases.								
	Remaining under treatment from previous year.	Admitted during the year.	Discharged.			Died.	Remaining under treatment at the close of the year.	Number furnished office relief.	Total treated in hospital and dispensary.
			Recovered.	Improved.	Not improved.				
Injuries.									
LOCAL INJURIES—Continued.									
Scalp wound:									
Bone not exposed		8	8					4	12
Bone exposed		1	1						1
Fracture of the vault of the skull		1				1			1
Concussion of brain	1		1						1
Compression of brain		1					1		1
Contusion of face		2	2					1	3
Wound of face		2	2					1	3
Fracture of facial bones		2	2						2
Contusion of the eye								1	1
Foreign body in cornea or conjunctiva								3	3
Wound of orbit		2	2						2
Contusion of pinna								1	1
Sprain of neck		1		1				1	2
Contusion of the chest		3	3					6	9
Fracture of the ribs		10	9	1				8	18
Wound of parietes of chest		2	1	1				1	3
Contusion of back	1	4	2	2	1			6	11
Sprain of back		6	5				1	15	21
Contusion of abdomen		2	2						2
Wound of parietes of abdomen		2			1	1			2
Contusion of pelvis		1		1					1
Wound of organs of generation		1	1						1
Fracture and dislocation of pelvis		3		2			1		3
Contusion of upper extremities	1	6	4	3				12	19
Sprain of the shoulder		6	4	2				15	21
Sprain of the elbow								2	2
Sprain of the wrist		2	2					12	14
Sprain of the fingers								1	1
Wound of the upper extremities		24	18	5	1			29	53
Wound of joint, upper extremities								1	1
Fracture of the clavicle		1	1					1	2
Fracture of the scapula		1	1						1
Fracture of the radius		5	2	2	1			2	7
Fracture of the ulna		3	2	1				3	6
Fracture of both bones of forearm		3	2			1		1	4
Fracture of carpus, metacarpus, and phalanges		2	1	1				2	4
Dislocation of the clavicle		1		1				1	2
Dislocation of the scapula								1	1
Dislocation of the humerus	1		1					1	2
Contusion of the lower extremities		14	12	2				25	39
Sprain of the hip		2	2					3	5
Sprain of the knee		3	2	1				8	11
Sprain of the ankle	1	18	12	6	1			9	28
Sprain of the foot		1					1	2	3
Wound of the lower extremities		13	8	3		1	1	18	31
Wound of joint, lower extremities								1	1
Fracture of femur	1	1	1		1			2	4
Fracture of cervix femoris		1	1						1
Fracture of patella		2		2					2
Fracture of leg, both bones	1	3	4						4
Fracture of tibia alone		2	1				1		2
Fracture of fibula alone		3	3						3
Dislocation of femur at the hip		1	1						1
AMPUTATIONS		1					1	2	3
Amputation of fingers								2	2
Resection of elbow-joint		1					1		1

TABLE VII.—*Tabular statement, by districts, of diseases and injuries, etc.*—Continued.

SOUTH ATLANTIC.

Diseases.	Number of Cases,								
	Remaining under treatment from previous year.	Admitted during the year.	Discharged.			Died.	Remaining under treatment at the close of the year.	Number furnished office relief.	Total treated in hospital and dispensary.
			Recovered.	Improved.	Not improved.				
TOTAL CASES	104	2018	1339	549	36	54	144	5869	7991
General Diseases	52	1029	697	282	18	16	66	2754	3833
Small-pox								1	1
Cow-pox		1			1			24	25
Measles		25	23	2				7	32
Whooping-cough								1	1
Mumps		3	2				1	10	13
Diphtheria		2	1		1			2	4
Simple continued fever		6	4	2				6	12
Enteric fever	3	17	15			2	3	1	21
Cholera, sporadic		1	1					4	5
Epidemic diarrhœa		1		1				2	3
Dysentery	2	34	27	4		1	4	60	96
Malarial intermittent fever	6	271	230	39	2		6	790	1,067
Malarial remittent fever	7	195	169	27		2	4	124	326
Malarial cachexia	2	38	29	6		1	4	134	174
Phagedæna		1		1				2	3
Erysepelas, simple		15	13	2				12	27
Syphilis:									
Primary	3	53	25	27	2		2	64	120
Secondary	6	87	11	66	1	1	14	228	321
Gonorrhœa		46	26	13	3		4	640	686
Filaria sanguinis hominis		1					1		1
Effects of heat								3	3
Scurvy		1	1					2	3
Alcoholism		2	2					3	5
Delirium tremens		3	2	1				2	5
Debility		9	5	3	1			37	46
Old age								1	1
Rheumatic fever	3	35	22	10		1	5	22	60
Rheumatism	5	119	85	31	1		7	502	626
Gout								2	2
Osteo-arthritis		1		1				2	3
Fibroma								1	1
Lipoma		2	1	1				2	4
Osteoma								1	1
Myoma								1	1
Adenoma								1	1
Warts		3	2				1	11	14
Condyloma								1	1
Carcinoma								1	1
Epithelioma								2	2
Tubercle of lung and other organs	12	49		40	5	6	10	33	94
Scrofula	2	2		3		1		8	12
Anæmia	1	2	1	1		1		4	7
Diabetes mellitus		2		1	1				2
Local Diseases	46	763	473	222	16	31	64	2847	3656
DISEASES OF THE NERVOUS SYSTEM	17	53	18	30	1	3	18	176	246
Congestion of cerebrum		2	1	1				3	5
Neuritis		1		1					1
Sclerosis								4	4
Apoplexy		2	1	1				2	4
Paralysis		1		1				1	2
Hemiplegia	2	4		4	1		1		6
Local paralysis		5		4		1			5
Anæsthesia								1	1
Spasm of muscle								2	2
Paralysis agitans		1		1					1
Neuralgia		8	4	4				48	56
Facial		6	4	2				48	54
Sciatica	1	5	5	1				12	18
Vertigo		1		1				11	12
Megrim		2		2				20	31
Epilepsy	1	8	1	6		1	1	10	19

TABLE VII.—*Tabular statement, by districts, of diseases and injuries, etc.*—Continued.

SOUTH ATLANTIC.

Diseases.	Number of Cases.								
	Remaining under treatment from previous year.	Admitted during the year.	Discharged.			Died.	Remaining under treatment at the close of the year.	Number furnished office relief.	Total treated in hospital and dispensary.
			Recovered.	Improved.	Not improved.				
Local Diseases.									
DISEASES OF THE NERVOUS SYSTEM—Cont'd.									
Hysteria								1	1
Hypochondriasis								4	4
Mania	11	1	1			1	10		12
Melancholia	2	4	1				5		6
Dementia		1		1					1
General paralysis of the insane		1					1		1
DISEASES OF THE EYE	2	10	12	3	1		2	48	66
Conjunctivitis:									
Catarrhal	1	5	5	1				22	28
Purulent		1		1				5	6
Phlyctenular								1	1
Chronic								2	2
Pterygium								1	1
Keratitis		4	3				1	3	7
Iritis		5	4	1				3	8
Atrophy of optic nerve								1	1
Inflammation of optic nerve		1					1		1
Cataract, lenticular	1				1				1
Myopia								1	1
Night-blindness								4	4
Stricture of nasal duct								1	1
Stye								1	1
Chalazion								3	3
DISEASES OF THE EAR		2	2					25	27
Inflammation of the external meatus:									
a. Acute								8	8
b. Chronic								1	1
Abscess of the external meatus								1	1
Accumulation of wax								4	4
Inflammation of the middle ear		2	2					7	9
Perforation of membrana tympani								1	1
Deafness								3	3
DISEASES OF THE NOSE		1		1				18	19
Epistaxis								3	3
Inflammation								3	3
Nasal catarrh		1		1				12	13
DISEASES OF THE CIRCULATORY SYSTEM	3	25		19	2	5	2	71	90
Hydropericardium								1	1
Pericarditis								1	1
Endocarditis	1					1		1	2
Valvular disease:									
Aortic	1	1		1			1	5	7
Mitral		15		10	1	3	1	29	44
Hypertrophy of heart								2	2
Degeneration of heart, fatty		1		1					1
Dilatation of heart		1		1				1	2
Angina pectoris		1		1				1	2
Palpitation and irregular action of heart								17	17
Degeneration of arteries								1	1
Dilatation of arteries		1		1					1
Aneurism of arteries		4		3		1		3	7
Phlebitis	1			1					1
Varix								9	9
Thrombosis of veins		1			1				1
DISEASES OF THE RESPIRATORY SYSTEM	3	126	73	30	3	15	8	531	680
Laryngitis:									
Acute		1	1					6	7
Catarrhal								1	1

TABLE VII.—*Tabular statement, by districts, of diseases and injuries, etc.*—Continued.

SOUTH ATLANTIC.

Diseases.	Number of Cases.								
	Remaining under treatment from previous year.	Admitted during the year.	Discharged.			Died.	Remaining under treatment at the close of the year.	Number furnished office relief.	Total treated in hospital and dispensary.
			Recovered.	Improved.	Not improved.				
Local Diseases.									
DISEASES OF THE RESPIRATORY SYSTEM—Continued.									
Bronchitis:									
Acute	......	40	36	9	2	1	1	376	425
Chronic	......	9	3	4	.....	1	1	77	80
Catarrhal	......	2	1	......	......	1	......	31	33
Spasmodic asthma	1	7	4	2	......	1	1	14	22
Hœmoptysis	......	5	3	1	......	.....	1	12	17
Pneumonia	......	35	18	7	......	10	......	7	42
Cirrhosis of lung	......	1	......	......	......	.....	1	......	1
Pneumonic phthisis:									
Acute	......	......	......	......	......	.....	......	9	9
Chronic	1	7	......	6	.....	1	1	7	15
Emphysema	......	......	......	......	......	.....	......	3	3
Pleurisy:									
Acute	1	9	7	1	1	....	1	6	16
Chronic	......	......	......	......	......	.....	......	2	2
Empyema	......	1	......	......	......	.....	1	...	1
DISEASES OF THE DIGESTIVE SYSTEM	4	131	87	34	1	5	8	1,021	1,156
Stomatitis	......	......	......	......	......	.....	......	13	13
Ulcerative stomatitis	......	......	......	......	......	.....	......	4	4
Thrush	......	......	......	......	......	.....	......	2	2
Abscess of the antrum	......	2	2	......	......	.....	......	....	2
Caries of dentine and cementum	......	......	......	......	......	.....	......	33	33
Necrosis of dentine and cementum	......	......	......	......	......	.....	......	1	1
Inflammation of dental periosteum	......	......	......	......	......	.....	......	1	1
Abscess of dental periosteum	......	......	......	......	......	.....	......	3	3
Inflammation of gums and alveoli	.....	1	1	......	......	..	.....	2	3
Ulceration of gums and alveoli	......	......	......	......	......	.....	......	1	1
Toothache	......	......	......	......	......	..	......	4	4
Inflammation of the tongue	......	......	......	......	......	..	......	2	2
Ulcer of the tongue	......	......	......	......	......	..	......	1	1
Elongated uvula	......	......	......	......	......	..	......	3	3
Sore throat	......	7	7	......	......	.....	......	45	52
Quinsy	......	3	2	......	......	.....	1	5	8
Follicular tonsillitis	......	13	13	......	......	.....	......	26	39
Ulceration of fauces	......	1	1	......	......	..	......	1	2
Sloughing sore throat	......	......	......	......	......	.....	......	1	1
Salivation	......	......	....	......	......	.....	......	1	1
Follicular inflammation of the pharynx	......	2	2	....	......	.....	......	40	51
Ulceration of pharynx	......	......	......	......	......	.....	......	3	8
Hæmorrhage of the stomach	......	......	......	......	......	.....	......	1	1
Inflammation of the stomach	......	3	1	......	......	1	1	15	18
Ulceration of the stomach	...	3	1	2	......	.....	......	1	4
Dyspepsia	....	7	5	2	......	.....	......	209	216
Gastrodynia	......	2	2	......	......	.....	......	12	14
Pyrosis	......	......	......	......	......	.....	......	1	1
Vomiting	......	......	......	......	......	.....	......	1	1
Catarrhal inflammation of the intestines	1	9	9	1	......	.....	......	15	25
Enteritis	1	......	1	......	......	..	....	.....	1
Colitis	......	......	......	......	......	.....	......	1	1
Obstruction of the intestines	......	2	1	1	......	..	......	....	2
Hernia	......	10	.....	8	....	2	......	90	100
Tænia solium	1	3	1	3	......	.....	......	3	7
Ascaris lumbricoides	......	......	......	......	......	.....	......	1	1
Diarrhoea	......	32	22	6	1	....	3	160	192
Constipation	.....	1	1	......	......	..	......	215	216
Colic	......	2	1	......	......	.....	1	17	19
Abscess of the rectum	......	......	......	......	......	.....	......	1	1
Ulceration of the rectum	......	......	......	......	......	.....	......	3	3
Piles:									
Internal	......	1	1	......	......	..	......	15	16
External	......	4	2	1	......	.....	1	28	32
Prolapsus of the anus	......	......	......	......	......	..	......	1	1
Fistula in ano	......	4	2	2	......	..	......	4	8
Fissure of the anus	......	2	1	1	......	.....	......	1	3

TABLE VII.—*Tabular statement, by districts, of diseases and injuries, etc.*—Continued.

SOUTH ATLANTIC.

Diseases.	Number of Cases.								
	Remaining under treatment from previous year.	Admitted during the year.	Discharged.			Died.	Remaining under treatment at the close of the year.	Number furnished office relief.	Total treated in hospital and dispensary.
			Recovered.	Improved.	Not improved.				
Local Diseases.									
DISEASES OF THE DIGESTIVE SYSTEM—Continued.									
Congestion of the liver		1	1					7	8
Hepatitis		4	3	1				1	5
Cirrhosis of liver		6	1	4		1		2	8
Jaundice		4	2	1			1	12	16
Inflammation of hepatic ducts and gall-bladder								1	1
Ascites	1			1				2	3
Peritonitis		2	1			1			2
DISEASES OF THE LYMPHATIC SYSTEM	3	76	50	25			4	127	206
Hypertrophy of the spleen								2	2
Hypertrophy of lymph-glands								2	2
Inflammation of lymph-vessels		1	1						1
Inflammation of lymph-glands	3	46	31	16			2	79	128
Suppuration of lymph-glands		29	18	9			2	44	73
DISEASES OF THE THYROID BODY								2	2
Goitre								2	2
DISEASES OF THE URINARY SYSTEM	1	27	6	18		3	1	67	95
Congestion of the kidney								1	1
Acute nephritis		10	3	6		1		10	20
Bright's disease		10		8		2		12	22
Calculus in kidney								1	1
Suppression of urine								1	1
Hæmaturia		3	3					1	4
Chyluria								3	3
Lithuria								1	1
Inflammation of bladder:									
Acute								11	11
Subacute		1		1				1	2
Chronic	1	2		2			1	10	13
Calculus of bladder		1		1				3	4
Irritability of bladder								11	11
Incontinence of urine								1	1
DISEASES OF THE GENERATIVE SYSTEM	6	120	70	31	1	3	12	336	462
Urethritis		1	1					4	5
Gleet								11	11
Stricture of urethra:									
Organic	1	13	3	5	1	2	3	36	50
Traumatic	1			1				1	2
Spasmodic		1	1					3	4
Urinary fistula	1	1		2					2
Hypertrophy of prostate gland								2	2
Œdema of the penis		1	1					1	2
Inflammation of glans penis								8	8
Ulcer of penis	2	64	47	9		1	9	204	270
Phimosis		4	3	1				2	6
Paraphimosis		3	2	1				2	5
Varicocele								5	5
Hydrocele of tunica vaginalis		2	1	1				11	13
Orchitis:									
Acute		16	9	7				14	30
Chronic		3		3				5	8
Epididymitis	1	10	10	1				18	29
Protrusion of tubuli		1	1						1
Cyst of testicle								1	1
Spermatorrhœa								4	4
Impotence								4	4
DISEASES OF THE ORGANS OF LOCOMOTION		14	12	1			1	24	38
Periostitis		1	1					3	4
Caries								2	2
Necrosis		3	3					1	4
Dropsy of joints								1	1

TABLE VII.—*Tabular statement, by districts, of diseases and injuries, etc.*—Continued.

SOUTH ATLANTIC.

Diseases.	Number of Cases.								
	Remaining under treatment from previous year.	Admitted during the year.	Discharged.			Died.	Remaining under treatment at the close of the year.	Number furnished office relief.	Total treated in hospital and dispensary.
			Recovered.	Improved.	Not improved.				
Local Diseases.									
DISEASES OF THE ORGANS OF LOCOMOTION—Continued.									
Synovitis:									
Acnto		3	3					1	4
Chronic		2	1	1				6	8
Loose cartilage								1	1
Dislocation of articular cartilage		1	1					1	2
Psoas abscess		1					1		1
Atrophy of muscles								1	1
Inflammation of tendons		1	1						1
Inflamed bursa		1	1					5	6
Thecal abscess		1	1						1
Bunion								1	1
Ganglion								1	1
DISEASES OF THE CONNECTIVE TISSUE	2	55	47	6			4	63	120
Œdema		2		1			1	6	8
Inflammation		16	16					18	34
Abscess	2	37	31	5			3	37	76
Undue formation of fat								2	2
DISEASES OF THE SKIN	5	117	87	24	7		4	318	440
Erythema		1		1				3	4
Urticaria								8	8
Eczema	1	4	4				1	48	53
Impetigo								6	6
Ecthyma		1	1						1
Pityriasis								1	1
Lichen								5	5
Psoriasis								3	3
Herpes		1		1				15	16
Zona								3	3
Acno		1	1					3	4
Sycosis								1	1
Chilblain								1	1
Frostbite		38	28	2	7		1	5	43
Ulcer	4	44	31	13			1	82	130
Boil		10	8	2				62	72
Carbuncle		7	4	3				4	11
Whitlow		9	6	2			1	22	31
Onychia								2	2
Corn								4	4
Cheloid								2	2
Wen								4	4
Pruritus								4	4
Ringworm		1	1					7	8
Tinea versicolor								5	5
Itch								14	14
Phthiriasis								3	3
Malingerer								1	1
Poisons		7	5	1		1		7	14
Alcohol		5	3	1		1		6	11
Sulphuric acid		1	1					1	2
Coal gas		1	1						1
Injuries	6	221	164	44	2	3	14	261	488
GENERAL INJURIES		19	14	2		2	1	15	34
Burns and scalds		12	8	1		2	1	12	24
Effects of cold								1	1
Sunstroke		1		1				1	2
Multiple injury		2	2						2
Exhaustion		4	4					1	5
LOCAL INJURIES	6	202	150	42	2	1	13	240	434
Strain of muscles		2		2				12	14

TABLE VII.—*Tabular statement, by districts, of diseases and injuries, etc.*—Continued.

SOUTH ATLANTIC.

Diseases.	Number of Cases.								
	Remaining under treatment from previous year.	Admitted during the year.	Discharged.			Died.	Remaining under treatment at the close of the year.	Number furnished office relief.	Total treated in hospital and dispensary.
			Recovered.	Improved.	Not improved.				
Injuries.									
LOCAL INJURIES—Continued.									
Foreign body in subcutaneous tissue	......	......	......	......	......	..	....	2	2
Contusion of scalp	......	......	......	......	......	...	......	1	1
Scalp wound:									
Bone not exposed	......	5	5	......	......	...	......	7	12
Bone exposed	......	1	1	......	......	...	......	......	1
Contusion of skull	......	1	1	......	......	...	......	1	2
Fracture of the base of the skull	......	1	1	......	......	...	......	......	1
Concussion of brain	......	2	2	......	......	...	......	......	2
Contusion of face	......	2	2	......	......	...	......	2	4
Wound of face	......	6	5	1	......	..	......	3	9
Fracture of facial bones	......	1	......	......	......	..	1	......	1
Contusion of the eye	......	1	1	......	......	..	......	1	2
Foreign body in cornea or conjunctiva	......	......	......	......	......	..	......	2	2
Wound of pinna	......	1	1	......	......	...	......	......	1
Contusion of the chest	......	14	11	2	......	...	1	14	28
Fracture of the ribs	......	2	1	1	......	...	......	1	3
Wound of parietes of chest	......	2	1	1	......	...	......	......	2
Perforating wound of chest	......	1	......	......	......	..	1	......	1
Contusion of back	......	6	5	1	......	..	......	5	11
Sprain of back	......	7	5	2	......	...	......	15	22
Wound of back	......	1	......	......	1	...	......	1	2
Fracture of spine	......	2	......	......	......	...	2	......	2
Concussion of cord	......	3	2	1	......	...	......	1	4
Contusion of abdomen	......	1	......	1	......	...	......	3	4
Contusion of pelvis	......	......	......	......	......	...	......	1	1
Wound of organs of generation	......	2	2	......	......	..	......	3	5
Contusion of upper extremities	1	5	2	4	......	...	......	20	26
Sprain of the shoulder	......	......	......	......	......	...	......	6	6
Sprain of the elbow	......	2	2	......	......	...	......	......	2
Sprain of the wrist	......	7	6	1	......	...	......	15	22
Sprain of the fingers	......	......	......	......	......	...	......	2	2
Wound of the upper extremity	1	42	37	5	......	...	1	55	98
Fracture of the clavicle	......	1	......	1	......	...	......	1	2
Fracture of the scapula	......	1	1	......	......	...	......	......	1
Fracture of the humerus	......	1	1	......	......	...	......	1	2
Fracture of the radius	......	......	......	......	......	...	......	3	3
Fracture of the ulna	......	1	1	......	......	...	......	2	3
Fracture of both bones of forearm	......	1	......	1	......	...	......	......	1
Fracture of carpus, metacarpus, and phalanges	......	7	3	3	......	...	1	3	10
Dislocation of the scapula	......	1	1	......	......	...	......	......	1
Dislocation of the humerus	......	2	2	......	......	...	......	1	3
Dislocation of the ulna	......	1	1	......	......	...	......	......	1
Evulsion of finger	......	1	1	......	......	...	......	......	1
Contusion of the lower extremities	......	14	12	2	......	...	......	32	46
Sprain of the hip	......	......	......	......	......	...	......	2	2
Sprain of the knee	......	1	......	1	......	...	......	2	3
Sprain of the ankle	......	16	13	2	......	...	1	11	27
Sprain of the foot	......	1	1	......	......	...	......	1	2
Wound of the lower extremities	3	21	16	5	1	...	2	14	38
Fracture of femur	......	4	2	......	......	...	2	......	4
Fracture of leg, both bones	1	3	1	1	......	1	1	......	4
Fracture of fibula alone	......	1	......	1	......	...	......	......	1
Dislocation of the foot at the ankle	......	2	......	2	......	...	......	......	2
Dislocation of the astragalus	......	1	......	1	......	...	......	......	1
Dislocation of the other tarsal bones	......	1	1	......	......	...	......	......	1

TABLE VII.—*Tabular statement, by districts, of diseases and injuries, etc.*—Continued.

THE GULF.

Diseases.	Number of Cases. Remaining under treatment from previous year.	Admitted during the year.	Discharged. Recovered.	Discharged. Improved.	Discharged. Not improved.	Died.	Remaining under treatment at the close of the year.	Number furnished office relief.	Total treated in hospital and dispensary.
TOTAL CASES	90	1603	1140	391	18	47	97	3372	5065
General Diseases	60	923	685	211	12	27	48	1480	2472
Cow-pox								5	5
Chicken-pox								1	1
Measles		3	3						3
Relapsing fever								1	1
Whooping-cough								2	2
Mumps		9	8	1				4	13
Simple continued fever		4	4					1	5
Enteric fever		8	6			2			8
Typho malarial fever		3	3						3
Yellow fever		4	4					2	6
Cholera, sporadic		3	3					1	4
Epidemic diarrhœa		1				1			1
Dysentery	7	44	42	7		2		47	98
Malarial intermittent fever	7	294	272	12	1	2	10	328	630
Malarial remittent fever	9	142	120	11		5	6	21	172
Malarial cachexia	1	26	23	2			2	138	165
Phagedæna								1	1
Erysipelas:									
Simple		2	1				1	2	4
Phlegmonous		1	1						1
Syphilis:									
Primary	7	75	53	23	2		4	65	147
Secondary	4	110	8	91	1	1	13	186	300
Gonorrhœa	1	24	19	6				295	310
Alcoholism		5	4		1			15	20
Debility		13	7	6				30	43
Rheumatic fever	2	17	17	2				52	71
Rheumatism	8	91	73	18	1	1	6	228	327
Gout								3	3
Osteo-arthritis								1	1
Hæmatoma								1	1
Fibroma								2	2
Lipoma		1		1				1	2
Adenoma		1		1				1	2
Angeioma								1	1
Warts								4	4
Carcinoma		2		1	1				2
Epithelioma	1	1		1		1			2
Tubercle of lung and other organs	13	36		20	5	12	6	40	89
Acute miliary tuberculosis								1	1
Scrofula		2		2				2	4
Anæmia		1	1					7	8
Local Diseases	24	524	348	143	5	19	33	1583	2131
DISEASES OF THE NERVOUS SYSTEM	6	52	24	23	2	4	5	105	163
Congestion of brain		2	2						2
Myelitis		2	1	1				1	3
Neuritis		5	1	3			1	5	10
Softening of brain or cord		1				1			1
Locomotor ataxy		5		2		1	2	3	8
Apoplexy	1	3		3		1		1	5
Paralysis								1	1
Hemiplegia		2		1		1		2	4
Paraplegia	1	2		1	1		1		3
Local paralysis		2		2				2	4
Wry-neck								1	1
Neuralgia	1	5	4	1			1	43	49
Facial	1	7	8					23	31
Sciatica		7	5	2				3	10
Vertigo		3	2	1				2	5
Megrim								3	3
Tetanus								1	1
Epilepsy	2	5	1	5	1			10	17

TABLE VII.—*Tabular statement, by districts, of diseases and injuries, etc.*—Continued.

THE GULF.

Diseases.	Number of Cases. Remaining under treatment from previous year.	Admitted during the year.	Discharged. Recovered.	Discharged. Improved.	Discharged. Not improved.	Died.	Remaining under treatment at the close of the year.	Number furnished office relief.	Total treated in hospital and dispensary.
Local Diseases.									
DISEASES OF THE NERVOUS SYSTEM—Cont'd.									
Hysteria	.....	.....	.....	....	.....	...	.....	2	2
Hystero-epilepsy	....	1	.....	1	....	...	.....	1	2
Hypochondriasis	.....	.....	.....	.....	....	...	.....	1	1
DISEASES OF THE EYE	.....	5	3	2	....	...	.....	28	33
Conjunctivitis:									
Catarrhal	.....	3	2	1	....	...	.....	13	16
Purulent	.....	.....	.....	....	.....	...	.....	6	6
Granular	.....	.....	.....	....	.....	...	.....	1	1
Pterygium	.....	.....	.....	....	.....	...	.....	1	1
Opacity of cornea	.....	.....	.....	....	.....	...	.....	1	1
Iritis	.....	.....	.....	....	.....	...	.....	1	1
Inflammation of optic nerve	.....	1	1	....	....	..	.....	.....	1
Day-blindness	....	.....	.....	.....	....	...	....	2	2
Neuralgia of eyeball	.....	.....	.....	.....	.....	...	.....	2	2
Stricture of nasal duct	....	1	.....	1	....	...	.....	1	2
DISEASES OF THE EAR	.....	2	1	1	.....	..	.....	14	16
Inflammation of the external meatus:									
a. Acute	.....	1	1	.....	.....	...	.....	4	5
Accumulation of wax	.....	1	.....	1	.....	...	.....	1	2
Inflammation of the middle ear	....	.....	.....	.....	.....	...	.....	6	6
Deafness	....	....	.....	.....	.....	...	.....	3	3
DISEASES OF THE NOSE	1	.....	1	..	...	...	.....	22	23
Epistaxis	.....	.....	.....	.....	.....	...	.....	1	1
Nasal catarrh	.....	....	....	.....	.....	...	.....	20	20
Ulceration	.....	.....	.....	.....	.....	...	....	1	1
Ozæna	1	....	1	.....	.....	..	.....	.....	1
DISEASES OF THE CIRCULATORY SYSTEM	1	21	4	12	.....	3	3	39	61
Pericarditis	.....	.....	.....	.....	.....	...	.....	1	1
Endocarditis	....	1	1	.....	.....	...	.....	.....	1
Valvular disease:									
Aortic	.....	1	.....	.....	.....	..	1	8	9
Mitral	.....	8	.....	5	.....	1	2	6	14
Hypertrophy of heart	.....	1	.....	1	.....	...	.....	2	3
Angina pectoris	.....	.....	.....	.....	.....	...	.....	2	2
Palpitation and irregular action of heart.	1	3	2	1	.....	1	.....	16	20
Aneurism of arteries	.....	4	1	2	.....	1	.....	2	6
Obstruction of arteries	.....	1	.....	1	.....	...	.....	2	3
Varix	.. ...	2	.....	2	.....	...	.....	.....	2
DISEASES OF THE RESPIRATORY SYSTEM	1	68	43	17	2	4	3	246	315
Laryngitis:									
Acute	.....	.....	.....	.....	.....	...	.....	4	4
Catarrhal	.....	.....	.....	.....	.....	...	.....	3	3
Ulceration of larynx	.....	.....	.....	.....	.....	...	.....	1	1
Bronchitis:									
Acute	.....	26	10	6	1	...	.....	151	177
Chronic	.....	3	1	2	.....	...	.....	24	27
Catarrhal	.....	.....	.....	.....	.....	...	.....	14	14
Spasmodic asthma	.....	3	.....	3	.....	...	.....	7	10
Hæmoptysis	.....	.....	.....	.....	.....	...	.....	3	3
Pneumonia	.....	23	16	1	1	2	3	7	30
Cirrhosis of lung	.....	1	.....	1	.....	...	.....	.....	1
Pneumonic phthisis, chronic	1	.....	.....	.....	.....	1	.....	2	3
Emphysema	.....	1	.....	.....	.....	1	.....	.....	1
Pleurisy:									
Acute	.....	9	6	3	.....	...	.....	28	37
Chronic	.....	2	1	1	.....	...	.....	2	4
DISEASES OF THE DIGESTIVE SYSTEM	1	90	70	15	.....	2	4	552	643
Stomatitis	.....	.....	.....	.....	.....	...	.....	3	3
Caries of dentine and cementum	.....	.....	.....	.....	.....	...	.....	37	37

THE GULF.

Diseases.	Number of Cases. Remaining under treatment from previous year.	Admitted during the year.	Discharged. Recovered.	Discharged. Improved.	Discharged. Not improved.	Died.	Remaining under treatment at the close of the year.	Number furnished office relief.	Total treated in hospital and dispensary.
Local Diseases.									
DISEASES OF THE DIGESTIVE SYSTEM—Cont'd.									
Abscess of dental periosteum								3	3
Inflammation of gums and alveoli								2	2
Toothache								13	13
Necrosis of palate		1		1					1
Hypertrophy of tonsils		1	1						1
Sore throat		3	3					24	27
Quinsy		1	1					3	4
Follicular tonsilitis		5	5					10	15
Salivation								2	2
Follicular inflammation of the pharynx		2	2					25	28
Ulceration of pharynx								1	1
Inflammation of the stomach		6	3	2		1		13	19
Dilatation of the stomach		1					1		1
Dyspepsia		1	1					119	120
Gastrodynia								1	1
Abscess in sub-peritoneal tissue		1	1						1
Obstruction of the intestines		1	1						1
Hernia		1		1				60	61
Fistula of intestines		1				1			1
Tænia solium		2	1	1					2
Ascaris lumbricoides								2	2
Diarrhœa		25	24	1				73	98
Constipation		2	2					106	108
Colic								9	9
Hæmorrhage of the rectum								1	1
Abscess of the rectum		1		1				1	2
Ulceration of the rectum	1		1					1	2
Piles:									
Internal		7	3	4				13	20
External		7	6				1	8	15
Fistula in ano		3	2	1				2	5
Pruritus ani		1	1						1
Hypertrophy of the liver		1	1					1	2
Congestion of the liver		4	3				1	10	14
Hepatitis		6	4	1			1		6
Perihepatitis		1	1					1	2
Cirrhosis of liver		2		2				1	3
Jaundice		3	3					3	6
Inflammation of hepatic ducts and gall bladder								2	2
Gallstones								1	1
DISEASES OF THE LYMPHATIC SYSTEM	2	65	46	13		1	7	54	121
Hypertrophy of the spleen								1	1
Induration and enlargement from ague								1	1
Congestion of the spleen								1	1
Splenitis		2	1	1				1	3
Hypertrophy of lymph-glands								1	1
Inflammation of lymph-glands	1	24	14	8			3	35	60
Suppuration of lymph-glands	1	38	31	4			4	14	53
Lymphadenoma		1				1			1
DISEASES OF THE URINARY SYSTEM	1	13	6	4		3	1	45	50
Acute nephritis								1	1
Bright's disease		4		1		2	1	9	13
Nephralgia								2	2
Diabetes insipidus								1	1
Suppression of urine								3	3
Hæmaturia	1	1	1	1				3	5
Inflammation of bladder:									
Acute		6	4	1		1		8	14
Chronic		1		1				8	9
Irritability of bladder								6	6
Retention of urine								1	1
Incontinence of urine		1	1					3	4

TABLE VII.—*Tabular statement, by districts, of diseases and injuries, etc.*—Continued.

THE GULF.

Diseases.	Number of Cases.								
	Remaining under treatment from previous year.	Admitted during the year.	Discharged.			Died.	Remaining under treatment at the close of the year.	Number furnished office relief.	Total treated in hospital and dispensary.
			Recovered.	Improved.	Not improved.				
Local Diseases.									
DISEASES OF THE GENERATIVE SYSTEM	2	100	75	28	1	1	6	167	278
Urethritis		3	3					1	4
Gleet								5	5
Stricture of urethra:									
Organic		30	20	8			2	28	68
Spasmodic		1	1					1	2
Inflammation of the penis								1	1
Inflammation of glans penis								2	2
Ulcer of penis	2	47	31	15			3	77	126
Gangrene of penis		1				1			1
Phimosis		3	3					1	4
Paraphimosis		1	1						1
Hydrocele of spermatic cord		1	1						1
Varicocele								2	2
Hydrocele of tunica vaginalis		2	2					7	9
Orchitis:									
Acute		15	10	3	1		1	9	24
Chronic		1		1				1	2
Epididymitis		3	2	1				13	16
Abscess of testicle		1	1						1
Spermatorrhœa								4	4
Impotence								4	4
Metrorrhagia								1	1
DISEASES OF THE ORGANS OF LOCOMOTION	2	19	9	9		1	2	15	36
Ostitis		1	1					1	2
Caries		2	1	1					2
Necrosis	1	6	3	4				4	11
Synovitis:									
Acute	1	1	2					2	4
Chronic		6	2	3			1	3	9
Abscess of joints		1				1			1
Ankylosis								2	2
Talipes valgus		1		1					1
Thecal abscess		1					1	3	4
DISEASES OF THE CONNECTIVE TISSUE	2	29	26	4			1	44	75
Œdema								1	1
Inflammation	1	11	10	2				10	31
Abscess	1	18	16	2			1	24	43
DISEASES OF THE SKIN	5	51	40	15			1	252	308
Erythema								3	3
Urticaria		1	1					3	4
Eczema		3		3				35	38
Impetigo								2	2
Ecthyma		1	1					8	9
Prurigo								9	9
Psoriasis								5	5
Miliaria								2	2
Herpes								2	2
Zona								1	1
Acne								1	1
Gutta rosea		3	1	2				2	5
Chilblain								37	37
Frostbite		10	10					6	16
Ulcer	5	18	13	9			1	47	70
Boil		8	8					28	36
Carbuncle		2	2					3	5
Whitlow		4	3	1				12	16
Onychia		1	1						1
Lupus								2	2
Cheloid								1	1
Wen								3	3
Pruritus								9	9
Hyperidrosis								1	1

TABLE VII.—*Tabular statement, by districts, of diseases and injuries, etc.*—Continued.

THE GULF.

Diseases.	Number of cases. Remaining under treatment from previous year.	Admitted during the year.	Discharged. Recovered.	Discharged. Improved.	Discharged. Not improved.	Died.	Remaining under treatment at the close of the year.	Number furnished office relief.	Total treated in hospital and dispensary.
Local Diseases.									
DISEASES OF THE SKIN—Continued.									
Tinea versicolor								2	2
Itch								25	25
Phthiriasis								2	2
Malingerer								1	1
Poisons		3	3					2	5
Lead		2	2						2
Alcohol								1	1
Morphine		1	1						1
Rhus								1	1
POISONED WOUNDS								1	1
Venomous animals								1	1
Injuries	5	153	103	37	1	1	13	297	455
GENERAL INJURIES		21	15	4		1	1	32	51
Burns and scalds		14	9	4		1		6	20
Effects of cold								24	24
Sunstroke		3	2				1	1	4
Multiple injury		2	2					1	3
Exhaustion		2	2						2
LOCAL INJURIES	5	132	88	33	1		15	263	402
Strain of muscles		1		1				2	3
Rupture of muscles								2	2
Strain of tendon								1	1
Foreign body in subcutaneous tissue								1	1
Contusion of scalp		2	1	1				3	5
Scalp-wound:									
Bone not exposed		2	2					10	12
Bone exposed		2	2					2	4
Concussion of brain		2	2						2
Contusion of face		2	2					3	5
Wound of face		2	1	1				13	15
Fracture of facial bones		2	1	1				1	3
Contusion of the eye								1	1
Wound of cornea								1	1
Wound of pinna								1	1
Foreign body in external meatus								2	2
Contusion of soft parts of neck								1	1
Contusion of the chest		5	4	1				11	16
Fracture of the ribs		3		2			1	3	6
Wound of parietes of chest								1	1
Perforating wound of chest								1	1
Contusion of back	1	8	6	2			1	11	20
Sprain of back		2	2					11	13
Wound of back		1	1					1	2
Concussion of cord		1	1					1	2
Contusion of abdomen		1		1				3	4
Wound of parietes of abdomen		1	1						1
Wound of organs of generation		1	1					2	3
Contusion of upper extremities	1	11	8	3			1	17	29
Sprain of the shoulder		1		1				11	12
Sprain of the elbow		1		1				1	2
Sprain of the wrist		3	2	1				6	9
Sprain of the fingers								1	1
Wound of the upper extremities		16	11	3			2	57	73
Fracture of the clavicle		1	1						1
Fracture of the humerus		2	1	1				1	3
Fracture of the radius		3	2	1				4	7
Fracture of the ulna								1	1
Fracture of carpus, metacarpus, and phalanges	1	2	2	1				5	8

TABLE VII.—*Tabular statement, by districts, of diseases and injuries, etc.*—Continued.

THE GULF.

Diseases.	Number of Cases.								
	Remaining under treatment from previous year.	Admitted during the year.	Discharged.			Died.	Remaining under treatment at the close of the year.	Number furnished office relief.	Total treated in hospital and dispensary.
			Recovered.	Improved.	Not improved.				
Injuries.									
LOCAL INJURIES—Continued.									
Dislocation of the clavicle		1	1						1
Dislocation of the humerus		1					1	1	2
Dislocation of the phalanges of thumb		1		1				1	2
Dislocation of the phalanges of fingers								1	1
Contusion of the lower extremities	1	17	12	5			1	28	46
Sprain of the hip								1	1
Sprain of the knee		3	1	1	1			5	8
Sprain of the ankle		2	1	1				12	14
Wound of the lower extremities		18	12	3			3	23	41
Wound of joint, lower extremities		2	2						2
Fracture of patella		1					1		1
Fracture of leg, both bones		3	1				2		3
Fracture of tibia alone		1	1						1
Fracture of fibula alone		1	1						1
Fracture of tarsus		1	1						1
Fracture of metatarsus	1						1		1
Dislocation of the femur at the hip		1	1						1
Dislocation of the knee		1					1		1
AMPUTATION	1		1						1
Amputation of arm	1		1						1

THE OHIO.

Diseases.	Remaining under treatment from previous year.	Admitted during the year.	Recovered.	Improved.	Not improved.	Died.	Remaining under treatment at the close of the year.	Number furnished office relief.	Total treated in hospital and dispensary.
TOTAL CASES	54	1237	840	350	17	26	58	3902	5193
General Diseases	21	531	358	143	6	9	36	1777	2329
Measles		5	4	1				1	6
Relapsing fever		1	1						1
Mumps		4	3	1				4	8
Simple continued fever		1	1						1
Enteric fever	3	44	37	2		2	6	1	48
Typho-malarial fever		4	2	2					4
Epidemic diarrhœa								3	3
Dysentery		15	11	2			2	24	39
Malarial intermittent fever	5	124	110	10	3	1	5	413	542
Malarial remittent fever		20	17	1			2	4	24
Malarial cachexia	1		1					13	14
Erysipelas, simple		7	7					1	8
Syphilis:									
Primary	1	31	16	14	1		1	134	166
Secondary	1	64	3	58			4	326	391
Gonorrhœa	1	16	12	3			2	316	333
Effects of heat		3	3					5	8
Alcoholism	1	15	13	1	1		1	16	32
Debility		2		2				45	47
Rheumatic fever		16	12	3			1	10	26
Rheumatism	1	126	104	18			5	389	516
Osteo-arthritis								2	2
Fibroma		1	1						1
Myxoma								1	1
Chondroma								1	1
Warts		1		1				7	8
Condyloma								1	1
Granulation tumors								1	1
Sarcoma								1	1
Carcinoma—epithelioma								1	1
Tubercle of lung and other organs	6	24		18	1	4	7	39	69
Scrofula	1	5		4		2		17	23
Diabetes mellitus		2		2				1	3

TABLE VII.—*Tabular statement, by districts, of diseases and injuries, etc.*—Continued.

THE OHIO.

Diseases.	Number of Cases.								
	Remaining under treatment from previous year.	Admitted during the year.	Discharged.			Died.	Remaining under treatment at the close of the year.	Number furnished office relief.	Total treated in hospital and dispensary.
			Recovered.	Improved.	Not improved.				
Local Diseases	25	541	340	178	11	17	20	1907	2473
DISEASES OF THE NERVOUS SYSTEM	5	22	12	6	1	4	4	71	98
Congestion of cerebrum								2	2
Inflammation:									
Of membranes of brain and spinal cord	1					1			1
Of cerebral membranes		1	1					2	3
Sclerosis		1					1		1
Progressive muscular atrophy		1			1				1
Apoplexy		3		1		1	1		3
Hemiplegia	3					2	1		3
Paraplegia		1		1					1
Local paralysis								1	1
Glosso-labio-pharyngeal paralysis	1			1					1
Spasm of muscle								2	2
Wry-neck		1	1						1
Neuralgia		1	1					28	29
Facial		5	4	1				14	19
Sciatica		6	5				1	12	18
Megrim								2	2
Epilepsy		2		2				3	5
Chorea								2	2
Hypochondriasis								3	3
DISEASES OF THE EYE		10	4	5			1	52	62
Conjunctivitis:									
Catarrhal		4	2	2				28	32
Purulent								5	5
Phlyctenular								2	2
Chronic								2	2
Granular		3		2			1	4	7
Ulcer of cornea								5	5
Iritis		1		1				2	3
Mydriasis								1	1
Shrunken eyeball		1	1						1
Amblyopia								1	1
Abscess of eyelid		1	1						1
Ptosis								2	2
DISEASES OF THE EAR		2		2				12	14
Inflammation of the external meatus:									
Acute								1	1
Abscess of the external meatus								1	1
Accumulation of wax								3	3
Inflammation of the middle ear		2		2				7	9
DISEASES OF THE NOSE	1	1	2					37	39
Epistaxis	1	1	2					3	5
Inflammation								17	17
Nasal catarrh								14	14
Ulceration								2	2
Ozæna								1	1
DISEASES OF THE CIRCULATORY SYSTEM	3	15	1	11	1	4	1	28	40
Valvular disease:									
Aortic	1	3		2		2			4
Mitral		7		4	1	1	1	9	16
Hypertrophy of heart		1		1					1
Degeneration of heart, fatty		1		1					1
Dilatation of heart		1		1				1	2
Palpitation and irregular action of heart								9	9
Aneurism of arteries		1				1		2	3
Varix	2	1	1	2				7	10
DISEASES OF THE RESPIRATORY SYSTEM	6	152	94	57	3	4		457	615
Laryngitis:									
Acute		3	1	1		1		9	12
Chronic								2	2

TABLE VII.—*Tabular statement, of districts, by diseases and injuries, etc.*—Continued.

THE OHIO.

Diseases.	Number of Cases.								
	Remaining under treatment from previous year.	Admitted during the year.	Discharged.			Died.	Remaining under treatment at the close of the year.	Number furnished office relief.	Total treated in hospital and dispensary.
			Recovered.	Improved.	Not improved.				
Local Diseases.									
DISEASES OF THE RESPIRATORY SYSTEM—Continued.									
Bronchitis:									
Acute	1	62	55	8				302	305
Chronic		8	3	5				17	25
Catarrhal								4	4
Spasmodic asthma		2		2				3	5
Passive congestion of lung		1	1						1
Pneumonia		31	28	1		2			31
Pneumonic phthisis:									
Acute		1		1				1	2
Chronic	5	35		39		1		90	130
Pleurisy:									
Acute		5	5					16	21
Chronic		3	1		2			12	15
Empyema		1			1				1
Adhesions of pleura								1	1
DISEASES OF THE DIGESTIVE SYSTEM	5	129	104	20	4	3	3	679	813
Stomatitis								3	3
Inflammation of the dental pulp								2	2
Ulceration of the dental pulp								1	1
Caries of dentine and cementum								10	10
Abscess of dental periosteum		2	2					1	3
Inflammation of gums and alveoli								1	1
Ulceration of gums and alveoli								1	1
Caries of the alveoli		1	1					1	2
Toothache								3	3
Ulcer of the tongue								1	1
Hypertrophy of tonsils								1	1
Sore throat		3	2				1	30	33
Quinsy		4	3	1				6	10
Follicular tonsilitis	1	7	6	1			1	12	20
Ulceration of fauces								3	3
Abscess of salivary glands								1	1
Salivation								1	1
Follicular inflammation of the pharynx.		1		1				56	57
Inflammation of the stomach		7	5	2				15	22
Ulceration of the stomach		1			1			1	2
Dyspepsia		2	2					170	172
Gastrodynia								2	2
Catarrhal inflammation of the intestines.	1	19	16	2		2		40	60
Enteritis								1	1
Typhlitis	1		1						1
Colitis		2	1				1		2
Hernia		3		3				40	43
Tænia mediocanellata		1	1						1
Diarrhœa	2	46	45	2	1			139	187
Constipation		2	2					71	73
Colic								6	6
Hemorrhage of the rectum		1	1						1
Abscess of the anus		1	1						1
Ulceration of the rectum								2	2
Piles:									
Internal		4	2	1	1			6	10
External		4	3	1				29	33
Fistula in ano		3	1	1	1			1	4
Fissure of the anus		2	2					1	3
Pruritus ani								2	2
Hypertrophy of the liver								3	3
Conjestion of the liver								3	3
Hepatitis		4	2	1		1		4	8
Cirrhosis of liver		3		3				1	4
Abscess of liver		3	2	1					3
Jaundice		1	1					4	5
Inflammation of hepatic ducts and gall-bladder		2	2					4	6

TABLE VII.—*Tabular statement, by districts, of diseases and injuries, etc.*—Continued.

THE OHIO.

Diseases.	Number of Cases.								
	Remaining under treatment from previous year.	Admitted during the year.	Discharged.			Died.	Remaining under treatment at the close of the year.	Number furnished office relief.	Total treated in hospital and dispensary.
			Recovered.	Improved.	Not improved.				
Local Diseases.									
DISEASES OF THE LYMPHATIC SYSTEM	1	37	23	13	2			51	89
Hypertrophy of the spleen		1	1						1
Hypertrophy of lymph glands		3	2	1				16	19
Inflammation of lymph glands		14	11	3				15	29
Suppuration of lymph glands	1	19	9	9	2			20	40
DISEASES OF THE URINARY SYSTEM		13	1	10		2		55	68
Acute nephritis		4		4				1	5
Bright's disease		5		4		1		7	12
Diabetes insipidus		2		1		1			2
Hæmaturia								2	2
Lithuria								1	1
Phosphuria								3	3
Inflammation of bladder:									
Acute								26	26
Sub-acute		1	1					2	3
Chronic		1		1				1	2
Irritability of bladder								10	10
Incontinence of urine								2	2
DISEASES OF THE GENERATIVE SYSTEM	2	88	53	30			5	231	321
Urethritis								2	2
Gleet								12	12
Stricture of urethra:									
Organic		14	5	7			2	36	50
Spasmodic		1	1					1	2
Hypertrophy of prostate gland								2	2
Acute inflammation of prostate gland		1		1				5	6
Œdema of the penis								1	1
Inflammation of glans penis		1	1					17	18
Abscess of penis								2	2
Ulcer of penis	2	52	33	20			1	100	154
Phimosis		3	3					1	4
Inflammation of the scrotum								1	1
Abscess of the scrotum								2	2
Varicocele		1		1				7	8
Hydrocele of tunica vaginalis								2	2
Orchitis:									
Acute		5	4	1				10	15
Chronic								1	1
Epididymitis		8	8					13	21
Spermatorrhœa								5	5
Impotence								9	9
Inflammation of the uterus								1	1
Catarrh of the uterus		1					1		1
Displacements of the uterus		1					1		1
Monorrhagia								1	1
DISEASES OF THE ORGANS OF LOCOMOTION	1	13	5	6			3	14	28
Ostitis		2		1			1		2
Necrosis		4	2	1			1	5	9
Dropsy of joints		1	1						1
Synovitis, acute		3	1	1			1	3	6
Dislocation of articular cartilage								1	1
Caries and necrosis of spine		2		2					2
Angular curvature of spine	1			1					1
Abscess of muscles								2	2
Inflammation of tendons								1	1
Inflamed bursa		1	1						1
Bursal abscess								1	1
Bursal tumor								1	1
DISEASES OF THE CONNECTIVE TISSUE		17	12	5				31	48
Inflammation		1	1					3	4
Abscess		16	11	5				28	44

TABLE VII.—*Tabular statement, by districts, of diseases and injuries, etc.*—Continued.

THE OHIO.

Diseases.	Number of cases. Remaining under treatment from previous year.	Admitted during the year.	Discharged. Recovered.	Discharged. Improved.	Discharged. Not improved.	Died.	Remaining under treatment at the close of the year.	Number furnished office relief.	Total treated in hospital and dispensary.
Local Diseases.									
DISEASES OF THE SKIN	1	42	27	13			3	189	232
Erythema								1	1
Urticaria		1	1					7	8
Eczema		1		1				36	37
Pityriasis		1		1					1
Lichen								2	2
Psoriasis								8	8
Herpes								11	11
Acne								7	7
Chilblain								2	2
Frostbite		3	1	2					3
Ulcer	1	24	16	7			2	31	56
Boil		1	1					30	31
Carbuncle		3	2	1				7	10
Whitlow		3	3					8	11
Onychia		1		1				2	3
Lupus								1	1
Pruritus		1	1					2	3
Hyperidrosis								4	4
Ringworm		1	1					8	9
Itch		2	1				1	20	22
Undetermined								2	2
Poisons		7	6	1				9	16
Carbolic acid								1	1
Alcohol		7	6	1				8	15
Injuries	8	158	136	28			2	209	375
GENERAL INJURIES	2	10	11	1				17	29
Burns and scalds	2	7	8	1				15	24
Effects of cold		1	1					2	3
Sunstroke		1	1						1
Multiple injury		1	1						1
LOCAL INJURIES	6	148	125	27			2	192	346
Strain of muscles								6	6
Foreign body in subcutaneous tissue		1	1					1	2
Contusion of scalp								1	1
Scalp wound:									
Bone not exposed		7	3	4				12	19
Bone exposed								1	1
Fracture of the vault of the skull								2	2
Concussion of brain		2	2						2
Contusion of face		1	1					4	5
Wound of face		5	3	2				6	11
Fracture of facial bones		1					1	3	4
Contusion of the eye		2	2					4	6
Foreign body in cornea or conjunctiva								8	8
Wound of eyelid		1		1					1
Wound of pinna		1	1						11
Contusion of the chest		4	4					9	3
Fracture of the ribs		3	2				1	2	5
Perforating wound of chest		1		1					1
Penetrating wound of pleura or lung		1	1						1
Contusion of back		5	4	1				3	8
Sprain of back		9	7	2				8	17
Wound of spine								1	1
Contusion of pelvis								1	1
Wound of organs of generation								1	1
Contusion of testicle		1	1						1
Contusion of upper extremities		5	5					13	18
Sprain of the shoulder								2	2
Sprain of the wrist		7	7					9	16
Sprain of the fingers		1	1					1	2
Wound of the upper extremities	1	25	22	4				37	63

TABLE VII.—*Tabular statement, by districts, of diseases and injuries, etc.*—Continued.

THE OHIO.

Diseases.	Number of Cases.								
	Remaining under treatment from previous year.	Admitted during the year.	Discharged. Recovered.	Discharged. Improved.	Discharged. Not improved.	Died.	Remaining under treatment at the close of the year.	Number furnished office relief.	Total treated in hospital and dispensary.
Injuries.									
LOCAL INJURIES—Continued.									
Fracture of the radius	......	......	......	......	......	...	......	1	1
Fracture of the ulna	......	1	1	......	......	...	......	1	2
Fracture of both bones of the forearm	......	2	2	......	......	...	......	......	2
Fracture of carpus, metacarpus, and phalanges	......	1	......	1	....	...	......	3	4
Contusion of the lower extremities	......	13	10	3	......	...	......	25	38
Sprain of the hip	......	1	1	......	......	...	......	1	2
Sprain of the knee	......	2	2	......	......	...	......	3	5
Sprain of the ankle	......	17	14	3	......	...	......	12	29
Sprain of the foot	......	4	4	......	......	...	......	2	6
Wound of the lower extremities	2	14	13	3	......	...	......	6	22
Wound of joint, lower extremities	1	2	2	1	......	...	......	......	3
Fracture of femur	......	1	1	......	......	...	......	1	2
Fracture of leg, both bones	1	4	5	......	......	...	......	2	7
Fracture of fibula alone	1	3	3	1	......	...	......	......	4

THE MISSISSIPPI.

Diseases.	Remaining under treatment from previous year.	Admitted during the year.	Discharged. Recovered.	Discharged. Improved.	Discharged. Not improved.	Died.	Remaining under treatment at the close of the year.	Number furnished office relief.	Total treated in hospital and dispensary.
TOTAL CASES	74	1325	966	294	9	67	63	2951	4350
General Diseases.	42	688	483	180	5	32	30	1451	2181
Measles	......	3	2	......	......	1	......	......	3
Mumps	......	......	......	......	......	...	......	2	2
Enteric fever	1	3	3	1	......	...	......	......	4
Typho-malarial fever	......	1	1	......	......	...	......	......	1
Cholera, sporadic	......	1	1	......	......	...	......	......	1
Dysentery	......	31	19	4	......	6	2	19	50
Malarial intermittent fever	13	220	207	16	......	4	6	473	701
Malarial remittent fever	......	34	28	1	......	4	1	......	34
Malarial cachexia	1	12	11	......	......	...	2	45	58
Phagedæna	1	......	1	......	......	...	......	......	1
Erysipelas:									
Simple	1	13	9	4	......	1	......	3	17
Phlegmonous	......	1	1	......	......	...	......	......	1
Syphilis:									
Primary	5	51	31	22	1	...	2	108	164
Secondary	6	106	28	80	2	4	3	200	312
Gonorrhœa	2	29	23	6	......	...	2	253	284
Effects of chemical agents	......	4	3	1	......	...	......	2	6
Alcoholism	......	14	12	2	......	...	......	12	26
Delirium tremens	1	2	2	......	......	1	......	......	3
Debility	......	4	3	1	......	...	......	3	7
Rheumatic fever	1	12	9	4	......	...	......	6	19
Rheumatism	4	103	90	19	......	...	3	260	372
Adenoma	......	......	......	......	......	...	......	2	2
Angeioma	......	1	......	......	......	...	1	......	1
Warts	......	......	......	......	......	...	......	3	3
Condyloma	......	3	3	......	......	...	......	......	3
Sarcoma	......	......	......	......	......	...	......	3	3
Carcinoma	......	1	......	......	......	...	1	......	1
Epithelioma	......	......	......	......	......	...	......	4	4
Tubercle of lung	6	31	......	18	2	10	7	32	69
Scrofula	......	1	......	1	......	...	......	2	3
Purpura	......	1	1	......	......	...	......	......	1
Anæmia	......	......	......	......	......	...	......	10	10
Leucocythæmia	......	1	......	......	......	1	......	......	1
Local Diseases	20	459	331	90	4	24	30	1249	1728
DISEASES OF THE NERVOUS SYSTEM	2	34	17	10	1	3	5	50	86
Of brain and its membranes	......	1	......	......	......	1	......	......	1
Of cerebral membranes	......	2	......	1	......	1	......	......	2

TABLE VII.—*Tabular statement, by districts, of diseases and injuries, etc.*—Continued.

THE MISSISSIPPI.

Diseases.	Number of Cases.								
	Remaining under treatment from previous year.	Admitted during the year.	Discharged.			Died.	Remaining under treatment at the close of the year.	Number furnished office relief.	Total treated in hospital and dispensary.
			Recovered.	Improved.	Not improved.				
Local Diseases.									
DISEASES OF THE NERVOUS SYSTEM—Cont'd.									
Abcesses of the brain		1	1						1
Locomotor ataxy		1	1						1
Paralysis		3		2			1		3
Hemiplegia	1	2		1		1	1		3
Paraplegia		1					1		1
Spasm of muscles								1	1
Paralysis agitans		1		1					1
Neuralgia		8	5	1	1		1	17	25
Facial	1	5	6					12	18
Sciatca		7	3	3			1	4	11
Vertigo		1		1				4	5
Megrim								5	5
Epilepsy								7	7
Hysteria		1	1						1
DISEASES OF THE EYE		8	2	2			4	30	38
Conjunctivitis:									
Catarrhal		3	1	1			1	10	19
Purulent		1					1	1	2
Phlyctenular								1	1
Granular								1	1
Pterygium		1	1						1
Keratitis								9	9
Iritis		1					1		1
Retinitis		1					1		1
Neuralgia of eyeball		1		1					1
Entropion								1	1
Chalazion								1	1
DISEASES OF THE EAR		1	1					6	7
Inflammation of the external meatus:									
Acute								1	1
Accumulation of wax								3	3
Inflammation of the middle ear		1	1						1
Hæmorrhage into labyrinth								2	2
DISEASES OF THE NOSE		1		1				13	14
Epistaxis								1	1
Nasal catarrh								8	8
Ozena								3	3
Necrosis of nasal bones								1	1
Necrosis of ethmoid		1		1					1
DISEASES OF THE CIRCULATORY SYSTEM	5	22	7	10	1	6	3	38	65
Hydropericardium								2	2
Pericarditis		1	1						1
Endocarditis								2	2
Valvular disease:									
Aortic	2	6		5		3		8	16
Mitral	2	7	3	2		2	2	13	22
Hypertrophy of heart								2	2
Palpitation and irregular action of heart		2	1				1	5	7
Aneurism of arteries		3		1	1	1		2	5
Varix	1	3	2	2				4	8
DISEASES OF THE RESPIRATORY SYSTEM		76	61	7		8		272	348
Laryngitis:									
Acute		1				1		1	2
Chronic								2	2
Bronchitis:									
Acute		22	21			1		216	238
Chronic		3	2	1				12	15
Catarrhal		1	1					8	9
Spasmodic asthma		2	1	1				3	5
Hæmoptysis								5	5

TABLE VII.—*Tabular statement, by districts, of diseases and injuries, etc.*—Continued.

THE MISSISSIPPI.

Diseases.	Number of Cases. Remaining under treatment from previous year.	Admitted during the year.	Discharged. Recovered.	Discharged. Improved.	Discharged. Not improved.	Died.	Remaining under treatment at the close of the year.	Number furnished office relief.	Total treated in hospital and dispensary.
Local Diseases.									
DISEASES OF THE RESPIRATORY SYSTEM—Continued.									
Pneumonia		37	28	3		6		3	40
Cirrhosis of lung								1	1
Pneumonic phthisis:									
Acute		1	1						1
Chronic		2		2				2	4
Pleurisy:									
Acute		7	7					14	21
Chronic								5	5
DISEASES OF THE DIGESTIVE SYSTEM	6	142	113	18	1	10	6	464	612
Stomatitis								1	1
Abcess of the antrum		1	1						1
Caries of dentine and cementum								5	5
Necrosis of dentine and cementum								1	1
Inflammation of dental periosteum								1	1
Abscess of dental periosteum		1	1					1	2
Hypertrophy of tonsils		2		2				2	4
Elongated uvula		1	1					4	5
Relaxed throat								1	1
Sore throat								6	6
Quinsy		4	3	1				2	6
Follicular tonsilitis		2	2					12	14
Follicular inflammation of the pharynx		1	1					24	25
Inflammation of the stomach	1	5	5	1				47	53
Ulceration of the stomach								1	1
Dyspepsia		1	1					52	53
Gastrodynia								1	1
Catarrhal inflammation of the intestines		41	34	1		5	1	85	129
Hernia		5		5				35	40
Tænia mediocanellata		1	1						1
Diarrhœa	3	41	37	3		1	3	55	96
Constipation		1	1					38	39
Colic		1			1			3	4
Abscess of the anus		1	1						1
Ulceration of the rectum		1	1					1	2
Piles:									
Internal		3	3					4	7
External		4	3				1	16	20
Prolapsus of the rectum								2	2
Fistula in ano								2	2
Fissure of the anus		1	1					2	3
Pruritus ani								1	1
Hypertrophy of the liver								4	4
Congestion of the liver		9	9					36	45
Hepatitis		2	1			1		1	3
Perihepatitis	1	2	2	1					3
Cirrhosis of liver		5		3		1	1	1	6
Abscess of liver	1	2	2			1			3
Jaundice		1		1				6	7
Inflammation of hepatic ducts and gall-bladder		2	2					11	13
Peritonitis		1				1			1
DISEASES OF THE LYMPHATIC SYSTEM	1	15	14				2	35	51
Induration and enlargement of the spleen from ague								2	2
Hypertrophy of lymph glands								1	1
Inflammation of lymph glands	1	4	5					15	20
Suppuration of lymph glands		11	9				2	17	28
DISEASES OF THE URINARY SYSTEM		13	3	9		1		20	33
Acute nephritis		4	1	2		1		2	6
Bright's disease		5		5				2	7
Hæmaturia								1	1
Lithuria								1	1

TABLE VII.—*Tabular statement, by districts, of diseases and injuries, etc.*—Continued.

THE MISSISSIPPI.

Diseases.	Number of Cases.								
	Remaining under treatment from previous year.	Admitted during the year.	Discharged.				Remaining under treatment at the close of the year.	Number furnished office relief.	Total treated in hospital and dispensary.
			Recovered.	Improved.	Not improved.	Died.			
Local D seases.									
DISEASES OF THE URINARY SYSTEM—Cont'd.									
Inflammation of bladder:									
Acute		1	1					4	5
Chronic		1		1					1
Irritability of bladder		1		1				9	10
Retention of urine		1	1						1
Incontinence of urine								1	1
DISEASES OF THE GENERATIVE SYSTEM	2	79	58	18	1	1	3	164	245
Urethritis								5	5
Gleet								6	6
Stricture of urethra, organic	2	25	16	9	1	1		32	59
Urinary fistula		1		1					1
Extravasation of urine		1	1						1
Acute inflammation of prostate gland		1	1						1
Inflammation of glans penis								2	2
Ulcer of penis		39	30	7			2	93	132
Phimosis		1	1						1
Chordee								2	2
Varicocele								2	2
Hydrocele of tunica vaginalis								2	2
Orchitis:									
Acute		8	8					7	15
Chronic		2	1	1					2
Epididymitis		1					1	8	9
Catarrh of the uterus								1	1
Displacements of the uterus								2	2
Metrorrhagia								1	1
Leucorrhœa								1	1
DISEASES OF THE ORGANS OF LOCOMOTION		9	5	3			1	10	19
Periostitis		2	1	1				3	5
Necrosis		1	1					1	2
Synovitis:									
Acute		2	2					1	3
Chronic		3	1	2				2	5
Anchylosis								1	1
Angular curvature of the spine		1					1		1
Inflammation of tendons								1	1
Contraction of tendons								1	1
DISEASES OF THE CONNECTIVE TISSUE	1	9	9	1				25	35
Inflammation		3	2	1				15	18
Abscess	1	6	7					10	17
DISEASES OF THE SKIN	3	50	41	11		1		122	175
Urticaria								2	2
Eczema		1		1				28	29
Impetigo		2	2						2
Lichen								1	1
Psoriasis	1			1				2	3
Miliaria								3	3
Herpes								10	10
Zona		1	1					2	3
Acne								1	1
Frostbite	1	13	12	2				5	19
Ulcer	1	26	19	7		1		30	57
Boil		3	3					18	21
Carbuncle		1	1					1	2
Whitlow		2	2					7	9
Onychia								2	2
Lupus								2	2
Pruritus								4	4
Anidrosis								1	1
Ringworm		1	1						1
Itch								3	3

TABLE VII.—*Tabular statement, by districts, of diseases and injuries, etc.*—Continued.

THE MISSISSIPPI.

Diseases.	Number of Cases.								
	Remaining under treatment from previous year.	Admitted during the year.	Discharged.			Died.	Remaining under treatment at the close of the year.	Number furnished office relief.	Total treated in hospital and dispensary.
			Recovered.	Improved.	Not improved.				
Poisons		2	2					8	10
Arsenic								1	1
Alcohol		2	2					1	3
Tobacco								3	3
Rhus								3	3
POISONED WOUNDS								1	1
Venomous animals								1	1
Injuri.s.	12	175	149	24			9	242	429
GENERAL INJURIES	1	7	7	1				14	22
Burns and scalds		5	4	1				13	18
Sunstroke		2	2					1	3
Exhaustion	1		1						1
LOCAL INJURIES	11	163	142	23		5	9	228	407
Strain of muscles		1	1					5	6
Scalp-wound:									
Bone not exposed		6	5	1				12	18
Bone exposed		1	1						1
Fracture of the vault of the skull		2	1	1					2
Fracture of the base of the skull		1				1			1
Concussion of brain		2	1				1		2
Contusion of face		1	5	1				1	2
Wound of face		5						6	11
Fracture of facial bones	1								1
Contusion of the eye		1	1					1	2
Foreign bodies in cornea or conjunctiva		1						1	1
Wound of eyelid								2	2
Wound of cornea		1		1					1
Contusion of pinna								1	1
Wound of pinna								1	1
Wound of neck		2		2					2
Contusion of the chest	1	3	4					8	12
Fracture of the ribs		2		2				2	4
Wound of parietes of chest	1	2	2			1			3
Penetrating wound of pleura or lung		1	1						1
Contusion of back		6	6					4	10
Sprain of back	2	6	6				2	17	25
Wound of back								1	1
Concussion of cord		2	1			1			2
Contusion of abdomen		4	4					2	6
Wound of parietes of abdomen		6	4	1		1		1	7
Contusion of testicle								3	3
Contusion of upper extremities		4	4					16	20
Sprain of the shoulder								1	1
Sprain of the elbow		1	1						1
Sprain of the wrist		5	4				1	6	11
Sprain of the fingers								4	4
Wound of the upper extremities	2	30	27	5				55	87
Fracture of the clavicle		3	2			1			3
Fracture of the scapula		1	1						1
Fracture of the humerus		2	1	1					2
Fracture of the radius		1	1						1
Fracture of the ulna	1		1					1	2
Fracture of both bones of forearm	1	1	2						2
Fracture of carpus, metacarpus, and phalanges		2	2					2	4
Dislocation of the humerus		1	1					1	2
Dislocation of the ulna		1	1						1
Contusion of the lower extremities	1	23	21	2			1	24	48
Sprain of the hip		2	2						2
Sprain of the knee		2	1	1				2	4
Sprain of the ankle		9	8				1	10	10
Sprain of the foot		1	1						1
Wound of the lower extremities		17	14	1			2	37	54

TABLE VII.—*Tabular statement, by districts, of diseases and injuries, etc.*—Continued.

THE MISSISSIPPI.

Diseases.	Number of cases.								
	Remaining under treatment from previous year.	Admitted during the year.	Discharged.			Died.	Remaining under treatment at the close of the year.	Number furnished office relief.	Total treated in hospital and dispensary.
			Recovered.	Improved.	Not improved.				
Injuries.									
LOCAL INJURIES—Continued.									
Fracture of femur	......	3	1	2	....	...	.....	......	3
Fracture of leg, both bones	......	2	1	1	.....	...	.....	1	3
Fracture of tibia alone	......	1	1	......	.....	...	.....	......	1
Dislocation of the patella	......	1	......	......	.....	..	1	......	1
Dislocation of the astragalus	1	.....	1	......	.....	...	.....	......	1
AMPUTATIONS	......	1	1	......	.....	...	.....	......	1
Amputation of leg	......	1	1	......	.....	...	.....	......	1

THE GREAT LAKES.

Diseases.	Remaining under treatment from previous year.	Admitted during the year.	Recovered.	Improved.	Not improved.	Died.	Remaining under treatment at the close of the year.	Number furnished office relief.	Total treated in hospital and dispensary.
TOTAL CASES	132	2	1506	747	45	72	177	9218	11765
General Diseases	61	10 5	582	400	18	30	76	4103	5209
Measles	......	7	6	1	......	..	......	1	8
Influenza	......	2	1	1	......	...	......	26	28
Mumps	......	4	2	......	1	....	1	10	14
Diphtheria	......	......	......	......	......	...	......	1	1
Simple continued fever	1	6	7	......	......	...	......	12	19
Febricula	......	7	7	......	......	..	......	5	12
Enteric fever	6	88	70	5	......	7	12	7	101
Typho-malarial fever	1	5	4	1	......	1	......	1	7
Cholera, sporadic	......	4	4	......	......	...	......	3	7
Epidemic diarrhœa	......	......	......	......	......	...	......	17	17
Dysentery	......	14	10	3	......	...	1	28	42
Malarial intermittent fever	3	77	70	4	1	1	4	302	382
Malarial remittent fever	1	32	26	5	......	2	....	40	73
Malarial cachexia	......	3	3	......	......	...	......	77	80
Erysipelas:									
Simple	......	11	11	......	......	...	......	19	30
Phlegmonous	......	2	2	......	......	...	......	4	6
Syphilis:									
Primary	1	33	5	28	......	...	1	130	:04
Secondary	19	207	43	161	1	1	20	1,046	1,272
Gonorrhea	......	58	40	11	1	...	6	927	835
Effects of excessive venery	......	......	......	......	......	...	......	1	1
Scurvy	1	......	1	......	......	...	......	......	1
Alcoholism	2	66	59	5	2	..	2	46	114
Delirium tremens	......	2	2	......	......	...	......	......	2
Effects of heat	......	1	1	......	......	...	......	2	3
Debility	......	20	23	3	1	2	......	209	328
Rheumatic fever	5	51	36	17	......	...	3	17	73
Rheumatism	8	231	137	87	3	..	12	894	1,133
Gout	......	1	......	1	......	...	......	......	1
Osteo-arthritis	......	1	......	1	......	...	......	1	2
Haematoma	......	......	......	......	......	...	......	2	2
Non-malignant new growth	......	12	9	1	1	...	1	26	38
Malignant new growth	1	6	2	......	2	2	1	1	8
Tubercle of lung and other organs	12	85	1	65	5	14	12	148	245
Scrofula	......	......	......	......	......	...	......	6	6
Purpura	......	......	......	......	......	...	......	1	1
Diabetes mellitus	......	......	......	......	......	...	......	3	3
Local Di cases	42	965	612	270	21	39	65	4416	5123
DISEASES OF THE NERVOUS SYSTEM	7	58	26	20	1	8	10	217	282
Congestion of cerebrum	......	2	1	1	......	...	......	2	4
Congestion of spinal cord	......	2	2	......	......	...	......	......	2
Inflammation:									
Of the brain	......	1	1	......	......	...	......	......	1
Of spinal cord and its membranes	......	1	......	......	......	...	1	......	1

TABLE VII.—*Tabular statement, by districts, of diseases and injuries, etc.*—Continued.

THE GREAT LAKES.

Diseases.	Number of Cases.								
	Remaining under treatment from previous year.	Admitted during the year.	Discharged. Recovered.	Discharged. Improved.	Discharged. Not improved.	Died.	Remaining under treatment at the close of the year.	Number furnished office relief.	Total treated in hospital and dispensary.
Local Diseases.									
DISEASES OF THE NERVOUS SYSTEM—Cont'd.									
Spastic spinal paralysis	.....	1	.....	1	.....	...	.....	.....	1
Locomotor ataxy	.....	3	.....	1	.....	...	2	1	4
Apoplexy	1	.....	1	.....	.....	...	.....	.....	1
Paralysis	1	1	.....	1	.....	1	.....	.....	2
Hemiplegia	3	3	.....	1	.....	3	2	....	6
Paraplegia	.....	1	.....	....	.....	1	....	.....	1
Local paralysis	.....	7	3	3	.....	.	1	4	11
Spasm of muscle	....	.....	.....	.....	.....	..	.....	1	1
Hyperæsthesia	.....	.....	.....	.....	....	...	.....	1	1
Neuralgia	.....	9	6	2	.....	..	1	145	154
Facial	.....	7	6	.....	.....	...	1	32	39
Sciatica	.....	8	2	4	.....	1	1	9	17
Vertigo	.....	1	.....	.....	....	...	1	9	10
Megrim	.....	.....	.....	.....	.....	..	.....	9	9
Epilepsy	1	3	2	2	.....	..	.....	3	7
Chorea	.....	3	.....	3	....	..	.....	1	4
Mania	1	2	2	....	.....	1	.....	....	3
Melancholia	.....	2	.....	1	1	..	.....	....	2
Dementia	....	1	.....	.....	.....	1	.....	....	1
DISEASES OF THE EYE	1	15	9	7	.....	...	.....	87	103
Hyperæmia of the conjunctiva	.....	.....	.....	.....	.....	...	.....	1	1
Ecchymosis	.....	.....	.....	.....	.....	...	.....	1	1
Conjunctivitis:									
Catarrhal	1	3	3	1	.....	...	....	44	48
Purulent	.....	.....	.....	.....	....	...	.....	11	11
Granular	.....	3	1	2	.....	..	.....	8	11
Keratitis	.....	1	.....	1	.....	..	.....	2	3
Ulcer of cornea	....	.....	.....	.....	.....	..	.....	1	1
Opacity of cornea	.....	1	.....	1	.....	...	.....	....	1
Iritis	....	4	2	2	.....	...	.....	7	11
Cataract: Lenticular	....	.....	.....	.....	.....	...	.....	1	1
Opacity of the vitreous	.....	.....	.....	.....	.....	...	.....	1	1
Amblyopia	.....	.....	.....	.....	.....	...	.....	1	1
Squint	....	1	1	.....	.....	..	.....	.....	1
Inflammation of lachrymal gland	.....	.....	.....	.....	.....	...	.....	1	1
Dacryocystitis	.....	1	1	.....	.....	...	.....	....	1
Epiphora	.....	.....	.....	.....	.....	...	.....	2	2
Blepharitis	.....	.....	.....	.....	.....	..	.....	2	2
Stye	.....	....	.....	.....	.....	...	.....	2	2
Abscess of eyelid	.....	....	.....	.....	.....	...	.....	1	1
Entropion	.....	1	1	.....	.....	...	.....	.....	1
Stricture and obliteration of puncta and canaliculi	.....	.....	.....	.....	.....	...	....	1	1
DISEASES OF THE EAR	....	6	6	.....	.....	...	....	32	38
Inflammation of the external meatus:									
Acute	.....	....	.....	.....	.....	...	.....	4	4
Abscess of the external meatus	.....	.....	.....	.....	.....	...	.....	1	1
Accumulation of wax	.....	....	.....	.....	.....	...	.....	10	10
Inflammation of the middle ear	.....	6	6	.....	....	...	.....	11	17
Ulceration of membrana tympani	.....	.....	.....	.....	.....	..	.....	1	1
Perforation of membrana tympani	.....	.....	.....	.....	.....	...	.....	2	2
Tinnitus	.....	.....	.....	.....	.....	...	.....	1	1
Deafness	....	.....	.....	.....	.....	...	.....	2	2
DISEASES OF THE NOSE	.....	2	.....	1	.....	...	1	83	85
Epistaxis	.....	.....	....	.....	.....	...	.....	3	3
Inflammation	....	.....	.....	.....	.....	...	.....	7	7
Nasal catarrh	....	2	.....	1	.....	...	1	72	74
Ozæna	.....	.....	....	.....	.....	...	.....	1	1
DISEASES OF THE CIRCULATORY SYSTEM	2	42	5	30	.....	4	5	96	141
Hydropericardium	.....	1	1	....	.....	...	.....	.....	1
Pericarditis	1	2	1	2	.....	..	.....	3	6
Endocarditis	.....	.....	.....	.....	.....	...	.....	1	1

TABLE VII.—*Tabular statement, by districts, of diseases and injuries, etc.*—Continued.

THE GREAT LAKES.

Diseases.	Number of Cases.								
	Remaining under treatment from previous year.	Admitted during the year.	Discharged.			Died.	Remaining under treatment at the close of the year.	Number furnished office relief.	Total treated in hospital and dispensary.
			Recovered.	Improved.	Not improved.				
Local Diseases.									
DISEASES OF THE CIRCULATORY SYSTEM—Continued.									
Valvular disease:									
Aortic	1	1		2				4	6
Mitral		15	1	8		3	3	30	45
Pulmonic								1	1
Tricuspid		1				1			1
Hypertrophy of heart		1		1				3	4
Inflammation of heart		2		2					2
Degeneration of heart, fatty		1		1				2	3
Dilatation of heart		1		1				6	7
Angina pectoris								1	1
Palpitation and irregular action of heart		3	1	2				24	27
Aneurism of arteries		4		2			2	4	8
Varix		10	1	9				17	27
DISEASES OF THE RESPIRATORY SYSTEM	9	176	110	45	7	15	8	1,236	1,421
Hay-asthma								1	1
Œdema glottidis								1	1
Laryngitis:									
Acute		1		1				68	69
Chronic		1	1					2	3
Catarrhal								6	6
Ulceration of larynx		1			1				1
Aphonia								1	1
Bronchitis:									
Acute	3	60	46	13	2		2	856	919
Chronic		10	4	4	1	1		121	131
Catarrhal		5	3	2				92	97
Spasmodic asthma	1	14	4	11				33	48
Passive congestion of lungs		1	1					1	2
Hæmoptysis		2	2					2	4
Pneumonia	1	45	30	3		10	3	6	52
Pneumonic phthisis, chronic	3	9	3	2	3	3	1	12	24
Emphysema		2		1			1	4	6
Pleurisy:									
Acute	1	18	14	3		1	1	26	45
Chronic		5	2	3				2	7
Empyema		1		1				2	3
Adhesions of pleura		1		1					1
DISEASES OF THE DIGESTIVE SYSTEM	2	175	128	34	7	4	4	1,265	1,282
Ulcer of the lips								3	3
Stomatitis								5	5
Ulcerative stomatitis								4	4
Cyst of the mouth								1	1
Ranula								1	1
Abscess of the antrum		1					1		1
Caries of dentine and cementum								16	16
Inflammation of dental periosteum								1	1
Abscess of dental periosteum		2	2					5	7
Ulceration of gums and alveoli		1	1					2	3
Caries of the alveoli								1	1
Toothache								4	4
Ulcer of the tongue								3	3
Hypertrophy of tonsils								1	1
Relaxed throat								1	1
Sore throat		2	2					58	60
Quinsy		4	4					19	23
Follicular tonsilitis		1	1					34	35
Ulceration of fauces		4	4					4	8
Abscess of salivary glands		1	1						1
Follicular inflammation of the pharynx								26	26
Ulceration of pharynx								1	1
Hemorrhage of the stomach								2	2
Inflammation of the stomach		10	8	2				11	21

TABLE VII.—*Tabular statement, by districts, of diseases and injuries, etc.*—Continued.

THE GREAT LAKES.

Diseases.	Number of Cases.								
	Remaining under treatment from previous year.	Admitted during the year.	Discharged.			Died.	Remaining under treatment at the close of the year.	Number furnished office relief.	Total treated in hospital and dispensary.
			Recovered.	Improved.	Not improved.				
Local Diseases.									
DISEASES OF THE DIGESTIVE SYSTEM—Cont'd									
Dyspepsia		26	13	11	2			257	283
Gastrodynia		1	1					3	4
Vomiting								1	1
Haemorrhage of the intestines								1	1
Enteritis		4	2	1			1	1	5
Abscess in the subperitoneal tissue								2	2
Hernia	1	14	8	5	1		1	124	139
Tænia solium		3	2		1			13	16
Ascaris lumbricoides								1	1
Diarrhœa		41	40	1				200	241
Constipation		5	4	1				246	251
Colic		3	3					26	29
Abscess of the rectum		2	2					2	4
Ulceration of the rectum		4	1	3				2	6
Piles:									
Internal		4	4					19	23
External		8	7	1				67	75
Proalpsus of the rectum		2	1		1			4	6
Prolapsus of the anus		1	1						1
Stricture of the rectum		1					1		1
Fistula in ano	1	13	11	1	2			3	17
Pruritus ani		1		1				5	6
Hypertrophy of the liver								1	1
Congestion of the liver		3	1	2				7	10
Hepatitis		4	1	2		1		3	7
Cirrhosis of liver		2		1		1		1	3
Jaundice		3	1	1		1		7	10
Gallstones		1	1						1
Biliary colic								4	4
Peritonitis		3	1	1		1		2	5
DISEASES OF THE LYMPHATIC SYSTEM	8	111	74	35	3		7	141	260
Induration and enlargement of the spleen from ague		1					1		1
Hypertrophy of lymph-glands								1	1
Inflammation of lymph-glands	4	44	25	16	2		5	105	153
Suppuration of lymph-glands	4	66	49	19	1		1	35	105
DISEASES OF THE URINARY SYSTEM	2	41	11	20	1	6	5	142	185
Congestion of the kidney								2	2
Acute nephritis	1	6	2	1		2	2	7	14
Bright's disease		14		8	1	4	1	14	28
Pyelitis		1		1					1
Diabetes insipidus								5	5
Suppression of urine		1	1						1
Hæmaturia		2		2				1	3
Inflammation of bladder:									
Acute		4	3	1				32	36
Subacute								4	4
Chronic	1	10	2	7			2	49	60
Calculus of bladder								1	1
Irritability of bladder		1	1					10	11
Retention of urine		1	1					2	3
Incontinence of urine		1	1					15	16
DISEASES OF THE GENERATIVE SYSTEM	4	166	126	34		1	9	630	800
Urethritis								4	4
Gleet		1		1				145	146
Stricture of urethra:									
Organic		37	23	10		1	3	76	113
Spasmodic		2	1	1					2
Urinary fistula		1		1				1	2
Hypertrophy of prostate gland								2	2
Œdema of the penis								1	1
Inflammation of the glans penis								16	16

TABLE VII.—*Tabular statement, by districts, of diseases and injuries, etc.*—Continued.

THE GREAT LAKES.

Diseases.	Number of cases.								
	Remaining under treatment from previous year.	Admitted during the year.	Discharged.			Died.	Remaining under treatment at the close of the year.	Number furnished office relief.	Total treated in hospital and dispensary.
			Recovered.	Improved.	Not improved.				
Local Diseases.									
DISEASES OF THE GENERATIVE SYSTEM—Continued.									
Abscess of penis		1	1					2	3
Ulcer of penis	1	66	54	11			2	271	338
Phimosis		8	8					4	12
Pharaphimosis		5	3	1			1		5
Abscess of the scrotum	1		1					1	2
Pruritus of scrotum		1	1						1
Inflammation of spermatic cord								1	1
Varicocele								10	19
Hæmatocele of tunica vaginalis								4	4
Hydrocele of tunica vaginalis		13	8	4			1	9	22
Orchitis:									
Acute	1	11	10	1			1	16	28
Chronic								2	2
Epididymitis		10	9	1				14	24
Spermatorrhœa		2	2					19	21
Impotence								10	10
Inflammation of the uterus		2	1	1				2	4
Catarrh of the uterus	1	1	1	1				3	5
Laceration of cervix uteri		1		1					1
Amenorrhœa		1					1		1
Menorrhagia								2	2
Leucorrhœa								6	6
Pregnancy		3	3						3
DISEASES OF THE ORGANS OF LOCOMOTION	2	38	24	10			6	40	80
Ostitis		2	2					2	4
Periostitis		1	1					3	4
Caries		2					2	2	4
Necrosis	2	11	7	5			1	6	10
Ununited fracture, or false joint		2					2	1	3
Dropsy of joints		1	1					3	4
Synovitis:									
Acute		8	7	1				4	12
Chronic		5	3	1			1	3	8
Ankylosis		1	1					1	2
Atrophy of muscles		1		1					1
Inflammation of tendons								9	9
Contraction of tendons		1		1				1	2
Inflamed bursa		1	1					1	2
Bursal abscess		1	1						1
Bunion		1		1				3	4
Ganglion								1	1
DISEASES OF THE CONNECTIVE TISSUE	2	47	38	7		1	3	75	124
Œdema		2		1		1		1	3
Inflammation		9	5	2			2	19	28
Abscess	2	36	33	4			1	55	93
DISEASES OF THE SKIN	3	88	55	27	2		7	432	523
Erythema		1	1					1	2
Urticaria		2		2				31	33
Eczema		10	3	7				72	82
Intertrigo		1		1				2	3
Impetigo		1	1						1
Ecthyma								2	2
Prurigo								1	1
Lichen								6	6
Psoriasis		1	1					7	8
Herpes								9	9
Zona		1	1					2	3
Acne		2	1	1				16	18
Sycosis		1	1					4	5
Melasma								1	1
Alopecia								7	7

TABLE VII.—*Tabular statement, by districts, of diseases and injuries, etc.*—Continued.

THE GREAT LAKES.

Diseases.	Number of Cases.								
	Remaining under treatment from previous year.	Admitted during the year.	Discharged. Recovered.	Discharged. Improved.	Discharged. Not improved.	Died.	Remaining under treatment at the close of the year.	Number furnished office relief.	Total treated in hospital and dispensary.
Local Diseases.									
DISEASES OF THE SKIN—Continued.									
Frostbite		3	3					14	17
Ulcer	3	45	30	14			4	94	142
Cicatrices								1	1
Fissures								1	1
Boil		1	1					49	50
Carbuncle		5	3	1			1	7	12
Whitlow		9	7				2	25	34
Onychia								8	8
Corn								2	2
Wen								5	5
Ringworm								10	10
Itch		3	2	1				46	49
Phthiriasis								8	8
Malingerer		1			1				1
Undetermined		1			1			1	2
Poisons		5	3	2				3	8
Lead		1		1				1	2
Mercury								1	1
Alcohol		3	3					1	4
Tobacco		1		1					1
POISONED WOUNDS		1	1					2	3
Venomous animals								2	2
Vegetable substances		1	1						1
Injuries	29	396	305	75	6	3	36	690	1115
GENERAL INJURIES	2	25	19	6			2	41	68
Burns and scalds	2	12	9	4			1	27	41
Effects of cold		4	4					11	15
Sunstroke		1	1					2	3
Multiple injury		7	4	2			1		7
Exhaustion		1	1					1	2
LOCAL INJURIES	27	371	286	69	6	3	34	649	1,047
Strain of muscles		13	12		1			65	78
Strain of tendon								5	5
Rupture of tendon		1					1		1
Contusion of scalp		2	2					1	3
Scalp-wound:									
Bone not exposed		15	14	1				22	37
Bone exposed		11	8	1	1	1		3	14
Contusion of skull		2	2					2	4
Fracture of the vault of the skull		2	1	1				3	5
Fracture of the base of the skull		1	1						1
Concussion of brain		7	3	1		1	2	1	8
Contusion of the brain	1		1						1
Contusion of face		4	3				1	3	7
Wound of face	2	10	10	2				14	26
Fracture of facial bones		12	11	1				1	13
Contusion of the eye		5	4	1				7	12
Foreign body in cornea or conjunctiva		1	1					4	5
Wound of eyelid		1	1					1	2
Wound of pinna								2	2
Contusion of soft parts of neck								2	2
Contusion of the chest	1	22	17	4			2	27	50
Fracture of the ribs		18	14	1			3	13	31
Perforating wound of chest		2	1				1		2
Contusion of back	1	18	18	1				42	61
Sprain of back	2	7	7				2	9	18
Wound of back		3	1	1			1	1	4
Contusion of abdomen								2	2
Wound of parietes of abdomen		1				1			1

TABLE VII.—*Tabular statement, by districts, of diseases and injuries, etc.*—Continued.

THE GREAT LAKES.

Diseases.	Number of cases.								
	Remaining under treatment from previous year.	Admitted during the year.	Discharged.			Died.	Remaining under treatment at the close of the year.	Number furnished office relief.	Total treated in hospital and dispensary.
			Recovered.	Improved.	Not improved.				
Injuries.									
LOCAL INJURIES—Continued.									
Contusion of pelvis		2	2					2	4
Wound of organs of generation								5	5
Wound of rectum								1	1
Wound of anus		1	1						1
Fracture and dislocation of pelvis								1	1
Contusion of testicle		1		1					1
Contusion of upper extremities		14	10	3			1	83	97
Sprain of the shoulder		2	1	1				4	6
Sprain of the elbow		3	2				1	4	7
Sprain of the wrist		6	2	4				28	34
Sprain of the fingers								4	4
Wound of the upper extremities	2	31	24	7	1		1	116	140
Wound of joint, upper extremities		1	1						1
Fracture of the clavicle	1		1					6	7
Fracture of the scapula		1	1					1	2
Fracture of the humerus		6	2	1			3	1	7
Fracture of the radius		7	3	1	1		2	1	8
Fracture of the ulna		2	1	1				1	3
Fracture of both bones of forearm		5	2	1			2	1	6
Fracture of carpus, metacarpus, and phalanges		6	4	1			1	5	11
Dislocation of the clavicle		1		1					1
Dislocation of the humerus		5	3	2				5	10
Dislocation of the radius								1	1
Dislocation of the radius and ulna		2	2						2
Dislocation of the carpus		1	1						1
Dislocation of the phalanges of thumb		1					1		1
Dislocation of the phalanges of fingers								1	1
Contusion of the lower extremities	1	36	28	4	1		4	65	102
Sprain of the knee		2	2					10	12
Sprain of the ankle	3	23	16	8	1		1	29	55
Sprain of the foot								1	1
Wound of the lower extremities		31	28	3				27	58
Wound of joint, lower extremities		1	1					1	2
Fracture of femur	4	3	4	3				1	8
Fracture of cervix femoris	1	2		3				1	4
Fracture of patella		1		1					1
Fracture of leg, both bones	3	7	4	5			1		10
Fracture of tibia alone	2	1	2	1				2	5
Fracture of fibula alone	1	3	2	1			1	2	6
Fracture of tarsus								3	3
Fracture of metatarsus								3	3
Fracture of phalanges of toes	1	3	3				1	2	6
Dislocation of the femur at the hip		1		1					1
Dislocation of the foot at the ankle	1	1	1				1	1	3
AMPUTATIONS		3	3					4	7
Amputation of fingers		2	2					4	6
Amputation of thigh		1	1						1

THE PACIFIC.

TOTAL CASES	104	1446	887	470	24	69	100	2447	3997
General Diseases	40	497	294	159	11	42	31	1095	1632
Small-pox		1	1						1
Cow-pox								208	208
Measles		13	11			1	1	3	16
Mumps		5	4	1					5
Cerebro-spinal fever		1	1						1
Simple continued fever		1	1					1	2
Febricula		1	1						1

TABLE VII.—*Tabular statement, by districts, of diseases and injuries, etc.*—Continued.

THE PACIFIC.

Diseases.	Number of Cases.								
	Remaining under treatment from previous year.	Admitted during the year.	Discharged.			Died.	Remaining under treatment at the close of the year.	Number furnished office relief.	Total treated in hospital and dispensary.
			Recovered.	Improved.	Not improved.				
General Diseases.									
Enteric fever		13	7			4	2	1	14
Typho-malarial fever		2	1			1			2
Epidemic diarrhœa		1	1					4	5
Dysentery		13	9	3	1			12	25
Malarial intermittent fever	3	40	36	5		2		59	102
Malarial remittent fever		16	11	4		1		4	20
Malarial cachexia		10	9				1	13	23
Erysipelas:									
Simple	1	6	6			1		4	11
Phlegmonous	1		1						1
Syphilis:									
Primary	1	23	15	9				30	60
Secondary	5	66	8	59		1	3	138	209
Gonorrhœa	2	38	22	14	1		3	232	272
Effects of excessive venery		1	1					1	2
Scurvy	1	7	5	2			1		8
Alcoholism		15	14	1				13	28
Delirium tremens		1				1			1
Debility	1	10	4	5		1	1	26	37
Rheumatic fever	3	34	26	5		1	5	2	39
Rheumatism	8	109	93	15	2		7	197	314
Gout								1	1
Osteo-arthritis	1	1	1				1		2
Lipoma		1	1					2	3
Myxoma		2	1	1					2
Chondroma								2	2
Neuroma								1	1
Angeioma								1	1
Warts								2	2
Condyloma		2	2					2	4
Carcinoma		2		2					2
Epithelioma								1	1
Scirrhus		3		1		1	1		3
Tubercle of lung and other organs	12	52		26	7	27	4	62	126
Acute miliary tuberculosis		3		3					3
Scrofula	1	2		2			1	4	7
Purpura		1		1				1	2
Anæmia		1	1					2	3
Local Diseases	34	643	331	246	13	25	42	1057	1744
DISEASES OF THE NERVOUS SYSTEM	6	46	21	20	5	1	5	81	133
Congestion, cerebral		1	1						1
Hæmorrhage, cerebral		1					1		1
Anæmia, cerebral		1	1						1
Spinal meningitis		1	1						1
Myelitis	1			1					1
Softening of brain or cord		1			1				1
Locomotor ataxy		3		1	1	1			3
Apoplexy		1		1					1
Hemiplegia	3	4		2	1		4	3	10
Paraplegia		1		1					1
Local paralysis		2		2				1	3
Glosso-labio-pharyngeal paralysis		1		1					1
Lead palsy	1			1				1	2
Hyperæsthesia								1	1
Neuralgia		9	8	1				36	45
Facial		3	2	1				9	12
Sciatica	1	7	5	3				9	17
Vertigo		2	2					1	3
Megrim								1	1
Epilepsy		6	1	4	1			15	21
Hypochrondriasis								2	2
Mania		1			1				1
Melancholia								2	2
General paralysis of the insane		1		1					1

TABLE VII.—*Tabular statement, by districts, of diseases and injuries, etc.*—Continued.

THE PACIFIC.

Diseases.	Number of cases. Remaining under treatment from previous year.	Admitted during the year.	Discharged. Recovered.	Discharged. Improved.	Discharged. Not improved.	Died.	Remaining under treatment at the close of the year.	Number furnished office relief.	Total treated in hospital and dispensary.
Local Diseases.									
DISEASES OF THE EYE	3	17	9	11				23	42
Conjunctivitis:									
Catarrhal		1	1					3	4
Phlyctenular		1	1						1
Chronic								1	1
Granular	1		1						1
Pterygium								1	1
Keratitis		4	2	2				2	6
Ulcer of cornea	1	3		4				4	8
Staphyloma								1	1
Iritis		5	3	2				3	8
Atrophy of optic disk		1		1				2	3
Cataract:									
Lenticular								1	1
Capsular	1			1					1
Shrunken eyeball		1	1						1
Diplopia								1	1
Amaurosis								1	1
Stricture of nasal duct		1		1					1
Blepharitis								2	2
Chalazion								1	1
DISEASES OF THE EAR		9	4	5				12	21
Inflammation of the external meatus:									
Acute								2	2
Abscess of the external meatus		1	1						1
Accumulation of wax		1	1					4	5
Inflammation of the middle ear		7	2	5				6	13
DISEASES OF THE NOSE		2		2				12	14
Inflammation								1	1
Nasal catarrh		1		1				7	8
Ulceration								3	3
Sebaceous cyst								1	1
Caries of nasal bones		1		1					1
DISEASES OF THE CIRCULATORY SYSTEM	1	33	2	25	2	8	2	25	61
Valvular disease:									
Aortic		13		8	1	3	1	9	23
Mitral	1	11		10	1	1		8	20
Tricuspid		1		1					1
Hypertrophy of heart								2	2
Degeneration of heart, fatty		1				1		1	2
Dilatation of heart		1				1			1
Palpitation and irregular action of heart		2		2				3	5
Degeneration of arteries								1	1
Aneurism of arteries		5	1	1		2	1	1	6
Varix		4	1	3					4
DISEASES OF THE RESPIRATORY SYSTEM	2	108	50	43	3	7	7	181	291
Laryngitis:									
Acute		1	1					9	10
Chronic		1	1					1	2
Bronchitis:									
Acute		26	16	7	1		2	107	133
Chronic		8	2	5	1			38	46
Catarrhal		5	3	2				4	9
Spasmodic asthma		4		4				6	10
Hemoptysis		1		1					1
Pneumonia		22	15		1	5	1	2	24
Abscess of lung	1	2		3				1	4
Pneumonic phthisis:									
Acute	1			1					1
Chronic		12		8		1	3	6	18
Emphysema		1		1					1

THE PACIFIC.

Diseases.	Number of Cases.								
	Remaining under treatment from previous year.	Admitted during the year.	Discharged.			Died.	Remaining under treatment at the close of the year.	Number furnished office relief.	Total treated in hospital and dispensary.
			Recovered.	Improved.	Not improved.				
Local Diseases.									
DISEASES OF THE RESPIRATORY SYSTEM—Continued.									
Pleurisy:									
Acute		14	9	5				4	18
Chronic		9	3	6				3	12
Empyema		2				1	1		2
DISEASES OF THE DIGESTIVE SYSTEM	2	115	71	34		4	8	238	355
Stomatitis		1		1				2	3
Ulcerative stomatitis								1	1
Caries of dentine and cementum								8	8
Abscess of dental periosteum		1		1				5	6
Ulceration of gums and alveoli								2	2
Toothache								1	1
Ulcer of the tongue								1	1
Hypertrophy of tonsils								1	1
Sore throat		1	1					19	20
Quinsy		11	10	1				2	13
Follicular tonsilitis		6	5	1				6	12
Ulceration of fauces		1	1					3	4
Inflammation of salivary glands		3	3						3
Follicular inflammation of the pharynx		2	1	1				16	18
Post-pharyngeal abscess		1	1						1
Inflammation of the stomach		15	8	4		1	2	9	24
Ulceration of the stomach		2		2				2	4
Dyspepsia		10	6	4				46	56
Gastrodynia		1	1					2	3
Catarrhal inflammation of the intestines		4	2				2	9	13
Enteritis								1	1
Colitis		1	1					1	2
Obstruction of the intestines		2	2						2
Hernia		2	1	1				34	36
Tænia solium		3	1	2					3
Ascaris lumbricoides								1	1
Diarrhœa	1	7	4	4				13	21
Constipation		7	6	1				31	38
Colic		1	1					1	2
Ulceration of the rectum		1		1					1
Piles:									
Internal		7	6	1				9	16
External		5	4	1				9	14
Fistula in ano		3	1	1		1			3
Fissure of the anus		1		1				1	2
Congestion of the liver		3	1	1			1	1	4
Hepatitis	1		1						1
Cirrhosis of liver		7		5			2		7
Abcess of liver		2	1			1			2
Fatty liver		1				1			1
Jaundice		1	1					1	2
Gallstones		1	1						1
Peritonitis		1					1		1
DISEASES OF THE LYMPHATIC SYSTEM	4	46	31	17			2	69	119
Congestion of the spleen		1					1		1
Hypertrophy of lymph-glands	1		1					10	11
Inflammation of lymph-vessels		1		1					1
Inflammation of lymph-glands	2	17	15	3			1	31	50
Suppuration of lymph-glands	1	27	15	13				28	56
DISEASES OF THE THYROID BODY								1	1
Goitre								1	1
DISEASES OF THE URINARY SYSTEM:	2	32	6	18	1	5	4	30	64
Congestion of the kidney		1	1						1
Acute nephritis		2	1	1				1	3
Bright's disease	1	18		12		5	2	17	36
Hæmaturia		2	2						2

TABLE VII.—*Tabular statement, by districts, of diseases and injuries, etc.*—Continued.

THE PACIFIC.

Diseases.	Number of cases.								
	Remaining under treatment from previous year.	Admitted during the year.	Discharged. Recovered.	Discharged. Improved.	Discharged. Not improved.	Died.	Remaining under treatment at the close of the year.	Number furnished office relief.	Total treated in hospital and dispensary.
Local Diseases.									
DISEASES OF THE URINARY SYSTEM—Cont'd.									
Inflammation of bladder:									
Acute	1	2		2	1			4	7
Sub-acute		4	1	1			2	4	8
Chronic		3	1	2				1	4
Irritability of bladder								2	2
Retention of urine								1	1
DISEASES OF THE GENERATIVE SYSTEM	5	107	70	36	1		5	193	307
Urethritis								1	1
Gleet								5	5
Stricture of urethra:									
Organic	3	35	18	18			2	44	82
Traumatic		1			1				1
Acute inflammation of prostate gland		2	1	1					2
Abscess of prostate gland		1	1						1
Inflammation of the penis								1	1
Inflammation of glans penis								7	7
Abscess of penis		1	1						1
Ulcer of penis	1	36	24	11			2	97	134
Phimosis		4	3	1				2	6
Paraphimosis		3	3					2	5
Varicocele								1	6
Hydrocele of tunica vaginalis		6	4	2					1
Orchitis:									
Acute	1	10	8	2			1	8	19
Chronic								7	7
Epididymitis		7	7					11	18
Abscess of testicle		1		1					1
Spermatorrhœa								7	7
Impotence								2	2
DISEASES OF THE ORGANS OF LOCOMOTION	2	26	13	10	1		4	15	43
Periostitis		2	1	1				2	4
Caries		1		1					1
Necorsis		7	3	4				1	8
Ununited fracture, or false joint	1		1						1
Synovitis:									
Acute		3	2		1			3	6
Chronic		4	1	2			1	4	8
Abscess of joints		1	1						1
Ankylosis	1	1	2						2
Loose cartilage		1		1					1
Degeneration of cartilage, and of the articular surfaces of bones		1					1		1
Lateral curvature of spine		2					2		2
Atrophy of muscles		1		1					1
Inflamed bursa		1	1					1	2
Thecal abscess		1	1					1	2
Bunion								3	3
DISEASES OF THE CONNECTIVE TISSUES	3	30	27	6				32	65
Œdema		1	1						1
Inflammation		4	3	1				4	8
Abscess	3	25	23	5				28	56
DISEASES OF THE SKIN	4	67	47	19			5	153	224
Urticaria		2	1	1				3	5
Eczema	1	10	9	2				19	30
Impetigo		1		1					1
Rupia		1		1					1
Pityriasis								1	1
Psoriasis	1	4	2	2			1	12	17
Miliaria								1	1
Herpes		2	2					10	12
Zona								1	1

TABLE VII.—*Tabular statement, by districts, of diseases and injuries, etc.*—Continued.

THE PACIFIC.

Diseases.	Number of cases. Remaining under treatment from previous year.	Admitted during the year.	Discharged. Recovered.	Discharged. Improved.	Discharged. Not improved.	Died.	Remaining under treatment at the close of the year.	Number furnished office relief.	Total treated in hospital and dispensary.
Local Diseases.									
DISEASES OF THE SKIN—Continued.									
Pemphigus								1	1
Acne								1	1
Sycosis		1	1						1
Ulcer	1	24	14	8			3	44	69
Boil		7	6				1	19	26
Carbuncle		4	3	1				8	12
Gangrene		1		1					1
Whitlow	1	8	8	1				11	20
Onychia								3	3
Wen		2	1	1				6	8
Pruritis								2	2
Hyperidrosis								1	1
Ringworm								4	4
Itch								4	4
Phthiriasis								1	1
Irritation by insects								1	1
Poisons		1	1					5	6
Iodine								1	1
Alcohol		1	1					1	2
Tobacco								2	2
Rhus								1	1
POISONED WOUNDS		2	2						2
Venomous animals		2	2						2
Injuries	28	301	236	63		2	26	280	609
GENERAL INJURIES	3	19	16	6				24	46
Burns and scalds		8	6	2				8	16
Effects of cold		1	1					14	15
Multiple injury	3	9	9	3					12
Exhaustion		1		1				2	3
LOCAL INJURIES	25	282	220	59		2	26	256	563
Strain of muscles	1	2	3					2	5
Rupture of tendon		1	1						1
Foreign body in subcutaneous tissue		1	1					1	2
Scalp wound:									
Bone not exposed		15	13	2				17	32
Bone exposed		3	2	1				1	4
Contusion of skull		1	1						1
Fracture of the vault of the skull		2				1	1	1	3
Fracture of the base of the skull	1	2		2		1			3
Concussion of brain		3	2				1		3
Contusion of face		1		1					1
Wound of face	1	7	7				1	6	14
Fracture of facial bones		4	4					2	6
Dislocation of the lower jaw								1	1
Contusion of the eye	1	2	2	1				3	6
Foreign body in cornea or conjunctiva								3	3
Wound of eyelid								1	1
Foreign body in external meatus								1	1
Wound of neck		2	2						2
Contusion of the chest		11	10	1				8	19
Fracture of the ribs		14	10	4				6	20
Wound of parietes of chest								3	3
Perforating wound of chest		1					1		1
Contusion of back		11	9				2	5	16
Sprain of back		3	2	1				5	8
Wound of back								1	1
Fracture of spine		1		1					1
Concussion of cord	1	1	1	1					2
Contusion of abdomen		3	3					2	5

TABLE VII.—*Tabular statement, by districts, of diseases and injuries, etc.*—Continued.

THE PACIFIC.

Diseases.	Number of Cases.								
	Remaining under treatment from previous year.	Admitted during the year.	Discharged.			Died.	Remaining under treatment at the close of the year.	Number furnished office relief.	Total treated in hospital and dispensary.
			Recovered.	Improved.	Not improved.				
Injuries.									
LOCAL INJURIES—Continued.									
Wound of parietes of abdomen		1	1						1
Contusion of pelvis		3	2	1				1	4
Wound of organs of generation		3	3					3	6
Foreign body in the rectum		1		1					1
Contusion of testicle		4	1	3				1	5
Contusion of upper extremities		11	8	3				22	33
Sprain of the shoulder								3	3
Sprain of the elbow		1	1					2	3
Sprain of the wrist		3	1	1				7	10
Sprain of the fingers								2	2
Wound of the upper extremities	4	31	25	7			3	68	103
Fracture of the clavicle		7	5	2					7
Fracture of the scapula								1	1
Fracture of the humerus		3	1	1			1		3
Fracture of the radius		1	1						1
Fracture of the ulna		4	3	1				1	5
Fracture of both bones of forearm	2	3	2	2			1	5	10
Fracture of carpus, metacarpus, and phalanges		6	2	3			1	7	13
Dislocation of the humerus		5	5					2	7
Dislocation of the radius								1	1
Dislocation of the radius and ulna		1	1						1
Dislocation of the carpus		1	1						1
Contusion of the lower extremities	2	28	22	7			1	28	58
Sprain of the knee	1	6	4	3				4	11
Sprain of the ankle	2	13	12	2			1	9	24
Sprain of the foot								3	3
Wound of the lower extremities	2	19	18	2			1	13	34
Fracture of femur	2	8	5	2			3		10
Fracture of cervix femoris	1						1		1
Fracture of patella		2	1	1					2
Fracture of leg, both bones	1	9	7				3	3	11
Fracture of tibia alone	1	7	5	2			1	1	9
Fracture of fibula alone	1	7	8						8
Fracture of metatarsus		1					1		1
Fracture of phalanges of toes		1					1		1
Dislocation of the femur at the hip	1	1	2						2
AMPUTATIONS	2	2	3				1		4
Amputation of fingers		1	1						1
Amputation of leg	1	1	1				1		2
Amputation of toes	1		1						1

QUARANTINE.

Diseases.	Remaining under treatment from previous year.	Admitted during the year.	Recovered.	Improved.	Not improved.	Died.	Remaining under treatment at the close of the year.	Number furnished office relief.	Total treated in hospital and dispensary.
TOTAL CASES		128	99	24		2	3	241	369
General Diseases		74	64	8		1	1	80	154
Small-pox		3	3					2	5
Enteric fever		4	4						4
Yellow fever		1	1						1
Dysentery		2	2					3	5
Malarial intermittant fever		11	9	2				31	42
Malarial remittent fever		23	20	2			1	2	25
Malarial cachexia		2	2					17	19
Syphilis:									
Primary		1		1				1	2
Secondary		2		2				6	8
Gonorrhœa		2	2					6	8
Alcoholism								2	2
Debility		19	19						19

TABLE VII.—*Tabular statement, by districts, of diseases and injuries, etc.*—Continued.

QUARANTINE.

Diseases.	Number of Cases.								
	Remaining under treatment from previous year.	Admitted during the year.	Discharged.			Died.	Remaining under treatment at the close of the year.	Number furnished office relief.	Total treated in hospital and dispensary.
			Recovered.	Improved.	Not improved.				
General Diseases.									
Rheumatic fever		1	1					2	3
Rheumatism		1	1					8	9
Elephantiasis		1		1					1
Tubercular meningitis		1				1			1
Local Diseases		43	28	13		1	1	138	181
DISEASES OF THE NERVOUS SYSTEM		1		1				11	12
Neuralgia		1		1				1	2
Sciatica								4	4
Vertigo								2	2
Megrim								2	2
Epilepsy								1	1
Hypochondriasis								1	1
DISEASES OF THE EYE		1	1					2	3
Conjunctivitis, catarrhal		1	1					2	3
DISEASES OF THE NOSE								1	1
Nasal catarrh								1	1
DISEASES OF THE CIRCULATORY SYSTEM		1		1					1
Pericarditis		1		1					1
DISEASES OF THE RESPIRATORY SYSTEM		6	3	3				29	35
Bronchitis, acute		3	2	1				24	27
Pulmonary apoplexy								1	1
Œdema of lung								1	1
Pneumonia								1	1
Pneumonic phthisis, chronic								1	1
Pleurisy, acute		3	1	2				1	4
DISEASES OF THE DIGESTIVE SYSTEM		8	7			1		57	65
Stomatitis								4	4
Caries of dentine and cementum								10	10
Abscess of dental periosteum								1	1
Necrosis of the alveoli		1	1						1
Sore throat								1	1
Inflammation of the stomach		1	1						1
Dyspepsia								11	11
Enteritis		3	3						3
Hernia		1				1		3	4
Diarrhœa								8	8
Constipation								16	16
Abscess of the anus								1	1
Piles, external		1	1					2	3
Hepatitis		1	1						1
DISEASES OF THE LYMPHATIC SYSTEM		3	2	1				2	5
Induration and enlargement of the spleen from ague								2	2
Suppuration of lymph-glands		3	2	1					3
DISEASES OF THE URINARY SYSTEM		2	1	1				1	3
Inflammation of bladder, acute		2	1	1				1	3
DISEASES OF THE GENERATIVE SYSTEM		4	2	2				8	12
Stricture of urethra:									
Organic		2		2				1	3
Spasmodic								1	1
Ulcer of penis		1	1					3	4
Hydrocele of tunica vaginalis		1	1					1	2
Pelvic cellulitis								1	1
Dysmenorrhœa								1	1

TABLE VII.—*Tabular statement, by districts, of diseases and injuries, etc.*—Continued.

QUARANTINE.

Diseases.	Number of Cases. Remaining under treatment from previous year.	Admitted during the year.	Discharged. Recovered.	Discharged. Improved.	Discharged. Not improved.	Died.	Remaining under treatment at the close of the year.	Number furnished office relief.	Total treated in hospital and dispensary.
Local Diseases.									
DISEASES OF THE ORGANS OF LOCOMOTION		2	1	1				1	3
Periostitis								1	1
Synovitis, acute		1	1						1
Angular curvature of spine		1		1					1
DISEASES OF THE CONNECTIVE TISSUE		3	2				1	3	6
Abscess		3	2				1	3	6
DISEASES OF THE SKIN		12	9	3				23	35
Eczema								2	2
Ecthyma								5	5
Prurigo								1	1
Herpes								2	2
Acne								3	3
Frostbite		9	8	1					9
Ulcer		1	1					3	4
Fissures								1	1
Boil								3	3
Whitlow								1	1
Pruritus								2	2
Malingerer		2		2					2
Poisons								3	3
Lead								1	1
Alcohol								2	2
Injuries		11	7	3			1	20	31
GENERAL INJURIES		3	2				1	1	4
Burns and scalds		1	1						1
Sunstroke		1	1						1
Multiple injury		1					1	1	2
LOCAL INJURIES		8	5	3				19	27
Contusion of skull								1	1
Contusion of face								1	1
Wound of face								1	1
Contusion of chest		1	1						1
Contusion of back		1	1						1
Sprain of back		1	1					3	4
Contusion of pelvis								1	1
Contusion of upper extremities		1		1				2	3
Sprain of the wrist								2	2
Wound of the upper extremities		1		1				7	8
Contusion of the lower extremities		1	1					1	2
Wound of the lower extremities		1		1					1
Fracture of cervix femoris		1	1						1

REVENUE STEAMER BEAR (ARCTIC CRUISE).*

May 25 to September 6, 1888.

TOTAL CASES									167
General Diseases									41
Malarial intermittent fever								2	
Erysipelas, simple								1	
Syphilis, secondary								2	
Gonorrhœa								7	

* This statement is not included in the foregoing tabulation.

TABLE VII.—*Tabular statement, by districts, of diseases and injuries, etc.*—Continued.

REVENUE STEAMER BEAR (ARCTIC CRUISE).

DISEASES.	NUMBER OF CASES.								
	Remaining under treatment from previous year.	Admitted during the year.	Discharged.			Died.	Remaining under treatment at the close of the year.	Number furnished office relief.	Total treated in hospital and dispensary.
			Recovered.	Improved.	Not improved.				
General Diseases.									
Alcoholism								2	
Debility								2	
Rheumatic fever								0	
Rheumatism								[illegible]	
Tubercle of lung								4	
Scrofula								2	
Anæmia								1	
Local Diseases									110
DISEASES OF THE NERVOUS SYSTEM									18
Hemiplegia								1	
Neuralgia								10	
Sciatica								1	
Megrim								6	
DISEASES OF THE EYE									8
Conjunctivitis, catarrhal								4	
Opacity of cornea								2	
Glaucoma								1	
Amblyopia								1	
DISEASES OF THE EAR									2
Inflammation of the middle ear								2	
DISEASES OF THE NOSE									11
Nasal catarrh								11	
DISEASES OF THE CIRCULATORY SYSTEM									1
Varix								1	
DISEASES OF THE RESPIRATORY SYSTEM									16
Larnygitis:									
Acute								2	
Chronic								1	
Bronchitis:									
Acute								6	
Chronic								5	
Hæmoptysis								1	
Pneumonia								1	
DISEASES OF THE DIGESTIVE SYSTEM									33
Caries of dentine and cementum								4	
Sore throat								1	
Inflammation of the stomach								4	
Dyspepsia								4	
Vomiting								2	
Hernia								1	
Constipation								11	
Colic								1	
Piles:									
Internal								1	
External								3	
Inflammation of hepatic ducts and gall-bladder								1	
DISEASES OF THE URINARY SYSTEM									4
Inflammation of bladder, subacute								3	
Irritability of bladder								1	
DISEASES OF THE GENERATIVE SYSTEM									3
Stricture of urethra, organic								1	
Ulcer of penis								1	
Orchitis, chronic								1	

TABLE VII.—*Tabular statement, by districts, of diseases and injuries, etc.*—Continued.

REVENUE STEAMER BEAR (ARCTIC CRUISE).

Diseases.	Number of cases.								
	Remaining under treatment from previous year.	Admitted during the year.	Discharged.			Died.	Remaining under treatment at the close of the year.	Number furnished office relief.	Total treated in hospital and dispensary.
			Recovered.	Improved.	Not improved.				
Local Diseases.									
DISEASES OF THE CONNECTIVE TISSUE	.....	.....	.....	.....	.....	...	.....	.....	1
Inflammation	.....	.....	.....	.....	.....	...	.....	1	.....
DISEASES OF THE SKIN	.....	.....	.....	.....	.....	...	.....	.....	13
Urticaria	.....	.....	.....	.....	.....	...	.....	2	.....
Ulcer	.....	.....	.....	.....	.....	...	.....	1	.....
Boil	.....	.....	.....	.....	.....	...	.....	2	.....
Carbuncle	.....	.....	.....	.....	.....	...	.....	1	.....
Whitlow	.....	.....	.....	.....	.....	...	.....	1	.....
Wen	.....	.....	.....	.....	.....	...	.....	1	.....
Itch	.....	.....	.....	.....	.....	...	.....	1	.....
Phthiriasis	.....	.....	.....	.....	.....	...	.....	4	.....
Injuries	.....	.....	.....	.....	.....	...	.....	.....	**16**
LOCAL INJURIES	.....	.....	.....	.....	.....	...	.....	.....	16
Scalp-wound, bone not exposed	.....	.....	.....	.....	.....	...	.....	1	.....
Contusion of face	.....	.....	.....	.....	.....	...	.....	1	.....
Wound of face	.....	.....	.....	.....	.....	...	.....	1	.....
Contusion of back	.....	.....	.....	.....	.....	...	.....	1	.....
Contusion of upper extremities	.....	.....	.....	.....	.....	...	.....	3	.....
Wound of the upper extremities	.....	.....	.....	.....	.....	...	.....	5	.....
Fracture of the radius	.....	.....	.....	.....	.....	...	.....	1	.....
Contusion of the lower extremities	.....	.....	.....	.....	.....	...	.....	1	.....
Sprain of the ankle	.....	.....	.....	.....	.....	...	.....	1	.....
Fracture of femur	.....	.....	.....	.....	.....	...	.....	1	.....

TABLE VIII.—*Tabular statement, by districts, of causes of mortality, among patients of the service during the year ended June 30, 1888.*

Causes of death.	Total.	Districts.								
		North Atlantic.	Middle Atlantic.	South Atlantic.	The Gulf.	The Ohio.	The Mississippi.	The Great Lakes.	The Pacific.	The quarantine stations.
Total Deaths from all Causes	468		86	54	47	26	67	72	69	2
FROM DISEASE	447	44	80	51	46	26	62	69	67	2
FROM INJURY	21	1	6	3	1	.....	5	3	2	.....
General Diseases	218	21	40	16	27	9	32	30	42	1
Small-pox	2	2	.....	.....	.....	.....	.....	.....	.....	.....
Measles	2	.....	.....	.....	.....	.....	1	.....	1	.....
Enteric fever	23	2	4	2	2	2	.....	7	4	.....
Typho-malarial fever	2	.....	.....	.....	.....	.....	.....	1	1	.....
Epidemic diarrhœa	1	.....	.....	.....	1	.....	.....	.....	.....	.....
Dysentery	11	1	1	1	2	.....	6	.....	.....	.....
Malarial intermittent fever	11	.....	1	.....	2	1	4	1	2	.....
Malarial remittent fever	19	3	2	2	5	.....	4	2	1	.....
Malarial cachexia	2	1	.....	1	.....	.....	.....	.....	.....	.....

TABLE VIII.—*Tabular statement, by districts, of causes of mortality, etc.*—Continued.

Causes of Death.	Total.	Districts.								
		North Atlantic.	Middle Atlantic.	South Atlantic.	The Gulf.	The Ohio.	The Mississippi.	The Great Lakes.	The Pacific.	The quarantine stations.
General Diseases.										
Erysipelas:										
Simple	3		1				1		1	
Phlegmonous	1		1							
Syphilis:										
Primary	1		1							
Secondary	8			1	1		4	1	1	
Delirium tremens	2						1		1	
Debility	5		2					2	1	
Rheumatic fever	4		2	1					1	
Rheumatism	1				1					
Malignant new growth	2							2		
Carcinoma	2	1	1							
Epithelioma	2	1			1					
Scirrhus	3	2							1	
Tubercular meningitis	1									1
Tubercle of lung and other organs	103	8	22	6	12	4	10	14	27	
Acute miliary tuberculosis	1		1							
Scrofula	3			1		2				
Anæmia	1			1						
Leucocythæmia	1						1			
Diabetes mellitus	1		1							
Local Diseases	228	23	40	34	19	17	30	39	25	1
DISEASES OF THE NERVOUS SYSTEM	32	6	3	3	4	4	3	8	1	
Inflammation:										
Of membranes of brain and spinal cord	1					1				
Of brain and its membranes	1						1			
Of cerebral membranes	2		1				1			
Softening of brain or cord	1				1					
Sclerosis	1	1								
Progressive muscular atrophy	1	1								
Locomotor ataxy	2				1				1	
Apoplexy	2				1	1				
Paralysis	1							1		
Hemiplegia	8		1		1	2	1	3		
Paraplegia	1							1		
Local paralysis	1			1						
Neuralgia	1	1								
Sciatica	1							1		
Epilepsy	2	1		1						
Chorea	1		1							
Mania	3	1		1				1		
Dementia	2	1						1		
DISEASES OF THE CIRCULATORY SYSTEM	47	9	8	5	3	4	6	4	8	
Pericarditis	2	1		1						
Valvular disease:										
Aortic	11	2	1			2	3		3	
Mitral	17	4	2	3	1	1	2	3	1	
Tricuspid	1							1		
Hypertr phy of heart	2	1	1							
Fatty degeneration of heart	1								1	
Dilatation of heart	2		1						1	
Aneurism of heart	2		2							
Palpitation and irregular action of heart	1				1					
Aneurism of arteries	7	1		1	1	1	1		2	
Obstruction of arteries	1		1							
DISEASES OF THE RESPIRATORY SYSTEM	70	3	14	15	4	4	8	15	7	
Laryngitis, acute	2					1	1			
Bronchitis:										
Acute	5	1	2	1			1			
Chronic	2			1				1		
Catarrhal	1			1						
Spasmodic asthma	2	1		1						
Pneumonia	41	1	5	10	2	2	6	10	5	

TABLE VIII.—*Tabular statement, by districts, of causes of mortality, etc.*—Continued.

Causes of Death.	Total.	Districts.								
		North Atlantic.	Middle Atlantic.	South Atlantic.	The Gulf.	The Ohio.	The Mississippi.	The Great Lakes.	The Pacific.	The quarantine stations.
Local Diseases.										
DISEASES OF THE RESPIRATORY SYSTEM—Continued.										
Pneumonic phthisis:										
Acute	3	.....	3	.....	.....	.....	.....	.....	.....	.....
Chronic	9	.....	2	1	1	1	.....	3	1	.....
Emphysema	1	.....	.....	.....	1	.....	.....	.....	.....	.....
Acute pleurisy	1	.....	.....	.....	.....	.....	.....	1	.....	.....
Empyema	3	.....	2	.....	.....	.....	.....	.....	1	.....
DISEASES OF THE DIGESTIVE ORGANS.	42	2	11	5	2	3	10	4	4	
Ulceration of the fauces	1	.....	1	.....	.....	.....	.....	.....	.....	.....
Inflammation of the stomach	6	1	2	1	1	.....	.....	.....	1	.....
Catarrhal inflammation of the intestines	7	.....	.....	.....	.....	2	5	.....	.....	.....
Fistula of intestines	1	.....	.....	.....	1	.....	.....	.....	.....	.....
Hernia	3	.....	.....	2	.....	.....	.....	.....	.....	1
Diarrhœa	3	.....	2	.....	.....	.....	1	.....	.....	.....
Constipation	1	.....	1	.....	.....	.....	.....	.....	.....	.....
Fistula in ano	1	.....	.....	.....	.....	.....	.....	.....	1	.....
Hypertrophy of the liver	1	.....	1	.....	.....	.....	.....	.....	.....	.....
Hepatitis	5	.....	2	.....	.....	1	1	1	.....	.....
Cirrhosis of liver	4	.....	1	1	.....	.....	1	1	.....	.....
Abscess of liver	2	.....	.....	.....	.....	.....	1	.....	1	.....
Fatty liver	1	.....	.....	.....	.....	.....	.....	.....	1	.....
Jaundice	1	.....	.....	.....	.....	.....	.....	1	.....	.....
Inflammation of hepatic ducts and gall-bladder	1	.....	1	.....	.....	.....	.....	.....	.....	.....
Peritonitis	4	1	.....	1	.....	.....	1	1	.....	.....
DISEASES OF THE LYMPHATIC SYSTEM.	2	.....	1	.....	1	.....	.....	.....	.....	.....
Lymphadenoma	1	.....	1	.....	1	.....	.....	.....	.....	.....
DISEASES OF THE URINARY SYSTEM	25	2	3	3	3	2	1	6	5	.....
Acute nephritis	4	.....	.....	1	.....	.....	1	2	.....	.....
Bright's disease	10	2	3	2	2	1	.....	4	5	.....
Diabetes insipidus	1	.....	.....	.....	.....	1	.....	.....	.....	.....
Acute inflammation of bladder	1	.....	.....	.....	1	.....	.....	.....	.....	.....
DISEASES OF THE GENERATIVE SYSTEM	6	.....	.....	3	1	.....	1	1	.....	.....
Organic stricture of urethra	4	.....	.....	2	.....	.....	1	1	.....	.....
Gangrene of penis	1	.....	.....	.....	1	.....	.....	.....	.....	.....
Ulcer of penis	1	.....	.....	1	.....	.....	.....	.....	.....	.....
DISEASES OF THE ORGANS OF LOCOMOTION	1	.....	.....	.....	1	.....	.....	.....	.....	.....
Abscess of joints	1	.....	.....	.....	1	.....	.....	.....	.....	.....
DISEASES OF THE CONNECTIVE TISSUE.	2	1	.....	.....	.....	.....	.....	1	.....	.....
Œdema	1	.....	.....	.....	.....	.....	.....	1	.....	.....
Abscess	1	1	.....	.....	.....	.....	.....	.....	.....	.....
DISEASES OF THE SKIN	1	.....	.....	.....	.....	.....	1	.....	.....	.....
Ulcer	1	.....	.....	.....	.....	.....	1	.....	.....	.....
Poisons	1	.....	.....	1	.....	.....	.....	.....	.....	.....
Alcohol	1	.....	.....	1	.....	.....	.....	.....	.....	.....
Injuries	21	1	6	3	1	.....	5	3	2	.....
Burns and scalds	5	.....	2	2	1	.....	.....	.....	.....	.....
Scalp wound, bone exposed	1	.....	.....	.....	.....	.....	.....	1	.....	.....
Fracture of vault of skull	2	.....	1	.....	.....	.....	.....	.....	1	.....
Fracture of base of skull.	2	.....	.....	.....	.....	.....	1	.....	1	.....
Concussion of brain	1	.....	.....	.....	.....	.....	.....	1	.....	.....
Wound of parietes of chest	1	.....	.....	.....	.....	.....	1	.....	.....	.....
Concussion of cord	1	.....	.....	.....	.....	.....	1	.....	.....	.....
Wound of parietes of abdomen	3	.....	1	.....	.....	.....	1	1	.....	.....
Fracture of clavicle	1	.....	.....	.....	.....	.....	1	.....	.....	.....
Fracture of both bones of forearm	1	.....	1	.....	.....	.....	.....	.....	.....	.....
Wound of lower extremities	1	.....	1	.....	.....	.....	.....	.....	.....	.....
Fracture of leg, both bones	2	1	.....	1	.....	.....	.....	.....	.....	.....

TABLE IX.—*Ratio of deaths from specific causes.*

Deaths from—	Per 100 from all causes.	Deaths from—	Per 100 from all causes.
General diseases	46.58	Diseases of the digestive system	8.97
Diseases of the nervous system	6.84	Diseases of the urinary system	5.34
Diseases of the circulatory system	10.04	Injuries	4.50
Diseases of the respiratory system	14.96	From all other causes	2.77

TABLE X.—*Ratio of deaths in each district.*

Districts.	Per 100 patients treated in hospital.	Districts.	Per 100 patients treated in hospital.
North Atlantic	3.53	The Mississippi	4.78
Middle Atlantic	4.80	The Great Lakes	2.83
South Atlantic	2.54	The Pacific	4.45
The Gulf	2.78	The quarantine stations	1.56
The Ohio	2.01		

TABLE XI.—*Comparative exhibit—Mortality per 100 patients treated, by districts, 1880 to 1888.*

Districts.	General average.	1880.	1881.	1882.	1883.	1884.	1885.	1886.	1887.	1888.
North Atlantic	3.30	2.19	2.84	4.00	3.50	3.50	3.95	3.09	3.04	3.53
Middle Atlantic	4.01	4.88	3.63	3.92	3.54	3.87	3.34	3.27	4.85	4.80
South Atlantic	3.18	2.89	3.22	3.05	3.97	2.86	3.05	3.54	3.53	2.54
The Gulf	3.50	2.90	3.94	4.98	3.49	4.10	2.40	2.96	3.82	2.78
The Ohio	3.79	3.69	4.38	5.64	5.50	4.83	2.43	3.05	3.06	2.01
The Mississippi	3.64	2.84	3.29	3.51	4.35	4.08	2.93	2.79	4.19	4.78
The Great Lakes	2.66	2.01	3.16	2.49	2.51	3.07	2.79	2.37	2.72	2.83
The Pacific	4.54	4.56	6.09	3.35	3.96	4.88	3.30	5.72	4.59	4.45

TABLE XII.—*Comparative exhibit—Ratio of deaths from specific causes, 1880 to 1888.*

Deaths from—	General average.	1880.	1881.	1882.	1883.	1884.	1885.	1886.	1887.	1888.
General diseases	47.90	47.35	46.15	51.75	50.00	48.67	46.61	48.40	45.63	46.58
Diseases of the nervous system	5.97	5.02	7.25	5.57	6.77	4.49	8.07	4.91	4.79	6.84
Diseases of the circulatory system	7.77	8.35	7.03	5.15	6.38	6.14	10.42	9.69	7.29	10.04
Diseases of the respiratory system	15.22	13.65	17.80	12.58	16.33	13.90	14.06	16.22	17.50	14.96
Diseases of the digestive system	9.41	10.87	8.13	12.99	10.16	9.20	9.90	7.37	7.08	8.97
Diseases of the urinary system	5.27	5.57	4.40	5.15	3.98	7.36	5.21	4.18	6.25	5.34
Injuries	5.35	5.85	6.60	4.54	3.99	5.94	3.39	5.41	7.92	4.50
From all other causes	3.11	3.34	2.64	2.27	2.39	4.30	2.34	4.42	3.54	2.77

TABLE XIII.—*Comparative exhibit—Average duration of treatment in hospital in each district, 1880 to 1888.*

Districts.	General average.	1880.	1881.	1882.	1883.	1884.	1885.	1886.	1887.	1888.
North Atlantic	26.59	26.64	22.07	24.86	26.60	30.13	30.22	26.56	23.80	27.76
Middle Atlantic	26.53	26.19	27.68	26.18	24.50	26.84	25.32	25.84	29.21	26.99
South Atlantic	25.55	28.52	23.80	23.20	23.70	23.46	26.06	26.72	27.99	26.53
The Gulf	22.84	24.55	23.00	35.25	20.19	19.97	18.63	19.43	20.82	23.24
The Ohio	24.11	24.57	23.88	29.22	26.50	22.56	23.18	23.61	21.87	21.62
The Mississippi	20.29	20.74	19.66	17.55	22.50	18.16	20.28	20.79	21.72	21.23
The Great Lakes	27.04	26.13	29.42	26.03	27.70	29.75	28.10	28.61	26.31	26.72
The Pacific	30.18	34.41	32.03	27.55	26.10	31.04	31.09	29.74	29.72	29.96

TABLE XIV.—*Statement of mortality of passengers on voyages from foreign ports to the United States, July 1, 1887, to June 30, 1888.*

Date.	Name of vessel.	Where from.	Male or female.	Age.	Cause of death as reported to the customs officer.
Sept. 19	Acapulco	Panama	Male	42	Unknown.
Mar. 8	Alsatia	Mediterranean ports	...do	25	Heart disease.
Oct. 4	Alesia	Marseilles	...do	23	Enteritis.
Do	...do	...do	Female	59	Inanition.
Do	...do	...do	Male	3	Cholera.
Do	...do	...do	Female	40	Do.
Do	...do	...do	Male	38	Enteritis.
June 1	Amalfi	Hamburgh	...do	46	Pneumonia.
Nov. 30	America	Bremen	Female	58	Apoplexy.
June 27	...do	...do	...do	43	Palpitation of heart.
Oct. 10	Arabic	Liverpool	...do	60	Exhaustion.
Oct. 3	Arizona	...do	Male	34	Concussion of brain.
Do	...do	...do	Female	22	Syncope.
Dec. 10	Assyrian	...do	Male	11	Croup.
Do	...do	...do	Female	8	Do.
Nov. 19	Australia	Hamburg	...do	13	Diphtheria.
July 26	Austrian	Glasgow	Male	65	Tubercle of lungs.
Feb. 4	Belgic	Hong-Kong	...do	31	Unknown.
July 12	Bohemia	Hamburg	Female	56	Heart disease.
Mar. 13	...do	...do	Male	2	Pneumonia.
Jan. 4	Bolivia	Mediterranean ports	Female	52	Intestinal obstruction.
Jan. 20	Brittania	...do	Male	35	Pneumonia.
Do	...do	...do	...do	60	Heart disease.
Apr. 6	...do	...do	...do	53	Apoplexy.
Nov. 22	British Princess	Liverpool	Female	9	Unknown.
Apr. 23	...do	...do	Male	22	Pneumonia.
Jan. 29	Burgundia	Marseilles	...do	33	Do.
June 2	Cachemire	Mediterranean ports	...do	43	Congestion of the brain.
Do	...do	...do	...do	43	Heart disease.
Apr. 4	Camorin	...do	...do	47	Apoplexy.
Do	...do	...do	...do	49	Gastric fever.
Sept. 1	Celtic	Liverpool	...do	25	Enteritis.
Dec. 24	Cephalonia	...do	...do	36	Delirium tremens.
May 21	Chateau Yquem	Mediterranean ports	...do	11	Tubercle of lungs.
June 23	City of Chicago	Liverpool	...do	41	Delirium tremens.
May 29	City of Pekin	Hong-Kong	...do	45	Unknown.
June 15	City of Rio de Janeiro	...do	...do	30	Do.
May 13	Cochar	Mediterranean ports	...do	25	Accident.
June 6	Colon	Aspinwall	...do	52	Tubercle of lungs.
June 25	Colorado	...do	...do	39	Congestion of lungs and paralysis.
Nov. 5	Dupuy de Lonce	Antwerp	...do	20	Tubercle of lungs.
May 2	Elve	Bremen	...do	80	Exhaustion.
Oct. 7	Ems	...do	...do	36	Blood poisoning.
Jan. 22	...do	...do	...do	26	Alcohol poisoning.
Oct. 17	Fulda	...do	...do	70	Uræmia.
Jan. 18	Gaelic	Hong-Kong	...do	17	Unknown.
Aug. 3	...do	...do	...do	40	Do.
Apr. 6	Gallia	Liverpool	...do	76	Heart disease.
Dec. 17	Gautemala	Panama	...do	36	Unknown.
Sept. 16	Germanic	Liverpool	Female	38	Pneumonia.
Feb. 24	...do	...do	Male	24	Delirium tremens.
May 18	Gothia	Stettin	...do	30	Unknown.
Apr. 17	Hammonia	Hamburg	...do	8	Meningitis.
Do	Hekla	Copenhagen	...do	22	Tubercle of lung.
Nov. 23	Hermann	Bremen	Female	16	Paralysis.
July 29	Hipparchus	Rio de Janeiro	...do	15	Small-pox.
Mar. 12	Historian	Liverpool and West Indies.	Male	26	Yellow fever.
Oct. 10	Indiana	...do	...do	55	Debility.
Oct. 30	...do	...do	...do	32	Delirium tremens.
June 7	...do	...do	Female	35	Apoplexy.
Sept. 4	Island	Copenhagen	Male	60	Pneumonia.
May 12	...do	...do	Female	22	Diphtheria.
May 18	Kansas	Liverpool	...do	18	Stomatitis, gangrenous.
Mar. 26	La Bretagne	Havre	...do	57	Heart disease.
Nov. 13	La Bourgogne	...do	...do	50	Exhaustion.
June 1	Lahn	Hamburg	Male	46	Pneumonia.
June 3	La Gasgogne	Havre	Female	28	Diphtheria.
Apr. 16	Leerdam	Rotterdam	...do	32	Apoplexy.
Dec. 7	Lord Gough	Liverpool	...do	60	Syncope.
Nov. 5	Main	Bremen	...do	30	Unknown.
May 22	Marathon	Liverpool	...do	20	Heart disease.
May 11	Martha	Mediterranean ports	Male	28	Meningitis.
Apr. 25	Neustria	...do	...do	27	Intestinal injuries.
Do	...do	...do	...do	35	Apoplexy.
Apr. 10	Nevada	Liverpool	...do	25	Suicide.
May 16	...do	...do	...do	35	Delirium tremens.
June 20	...do	...do	...do	27	Bronchitis.

TABLE XIV.—*Statement of mortality of passengers on voyages from foreign ports to the United States, etc.*—Continued.

Date.	Name of vessel.	Where from.	Male or female.	Age.	Cause of death as reported to the customs officer.
May 5	Olympia	Mediterranean ports	Male	41	Tubercle of lung.
Dec. 6	Parisian	Liverpool	Female	60	Bronchitis.
Apr. 29	P. Caland	Rotterdam	Male	26	Congestion of lungs.
Sept. 20	Polynesia	Hamburg	Female	22	Peritonitis.
May 7	Republic	Liverpool	Male	21	Epilepsy.
Nov. 15	Rhaetia	Rotterdam	...do	55	Heart disease.
Do	...do	...do	...do	22	Diphtheria.
May 4	...do	Hamburg	...do	34	Apoplexy.
Do	...do	...do	...do	48	Pneumonia.
July 13	Rhein	Bremen	Female	50	Do.
May 18	Rugia	Hamburg	...do	38	Apoplexy.
Nov. 17	Slavonia	Stettin	Male	45	Tubercle of lungs.
May 13	Sorrento	Hamburg	Female	17	Croup.
June 21	State of Indiana	Glasgow	...do	20	Meningitis.
July 29	State of Pennsylvania.	...do	...do	33	Pregnancy.
Mar. 14	"The Queen"	Liverpool	Male	24	Pneumonia.
Apr. 27	Thingvalla	Antwerp	Female	42	Unknown.
Apr. 1	Trave	Bremen	...do	25	Tubercle of lungs.
May 24	...do	...do	Male	26	Delirium tremens.
Apr. 22	Umbria	Liverpool	...do	50	Heart disease.
Dec. 21	Utopia	Mediterranean ports	...do	37	Apoplexy.
Nov. 30	Werra	Bremen	Female	24	Heart disease.
Apr. 18	Westernland	Antwerp	...do	58	Angina pectoris.
Nov. 4	"W. G. Irwin"	Honolulu	Male	36	Unknown.
Apr. 2"	Wieland	Hamburg	...do	57	Marasmus.
Nov. 16	Wisconsin	Liverpool	...do	15	Pneumonia.
Oct. 29	Zaandam	Amsterdam	Female	29	Hæmorrhage, internal.

SELECTED CASES FROM HOSPITAL PRACTICE.

REPORT OF OPERATIONS FOR THE RADICAL CURE OF HERNIA.

By Surgeon W. H. Long, M. H. S.

In the annual report of the Surpervising Surgeon General, U. S. Marine-Hospital Service, for 1887, I reported three operations for the radical cure of hernia, and I wish to make a statement in regard to them before entering on the particulars of subsequent operations. As stated in that report, Case I was killed a few months after the operation. Case II was re-admitted to hospital November 1, 1887, with a return of his hernia, which had remained apparently cured for nine months. He did not wear his truss as directed, and while lifting logs a sudden break occurred. This was a very large scrotal hernia before the first operation, and when re-admitted the hernia had become scrotal again. A second operation was performed January 30, 1888. He was admitted to hospital July 30, 1888, with pneumonia, and died August 11. A careful dissection of his hernia was made, and the results will be given in connection with the report of the secondary operation in this paper. Case III was examined July 10, 1888, and the cure seemed permanent.

Case IV.

Frank Morgan; aged thirty-two; born in New York; admitted to United States Marine Hospital, Detroit, June 17, 1887, with inflammation of inguinal lymphatic gland, and re-admitted September 24, 1887, with right oblique inguinal hernia, a simple bubonocele of three years' duration. The operation was performed under chloroform September 23, 1887. There was no rise of temperature in this case and no unfavorable symptoms. The external wound healed by first intention and the drainage tube was removed in four days. The patient was discharged in twelve days, apparently cured. He is now in hospital with rheumatism, and there seems to be some signs of the hernia returning, but it will require further observation before being able to give a definite opinion as to the cure.

Case V.

John Bulger; aged thirty-eight; born in Ireland, admitted to Marine Hospital, at Detroit, October 6, 1887, with inflammation of inguinal gland and right oblique inguinal hernia. The operation was made two days after his admission. The sac and hernia followed the cord almost to the testicle. The sac was amputated and the ring sewed up. There was no rise in temperature, and the patient was discharged October 28, 1887, cured.

CASE VI.

Dennis Dwyer; aged forty-two; born in Ireland; admitted to Marine Hospital, Detroit, October 10, 1887, with lacerated wound of leg, and right oblique inguinal hernia about the size of a hen's egg. This case was operated on October 11. The sac was returned and the edges of the ring brought together as usual. Union was rapid and there was no elevation of temperature. He was discharged November 15, 1887, cured. When last seen, in February, 1888, the cure seemed permanent.

CASE VII.

Jacob Bundy; aged forty; born in Michigan, of French parentage; admitted to Marine Hospital, Detroit, October 5, 1887, with left scrotal hernia. He was put under treatment for the improvement of his general condition, and the operation was not performed until November 21. The sac was carefully dissected from the cord and testicle and measured over 5 inches in length. Double ligatures of catgut were put around the sac at the ring and then cut off and some traction was made on the sac while the ligatures were being applied. After the sac was amputated it dropped through the ring, and, in attempting to recover the stump, the ligatures were pulled off. This not only left a large opening into the peritoneal cavity, but, as the peritoneum was quite vascular, a large amount of blood was poured out at once. Fortunately the bleeding margin of the peritoneum was secured and stitched into the ring. At 8 p. m. his temperature was 38° C.; November 22, 8 a. m., temperature 38°; 6 p. m., 39°. November 23, a. m., 39°; p. m., 40°; no tenderness over abdomen. November 24, a. m., 38.3°; p. m., 39°. November 25, a. m., 38°; p. m., 39°. November 26, a. m., 37.4°; p. m., 37.3°. The evening temperature on the 28th and 29th was 38°; afterwards there was no rise at all. The pulse was at no time higher than 106. There was considerable scrotal swelling and the wound healed by granulation. He was discharged February 5, 1888, but was kept longer than necessary, for purposes of observation. Three months later the cure seemed permanent. In this case there was partial atrophy of the left testicle, probably due to damage done to the cord when separating the sac, or to the nerve while attempting to get control of the bleeding edges of the peritoneum.

CASE VIII.

Jos. Kane; aged twenty-one; born in Massachusetts; admitted to U. S. Marine Hospital, Detroit, January 1, 1888, with left scrotal hernia. He was operated on January 25 and a departure from the usual method of dissecting out the sac was made. The neck of the sac at the ring (as recommended by Professor Gross*) was exposed, unligated, allowing the stump to fall back in the ring and leaving the empty sac in situ. The usual antiseptic cautions were observed, but the wound did not heal by first intention and suppuration of the empty sac occurred. On the evening of the operation his temperature was 38° C.; January 26, a. m., 37.2°; p. m., 38°. January 27, a. m., 37.2°; p. m., 38°. On the 28th his temperature was normal morning and evening and did not rise again until February 6, when a free incision was made into the suppurating sac. Februay 7, a. m., 38.4°; p. m., 39°. February 8, a. m., 37.3°; p. m., 38°. His pulse at no time exceeded 100. There was no further rise in temperature and he made a good recovery with a depressed cicatrix over the site of the ring, and was discharged

* Gross's Surgery, Vol. II, p. 514.

April 2. The suppurating sac gave much more trouble than the wound at the ring.

CASE IX.

John Wilson; aged thirty-seven; born in Pennsylvania; admitted to Marine Hospital, Detroit, January 1, 1888, with right scrotal hernia. The operation for removal of the sac and sewing up the ring was made January 27. On the evenings of the 28th and 29th his temperature was 38° C. There was no subsequent rise and the wound healed rapidly. He was discharged March 13, apparently cured, and has not been under observation since.

CASE X.

George Smith; aged fifty-four; born in Germany; admitted to Marine Hospital, Detroit, January 25, 1888, with a very large hydrocele of left cord and tunica vaginalis. He was afterwards found to have a right scrotal hernia, and a double operation was performed January 29. The hydrocele was first laid open and the cavity packed with carbolized tape, after which all the parts were washed with mercuric chloride solution (1 in 1,000), and the herniotomy performed, the sac being removed, followed by stitching, inserting drainage tube, and antiseptic dressing as usual. There was a slight rise in temperature on the morning of the 30th, and at 6 p. m. it was 39° C.; February 1, a. m., 38°; p. m., 37.3°, and no subsequent rise. The hernia wound healed rapidly, and was practically well by February 12, but the hydrocele required a much longer time. He was discharged April 2, having recovered perfectly from both operations and with no signs of hernia.

CASE XI.

Major Shelby (colored); aged forty-eight; born in Mississippi (the case referred to in the beginning of this report as Case II); admitted to Marine Hospital, Detroit, November 1, 1887, with a return of the hernia operated on the previous January. There had been no sign of a return until brought on, a day or two before his admission, by heavy lifting. While the second sac had descended into the scrotum, it was very small in comparison with the first. His general condition was very bad and it was not judged advisable to operate before January 30, 1888, when he was much improved. The sac was again amputated and the ring sewed up with the stump between the pillars of the ring. The external wound was not brought together in this case, but left open to heal by granulation and thus strengthen the parts. The only rise in temperature noted was on the second day, when 38° C. was recorded. He made good progress with a large granulating wound, and was discharged April 22, apparently cured, with a large amount of cicatricial tissue over the site of the ring. He was readmitted July 30, 1888, with pneumonia, and died August 11. The dissection showed quite an amount of cicatricial tissue occupying the site of the ring and slightly depressed. Much of it had been absorbed since his discharge in April. The pillars of the ring were adherent, but the adhesions were broken without much difficulty. There was no sign of stump between the pillars, nor was the peritoneum adherent to any portion of it, except the inner surface, lightly by connective tissue. When fully opened, the peritoneum beneath was found cone-shaped (with the top of the cone cut off) and very much thickened. The top of the cone was 1 inch in diameter, one-fourth of an inch thick, and simply rested against the inner opening of the ring. He had worn his soft truss but little since the last operation.

CASE XII.

Robert Mahan; aged twenty-two; born in Ireland; admitted to Marine Hospital, Detroit, January 30, 1888, with right oblique inguinal hernia, of a few months' duration. This patient was operated on under chloroform, February 1. The hernia was a simple bubonocele. The sac was returned and the pillars brought together in this case. Union by first intention was secured, the drainage tube being removed on the 4th. There was no elevation of temperature, and he left the hospital of his own accord, February 13, apparently well. He has not been under observation since that date.

CASE XIII.

John Kelly; aged forty-one; born in Ireland; admitted to Marine Hospital, Detroit, March 12, 1888, with an old right scrotal hernia. The office had been furnishing him with a truss every few months for years, but consent for an operation could not be secured until this time. It was performed March 14. This hernia was of considerable size, and, as the parts were much thickened and changed by long wearing of trusses, the dissection of the sac was more difficult than usual. The sac was amputated at the ring and the stump included in the sutures. On the morning of March 15 the temperature was 38° C. and at 6 p. m. 39°; March 16, a. m., 38°; p. m., 38.2°; March 17, normal, and there was no further rise and no unfavorable symptoms. Union by first intention was secured, and he was discharged, cured, April 30, 1888. He reported at the hospital August 20, and the cure seemed permanent.

CASE XIV.

Chester Carpenter;* aged twenty-one; born in Ohio; admitted to Marine Hospital, Detroit, May 15, 1888, with right scrotal hernia of several years' duration. The operation for radical cure was performed May 18, the sac amputated and stump treated as in former cases. On the 19th morning and evening temperature 38° C.; May 20, a. m., 38°, p. m., normal, and there was no further rise. There was a failure to obtain union of the external wound by adhesion and it healed by granulation—which was slow. He was discharged July 1, 1888, apparently cured.

In all these cases drainage tubes and antiseptic dressings were used. The danger to life seems very small, there being not even an expected amount of constitutional disturbance.

---

* This case was exhibited to the Detroit Academy of Medicine.

CASE OF ANKYLOSIS OF LOWER JAW RELIEVED BY MAKING A FALSE JOINT.

By Surgeon W. H. Long.

Andrew Johnson; aged fifty-six; born in Ireland; was admitted to the Marine Hospital, port of Detroit, December 19, 1877, with ankylosis of the lower jaw, the right joint only being affected. His teeth were tightly closed, and he was able to make no movement whatever of the lower jaw. This condition had existed for over eight years. There was found on examination considerable enlargement of the articular process of the bone on the right side, and it was believed the disease was malignant, and the patient was placed under observation. Only liquid foods could be taken or had been for several years.

There was no history of injury to the joint, of syphilis, or rheumatism, with the possible exception of rheumatic arthritis of this joint; that is not at all clear. In March, 1888, the patient was given chloroform as a means of diagnosis, but while under full anæsthesia the jaw could not be moved, and from other circumstances the theory of malignant disease was abandoned. On April 4 an operation was made for his relief. It was found when the joint was exposed that bony union had taken place between the articular process and the glenoid cavity, with considerable thickening of the head of the bone.

As any operation would necessitate a separation of the continuity of bone, it was thought best to go lower down and form a false joint in the smallest part of the shaft of the process.

The operation was a complete success, and the mouth opened to its full extent as soon as the bone was divided. He was discharged April 26, recovered. He was heard from about July 20, when the false joint was working perfectly, and he could masticate all kinds of food.

The inclosed diagram gives all the steps of the operation. There was less than 15 cubic centimeters of blood lost, and no injury done to any nerve. A Hey's saw was used for the division of the bone.

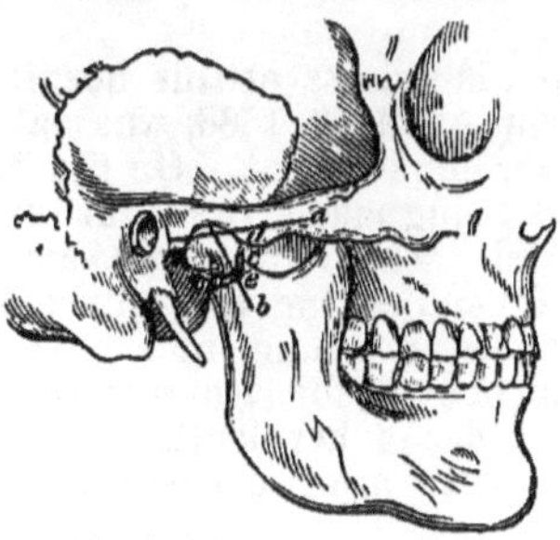

a—First incision.
b—Second incision.
c—Where the bone was sawed through.
d—Upper fragment as rounded off.
e—Lower fragment as hollowed out.

OEDEMA OF THE GLOTTIS—LARYNGOTOMY.

By Surgeon W. H. Long, M. H. S.

James Robinson; aged twenty-two; nativity, Illinois; was admitted to the U. S. Marine Hospital, Detroit, Mich., May 7, 1887, suffering from quinsy. Both tonsils were much swollen, and the tongue sore. Gargles, and frequent application of steam by means of the spray apparatus, seemed to give great relief from the pain and tenderness. On the morning of May 9 the tonsils were incised freely, with quite a free discharge of pus from the right one following. Temperature, 39° C., pulse 110, at 8 a. m. Relief of all uncomfortable symptoms followed; temperature at 6 p. m., 37.4°, pulse 90. At 12 (midnight), I was called by the night nurse, who said that Robinson was dead. Suspecting the cause to be œdema of the glottis, I ordered the nurse to call the assistant surgeon and bring the case of instruments to the ward. Going at once to the man, I found him apparently dead. No pulse at the wrist, and but a feeble flutter of the heart could be detected. No air could be forced in or out of the lungs by means of artificial respiration. The assistant surgeon and nurse, with instruments, came at this moment, and I sent the former for the tracheotomy-tube, while I made an opening into the larynx through the crico-thyroid membrane. The assistant had to go down one flight of stairs to the dispensary, and not being able to find the tube, aroused the steward to get it. He returned as quickly as possible, but in the meantime several minutes had elapsed, and no action of the heart could be heard. The tube was inserted, but no effort at breathing was made. Artificial respiration was at once resorted to, and continued for fifteen minutes, when a feeble gasp was made, and in a few minutes respiration was established and the heart's action discernible. A short time after the pulse could be felt at the wrist, and in half an hour consciousness returned. Improvement was steady. The tube was removed May 23, and the patient discharged May 31, entirely well. There was no impairment of the voice after the healing of the wound.

NOTE.—Mary Cragon, laundress at this hospital, was subject to attacks of quinsy, and on April 19, 1888, was taken with the sixth or seventh attack since her employment. On the 20th, while an examination of her throat was being made, the right tonsil opened and a free discharge of pus followed. The night nurse saw her at midnight, when she was breathing freely and feeling very much relieved and comfortable. He visited her again at 4 a. m., and found her dead in her bed. She had been dead long enough for *rigor mortis* to take place. Œdema of the glottis was the cause of her death. While this complication is not common in quinsy, here are two cases occurring in this hospital within one year.

SEAMAN JOHN BACKLUND.

Re-amputation of left leg, superior third, circular; pneumonia; pyæmia; recovery. By Surgeon Henry W. Sawtelle, U. S. Marine Hospital Service.

UNITED STATES MARINE HOSPITAL.
San Francisco, Cal., January, 1888.

RE-AMPUTATION LEFT LEG AT SUPERIOR THIRD FOR ULCER AND NEURALGIA OF STUMP—PNEUMONIA—PYÆMIA—RECOVERY.

By Henry W. Sawtelle, Surgeon, U. S. Marine Hospital Service.

Seaman John Backlund, aged thirty-eight years, nativity Finland; admitted to U. S. Marine Hospital, San Francisco, Cal., August 14, 1886, suffering from a compound comminuted fracture of tarsal and metatarsal bones, extensive laceration of the leg and foot, with gangrene, resulting from an injury received August 10 by a cable car-wheel passing over the limb. Passed assistant surgeon H. W. Yemans amputated the leg at the middle third, by Sedillot's method, August 16, 1886. Secondary hæmorrhage supervened. A portion of the outside flap sloughed off. He was discharged, by request, June 6, 1887. At this time there was a small central ulcer in the stump, which no treatment seemed to affect, together with neuralgic pains, more or less persistent though not particularly severe. The stump continued to trouble him more and more, and he again applied for relief after a few days' absence in the city. Upon re-admission the ulcer seemed to be about the same as when he was discharged, but there was, in addition, considerable inflammation of the surrounding parts, and the pain was so disproportionately great as to compel the conclusion that nerve filaments were involved in the dense mass of cicatricial tissue on which the ulcer was seated. The ulcer proved utterly rebellious to all treatment instituted, and at the patient's urgent request it was decided to re-amputate as the only hope of giving the man a useful stump. On July 25, 1887, the patient was etherized, and I reamputated the limb at the superior third, by the circular method, aided by assistant surgeon W. D. Bratton, Marine Hospital Service. An examination of the amputated extremity of bone showed about 2 centimeters thickness of dense fibrous tissue between it and the floor of the ulcer. The bone itself appeared to be in a state of healthy proliferation. Notwithstanding every precaution a slow oozing distended the flaps, and on the third day it was necessary to remove the sutures, turn out a mass of clots, wash and pack the cavity beneath the flaps. Suppuration followed. But finally the result was all that could be desired—the flaps perfect. In the mean time certain complications, constituting the interesting features of the case supervened. The temperature after the operation was above normal every evening, but about one week thereafter a stitch in right side, cough, and fever indicated what further examination revealed was pleurisy. This, in a few days, developed into pneumonia of the lower lobe of the right lung, which progressed slowly to a favorable termination. But while the pneumonia thus underwent resolution, the abnormal temperature persisted with much the range of septic fever. No cause could be assigned for this until accidentally quite an abscess was discovered in the right fore-arm. The patient was an intelligent man, yet he had never called attention to it. It was now a month after the operation, and there was some doubt whether to ascribe the abscess to an injection hypodermically at that point during the operation. A quantity (50 cubic centimeters) of ill-formed but not fœtid pus was evacuated, and the abscess cavity soon closed up; but the febrile movement still continued, and now a slight dullness over the right apex, increased vocal fremitus, and harsh respiratory sounds, which had been observed for some time, became more marked. There was a short hacking cough and a thick sputum, with shreddy opacities. These signs taken together with average temperature of 38° C., a. m., and 39° C., p. m., appeared to be the forerunner of a serious lesion of the lung. A few days later some pain and swelling was complained of in Scarpas triangle of the amputated limb. The stump was at once examined, but found perfectly healthy. The application of poultices seemed to suppress the inflammation, but about September 20 it recurred in the same place, and went on to suppuration. As the abscess was large and deep-seated, involving the tissues about the great vessels in that region, it was promptly opened and 250 cubic centimeters of pus and blood clots were liberated. The cavity was then distended and irrigated with a solution of carbolic acid, and afterwards injected with iodoform and glycerine. The temperature now rapidly sunk to normal. The injection of iodoform and glycerine was several times repeated, and the discharge soon assumed a serous character, and very much diminished in quantity. Simultaneously the cough ceased, there were no more sweats and fever, and the signs of consolidation noticed about the right upper lobe of the lung cleared up almost entirely.

October 19.—The sinus leading to the abscess is still kept open, allowing a few drops of serum to escape.

November 1.—Abscess cavity entirely closed. During convalescence the patient made a peg leg for himself, and he was discharged November 19, 1887, with a firm and well-formed stump.

The accompanying photograph shows the stump to good advantage.

NOTE.—For report of re-amputation of leg, superior third—case of John Backlund—reported January 23, 1888.

This man walked to the hospital a few days ago, a distance of 1½ miles, on his wooden peg. He stated that he had followed his new vocation, that of attending a hog-ranch, constantly since his discharge from hospital without experiencing any pain or other trouble on account of the limb. The stump was firm and healthy; use of knee perfect.

CEREBRAL HEMORRHAGE—RIGHT HEMIPLEGIA—APHASIA—FROM MULTIPLE INJURY—RECOVERY.

BY HENRY W. SAWTELLE, SURGEON, U. S. MARINE HOSPITAL SERVICE.

Seaman Arthur Ingray; aged nineteen years; nativity, England; was admitted to the U. S. Marine Hospital, San Francisco, in the afternoon of April 23, 1887, from the British ship *Earl Derby*.

History.—I learned from the captain of the ship that on the morning of April 21, two days and one-half prior to admission, the boy fell a distance of 13 feet between decks; that when picked up he was insensible and bleeding from the mouth and nose, and had since been unconscious. I was unable to learn that there had been any discharge from the ears. He was brought to the hospital in an open wagon a distance of 5 miles.

Upon admission the patient was comatose, together with complete right hemiplegia, lateral deviation of head and eyes to left; incontinence of urine; difficult deglutition; constipation; respiration a little slower than normal; pulse 68; pupils normal as to size; right cornea apparently insensible to touch; ptosis right side; jaws clenched; mouth dry and stained with blood, but no wound of buccal cavity; no wound about head; no discharge from ears; large ecchymosed spot over right scapular region. Left parietal and occipital scalp œdematous to such an extent that the head presented a shapeless and an unsightly appearance. The condition of the patient pointed to a hemorrhage into the left motor area, or the so-called excitable area of the cortex described by Ferrier and Bastian. A fracture at the base of the skull located at the anterior fossa was also suspected, but later on this was excluded as one of the lesions. Ordered hair clipped and cool applications to head; 0.06 cubic centimeter ol. tiglii on tongue produced no effect. Administered 0.5 gm. each of hydr. chlor. mite and soda bicarb., followed in five hours by an enema. Result, free evacuation. Restlessness relieved by a solution of chloral hydr. and kali. brom. Nutriment, milk and beef tea.

April 24.—Head turned sharply to the left, and when moved to natural position it appears to give pain, and if unrestrained resumes its former unnatural position. Tongue dry and brown; sordes on teeth; left limbs move incessantly. Ordered extr. ergot fld. 4 cubic centimeters.

April 25.—Extremities cold; condition otherwise the same; heat applied to feet.

April 26.—Tendency to move body to the left, from the paralyzed side, and he would slip out of bed if not properly guarded.

April 27.—Exploration made by incision at boggy point in left parietal region; no fracture of vault; 120 cubic centimeters blood allowed to escape. Patient at once appeared easier; deglutition improved.

April 29.—More sensible; attempts articulation; involuntary movements of left limbs subsided.

April 30.—On protrusion of tongue to-day for the first time it was found to deviate to the right. A second incision this time at a boggy point near vertex, 120 cubic centimeters blood allowed to escape, which resulted as before in relief of restlessness; deglutition improved so that now he takes liquid nourishment by means of a tube quite readily.

May 2.—Ordered kali. iodid. 0.6 gm., hyd. bichlor. 0.003 gm. thrice daily.

May 3.—Another incision in scalp near the last gave further relief. In answer to a question patient indistinctly pronounced the words "All right."

May 6.—Drowsy; takes less nourishment. A swelling over the right mastoid process the size of a hen's egg was to-day freely incised and about 60 cubic centimeters of blood liberated. Sensation improved on the right side. Motion still impossible. Free and continuous discharge from incision near vertex.

May 7.—Better; variation of pupils thus far very slight. This morning for the first time the right pupil is more contracted than the left.

May 9.—A fly traversed the right cornea without exciting reflex action of any kind. Somewhat noisy delirium, alternating at times with weeping and moaning; very slight difference in pupils; both respond to light.

May 11.—Right conjunctiva now somewhat sensitive; some protrusion of right eye from paralysis of ocular muscles; slight tension of eye-ball. Leech applied to right temple, heat to feet; scalp well drained and doing well.

May 13.—Conjugate deviation disappeared; urine and fæces still passed involuntarily. Patient more quiet; mental condition improved. He now recognizes his attendant, and weeps when left alone. Kali. iod. increased from .6 gm. to 1.4 gm. ter in die.

May 16.—Ptosis on the right side still continues; eye-ball bulges yet, but less than formerly.

May 18.—Kal. iod. increased to 2.5 gm. ter in die. Mental condition much more favorable; speech greatly improved; can answer sufficiently to simple inquiry as to his wants; paralysis of limbs and face the same.

May 20.—Temperature for the last week a little subnormal. Faradic current begun on right side. The ptosis heretofore observed has disappeared. Small abscesses containing laudable pus have been opened at base of skull and in the region of the occiput.

May 22.—Power over sphincters of bladder and rectum restored.

June 9.—Steady but gradual improvement in comprehension and power of articulate speech.

June 22.—A gradually developed swelling in the scalp at the vertex was to-day opened and a small amount of pus evacuated; warm applications to feet now seldom required; sensation restored in paralyzed limbs.

June 26.—Kal. iodid. and hydr. bichlor. stopped; electricity continued.

July 6.—Scalp wounds healed; paralysis complete.

July 15.—Slight clonic spasms of ankle of affected limb have occurred occasionally upon touching the foot to the floor; arm reflexes exaggerated; extensors of leg and flexors of thigh are the only muscles of limbs whose function is restored, and the degree of impairment is considerable in these. Recovery from facial paralysis; no deviation of tongue. Patient bright; appetite good, and bowels regular. There is some impairment of memory, mainly of words. He understands anything spoken. Aphasia was at first complete; there was loss of memory of written and spoken language, and inability to articulate. Now memory of spoken language has been regained and the power of articulation and recognition of written words are rapidly increasing.

July 20.—Reads much better; paralysis the same, except that he can now semiflex the forearm on the arm, and slightly flex the foot on the leg; no command over fingers and toes.

July 25.—Slight contracture of forearm.

September 12.—For the last month a daily hypodermic of one-forty-eighth grain (.0014 gram) strychnine sulphate has been given in the fore-arm, chiefly with the result that he can flex and extend the hand, though the fingers are scarcely movable. He has been able to walk about rather stiffly for weeks. Electricity has been continued. Contracture of muscles of forearm, which at one time was quite marked, fast disappearing; clonic spasms of ankle have ceased. The muscles preserve nearly their normal size as compared with uninjured side. Ability to speak and read nearly fully restored. General health good.

September 14.—Discharged and sent home (to London) by British consul.

Range of temperature: Morning, 36° 4 C. to 37 .8° C.; the lowest on April 26, the highest April 24. Evening, 36 .5° C. to 39° C.; the lowest April 25, the highest April 30.

The temperature of right or paralyzed side exceeded that of the left or sound side, on several occasions during the first week, from two-tenths to four-tenths of a degree, after which there was scarcely a difference between the two sides. The steady progress made under treatment gave promise of perfect restoration, ultimately, notwithstanding the unfavorable manifestations of contracture noted during the last two months' stay in hospital. In view of the patholical changes succeeding cortical lesions of the brain, frequently mentioned by various authors, it is to be regretted that the return of the young man to his home in England precluded further observation in the case.

COMPOUND COMMINUTED FRACTURE BOTH BONES LEFT LEG—LACERATED WOUNDS OF FACE—RECOVERY.

By Surgeon Henry W. Sawtelle, U. S. M. H. S.

John Michaels; aged thirty-seven years; nativity, Sandwich Islands; a strong, robust man; was admitted to the U. S. marine hospital, San Francisco, Cal., February 3, 1888, from the steamer *City of Stockton*, with the following history: On the evening previous to admission, while the sailor was descending from aloft in the boatswain chair, the rope broke and he was precipitated feet foremost through the skylight into the cabin below, a distance of about 50 feet. When picked up he was unconscious and remained so for about seven hours. Soon after the arrival of the vessel in port, the following morning, he was placed in a carriage and brought to the hospital with simple wet dressings to the wounds. Upon examination I found a compound comminuted fracture of both bones of the left leg at the middle third. The tibia was fractured obliquely. I removed several spiculæ of bone at once, and irrigated the wound thoroughly with a solution of mercuric chloride 1-2000. The wound was dressed with Balsam Peru and the limb placed in a fracture box filled with bran. No untoward symptoms supervened, and on March 1 the wounds had entirely closed, whereupon a plaster of Paris bandage was applied. On removing the bandage about the 1st of April, it was ascertained that the fibula had united perfectly, but there was was some motion of the tibia at the seat of fracture. Splints were then applied for some time without benefit.

On April 27, 1888, the patient was etherized, the bone exposed by incision at the point of fracture, the extremities of the fragments were perforated with Brainard's drill, and two iron-wire nails about 4 centimeters in length were inserted into the fragments, thus bringing the bones closely and firmly together. The wound healed rapidly with no unfavorable signs, the nails remaining in the bones, and by the middle of June following the union was firm and the patient was able to walk without a stick. He was discharged June 30, 1888, with some thickening about the fractured tibia, but there was no tenderness whatever.

TWO INTERESTING CASES OF UNUNITED FRACTURE, ONE OF NINE YEARS' DURATION, SUCCESSFULLY OPERATED ON.

By Surgeon W. H. Long, M. H. S.

Case I.

George Williams; aged twenty-one; nativity, Michigan; admitted to U. S. Marine Hospital, Detroit, Mich., October 24, 1887, with compound comminuted fracture of both bones of the leg.

This injury was produced October 10 by the leg becoming entangled in a coil of rope which was tightened up by the moving vessel. Much injury was done to the soft tissues, and when he arrived at Detroit (having been transferred from Saint Ignace, where he had been under treatment for two weeks) the sloughing had left the fragments of bone bare. Although it looked as if amputation were almost inevitable, a conservative and antiseptic line of treatment was adopted. November 18 chloroform was administered, the loose fragments of bone removed, and the limb encased in a plaster-of-Paris splint, a fenestrum being left to allow the continuance of the antiseptic dressing of the wound. Healthy granulations gradually replaced the lost tissues and the wound healed perfectly. On removing the splint, however, it was found that nothing but ligamentous union had been secured between the fragments of the bones. On April 7, 1888, the patient was again put under chloroform and ether, the bones cut down upon, and their ends freshened (after dividing the ligamentous union) and the fragments brought together by silver wire, eight strands being twisted together. Shortly thereafter erysipelas unfortunately appeared and for sometime it was feared that the patient would lose his leg and possibly his life. Tinctura ferri chloridi, quinine, stimulants, and nourishing diet sustained his strength, and, with the local use of charcoal poultices, caused the erysipelas to subside gradually. A plaster-of-Paris splint was applied again, May 25, and when removed, early in July, perfect union had taken place. When discharged, August 9, he was rapidly recovering use of the limb.

Case II.

Frank Jarmey, aged thirty-one; nativity, Canada; admitted to U. S. Marine Hospital, Detroit, April 5, 1888, with ununited fracture of both bones of left forearm, which had existed for nine years.

This patient was put on preparatory treatment for improvement of his general condition. June 4, chloroform was administered; a short longitudinal incision was made on each side of the forearm over the seat of the fracture. A single strand of silver wire was found—evidence of an unsuccessful operation performed several years before. The ends of the fragments of both bones were sawed off and wired together, as in Case I. The wound was closed and treated antiseptically. A very large amount of callus was thrown out. This patient is still under treatment, and a perfect success is anticipated. The limb, however, will be nearly 3 inches shorter than its fellow.

LACERATED WOUND OF KNEE—RUPTURE OF INTERNAL LATERAL LIGAMENT.

By Passed Assistant Surgeon W. A. Wheeler, M. H. S.

William C.; aged twenty-four; nativity, United States; was admitted to marine ward, Sister's Hospital, Buffalo, N. Y., October 19, 1887.

His knee had been caught in the bight of a tow-line and he saved himself only by falling forward and thus disengaging the leg. The knee joint was opened and a large amount of synovial fluid escaped. The internal lateral ligament was torn from the head of the tibia. The wound was between 6 and 7 inches in length and about 4 inches in breadth throughout.

The wound was thoroughly cleaned and irrigated with a bichloride solution, 1–2,000; a dressing of iodoform gauze applied, and a side splint put on having a slight angle. The position of the wound prevented the use of a posterior splint. Ankylosis was expected, fibrous at least. The first dressing was changed at the end of three days because of the discharges. After that they were allowed to remain longer. At no time did the temperature exceed 37.5 C., or the pulse beat faster than 92 per minute. A bit of the torn ligament sloughed away. The wound slowly closed by granulation, the ligament became attached to the tibia, and the man made a good recovery. Before the wound was closed passive motion was practiced, which undoubtedly retarded the healing process, and also without doubt prevented ankylosis, which was very slight when he left the hospital, April 4, 1888.

STUDIES IN SERVICE STATISTICS.

SYPHILIS, PNEUMONIA, AND TYPHOID FEVER.

By Passed Assistant Surgeon Charles E. Banks, U. S. Marine Hospital Service.

The application of mathematics to medicine has its legitimate uses in defined limits. It is not possible to diagnosticate disease by the "rule of three," but we can forecast its results from the theories of percentage. The recorded reports of disease as treated by the officers of the Marine Hospital Service are of the greatest value to medical statisticians, and yet they are but seldom utilized. During the period of 1875 to 1885, inclusive, over 300,000 cases were treated, and records of each one made and the results reported. This constitutes a basis of information nearly unequaled in the annals of medicine in this country; but it is a matter of common observation that articles in encyclopædias written by the leaders of medical literature are often dependent for their conclusions upon the statistics of a few hundred cases of a localized character. The following examples of a casual study of the service statistics were undertaken to show the value of gleaning in this unworked field.

SYPHILIS.

From 1877 to 1885, inclusive, there were treated by this service 45,118 cases of syphilis, of which 20,415 were of the primary lesion, and 24,073 of the secondary type. Of the 20,415 cases of primary syphilis, 3,637 were classified as hard chancre, equivalent to 17.8 per cent., and 16,778 as soft chancre, equivalent to 82.2 per cent., a little less than 1 to 5 as the relative proportion of hard to the soft variety. Cornil, Syphilis (Simes and White, editors), page 85, says: "Puché, whose statistics were based upon the immense number of 10,000 chancres, found one indurated chanchre to four simple chancres." It will be noted that our experience practically tallies with Puché upon a basis of what Cornil might well call the doubly immense number of 20,000 chanchres, and it is gratifying to find ourselves in touch, as it were, upon the question of diagnosis with these distinguished Frenchmen, who may well be called the classical experts in veneral diseases. From a study of these statistics the following tabulations have been made:

I.—*Hard chancres.*

Districts.	1877.	1878.	1879.	1880.	1881.	1882.	1883.	1884.	1885.
North Atlantic	12	23	24	24	29	34	16	45	27
Middle Atlantic	17	31	104	106	36	25	22	56	18
South Atlantic	37	32	47	49	57	71	85	94	55
Gulf	22	4	23	23	26	28	43	57	38
Ohio	1	3	32	33	74	65	75	88	44
Mississippi	21	7	97	100	112	72	59	42	22
Great Lakes	5	21	91	97	169	199	170	204	79
Pacific	24	6	11	11	10	9	34	74	36
Total	139	127	429	443	513	503	504	660	319

II.—*Soft chancres.*

Districts.	1877.	1878.	1879.	1880.	1881.	1882.	1883.	1884.	1885.
North Atlantic	45	48	140	142	110	118	120	230	101
Middle Atlantic	104	118	262	273	165	206	205	393	246
South Atlantic	101	119	295	400	284	356	325	576	350
Gulf	113	119	205	208	223	182	191	333	204
Ohio	126	140	320	333	382	413	354	566	298
Mississippi	148	134	207	214	254	323	352	348	175
Great Lakes	89	108	335	321	414	412	395	709	257
Pacific	98	111	109	113	99	83	89	103	58
Total	824	897	1,953	2,004	1,930	2,093	2,121	3,258	1,698

III.—*Secondary.*

Districts.	1877.	1878.	1870.	1880.	1881.	1882.	1883.	1884.	1885.
North Atlantic	35	54	74	77	149	164	191	322	187
Middle Atlantic	126	114	295	299	326	436	349	697	256
South Atlantic	77	64	301	303	425	475	382	1,031	466
Gulf	78	73	155	158	336	337	360	608	380
Ohio	140	108	296	309	477	565	487	736	393
Mississippi	119	105	209	215	378	366	288	425	287
Great Lakes	79	101	518	525	675	745	983	2,143	1,109
Pacific	38	56	138	142	225	159	203	482	294
	692	675	1,986	2,028	2,991	3,247	3,248	6,464	3,372

IV.—*Consolidated table.*

	1877.	1878.	1879.	1880.	1881.	1882.	1883.	1884.	1885.	Total.
Hard chancre	139	127	429	443	513	503	504	660	319	3,637
Soft chancre	824	897	1,953	2,004	1,930	2,093	2,121	3,258	1,698	16,778
Total (primary syphilis)	963	1,024	2,382	2,447	2,443	2,596	2,625	3,918	2,017	20,415
Secondary syphilis	692	675	1,986	2,028	2,991	3,247	3,248	6,464	3,372	24,703
Total cases of syphilis	1,655	1,699	4,368	4,475	5,434	5,843	5,873	10,382	5,389	45,118
Number of cases of all diseases treated	15,175	18,223	20,922	24,860	32,613	36,184	40,195	44,761	41,714	304,464
Rates of syphilis to all cases	10.91	9.32	20.70	18.01	16.66	15.82	14.40	23.19	12.91	14.80

The above tables may perhaps be left to convey their own varied lessons without comment from me. The grand ratio of 14.8 cases of syphilis, primary and secondary, to the hundred of all classes treated will enable our medical officers to correct accurately the universal and erroneous impression obtaining in the public mind that our professional work is exclusively confined to venereal disease, which is ordinarily assigned to Jack as his particular brand by right of eminent domain.

PNEUMONIA.

The Medical News, of Philadelphia, in an editorial upon the subject of pneumonia in its issue of December 11, 1886, stated that "the ratio of mortality in the large general hospitals of this country is rarely below, more often above, 25 per cent., which represents about the average death rate from disease in the Northern and Southern armies during the civil war." In an article upon the same disease, entitled "Notes on the past and present mortality and treatment of pneumonia," Dr. Henry Hartshorne establishes by the proofs of percentage that the death rate from pneumonia has trebled during his personal observations, extending over nearly half a century. In the Pennsylvania Hospital during the three years 1845, 1846, 1847, it was 6.25 per cent.; in the years 1865, 1866, 1867, it was 18.50 per cent.; in 1884, 1885, 1886, it was 31 per cent., an increase of over 500 per cent. in forty years. It occurred to me that the author had passed by a most valuable set of statistics in his various sources of information, as nothing therein appeared relating to the mortality from pneumonia in the Marine-Hospital Service. My interest in the subject led me to compile the following table, exhibiting the experience of this disease as it occurs among seamen who are treated in our marine hospitals. If the statements quoted above as to the growing mortality from pneumonia are correct it will be seen that Jack fares well with us when sick with that disease. The table is arranged by years and geographical districts, and the figures show the death rate.

Year.	Districts.								
	North Atlantic.	Middle Atlantic.	South Atlantic.	Gulf.	Ohio.	Mississippi.	Great Lakes.	Pacific.	Average.
1880	13.9	18.7	23.1	11.8	22.5	9.1	25.0	31.3	18.8
1881	19.0	16.7	27.7	17.0	15.4	35.8	21.0	16.6	20.9
1882	20.0	33.3	22.5	31.5	20.6	14.6	20.8	11.8	20.9
1883	33.3	23.8	22.6	6.3	18.1	23.0	30.0	0.0	21.5
1884	4.4	33.3	15.0	16.6	7.0	19.2	31.5	11.8	15.2
1885	29.2	23.1	11.3	10.5	12.5	9.5	16.6	10.5	15.1
1886	21.0	9.1	22.9	19.3	12.5	25.8	23.8	57.1	21.4
1887	15.0	36.8	7.4	21.0	23.8	20.0	16.6	33.3	20.2
	16.4	24.1	18.9	16.9	15.4	20.4	22.2	18.0	16.4

The following table shows the number of cases and deaths in the same period, 1880–1887, inclusive, from this disease in each district:

District.	Cases.	Death.
North Atlantic	194	32
Middle Atlantic	145	35
South Atlantic	307	58
Gulf	183	31
Ohio	260	40
Mississippi	278	57
Great Lakes	171	38
Pacific	111	20
Total	1,649	311

Reports of the service since 1872, exclusive of three years which are not in this hospital library, show a total of 3,011 cases and 496 deaths, being a ratio of 16+ per cent., the same as shown above in the consolidated table.

ENTERIC (TYPHOID) FEVER.

It occurred to me that a similar examination of the statistics of typhoid fever as embodied in the Service reports might also be of value, not for purposes of invidious comparison, but as a guide to the results of our own work among a homogeneous class of men, living under well-known and clearly defined conditions. I quote from Pepper's "System of Medicine," Vol. I, page 310, article "Typhoid fever," by James H. Hutchinson, M. D. "During the twenty years from January 1, 1862, to December 31, 1881, 621 cases of typhoid fever, 121 of which were fatal, were admitted into the Pennsylvania Hospital." This may be taken as a sample of the results of treatment in one of the best of our civil hospitals, where skillful practitioners, with the aid of trained nurses, can utilize all the adjuncts of modern medicine for the benefit of their patients. The results as averaged from the figures quoted represents a death rate of 19.5 per cent. The following tables of statistics from the records of the Service show the results of treatment of this disease among sailors in marine hospitals:

Year.	Districts.								
	North Atlantic.	Middle Atlantic.	South Atlantic.	Gulf.	Ohio.	Mississippi.	Great Lakes.	Pacific.	Average.
1880	9.2	16.7	11.1	100.0	26.3	31.2	7.1	16.6	16.5
1881	16.7	27.3	20.0	33.3	37.5	21.3	15.0	25.0	23.1
1882	17.8	10.7	19.5	14.3	7.1	25.0	7.0	0.0	11.6
1883	9.5	19.2	12.5	7 1	15.7	15.0	8.4	25.0	14.9
1884	4.9	20.5	14.3	0.0	7.7	25.0	10.4	17.4	13.1
1885	9.1	20.0	21.4	25.0	31.2	33.3	11.8	0.0	16.0
1886	6.2	11.1	11.3	33.3	26.0	26.6	16.1	10.0	16.3
1887	7.7	16.6	21.7	75.0	18.0	12.5	8.6	40.0	15.1
	8.9	17.3	17.6	41.6	21.2	23.6	10.9	16.9	14.9

The following table shows the number of cases and deaths in the same period, 1880–1887, inclusive, from this disease in each district:

District.	Cases.	Deaths.
North Atlantic	304	27
Middle Atlantic	251	44
South Atlantic	176	31
Gulf	36	15
Ohio	174	37
Mississippi	114	27
Great Lakes	502	55
Pacific	77	13
Total	1,637	249

The records of the service since 1872, with the excepted years mentioned above, show a total of 2,503 cases and 374 deaths; an average of 14.9 per cent.

NECROSIS OF CLAVICLE AND TIBIA.

By Passed Assistant Surgeon S. T. Armstrong, M. H. S.

The following case is reported on account of the presence of a necrosed bone for many years without causing any marked irritation.

J. Curtis; aged thirty; a native of Virginia; was admitted to the U. S. Marine Hospital, New York, on January 24, 1888, for ulcers of the skin of the legs. He stated that in 1882 he knocked his shins against the ratlines, abrading the skin, and subsequent ulceration occurred. The ulcers healed, but have since been liable to recurrence on the slightest traumatism, and now have an unhealthy, indolent appearance. He had a chancre in 1880, and within a year a papular syphilitic eruption. He was placed on constitutional treatment, and bromine water applied to the ulcers. The latter became cleaner under this treatment, and on the 26th a sinus was noticed in the ulcer on the right leg; with the probe necrosis of the tibia was detected. On January 30 the patient was anæsthetized with chloroform, and, assisted by Surgeon Wyman and Assistant Surgeon Kinyoun, a straight incision was made along the crest of the tibia, the superficial necrosed bone chiseled out, and some pockets of pus infiltrated cancellous structure chiseled away. The leg was made bloodless by applying Esmarch's tourniquet, and the bone was packed with carbolized lint, so very little blood was lost. While he was under the anæsthetic Assistant Surgeon Kinyoun noticed a projection of necrosed bone from the center of the left clavicle. An examination showed that there had been an old fracture of the clavicle, with vicious union. Over an inch of the bone belonging to the internal fragment projected from the skin, which was red and granulating about the base of the necrosed bone. The skin was incised, the superficial fascia reflected back, and the necrosed bone, which extended to the sternal articulation, removed with bone forceps. The wound was united with catgut ligatures, and it and the tibia dressed antiseptically.

When the patient had recovered from the anæsthetics he stated that when he was seven years old, while seesawing, he fell to the ground and the plank on which he had been playing struck his left clavicle, fracturing it. He could feel the ends of the bones rub against each other; he does not know how long the arm was incapacitated, but he has never since been able to use the left arm as well as the right. Two years ago, while lifting a load of coal, he suddenly turned his head to the right and the bone perforated the skin; it had caused him no special inconvenience and he has never consulted a surgeon about it.

Although each wound suppurated freely, his general condition improved under tonic treatment, and on the 6th of February he was allowed to sit up. Several small shavings of necrosed bone were chiseled away from the tibia during the granulation repair. By the 29th of March the wound over the clavicle had healed. On the 2d of May the right leg was almost healed, and the patient, who had been assisting in the ward for some weeks, was discharged in order that he might fill a position.

MALFORMATION OF HAND—UNSUCCESSFUL SEPARATION OF WEBBED FINGERS.

By Passed Assistant Surgeon S. T. Armstrong, M. H. S.

Plastic surgery is a matter of such interest that the details of the following case seem worthy of record.

George Van Tassel; aged forty-five years; a native of New York; was admitted to the U. S. Marine Hospital, New York, February 27, 1888. On the 15th instant his hands were frostbitten while at sea. He applied ice at the time, but was unsuccessful in preventing the trouble. When admitted to the hospital his fingers were painful, and blisters had formed under the skin. His right hand was congenitally deformed, presenting the appearance shown in the accompanying photograph. The thumb is normal; there is hypertrophy of the index finger; the middle finger is absent, and the ring and little finger are webbed, with contraction of fascia, so that they can not be extended. The metacarpal bone of the middle finger is present, articulating with the phalanx of the ring finger. The extensor tendons are distinct and well marked; the ring finger being supplied with the one which should have gone to the middle finger. As a matter of interest regarding maternal impressions on the fœtus in utero, the patient stated he had heard that his mother, while pregnant, had been horrified on seeing the hand of a man who had the middle finger amputated.

The patient recovered slowly from the frostbite, but as soon as it was supposed the vitality of the fingers was restored, he acceded to having the webbed fingers separated. The operation was urged, even at his age, because he virtually had only three fingers, and the webbed ring and little finger was so contracted that its usefulness was limited. By separating them the normal condition of the tendons and bones promised two serviceable members; and as it was the right hand, the addition of another finger would be quite desirable. On March 29, after thorough cleansing of the hand, the web was cocainized, an Esmarch's compress wound about the wrist, and a tongue of skin was dissected up from the dorcal surface of the web. The latter was then incised from behind forward. To my chagrin I found the elasticity of the skin had been lost, and that the fingers could only be extended by making transverse incisions on the palmar digits. If this was done cicatrization would cause recontraction, and the condition be unimproved. The patient was asked for his consent to a dissection of the skin of the chest, and suturing of the flaps to the wounded edges, binding the arm to the chest until the vitality of the flap was assured, and then cutting off the pectoral attachment of the flap; but to this he would not accede. The density of the web prevented suturing the incised edges of the skin,

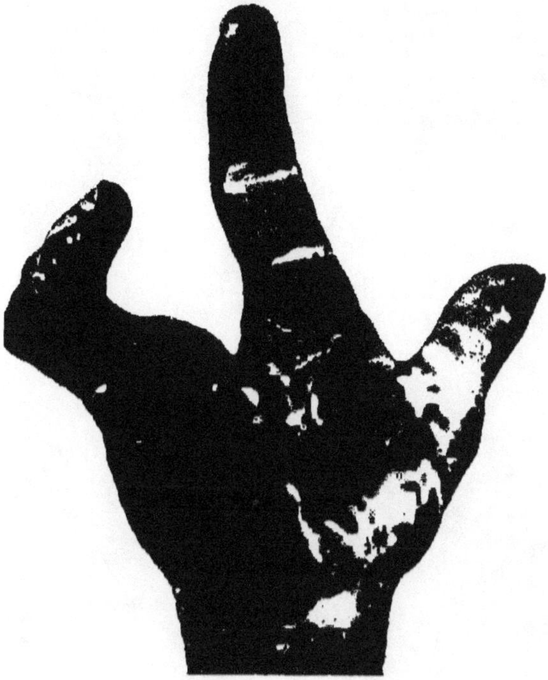

MALFORMATION OF HAND.—UNSUCCESSFUL SEPARATION OF WEBBED FINGERS.

and after controlling the hemorrhage by hot water, the wound was dressed antiseptically. So great was the pain in the hand during the night that he had to have morphine.

April 1.—Dressed the hand; no pus formation; 11th, applied skin grafts to granulating surfaces; the fingers are dresssed separately; 14th, placed a band about the wrist, attaching a rubber band to it so as to bring it over the commissure of the fingers and thus exercise traction on the granulating surface to prevent the adhesion of the granulating surface and gradual formation of the web; 16th, applied four skin grafts to granulating surface; 19th, the pain in the commissure is so great that the rubber band has to be dispensed with.

May 5.—The web is reforming; there is a severe neuralgia in the hand, which is not attributable to any condition present in it. Immersion in hot water was ordered. Going on leave of absence, the subsequent treatment of the case was in the hands of several officers. Granulation progressed slowly, and after it was accomplished the web was almost equal to its old dimensions. The neuralgia in the hand was so persistent that he was under treatment for it for almost a month, being discharged June 5, 1888. He would not assent to another operation.

The various methods of operating, according to Dr. J. A. Fort (Des difformités congénitales et acquires des doigts) for the relief of webbed fingers are (1) incision; probably the oldest procedure; (2) compression; Dupuytren advising compression over the commissure of the web; Maisonneuve, compression of the two surfaces of the web; and Delore, lead wire held by a band of elastic; (3) cauterization; Séverin advising caustic threads to destroy the web; (4) ligature; Ruttorffer employed lead wire at the commissure of the fingers and consecutive incision of the web; Chelins, a lead thread with bullets pendent from either end so as to cut the web by the tension of the wire; Beck employed a thread, replaced by a leaf of lead; (5) excision of cicatrix; Delpech advocated this procedure where the membrane had reunited; (6) destruction of cicatrization; Amussat burned the commissure with nitrate of silver; (7) Suture; Velpeau used a suture at the level of the commissure, with subsequent incision; Follin applied sutures to the lateral faces of the fingers and then incised; (8) autoplastic: Zeller cut a triangular flap from the dorsum of the web, incised the latter, and bringing this tongue of skin over the commissure, sutured it to palmar skin; Morel-Lavallee cut triangular flaps from dorsal and palmar surface of the web and united them at the commissure; Dieffenbach incised the palm, detached four flaps, and sutured laterally; Deces, reversing Zeller's method, cut a flap from the palmar web; Didot made an incision equal to the length of the web in the middle of the dorsal surface of one finger and the middle of the palmar surface of the other and dissected each flap from the finger and web and brought it around the exposed surface of the finger to which it remained attached. The procedure employed in this case was Zeller's, with subsequent application of Velpeau's compression at the commissure.

FRACTURE OF THE ISCHIUM.

By Passed Assistant Surgeon S. T. Armstrong, M. H. S.

The comparative rarity of fractures of this bone will probably be a sufficient excuse for recording the history of the following case:

Ben Olsen, aged thirty-eight, a native of Norway, was admitted to the U. S. Marine Hospital, New York, on November 14, 1887. He stated that fourteen days previous to his admission to the hospital, while clearing a line on board his vessel, he slipped and fell into the hold, a distance of 10 feet. He struck on the floor beneath, with the right thigh extended and receiving the shock of the impact. He was unable to rise, and after being taken to his bunk the thigh commenced to swell; the mate applied kerosene oil to relieve this condition. By the eighth day after the accident the thigh had returned to its natural dimensions.

When admitted he was examined by Interne W. P. Spratling, who noted that a "thorough examination revealed no fracture of any portion of the femur or pelvis. There seems to be a deep-seated bruise of the gluteal muscles, and there is tenderness on pressure over the knee-joint."

On the 5th the note was made on the history sheet: "Patient can put almost normal amount of weight upon the foot while standing; the tenderness about the hip joint is disappearing." The diagnosis of contusion of the thigh was made, though I understood that one medical officer who saw the case believed it to be an impacted fracture of the femur. On the 11th, the case having come under my charge, a very thorough examination was made, as the persistence of pain in the right hip seemed scarcely in consonance with a contusion. The usual manipulations of the thigh were made, forced flexion causing pain referred to the region of the head of the femur. Similar pain was caused by rotation outward. The pain was not sharp, as it would have been in case of fracture of the neck of the femur, nor was the foot everted when the patient lay upon his back; so any injury to the femur was excluded. Passing the index finger of the right hand into the rectum and feeling along the ramus of the right ischium, an unevenness was detected. When the thigh was flexed or rotated, motion could be felt at this point; the line of fracture was transverse. The patient was examined by the other officers on duty at the hospital and the diagnosis confirmed.

The patient was put upon his back, with support to the right leg to secure immobility. He was not very intelligent and was willful, the nurse informing me that he would move whenever possible. In consequence, on the last of December motion was still detected at the site of fracture. He was allowed to sit up and walk with a crutch, as it was believed that the thigh would make extension on the bones and the motion excite the deposit of new bone. January 30 he was returned to bed, and on the 5th of March he was allowed to sit up, as there seemed to be bony union then.

The use of the lower extremity was regained very slowly, and when he dispensed with his crutches he had a decided limp on account of shortening of the leg. He was discharged from the hospital July 5.

All works on general surgery refer to this fracture as unusual. Gross (Surgery, vol. I, p. 961) states that there may be either shortening or retention of natural length of the lower extremity. In Hamilton's excellent monograph on fractures he refers to the necessity of rectal, or in females of vaginal, examination. The history of this case, it is believed, will show the necessity of making a rectal examination in all cases of injury to the thigh where fracture of the femur is suspected but not present.

PYÆMIA CONSEQUENT UPON WOUND OF TOE—DEATH—ILLUSTRATING THE NECESSITY OF ANTISEPSIS.

By Passed Assistant Surgeon S. T. Armstrong, M. H. S.

It is believed that the following case clearly illustrates the necessity of careful antisepsis in the treatment of all wounds, however seemingly unimportant.

Carl Willers, aged forty-two, a native of Germany, was admitted to the U. S. Marine Hospital, New York, January 5, 1888. He stated that upon January 3 a block fell upon the right foot, lacerating the great and second toe. He was taken to Long Island College Hospital, and there a bandage was applied to the foot. When he was admitted to the Marine Hospital his foot was covered with a dirty, blood-stained dressing, the odor from which was very bad. Removing the dressing, dead skin covered with dirt was found over the surface of the wound; the foot was cleansed as much as possible by washing, and poultices were applied during the night. On the 6th his foot was kept in a hot brominated solution all day.

January 7.—There is so much sloughing tissue about the end of the great toe that amputation is necessary; the base of the toe was constricted with a rubber band, cocaine introduced, and the toe amputated; the artery was closed by torsion, capillary hemorrhage staunched with hot water, and the flaps united by catgut sutures. After the operation he felt considerable pain in the stump, and after the ward visit in the evening he had a chill and fever during the night.

January 8.—He complained of pain in the toe and foot; his pulse was 126; temperature, 38.8° C. His facial expression was anxious. Quinine, .30 gm., was ordered every three hours. He felt no better in the evening, and the medicine was continued during the night.

January 9.—He felt better this morning. The foot was not swollen, nor was it painful except on a pressure. Fever was not present, but commenced during the day, and in the evening iron was added to the quinine.

January 10.—He felt nauseated this morning. The skin posterior to the toe was red, and the leg was painful upon pressure. Carbolic acid was applied to the leg, and he was removed from the surgical ward. The morning temperature was 38.8°, pulse 110, respiration 24; in the evening the temperature was 39.2° C., pulse and respiration as in the morning. Acetanilide, .30 gm., was ordered every two hours.

January 11.—Temperature 38.5° in the morning, 39.3° in the evening. The entire leg was very painful along the line of the lymphatics.

January 12.—Temperature 38.6° in the morning, 39° in the evening. Patient weaker and delirious; moans about the pain in his leg. He will eat nothing; stomach irritable. Brandy ordered every two hours.

January 13.—Temperature 38.7° in the morning, 39.4° in the evening. He rested very badly last night; delirium increasing. The wound of the toe has been dressed openly since the 10th; there is but little discharge, but the tissues are gangrenous. The patient died on the 14th.

The necropsy was made fifty-four hours *post mortem*. *Rigor mortis.* Livores. Amputation wound of right great toe with sloughing of the adjacent tissue, the sloughing extending along the sole of the foot to the external malleolus of the ankle. The lymphatic ducts along the leg and thigh were found filled with pus.

There were old pleuritic adhesions about each lung. Heart and abdominal viscera were normal.

The treatment of the case was antiseptic *ab initio*, and the fact that the chill occurred a few hours after the operation goes far towards proving pyæmic infection of the leg at that time. A careful review of the dressings showed no extraneous source of infection, and the foul condition of the wound when first treated points to original wound infection.

THE CURE OF BUNION BY RESECTING THE FIRST METATARSAL BONE.

By Passed Assistant Surgeon S. T. Armstrong, M. H. S.

While it is not believed that bunions are more frequent among seamen than among any other class of laborers, yet it is believed that the experience of the officers of this Service will testify to their prevalence among the class of men coming under their observation. Rarely, however, is any special treatment requested, as an aperture cut in the boot or shoe, while not adding to the appearance of that article of apparel, will yet suffice to relieve the discomfort of the enlarged joint. The bunion is generally accepted as something that is inevitable, and rarely does a patient ask to be relieved of this discomfort.

In a paper presented to the Tennessee State Medical Society (*vide* Transactions, 1888), the writer reviewed the history of resection of the head of the first metatarsal bone for the relief of this condition, and advocated a more frequent resort to an operation, which, if properly performed, is painless and as free from danger as is any operation which involves the solution of continuity of the tissues. Only one fatal case was reported (Dr. Pooley: Medical Record, 1875, page 372), and in this instance the patient was seventy-five years of age; there was sloughing tissue in the joint at the time of operation, and the death in eight days was undoubtedly due to septicæmia existing at the time of operating.

The method of operating which has been employed is first a thorough cleaning of the foot with a nail-brush, and warm bichloride of mercury solution. The blood vessels of the foot are controlled by a piece of rubber tubing, or Esmarchs's contractor, applied about the ankle, and from 30 to 60 minims of a 4 per cent. solution of cocaine is injected about the joints. An incision is made over the joint, along the internal border of the foot, the tissues held apart by sharp-pronged retractors, the periosteal tissues separated from about the bone, and the head of the first metatarsal bone resected with Wyeth's exsector. In lieu of this latter instrument Hays's saw may be used, although it will not prove to be so convenient. The ligaments are cut with the knife and the bone removed. The constricting tubing is released and a little bleeding encouraged, any spurting vessel being seized in hæmostatic forceps. A generous use of hot water will soon staunch the capillary hemorrhage, and the wound can be dressed with iodol, the edges satured, a wad of cotton placed between the toes so as to approximate the base of the great toe to the stump of the metatarsal bone, and the wound dressed antiseptically. There is rarely secondary fever, and the wound heals by granulation. It is desired to refer in this paper to two points which were not appreciated at the time of writing the former paper, viz, the necessity of resecting the head of the bone sufficiently far back; and, secondly, of removing the sesamoid bone in the flexor brevis pollicis. The reasons for these are that there is the possibility of exostosis of the former, and in the latter there is a tendency to hypertrophy of the sesamoid bones, rendering the subsequent condition of the patient but little better than before the operation. The history of the following case will demonstrate this:

John Quinn; aged forty-five; a native of New York; a steam ship fireman; was admitted to the U. S. Marine Hospital, New York, December 24, 1887. He had suffered from bunions on each foot for six or seven years. Some months previous to his admission to the hospital the skin over each bunion became perforated and a sticky white fluid was discharged. On the right metatarso-phalangeal articulation there was a round, unhealthy looking ulcer about three-fourths of an inch in diameter; there was marked hollax valgus. Over the left metatarso phalangeal articulation there was a small aperture, exuding a glairy fluid. As he had a history of venereal disease, he was placed on constitutional treatment, with local applications to the bunions. No improvement followed this plan of treatment, and on January 20, 1888, having consented to an operation on the right foot, the head of the first metatarsal bone was resected as described. There was no subsequent trouble with the wound, healing by granulation occurring. About the last of January the left bunion became worse, and the necessity of operative treatment was so manifest that on Februry 9 it was operated on similarly. The case was discharged from treatment March 17, and he was able to walk very well. After he had been on his feet for some time he noticed that there was swelling about the right metatarsal joint, the inconvenience becoming so great that he called at the out-patient office, and received treatment. But the condition did not improve, and he sought re-admission to the hospital for relief. Less bone had been removed in the operation on the right than in that on the left bone; the latter had caused him no trouble, and the articulation was good. Examination of the right joint showed inflamed skin, and a condition of exostosis of the head of the first metatarsal bone. The necessity of a second operation was explained to him, and he greatly desired it. The operation was the same as before, except that the sesamoid bones, which were found hypertrophied, were removed. Those under the left great toe were removed at the first operation, on account of necrosis. The temperature chart showed no pyrexia, the dressings were changed every other day, and the wound healed by granulation. Examination of the piece of metatarsal bone removed showed that it was covered with cartilage and the exostosis was caused by inflammatory hypertrophy.

The period during which the patients are confined is comparatively short, and it is believed the comfort with which the boot may be worn compensates for the time consumed by the treatment.

EXCISION OF TUNICA VAGINALIS FOR THE CURE OF HYDROCELE.

By Passed Assistant Surgeon S. T. Armstrong, M. H. S.

In a consideration of the treatment of hydrocele of the tunica vaginalis, the records of this service show that 172 cases have been treated from 1881 to 1887; of these 108 were treated with iodine, 2 presumably successfully; 2 treated with iodine failed; 3 were undetermined. Of 10 treated by carbolic acid injection, 1 was successful. This leaves 49 cases undetermined. The proportion of successful cases treated by iodine injection is very gratifying, and would seem to indicate its efficiency.

Year.	Number of cases.	Tincture iodine treatment.
1881	20	8, incised and packed with lint, 1.
1882	22	15, carbolic acid, 3.
1883	18	6, carbolic acid, 6.
1884	26	22, carbolic acid 1, unsuccessful.
1885	26	21, successful; 2 failures; 3 undetermined.
1886	32	16, tapped, 11.
1887	28	20
Total	172	108

In the following case, injection of tincture of iodine twice failed to cure a hydrocele, and excision of the sac had to be resorted to:

William Plumette; aged twenty; a native of France, a quadroon, was admitted to the U. S. Marine Hospital, New York, on February 14, 1888. About the first of January the patient acquired a case of gonorrhea; and about the same time he noticed an enlargement of the right testicle, which inconvenienced him so much that he secured admission to the hospital. He was treated at first by Assistant-Surgeon J. J. Kinyoun, who tapped the sac on February 15 with a sterilized instrument, removing about 200 cubic centimeters of clear fluid. The character of the fluid was such that it was employed for bacteriological cultivations; thus showing only an indirect connection, if any, between the hydrocele and the gonorrhea. The scrotum was supported in a suspensory bandage.

February 22.—The hydrocele having refilled, it was tapped and tincture of iodine injected.

February 29.—Patient transferred to my wards. The right scrotum was as large as a goose egg. In introducing the needle of an exploring syringe, the tunica vaginalis was so tough and thickened that it was thought the testicle was penetrated; 150 cubic centimeters of flocculent fluid was evacuated, and 3 grams of tincture of iodine injected. Severe pain and burning followed the injection.

March 3.—The inflammatory action resulting from the injection of iodine was so severe that applications of lead and opium wash were made and the scrotum supported. By the 7th the lotion was discontinued, but the patient was kept in bed. Ung. hydrarg. and ichthyol ointment (60 per cent.) were used externally in the vain hope of securing absorption.

April 2.—The hydrocele was tapped and a few cubic centimeters of fluid evacuated. The sac was so thick that it was evidently impossible for an adhesive inflammation to occur, and its removal was urged upon the patient.

April 9.—The patient was chloroformed, the pubes and scrotum cleansed with a bichloride solution, and an elliptical incision made in the skin of the scrotum; the sac was dissected away from the connective tissue, incised, and cut away close to the testicle; the covering of the testicle was scraped, a few small blood-vessels ligated, the capillary hemorrhage controlled by hot water, a drainage tube introduced, and the wound united by catgut sutures. The dressing was thoroughly antiseptic.

April 10.—Pulse and temperature good; in the evening the temperature was 38° C.

April 11.—Temperature, a. m., 38.5°; p. m., 38.1°. Quinine, 30 grains given every two hours during the day. The wound was dressed; free purulent discharge from the drainage tube.

April 12.—Temperature, a. m., 39°; p. m., 37.8°; carbolized compresses were applied to the scrotum every two hours during the day.

April 13.—Temperature, a. m., 38.6°; p. m., 38.1.° Wound doing very well.

April 14.—Temperature, a. m., 37.9°; p. m., 37.9°. The wound had united by first intention, excepting at the upper and lower angles, from each of which there was purulent discharge. The temperature after this date varied, occasionally reaching 39°, though usually about 37.4°. By the 30th the scrotum was almost normal in size and the purulent discharge small in quantity. He was discharged, recovered, May 14.

It is fortunate that hydroceles of this character are rarely met with in this country, though Sir Joseph Fayrer in a discussion before the Royal Medical and Chirurgical Society last February stated "that hydroceles were common in India and that they had thicker walls and were larger than those seen in England; he had been inclined to consider them as part of a constitutional state, as being at least connected with, if not caused by malarial fever; the sac was rigid with cartilaginous plates; for such cases no treatment availed except excision." If malarial fever has any pathogenical relation to the development of hydrocele, this latter disease should be much more prevalent in the semi-tropical portion of the Mississippi Valley than my experience shows it to be. This opinion is supported by the statistics of Charity Hospital, New Orleans, in which from 1880 to 1885, inclusive, 38,806 patients were treated, and there were only 31 cases of hydrocele in whites and 10 in negroes.

Excision of the sac of a hydrocele is a reversion to a primitive method of treatment. Celsus (Lib. VII, Cap XXI) says: In humoral collections in the scrotum let it out and cut away any membrane which may contain it. This practice was also in vogue among the Arabians, as Abal Kassem (Chirurg. lib. II, § 62) advises the extirpation of the sac when possible. Within recent years the general treatment of hydrocele by this method has been recommended, because no relapse would follow. Bergman has notably supported it, and W. W. Keen (Medical News, April 7, 1888), in reporting a case of radical cure by excising the parietal portion of the sac, recommends it. Yet Henry Morris (British Medical Journal, 1888, Vol. I, p. 466) reports two cases of hydrocele in which he excised the sac, with subsequent recurrence of the hydrocele. Even this operation, then, is not uniformly successful.

Volkmann (Berlin Klin. Woch., January 17, 1876), in a paper on the antiseptic method in the treatment of hydrocele, advises incising the scrotum and the sac, securing bleeding vessels, and syringing the sac with a 3 per cent. solution of carbolic acid. This is a modification of the treatment employed by Galen (Meth. Med., lib. XIV), who introduced a seton; and analogous to that of Paulus Arginetus (Lib. VI, c. 62), who not only incised the tunica but occasionally cauterized it. Rhazes' recommendation to incise the sac every time it refilled, shows that this operation was not always successful; Jean de Vigo (Sprengel, T. VII, page 193) opened old hydroceles twice a year—in the spring and autumn; and in two hundred and fifty-four cases of this operation by Volkmann, Kuester, Weir, Englisch, Albert, Lister, and Jacobson, reaccumulation occurred in three, and one died of septicæmia, and one of pyæmia (Medical News, May 3, 1884).

Presumably it was on account of reaccumulation of fluid after operating that other treatment was sought for; as early as 1677 Jean Lambert (Les Comment. et Beav. Chir.) advised the injection of strong solutions of corrosive sublimate. James Earle (Treatise on Hydrocele, 1791) used port wine with a decoction of rose leaves. Sir Ranald Martin (Lancet, April 30, 1842) advocated the injection of tincture of iodine, and his method has given general satisfaction. With this method as competent a surgeon as Billroth (Weiss, Wien. Med. Woch., No. 4, 1884) in one hundred and sixty-six cases had six recurrences and five cases of suppuration. The priority of using injections of carbolic acid has not yet been decided, I believe, but it is for several reasons preferable to the iodine.

All methods employed show in their statistics a percentage of recurrences, and as the injection method is less dangerous to the patient, it should be recommended by the surgeon unless he is afflicted with a *cacoethes scribendi.*

In cases of recurring hydrocele, in which changes have occurred in the character of the sac, treatment by excision will find a legitimate field.

ANEURISM ABDOMINAL AORTA, SACCULAR—RECOVERY.

By Passed Assistant Surgeon P. C. Kalloch, U. S. Marine-Hospital Service.

Fred. Charleston; aged twenty-seven years; nativity, Finland; admitted to the U. S. Marine Hospital, San Francisco, Cal., March 22, 1888.

In 1879 he was treated in an hospital at New York for venereal sores, four in number, the scars of which remain, one of them being on the skin midway of the penis; also a swelling in each groin appearing one month after the sores, both suppurating. Secondary eruption then occurred, for which medicine was taken during six months.

He was well until Sepember, 1886, when he was admitted to hospital at Sydney, Australia; diagnosis according to his statement being dyspepsia and neuralgia of chest. The only sympton was a steady burning pain confined to the side and back. "The examinations were very superficial." He was not benefited by the treatment at Sydney, but the pain afterwards subsided and was entirely absent during one year, when it began again gradually.

When admitted to the hospital here, he had slight pain through the day; getting severe after supper about 5 p. m., continuing up to 2 a. m., when he would fall asleep. Upon waking up in the morning, he would have no pains until after breakfast, when it would be slight, as stated above. The severe pain alluded to was of a burning character, and when it was greatest, he was unable to lie quietly in bed, but felt that he must get up and move about.

Upon examination, the patient in a recumbent posture, a distinct pulsating tumor is noticed in the gastric region, to the left of median line and 6 centimeters below the ensiform appendix. The pulsations, which are expansive in character, are felt over an area of 7 centimeters. A bruit is distinctly heard.

Treatment.—Iodide of potassium was given continuously in doses of 10 grains, *t. i. d.* A light diet, consisting of milk, beef tea, toast, and mush, restricted somewhat in quantity. The patient was placed in a plaster dressing, applied in the usual manner, extending from the nipple line to the knees, leaving openings sufficient for the performance of natural functions.

The application of the plaster was used to enforce perfect quiet, thus avoiding the natural increase of the heart's action attending movements of the body.

June 7, 1888.—*Result.*—The pain gradually disappeared, so that five weeks after the application of the plaster it was entirely gone, and has not been felt since. The pulsation and bruit have also disappeared entirely. There is a hard, ill-defined tumor about 8 centimeters in diameter at the aneurismal site. The abdominal walls are thicker from accumulation of fat during the patient's treatment. He was discharged June 16, 1888.

NOTE.—*Vide* case of abdominal aneurism treated by rest successfully by Passed Assistant Surgeon John Guiteras, Marine-Hospital Service, New York, Medical Journal, December 25, 1886.

A CASE OF RUPTURE OF TENDON OF QUADRICEPS EXTENSOR FEMORIS—RECOVERY.

By Passed Assistant Surgeon P. M. Carrington.

John Miller; aged sixty-five years; a native of Germany; was admitted to the U. S. Marine hospital, San Francisco, Cal., on November 25, 1887, and gave the following history: "Six days ago, November 19, while walking rapidly on a plank sidewalk, one of the boards broke under my weight, throwing me to the ground. I caught on the right knee, squarely and forcibly, and heard and felt something snap just above the knee cap. I was unable to rise, and was taken up and carried on board by the crew."

An examination showed that a rupture existed just above the patella. The muscle was retracted several inches, and there was a deep sulcus between it and the patella. There was found to be fluid exuded at the seat of rupture; it was removed by aspiration—about 75 cubic centimeters sero-sanguinolent. The ruptured ends were brought into apposition and retained by bandages and posterior splint. Later on the leg and thigh were put up in plaster, and by January 20, 1888, firm union had taken place. The patient was now allowed to walk about using crutches, but, being of a very nervous, excitable nature, he, on January 29, had another fall, injuring the knee and bringing about an effusion, which was again relieved by aspiration, 25 cubic centimeters of bloody fluid being removed. The tendon was not again ruptured. He recovered slowly from the last injury and was discharged June 11, 1888.

Though permanently disabled for further sea service, he is able to walk quite well with the aid of a stick, and can perform light work.

In 1874 this man ruptured the left quadriceps extensor tendon by a similar accident. From this he recovered, but three months later had a fall and reruptured the tendon, the final result being imperfect union and permanent lameness.

This case is thought worthy of report, as a rare form of injury which has occurred twice to the same man.

TWO INTERESTING CASES OF ENTERIC FEVER.

By Assistant Surgeon F. C. Heath, M. H. S.

Case I.

William Sykes; age twenty-three; nativity, Canada; admitted to U. S. Marine Hospital, Detroit, Mich., June 12, 1888.

This case is interesting because of its long course, the continued high temperature during the third week of the fever (see accompanying chart), the character and duration of the delirium, and an accident which occurred during the delirium.

History.—The patient had been sick two weeks before his admission to hospital, and over seven weeks more elapsed before his temperature reached normal for two successive days. At 6 p. m., June 12, it was 39.8° C., pulse 100, respiration 24, tongue covered with a white coating, abdomen tender on palpation, with gurgling at ileo-cæcal valve, rose-spots, diarrhœa, anorexia, and headache—a clear case of enteric fever at the end of the second week. For the greater part of the week following his temperature was 40° C., or over, and at 6 p. m., June 17, it reached 40.6°. The delirium began about the middle of the third week and continued for nearly three weeks. At times it was difficult to keep the patient in bed, and men were detailed for that purpose, night and day—later, although quiet most of the time, he would tear his bed-clothes at night into many pieces. On the morning of June 26 he swallowed the clinical thermometer which the nurse had put under his tongue. He was given mustard for emesis; this failing, oleum ricini was administered, in the hope of facilitating the passage of the thermometer through the bowels. It remained in, however, until July 8, a period of twelve days, when it passed through the anus unbroken, the mercury registering 10.4° F. As shown by the chart, the patient's temperature was normal when he swallowed the thermometer, rose next day to 38°, and with one exception never went below that until after the instrument passed out and seldom thereafter went above it. This patient was very weak at times, but when discharged was gaining strength and flesh rapidly. The line of treatment pursued in this case (except a little opium and potass. bromidi to control delirium) was milk and whisky every three hours and frequent spongings with dilute alcohol—a course much relied upon at this station and more than justified by its fruits, the mortality from enteric fever being but one in forty cases from January 1, 1887, to January 1, 1888.

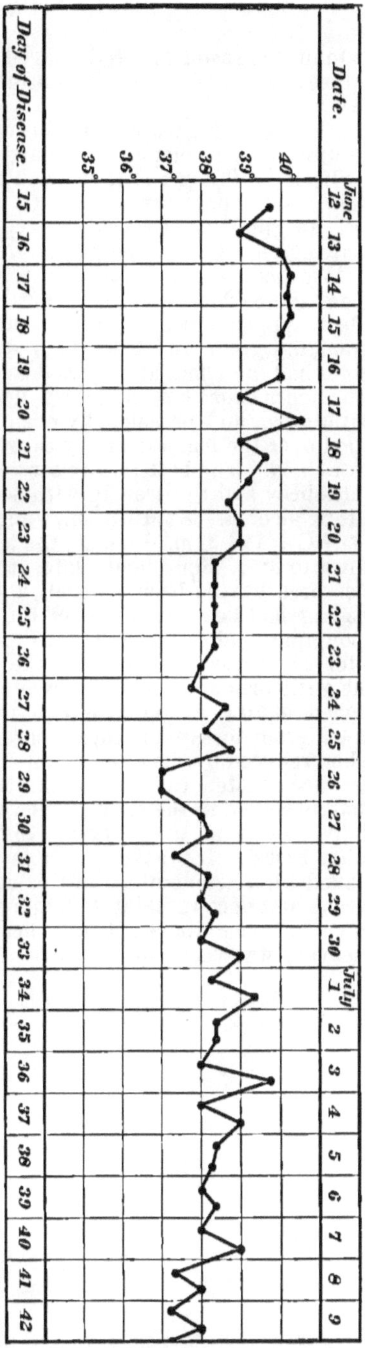
Date.
June 12
13
14
15
16
17
18
19
20
21
22
23
24
25
26
27
28
29
30
July 1
2
3
4
5
6
7
8
9
Day of Disease.
15
16
17
18
19
20
21
22
23
24
25
26
27
28
29
30
31
32
33
34
35
36
37
38
39
40
41
42
35°
36°
37°
38°
39°
40°

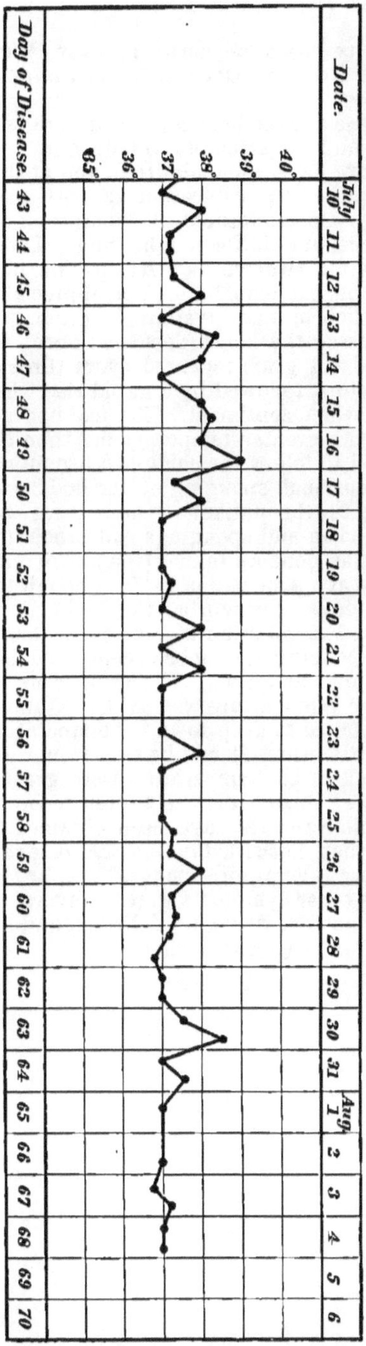
Date.
July 10
11
12
13
14
15
16
17
18
19
20
21
22
23
24
25
26
27
28
29
30
31
Aug. 1
2
3
4
5
6
Day of Disease.
43
44
45
46
47
48
49
50
51
52
53
54
55
56
57
58
59
60
61
62
63
64
65
66
67
68
69
70
35°
36°
37°
38°
39°
40°

CASE II.

John Ferguson (colored); aged twenty-two years; nativity, West Indies; admitted to U. S. Marine Hospital, Detroit, Mich., June 13, 1888.

The interesting features in this case are the long-continued high temperature (see accompanying chart) and the attempts to reduce it.

History.—Patient had been sick five days when admitted, and at that time his temperature was 40° C., pulse 90; respiration 22, with diarrea, gurgling at ileocæcal valve, some tenderness on pressure over that region. Coated tongue, ear-ache, and dullness of hearing. Later, he lost his hearing almost entirely for two weeks. Antipyrine in 1 gram and 0.66 gram doses relieved his ear-ache, but had no appreciable effect upon his temperature. Antifebrin was given in 0.2 gram, 0.33 gram, 0.4 gram, and 0.66 gram doses—the latter dose but once; 0.2 gram had no effect at all; 0.33 and 0.4 gram repeated every three or four hours caused a temporary decline, followed by a rapid rise when withdrawn, and occasionally even when continued. The ice bag applied over the femoral artery caused a greater temporary fall than the antifebrin. The best results seemed to follow the combined use of the antifebrin and the ice-bag with occasional sponging of the body with dilute alcohol. At 10 p. m., June 24, the patient's temperature was 40.4° C.; at 4 a. m., June 25, the ice bag and spongings had brought it down to 38°. Four hours later it had gone up to 39° (the antipyretic measures having been omitted), and at 6 p. m. it was 40.8°, although the ice-bag had been used part of the day. Antifebrin, the ice-bag, and spongings had reduced it to 37° at 1 a. m., June 26, but seven hours later it had risen again to 40.8°, the sponging having been continued, but the antifebrin and ice-bag were stopped at 1 a. m. The latter were resumed at 10 a. m. and at 6 p. m. the temperature was 38° C. Quinine in 0.2 gram doses every three hours failed to keep down the temperature when reduced by the ice-bag and antifebrin. It will be seen from what has been stated that the fluctuations of the temperature were greater than is shown in the chart, which was made from the figures recorded daily at 8 a. m. and 6 p. m. Similar results have been obtained in other cases. It was remarkable that, notwithstanding the long-continued high temperature in this case (averaging about 40° C. for two weeks and once reaching 41.2°), his other symptoms were so favorable, pulse but once above 100, diarrhea not excessive, no delirium, and his recovery was very rapid after the fever began to decline.

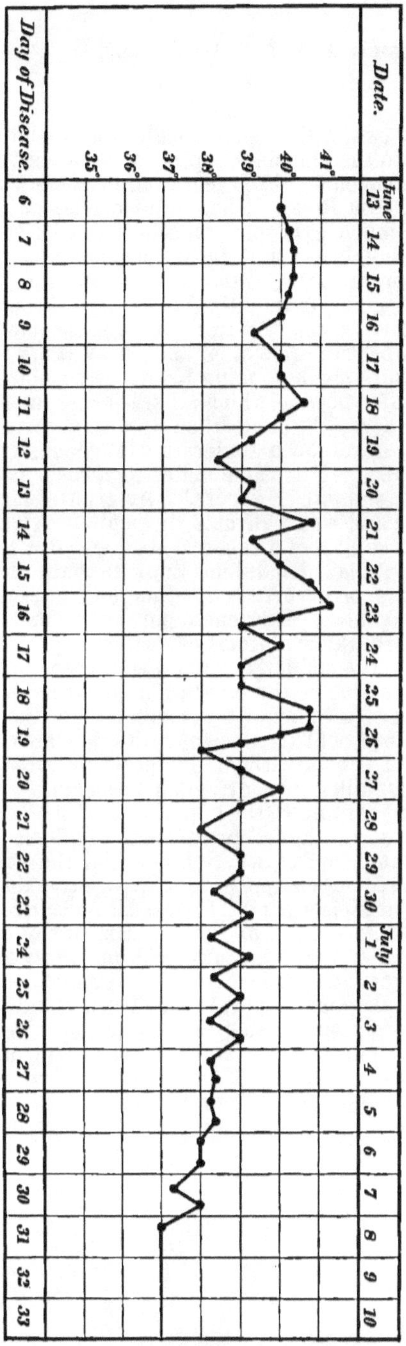
Date.
Day of Disease.
35°
36°
37°
38°
39°
40°
41°
June 13
14
15
16
17
18
19
20
21
22
23
24
25
26
27
28
29
30
July 1
2
3
4
5
6
7
8
9
10
6
7
8
9
10
11
12
13
14
15
16
17
18
19
20
21
22
23
24
25
26
27
28
29
30
31
32
33

MULTIPLE NEURITIS.

By T. M. Holmes, A. A. S. M. H. S., Rome, Ga.

G. H. M.; aged twenty-two, a Georgian; made application October 18, 1886, for admission into the Marine Hospital at this port, with the following history: He had been for three years acting as clerk upon the steam-boats plying the Coosa River. The nature of the position was such as to subject him to much exposure, especially during the winter months, when freights were heavy and the atmospheric changes extreme. He was of an imprudent disposition and was constantly exposing himself unnecessarily, going frequently during the coldest weather without his coat, and at times, when very tired, falling asleep in the open air, where the rain would beat in upon him, and on awaking would be so stiff and cold as to require much rubbing before being able to move. Moreover, owing to the influences to which all sea-faring men are subject in a greater or less degree, he had fallen into intemperance, and though he had probably never been under the influence of alcoholic spirits in an extreme degree, yet he came under that large and unfortunate class commonly denominated "topers." As a natural result he had become much bloated and was a chronic dyspeptic. Again, about five years ago, he was the subject of a venereal sore, and was treated by the town charlatan for syphilis. He did not know that the charlatan's diagnosis was a correct one, or if correct, whether he had received the proper treatment, but had never experienced any inconvenience from the trouble or noticed any of the symptoms of tertiary syphilis.

For some weeks prior to the sudden onset of his disease, he had been complaining of persistent pains in the muscles of his arms, back, and legs, which seemed to be of a rheumatic character. For these, I had been treating him in the out-patient department with salicylate of sodium, but with only partial relief, when, without any other prodromic symptoms, he experienced an inability to control his lower limbs. He had started to ascend the steps leading to the upper deck of the boat, when suddenly his legs gave way, and he fell prostrate to the floor. He was immediately carried to the hospital, where I saw him the succeeding day. I found him in the recumbent position with an utter inability to move himself or any part of himself, in the least. He had "drop wrist" and "drop feet," and had no control of the muscles of volition. He could not change his arms or legs from any position into which they might helplessly fall. Every muscle in his body seemed to share in a greater or less degree in this general paralysis. Even the diaphragm was apparently totally paralyzed, causing the respiration to be entirely thoracic, about thirty per minute, deep and labored. The pulse was quick and small and numbered 130 to 135 per minute. Hyperæsthesia and hyperalgæsia were prominent symptoms, it being almost impossible to even touch him, as in the changing of his position for his comfort, without giving him great pain. There were constant and almost unbearable pains in his feet, legs, and hands, characterized by a tingling sensation, paræsthesiæ and formication. These pains were so great as to produce insomnia, and these two symptoms were the bane of his existence, from which he never failed to pray me at each visit for relief. They were also to him unfailing barometers, always increasing in intensity a few hours antecedent to a change of the atmosphere to a state of greater humidity. His extremities were warm to the touch, but warm applications would relieve the pains momentarily. There was almost continually on the patient's face an expression that betrayed his inner feelings of discomfort. Every muscle in his body was a "touch-me-not," which, when pressed upon, caused the patient to give quick exclamations of pain.

Delayed sensation was a prominent sympton, the prick of a pin not being felt for some seconds. The "tendon reflex" was totally absent, and he was troubled with diplopia for several days after his prostration, objects on the wall appearing double. He was totally without strength in any way whatever, even the grasp of his hands being scarcely perceptible. His appetite was at first somewhat impaired, but it gradually grew to be enormous, and, strange to say, his digestion improved correspondingly. His bowels, however, were constipated, and he voided his urine only at long intervals. This, I think, was due to as many as three causes: (1) To the lack of nervous force; (2) to the effect of the opiates necessary for the relief of pain; (3) to the dread incident to his utter helplessness. Besides these annoyances, profuse night-sweats added greatly to his discomfort. His brain evidently shared to a certain extent in the general nervous derangement, as his memory was much impaired. He had no idea of time. On being asked, about the sixth week of his illness, how long he had been in bed, he replied, "About a week."

He frequently repeated a question to me the third or fourth time during one of my visits with as much complacency as at first. After several months of illness, when his condition was much improved, he discovered that the middle finger of his left hand, on being elevated a little, would enter into the most amusing gesticulations, resembling very much the actions of a little automatic limber-jack. He was very fond of displaying this to every visitor, and sometimes did so with equal pleasure two or three times during a single visit, making the same comments upon it each time.

As the weeks passed, the most of his symptoms improved very slowly but perceptibly, with two notable exceptions, the atrophying of the muscles, and the drawing of the muscular tendons. These caused the arms and legs to become exceedingly flat and thin, and the fingers and toes to be flexed to their utmost. The nails became hard and brittle and thick in the middle, tapering towards their ends, presenting a falcon-like appearance—the so-called "hob nail." The wrist, elbow, ankle, and knee joints were in the same flexed and fixed condition that the fingers and toes were. For weeks after his confinement, this general tendency to contraction caused the feet and legs to draw up in bed, and he had no power to force them down again. An attempt to forcibly correct this deformity in any of the parts gave great pain.

Dr. M. Allen Starr (whose graphic lectures during the winter of 1886 and 1887 before the New York Pathological Society on multiple neuritis were read with so much interest) divides the etiology of this disease into three distinct classes: (1) "Toxic cases, due to poisoning by alcohol, arsenic, and bi-sulphide of carbon; (2) infectious cases, due to the direct action upon the nervous system of the infectious agents, producing diphtheria, variola, typhoid and typhus fevers, severe malarial fever and tuberculosis, to which must be added the agent causing the epidemic form of neuritis known as kake or beriberi; (3) spontaneous cases, due to uncertain causes, among which cold and exposure to damp and wet and to overexertion may find a place." I feel satisfied that alcohol and exposure to cold were the prime if not the sole factors in the production of this case.

The literature of multiple neuritis is of such recent date that but little is known of the disease, especially in this country. It has always been confounded with locomotor ataxia and other paralyses, and not until recently has its pathology been truly understood and the disease given its proper and distinctive place in the nosology of diseases. Instead of being a disease of the spinal cord, as one would naturally suppose from the universal paralysis, the pathologists of recent years have demonstrated the fact that in cases presenting the above symptoms the pathological condition really exists in the peripheral nerves. On dissecting the nerves of subjects that have died with these symptoms, and subjecting them to a careful microscopical examination, they have been found to be in various stages of degeneration. The axis-cylinders near the nerve roots have been found increased in numbers or entirely destroyed, the medullary sheaths being broken up into fatty fragments, the myelin dividing into large and small drops containing fat granules, and the degenerative mass within the Schwann sheath, consisting of myelin and axis-cylinder, has been found in various stages of absorption, the conditions varying in different subjects (Starr). Sometimes only certain pheripheral nerves are affected, while in this case we have unmistakable evidence that the sensory, motor and the (involuntary) nerves to a certain extent were implicated, the general paralysis, perverted sensation, and condition of the respiratory organs amply attesting this fact.

Treatment.—Owing to the fact that there was great tenderness over the whole length of the spinal region, a fly blister, about 4 inches broad, was applied from the seventh cervical vertebra to the coccyx, for the purpose of relieving the congestion and promoting absorption. He was put upon a digestive tonic composed of Sheffer's pepsin, muriatic acid, and Bower's glycerine. Iodide of potassa, in compound tincture of gentian, was given three times a day, at first in 10-grain doses, gradually increased to 100 grains a day. This salt was given for its absorbent and alterative effect, and was continued in these maximum doses for weeks, with an occasional intermission of several days' duration, in order to allow the stomach and heart a rest. Strange to say that notwithstanding the patient was a chronic dyspeptic, these large and continued doses of iodide of potassa did not impair his digestion, but it improved rapidly.

Opiates were given, when necessary, for the relief of pain and insomnia. These were administered hypodermically as it was soon discovered that when given any other way it required hours to secure their good results.

After weeks of the above constitutional treatment, elixir of the phosphate of iron, quinine, and strychnia, and the comp. syr. hypo. were alternately employed. Besides these efficient nerve foods, the constant electrical current was often used, but with doubtful results. At first this gave great pain, but failed to produce the natural muscular contractions, the whole muscular mass of any part seeming to be one soft, flabby muscle without tonicity. Brandy, in moderate quantities, was administered at regular intervals as a stomachic and cardiac stimulant. The extracts of malt and the wine of cocoa were also used to good advantage. After several months of this line of treatment, when the hyperesthésia and hyperalgæsia had abated to a great extent, massage constituted the main treatment. This was pushed vigorously, and was followed by the most satisfactory results. The thin arms and legs soon began to thicken and to increase in volume, so that within a few weeks they would not have been recognized as the same limbs. The patient continued to improve to the eighth month of his confinement (June 13, 1887), when he refused to comply with the regulations of the U. S. Marine-Hospital Service, relative to being transferred to the nearest marine hospital, Mobile. Owing to this refusal, he was dropped from the service, and thus failing to receive the necessary continuous treatment, he found after several months that his case was not progressing very rapidly toward a final recovery. He, therefore, concluded that he would like to be restored to the service, and transferred to Mobile. He was accordingly re-instated, by order of the Surgeon-General, on the 31st day of December, 1887. He was taken to Mobile February 11, 1888, greatly improved by his forty days of recent treatment with massage. It had now been nearly fourteen months since the patient had fallen into my hands, the most helpless and pitiful specimen of suffering humanity I had ever seen. I had watched the case with a peculiar interest, as it was the first of the kind I had ever seen, and I had never known of a similar case reported from the South. Nor had I ever seen a word of literature upon the disease in any medical work. I was indebted to Dr. M. Allen Starr's lecture alone for my information upon the newly discovered disease. The patient was able to walk, with the aid of a stick, around his bed and into an adjoining room two or three weeks before his departure, and was able to sit up nearly all the way to Mobile. He returned to Rome, however, within less than sixty days greatly reduced. The climate of the Gulf coast had a very debilitating effect upon him, and from some cause his digestion gave way and he frequently vomited his food. He was seized with the most severe attacks of angina pectoris, recurring every few days. I saw him in two of these attacks after his return which were very distressing, and in which he suffered exceedingly. They were promptly relieved by hypodermics of morphia, and disappeared altogether after a few days of dieting and total prohibition of medicine. He now enjoys good health and is able to walk over the city and to do light work, such as drawing water, etc.

REPORTS OF FATAL CASES, WITH NECROPSIES

REPORTS OF FATAL CASES, WITH NECROPSIES.

[NOTE.—The names of complications occurring in the progress of a case are inserted under the case number.]

MEASLES—ŒDEMA OF LUNGS.

R. T.; born in Indiana; aged twenty-seven years; admitted to the U. S. Marine Hospital, Cairo, Ill., February 24, 1888. Died February 28.

History.—This patient had been seriously ill at a sailors' boarding-house for some eight days before admission to hospital. He had employed only domestic remedies, principally purgatives, and only sought medical relief when too weak to help himself. On admission he was very dirty and covered with vermin. Temperature, 36.5° C.; respiration, 12; pulse, 110; cough troublesome, eyes intolerant of light; eruption suppressed. No information gained on auscultation. He was placed at once in bed, bottles of hot water placed to feet, thighs, and armpits, and free stimulation with whisky and liquor ammonii acetatis begun. He rallied promptly. Beef tea, milk, eggs, and stimulating broths were freely given. The next day a hot bath was given, after which treatment was resumed. He was extremely reticent, and could with difficulty be made to answer questions. His improvement was satisfactory until an hour before his death, when he beckoned the nurse, who answering immediately found him insensible.

Necropsy (twelve hours after death).—Body that of a slender, muscular young man. *Rigor mortis* well marked. Hypostatic congestion noted. Nothing abnormal was found on examination, except that both lungs were moderately full of serum, and each side of the heart filled with firm *ante-mortem* clots.

ENTERIC FEVER.

CASE 1.

A. W. J.; aged twenty-four; nativity, Sweden; admitted to U. S. Marine Hospital, Port Townsend, Wash., July 6, 1887; died July 9, 1887.

Necropsy (eighteen hours after death).—Rigor mortis absent.—The heart contained a small and semi-liquid *post-mortem* clot in the left ventricle which engaged the cordæ and columnæ. The valves were normal.

The lungs were normal in tissue, but the whole posterior plane for the depth of about 30 millimeters was congested and sank immediately when they were placed in water.

The intestine: The principal change noticeable was due to ulceration located in Peyer's patches. They were more frequent in the immediate neighborhood of the ileo-cæcal valve and diminished in depth of ulceration and in number from that termination. The entire mucous membrane for several feet above the valve was deeply congested, and a number of the solitary glands presented points of ulceration. During the examination it was noticed that the escaped blood did not readily coagulate, but remained almost fluid. Examination of the kidneys gave no result beyond slight congestion of the cortical portion.

CASE 2.

Lobular pneumonia.

O. J.; aged twenty-two; nativity, Norway; admitted to U. S. Marine Hospital, New York, August 24, 1887; died September 1, 1887.

Necropsy (twenty hours after death).—Lungs hypostatically congested, and lobular pneumonia present in both lungs. Heart and membranes normal. The ileum for about 1 meter was ulcerated; general injection of the peritoneum; mesenteric glands enlarged.

CASE 3.

Enteric fever.

P. O.; aged thirty two; nativity, Norway; admitted to Marine Hospital, Boston, Mass., October 3, 1887; died October 11.

Necropsy—(eight hours after death).—Rigor mortis present. Pericardium contained 25 cubic centimeters of clear serous fluid. Lungs were normal. Peritoneum highly inflamed, both on visceral and abdominal surfaces. Abdominal cavity full of gas. Bowel distended with gas and containing a bright yellow fluid. Perforation through small intestine about 12 inches from the ileo-cæcal valve.

CASE 4.

G. B.; aged twenty-seven years; nativity, United States; was admitted to the Sisters' Hospital, Buffalo, N. Y., October 10, 1887; died October 27, 1887.

When admitted, patient had been sick some ten days; was much emaciated; complained of considerable pain in the abdomen, and said he had been injured there in a quarrel ten days before; considerable diarrhea, which resisted treatment; epistaxis occurred several times after admission.

Necropsy (three hours after death).—Body greatly emaciated. Abdomen contained about 1,500 cubic centimeters of dark serum. Stomach was congested. The ileum, cæcum, and ascending colon were the seat of a violent inflammation, and their glands, solitary and agminated, were ulcerated or swollen. Spleen was enlarged, and weighed 1,500 grams. The kidneys were healthy. Peritoneum in many places was adherent to the intestines. Heart and lungs normal. No further examination made.

CASE 5.

N. B. (negro); aged twenty-two years; nativity, Maryland; admitted to the U. S. Marine Hospital, Baltimore, Md., November 17, 1887; died December 7, 1887.

From statements made by the patient, he was supposed to have been sick about three weeks before his entrance to hospital. Information elicited from him was contradictory and indefinite. The case was supposed to be one of malarial fever. With the exception of the temperature, this case presented more of the marked characteristic symptoms of typhoid fever; eruption, diarrhea, tenderness over abdomen, and gurgling in the right ileo-cæcal region did not occur.

Two days before death the patient passed a few drops of clear blood; there is some doubt if this proceeded from the diseased gland found in the autopsy, as hemorrhoids existed.

Treatment.—The patient was put on milk diet, and sulphate of quinine given during the whole of the disease, 1.3 grains a day being the excess given. Restlessness and prolonged wakefulness were somewhat relieved by sulphate of morphia and hyoscyamus. Beef extracts and stimulants were given.

Necropsy (eighteen hours after death).—*Rigor mortis* well marked. Heart contained large amount of fluid blood, and an *ante-mortem* clot; valves and tissue normal. Lungs slightly œdematous. Liver normal. Kidneys normal.' Spleen enlarged, soft, and congested. Small intestines: Ileum contained small ulcers of recent date, having excavated edges, the base being formed by the muscular coat of the bowel. No perforations. Bowel well filled with more or less fluid mass of fæces, of yellow color and offensive odor. Large intestines: About the caput coli were found a few ulcers similar to those above described.

CASE 6.

Lobar pneumonia.

S. M.; aged twenty years; born in Michigan; admitted to the U. S. Marine Hospital, Chicago, Ill., December 2, 1887; died December 9, 1887.

History.—States that he has had a prodromal period of three or four days; malaise, frontal headache, epistaxis, anorexia, and slight diarrhea. On the night of the second day he had from eight to twelve rice-water stools.

December 3.—The abdomen was flaccid, but there was intense pain and gurgling on manipulation; twelve roseola spots on abdominal skin. Face characteristic; skin flushed; eyes sunken, etc.; tongue red and pointed; blackish fur on dorsum; some sordes on teeth; stomach intensely irritable, ejecting even melted ice, given in small quantities. Temperature 38.5° C.; pulse, 100. Constitutional depression very marked; much subsultus and general nervous tremor. Heart's action weak. Lungs give no indication of commencing trouble; quinine, digitalis, and am. carb. used. At the evening visit the temperature was 40° C.; pulse, 100; antipyr. given in gram doses every two hours; stools, ten in number; lead and opium given.

December 4.—Condition about the same, but the lungs show a commencing pneumonia. Tincture strophanthus in five-drop doses and rectal feeding now commenced.

December 5.—Still continues very sick. Morning temperature, 39° C.; evening, 40° C.

December 6.—Temperature the same as the day before. It is impossible to keep anything on the stomach or in the rectum.

December 7.—Temperature, a. m., 38.5° C.; p. m., 39.4° C.

December 8.—Temperature remains the same. At 10.30 p. m. the pulse can hardly be counted.

Died at 8.30 a. m., December 9. 1887.

Necropsy.—*Rigor mortis* well marked; body somewhat emaciated. Pleura adherent to right lung surface. Middle and upper lobes of right lung consolidated (red hepatization); lower lobe congested. Mesentery much congested. Some folds of small intestine of a dark purple color. Mesenteric glands enlarged to pea size. About 12 feet of the intestine, including the ileo-cæcal valve, was tied off and opened; about 5 feet from the valve there was a diverticulum of the intestine, forming a pocket 4 inches in length. The vessels of the gut were intensely engorged; the mucous membrane swollen and covered with patches of lymph. The first patch was in the wall of the diverticulum mentioned, and as large as a half dollar; below this and approaching the valve they were frequently seen, and the neighboring glands were very large. At the valve there was a cluster of four glands as large each as a pigeon's egg and firmly adherent to the jejunum, cæcum and appendix, and abdominal wall; an immense Peyer's patch was seen just within the valve. The glands forming this cluster were cheesy, and one was on the point of rupture. Death from typhoid fever. Liver and spleen enlarged.

CASE 7.

Pneumonia.

A. P.; aged twenty-four years; born in Sweden; admitted to marine ward, German Hospital, Philadelphia, Pa., December 14, 1887; died December 25, 1887.

History.—Patient was markedly cyanotic on admission. Temperature, 40° C.; pulse, 116; respiration, 34. He could scarcely be aroused, and could not be induced to speak. It was, however, ascertained from the person who brought him to hospital that he had been sick for twelve or fourteen days. There was no eruption, but the entire surface was of a dusky blue color, most marked on the face, neck, and hands. Stools passed involuntarily and were very offensive. The urine was high-colored, passed involuntarily, and did not contain albumen. Physical examination of the chest revealed some moist râles, but no evidence of congestion was found. Abdomen slightly tympanitic.

Treatment.—Wet cups were applied on admission. Tartar emetic, .002 gms. every half hour until sweating ensued; also antifebrin in .065 gm. doses hourly to reduce the temperature.

December 15.—Ol. terebinthinæ were given in emulsion, and stupes of the same were applied over the abdomen. This plan of treatment was followed, with the addition of stimulants, but without any appreciable beneficial effects. The patient steadily grew worse, and died at 7.15 a. m. on above date.

Autopsy (*fifty hours after death*).—Body not extremely emaciated. (*Rigor mortis.*)

Thorax: Lungs showed congestion of both lower lobes and also middle lobe of right lung in state of red hepatization; no adhesions. Pleura normal. Heart pale and flabby. Right cavity contained fluid blood, as did also the large veins.

Intestines: Peyers's glands characteristically inflamed and enlarged with ulceration, some measuring as much as an inch and a quarter by three-quarters inch in size. Liver large and pale; weight 2450 grams; spleen, weight 230 grams; right kidney, weight 230 grams; left kidney, weight 250 grams.

CASE 8.

Pneumonia.

G. G.; aged twenty two years; nativity, Norway; admitted to U. S. Marine Hospital, Stapleton, N. Y., January 9, 1888; died January 16.

Necropsy.—*Rigor mortis* marked; body slightly emaciated. The thorax was opened and the heart removed; a considerable quantity of serum was found in the pericardium; the heart was flabby; the valves normal; the cavity was filled with *post mortem* clots. Hypostatic congestion was present in the lungs; a circumscribed lobular pneumonia was found on the anterior surface of the lower lobe of the right lung. The liver was normal to all appearance. The spleen was enormously congested, and soft and pultaceous. The mesenteric glands were considerably enlarged, and the mesentery injected; the glands situated near the junction of the ileum with the cæcum were broken down and filled with cheesy pus. The large intestine was filled with fæces. The ileum for 20 centimeters or more above the cæcum was found to be ulcerated. The ascending, transverse and descending portions of the colon as far as the sigmoid flexure were one mass of small ulcers, penetrating the mucous membrane and the submucous also. The kidneys were enlarged and congested. The other organs were normal.

CASE 9.

C. O'D.; aged twenty-six years; nativity, Ireland; admitted to the marine ward, Mercy Hospital, Pittsburgh, Pa., March 30; died March 31, 1888.

History.—This patient left Pittsburgh on the steamer *Raymond Horner*, five weeks ago; was taken sick one week later with fever and diarrhea, but continued at work, taking medicine as directed by the captain; he staid by the vessel during the trip to New Orleans and until she reached Vicksburg, Miss., on her return trip March 28, at which time he took the train for Pittsburgh, arriving on the 30th and going at once to hospital. Patient very weak and emaciated (says he has lost 40 pounds in weight); pulse about 100; temperature 38.1° C.; slight tenderness on pressure over abdomen, but no decided pain when quiet. No eruption, but general condition indicated enteric fever. Tympanitis was not marked.

Necropsy (seven hours after death).—*Rigor mortis* present. On opening the abdominal cavity fetid gas escaped, and the cavity contained a quantity of purulent fluid; the great omentum was matted down to the intestines, which were in spots almost gangrenous, the peritoneal coat destroyed, and the gut dark red. There were numerous ulcers in the lower part of the ileum, several extending through to the peritoneal coat; one situated about 12 inches from the ileocæcal valve had completely perforated the gut. The perforation was one-half inch in diameter and had evidently existed for several days. The large intestine was also much inflamed, and the mesentery greatly thickened. Heart flabby, and the right auricle contained a fibrinous clot. There was some congestion of the lungs, which by their color proved this man to have been a resident of the coal region. The surface of the liver was also black, but the organ was otherwise normal in appearance. Kidneys normal.

CASE 10.

I. P. L.; aged twenty-three years; nativity, New York; admitted to U. S. Marine Hospital, New Orleans, La., May 6, 1888; died May 18, 1888.

Clinical history.—Admitted from United States ship *Galena*, with following history:

Taken sick April 27, 1888; had suffered an attack of colic on previous night, for which a cathartic was given; next morning (28th) his temperature was $38\frac{3}{5}^{\circ}$ C., pulse 98 per minute; from this to time of admission temperature ranged from 38° C to $39\frac{3}{5}^{\circ}$; pulse from 80 to 98 per minute; from 2 to 5 thin, watery, ocher-colored stools daily; urine normal, high colored; frontal headache; no other pain except in left shoulder.

When admitted to Marine Hospital May 6, 1888, temperature 40°, pulse 120 per minute and weak; subsultus tendinum; slight delirium; diarrhea, 3 to 5 stools during next few days; temperature range, morning 38°, evening $39\frac{3}{5}$. Gurgling and tenderness on pressure in right iliac region. No rose-colored spots on body. Hemorrhage from bowels. On afternoon of 9th of May, ergot and turpentine given; 2 more slight hemorrhages took place during the evening of same day. No hemorrhages after this date. Temperature did not go above 39°, but occasionally as low as 37°. Died on the night of May 18, the twenty-first day of sickness.

Necropsy (*eight hours after death*).—*Rigor mortis.* Body small, emaciated; bed-sore developing over sacrum. Thoracic cavity: left pleura adherent, slight hypostatic congestion with one or two patches of pneumonic consolidation in posterior inferior portions of both lungs. Otherwise lungs appeared normal. Heart small and empty, except *ante mortem* clot in pulmonary aorta; heart tissue pale; valves flabby. Stomach filled with undigested fluids or, rather, semi-fluids. Liver congested, tissue easily torn. Spleen large and soft; kidneys somewhat congested. Intestines: at junction of small and large and several inches of ilium the characteristic pathological changes of Peyer's patches were visible; ulcerations in several places had destroyed the mucous and muscular coats of the intestines, but no perforation had taken place. For several feet the small intestines were intensely congested. Ulcerations here and there, near the ileo-cæcal valve. Bladder normal. Brain not examined.

CASE 11.

G. N.; aged thirty-two years; nativity, Norway; admitted to U. S. marine hospital, New Orleans, La., May 29, 1888; died June 13, 1888.

Clinical history.—At time of admission temperature was $40\frac{3}{5}^{\circ}$ C.; pulse, 100 per minute; respiration, 40 per minute. Complained of slight pain, with gurgling, on pressure in right iliac region. Diarrhea, from two to four thin ocher-colored stools per day. No delirium. Slight cough; bronchial rales; normal vesicular respiration over space occupied by lungs; slight regurgitant murmur heard at apex; induction—"mitral insufficiency;" moderate tympanites. Disease ran usual course of enteric fever. Evening temperature averaged two-fifths degrees C. higher than the morning for first week, 40 and $40\frac{1}{5}^{\circ}$ p. m., $39\frac{3}{5}$ and $39\frac{1}{5}^{\circ}$ p. m. Sponging the body with water and alcohol, administration of antipyrine at night, with occasional full doses of sulph. quinine, and astringents for the diarrhea, was the plan of treatment adopted.

June 10, 1888.—Temperature $38\frac{1}{5}°$ a. m.; pulse dicrotic; during the day he had two large hemorrhages from the bowels; ergot and turpentine, with ice, controlled it to some extent; temperature p. m. 37° C.; pulse, 112.

June 11 *a. m.*—Hemorrhages.

June 12 *a. m.*—Hemorrhages twice during forenoon.

Died during the afternoon of 13th.

Necropsy (*fourteen hours after death*).—Body of large size, well developed, muscular, fairly nourished. *Rigor mortis.* Moderate.—Posterior aspect of trunk: Limbs, neck, and arms discolored by *post mortem* ecchymosis. Cutis peeling from ankles where sinapisms had been applied. Back of right hand had the figure of a ship pricked into skin, with some coloring matter, presumably India ink. Cicatrix in right groin, about 4 centimeters long. Abdomen greatly distended with gas. Mucous membrane of larynx and trachea congested. Thoracic cavity: Pleura not adherent; pericardium contained about 100 cubic centimeters serous fluid; heart contracted and empty, of medium size, its tissues pale; valves flabby; mitral valve had a few recent vegetations. Aortic valves also contained vegetations, and showed signs of acute inflammatory exudations. Both systemic and pulmonary aorta appeared to have suffered (intima) from inflammation for about 3 centimeters from orifice, inclusive; the inner coat of these vessels was of a *deep pink* color with a slight exudate. Bronchial tubes: Mucous membrane inflamed and coated with mucopurulent fluid. Both lungs acutely congested in their posterior superior portions. Œdema of inferior portion of lungs. One or two small areas of tubercle in upper lobe of left lung. Abdominal cavity: Spleen large, dark in color, and soft; capsule of spleen contained numerous spots of amyloid degeneration, size grain of sago; "sago spleen" in this part. Liver large and pale, reaction to gross test, iodine, of amyloid degeneration. Area of inflamed substance about 3 centimeters in diameter around hepatic vein; no embolism discoverable. Mesenteric glands tubercular, cheesy in places, breaking down in others, purulent. Intestines enormously distended with gas. Near the ileo cæcal valve and for some distance in the small intestine a number of indurated and many ulcerated Peyer's patches were found; some of these ulcers were 3 centimeters in diameter, destroying mucous and muscular coats; gut tore in removing, but no perforation was discovered. The ulcers of the intestine partook in part of the nature of *tubercular* lesions inasmuch as they followed the *circular course* of blood vessels around the gut, their diameter was such (3 centimeters) as to justify the diagnosis characteristic pathological lesions of glands of Peyer and hyperæmia of solitary glands found only in enteric fever. Mesentery also hyperæmic. Kidneys large and pale. Capsule of kidney thickened and peeled easily from the surface.

CASE 12.

Peritonitis.

T. M.; aged twenty-three years; nativity, Germany; admitted to U. S. Marine Hospital, San Francisco, Cal., June 4, 1888; died, June 16, 1888.

History.—There was very little tenderness of the abdomen when the patient was admitted, and the symptoms of typhoid were not well marked until two days later. Extreme pain and tenderness over abdomen; vomiting; and a fall of temperature indicated perforation and peritonitis forty-eight hours before death.

Necropsy (three hours after death).—Upon opening the abdomen about 500 cubic centimeters of flocculent yellow fluid escaped, with some very offensive gas.

The surface of the intestines was covered with dark-colored (almost black) inflammatory lymph. They were distended with gas and contained a small amount of liquid fæces. There were several small ulcers in the large intestine near the ileo-cæcal valve, and two large ulcers, both communicating with the peritoneal cavity in the ileum a few inches from its junction with the cæcum. The spleen was enlarged and soft; the kidneys red, with suffused blood, and the liver not markedly changed in appearance. The lungs were adherent at their apices, but no signs of tubercle were present. The heart was fatty. The pericardial cavity contained about 75 cubic centimeters of fluid.

CASE 13.

C. M.; seaman; aged forty-five; nativity, Ireland; admitted to the marine ward, Sisters' Hospital, Buffalo, N. Y., June 23, 1888; died June 30, 1888.

When admitted he said he had been sick two weeks, and had been drinking heavily besides. He was very weak and emaciated, with a temperature of 40° C., a pulse of 108 per minute, and a dry parched tongue. He stated that he had had a bad diarrhea, but he had stopped it with brandy. His condition did not improve, but remained about the same until June 29, when his heart weakened very rapidly, his condition growing worse, till June 30, when he died.

Necropsy (six hours after death).—Peritoneum healthy; contained about 200 cubic centimeters of serum. Stomach slightly congested. Small intestine normal until near the cæcal region, where it was the seat of inflammation. The glands in this region were in various stages of inflammation; some ulcerated, others partially covered with granulation; some of them, however, diseased to the extent of perforation; nor was there evidence of hemorrhage, though the last two movements of the bowels were slightly tinged with bright blood. All other abdominal organs were found to be healthy. The thorax was not opened, nor the cranium.

TYPHO-MALARIAL FEVER.

CASE 1.

Perforation of intestine.

H. K.; aged thirty-three; born in Norway; was admitted to the U. S. Marine Hospital, New York, July 15, 1887; died August 26.

Necropsy (six hours after death).—*Rigor mortis* not well established; body emaciated; abdomen retracted. There was an extensive peritonitis in some places, matting the intestines together; this was found to be due to a perforation of the ileum, about 25 cubic centimeters from the pylorus. The whole intestinal tract was the seat of inflammation.

Peyer's patches enlarged and ulcerated; enlargement of the mesentric glands. The spleen was very much enlarged and pigmented; other organs normal. Sections were made from the spleen, Peyer's glands and mesenteric glands, and on staining them, short bacilli were found, corresponding in all respects to that described by Gaffky.

CASE 2.

J. A.; aged twenty-four years; nativity, Azores Islands; admitted to the U. S. Marine Hospital, San Francisco, Cal., November 26, 1887; died December 5.

Necropsy.—Liver adherent to the diaphragm by firm band, and greatly enlarged. Tissue pale on section and harder than normal. Spleen enlarged to three times its normal size, and tissue very soft. Small intestine: Mucous membrane of ileum reddened, and extensive ulceration of Peyer's patches on lower portion. Large intestine: Ulceration of solitary glands very extensive in the cœcum; also a few ulcerations in first part of ascending colon. Mucous membrane of entire colon very red, and the colon contained 300 cubic centimeters of dark-colored blood. Kidneys were normal. The mesenteric glands were very much enlarged.

CASE 3.

M. W. (colored); aged thirty-two; a native of Alabama; admitted to the Marine Hospital, Mobile, Ala., on January 14, 1888; died March 5.

History.—When admitted he was suffering from fever of a remittent type, which continued for thirty-two days. Convalescence then seemed established, and for about two weeks, while there was little physical improvement, he had no fever. About this time complaint was made of pain in the hypogastrium, followed by profuse diarrhea and a recurrence of fever. General prostration supervened and death.

Remarks.—At no time in its history were the prominent symptoms of enteric fever present in this case, nor during the last week; hence there was no change made in the original diagnosis.

Necropsy (*twelve hours after death*).—Emaciation extreme. *Rigor mortis* not prominent. Abdominal walls distended. Same œdema of ankles. Abdomen opened, whence a quantity of foul gas escaped. Peritoneum and omentum adherent and included in incision. The intestines presented a dry, glistening appearance, and were distended. The mesentery was engorged; glands enlarged and very soft. At the coecum the folds of intestine were matted together, forming a pouch into which there had drained some 300 cubic centimeters of yellowish fluid, from a rupture in the coats of the ileum, 5 centimeters from its juncture with the caecum. One meter of ileum, nearest the valve, was removed and laid open. Numerous Peyer's patches were enlarged and softened, but in only two was there ulceration, one of which had perforated as above mentioned. There was no hemorrhage from this perforation. Liver pale and enlarged. Spleen very large and soft, breaking down under the hand into a black, grumous pulp. Muscle of the heart not microscopically fatty.

DYSENTERY.

CASE 1.

F. W. B.; aged twenty-five; born in Finland; admitted to the marine ward of the German Hospital on June 22, 1887; died June 24.

History.—Nothing could be definitely learned of his family or personal history. On the day of his admission the temperature rose to 40° C., and during the night he had over ten stools, which were all very bloody. The following day he had twelve stools and his temperature was nearly

40.5° C. During the time he was in the hospital he seemed to suffer very much, as he was very restless. He died Sunday morning, June 24, at about 2 o'clock. He was subjected to the following treatment: Hydrarg. Chlorid. mit. .016 grams; pulv. opii, .0324 grams; pulv. ipecac, .065 grams. He was given this powder every two hours; also ergotin., .32 grams every four hours, and brandy 250 cubic centimeters.

Necropsy (thirty-one hours after death).—Body well nourished, adipose tissue abundant. His heart was normal; all the cavities were full of uncoagulated blood; right lung was considerably smaller than left. Right lung weighed 350 grams; the left, 470 grams; the right lung was a little congested; right cavity of the heart was occupied by organized clots which intervened among the leaflets of tricuspid valve.

Rectum was congested, and here and there were junctiform hemorrhages.

The mucous membrane of the ilium and colon was much congested, while that of the stomach and upper portion of the small intestine was normal.

CASE 2.

E. D. H. (colored); aged forty-three; a native of Kentucky; was admitted to the Marine Hospital at Memphis, Tenn., August 13, 1887; died August 23.

History.—He said he had twenty or more dejections daily, accompanied by griping pain. The stools were not bloody at first. Appetite poor. He improved rapidly under treatment till he had only one dejection daily. For some reason, inexplicable, at the end of ten days he again grew worse; the griping pain returned; the pain was located in the course of the colon; his stools now contained blood and coarse shreds of mucus; his failure was constant and the dejections uncontrollable.

Necropsy.—Body much emaciated. *Rigor mortis* well marked. Scars on right arm and on both legs, on anterior surface. On the mucous surface of the colon there were a large number of ulcers of various sizes. The length of the ulcer was at right angles to the axis of the intestines. A square inch of normal mucous membrane could not be mapped out on the mucous surface of the colon. The edges of the ulcers were indurated and abrupt. The ulcer was covered with brownish black mucus and detritus. At one point, only the peritoneum formed the base of the ulcer. At this point the peritoneum was congested and covered with recent fibrin. The mesenteric glands were very much enlarged.

Weight of organs.—Right lung, 404; left, 270; heart, 275; spleen, 176; right kidney, 145; left, 149; liver 1,364 grams.

CASE 3.

J. K.; aged twenty-eight; nativity, Massachusetts; admitted to Marine Hospital, Boston, Mass., September 14, 1887; died September 21.

Necropsy (twenty-one hours after death).—*Rigor mortis* present. Body greatly emaciated. Pleural cavity contained normal amount of fluid. Both lungs congested in lower lobes. Right upper lobe much affected by tuberculosis. Left upper lobe showed some points of degeneration. Liver weighed 3,650 grams. A small calcareous concretion (inspissated pus) found in left lobe. Mesenteric glands enlarged. Mucous membrane destroyed throughout the colon; many ulcerated patches, and a perforation at junction with the sigmoid flexure. Kidneys normal.

CASE 4.

J. L.; aged forty years; nativity, Wisconsin; admitted to the U. S. Marine Hospital, Cairo, Ill., September 13, 1887; died October 3, 1887.

History.—On admission he suffered from diarrhea, nausea, loss of appetite, and slight fever; these symptons gradually assumed a dysenteric type, with frequent bloody stools containing shreds of mucus and small portions of fecal matter. The stools increased greatly in number and the patient's strength rapidly declined in spite of active medication.

Necropsy.—Slight pleuritic adhesions near apex of right lung; lungs healthy; heart small and contracted; valves normal. Liver congested and softened; stomach and spleen normal. Small intestines distended with gas, vessels congested, mucous membrane thickened and coated with tenacious mucus. Large intestines: Bowels markedly congested; walls thickened and œdematous, particularly throughout the sigmoid flexure and rectum; the mucous membrane was easily detached in many places, while at other points it was ulcerated; slight adhesions from beginning of peritonitis were noticed atvarious places about the lower part of the large intestine.

CASE 5.

T. T.; aged thirty-six; nativity, Norway; admitted to the U. S. Marine Hospital, New York, December 4, 1886; died October 3, 1887.

Necropsy (thirty-six hours after death).—Body emaciated. Lungs hypostatically congested, and contained tubercular deposits at both apices. Heart and blood vessels small and pale. Kidneys small and degenerated. Spleen contracted; stomach empty; mucous membrane healthy. The colon, from the cœcum to the rectum, was one continuous ulceration; also large cicatrices, sets of others that had healed (the diameters of the ulcers were .5 to 1 centimeter and about .5 centimeter deep). The muscular coats of the large intestine were greatly thickened. There were about 500 cubic centimeters of serum in the abdominal cavity. Liver, cirrhotic and adherent to the surrounding tissues.

Weight of organs.—Heart, 170 grams; right lung, 300 grams; left lung, 280 grams; liver, 800 grams; right kidney, 125 grams; left kidney, 130 grams; spleen, 235 grams; stomach, 125 grams.

CASE 6.

G. P.; aged thirty-nine years; nativity, Finland; admitted to the U. S. Marine Hospital, Baltimore, Md., with malarial cachexia, September 12, 1887; re-admitted with dysentery, September 27, 1887; died October 3, 1887.

History.—The patient, by his statement, several times during the summer had attacks of diarrhea which he attributed to unhealthy water. This, with the malarial fever, rendered him anæmic and in a weak condition when entering hospital. Exposure to cold, together with the immoderate use of ice-water, is assigned as the cause of the last attack, which from the beginning was characterized by tormina, tenesmus, and frequent stools of mucus and blood. Constitutional disturbance, such as fever and emaciation, was marked. The patient presented at times seeming improvement, but it did not continue long enough to allow him to rally. A general state of apathy, persistent hiccough, collapse, and exhaustion terminated the case.

Treatment.—On the first appearance of the disease the patient was put on milk diet and given 30 cubic centimeters castor oil with 1.3 cubic centimeters of tincture of opii. Pepsin, opium, and bismuth were given after meals; later, pills of acetate of lead and powdered opium, with stimulants. Enæma of starch and tincture of opium, and a solution of nitrate of silver .6 gm. to 30. cubic centimeters were injected into the colon.

Necropsy (fifteen hours after death.)—*Rigor mortis* moderate. Heart normal. Lungs normal with exception of slight pleuritic adhesion at right apex. Liver slightly anæmic; otherwise healthy. Spleen normal. Kidneys normal. Small intestines normal, with exception of some roughening of mucous surface in lower part of ileum. Large intestines presented greatest changes about splenic and hepatic flexures and about the sigmoid flexure consisting of an infiltration of a reddish semi-solid nature, forming irregular elevations on the mucous surface, which had in places broken down, leaving ragged shallow ulcers, covered with shreds of whitish stringy lymph. Entire track more or less congested. No perforation. Peritoneum normal.

CASE 7.

J. H.; aged fifty-five; native of Ireland; admitted to hospital October 5, 1887; died October 12, 1887.

Necropsy (six hours after death).—Body much emaciated and shrunken; the deposits of fat in the orbits and perineal spaces much diminished. The tissues all seemed abnormally dry on section. The serous cavities were devoid of lubricating material, except the pericardial sac, which contained about 60 cubic centimeters of fluid. The heart was small, pale, and flabby. The mitral valve was thickened. In the upper lobe of left lung were found small bodies, apparently miliary tubercles; the lung was otherwise normal. Liver normal. The mesenteric glands showed no change. The large intestine, for about 6 inches in the region of its splenic flexure, was bluish-red in color; its walls were much thickened and the size of the gut somewhat diminished. Two small ulcers, apparently only involving the mucous membrane lining of the gut, were also found in this region. The suprarenal capsule of the left kidney was greatly thickened, and presented a globular appearance; it was filled with a dark substance resembling coffee grounds, probably the result of *post mortem* disintegration of the medullary substance.

CASE 8.

C. J. (colored); aged thirty-six years; a native of Tennessee; was admitted to the Marine Hospital, Memphis, Tenn., September 13, 1887; died October 26, 1887.

History.—Frequent and bloody stools, accompanied by griping pain and tenesmus. Pain along the colon when pressure was made. Slight fever. Under treatment his recovery was rapid. He was discharged at his own request and contrary to advice, September 16, 1887. He was again admitted October 15, 1887. His stools were very frequent, bloody, and contained long shreds of mucus. They were very offensive. Under treatment stools became less frequent, being reduced to five or six daily. He failed rapidly, and died October 26, 1887.

Necropsy.—*Rigor mortis* well marked. Scars on both legs. All viscera healthy. The mucous surface of the colon was covered with ulcers, varying in size from two to five centimeters in length and as many in breadth.

The edges of the ulcers were abrupt. Each ulcer was surrounded by an areola of red tissue, as if an effort was being made to heal the ulcerated surface. All mesenteric glands were enlarged and caseous. The intestines were very tender, and would not bear one-third of a meter of their length.

Weight of viscera.—Spleen, 160; liver, 1,295; pancreas, 46; right kidney, 121; left, 129; right lung, 313; left, 324; heart, 267.

Case 9.

E. J. (colored); aged thirty-nine years; a native of Alabama; was admitted to the Marine Hospital at Memphis, Tenn., November 2, 1887.

History.—Pain in abdomen; frequent dejections; stools at first containing mucous and fecal matter; later they became bloody; stools offensive; appetite poor; pain along course of colon; all plans of treatment failed to control the dejections; opium until drowsiness was caused availed nothing.

Necropsy.—Scars on both legs; enlarged glands in both groins; all organs healthy except colon. In the colon there was not the slightest trace of normal mucous membrane from the ileo-cæcal valve to the anus. The whole inner surface was covered with shreds of sloughing mucous membrane. One piece was 15 centimeters long. The mesenteric glands were enlarged and cheesy.

Weight of viscera.—Liver, 1,409; left kidney, 132; right, 128; right lung, 272; left, 215; heart 315; spleen, 95 grams.

Case 10.

W. T. (colored); aged thirty-six years; a native of Kentucky; was admitted to the Marine Hospital at Memphis, Tenn., December 8, 1887.

History.—He complained of pain in the belly, and had frequent dejections, which contained no blood. There was pain and tenderness around navel; pain not marked around colon. Appetite poor; some fever. The pain increased and the face assumed an anxious expression. The stools contained much mucus, and were very offensive. He failed rapidly, and died on the 18th of December, 1887.

Necropsy.—All the intestines were matted together by recent lymph. In the left loin there was a perforation of the colon, through which fecal matter had escaped into the peritoneum. The colon was very tender, tearing when the slightest tension was put upon it. When the colon was removed and cut open it was difficult to tell which was the proper lumen of the colon, as there were bands of necrosed mucous membrane and ropy mucus extending across the lumen of the colon. Viscera normal; not weighed.

Case 11.

W. H. S. (white); aged thirty-two; a native of Ohio; admitted to U. S. Marine Hospital, Memphis, Tenn., January 18, 1888. Died January 21, 1888.

History.—He has frequent and bloody stools, accompanied by much pain. His abdomen is very tender over the whole length of the colon. He is much emaciated, pale, and delirious. He has nausea and occasional vomiting. Stools every half hour; pulse 130, and feeble. Breath offensive, having a fecal odor.

January 19.—Vomited milk, but retained it when mixed with an equal quantity of lime water. Given morphia and bismuth.

January 20.—Stool every third hour; pulse 140 and more feeble than yesterday.

January 21.—Patient died of exhaustion.

Necropsy.—Body much emaciated. Abdomen blue, from decomposition, over the colon. Organs normal, except the colon. The mucous membrane of the colon was black and sloughing. Mesenteric glands much enlarged.

CASE 12.

Peritonitis.—Foreign body (match) in ileum.

J. D. (colored); aged twenty-seven, a native of Alabama; was admitted to the Marine Hospital, Memphis, Tenn., January 27, 1888.

History.—Has been sick three weeks; frequent stools, with severe griping all the time; no appetite; feels very weak. The stools contained much blood and mucus, and were very offensive. Under treatment he improved slowly. March 1 the number of stools were two daily. His appetite improved and he seemed on the road to recovery. In a few days he began to fail. The stools became more frequent; his appetite failed, and only by the use of stimulants was he kept alive. Died March 30, 1888.

Necropsy.—No *rigor mortis.* Body much emaciated. No subcutaneous fat. No fat in the omentum. The mucous membrane of the colon was black and sloughing. In the right iliac fossa the intestine for about 10 centimeters above the ileo-cæcal valve was adherent to the peritoneum. The omentum was also adherent. When the adhesions were torn a small amount of pus was found confined by the adhesions. The ileum was cut 20 centimeters above the adhesions, and water poured in. Water flowed through an opening into the old cavity occupied by the pus. On section one-half of a match was found lying across the lumen of the gut. In several places near the match only the peritoneal coat remained. Both pleural cavities were obliterated by old adhesions, so firm that the lungs could not be removed. The pericardial sac was also obliterated. The left lobe of the liver was firmly adherent to the spleen. Liver, 1,360; spleen, 237. The second attack of dysentery was due to the match.

INTERMITTENT FEVER.

CASE 1.

A. J. (colored); aged forty-five years; nativity, Virginia; admitted to Mercy Hospital, marine wards, June 28, 1887; died July 2, 1887.

History.—When admitted he was suffering from profuse diarrhea. He was weak and emaciated; his temperature 38° C.; the skin cold and moist; pulse rapid and weak. He had been ill several days before leaving the river, and had rough usage for two or three days on shore before going to the hospital.

Necropsy.—The lungs were congested but crepitant throughout. Heart normal in size, soft and friable in texture; no clots on valvular lesions.

Liver enlarged, of a deep slate color; soft, yielding to pressure of the finger; surface smooth and the capsule is easily removed.

Spleen is greatly enlarged, black in color; has the appearance of a mass of blood, and it is softened; kidneys slightly enlarged, pale and softened.

DIAGRAM.

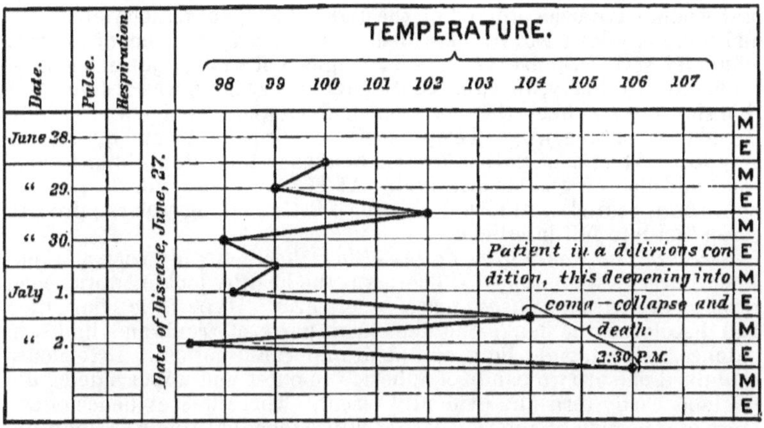

Notes on autopsy held upon the body of A. J. (colored), July 3, 1887.—Abdominal and thoracic cavities only examined. Lungs deeply congested, though crepitant throughout. Heart about normal in size, but soft and friable in texture. No blood or clots in heart. No valvular lesion. Liver enlarged, of a deep coppery or slate color; soft, yielding to the finger; smooth over surface, and capsule easily removed. Spleen greatly enlarged, black, and gave an appearance of a huge mass of blood; somewhat softened. Kidneys slightly enlarged, pale, and softened; relation of cortex to parenchyma not altered. Prima via presents no marked abnormality.

CASE 2.

Fatty degeneration of the liver and heart.

P. N.; aged thirty-five years; nativity, Denmark; admitted to U. S. Marine Hospital, San Francisco, Cal., July 22, 1887; died July 24, 1887.

History.—This man came in July 22, about 11 a. m. He stated he had been well up to five days before, when he became constipated and gradually weak. He had several slight chills, but was not aware he had fever; says he never had malaria, but years ago had yellow fever at Panama. When sickness came on, was aboard pilot-boat off the bar. He applied at office, custom-house, for relief, and for a day or two was treated for intermittent fever, and, with other callers there, was vaccinated. A day or so before admission his bowels were moved by oil and pills. Upon admission, temperature 38.8° C.; patient quite weak; thirst considerable; tongue dry, swollen, cracked, some sores; mind clear, no pain in head or elsewhere, and results of examination were perfectly negative. In fact, beyond febrile movement, nothing was evident. The pulse being full, strong, and regular, no stimulant was thought advisable, and rest, with abundance of milk in small quantities, at short intervals, was thought to be sufficient to combat the exhaustion complained of. Quin. sul. 0.75, ac. hydrobrom d 1 cubic centimeter, t. i. d., was ordered, with the result that temperature gradually fell to 38° C. some five hours before death. Meanwhile, increasing weakness was complained of, and the pulse became less full and strong, though still by no means so bad as subjective feeling of weakness would lead one to expect. Stimulant would have been ordered on the night of 23d, but patient fell asleep and was not allowed to be disturbed. Next morning his condition was evidently serious, pulse very weak, tongue not so dry, but exhaustion profound. Whisky, 15 cubic centimeters every hour, was ordered, but this showing no effect, the dose was doubled and atropine and brandy injected subcutaneously. Temperature a. m. was 38° C. and quinia was stopped. At 11 a. m. patient's pulse weakened further, his breath came short and shallow and his face livid. At 11.30 he died. For the last few hours he appeared semi-torpid, and some little shaking was required to rouse him into full intelligence.

Necropsy four hours after death.—Rigor mortis already very marked. Body fairly well nourished. There was the healthy looking abrasion of recent vaccination at usual place on left arm. Hypostatic congestion had discolored the flanks and dependent parts of trunk and limbs, in patches. Chest, right lung, and pleura appeared normal. Left pleura contained one or two bands of adhesion to outer and upper side of upper lobe, easily torn and evidently recent. There was evidence of collapse of a portion of anterior part of upper lobe, but this was doubtful, and at most the lesion was limited in extent. Some hypostatic congestion of both lungs. Heart was about normal in size; the left ventricle firmly and the other cavities scarcely at all contracted. There were no clots, except a few small soft fibrinous masses in right ventricle, and a similar smaller clot in the pulmonary artery attached to the valves. But both auricles were full of fluid blood of the color, and nearly the consistence, of black ink. The cardiac valves were tested and found sufficient, except possibly the mitral, which, at times, allowed some regurgitation. All the valves appeared thinned, but not diseased. The whole organ was fatty. The muscular tissue in left ventricle was perhaps hypertrophied, but everywhere was yellow, soft, and friable. Abdomen: Peritoneum appeared normal. The whole intestinal tract was examined, but beyond a rather unusual amount of doughy fæces in colon nothing abnormal was seen. Bladder was moderately distended. Liver was about normal in size, and far advanced in fatty degeneration. There was a small amount of bile in the gall-bladder. The capsule of liver peeled away with the utmost ease. Spleen was likewise normal in size, but extremely dark in color. In consistence it was a mere grumous pulp. Kidneys were of normal size, rather pale, though quite firm; the extreme facility with which the capsule stripped off argued a degree of fatty degeneration which a slight shade of yellow in the pale vortex seemed to confirm. Brain: Upon removing the calvarium and incising the dura quite an amount of serum escaped. This seemed due to an œdematous state of the membranes. There was no great congestion of the veins of the pia, nor of the sinuses. The brain itself appeared perfectly healthy, and numerous sections revealed no lesion. The amount of fluid in the ventricles was scarcely abnormal. The œdema of the membranes referred to was either a post-mortem occurrence or supervened a few hours before death, for the symptoms up to a short time before death negatived the possibility of such a condition. The blood, after all, arrested most attention. From the heart and great vessels it poured, an inky stream at first, fluid and noncoagulable. As it spread out over the table, the surface soon appeared covered with an iridescent film, a bluish purple color being most permanent. Some of the blood reddened after exposure to air, especially where it thinly covered the table, but most of it remained dark, in places becoming tarry as it feebly attempted to coagulate. Under the microscope the blood seemed far less changed than its gross appearance had given reason to expect. The red corpuscles were unusually pale, but for the most part normal in size and shape. But they appeared less clear in outline and firm in consistency than normal, and slight pressure seemed to agglutinate them in masses. The white corpuscles were scarce, but pale corpuscular cells, from a size scarcely visible to that of a red corpuscle, were abundant. There was a great deal of granular detritus deeply stained with blood pigment, and oil globules in considerable numbers were seen.

Case 3.

J. H.; aged twenty-three years; nativity, Finland; admitted to marine ward, German Hospital, Philadelphia, Pa., August 9, 1887; died August 12.

History.—His condition on admission indicated serious disease, but being a Fin and no one available to converse with patient an accurate statement could not be obtained. Temperature on evening of admission, 39° C., and next morning had dropped to 37° C; evening temperature, 38.5° C. During the day patient appeared to be very sick, and the evening temperature 41° C., rising to 41.2° C. at midnight. Morning temperature on the 12th was 41.1° C.

Treatment.—At once three com. cath. pills, and sulph quinia .03 gm. at night. This was followed next morning by calomel and soda powder and quinine repeated. On the 11th quinine was continued, and on the 12th whisky and tincture of digitalis were given hypodermatically and turpentine stupes applied. Becoming cyanosed 250 grams of blood was drawn from the right arm. Patient did not rally, and died quietly at noon of 12th.

Autopsy.—Body of a large and well developed man, well nourished. Lungs crepitant, but on section contained much venous blood, otherwise in good condition. Heart normal; contained only small clots. Liver slightly congested and somewhat larger than normal; gall bladder moderately distended. Spleen pultaceous; weighed 600 grams. Kidneys normal. Mesenteric glands large and pale color.

Brain: Skull very thin; dura mater adherent at vertex with marked evidence of inflammation found upon removal of membrane. Weight of brain 1,585 grams.

Case 4.

Cirrhosis of liver and kidneys.

R. A. H.; aged fifty years; nativity, Ohio; admitted to the marine ward, Evansville City Hospital, Evansville, Ind., July 30, 1887; died September 28.

When admitted had been suffering from diarrhea for over six weeks and was much emaciated and very weak. The diarrhea was checked by the use of opium and copper sulphate; the patient was re-admitted August 24, for malarial fever, intermittent. He had suffered from a severe attack of fever, lasting two months previous to his attack of diarrhea. He now had a hard chill every other day, followed by high fever, the evening temperature on the day of the chill often running up to 40° C. Quinine was given in large doses, and the chills and fever were materially lessened, but never entirely subdued. In the latter part of August the feet became swollen and œdematous, and later on the abdomen became distended with serum, while the veins on the surface were swollen and tortuous. Having been for years a hard drinker cirrhosis of the liver was diagnosed. The urine was then examined and found to be loaded with albumen, and to make matters worse the old diarrhea returned and the slight cough now became severe and distressing. On examining the lungs the existence of a small cavity was detected at the apex of the left lung, and there was marked dullness over the apex of the right. From such a complication of diseases it was but natural to anticipate an unfavorable termination, and death occurred September 28.

Necropsy (*ten hours after death*).—*Rigor mortis* well marked; body emaciated; abdomen distended and legs much swollen. Left lung, small cavity at apex; surrounding tissue consolidated and infiltrated with small tuberculous masses. Right lung, apex consolidated; condition same as that of left. There were old pleuritic adhesions over the surface of both lungs. The heart was small and valves intact. The liver very small; surface rough and nodulated; tissue firm, bloodless, and difficult to cut; color, light yellow. The spleen was large, soft, friable, and its capsule much thickened. The kidneys were small and contracted, surfaces rough, capsules adherent, cortical substance almost entirely gone, and the tissue extremely dense and of fibrous character. The cæcum, or rather the mucous membrane lining it, was a ragged mass of ulcerations which extended half way up the ascending colon, and the ileo-cæcal orifice was so constricted that its diameter was less than that of an ordinary lead pencil. The mesenteric glands were much enlarged, especially those in the neighborhood of the cæcum, and some of them were broken down, forming a soft caseous mass. The small intestines were normal. The brain was not examined.

CASE 5.

Abscess of liver.

M. Mc.; aged forty-two years; a native of Ireland; admitted to U. S. Marine Hospital, San Francisco, Cal., November 14, 1887; died November 22.

Necropsy (*twelve hours after death*).—Pronounced *rigor mortis.* Tissues flabby, but not much emaciated. Considerable subcutaneous fat. Thorax: Pleural cavities and lungs were apparently normal; the lungs were somewhat congested, particularly in dependent portions, and were not quite so much collapsed as usual; there may have been slight emphysema. Heart was flabby, fatty, and somewhat dilated. The left heart was empty, but in the aorta, beginning at the valves, was a fibrinous clot some 1 centimeter in diameter, extending cord-like at least to the first branches of the arch. The right auricle was full of fibrinous clot, which was continuous through the tricuspid orifice, with a similar clot in the right ventricle; thence the clot, passing through the pulmonary valves and half filling the caliber of the artery, ended beyond the pulmonary bifurcation in soft blood clots. Abdomen: The walls of the abdomen and the omentum and mesentery contained considerable fat. Liver was at least twice the normal size, the increase in bulk being due mainly to thickening. The organ was deeply congested, but its tissue proper was yellowish, pale, and friable, especially in left lobe. It was no doubt fatty. In the right lobe, the appearance was somewhat similar, but several sections gave the genuine nutmeg appearance. In the under part of the right lobe, just posterior and partly external to the gall bladder, was an irregular loculated abscess in the substance of the liver, which discharged when ruptured about 100 cubic centimeters of thick, creamy, inodorous pus. Above the abscess and externally there was at least 5 centimeters thickness of liver tissue, and the abscess would have pointed directly downward toward the kidney, as here only a softened layer of about 5 centimenters in thickness walled in its contents. The abscess was clearly of recent formation. Spleen was two and a half times the usual size, nearly, and was a mere purplish pulp. Kidneys were perhaps one and a half times their normal size. They were quite pale and the capsule was readily detached; their substance was friable and cut easily; the section revealed a marked fatty pallor of pyramids as well as cortex. Several small retention cysts were found in the cortex and under the capsule.

CASE 6.

Pneumonia.

W. D. (colored); aged thirty-one; a native of Kentucky; was admitted to the Marine Hospital, Memphis, Tenn., January 13, 1888; died January 18, 1888.

History.—Had been sick several days; had a chill every second day; there was no pain in any part of his body; he had no cough; the chills were stopped by .3 grams of quinine every fourth hour. On the 16th he became delirious; he would answer questions intelligently, but was always muttering. On the evening of the 16th, about 7 p. m., while sitting near the radiator with the other patients, he ran out of the ward in his night-shirt. There was snow on the ground. That night his delirium became violent; he tore his sheets and shirt. Restraining cuffs were put on him. Nothing could be done with him on the 17th. He failed rapidly. On the 17th there were symptoms of pneumonia.

Necropsy.—*Rigor mortis* not well marked. Many scars on lower part of right side of chest. Both pleural cavities completely obliterated by old adhesions. The right lung normal, as was the upper lobe of the left. The lower left lobe was entering the stage of red hepatization. Heart normal; pericardial sack obliterated by firm old adhesions; spleen enlarged and friable; capsule easily detached; liver enlarged and congested.

Diagnosis from necropsy.—Old pleurisy, pericarditis, recent malarial fever and pneumonia.

Weight of viscera.—Liver, 2,350 grams; spleen, 452; right lung, 575; left lung, 1,875; left lower lobe, 1,390; right kidney, 215; left, 220; heart, 425.

CASE 7.

Dysentery.

H. F. G. (white); aged forty-five; a native of Missouri; admitted to the U. S. Marine Hospital, Memphis, Tenn., December 11, 1887; died February 25, 1888.

History.—For a week before admission he had a chill every second day, poor appetite, loss of flesh and strength. He recovered from the chills and was then taken with dysentery. He failed rapidly and became very weak. He recovered from the dysentery, and for four weeks before he died he had only one stool daily. It was impossible to find anything that he cared to eat; his dislike of food was extreme and peculiar. He died February 25, 1888, of inanition.

Necropsy.—All organs healthy but small. His whole system was extremely emaciated.

Case 8.

Pneumonia.

J. H.; aged twenty-four years; born in Illinois; admitted to U. S. Marine Hospital, Cairo, Ill., March 16, 1888; died March 26, 1888.

History.—On admission the patient was greatly reduced in strength and was scarcely able to crawl to the hospital. He had been ill with malarial fever for the preceding five months. Quinia, with whisky, milk and food, antipyrine, and, upon the development of pneumonia, an oiled silk jacket was used. The illness assumed from the first a typhoid character, and with some few rallies he sank rapidly.

Necropsy (four hours after death).—Body that of a slender tubercular young man, badly nourished and emaciated. *Rigor mortis* well marked. Hypostatic congestion throughout. Both lungs solidified throughout, and about breaking down except the superior lobe of the left lung, which was but slightly congested. Plural cavities obliterated. Liver and spleen greatly enlarged and hardened.

REMITTENT FEVER.

Case 1.

L. H.; aged twenty-eight years; nativity, Ohio; admitted to the U. S. Marine Hospital, Saint Louis, Mo., July 11, 1887. He died immediately on being taken into the ward.

History.—But little could be learned of patient's sickness, as he was delirious when first seen, and no information could be had, except that he had been sick for a few days from chills, fever, and diarrhea.

Necropsy (seventeen hours after death).—Body emaciated; skin of a tawny color; *rigor mortis* slight. Brain meninges, congested. Pleuræ, normal. Lungs, slightly congested, otherwise normal. Heart, normal. Stomach contained some bile, otherwise healthy. Liver and spleen, both enlarged and very much congested with dark blood; gall-bladder distended with bile, some of which had been extravasated into the surrounding structures. Other organs not examined.

Case 2.

Peritonitis.

Mrs. G. Y.; aged forty-eight; nativity, Scotland; admitted to U. S. Marine Hospital, Detroit, Mich., August 2, 1887; died August 21, 1887.

History.—The patient was unable to give a correct history of her case. In the spring she had suffered from liver trouble. When admitted to hospital she was very weak, much emaciated, and had considerable fever, which began with a chill and was marked by occasional sweats and attacks of vomiting. No evidence of organic disease could be found. The fever was soon controlled by moderate doses of quinine, but a severe diarrhea soon set in, upon which bismuth subnitrate in large doses, opium, and lead acetate, either alone or combined, had no effect. It was checked somewhat by ergot, and finally controlled by a pill containing the sulphates of copper, morphine, and quinine. Still the patient continued to fail quite rapidly, although taking considerable nourishment in the form of beef tea, toast, milk, chicken broth, and milk punch. She never complained of much pain, but firm pressure over the region of the liver revealed a slight tenderness. During the last week of her illness she had some cough and expectoration; there was marked œdema of the right lower extremity and abdominal enlargement, partly from liquid and partly from gas.

Necropsy (eleven hours after death).—Rigor mortis slight; emaciation extreme; heart and lungs normal but considerable liquid in pleural cavities and pericardial sac. Liver large; tissue softer than normal; weight, 1,220 grams. Spleen and kidneys below normal size. Stomach and intestines distended with gas. Considerable liquid in peritoneal cavity. Lymph deposits were abundant over various parts of the peritoneum, notably that covering the liver and intestines. Some white masses were found to the left of the vertebral column, which, upon examination, proved to be medullary carcinoma.

Case 3.

Lobular pneumonia.

J. P.; aged eighteen years; born in Ireland; admitted to the U. S. Marine Hospital, Chicago, Ill., September 3, 1887; died October 1, 1887.

History.—Entered hospital quite sick with fever; states that he has been too sick to work for several days; complains of headache, pains in back, and some sore throat; tongue dry and heavily coated with a dirty brown scum, also tremulous; skin thick and muddy looking; bowels said to be constipated; nausea and some vomiting; abdomen tender, no gurgling; temperature 40° C., pulse 120. The bowels were opened and quinine given in 6 grain doses at short intervals; sponge baths, ice and milk-punch freely. On next visit the quinine had so affected his hearing that it was difficult to make him understand. It was stopped and antipyrine used during the entire case with sponging. On second day the throat became much inflamed; the tonsils were swollen and ragged; palatal arch and pharynx were intensely inflamed. Remedies were at once used to check this, but it became very troublesome. The Eustachian tube and middle ear became involved, and early perforation of the membranal tympani took place. The general condition at this time was precarious. The temperature ranged high; the nervous system became profoundly affected; subsultus was at times noticed, tongue was tremulous, dry, and cracked; teeth and gums covered with sordes, and sleeplessness marked. Added to this was a lobular pneumonia induced by inhalation of material from the diseased pharynx and post nasal cavities, or a descent of the inflammation, for there was a general acute bronchitis. The pneumonic spot was apparently located in the right middle lobe. There was localized dullness, with absence of vesicular murmur, and the presence of bronchial breathing and increased vocal resonance. During this period a fatal termination was expected, but he rallied from this low state. The pharynx and nose improved; the bronchitis became subacute; the lung seemed to be clearing up; he ate heartily of all that was allowed him; his improvement was indeed marked, yet the liver remained large and tender, and the spleen was also enlarged. Treatment directed mostly to the lung affection, and to keep up the heart power digitalis and am. carb. were given. and whisky was used freely at all times. In spite of such hopeful signs the heart's action was noticed to decline, and, although stimulation was increased, the lungs slowly became clogged, and he died of heart failure.

Necropsy (*fourteen hours after death*).—*Rigor mortis* marked; body much emaciated. Pleuræ found intact. Right lung contained a pneumonic spot, as large as the closed fist, in its lower lobe. The middle lobe was a mere wedge between the larger upper and lower lobe. The entire lung was greatly engorged. Left lung also contained several small spots of inflammation (lobular pneumonia), not discovered before death. Pharynx not seen. Liver was much enlarged, of a pale brown color, and heavily pigmented on the under surface; it was not friable, fatty, or lardaceous; weight 3,150 grams. Spleen was large and friable; medullary portion was diffluent on manipulation; much pigment noticed; weight 650 grams. The folds of the mesentery were congested and the glands stood out sharply as small, pea-like pigmented masses thickly scattered throughout the omental folds. A portion of small intestine was carefully examined, but not a sign of ulceration or an enlarged patch could be found; not even a solitary gland enlarged. Although at times the diagnosis was questioned, yet this was not *typhoid fever*.

CASE 4.

J. F., aged thirty-four years; nativity, Maine; admitted to Marine Hospital at Boston, Mass., December 5, 1887; died December 5.

The patient contracted his disease on the island of Java.

Necropsy (*twelve hours after death*).—*Rigor mortis* present. There was an extensive effusion of serum into the pleural and abdominal cavities. The liver was congested, and the spleen enlarged, dark colored, and hard. The kidneys were congested and dark in color.

CASE 5.

B. B.; aged thirty-seven years; nativity, Mississippi; admitted to U. S. Marine Hospital, New Orleans, La., January 1, 1888; died January 7.

Necropsy (*eight hours after death*).—Body fairly nourished; ecchymosis unusually marked on dependent parts. Pericardial fluid was clear and of normal quantity. Heart was pale, soft, and fatty. Ventricles contained small *ante mortem* clots. Valves were normal. Lungs: There were a few slight adhesions at the apex of the left lung, but the right lung had firm adhesions at apex and base; hypostatic congestion was well marked over posterior parts of both lungs. The lower lobe of right lung was adherent to the lobe above it by recent and soft adhesions. Liver was enlarged and very soft (almost pulpy). It was easily penetrated by the finger. Gall bladder contained about 30 cubic centimeters of very dark bile. Spleen was about eight times its normal size, and was of the consistence of a soft blood clot. There was a fissure across its middle on the superior surface, extending about half way through. Kidneys were congested. Bladder contained about 100 cubic centimeters of dark-colored urine. Intestines empty and normal. They were examined carefully, but no *typhoid* lesions could be found. Mesenteric glands were normal. Vermiform appendix rather long and perfectly empty.

Brain: Over the vertex the dura mater was adherent to the pia mater by recent lymph in small patches. About the occiput on left side the same condition existed. Surface of brain was much congested.

Case 6.

Pneumonia—Peritonitis.

J. L. (colored), aged thirty-eight; a native of Tennessee; admitted to the U. S. Marine Hospital, Memphis, Tenn., February 18, 1888; died February 22.

History.—He was taken sick February 15, on which day he had a severe chill, and on the 17th he had another. Pain along border of ribs, tenderness over the stomach and left lobe of the liver; conjunctivæ yellow. Area of liver dullness enlarged. No cough or pain in chest; pulse, 90 and weak; respiration, quick and shallow; temperature, 38° C.

February 19.—Complains of slight cough and a pain near the middle of the sternum; dullness and crepitant râles over right apex; moist râles over chest on right and left sides.

February 20.—Pain in the abdomen same as yesterday, only more general. Pulse 100, fuller, and temperature 37.5° C.

February 21.—Respiration very shallow, and abdomen very tender; no anxious expression about the face; pulse, 100 and weak; respiration, 40.

February 22.—Pulse, 140, thready; temperature, 39; the temperature never went above 39° C., nor below 37.5° C.; eyes and skin, yellow.

Necropsy.—Small intestines glued together by recent fibrinous material and easily separable; mucous membrane of appendix vermiformis was inflamed. The appendix was free; no cause for peritonitis found; right apex solidified, in condition of red hepatization; heart covered with a false membrane easily detached and covered with villi; 200 cubic centimeters of fluid in pericardium; valves efficient, and orifices normal; heart cavities filled with *ante mortem* clots.

Weight of viscera in grams.—Left lung, 255; right, 863; left kidney, 218; right, 198; heart, 438; heart clot, 72; liver, 2,126; spleen, 278; spleen pulp very soft; liver congested and substance soft; no stains of bile in liver.

MALARIAL CACHEXIA—MITRAL REGURGITATION—SUBACUTE INFLAMMATION OF THE BLADDER.

L. W.; aged thirty-seven; born in Maine; admitted to the U. S. Marine Hospital, Vineyard Haven, Mass., April 6; died April 20, 1888.

History.—On entering the hospital he was found to be in a very low condition. There was great emaciation, marked mitral regurgitation, hæmaturia, subacute inflammation of the bladder, and a history of daily periodical chills or rigors for the preceding three months. He had been under treatment at various times, but received no relief. His temperature on admission was 38° C. The next morning normal, and the following evening 39.4° C. This variation in the temperature continued till the day before his death, when it dropped to 36. He possessed little or no assimilating power, gradually growing worse. Seven days after admission a violent epistaxis occurred, followed in a few hours by marked points of hæmorrhagic extravasation scattered all over the body and extremities. Just prior to death a large quantity of blood escaped from the bowels. After death I elicited from his family the history of a hæmorrhagic diathesis.

Necropsy (*examination made thirty two hours after death*).—*Rigor mortis* well marked. Great emaciation. Spots of suggillation were noticed all over the body and extremities, and the skin had a marked yellow hue. A yellow discoloration was observed, particularly in the costal cartilages, and somewhat throughout all the internal organs. On opening the pericardium the surface of the heart was found to be covered with pus, the veins distended, and its muscular structure soft and œdematous. The cavities of the heart were filled with *ante mortem* clots, while two large vegetations were found on the mitral valves extending 1.875 centimeters into the ventricle, and being .625 centimeters wide at the point of attachment. Some pus was found in the ascending portion of the aorta. Slight pleuritic adhesions in both pleural cavities; hypostatic congestion, emphysema, and slight œdema of the lungs. Gall bladder distended. Liver enlarged, congested, firm, and hard; weight, 2,750 grams. Capsule adherent. Spleen very much enlarged; size, 15 centimeters by 15 centimeters by 7.5 centimeters; weight, 375 grammes. Both kidneys were enlarged, congested, and capsules adherent, with clotted blood in the pelvis. Omentum congested. Bladder distended with bloody urine.

PERNICIOUS MALARIAL FEVER.

S. P.; admitted to the U. S. Marine Hospital, New York, August 2, 1887; died on August.3.

History.—At the time of the patient's admission he was in a semi-unconscious state and no intelligible history was obtained.

Necropsy (*eighteen hours after death*).—*Rigor mortis* slight; body fairly nourished. The skin was jaundiced, lungs greatly œdematous; pleural cavity containing a great quantity of serum; pleura pigmented; heart in diastole, heart muscle pale; valves normal, liver enlarged, pigmented, and of a chocolate hue; spleen greatly enlarged, friable, melanotic. Mesenteric glands enlarged; other organs normal.

ERYSIPELAS.

Thrombosis of longitudinal sinus.

G. L. (colored); aged thirty-two; a native of Kentucky; was admitted to the Marine Hospital, Memphis, Tenn., March 2, 1888.

History.—He had been sick a week; had pain and a burning feeling in the right side of his face; some fever but no chill; appetite poor, tongue coated; right side of face and scalp badly swollen; right eye was closed and he could with difficulty open his mouth. Temperature 39.5° C.; pulse 120 and weak. He was brought to the hospital in the rain in an express wagon. The day after his admission he became delirious. March 4 he was troubled with nausea and vomiting; temperature, 40; pulse 130 and weak. He failed steadily and died on the 6th.

Necropsy.—Body that of a well-developed man, who would weigh 80 kilograms. *Rigor mortis* well marked. All of one side of the head swollen and œndematous; upper lip hard and thick; dura mater dull looking. There was a large clot in the longitudinal sinus, and about 4 centimeters from the torcular herophili there were vegetations over a surface the size of a nickel. To this was attached a fibrinous clot. The veins of the pia were distended, showing all the finer ramifications. The lateral sinuses were full of blood, due probably to pressure of the swollen tissues on the internal jugular. There were several metastatic abscesses in various parts of the right lung. Some were as large as a pea, some as large as a celery seed. The liver was soft and friable; the left pleural cavity was obliterated by old firm adhesions; heart normal.

Weight of viscera, etc.—Brain, 1,502; liver, 1,909; right, lung, 652; left, 429; heart, 334; spleen, 210.

SEPTICÆMIA.

C. W.; aged forty-two; nativity, Germany; admitted to U. S. Marine Hospital, Stapleton, N. Y., January 5, 1888; died, January 14.

Necropsy (fifty-four hours after death).—*Rigor mortis* was marked; livores were present. There was sloughing of the skin of the right leg. There was an amputation wound of the right great toe. On incising the skin of the foot necrosed tissue was found extending along the sole of the foot and about the external malleolus. On incising the thigh the lymphatics were found filled with pus. The viscera were found normal, except for pleuritic adhesions, which were present on both sides of the chest.

PRIMARY SYPHILIS.

(*Suicide—internal injuries—shock.*)

A. W.; aged twenty-two years; born in Norway; admitted to marine ward of the German Hospital on February 15, 1888.

History.—When admitted he was suffering from venereal ulceration of the prepuce, for which he received ordinary treatment. He was morose and reticent with the other patients, and on the day following admission, at about 11.30 a. m., he deliberately jumped from the window of the ward, which, being on the third floor, made a descent of at least 40 feet. He struck the eaves of an adjacent lower building and thence to the pavement below. On being picked up he was found to have a compound comminuted fracture of the right femur at the lower end of the middle third, and was suffering very profoundly from shock. There was a fracture of the inferior maxilla, which was also compound. The tops of several teeth were broken off, and there were lacerated wounds of lower lip and face; there was also a compound fracture of right elbow joint, with more or less general contusions over the body. When the patient had rallied sufficiently he was etherized, and a resection of an inch and a half of the femur was made, the ends wired, and the limb put up in plaster of Paris. He came well out of the ether, but never fully rallied from the original shock, and died February 17, 8 p. m.

Necropsy (Twenty-six hours post mortem).—Body well nourished; thoracic viscera were normal. Stomach showed inflammation of both internal and external coats. The liver was congested and very dark in color. Both kidneys were very much congested. Ulna of right forearm was fractured in several places about the joint, transversely and longitudinally. In the fracture of femur which was operated upon the wire had broken.

SYPHILIS.

CASE 1.

Cerebral.

C. M.; aged thirty-five years; born in Germany; admitted to the U. S. Marine Hospital, Portland, Me., August 11, 1887; died August 15, at 3 p. m.

History.—Three days before his admission, while at work as cook and steward on a small yacht, he suddenly became morose, taciturn, and without warning threw himself overboard. He fought desperately with his rescuers, and was gotten aboard with great difficulty. As soon as possible, he was transferred in handcuffs, with ankles lashed together, to this hospital, requiring the exertions of two men to control him. Treatment was palliative; large doses of bromide of potash, chloral hydrate, and morphia (hypodermically) seemed to have little or no effect. He had occasional semi-lucid intervals, during which he was taken out of the straight-jacket, washed, dressed, and fed. He would occasionally accept food, port wine, tea, and milk. Towards the end he sank into coma. A noticeable feature was that although violently screaming and raving most of the time, in English and German, he did not use any profane or vulgar language whatever.

Necropsy (nineteen hours after death).—Body that of a musular man in the prime of life, and well developed, though emaciated. *Rigor mortis* very marked; hypostatic congestion very marked, the body being greatly discolored. Base of brain congested; summit of cerebrum exhibited on either side of longitudinal fissure a patch of syphilitic deposit, about 2 centimeters in width each, extending posteriorly 7 centimeters from the vertex. Lungs adherent to chest wall at apices; otherwise normal. Heart empty, relaxed, valves softened. Liver weighed 1,400 grams, was adherent to diaphragm, congested, and cirrhosed; gall-bladder enlarged, and distended with fluid, black bile; kidneys contracted and cirrhotic; spleen friable and jelly-like. Dura mater closely adherent to skull, cerebellum softened.

CASE 2.

G. C.; aged fifty years; nativity, Scotland; admitted to U. S. Marine Hospital, Cleveland, Ohio, May 11, 1888; died June 8.

History.—When admitted he was delirious; had pain in the head and syphilitic iritis. On the subsidence of the delirium he was stupid and indifferent. Although the fact was elicited that he had suffered with syphilis, it was impossible to obtain any satisfactory history in consequence of the dullness of his intellectual faculties. Anti-syphilitic remedies were not well borne, and made no appreciable impression on his condition, which fact was attributable to lack of assimilation, the general system being so broken and disordered as to be incapable of appropriating either supporting or specific treatment.

Necropsy (sixteen hours after death).—The brain was above the average size; the surface of the brain was much congested, but on section its interior was normal in appearance. The dura mater was slightly thickened and its internal surface roughened a little, but no new formations were observed, and the dura mater was abnormally adherent to the skull. The pathological conditions revealed by the *post mortem* examination of the head were not marked, except the congestion of the surface of the brain, and were so totally inadequate to account for his nervous symptoms during life that it would seem proper to class this case among the cases of syphilis of the brain, *sine materiâ.*

The stomach was affected with catarrhal inflammation. The liver was hyperæmic and of a brownish-red color, and apparently in the incipient stage of cirrhosis.

CASE 3.

Tubercle of lungs.

G. W.; aged forty-seven years; a native of South Carolina; admitted to the Marine Hospital at Memphis, Tenn., September 20, 1887.

History.—This patient's legs below the knees were covered with ulcers of various sizes; some were 3 and some 10 centimeters long. He had had these several months. He had the initial lesion of syphilis and the secondary efflorescence several years previous to his admission. He said his usual weight when well was 68 kilos. When admitted he weighed a little over 36 kilos. Appetite poor and fickle. The ulcers did fairly well under treatment and had healed before his death. After the ulcers healed he had occasional attacks of catarrhal inflammation of the bowels. These yielded readily to treatment. Then came evidences of consolidation of left lung with muco-purulent expectoration. He was too weak to raise the sputa, and so was drowned in the pus from his own lung. He died November 24, 1887.

Necropsy.—*Rigor mortis* well marked. Scars over both legs. No scar in either groin. Emaciation extreme. Mesenteric glands much enlarged. Recent adhesions in left pleural cavity. There was consolidation of left lower lobe. There was inflammation of peri-bronchial glands, some of which had undergone caseous degeneration; some had broken down and discharged their contents into the bronchi by ulceration.

Weight of viscera.—Heart, 187; right lung, 710; left, 494; liver, 1,464.

CASE 4.

Pneumonia.

S. D. (colored); aged nineteen years; native of Georgia; was admitted to the hospital at Memphis, Tenn., April 11, 1888.

History.—He complained of severe pains in all his bones. These pains are very severe at night. He says he has not had anything to eat for two weeks, except now and then a small piece of bread. His legs from his knees to the ankles were covered with scabs. He had chancres and ulcers of penis (chancroids) and suppurating lymph glands. He did not fail very much, for he was nearly dead when admitted. He died April 19, 1888.

Necropsy.—Upper lobe of right lung solidified. Mesenteric glands enlarged and caseous.

DEBILITY.

Cerebral tumor.

E. B.; aged sixty-three years; native of the United States; was admitted to Grace Hospital, Seattle, Wash., November 22, 1887; died December 19, 1887.

History.—The patient when admitted to the hospital was very much emaciated and weak, apparently suffering from debility. He was quite deaf, and also somewhat demented, so that it was impossible to get a satisfactory history from him at that time. He was put on tonics, and for a time improved, both physically and mentally. He complained of severe frontal headache, which he claimed to have had for nearly ten years. There was no history of syphilis. Two weeks after being admitted he had a relapse and rapidly grew weaker. Paralysis of bladder and bowels occurred, and also slight paralysis of the lower extremities; the latter, however, was not constant. At times there was a slight tremor of the head and hands on voluntary motion. Several times there was a change for the better, but only to be followed by a relapse, each time sinking lower than before. He had no fever until the day of his death, when his temperature increased to 39° C. Several days before death the paralysis became general, and the day before the muscles became rigid: death ensuing from spasm of the respiratory muscles.

Necropsy (twenty hours after death).—*Rigor mortis* marked. The dura mater presented a healthy appearance. Pia mater showed signs of slight congestion, except over the right frontal region, where it was quite pale. The brain substance of the superior convolutions of the right frontal lobe was in a very soft, almost fluid state, from the pressure of a tumor which was found in the inferior part of the lobe. This tumor was the size of a hen's egg, and on section presented a tubercular appearance, with a small pus cavity in the center. No other signs of tubercle were found.

DELIRIUM TREMENS.

G. L.; aged thirty-nine years; native of New York; was admitted to marine ward Grace Hospital, Seattle, Wash., April 9, 1888; died April 18, 1888.

History.—He had been drinking heavily for three weeks, and became delirious three days defore his admission to the hospital. Four days after he became comatose, and gradually sank until his death.

Necropsy.—The vessels of the dura mater and pia mater were much distended. On section blood oozed freely from the cut surface of the cerebrum. The ventricles were distended with serum. Other organs not examined.

RHEUMATIC FEVER.

CASE 1.

Pleurisy.

A. P. W. (white); aged twenty-three years; native of Louisiana; admitted to the Marine Hospital, Memphis, Tenn., November 28, 1887.

History.—He complained of pain, which was located in various joints. The worst pain was in his right knee. This was considerably swollen, hot, and tender to the touch. The capsule was much distended. The joint was aspirated and 250 cubic centimeters of fluid withdrawn. Hot dressings with compression were applied. The joint refilled twice, and was twice aspirated, withdrawing less fluid at each aspiration. With sodium salicylate and iodide of potash the rheumatism disappeared. He was then given citrate of iron and quinine. His skin was very pale. This pallor was at first attributed to the rheumatism. He did not seem to improve. On careful examination there were found venous hum in the neck, dyspnœa, an enlarged spleen, and an increase of white corpuscles in the blood. The relative increase to red could not be determined without counting. There was no albumen in the urine. His failure was constant, but gradual.

Necropsy.—Body much emaciated. Fluid in all cavities. Lungs crepitant everywhere. Old pleuritic adhesions on right side. Heart normal and valves efficient. Two liters of fluid in each pleural cavity and 200 cubic centimeters in the pericardium. Intestines normal; mesenteric glands enlarged. The liver had on its surface six cicatrices, one of which extended two centimeters into its substance. The surface had a granular appearance. The liver was normal in size. To the eye Glisson's capsule was thickened. The spleen was large but normal in appearance. It was firm. The lymph glands of mediastinum were enlarged.

Weight of viscera in grams.—Right lung, 975; left, 835; left kidney, 197; heart, 420; spleen, 834; liver, 911.

Microscopically the liver shows much thickening of interstitial tissue, and liver cells very granular.

CASE 2.

Pericarditis-myocarditis—enlarged liver.

J. N.; aged twenty-six years; nativity, Germany; admitted to U. S. Marine Hospital, San Francisco, Cal., February 6, 1888; died February 15, 1888.

History.—The elbows and shoulders were the joints affected, and though quite painful were not much swollen. There was decided increase in the area of liver dullness, and the heart's action was somewhat irregular and feeble, but there were no friction sounds, and no pain was complained of in the precordial region. He was taken suddenly worse on the evening of the 14th; the heart failed rapidly, and death was occasioned by heart clot.

Necropsy (twenty-four hours post mortem).—Pericardium found adherent to the lung and diaphragm; to the latter by old and very firm adhesions; so very firm, that it was necessary to disect it up. The cavity of the pericardium was completely obliterated by adhesions of the two surfaces from old inflammation, except over the left ventricle, where the adhesions were more recent, and in this locality there was inflammation of the substance of the heart. The left ventricle was somewhat dilated and the mitral valve very much thickened. *Ante mortem* clots in both auricles extending into the ventricles and great vessels. There were some old pleuritic adhesions on the left side. The lungs were compressed but normal in structure. Liver much congested and soft, weight a little over 2½ kilos.

CASE 3.

Endocarditis.

G. J.; aged twenty-five years; nativity, Germany; admitted to U. S. Marine Hospital, Stapleton, N. Y., March 24, 1888; died March 31.

Necropsy (thirty-five hours post mortem).—Body of a healthy, well developed male. *Rigor mortis;* livores. The heart contained clots in all its cavities; valves were normal; endocardium of left ventricle was injected. Left lung was œdematous; the pleura of the upper lobe was covered with small, irregular, suppurating foci. Right lung was œdematous; it was attached by old adhesions. Right kidney contained pus in the pelvis and purulent foci in the pyramids. Left kidney contained pus in the pelvis and purulent foci in the cortex. The liver was normal. Spleen normal. Mucous membrane of the bladder was congested; bladder contained purulent urine. The urethra was congested. As the patient had an erysipelatous blush of the feet before death, though these members appeared normal, a knife was passed into right leg above internal malleolus; pus foci were found; like foci were found in the left leg and in the deltoid muscles. The blood-vessels of the brain were congested; there was softening of right tempero-sphenoidal lobe at the beginning of the sylvian fissure.

RHEUMATISM.

Atheroma.

W. H. (colored); aged eighty-four years; nativity, Virginia; admitted to the U. S. Marine Hospital at Baltimore, Md., March 14, 1888; died April 17, 1888.

Necropsy (fourteen hours after death).—Rigor mortis well marked. Body well developed, but poorly nourished. Heart under usual size, with considerable fat on the surface; blood in the cavities fluid; aortic valves had a few atheromatous nodules near attached border. Aorta gave evidence of beginning calcareous change. Both lungs adherent to chest walls; entire lung tissue extremely œdematous. Liver was fatty in places. Spleen enlarged, dark, with atheromatous vessels, and patches of the same calcified matter on the surface. Kidneys slightly granular. Small intestines normal, but more or less devoid of any contents. Large intestines contained hard scybalous masses of a dark green color. Brain not examined.

CARCINOMA.

CASE 1.

Epithelioma—face.

J. S.; aged sixty-seven years; nativity, Ireland; was admitted to the U. S. Marine Hospital, port of Boston, August 4, 1886; died July 4, 1887.

History.—When the patient was first examined at the hospital he stated that the disease appeared upon his lip about two years and six months prior to that date, and that about one year before, an operation was performed in New York, removing a considerable portion of the lower lip. His mouth was somewhat contracted by the operation, and the disease had recurred involving the old cicatrix, the integument beneath the lower jaw and the sublingual glands. An operation was made shortly after his admission to the hospital, cutting wide of all diseased tissues, removing considerable of the left cheek and the lower lip. The wound united and nearly closed, but there was a recurrence of the disease about three months later, involving the cheek, parotid gland and sublingual glands. He suffered constant and excruciating pain, which was mitigated by the administration of large doses of morphine and the local application of cocaine. The discharge from the diseased surface and the saliva, which could not be retained, were profuse and the odor very offensive. The patient died from exhaustion on July 4, 1887.

Necropsy (*twenty-four hours after death*).—Body greatly emaciated and *rigor mortis* present. The left cheek, the lower lip, the skin over the left parotid and beneath the chin were destroyed, freely exposing the submaxillary bone and the large vessels of the neck and face. The facial artery was destroyed, although there had been no hemorrhage during the course of the disease. Small cysts were found in each kidney. Other organs normal.

CASE 2.

Epithelioma—face.

J. D.; aged fifty-five years; nativity, Newfoundland; admitted to the U. S. Marine Hospital, Portland, Me., November 14, 1887; died January 7, 1888.

History.—Had previously been a patient at the hospital, September 5 to October 17, 1887, for epithelioma, and was discharged with mark of "recovery." An operation had been performed September 9 for the complete removal of the cancer by my predecessor, with the result as stated. Recurrence of the growth in situ followed with infiltration and enlargement of the cervical glands, and he was re-admitted a month later and treated symptomatically until his death, which occurred eight weeks after his re-admission.

Necropsy (*twenty-eight hours after death*).—*Rigor mortis* present, but probably due in part to extreme cold weather. Body emaciated. At site of operation a deep ulcerated surface, exposing the inferior maxilla. The cervical glands on both sides were hypertrophied and ulceration had progressed in one. The visceral organs were all found to be normal in size, position, and constitution. The heart contained organized clots in both ventricles extending up into the vessels leading therefrom. The right ventricle was completely filled with a large fibrinous clot. These organized clots are, however, commonly found in cases characterized by a gradually weakening circulation.

CASE 3.

Scirrhus of stomach.

F. S.; aged forty years; nativity, Ohio; admitted to the U. S. Marine Hospital, Saint Louis, Mo., September 6, 1887 (a new permit issued and diagnosis changed October 29); died November 26.

History.—Patient had been complaining for a number of months previous to his admission to the hospital with dyspeptic symptoms. At the time of his admission the diagnosis of diarrhea and malarial fever, intermittent, was made. After several weeks treatment the diarrhea and symptoms of intermittent fever disappeared, but jaundice supervened, with continued distress about the præcordia, some tenderness over the liver, and frequent nausea and vomiting. The diagnosis was then changed to hepatitis with jaundice. Notwithstanding varied treatment he gradually became more emaciated, the jaundice increased, the pain in the epigastric region continued, and he was troubled with persistent vomiting, the vomited matter resembling coffee-grounds for a few days prior to death. He could not retain any food, liquid or solid, and a few hours before death vomited about a pint of blood.

Necropsy (*twenty hours after death*).—*Rigor mortis* well marked; body much emaciated; skin of a tawny color, and all the internal organs and tissues deeply stained by bile pigment. Pleuræ, slight adhesions on left side; lungs, both collapsed but not consolidated, readily floating, a few calcareous nodules were found in both lungs about the size of a pea; heart, muscular substance tinged yellow, normal in other respects; liver, much enlarged and discolored yellow; biliary ducts greatly distended with bile; gall-bladder about half normal size, its walls thickened and contained two gall stones, each about the size of a hazel-nut, but contained no bile. The ductus communis choledochus and the cystic duct were both impervious. Stomach distended with gas, and contained a dark bloody fluid; the walls were deeply stained, the lining membrane thickened and somewhat softened in one place, showing indications of the point whence the hemorrhage came. At the pylorus this thickening was greatly increased, and the opening into the duodenum seemed to be entirely occluded. In this situation was also found a tumor of undoubtedly malignant character (best classed under carcinoma, variety scirrhus), which included the pyloric portion of the stomach, the head of the pancreas, upper portion of the duodenum, and the hepatic, cystic, and common bile ducts. On section the tumor was dense, with no signs of ulceration. Kidneys appeared to be normal, except the deep discoloration which pervaded the entire organ. Other organs as far as examined showed no marked pathological conditions.

CASE 4.

Stomach, pancreas and mesentery.

O. R; aged fifty-eight years; nativity, Ireland; admitted to U. S. Marine Hospital, Stapleton, N. Y., January 18, 1888; died March 28.

Necropsy (*twenty hours post-mortem*).—There was pleuritic thickening at the apex of the left lung, and thickening of the pleura of the right lung; hypostatic congestion was present in both lungs. There was thickening of the mitral valve; sclerosis of the vessels of the heart was present, and thickening of the pericardium in plaques. The capsule of the spleen was thickened, and the organ was found hard on section. A cyst was found in the left kidney at its external border; otherwise it was normal. The right kidney was lobulated but normal. The liver was soft, with fatty degeneration. The stomach was carcinomatous; a cancerous mass existed along the entire lesser curvature. The pancreas was carcinomatous. The cancerous masses resembled bunches of grapes. The mesenteric glands were cancerous. Cancerous deposits were found in the peritoneum.

CASE 5.

Stomach, liver, and peritoneum.

J. H.; aged forty-four years; nativity, Canada; admitted to U. S. Marine Hospital, Detroit, Mich., April 9, 1888; died April 21.

History.—This patient was first admitted to hospital on February 2, 1888, with cirrhosis of the liver, and was re-admitted April 9 with carcinoma of stomach. Physical examination showed the liver to be diminished in size. He gave a history of having suffered several times before with liver disturbance and had been tapped once for ascites. He had been addicted to the use of alcohol to excess when first admitted, he was troubled with constipation, slight jaundice, occasional vomiting, and some pain over the liver and stomach, which later on increased in intensity. Ascites was not marked until the last few weeks of his life. He was tapped April 16, 1888, and 5,000 cubic centimeters of fluid withdrawn. He died of asthenia, April 21, 1888, at 10 a. m.

Necropsy, (ten hours after death).—*Rigor mortis* not marked; body emaciated. Lungs, normal. The mitral and tricuspid valves of the heart were thickened. Spleen enlarged, and liver diminished in size and nodulated; the former weighing 402 grams, the latter 1,500. Considerable cancerous matter was found in the stomach, liver, duodenum and different parts of the peritoneum. Kidneys normal.

CASE 6.

Scirrhus of pancreas and pylorus.

F. G.; aged fifty-four years; native of Germany; admitted to U. S. Marine Hospital, San Francisco, Cal., October 17, 1887; died November 21.

Necropsy (eight hours after death).—*Rigor mortis* present; great emaciation; no jaundice. Only the abdomen was examined. The intestines were nearly empty, and collapsed. The stomach was greatly distended with a mass of ingesta, and partly with gas. The capacity of the inflated organ was not measured, but was near 2,000 cubic centimeters. The color of contents—a grumous brownish, almost fluid, matter—did not seem due to blood, as no ulcerations were seen. Fragments of articles of food were recognized. The pylorus, head of pancreas, and a number of infected glands were matted inextricably together, and constituted a tumor of irregular shape, the size, perhaps, of a small orange. The stomach was slit up along the greater curvature, through the pylorus, after it had been ascertained that the orifice of the latter just admitted the end of the little finger. It was then seen that the pylorus and the stomach together were involved to the extent of some 2 inches, and that the cancerous growth was not very thick but extremely dense and firm. The inner surface was extensively eroded, but there was no indication of there ever having been hemorrhage. The mucosa (as well as the other layers of the stomach wall) was pale and thin, and covered with glairy mucus. It was difficult to separate the head of the pancreas from the mass of glands and infected connective tissue with which it was bound up, but it was sufficiently shown to be cancerous, and fused by the neoplasm into the lower wall of the pylorus. The body of the pancreas, for an inch or two from the head, contained nodules of scirrhus. The liver was displaced to the right by the enlarged stomach, but did not appear to contain any nodules. The spleen was some two-thirds only of its normal bulk, but likewise was not found to be infected. Nothing else worthy of note was observed, except the very extensive lymphatic involvement, not only in the immediate vicinity of the primary trouble, but throughout the upper mesentery.

CASE 7.

Liver and omentum.

Mrs. I. D. (cook); aged forty-two years; nativity, Michigan; admitted to U. S. Marine Hospital, Detroit, Mich., March 16, 1888; died April 8.

History.—She first entered the hospital February 22, 1888, with malarial cachexia, from which she recovered, and was re-admitted March

16, with carcinoma of the liver. Ascites was a very prominent symptom in this case, and gave her much discomfort. She was tapped three times, and about 10,000 cubic centimeters of fluid withdrawn each time. She had occasional attacks of severe pain over the right hypochondriac and epigastric regions. A tonic and supporting method of treatment was pursued, but in spite of it she failed rapidly and was much emaciated at the time of her death, which occurred April 8, 1888, at 5 p. m.

Necropsy (*fifteen hours after death*).—*Rigor mortis* slight, body much emaciated. Heart and lungs normal. Kidneys and spleen somewhat enlarged; weight of right kidney, 197 grams; left, 192; spleen, 320; liver, 1,497. Cancerous matter was found in the liver and omentum and a gall-stone about the size of a pigeon's egg in the gall-bladder.

Case 8.

Omentum and peritoneum.

N. J.; aged fifty-three years; native of Norway; admitted to U. S. Marine Hospital at Boston, Mass., April 3, 1888; died April 16.

History.—Patient stated that he had a hemorrhage from the stomach and bowels four years ago, but has had no recurrence. Three months previous to admission he had a fall on shipboard, striking on the left side, but soon recovered from this. He was apparently in good health until twelve days previous to admission, when the abdomen began to swell, and with the exception of a few scybalæ, he had no movement of the bowels for ten days. Considerable fluid in abdomen, intestines tympanitic, liver pushed up as high as nipple; no fever; pulse good, but considerable pain in epigastrium. After vainly trying for three days various purgatives and injections through the rectal tube, and patient's condition growing rapidly worse, exploratory laparotomy was decided upon. With this intention attempts were made on the night of the 6th of April to anæsthetize the patient, but had to be abandoned, both ether and chloroform affecting the respiration and circulation in an alarming manner. The aspirator was introduced and 6,000 cubic centimeters of blood-stained serum removed. This rendered the patient more comfortable that night and next day, during which time stimulants were freely used, so that when night came he was in a condition allowing the operation. Ether was administered and an incision 10 centimeters in length was made in the linea alba between the umbilicus and pubis, and the abdomen opened in the usual manner. A considerable quantity of serum escaped, and on introducing the hand extensive cancerous deposits in the omentum and peritoneum were disclosed. The omentum was very thick and hard, and of a dark red hue. Portions of the small intestines were deeply injected and the convolutions more or less matted together from peritonitis. Further operative procedures were deemed inadvisable; a drainage tube was inserted, the abdominal wound was closed with silver sutures and dressed antiseptically. Though suffering from profound shock at the close of the operation, the patient rallied; the bowels moved several times the following day; the vomiting ceased, nourishment was retained, and his general condition was much improved. There was very little febrile reaction, and the sutures were removed by the seventh day, the wound having healed by first intention except at the site of the drainage tube. A day or so later hiccough became annoying, the face anxious, the pulse flagging, and the patient gradually sank into death.

Necropsy (*ten hours after death*).—Right lung weighed 560 grams; left lung weighed 500 grams; both normal except a few hyperaemic patches.

Heart weighed 380 grams and was normal. Peritoneum was studded with cancerous nodules. The omentum, stomach, and intestines were matted together by extensive cancerous deposits and inflammatory adhesions and could not be separated without tearing the organs. The omentum was from 1 to 3 centimeters in thickness and completely occupied by a hard cancerous growth. Liver weight, 1,980 grams; lower portion of right lobe contained a carcinoma of the size of an orange, yellowish white in appearance and tough in texture. The upper part of the right lobe contained a similar growth as large as a walnut. The abdominal cavity contained about 1,000 cubic centimeters of reddish serum. The laparotomy wound had healed by primary union except at the site of the drainage tube. There was a minute abscess in the sheath of the right rectus muscle at the site of the sutures.

GENERAL TUBERCLE.

CASE 1.

J. S.; aged thirty-one years; nativity, Pennsylvania; admitted to U. S. Marine Hospital, New Orleans, La., November 9, 1887; died January 30, 1888.

History.—When admitted he complained of a moderate sciatica of the left leg. The glands of the neck were swollen, especially those of the posterior triangle; glands in left axilla and supra-clavicular region also enlarged and painful. Patient states that this was the case about a year and a half ago, but that the glandular swelling subsided. General appearance good. Diagnosis as above recorded was made with some diffidence after observing the case for sixteen days. November 18, 1887, he complained of difficulty in swallowing and sore throat; cough severe; physical signs of phthisis increasing. In December two cervical glands on the left side were suppurating and discharging; considerable cachexia. Sciatica well. Sore throat improving. Died January 30, 1888.

Necropsy (seven hours after death).—Body small, lightly built; emaciated; skin of a waxy color; an opening made by knife was seen on each side of the neck; bed-sore over sacrum. Larynx contained tubercular ulcers. Thorax, no extra fluid in pleural cavities; both pleura adherent to lungs and chest wall; pleura thickened and tubercular; heart small; tissues pale, its valves contracted from chronic fibrinous endocarditis. Lungs infiltrated with tubercle (disseminated tuberculosis). Tubercular nodules projecting from cut surfaces; these nodules also seen along the courses of the blood and lymphatic vessels. Signs of desquamative pneumonia; bronchial glands caseous; glands of neck caseous and broken down by suppuration. Abdominal cavity, liver pale, large, and fatty; spleen tissue inelastic, amyloid; organ enlarged. Kidney presented microscopical appearance of "large white kidney of Bright;" capsule peeled easily; cortical and medulary line well defined. The intestines presented no unusual appearance except in descending colon. In this portion of colon a couple of pouches as large as an egg, tortuous between, where the gut had apparently turned slightly on its axis and became adherent; bladder distended and full of urine; mesenteric glands caseous. Pathological diagnosis, disseminated tubercle.

CASE 2.

C. M.; aged twenty-three years; nativity, Cape de Verde Islands; admitted to the U. S. Marine Hospital, New York, October 19, 1887; died October 26.

Necropsy (*twenty-four hours after death*).—*Rigor mortis* marked; body much emaciated; a white surface, 5 by 8 inches, on the right side extended from the umbilicus to the median axillary line, which had the appearance of having been formerly the site of a blister. Thorax and abdomen opened by an incision from the sterno clavicular articulation to the pubes. Heart firmly contracted; pericardium contained about 50 cubic centimeters of flocculent serum; all heart valves normal. Right lung (weight, 870 grams) adherent to all surfaces; covered with a fibrinous deposit, and contained a great number of small, recent tubercles; on section the lung was found to be infiltrated with turbercles. Left lung (weight, 650 grains), pleural surfaces adherent by a thick fibrinous layer from 1.25 to 1.88 centimeters in thickness, and tubercular. The lung was compressed upwards and backwards by the presence of a large cavity situated in the lower portion of the left pleural cavity, and it was filled with 1,200 cubic centimeters of straw-colored serum. This was walled in by layers of well-organized lymph, showing that the general infection must have arisen from this old pleurisy. Liver pale and waxy, and covered on its free border with gray tubercle; on section tubercle was found in the body of the organ, but situated along the course of the large vessels. Spleen (weight, 285 grams), surface a violaceous color and thickly studded with tubercles of differ-nt ages; the whole organ was infiltrated with tubercular manes. The kidneys, mesenteric glands, and intestines contain many tubercles. Brain not examined.

TUBERCLE OF LARYNX AND LUNGS.

CASE 1.

F. C.; aged thirty-six years; born in Germany; admitted to the U. S. Marine Hospital, Chicago, Ill., August 18, 1886; died October 10, 1887.

History.—General history and physical examination proved that there was a tuberculous deposit in the lungs. Tubercular laryngitis was also developed, which gave great pain and suffering.

Necropsy.—Body very much emaciated. Apex of right lung a mass of blackened tubercles, with pus sacs throughout; a small abscess was found in lower lobe. Pus cavity in apex of left lung; purulent infiltration of the remains of this lung. Pleuræ adherent.

CASE 2.

W. Mc C.; aged forty-seven years; nativity, Illinois; admitted to U. S. Marine Hospital, San Francisco, Cal., October 10, 1887; died October 15.

Necropsy (*six hours after death*).—Body warm; *rigor mortis* marked; emaciation very great. Lungs were both loosely bound at various points by recent adhesions of no great extent, particularly over apices and upper lobes. Both lungs were strewn throughout with granular tubercle, aggregated at many points into nodes and nodules, some of which had broken down; some apparently had discharged their contents and were in process of cicatrization, while in some, extension of ulceration had produced cavities of some size; the largest of these, situated at left apex, would contain a hen's egg, and there was one of one-third this size at the right apex; but between the granulations the greater part of the lung was in apparently fair condition. Pericardium contained about 30 cubic centimeters of serum. Heart was small, fatty, but the muscular fiber was not greatly degenerated. In the right ventricle was a firm *ante-mortem* fibrinous clot passing into the pulmonary artery and ramifying with the distribution of that vessel, ending in soft, dark clots, which must have occluded the vessels. In the left ventricle was a similar clot, passing into the aorta and vessels of the arch. It was smaller than the pulmonary clot, occluding perhaps one-third the caliber of the aorta. Abdomen: No peritonitis. Through the greater part of ileum were numerous ulcerations of patches of Peyer, differing from lesions of typhoid fever only, apparently, in that the mesenteric glands presented about their normal appearance. There was no indication of the existence of these ulcers till shortly before death. The larynx was next exposed by longitudinal incision and the tongue drawn down through an incision in the floor of buccal cavity so as to expose the epiglottis. The latter was found to be destroyed by ulceration, there remaining only a mere stump, thickened and rigid. The whole larynx, including false and true cords, was eroded and ulcerated, but not very deeply at any one place; but the mucous membrane was entirely gone, and a thin purulent matter covered the bare fibrous tissue or granulations beneath.

CASE 3.

W. C.; aged, forty years; a native of England; admitted to U. S. Marine Hospital, San Francisco, Cal., November 7, 1887; died November 26.

Necropsy (*fourteen hours after death*).—*Rigor mortis* well marked; body greatly emaciated. Chest: Extensive old pleuritic adhesions on both sides, but especially so on right side. Lungs both filled with tubercular deposits, some of which had undergone cheesy, and others calcareous, degeneration. There was a cavity, large enough to admit a man's fist, in the right apex, and one about one-third that size in the left apex. Heart flabby, right side fatty, but otherwise normal. Larynx: Ulceration posteriorly, and several small tubercles anteriorly. No other organs examined.

TUBERCLE OF LUNGS.

CASE 1.

T. J.; aged twenty-two years; nativity, Norway; admitted to U. S. Marine Hospital, San Francisco, Cal., June 28, 1887; died July 4.

Necropsy (*twenty hours after death*).—Great emaciation; moderate *rigor mortis*. No clubbing of nails. Abdomen somewhat distended with gas. Chest: There were several pleural adhesions on the right side, at the base and outer border of lower lobe and the outer surface of upper lobe, but very little effusion in the cavity of pleura. Right lung was hepatized throughout the upper lobe, with one or two small cavities; there was the red hepatization of croupous pneumonia, with congestion and œdema. Pieces of the lung tissue sank in water. The lower lobe was intensely congested and œdematous, while the middle lobe was likewise œdematous, but emphysematous and not much congested. Left lung was with difficulty extracted, because of firm and uniform pleural adhesions literally obliterating the sac of that side. The whole lung was consolidated, but the upper two-thirds had broken down centrally and was now almost a pultaceous mass of pus, granules, and masses of cheesy matter. The lower anterior portion was a firm resistant mass of cheesy matter. Nothing was observed of discrete granulation, nor was any positive evidence of tubercle to be found. The appearances were rather those of pneumonic phthisis. Heart was flabby and anæmic to a degree; its walls were pale and somewhat thinned; its size nearly normal and the coronary vessels showed fatty degeneration in their walls. Pericardium smooth and pale, and contained 75 cubic centimeters of reddish, straw-colored serum. Abdomen: This was somewhat distended, partly with intestinal gas, partly from the unusual size of some of its organs. The vessels of the great omentum were injected, and numerous strong, but thin and membranous adhesions connected it with the parietal peritoneum. There were no adhesions elsewhere, and little or no fluid in the cavity. Liver was much enlarged, pale, somewhat yellowish and friable, no doubt fatty. Spleen was some three times its normal size, dark in color, grumous and pulpy in consistence, like a black mass of disorganized blood clot. Kidneys were normal in size and other respects, but somewhat anæmic. Small intestine was injected, or inflamed, from the lower third of jejunum to the ileo-caecal valve. The foci of inflammation were the solitary and agminated glands, which were everywhere the seat of ulceration and dark hemorrhagic congestion. In some places numerous small ulcers were aggregated, so as to give a honeycomb appearance. It was noted that the ulcers were the same in appearance throughout the whole tract involved, as though the process was everywhere in the same stage; also that there was little or no infiltration around them, and nowhere was simple infiltration of solitary glands or patches of Peyer found. The ulcers discharged a dark, sloughy matter, and none of them showed any tendency to cicatrize. Several had nearly perforated the peritoneum, one had actually done so, but there being only a small amount of soft, yellow fæces none had escaped into the cavity. The absence of the usual typhoid fever infiltration and other characters has been noted, but on the other hand the absence of any infiltration, or even of scattered tubercle (except that one or two possibly tuberculous granulations were seen), makes the demonstration of tubercular intestinal ulcer difficult. There was very generally a pigmentary discoloration of the intestinal mucous membrane, in the shape of a fine granular deposit. Lymph glands of the mesentery were much enlarged, hard, cheesy on section. Laryngeal mucous membrane pale, with superficial erosions. The vocal chords were thickened and fibrous, pale and denuded of membrane, and between their anterior attachments was a deep ulceration about two-thirds by one-third centimeter, which nearly perforated the anterior wall.

NOTE.—This patient was very low when admitted; he had been sick on board ship at sea for several months, without medical treatment or proper nutriment.

CASE 2.

C. A.; aged twenty-six years; native of Sweden; admitted to U. S. Marine Hospital, Boston, Mass., June 23, 1887; died July 5.

Necropsy.—Body greatly emaciated; lungs solidified and adherent to chest walls. Cavities existed in the upper lobe of right lung. The heart was small. An organized clot nearly filled the right auricle and extended into the right ventricle. The liver, spleen, and kidneys were normal. The mesenteric glands were greatly enlarged.

CASE 3.

Oedema.

J. G.; aged fifty-one years; nativity, Ireland; admitted to U. S. Marine Hospital, San Francisco, Cal., June 7, 1887; died July 26.

Necropsy (*twenty-four hours after death*).—*Rigor mortis* still persistent. Great emaciation. Only the thorax was examined. Left pleura was entirely obliterated by adhesions so old and firm that it was impossible to separate the lung completely, The left lung was a mass of tubercle, with extensive cavities in upper lobe, smaller ones in lower lobe. The adhesions in right pleura were equally extensive with those in the left side, but more recent and easily torn. The right lung was greatly congested and œdematous, but tubercular granulations were few and scattered. The heart was extremely fatty; it was flabby, and the ventricles were almost collapsed, and the right ventricle not distended with blood as might have been expected.

CASE 4.

C. C.; aged twenty-five years; nativity, Germany; admitted to U. S. Marine Hospital, San Francisco, Cal., March 11, 1887; died July 31.

Necropsy (*eighteen hours after death*).—*Rigor mortis* marked. Emaciation extreme. The visceral layer of left pleura almost entirely obliterated anteriorly; only two fibrous strips of it remained, which crossed the cavity from side to side. The left lung was entirely destroyed, and in its stead was found about 500 or 600 cubic centimeters of ichorous pus of fetid odor, and some detritus of lung tissue. The right pleura was strongly adherent to the lung. The right lung was partly solidified, and studded throughout with tubercles. Numerous sections through the organ opened up many small cavities, little larger than a pea, containing pus. The heart was small and contracted. Other organs not examined.

CASE 5.

J. M.; aged thirty-nine years; nativity, New York; admitted to the U. S. Marine Hospital, Saint Louis, Mo., June 15, 1886; died August 4, 1887.

History.—Patient suffered from cough, continued loss of weight and strength, night sweats, hæmoptysis, etc.

Necropsy.—Body greatly emaciated. Lungs small and contracted, filled with small, cheesy tubercles of a grayish-white color, and semisolid consistence. Pleuræ: Both pleuræ were completely adherent everywhere to the chest walls; the pleural cavity was almost entirely obliterated. Other organs not examined.

CASE 6.

D. S.; aged forty-three years; nativity, Ireland; admitted to U. S. Marine Hospital, San Francisco, Cal., December 7, 1885; died August 15, 1887.

Necropsy (*three hours and a half after death*).—Body still warm, rigor had not set in; emaciated, but not extremely so. Chest: Both pleuræ obliterated by adhesions—those on right side being more recent and easily torn, while on left they were so strong that the lung could not be torn away. The left lung was, therefore, not thoroughly examined, but was felt to be shrunken and cirrhosed throughout. The right lung had one shrunken cavity at the apex, where it was strongly adherent to the pleura, and the rest of this organ was intensely congested and crowded with miliary tubercles. Heart: The pericardial sac was obliterated, the walls were the seat of adhesive inflammation, and when they were forcibly separated numerous miliary granulations could be seen and felt in both layers. The heart itself was rather small and flabby. Abdomen: When opened contained some 100 cubic centimeters of serum, probably due to localized peritonitis excited by several tubercular ulcers of the ileum. Liver: Was about one and one-half times normal size, firm, dense, with the appearance of advancing fibrosis. Spleen: Some three times the normal size, rather softer than usual, and much congested. Kidneys: At least twice the normal size, and considerably congested. Capsule peeled off without difficulty. Right kidney contained, superficially, one or two small cysts. Both organs were probably fatty, the cortices of both being of a general yellow, fatty hue, with numerous spots more fatty still. Brain: The membranes, though congested, were not extremely so. On either side of longitudinal sinus, in the region of vertex, the pia was inflamed and adherent to dura, for an area altogether of 7 by 2 centimeters. At several points the pia was adherent to cortex of brain, but the latter did not appear inflamed. At the vertex, bordering the longitudinal fissure, there was an area of softening of about 1 centimeter square, involving the thickness of the cortical layer. There appeared to be no basal meningitis. The inflammation over vertex appeared to be of a simple sero-plastic nature—at least only one undoubted miliary tubercle was found in the pia mater. There was a good deal of fibrinous exudation, while the amount of serum between the membranes and in the ventricles must have been 50 to 75 cubic centimeters. The cranial nerves and optic bulbs were all softened by this fluid. Sections of the brain revealed nothing beyond fluid in ventricles and injection of choroid plexus.

CASE 7.

J. R.; aged sixty years; nativity, Austria; admitted to marine ward of St. Francis Xavier's Infirmary, Charleston, S. C., on August 18, 1887; died August 23. Diagnosis tubercle of lung.

History.—Patient gave no connected account of his illness. He presented all the external symptoms of pulmonary tuberculosis, and the apices of both lungs were found dull on percussion. His form was considerably attenuated, his chest contracted, and the scapulæ quite prominent. He died suddenly of hæmoptysis on the evening of August 23.

Necropsy (fifteen hours after death).—*Rigor mortis* well marked. Body much emaciated. Abdomen greatly distended with gas, and a deep and dark discoloration in the right inguinal region, where a hernia appeared. On account of the firm adhesions of the pleuræ and diaphragm to the sternum and costal cartilages, difficulty was experienced in opening the thorax. The heart was first examined. It was firmly attached to the greater part of the surface of the hpericardium, was normal in size but dilated. The substance was pale, easily torn, and was in a condition of fatty degeneration. The aorta (ascending portion) was large in caliber, and a small calcareous nodule was found in its transverse portion. Both right and left ventricles were dilated. Valves normal. On account of its strong attachment to the pleura the lung (right) was removed with great difficulty. Throughout the upper lobe were scattered numerous tubercular nodules, and calcified particles were found filling the air-cells. The lower lobe was less marked by disease, but contained a large number of tubercular deposits. The left pleura covering the lung had formed adhesions to the upper ribs near the sternum, and the lung could not be removed in its entirety. Extensive ulceration had taken place in the parenchyma of the upper lobe and several cavities were visible. The hemorrhage had evidently issued from this lobe of the left lung. The middle lobe, although not containing cavities, retained a number of nodules, which extended into the lower lobe. The other organs were not examined. No microscopical examinations made.

CASE 8.

J. N.; aged forty-nine years; nativity, Sweden; admitted to the U. S. Marine Hospital, Chicago, Ill., July 19, 1887; died August 24, 1887.

History.—He entered hospital suffering from bronchitis of five years' duration. Auscultation gave only the harsh respiration and small rales of a chronic bronchitis; this was general. No dullness on percussion. He complained of soreness and "dry cough," with much weakness. Tongue clean; appetite good. Skin of a peculiar muddiness. Heart sounds normal, but showing weakness. Placed on regular treatment and good diet. Lost ground rapidly. Very soon the expiration became lengthened and very harsh. Dullness over the right apex, not so dull over left. All symptoms denoted a rapid deposition of tubercle and marked labor of heart's action. Up to the day of his death he was up and around. Died quietly of heart failure, due to intense venous pressure.

Necropsy.—*Rigor mortis* not marked; body poorly nourished. There were adhesions only at each apex; most at right. Entire lung surface studded with tubercle; no cheesy deposits or abscesses. At left apex there was a small, perfectly clean cavity, as large as an English walnut; did not communicate with bronchus; decolorized lymph lined its sides. Sections of the lung floated low in water bath, and the tissue was full of serum from the engorged vessels. None of the tubercle has broken down; evidently a recent deposit. The heart was slightly enlarged; much fatty degeneration.

CASE 9.

P. C.; aged twenty-eight years; nativity, Ireland; admitted to the U. S. Marine Hospital, New York, August 15, 1887; died September 1, 1887.

Necropsy (*twenty hours after death*).—Body extremely emaciated; *rigor mortis* slight. Pleural adhesions found on both sides of the chest; lungs studded with recent deposits. A portion of right lung was the seat of lobular pneumonia, due to tubercular deposit. Mesenteric glands in the right iliac region much enlarged. Heart and other organs normal.

CASE 10.

G. B.; aged thirty-three years; nativity, Canada; entered the U. S. Marine Hospital, Chicago, Ill., July 18, 1887; died September 5, 1887.

History.—Physical examination showed him to be in the last stage of the disease. Both lungs dull on percussion, save the left apex, which was cavernous. Auscultation gave the grossest signs of rapid disintegration of left lung. Right gave only a limited amount of vesicular breathing with prolonged expiration.

Necropsy.—Body much emaciated; very slight rigor. Left lung found completely destroyed. A small quantity of pus was found in the right apex and the remaining tissue was very thickly studded with tubercle. Heart normal; other organs not examined.

CASE 11.

S. F.; aged thirty-six years; nativity, Finland; admitted to U. S. Marine Hospital at Port Townsend, Wash., January 23, 1887; died September 9, 1887.

Necropsy (eighteen hours after death).—Rigor mortis marked. Inspection: Chest walls retracted; abdominal walls relaxed, protuberant and pit upon pressure. Upon examination a cavity was found in the apex of the right lung a little larger than a walnut, partly filled with a semi-purulent fluid. The walls of this cavity were composed of lung tissue, solidified by inflammatory exudations. Several smaller cavities were found scattered through the upper and middle lobes of the right lung. Left lung: Almost the entire substance of the upper lobe was involved in one large cavity, and the lower lobe presented very generally points of tubercular ulceration. The heart: The ventricles were filled with blood of semi fluid consistency and no clot was present. The liver and kidneys seemed normal, but the pancreas presented, especially near its head, several well-marked points of tubercular ulceration. The patient died from exhaustion.

CASE 12.

E. W.; aged forty-six years; nativity, Ireland; admitted to U. S. Marine Hospital, Chicago, Ill., December 1, 1886; died September 9, 1887.

History.—Before admission the patient had been troubled with cough, profuse expectoration, night sweats, etc., and these symptoms continued to the end, with only slight remission. Physical examination gave evidence of general tubercular infiltration of lungs. There was much emaciation and the patient subject to severe headache and other symptoms of meningeal inflammation.

Necropsy.—No *rigor mortis* after sixteen hours; body much emaciated. Lungs infiltrated with tubercle, large and yellow; each apex was a dense nodular mass with cheesy centers; small abscesses in various places throughout the lungs. Left lung much contracted and pigmented. Other organs normal, save the liver, which was slightly enlarged, of a light-brown color, friable, breaking in the fingers easily and giving a dull, granular surface; the tissue was tough, cutting harshly under the scalpel. Vessels of brain full of dark blood; pia mater and arachnoid membranes matted together in a thick layer of lymph over the surface of temporal and occipital lobes of either hemisphere, but did not extend to frontal lobes on either side. Membranes at the base adherent and inflamed. Brain substance microscopically normal. Could detect no tubercles.

CASE 13.

N. W.; aged twenty-eight years; nativity, Norway; admitted to the U. S. Marine Hospital, Baltimore, Md., January 31, 1887; died September 14, 1887.

History.—On entering hospital the patient gave a list of symptoms of a previous sickness that seemed to indicate a severe attack of pneumonia, which had occurred about a year previous. For some months he had persistent cough, with expectoration, shortness of breath, emaciation, together with hectic fever, night sweats, and occasional diarrhea. The morbid sounds of the thorax, on examination, showed a diseased condition of the lungs, with considerable loss of tissue in the right. Treatment: Tonics, cod liver oil, hypophosphites, occasional treatment, as required, for diarrhea and night sweats, was prescribed.

Necropsy (nineteen hours after death).—Rigor mortis feeble. Body much emaciated. Lungs: Right lung very adherent to pleura, and, when removed was entirely surrounded by an adventitious coat of connective tissue; lung filled with cavities, containing pus and broken-down tissue; left lung less firmly adherent, but tissue was in a similar condition to that of the other. Heart: Pericardium contained about 50 cubic centimeters of straw-colored serum; all the cavities of the heart were entirely filled, with dark soft clots; slight atheromatous patches on aortic and pulmonary valves; otherwise normal. Liver congested and soft.

CASE 14.

L. A.; aged twenty-two years; nativity, Norway; admitted to U. S. Marine Hopital, Wilmington, N. C., July 20, 1887; died September 14.

Necropsy.—Body greatly emaciated. Decubitus on left hip. Right lung: In opening the thorax a large pus cavity was ruptured. Pleural cavity was obliterated; lung could not be separated into lobes. No air present. The whole mass was riddled with pus cavities and all the solid portion was composed of tuberculous nodules. Left lung: Abundant recent adhesions of pleural surfaces; at apex of this lung was found the nearest approach to normal lung tissue, comprising the upper third of upper lobe. The remainder of this lobe contained no air and consisted of tubercles and small pus cavities. Lower lobe, abundance of miliary tubercle; air entered in places. No macroscopic evidences of tubercle in other organs. Pericardial surface covered with a whitish, soft deposit from pericarditis, of which, however, there was no evidence in life, obscured, perhaps, by the extreme condition of the left lung. Heart otherwise normal in appearance.

Weight of organs.—Left lung, 755 grams; right lung, 780; liver, 1,430; left kidney, 190; right kidney, 130; spleen, 190.

CASE 15.

G. F. D.; aged thirty-two years; native of Portugal; admitted to U. S. Marine Hospital, Boston, Mass., October 5, 1886; died September 20, 1887.

Necropsy (thirty-six hours after death).—Rigor mortis slight; body greatly emaciated; bed-sore on left thigh near great trochanter. There was an abnormal amount of fluid in the pericardial cavity. Both lungs were filled with tubercle, the right lung being adherent to chest-wall and diaphragm. The right lung contained three large cavities. The bronchial glands had undergone cheesy and calcareous degeneration. Other viscera normal.

CASE 16.

S. A.; aged twenty-eight years; nativity, Australia; admitted to U. S. Marine Hospital, San Francisco, Cal., July 5, 1887; died September 29.

Necropsy (twenty-seven hours after death).—Rigor mortis persistent; extreme bodily emaciation. Lungs: Both a mass of dense tubercle, broken down at numerous points into small circumscribed abscesses, and containing many small cheesy nodules. Pleuræ everywhere adherent, but not firmly except at apices. Heart: This was nearly normal in size, anæmic, but of good fiber, although the coronary vessels were fatty. Intestines: At various points in the ileum there were inflammatory areas corresponding to the patches of Peyer, but no thickening or ulceration.

CASE 17.

Meningitis.

W. S.; aged forty-three years; nativity, Scotland; admitted to U. S. Marine Hospital, San Francisco, Cal., February 23, 1887; died September 29.

Necropsy (*twenty-one hours after death*).—*Rigor mortis* well marked; bodily emaciation extreme. Before death the symptoms for some days indicated meningitis followed by œdema. Brain: Upon removing the calvarium the vessels of the meninges were found engorged, the sinuses and veins particularly, and the membranes were œdematously swollen. Considerable fibrinous exudation, moreover, was found over the convexity of the brain, and at several points this caused adhesion of the membranes to each other. The brain tissue itself appeared anæmic. Beneath the pia and in all the ventricles was a great collection of serous exudation. There was considerable tubercular enlargement of both epididymes with hydrocele of the tunica vaginalis. There was an organic urethral stricture, admitting No. 11 E. scale. The lungs were not examined, owing to a cut on the finger of operator. But the only point of interest in the diagnosis had been verified, and the *post mortem* itself could not have increased the certainty that the ultimate or prime cause of death was extensive tubercular deposit in both lungs, with formation of cavities and extensive pleuritic adhesion.

CASE 18.

A. L.; aged thirty years; nativity, Sweden; admitted to the U. S. Marine Hospital, San Francisco, October 6, 1887; died October 16.

Necropsy (*six hours after death*).—*Rigor mortis* pronounced. Body excessively emaciated. Thorax: Left lung atrophied; apex filled with cavities the size of buckshot; the remaining portion of the lung full of miliary tubercles; right pleura adherent over lowest lobe of corresponding lung. Right lung devoid of cavities, but thickly strewn with gray tubercle. The base and lowest lobe, when cut into, were found of a bright red color. Pressure brought out a vermilion hue and pasty exudation, which gave a peculiar bright red appearance to the freshly cut surface. Abdomen: The liver, normal in size, was of pale pinkish hue and thickly covered with minute punctiform yellowish dots. There were two nodular elevations on the anterior surface of the transverse lobe, which, when cut into, were found to be normal tissue. The spleen was apparently natural; duodenum darkly discolored. At two points on exterior surface of small intestines rounded circumscribed spots of inflammation indicated interior ulceration. The canal contained only a small quantity of yellowish fluid matter. Duodenum coated with dark greenish moss-like substance, which accounted for dark external appearance. There were eight points of ulceration found throughout the intestinal canal. These were, with one exception, seated opposite the attachment of the mesentery. In the majority of instances the direction of the ulcer was transverse; a few were longitudinal, one circular, and in another case, by coalescence, one of mixed type was found. In two places necrosis of the serous coat had progressed nearly to perforation. In the lower portion of the descending colon the folds of mucous membrane were puffy and highly injected. Numerous small ulcer-like depressions dipped between the folds, giving the surface a honey-comb-like appearance. Only in a few localities were the mesenteric glands found enlarged. Bladder walls thickened. On superior surface two small caseous nodules the size of buckshot were found. When the wall was incised cloudy and offensive urine flowed out, soon followed by thick gray pus. The inner surface about the fundus was greatly thickened, irregularly granular, and covered with pus. Incision into the pars prostatica liberated considerable ichorous pus. The prostate was almost destroyed, and around it was found a pus cavity, which showed no communication with the rectum.

Case 19.

Congenital perforation of semi lunar valve.

I. A. (mulatto); aged twenty-five years; nativity, Louisiana; admitted to the U. S. Marine Hospital, Cairo, Ill., June 23, 1887, suffering from tubercle of the lungs; died October 18.

Necropsy.—Body emaciated. Left lung contained numerous cavities, and was extensively infiltrated with tubercle; pleural adhesions were numerous. The right lung was almost entirely destroyed, and so firm were the adhesions between the pleural surfaces that it was impossible to remove the lung in its entirety. The heart was large and dilated, and the base of one of the semilunar valves of the aorta was perforated by an opening about the size of a crow quill; the margins of the opening and general appearance pointed to a congenital origin of the abnormality. The omentum was wasted, and one or two narrowed portions of intestine were found in the ileum. The other viscera were healthy.

Weight of viscera.—Heart, 512 grams; left lung, 1,024; liver, 2,272; spleen, 321; pancreas, 128; right kidney, 112; left kidney, 224.

Case 20.

F. A.; aged thirty-nine years; nativity, Finland; admitted to hospital Galveston, Tex., July 8, 1887; died October 19.

Necropsy (*twelve hours after death*).—*Rigor mortis* well marked. The lungs were closely adherent to chest wall throughout the whole extent of their contiguous surfaces and were removed with much difficulty. The pleural cavities were entirely destroyed. The left lung contained numerous tubercular deposits; in the right lung were found several cavities, varying in size; some filled, others partially filled, with pus. Heart and liver normal. No tubercular deposits in glands of the mesentery.

Case 21.

R. H.; aged fifty-seven years; nativity, United States; admitted to hospital, Galveston, Tex., August 31, 1887; died October 21.

Necropsy (*fifteen hours after death*).—The right lung presented numerous tubercular deposits in its upper lobe; the lower lobe was in the stage of red hepatization. The left lung was closely adherent to the chest wall, and was marked by emphysema throughout. The walls of the superficial arteries were extensively calcified. Small plates of lime salts were found in several spots on the walls of the heart, at the bases of segments of the aortic valve and around the coronary artery. Left ventricle of heart dilated and walls thinned. Liver was of a pale yellowish color, and gritty on section. Kidneys normal. The costal cartilages and the cartilages of trachea and bronchi were calcified.

Case 22.

Pleurisy.

A. C.; aged twenty-three years; nativity, Rhode Island; admitted to the U. S. Marine Hospital, New York, August 2, 1887; died October 24.

Necropsy (forty-eight hours after death).—Body much emaciated. Right lung: Nearly the whole of the upper and middle lobes solidified with tubercular masses in different stages; some small cavities. Left lung: Small, contracted, and thoroughly infiltrated with tubercle. Left pleuræ: Cavity contained about 200 cubic centimeters of sero-purulent fluid. Other organs normal.

Case 23.

L. R.; aged forty-eight years; nativity, Louisiana; admitted to hospital, Galveston, Tex., October 29, 1887; died October 29.

Necropsy (eighteen hours after death).—The apex of left lung was found to be completely solidified, with cavities varying in size from a buckshot to a hen's egg. Tuberculous deposits all through left lung. Right lung: Lower lobe filled with tuberculous deposits. Heart, liver, and kidneys normal.

Case 24.

G. F.; aged fifty-one years; nativity, Germany; admitted to the U. S. Marine Hospital, Saint Louis, Mo., October 10, 1887; died November 6.

History.—On being admitted to the hospital he complained of having lost much in bodily weight; great exhaustion; loss of appetite; troublesome cough, the expectorated matter being of a yellowish, lumpy, viscid character; occasional morning chills; night sweats, etc.

Necropsy (fifteen hours after death).—*Rigor mortis* moderate. Body very much emaciated, the abdomen was so much collapsed that the outline of the spinal column was seen. Superficial ulcers, about 5 centimeters in diameter, were seen on each leg. Pleuræ: Pleural surfaces adherent throughout; pleural cavity almost entirely obliterated. Lungs contracted, rough and knotty in external appearance. On section, cavities large enough to admit a marble, and filled with viscid, yellow pus.

In some places the lung substance was very soft and fragile; in others a semi-solid, cheesy matter exuded on pressure. The apices of the lungs were more affected than the bases. Heart small and fatty. Valves all normal. Stomach: An old cicatrix was observed near the pylorus, and the walls were thickened and "gristly" at that point. Spleen slightly enlarged. Liver normal in color and size. Gall bladder distended with bile, but contained no stones. Intestines apparently in normal condition. Mesenteric glands were enlarged in places, and contained a grayish, yellow mass. Other organs apparently normal.

Case 25.

Pulmonary hemorrhage.

P. M.; aged thirty-one years; nativity, Wisconsin; admitted to the U. S. Marine Hospital, Chicago, Ill., June 4, 1887; died November 7.

History.—Physical examination revealed well-marked signs of tubercular infiltration. The usual symptoms of the disease were present. Patient had been improved by the use of Bergeon's method of rectal injections of sulphuretted hydrogen, but soon declined. Death ensued from hemorrhage.

Necropsy.—Body greatly emaciated; slight rigor. Pleuræ adherent on either side; right lung deeply pigmented; apex adherent, firm, and nodulated; only a few pus collections; remainder of this lung studded with tubercle undergoing cheesy degeneration. The left lung was hard and blue-black in color on its surface; it was so firmly adherent that it could hardly be dislodged. A large cavity was found in the center filled with pus and clotted blood, evidently the seat of the hemorrhage.

CASE 26.

W. B.; aged thirty-one years; nativity, Ireland; admitted to the U. S. Marine Hospital, San Francisco, Cal., November 5, 1887; died November 9.

Necropsy (*twenty hours after death*).—*Rigor mortis* and emaciation marked. Pleuræ: The right pleural cavity was obliterated by old and firm adhesions; the left was almost normal. Lungs: The right was densely nodulated with tubercle. There were many small cavities and numerous cicatrices and depressions on the surface, indicating disease of long standing; the left lung was thickly sown with granular tubercle, nodulated in places. The infection was comparatively recent. The lung was greatly congested and œdematous.

CASE 27.

P. J.; aged forty-eight years; nativity, Denmark; admitted to U. S. Marine Hospital, San Francisco, Cal., November 14, 1887; died November 15, 1887.

Necropsy (*twelve hours after death*).—*Rigor mortis* present; emaciation not as great as usual. Enlarged veins coursed over right upper chest; face dusky and livid. Thorax pleuræ were both nearly obliterated by numerous and strong adhesions, more markedly so as regards the left cavity. There were strong adhesions to diaphragm and pericardium. Lungs were both full of thickly-strewn granular tubercle, and the whole intervening tissue was congested and œdematous. The left lung contained some nodules and small cavities in the apical region. Pericardium was torn in extracting left lung, and a considerable quantity of clear fluid escaped. Heart was dilated considerably, and its tissue flabby and friable. Abdomen contained a liter or so of serum, for which no cause could be found unless in the condition of the liver, presently to be noted. Liver was about normal in size, pale, slightly yellowish, in tint, and decidedly firmer in texture than normal. On section it appeared mottled with pale yellow spots on a ground of pale brown. The organ was anæmic, and in general hue much lighter than normal. Spleen about one and a half times the usual size, not congested, rather lighter colored than normal. Kidneys were both remarkably large, the left nearly twice the natural size, the right somewhat smaller. But neither on section nor in general character was anything abnormal detected, except that the pyramids in both were congested, and in the left organ the peripheral cortical substance was rather thin, though it was unusually abundant between pyramids. Bladder moderately distended with urine.

Case 28.

G. H.; aged nineteen years; nativity, Sweden; admitted to U. S. Marine Hospital, San Francisco, Cal., October 11, 1887; died November 17, 1887.

Necropsy (three hours after death).—*Rigor mortis* present; body emaciated. Thorax pleuræ. On both sides there were many firm adhesions of the opposing surfaces, likewise to the diaphragm and pericardium. Lungs: Both filled with tubercular deposits of variable size, many of which had begun to break down. Heart not examined. Abdomen: A small quantity of sero-purulent fluid found in the abdominal cavity, and the peritoneum was thickened and opaque. There were spots of ulceration at various points in the small intestines; the surrounding mucous membrane was highly congested. There was slight enlargement of the mesenteric glands. Kidneys: Both greatly enlarged and the cortical substance had almost wholly undergone fatty metamorphosis. Larynx: There was found extensive, though superficial, ulceration of the larynx, extending from the cricoid cartilage below to the arytenoid cartilage above, and laterally, involving the posterior portion of the vocal cords.

Case 29.

C. K.; aged fifty-six years; nativity, Sweden; admitted to the U. S. Marine Hospital, New Orleans, La., October 10, 1887; died November 19, 1887.

History.—The patient had been sick about sixteen months and confined to his bed about four and one-half months, being sent to this country from Almeria, Spain, by the consul. His case presented the usual symptoms and signs of pulmonary tubercle, with profuse diarrhea breaking out intermittently.

Necropsy (twelve hours after death.)—Body much emaciated; old syphilitic scars in various parts. Left lung adherent over the apex; old, firm adhesions, adherent also over posterior portion, with soft, recent adhesions. Right lung generally adherent, with firm adhesions; the pulmonary tissue here is so much decomposed that the lung breaks down on attempting to detach it. Pericardial fluid normal. Heart small, very devoid of fat outside, yet evidently in well-marked, fatty degeneration; valves normal, although aortic valves are a little roughened. Great vessels normal. Right lung a mass of putrilage; pus, cheesy matter, and inflamed lung tissue mixed in every conceivable proportion; no large, well marked vomica. Left lung has a large vomica with firm walls in the apex, and general hypostatic pneumonia, breaking down into pus of the lower posterior portion. Liver enlarged and fatty; gall bladder enormously distended, contains 200 cubic centimeters of fluid; but all ducts are patent. Kidneys, both of them enlarged and congested. The mesenteric glands are generally enlarged and cheesy, a few have suppurated but not broken their capsules. A small amount of flocculent fluid in the peritoneal cavity; this is distinctly purulent in the more depending portions. There are many ulcers, all small, however, in the ileum and first part of the colon; these are evidently tubercular.

Case 30.

T. O'D. (colored); aged twenty-four years; nativity, Louisiana; admitted to the U. S. Marine Hospital, Saint Louis, Mo., October 5, 1887; died November 20, 1887.

Necropsy.—Emaciation of body very marked. Pleuræ almost completely adherent. Lungs: Left lung full of cavities from which exuded on section a cheesy matter, in some places almost of solid consistency. On right side the lung was small, contracted, and had several small cavities near the apex, containing a similar material to those on the left side. Heart small and fatty; valves normal. Spleen enlarged and congested; very dark in color. Liver enlarged and congested. Other organs were found to show no pathological changes.

CASE 31.

C. E.; aged twenty-eight years; nativity, Norway; admitted to U. S. Marine Hospital, San Francisco, Cal., August 10, 1887; died November 13, 1887.

Necropsy (seventeen hours after death).—Though the air was rather cool, the body was still warm, and there was little or no rigor. Emaciation was marked, but extreme. Thorax: Left lung bound down laterally and about upper lobe by pleuritic adhesions. The upper lobe was full of tubercle containing several small cavities and the rest of the lung was strewn with tubercle. Right lung was bound down similarly to the left, and the pleural cavity contained a small amount of fluid, which was not estimated. The whole upper lobe was an immense abscess, cavity the size of an orange, and there were other large ones in the neighborhood of this. The rest of the lung was tubercular. Heart was dilated, flabby, fatty, and almost collapsed. Abdomen contained 1,000 cubic centimeters, estimated, of serum, but no evidence of peritonitis—adhesions, plastic, or purulent exudation, etc.—beyond injection of peritoneal coat of intestines. Intestines were distended with gas in some places, and altogether collapsed in others, perhaps immediately adjoining. The explanation of this peculiar difference seemed to be that where the distended spots were the intestinal wall had undergone ulceration and wasting, in some places nothing but the peritoneal coat being left. On opening the small intestine this condition of things was more plainly apparent; at some points were ulcers, at others were intensely congested vessels which had given way and caused hemorrhage, whilst almost everywhere the mucous coat was the seat of superficial erosion or widespread maceration, resulting in almost total destruction of the valvulæ conniventes and glandular structures. Liver very large, much conjested. Its tissue was firm, pale, and indurated. Spleen nearly natural. Kidneys enlarged, somewhat congested. Cortical portion pale and probably fatty.

CASE 32.

Pulmonary hemorrhage.

F. E.; aged thirty-eight years; nativity, Germany; admitted to the U. S. Marine Hospital, Chicago, Ill., November 6, 1887; died November 25, 1887.

History.—Was admitted to hospital for hemorrhage of lungs. Stated that he had been subject to a "cough" for sometime, but had never been treated for it. Two days before he had applied for office relief. When admitted there was marked haemoptysis. Was put to bed and ergot given hypodermatically; but soon after there occurred a copious hemorrhage, possibly 600 cubic centimeters. Patient was almost exsanguinated, and rallied slowly. Whisky was given with the greatest care. On the fourth day the chest was examined. Right lung was dull at apex and almost flat in lower portions; auscultation located the hemorrhage from the lower right lung; crepitant rales at apex, expiration harsh and prolonged. Temperature 36.4° C.; pulse 126. Ergot was given continuously and dorsal decubitus enforced. On the 13th he again had a profuse hemorrhage; about 500 cubic centimeters. He had not risen from bed even to reach the stool-chair. Ergot was given freely; still as often as the heart's action rallied the plug was driven out and the bleeding would recommence. He bled to death at 2 o'clock a. m., November 25, 1887.

Necropsy.—Body fairly nourished; marked *rigor mortis.* Right pleury adherent and lung removed with difficulty. The tissues were thickla infiltrated with tubercle and at various points these were massed together and broken down into cheesy masses. The middle lobe was very much indurated as with interstitial inflammation, and at one point there was a cavity as large as a walnut opening into an enlarged tube; this was full of pus and clotted blood. Left lung contained a few gray nodules at the apex only.

CASE 33.

W. P. G.; aged thirty-nine years; nativity, New York; admitted to the U. S. Marine Hospital, San Francisco, Cal., September 10, 1887; died November 26, 1887.

Necropsy (twelve hours after death).—*Rigor mortis* present. Great emaciation. Superficial bedsore over sacrum. Thorax: Right pleura was pretty well bound down with adhesions. Left contained several bands crossing the lower two-thirds of the cavity, while the upper lobe was entirely bound down. No fluid in either cavity. Both lungs were full of disseminated tubercle, and the upper lobes were densly infiltrated with them. Cavities the size of a large egg were found in each apex. Considerable emphysema of lower lobes of each lung. Heart flabby and fatty, but otherwise normal.

CASE 34.

J. S.; aged thirty-five years; nativity, New York; was admitted to the U. S. Marine Hospital, New York, on November 22; died November 27, 1887.

The necropsy was made thirty-four hours *post mortem. Rigor mortis.*

The entire right lung was attached by old adhesions; it weighed 910 grams. The upper lobe was tuberculous and filled with small cavities, in one of which was a blood coagulum the size of a walnut; the middle and lower lobes contained tubercles. The left lung also was adherent; it weighed 910 grams; a few cavities were found in the apex, and tubercles distributed throughout the lung. The heart weighed 320 grams; thickening of the pericardium in plaques; all valves normal. The liver was fatty; weight 1,790 grams. The spleen weighed 120 grams; parenchyma soft. The right kidney weighed 135 grams; the left, 145; both were normal. The stomach, intestines, and bladder were normal.

CASE 35.

Pleurisy.

J. H. T.; aged thirty years; nativity, New York; admitted to the U. S. Marine Hospital, New York, October 10; died November 27, 1887.

History.—When admitted the patient gave a history of ill health for three months, and examination revealed the presence of tubercular deposit in the lungs. The necropsy was made twenty-five hours *post mortem*. *Rigor mortis.* Skin pale; œdema of lower extremities.

The right lung was attached by recent fibrinous adhesions, and the lung was covered with a yellow, plastic exudate. The pleural cavity contained 100 cubic centimeters of serum. The lung weighed 1,790 grams. The apex was filled with cavities; small cavities in the lower lobe, fatty degeneration of the parenchyma, and interstitial thickening. The left lung weighed 1,090 grams. It was attached to the pleura by a few old adhesions, and a small cavity was found in the apex; the lung was in the same pathological condition as the right. The pericardial sac contained about 150 cubic centimeters of clear fluid. The heart weighed 320 grams; normal. The liver weighed 1,760 grams, and was fatty. The spleen weighed 150 grams, and was normal. The right kidney weighed 160 grams; the left 180; both were normal. The intestines, stomach, and bladder were normal.

CASE 36.

O. L.; aged thirty years; nativity, Sweden; admitted to Marine Hospital at Boston, Mass., May 9, 1887; died November 28, 1887.

History of tubercle of lung, with high evening temperature, gradual emaciation, etc.

Necropsy (*thirty hours after death*).—*Rigor mortis* present; body much emaciated. Lungs adherent to pleura in many places; full of cavities, large and small, filled with pus, showing a general breaking down of the lung texture. A microscopical examination showed the presence of the tubercle bacillus. The pericardium was adherent to the inner surface of the pleura, showing an old pericarditis; heart normal. The peritoneal cavity contained about 400 cubic centimeters of serous fluid. The mesenteric lymph-glands were cheesy.

CASE 37.

J. M.; aged forty-seven years; nativity, Ireland; admitted to the U. S. Marine Hospital, New York, November 10, 1887; died December 24, 1887.

Necropsy (*thirty-eight hours after death*).—Body extremely emaciated; *rigor mortis* slight; body covered with small copper-colored spots, resembling a specific eruption. Blood-vessels of heart enlarged and tortuous. Both lungs filled with tuberculous material, and a large cavity was found at the left apex. Kidneys small and contracted. Other organs normal.

CASE 38.

W. A.; aged forty-three years; nativity, England; entered the U. S. Marine Hospital, Chicago, Ill., December 23, 1887; died December 25, 1887.

History.—This case was admitted August 10, 1887, as a "chronic," having been treated for rheumatism, pleurisy, and lung disease in this hospital within the past few years. Chronic bronchitis was the diagnosis on admission, but it soon became evident that there was a tuberculous deposit; hence the re-admission. Patient remained quite comfortable for several weeks, but was soon troubled with the usual symptoms of the disease: increased cough and expectoration, pain in the chest, night sweats, emaciation, and marked debility. Death came from exhaustion.

Necropsy.—Rigor mortis well marked; considerable emaciation; skin of an unusually yellow hue. Pleuræ adherent on either side. Right lung was a mass of tubercular deposit, with two or three very small abscesses. Left lung deeply pigmented, but almost free of tubercles. Kidneys abnormal; weight of right only 120 grams; left, 450. Liver slightly enlarged. Other organs normal.

CASE 39.

Pleurisy.

A. S.; aged forty-nine years; nativity, Denmark; admitted to the U. S. Marine Hospital, New York, December 12, 1887; died December 26.

Necropsy (ten hours after death).—Rigor mortis well established; body fairly nourished; pericardium contained about 50 cubic centimeters of flocculent serum; heart cavities filled with *ante mortem* clots; valves, normal; weight, 205 grams. Left lung adherent at its apex by recently organized bands of connective tissue. The left pleural cavity contained about 1,200 cubic centimeters of flocculent serum, and this was sacculated; the walls were made up of a large amount of fibrinous material, in layers, and contained many tuberculous foci. The whole lung was filled with miliary tubercles; weight, 1,205 grams. The right lung was emphysematous; weight, 2,030 grams; on section there was a large amount of cicatriciae tissue; no tubercles. The liver weighed 2,105 grams, slightly enlarged and cirrhotic; kidneys slightly fatty; other organs normal.

CASE 40.

Mitral insufficiency.

W. C.; aged twenty-nine years; nativity, England; was admitted to the U. S. Marine Hospital, Boston, Mass., December 27, 1887; died January 2, 1888.

Clinical history.—Patient was troubled with cough about one year, this being the second time that he had been admitted for treatment at this hospital for phthisis pulmonalis. When admitted to hospital his cough was very distressing, expectoration slight and mucous; dullness over upper lobes both lungs and mitral regurgitant murmur heard at apex of heart. There was no albumen in his urine and no œdema of any part of the body. Twenty-four hours before dissolution he had a severe convulsion, lasting several minutes. This was shortly afterwards followed by coma, which continued until his death.

Necropsy (twenty-two hours after death).—Rigor mortis present; body small, emaciated, and showed livid patches over dorsum; upper lobes of both lungs nearly solidified, containing claret-colored serum. Tubercular deposits were found in each lung near the apices. An *ante mortem* clot, about 3 inches long and the diameter of a lead-pencil, extended through the auriculo-ventricular openings on each side of the heart. The mitral valves were rough and fringed at their free margins. The heart was in systole and hypertrophied. Both kidneys were small, contracted, rough upon the surface, and the capsules adherent. The color of the kidneys was white and the cortical substance was very thin. Weight of right kidney 65 grams, left 95. Brain: The vessels of the pia mater were congested and the lateral ventricals contained considerable fluid.

CASE 41.

W. J. G.; aged thirty-two years; nativity, Ireland; admitted to the U. S. Marine Hospital, San Francisco, Cal., November 7, 1887; died January 9, 1888.

Necropsy (eighteen hours after death).—Slight *rigor mortis;* emaciation extreme. Pleuræ: Extensive and firm adhesions on right side so that the lung could not be removed without much laceration. The left pleura was adherent to the diaphragm and pericardium. Lungs: Small abscesses were found in each apex and both lungs were strewn throughout with tubercle. Heart fatty. Considerable fluid in cavity. No other organs examined.

CASE 42.

Aneurism—arch of aorta.

J. A.; aged fifty-one years; nativity, China; admitted to U. S. Marine Hospital, Stapleton, N. Y., November 28, 1887; died January 10, 1888.

Necropsy (thirty-seven hours post-mortem.)—Body fairly well nourished. *Rigor mortis* slight. The heart was pushed to the left side; a large tumor was found in the median line adherent to the sternum; the osseous tissue was eroded to a considerable extent at the junction of the manubrium and gladiolus. This tumor was removed and was found to be a large sacculated aneurism of the arch of the aortá, situated on the ascending and transverse portions. Both lungs contained cavities and the lung tissue was filled with tubercles. The valves of heart were thickened. The heart was small; left ventricle hypertrophied. The other organs were normal.

CASE 43.

*Diabetes.**

G. F. M.; aged thirty-one years; nativity, Delaware; admitted to the marine ward of the German Hospital, Philadelphia, January 4, 1888; died January 21, 1888.

History.—He stated that he had been more or less ailing ever since he left the hospital in May last, and on readmission his general appearance was bad. He had considerable œdema of the lower extremities. His weight was 128 pounds. Examination showed advanced tubercular disease of both lungs. The upper lobes of both organs giving evidence of a destruction of tissue resulting in cavities varying in size. He was passing an average of 4,800 grams of urine daily, containing sugar to the amount of .324 to 30 grams. His treatment was palliative and addressed mainly to the relief of symptoms, no regular course of diabetic treatment being essayed. Morphia sulphate in doses varying from .008 to .032 grams being administered p. r. n. Also fluid extract jaborandi 1 cubic centimeter every two hours to relax the circulation and produce diaphoresis. Patient grew gradually weaker and expressed himself as having fully lost all hope of recovery. He lingered until the 21st of January, when he died.

Necropsy (forty five hours post-mortem).—Body extremely emaciated. *Rigor mortis* well marked. Thorax: About 960 grams serous fluid in right pleural cavity, recent and old adhesions. The whole right lung showed

---

* See Annual Report M. H. S. for 1887.

evidences of advanced pneumonic phthisis, many cavities varying in size from that of a pea to that of a walnut. No normal lung tissue was left. The upper lobe of the left lung was in about the same condition as the right lung. Lower lobe contained circumscribed spots of degenerated tubercle; very little normal tissue being left. The heart was apparently normal, contained small amount of fluid blood, and weighed 260 grams. Weight of liver 900 grams, spleen 375. Both kidneys showed parenchymatous nephritis; right weighed 250 grams; left 250; stomach slightly congested.

CASE 44.

Chronic nephritis.

E. B. (female); aged nineteen years; nativity, Pennsylvania; was admitted to the marine ward, Mercy Hospital, Pittsburgh, Pa., on December 27, 1887; died January 22, 1888.

History.—Symptoms: Cough, expectoration of purulent matter, and diarrhœa; she was pale and emaciated; there were physical signs of phthisis pulmonalis, and the urine contained a large proportion of albumen.

Necropsy.—Length of right kidney, 18 centimeters; breadth, 8 centimeters; estimated weight, 450 grams. Left kidney, length, 14 centimeters; breadth, 8 centimeters; estimated weight, 300 grams. Color of kidney substance, whitish gray. The enlargement of these organs was shown principally in the septi bertini, the cortex being quite narrow. The pelvis in each kidney was of purple color. The apex of each lung contained several small cavities, surrounded by tubercular inflammatory products. Both lungs were extensively fastened by their pleural surfaces to the chest-wall.

CASE 45.

Tubercular disease of knee joint.

W. L.; aged twenty-five years; nativity, Norway; admitted to the U. S. Marine Hospital, New Orleans, La., October 29, 1886; died January 27, 1888.

History.—Tubercular disease of the right knee-joint developed some months before his death. His leg was amputated September 6, 1887, and after the loss of his leg his system seemed to rally, and he gained flesh for a short time.

Necropsy (twelve hours after death).—Body was of medium size and emaciated. Stump of recent amputation of right thigh nearly healed. There were ulcers on the upper and posterior portion of the right shoulder; hypostatic congestion and *post-mortem* discolorations of skin and muscles of back; scars on the temple from blisters, and bed-sores over the sacrum. *Rigor mortis* well marked. Thoracic cavity: left pleura adherent throughout, but the right one only adherent on posterior portion. There was no effusion in the pleural sacs. Right lung: Upper lobe was infiltrated with tubercle; the middle and lower lobes were œdematous, but otherwise normal. Left lung was atrophied and tubercular; weight of left lung was 120 grams; of right lung, 1,120. Heart was pale; its valves flabby, but otherwise normal. Abdomen: Liver large, pale, and giving evidence of fatty degeneration. Spleen was hypertrophied and very much congested. Its tissue was soft and easily torn. A supernumerary spleen, the size of a common chestnut, was attached. Left kidney was lobulated, its capsule easily torn; the line between cortical and medullary substance well marked. It was slightly amyloid. The right kidney seemed to be in a similar condition. The intestines were congested and distended with gas. Descending colon crossed over the upper part of the pelvis, the sigmoid flexure lying in front and above the bladder, and the rectum therefore descended on the right side of the pelvic cavity. At the splenic end of the transverse colon (at the point where it becomes descending colon) the caliber of the gut was suddenly contracted to one-third its normal size for a distance of 8 or 10 centimeters. Bladder was normal. Brain tissue pale and œdematous; dura mater thick and adherent; ventricles distended with fluid; pia mater at the base contained small granular bodies, the size of hemp seed, which were probably tubercles.

CASE 46.

Valvular disease of heart.

F. R.; aged sixty-two years; nativity, Spain; admitted to the U. S. Marine Hospital, New Orleans, La., January 30, 1888; died February 3.

History.—When admitted he suffered from excessive dyspnœa, and expectorated purulent matter. The intercostal spaces on the right side were obliterated. The vessels in the neck pulsated strongly. He had been ailing for some time, but his present attack dated three weeks back.

Necropsy (*twelve hours after death*).—Body was stout, well-nourished, and cyanosed. Pleuræ, both right and left, had old, tough adhesions; the fluid in the sacs was normal in amount and character. Heart was hypertrophied and fatty; was in diastole and filled with soft blood-clots. Mitral valve was normal. Aortic valves had two cusps firmly adherent for about one-third of their entire length, and they were all stiff with atheromatous deposits. The left ventricle and the aorta (for about 3 centimeters) were filled with a fibrinous clot. The left lung was so broken down that no lung tissue seemed to be available for breathing purposes. Right lung: The lower lobe almost solid, and the upper lobe studded with tubercles. Other organs not examined.

CASE 47.

Peritonitis.

C. M.; aged twenty-eight years; nativity, Kentucky; admitted to the U. S. Marine Hospital, Cairo, Ill., February 1, 1888; died February 5.

History.—This patient had been failing in health for some two months prior to his admission to hospital, having suffered much with "chills and fever." He sought relief for "shortness of breath." Auscultation revealed greatly reduced air-space, and percussion showed decided solidification in both lungs. Temperature axilla, 38.5° C.; cough slight; respiration shallow, hurried; skin bathed in sweat; could not lie down. A tonic and stimulating treatment was begun. He sank rapidly.

Necropsy (*twelve hours after death*).—Body that of a muscular young mulatto, much emaciated. *Rigor mortis* marked. Abdominal cavity containing bloody serum. Peritoneum congested and showing peritonitis. Spleen enlarged; congested; weight, 140 grams. Liver, weight, 2,750 grams. Bladder walls hypertrophied. Pericardium containing 100 cubic centimeters bloody serum. Heart: Both ventricles filled with tarry blood. Aortic valve somewhat deficient. Left pleura filled with tough, fibrinous formation. Lungs throughout filled with masses of cheesy tubercle, with pus and blood.

CASE 48.

G. T. W. (negro); aged thirty years; nativity, Delaware; admitted to the U. S. Marine Hospital at Baltimore, Md., January 1, 1887; died February 8, 1888.

Necropsy (*seventeen hours after death*).—*Rigor mortis* fairly developed. Body extremely emaciated. Heart small and flabby, valves normal. Lungs were bound down to chest walls by firm old adhesions and lung-tissue was lacerated in any attempt to remove these organs. Cavities varying in size from that of a pea to that of a walnut were distributed through both lungs, especially in upper lobes; cavities contained a gray muco-purulent matter. Liver showed many small abscesses near the surface filled with thick yellow pus. Spleen very small and soft, but contained no abscesses. Kidneys somewhat atrophic, otherwise normal. Intestines, both large and small, had the remains of old as well as new tubercular ulcers. Brain not examined.

CASE 49.

T. C.; aged thirty-seven years; nativity, United States; admitted to U. S. Marine Hospital, Stapleton, N. Y., January 9, 1888; died February 15.

Necropsy (*twenty-six hours after death*).—*Rigor mortis* marked. Body extremely emaciated. The right lung was adherent to the costal parieties in its upper portion. The left lung was slightly adherent at its apex. The right lung was the seat of cavities, and there was general breaking down of its entire substance. The left lung was solidified by recent tubercle. The tissue in the region of the larynx was swollen and œdematous; on removal there were found two glands of considerable size situated just below the os hyoides, that had undergone caseous degeneration and set up perichondritis. All the other organs were normal.

CASE 50.

R. B.; aged thirty years; nativity, Ireland; admitted to U. S. Marine Hospital, San Francisco, Cal., February 6, 1888; died February 19.

Necropsy (*ten hours after death*).—*Rigor mortis* present. Body very much wasted. Chest: Both lungs studded with tubercle, some of it in a state of cheesy degeneration, others completely broken down. One very large cavity occupied the entire right apex, and there were numerous smaller ones in both lungs. Heart: There was about 100 cubic centimeters of fluid in the pericardium, and the heart was of very small size, even for so small a man as the subject. The aorta was slightly dilated. Abdomen: Numerous tubercular ulcerations were found in both the large and small intestine, in several places the gut was almost perforated. The mesenteric glands were considerably enlarged. The kidneys and spleen were of normal size and structure. Liver a little larger and rather harder than normal.

CASE 51.

J. M.; aged thirty-six years; nativity, Virginia; admitted to U. S. Marine Hospital, New Orleans, La., February 2, 1887; died March 1, 1888.

Necropsy (*eighteen hours after death*).—*Rigor mortis* well marked. Body very much emaciated. Upon opening the thoracic cavity the lungs seemed to fill the entire space and were firmly adherent to the chest walls; both lungs were studded with gray tubercle. In the left lung, upper lobe, a cavity 5 by 5 centimeters existed; heart small, valves normal; liver large, congested, granular, or parenchymatous degeneration evidently going on; spleen large, infiltrated with small grayish, granular bodies, similar to the condition seen in the liver; kidneys showed signs of chronic congestion, large and hard, cortical portion thickened and dark red; intestines normal; stomach normal; brain not examined.

CASE 52.

R. K.; aged thirty-six years; nativity, Denmark; admitted to the marine ward of the German Hospital, Philadelphia, on March 26, 1887; died March 3, 1888.

History.—He was first admitted on the above date, suffering from an attack of irregular intermittent malaria fever, and was discharged as cured on April 19, 1887; on which date he was re-admitted. Diagnosis: Tubercle of lungs, for which he was treated and discharged again as improved. He was again re-admitted on May 23, 1887, with the same diagnosis as when admitted last time. He remained in the hospital from this date to the day of his death. During his stay in hospital he was one of a number who were subjected to the so-called "gas treatment," but was no more benefited than the others, his disease going on in the usual course to the destruction of pulmonary tissue and the formation of vomicae. His muscular system wasted to a minimum. A few days before his death an obstinate diarrhœa set in, together with an idiopathic facial erysipelas.

Necropsy (*March* 5, 1888).—Emaciated extremely. Both lungs adherent to thoracic walls; upper lobes of both destroyed and occupied with cavities, large and small, and nodules in all stages of degeneration; lower lobes also affected. Mesenteric glands all enlarged. Bowels showed signs of enteritis and colitis.

CASE 53.

H. C. (colored); aged thirty years; native of Kentucky; admitted to the Marine Hospital, Memphis, Tenn., February 5, 1888; died March 3.

History.—He had been sick more than a year before admission. He had a severe cough, pain in chest, poor appetite, loss of flesh, and strength. Dullness over lower lobes of both lungs. Coarse râles with amphoric respiration, tympanitic resonance over both apices. He failed steadily and died March 3, 1888.

Necropsy.—Large cavity involving the upper lobes of both lungs. Many small cavities in other parts of both lungs. The middle lobe of right lung in fair condition. Numerous foci of tubercular deposits in the spleen. Mesenteric glands enlarged and caseous.

Weight of viscera in grams.—Right kidney, 177; left, 169; heart, 267; right lung, 670; left, 690; spleen, 227; liver, 1,355.

CASE 54.

C. K. (colored); aged twenty-three years; nativity Tennessee; admitted to the U. S. Marine Hospital at Saint Louis, Mo., October 21, 1887; died March 9, 1888.

Necropsy (*seven hours after death*).—Cadaveric rigidity slight; body considerably emaciated. Brain not examined. Thoracic cavity, pleuritic adhesions extensive on both sides. Lungs, both contained numerous tubercles, especially about the apices; no cavities discovered. Heart normal, excepting a large deposit of fat about the auricles. Abdominal cavity; liver, rather small, but apparently normal. Intestines, numerous inflammatory, ulcerative patches in the lower part of the small intestines, which contained a large amount of pus. Pus was also found in the peritoneal cavity; no opening in the intestinal walls could be found; mesenteric glands enlarged and inclined to soften. Stomach and spleen normal. Left kidney enshrouded in a thick fibrous capsule, on the outside of which was a collection of a clear jelly-like material which was friable and easily detached. This material was also noticed in several places attached to the omentum and mesentery. Right kidney normal, as was also the bladder.

CASE 55.

E. A. (colored); aged forty-three years; nativity Alabama; admitted to the U. S. Marine Hospital, Saint Louis, Mo., March 17. 1888; died March 18, 1888.

History.—On admission patient stated that he had been sick for about two months previously from a persistent bloody diarrhœa. There was great emaciation and prostration, a slight cough, and a fetid diarrhœa, stools containing muco-pus mixed with an occasional small amount of blood. There was dullness over both lungs, diminished respiration, and moist rales throughout both lungs. Body covered with a cold, clammy sweat. Death occurred seemingly from asthenia.

Necropsy (*eighteen hours after death*).—*Rigor mortis* present; body very much emaciated. Lungs congested and filled with small yellow tubercular masses, in various stages of softening. Heart, right side dilated and full of blood-clots. Stomach and spleen both normal. Liver congested. Intestines, injected at middle part; in the lower part of the ileum were soft yellow bodies, averaging about the size of a pea, and attached to the internal tunic of the intestine; several firm ragged ulcers were found near the ileo cæcal valve, extending usually transversely around the intestine. Two small holes were noticed in the wall of the cæcum. There was a small amount of pus in the abdominal cavity. The peritoneal surfaces were adherent in spots. Other organs were not examined.

CASE 56.

A. H.; aged twenty-five years; nativity, Norway; admitted to U. S. Marine Hospital, San Francisco, Cal., December 5, 1887; died March 23, 1888.

Necropsy (*thirteen hours after death*).—Body extremely emaciated. Thorax: Both lungs bound down more or less firmly by adhesions. An abscess the size of an orange occupied apex of left lung. The rest of this lung was strewn with tubercular granules and deeply congested. The right lung was full of miliary tubercle.

CASE 57.

Fatty heart.

B. S.; aged twenty-eight years; nativity, South Sea Islands; admitted to U. S. Marine Hospital, San Francisco, Cal., November 30, 1887; died March 27, 1888.

Necropsy (*eight hours after death*).—*Rigor* pronounced. Very great emaciation. Thorax only was examined. Left lung was so much broken down, so bound down by adhesions, and so much encroached upon by the heart and pericardial sac, that it could not be closely examined. Right lung was full of disseminated tubercle. At the outer side the pleural walls were weakly adherent by means of a gelatinous, villous lymph exudation, quite peculiar, and identical with that to be mentioned as found in the pericardium. Pericardium contained 300 cubic centimeters serum. The walls were greatly thickened and covered with the peculiar lymph just mentioned. At the outer side of the left ventricle, just above the apex, the visceral and parietal layers were adherent over an area of 3 centimeters square. The heart was very fatty and flabby, somewhat hypertrophied, and very considerably dilated. Nothing wrong was noted about the valves.

Case 58.

Tubercular disease of testicle; cystitis.

J. R. H.; aged sixty years; nativity, United States; admitted to U. S. Marine Hospital, Stapleton, N. Y., December 19, 1887; died March 27, 1888.

Necropsy (*thirty-five hours post mortem*).—*Rigor mortis.* Right arm tattooed with brigatine in full sail, and left arm with United States flag. The right lung was adherent to the costal pleura by old fibrinous bands; it was filled with tubercles in cheesy degeneration. The left lung was attached by one or two bands; there was a little fluid in the pleural cavity, and the lung was filled with tubercles in a state of cheesy degeneration; there was a small cavity filled with pus in the apex. Heart was normal. Liver was enlarged; gall bladder distended. Pancreas was normal. Pelvis of each kidney was inflamed and pus corpuscles were present; the kidneys were cirrhosed. Stomach and intestines were normal. Bladder was slightly distended and contained urine and a large quantity of pus; the wall of the bladder was reticulated, containing numerous pockets. Prostate was hypertrophied, with a bilateral projection extending into the bladder. In front of the prostate the urethra was sacculated. Left testicle was degenerated, and the epididymis contained some cheesy pus. Tuberculous deposits were present in the right testicle.

Case 59.

J. J. D.; aged forty-five years; nativity, New York; admitted to the marine ward of the German Hospital, Philadelphia, October 17, 1887; died March 29, 1888.

History.—He was admitted on the above date, giving a history of considerable previous ill health. He stated that his lung had been affected more or less for two or three years. Examination showed advanced tubercular disease of both lungs. He was subjected to the ordinary treatment ol. morrhuæ p. r. n., stimulants, etc., and sol. cocaine hydrochl. for the distressing laryngeal symptoms. Repeated examination of the larynx were made, but never was there any localized ulcerations made out. His muscular and adipose development were maintained to a surprising degree.

Necropsy (*thirty-two hours post mortem*).—Body well nourished, fat abundant everywhere. Both lungs closely adherent to thoracic wall; adhesions evidently of long standing and very firm. Both organs riddled with cavities varying in size. Caseous degeneration of lungs.

CASE 60.

Meningitis.

P. M.; aged fifty-five years; nativity, Ireland; admitted to the U. S. Marine Hospital, Saint Louis, Mo., March 10, 1888; died April 5, 1888.

History.—Patient was suffering from symptoms of pneumonia at the time of his admission, and occasional chills, followed by fever, sweating, and prostration; about twenty-four hours before death he fell into a comatose state, from which it was impossible to arouse him.

Necropsy (twenty hours after death).—Body emaciated; *rigor mortis* moderate. Brain: Meninges deeply injected and thickened, and adherent to the surface of the brain on its superior surface to a small extent. The surface vessels of the brain also congested; intracranial fluid increased in quantity and contained small, white flaky bodies. Brain substance increased in consistency. Lungs: Pleuritic adhesions almost complete on right side. Right lung ulcerated in several places, and partly filled with a yellowish tubercular matter of soft consistence, sections readily sinking when placed in water. Left lung congested and filled with a frothy fluid. Heart: Right side very fatty, some yellow clots found in right auriculo-ventricular opening. Valves normal. Liver greatly enlarged and in an advanced stage of fatty degeneration.

CASE 61.

J. T.; aged fifty-four years; nativity, Denmark; admitted to U. S. Marine Hospital at Chicago, Ill., March 19, 1888; died April 6, 1888.

Necropsy.—*Rigor mortis* well marked. Body greatly emaciated. Skin dark and sallow and drawn tightly over the skeleton. Left pleura bound to parieties of chest and to diaphragm by numerous old adhesions. Parietal and visceral layers of right pleura adherent throughout and greatly thickened. Right lung apparently atrophied and shrunken. Upon section of upper lobe numerous miliary tubercles were found throughout the substance of the lung. Right lung also contained some small miliary nodules. No cavities were discovered in either lung. Heart: Left auricle and ventricle contained *ante-mortem* clots extending into vena cava. Mitral valves thickened. Abdomen: Mesenteric glands greatly engorged. Portal vein and branches greatly distended with thickened tarry blood. Kidneys somewhat larger than normal, but otherwise showed no appearance of any pathological change.

CASE 62.

Mitral insufficiency—Fatty kidneys.

E. F.; aged thirty-six years; nativity, New York; admitted to U. S. Marine Hospital, San Francisco, Cal., March 14, 1888; died April 12, 1888.

History.—The symptoms in the case were those of phthisis, and during the last weeks of his life there was considerable œdema of the lower extremities. His urine contained a large amount of albumen; was voided frequently, and he passed about 2,000 cubic centimeters in twenty-four hours. On April 11, he complained of having vomited his food for several days. On the following day there were several attacks of general convulsions and unconsciousness, in one of which he died.

Necropsy.—There was considerable emaciation. The omentum and mesentery contained considerable fat. The small intestines showed some inflammation, and one enlarged gland contained purulent matter, probably from softened tubercle. The spleen and liver were normal in appearance. The kidneys were somewhat smaller than normal size; the capsules firmly adherent; their color outside whitish with red patches from inflammation. The backs of the kidneys were rounded (typical "pig-back") and both surfaces somewhat irregular in outline. Upon section the kidney structure was white in color; the cortex narrowed, the pyramids occupying about half their usual space. These changes were apparently due to fatty degeneration. The heart had considerable surface fat; its walls were quite firm and of normal thickness. The right ventricle contained *ante mortem* clots attached to the surface and extending into the pulmonary artery. The mitral valves were thickened and their edges drawn, from fibrinous contraction. At the apex of the left lung a cavity sufficiently large to contain 50 cubic centimeters was found. The upper part of this lung contained extensive tubercular deposits; its base was red with suffused blood. The right lung was fastened in every direction to the costal pleura. Its color upon section was gray, with black spots of coal pigment distributed throughout. Its consistence was tough from induration.

Case 63.

J. K.; aged forty-four years; nativity, England; admitted to the U. S. Marine Hospital, Stapleton, N. Y., February 1, 1888; died, April 18.

Necropsy (fifty four hours after death).—Body emaciated. There was a serous effusion, tinged with blood, in the pericardium. The external veins of the heart were engorged; clots were present in its right side, and an *ante mortem* clot was found on the left side extending into the aorta. The lungs were firmly adherent to the chest walls. The right lung was thickly studded with tuberculous masses and was somewhat consolidated. The left lung was in the same condition, and contained also cheesy masses undergoing softening. The liver was normal. The spleen was soft and friable. The left kidney was tough on cutting and congested; the right kidney the same. The other organs were normal.

Case 64.

D. B. (colored); aged twenty-eight years; nativity, Tennessee; was admitted to the Marine Hospital, Memphis, Tenn., March 12, 1888.

History.—Has had a cough one year or more, expectoration scanty. Has lost much flesh and strength. Appetite very poor. Has night-sweats and fever every afternoon. Physical examination shows large cavities in both lungs. His cough was much improved by cod-liver oil. On the 5th of April a troublesome diarrhœa began, and he failed rapidly. The diarrhœa could be checked but not controlled. He died on the 20th of April.

Necropsy.—*Rigor mortis* slight; great emaciation; many cavities in both lungs; strong pleuritic adhesion over both lungs: colon intensely congested; mesenteric glands enlarged and caseous.

Case 65.

T. T.; aged twenty-eight years; nativity, Denmark; admitted to U. S. Marine Hospital, San Francisco, Cal., February 27, 1888; died April 25, 1888.

Necropsy (eighteen hours after death).—The left lung was everywhere adherent to the chest wall, except over a space about 10 centimeters square outside the nipple line, where the pleural sac had become a pus-secreting cavity, communicating with the lung by several ragged openings. The flattened lung was filled with tubercle, and there were several small cavities in the lung structure. The upper lobe of the right lung was also filled with tubercle and had several small cavities. The kidneys were larger than normal and fatty.

CASE 66.

Peritonitis.

B. B.; aged thirty-three years; nativity, Iceland; admitted to U. S. Marine Hospital at Boston, Mass., April 6, 1888; died May 3.

History.—Patient gave a history of good health till eight months previous to admission, when he began to suffer from fever, cough, and dyspnœa on exertion. These symptoms increased in severity, and later on the abdomen began to swell. On examination exaggerated respiration was heard over the upper portion of both lungs, dullness over both bases and weak respiratory sounds, a murmur with the second sound of the heart was audible, most distinct at the base, and the abdomen was moderately distended with fluid. Patient was aspirated several times, both from the peritoneal and pleural cavities, the fluid withdrawn aggregating 5,000 cubic centimeters, but with only temporary relief. Cough, dyspnœa, with elevation of temperature in the evening, steadily progressed till death.

Necropsy (four hours after death).—No cadaveric rigidity; considerably emaciated; enlarged glands in the anterior mediastinum; heart displaced upward and to the right. Heart: weight, 360 grams; slight hypertrophy; *ante mortem* clot in right ventricle, and small plaque on one segment of the tricuspid valves. Right lung: weight, 630 grams; adherent and removed with difficulty; greater part of pleural cavity obliterated; lung impregnated with gray tubercle throughout. Left lung: weight, 790 grams; œdematous; lower lobe congested; apex and upper lobe infiltrated with fine tubercle. Peritoneum thickened, studded with tubercle and universally adherent; peritoneum, omentum, and intestines united in an undistinguishable mass of adhesions, forming saccules containing a good deal of fluid. Liver: weight, 1,940 grams; normal in appearance but firmly adherent to diaphragm by its upper surface; posterior portion of right lobe contained tubercle. Right kidney; weight, 200 grams; left kidney, weight 190 grams, both normal. Spleen: weight, 280 grams; normal in appearance.

CASE 67.

J. S.; aged thirty-five years; nativity, Norway; admitted to U. S. Marine Hospital, Chicago, Ill., October 14, 1887; died May 3, 1888.

Necropsy.—*Rigor mortis* slight; body fairly nourished; lower extremities œdematous. Right lung consolidated throughout upper lobe. Near the apex was seen a small cavity that would contain about 5 cubic centimeters. Left lung firmly adherent to pleura throughout; upper lobe consolidated; near apex of upper lobe were several small cavities, each of from 5 to 15 cubic centimeters capacity. Two of these cavities were filled with recent clots, showing the seat of *ante mortem* hemorrhage. Pericardiac sac contained about 75 cubic centimeters of serous fluid. Large *ante mortem* clot in right ventricle extending into pulmonary artery. Left ventricle of heart contained a few *post mortem* clots.

Case 68.

M. A.; aged twenty-six years; nativity, Norway; admitted to the U. S. Marine Hospital, San Francisco, Cal., April 14, 1888; died May 10.

Necropsy (twelve hours after death).—The mesenteric glands were enlarged. There were several ulcers in the small intestines, one of them being 1½ centimeters in diameter; probably tubercular. The kidneys were slightly enlarged, the margins rounded, presenting internally the appearance of fatty degeneration. The liver was much enlarged and pale in color. The right pleural cavity contained 500 cubic centimeters of fluid. The lung on this side was flattened and contracted to one-third its natural size; its tissues were fibrous and contained an abundance of tubercle, with the bronchi thickened and calcareous. This lung was fastened by two thick fibrinous bands to the chest wall. The left lung was filled with miliary tubercle and contained several small cavities. The pericardial cavity contained about 100 cubic centimeters of fluid. The pericardium was of pearl color. There was no valvular disease.

Case 69.

Cirrhosis of the liver.

D. M.; aged forty-one years; nativity, Canada; admitted to U. S. Marine Hospital, Cairo, Ill., March 14, 1888; died May 18.

History.—Patient was admitted with pneumonia, from which he apparently entirely recovered, his later symptoms pointing to cirrhosis of liver. After the diagnosis was so changed, March 26, 1888, he gradually sank into an adynamic state, without pain, dying of exhaustion.

Necropsy (twenty six hours after death).—Body a dark yellow; much emaciated; ecchymosed; bed-sores on sacrum and hips. Thorax: Pleural cavities obliterated; both lungs completely solidified and filled; masses of gray tubercle beginning to break down. Pericardium thickened. Heart fatty, flabby. Liver small, pale, nodular; weight, 1,575 grams. Spleen, currant-jelly like; friable. Kidneys fatty; left kidney containing pus. ' Intestines studded with tubercles.

Case 70.

J. S.; aged thirty-two years; nativity, Germany; admitted to the U. S. Marine Hospital, Chicago, Ill., December 29, 1887; died May 23, 1888.

Necropsy.—*Rigor mortis* well marked. Body very much emaciated. Right lung full of small tubercular deposits. Upper lobe contained one small cavity which was filled with pus. Upper lobe of left lung contained two small cavities which were filled with pus. Heart walls very flabby. Large *ante-mortem* clot in left auricle and ventricle. Dark clots of blood in right side of heart. The kidneys were very much congested. Other organs normal.

Case 71.

Syphilis, secondary.

J. T.; aged twenty years; nativity, Tennessee; admitted to U. S. Marine Hospital, New Orleans, La., February 10, 1888, suffering from secondary syphilis; died May 27.

History.—Shortly after admission began to cough. Examination of chest developed signs of incipient phthisis. History of syphilis undoubted. Anti-syphilitic treatment exerted no influence over lung trouble, rendering it improbable that a diagnosis of syphilitic phthisis solved both questions. The tubercular trouble ran a moderately rapid course, ending in death May 27, 1888.

Necropsy (fourteen hours after death).—Body, medium size, slight build. Emaciated. *Rigor mortis* present. Bed sore over sacrum. Both pleuræ adherent. A cavity the size of the closed fist was found in the apex of the left lung; balance of left and upper portion of right lung infiltrated with tubercle. Heart unusually small, its tissue pale and anæmic. Valves flabby and soft. Liver in first stage of amyloid degeneration. Spleen enlarged, dark in color, soft, and easily torn. Kidneys large; tissuepale; capsule easily stripped; line between cortical and medullary substance not well defined. Brain and cord not examined.

CASE 72.

A. W.; aged nineteen years; nativity, Scotland; admitted to U. S. Marine Hospital, San Francisco, Cal., March 23, 1888; died June 11.

Necropsy (eighteen hours after death).—The body was extremely emaciated; the heart contained a fibrinous clot; the valves were competent; the surface of the heart presented at the auriculo ventricular junction a jelly-like mass of fat; the entire surface was pale in color. The lungs were everywhere adherent to the chest walls. They were dense and fibrous in structure, showing an abundance of pus from the thickened bronchial tubes; there were many spots of yellow degenerated tissue (tubercular). The other organs presented normal appearances.

CASE 73.

F. G.; aged twenty-eight years; nativity, Sweden; admitted to U. S. Marine Hospital, San Francisco, Cal., March 8, 1888; died June 13.

Necropsy (thirteen hours after death).—The body was extremely emaciated; the lungs were universally adherent to chest walls; they were filled throughout with miliary tubercles; nearly the whole of the right lung had disappeared by ulceration, leaving only the thickened pleura and a small portion of the lower lobe.

CASE 74.

Tubercle of lungs.

K. B.; aged twenty-six years; nativity, Norway; admitted to U. S. Marine Hospital, San Francisco, Cal., April 18, 1888; died June 18.

Necropsy (seven hours after death).—The body was considerably emaciated. Both lungs were firmly adherent to the chest walls, both contained miliary tubercles throughout. There was a cavity at each apex, that on the right side occupying the greater part of the upper lobe; the cavity at the left side was comparatively small. The kidneys presented the appearance of fatty degeneration.

CASE 75.

Enteritis—Perforation of colon.

A. C. (colored); aged twenty-seven years; nativity, Florida; was admitted to the Marine Hospital, Memphis, Tenn., June 14, 1888.

History.—He had been previously treated in the hospital for yellow tubercle of the lung. This time he complained of severe pain in the right side of belly and frequent stools. The stools contained mucus and watery fæcal matter. While he had so many stools, cough and hæmoptysis did not trouble him. Died on the 27th.

Necropsy.—Cavities in both lungs; in the apex lobe the size of a large orange. Old pleuritic adhesions. In the right loin there were several perforations of the colon; some were quite large. The colon was firmly attached to peritoneum of anterior abdominal wall. In the cavity formed by adhesions was 50 cubic centimeters of purulent fluid, containing fæcal matter. From cæcum to anus there was not a patch of normal mucous membrane; all were black and sloughing.

Weight of viscera.—Left lung, 491; right, 521; spleen, 124; liver, 1,750; left kidney, 175; right, 180; heart, 290.

INFLAMMATION OF THE BRAIN AND ITS MEMBRANES.

S. A. (colored); aged forty-five years; nativity, Virginia; occupation, deck-hand; was admitted to the U. S. Marine Hospital at Saint Louis, Mo., April 6, 1887; re-admitted for new disease December 29, 1887; died December 30, 1887.

History.—Patient entered the hospital with facial neuralgia, and shortly showed symptoms of paralysis of the left side of the face, with increased pain, which resisted all remedies. Pain in the internal ear, with vertigo, occurred at about this time, so that the patient was unable to walk without falling down, and "auditory vertigo" was added to the diagnosis. Some time after the occurrence of these symptoms he fell into a semi-comatose condition, which continued for a number of weeks, with partial paralysis of the left side of the body. On rallying from this trouble there remained ptosis of the left eye, slight facial paralysis, with mild involvement of the tongue and impaired use of the left arm. These symptoms remained present during the interval between the first and last attacks of semi-consciousness (a period of about six months), together with progressive weakness of the mind and memory, the patient acting in a stupid manner. He denied ever having had syphilis, yet it is believed that he did have this disease years before. About a week prior to his death he complained of great debility and an increase of the pain in his face, and it was noticed that the facial paralysis was much more marked. He became unable to sit up, and was soon prostrated, being unable to speak or swallow. There was no paralysis of either arms or legs. The urine and fæces were discharged involuntarily; the pulse was very rapid and weak; respiration slow and labored; temperature about normal; urine acid, of high specific gravity, and contained no albumen or sugar.

Necropsy (six hours after death).—Cadaveric rigidity moderate. Body well nourished. Cranial cavity: Membranes thickened, congested, opaque, and adherent to each other. These conditions were especially marked about the base of the brain, where the membranes were very much thickened. Brain: Patches of lymph were observed at various places on the external surface; on section spots of marked congestion were noted, and the consistence of the organ slightly increased, cutting almost as if hardened in alcohol; the cut surface was of a reddish tint in points, and fluids rather increased; anterior pyramids of medulla oblongata and upper portion of cord were very much hardened in consistence. Lungs somewhat congested, but otherwise normal. Heart slightly fatty; valves, etc., normal. Liver and spleen congested. Kidneys congested, and contained increased amount of white connective tissue. Other organs apparently normal so far as examined.

INFLAMMATION OF CEREBRAL MEMBRANES.

Case 1.

A. D.; aged thirty years; nativity, New York; entered the U. S. Marine Hospital, Chicago, Ill., August 8, 1887; died August 18, 1887.

History.—General appearance that of robust health. Has been temperate in every way. Seven years ago he received a sunstroke, which prostrated him for two months. The next summer he had another stroke on ship board, and the following summer one on land, when he suffered very severely with pain in the base of brain, prostration, muscular spasms, etc.; he was perfectly demented for several days at a time, and at other times suffered in a milder degree. A few days before admission he had been exposed to great heat. When admitted he complained of headache, even touching the hair gave pain; conjunctival vessels were engorged; pulse and temperature normal; all viscera seemed to be in a normal condition. Patient was peevish and petulant.

August 8.—Hair shaved from neck and temporal bone and a blister applied; ℞: Elaterium .06, pil. hydrag. 1, M. ft. caps. No. iv.; sig.; one every two hours until bowels were moved freely. ℞: Pot. brom. sol. 50 per cent.; sig., 4 c. c. every three hours.

August 9.—He had a spasm of apparently of every muscle in his body; he was rigid; eyes half closed, but he was conscious. Previous to the spasm, the basilar pain and injected condition of the eyes had disappeared, but he complained of great pain and soreness in the muscles afterwards. Spasm lasted five minutes. Bowels not open. Full doses brom. potash were given, and elaterium with ol. tiglii until bowels were moved.

August 14.—Patient had steadily improved to date, when another spasm occurred, which left him very weak, and stimulants were ordered.

August 16.—Patient has been drowsy for the last two days, but is easily aroused. Occasional spasms and extreme weakness, though the latter not indicated by the heart's action. He eats freely of eggs, milk, etc.

August 17.—Pulse full and equable, but quicker. Temperature 37.2° C., the first time it had been above 37° C.; 6 p. m., unconscious since 11 a. m.; urine passed in bed; pupils dilated, do not respond to light. Carbonate of ammonia, spirits frumenti, iodide potassium given freely; 8 p. m., breathing shallow and jerky, showing that pressure of meningeal fluid had extended.

August 18.—Death.

Necropsy.—Five hours after death.—Body in good condition, muscular, and well proportioned. *Rigor mortis* very marked. Much dark fluid blood in vessels of scalp. Dura mater subacutely inflamed, and when removed presented a roughened, opaque surface with inflammatory thickening. The sinuses were engorged with black fluid blood. Cerebrospinal fluid much increased in quantity and of dark color. Pia mater and arachnoid intimately adherent and attached to surface of brain by plaques of recent lymph. Vessels of pia mater immensely distended with dark fluid blood. Sections showed the vessels of the brain also engorged. No appreciable change in brain substance. Lateral ventricles filled with fluid of a dirty appearance. The amount of fluid pressing on the floor of the fourth ventricle was evidently the immediate cause of death from paralysis of the centers of respiration. All evidences showed the total want of æration of the blood. The black fluid blood in the cavity after removing the brain was about 500 cubic centimeters.

CASE 2.

Tubercular.

O. B.; aged eighteen years; nativity, Norway; admitted to U. S. Marine Hospital, Stapleton, N. Y., January 24, 1888; died January 31.

Necropsy (forty eight hours after death).—*Rigor mortis* marked. Body slight and fairly nourished. Depression of the left side of the chest. The calvarium was removed; the dura mater was adherent in places by recently formed fibrinous deposits. Situated in the superior longitudinal sinus was a large aggregation of tubercular masses about the size of shot. At the base of the brain, extending from the medulla upward over the pons varolii, was a large deposit of fibrin, studded with tubercle. The arachnoid in this vicinity was inflamed and the seat of tubercular nodules. The ventricles were filled with fluid; the brain substance was congested, and in some of the veins there was a commencing inflammation. In the left lenticular nucleus there was a large area of red softening, giving rise to paralysis during the last two days of life. No thrombi or emboli were found. The lungs were both adherent to the costal parieties. The left lung was small, contracted, and filled with tubercle. The right was also filled with tubercles, but not contracted. The heart was filled with *ante-mortem* clots. The other organs were normal.

CASE 3.

T. H. (colored); aged twenty years; nativity, Mississippi; was admitted to the Marine Hospital, Memphis, Tenn., June 26, 1888; died June 29.

History.—His friends said he had been sick ten days before he was admitted. He complained of a severe pain in his head; could not sleep, but was continually tossing from one side of the bed to the other. The day before his admission, they said, a doctor had given him a hypodermic of morphia, since which he had lain in a stupor. When admitted he was comatose; he could not be aroused and did not move, except when tickled or pricked with a pin. He would drink when water was offered to him. Pupils did not react to light and were equal in size. Pulse, 100 and weak; it was difficult to count the pulse on account of the constant working of the fingers. Temperature, 37.5°. Diagnosis: Patient in stage of effusion of acute meningitis. He was just alive when admitted. There was no reaction to stimulants. He died June 29, 1888.

Necropsy.—Dura mater adherent along each side of longitudinal sinus to the pia mater. The dural veins were distended. Blood clots in longitudinal, lateral, and cavernous sinuses. The pia mater could not be separated from the brain without tearing. The veins of pia mater much distended. The convolutions were flattened by pressure. There was an increase of fluid in all the ventricles and between the dura and pia maters. Weight of brain, 1,482 grams.

CASE 4.

Hemorrhage.

B. W.; aged twenty-two years; nativity, England; admitted to the U. S. Marine Hospital, New York, August —, 1887; died August 29, 1887.

History.—This patient was from the U. S. revenue bark *Chase*; he was sent down from Gardiner's Bay on board one of the Sound steamers, from which he was taken off and brought to the hospital in the ambulance. On admission he was in a profound stupor, as if he had been taking a narcotic; soon afterwards he was roused, and became rational. His chief trouble seemed to be a constant twitching of the muscles of the body, in all respects resembling chorea, these occurring only when the patient was awake. The patient stated that he had never had any attacks like this before; that the attack came on suddenly, on board the vessel, and he was for a time unconscious; that he suffered no pain, only the inconvenience of not being able to control his legs and arms. He was during the first five days perfectly quiet when asleep, but after that time the muscular twitching became worse and more constant. He then sank into a deep sleep, from which he could not be aroused; this continued until the date of death, August 29, 1887.

Necropsy (*eighteen hours after death*).—Body fairly nourished; sordes upon teeth; some discoloration about the nates. Thorax and abdomen examined; organs normal. Calvarium removed. The dura mater and arachnoid were congested over the region of the antrum lobes. The superior longitudinal sinus was completely occluded by a finely organized thrombus; the walls of the sinus were infiltrated with inflammatory deposit. At the site of the thrombus there was a large blood clot of about 7 cubic centimeters thick and 4 cubic centimeters in diameter. This was the cause of the muscular convulsion. Strange to say that, just situated over the moter area, it caused no paralysis. Spinal cord removed; found normal.

Case 5.

Abscess, body of sphenoid bone.—Laryngitis.

H. G.; aged twenty-one years; nativity, England; was admitted to marine ward, Grace Hospital, Seattle, Wash., May 17, 1888; died May 27, 1888.

History.—When admitted to the hospital the patient gave a history of failing strength for over a week, accompanied by increasing headache and profuse diarrhœa. He had a typhoid appearance, swollen and furred tongue, sordes on teeth, diarrhœa, some tympanites; temperature 39.4° C., but no abdominal tenderness or eruption. He was put on milk alone, with an ice-bag to his head. For four days the temperature ranged from 38.2° C. morning, to 39° C. evening, and the number of stools became less, but the headache continued to increase, together with a severe pain in the back of neck. On the 21st he had a severe chill, and the temperature rose to 40.4° C. in the evening. Large doses of tinct. ferri chlorid. and quin. sulph. were given.

May 22.—Had another chill. Severe pharyngitis and difficulty of swallowing; 23d, another chill; 24th, no chill; 25th, no chill; pharynx more swollen, but no fluctuation or pointing detected; some laryngitis.

May 26.—Laryngitis increased rapidly; external applications and steam inhalations gave no relief.

May 27.—Œdema of larynx came on during the night. Face cyanosed and respiration very labored. Seven a. m., laryngotomy was performed, after which the breathing was much easier, but the heart failed rapidly, and he died at 10.30 a. m. A few hours before death temperature rose to 42.2° C. No delirium except during high fever. Two days before death the eyes protruded some, and there were sharp shooting pains through the face. No diarrhœa for several days before death.

Necropsy.—The pharynx and larynx showed evidence of severe inflammation, but no pus was found in the tissues. The brain membranes were much congested, and several points of pus were found on their surface. In the left middle lobe of the cerebrum was found a small collection of pus just beneath the pia mater. There was a small quantity of pus in the apex of each orbit. The upper surface of the body of the sphenoid bone was denuded of its periosteum and the cancellous tissue within filled with pus.

SOFTENING OF BRAIN.

Capt. P. J. D.; native of Holland; was admitted to the Marine Hospital, Mobile, Ala., on April 19, 1888; died April 24, 1888.

History.—He was the master of the Dutch bark *Pauline.* Whilst at Pascagoula, Miss., he was observed to be acting "queerly." There was insomnia with loss of appetite and clouded intelligence. He refused to seek medical aid, and on the sixth day of the disease the mate of the ship, without his consent, obtained the services of a physician, and he was pronounced insane. He was taken into the hospital on May 19 by request of the vice-consul at this port. Status on admission: Sits listlessly in his chair; countenance apathetic; answers questions with difficulty and unintelligently. A peculiarly offensive odor emanated from his person; tongue, coated; temperature, 38° C.; pulse, 94; bowels, loose; dejecta, black and fetid; urine, coffee-colored. He was ordered a warm bath and put to bed. Soon after he was seized with tonic spasms of short duration, simulating electric shocks; active delirium, exalted temperature and pulse rate continued until death.

Necropsy.—*Rigor mortis* marked. Body well nourished. Calvarium removed. Sinuses full of dark blood; meninges also engorged; no signs of preceding meningitis; vessels of pia of dark-blue color and very full. Brain with great difficulty removed, as it was too soft to be readily handled. It presented a peculiarly blanched surface, quite in contrast to what was expected from the engorged pia mater. On section the gray substance of the cortex and ganglia was scarcely appreciable; it was one dead white from center to periphery. There was no appearance of localized softening from pressure of a tumor or extravasated blood; no signs of syphilis; no occlusion of the larger basic vessels—it seemed a simple general softening. The total lack of the personal history of this case was highly appreciated in the formation of a diagnosis and in the institution of treatment, and especially is it regretted in the light of the disclosures of the necropsy. Absolutely no history could be gained from those about the man except that he was "queer." Other organs of thorax and abdomen were found normal.

HEMORRHAGE—CEREBRAL.

W. T. (colored seaman); aged forty years; nativity, Alabama; was admitted to the U. S. Marine Hospital at Mobile, Ala., at 8.20 a. m., July 11, 1888; died at 9 o'clock—forty minutes later.

History.—His captain states that this is the second attack of the kind which he has experienced, the first occurring two years ago and presenting all the symptoms of intracranial hemorrhage. The patient complained of cramping pains in the muscles of the calves and thighs during the day preceding admission to hospital. This was considered to be "cramp," and some remedies were administered by an officer of the steamer. During the night he became comatose and when admitted to hospital was *in articulo mortis*. Pupils widely dilated and insensible to light. Respirations 10 to the minute; stertorous and shallow. Heart's action excited; pulse 114; temperature 37° C. Heart action failed with the paralysis of the respiratory center, and it could scarcely be decided whether death resulted from apnœa or cardiac failure.

Necropsy.—Body that of a fully developed man in good condition. No appearance of external injury. Calvarium removed. A large quantity of bloody serum escaped from a puncture in the dura mater. Before the brain was removed there was seen a ragged rent of the cortex about the middle, or temporo-sphenoidal lobe, of the right hemisphere, from which a blood-clot protruded, and through which the blood serum had drained into the membranes. The displaced clot weighed 50 grams and exposed a clot cavity as large as a walnut, the walls of which, from pressure, were diffluent. The central ganglia were softened, and there was evidence that the lateral ventricle had been encroached upon before the peripheral rupture relieved the pressure. The thalamus opticus was diffluent. Section of the pons revealed a clot of the size of a split pea at its center.

HEMIPLEGIA.

CASE 1.

J. H.; aged forty years; nativity, Newfoundland; admitted to U. S. Marine Hospital, Detroit, Mich., August 14, 1887; died September 18, 1887.

History.—Patient had generally enjoyed good health, but had acquired syphilis about five years ago. On August 6, 1887, he fell suddenly; was unconscious a short time, and on recovering consciousness found that he had lost the use of his left upper and lower extremities, the muscles of the face being also slightly affected. When admitted to the hospital he had so far improved that his facial muscles were under control and he could walk a little with assistance, but had no power over the muscles of his left upper extremity, although sensation was not lost. This loss of power continued to the end, while the lower extremity improved for a time so that he could walk quite well with a cane. September 10 he fell again and failed gradually from that time, never regaining control of muscles of left side, swallowing and articulating with difficulty and apparently unconscious most of the time.

Necropsy (five hours after death).—*Rigor mortis* slight. Body showing scars of syphilitic ulceration. Membranes of brain slightly thickened, especially pia mater, and its vessels deeply congested; considerable serum in both lateral and fifth ventricles; softening of tissue along the margins of the longitudinal fissure and in portions of the right hemisphere, also noticeably in both corpora striata. A cavity containing about 15 cubic centimeters of pus was found in right corpus striatum.

CASE 2.

Cysts in lateral ventricles.

J. C.; aged fifty-three years; nativity, Ohio; admitted to Marine Hospital, Louisville, Ky., July 3, 1885, with hemiplegia; died February 29, 1888.

History.—Case of general failure from the beginning. Previous history uncertain, except that patient was addicted to strong drink at times.

Necropsy (*fifteen hours after death*).—Skull-cap symmetrical, heavy, in places translucent; diploe lacking; dura mater thickened and dense, especially along superior longitudinal fissure, and part covering frontal lobes. Pacchionian bodies quite numerous. Pia mater denser than normal, cloudy, vascular, easily removable, particularly over anterior part of hemispheres. Brain seemed to be flattened and depressed along each side of superior longitudinal fissure, the point of greatest meningeal thickening. In right lateral ventricle, beginning at posterior extremity of choroid plexus, was a cyst about 2 centimeters in diameter, containing serous fluid and minute calcareous bodies or masses. On left side was similar cyst without masses. Blood-vessels apparently healthy. Spinal cord removed entire. Dura greatly thickened in places, especially in cervical and lumbar portions, and by what seemed repeated layers of fibrous material. At one point, between the layers in the lumbar region, there was a dark-brown, semi-dry blood-clot. Naked-eye appearance of pia and arachnoid normal. Partial microscopical examination showed localized increase of connection tissue in pia mater of cord, with prolongations between the fissures. At certain points this increase was puripheral; at others, mostly in the dorsal and lumbar regions, it showed plainest in the lateral columns corresponding to the crossed pyramidal track. Other organs not examined.

CASE 3.

Softening of brain.

J. A.; aged sixty-five years; nativity, United States; was admitted to Sisters' Hospital, Buffalo, N. Y., June 17, 1885, suffering from hemiplegia, which was apparently the result of an attack of apoplexy.

History.—Left side affected. His condition improved very little at any time during his stay in hospital, nor was there any change for the worse until August, 1887, when his intellect became impaired and he lost power of speech. He remained in this condition till his death, October 1, 1887.

Necropsy (*thirty-six hours after death*).—Brain generally softened. On puncturing the membranes about 200 cubic centimeters of serous fluid escaped. The arteries were the seat of atheroma, notably the middle meningeal and vertebral. All organs in the throat were sound. In the abdominal cavity the kidneys and liver were contracted, otherwise healthy. Other viscera appeared normal.

CEREBRAL EMBOLISM.

Middle and right anterior cerebral.

W. H.; aged thirty-two years; nativity, United States; admitted to U. S. Marine Hospital, Stapleton, N. Y., January 2, 1888; died January 8.

Necropsy (*sixteen hours post mortem*).—*Rigor mortis;* livores of the recumbent surface of the body; scars on the scalp and skin of the leg. The calvarium was of normal thickness; the dura mater was easily detached; there was no evidence of a bone lesion. The dura mater was attached to the superior longitudinal sinus. On the right hemisphere, over the second and third frontal convolutions, there was a deposit of lymph. All the blood vessels were congested, most intensely so in the left hemisphere. On section the brain tissue was found normal excepting in the occipital lobe, where there was softening of the gray matter. There was an embolus at the bifurcation of the middle cerebral artery. There was an embolus of the right anterior cerebral artery, and softening, with necrosis, of the white substance of the inferior frontal convolution. The heart was normal. There was hypostatic congestion of the lower lobe of each lung. The abdominal viscera were normal.

SCLEROSIS—BRAIN AND SPINAL CORD.

C. M.; aged thirty-nine years; nativity, Germany; admitted to U. S. Marine Hospital at Boston, Mass., September 24, 1887; died February 14, 1888.

History.—No history could be obtained of patient's condition previous to admission, and the few words spoken by him were not intelligible. He comprehended questions imperfectly, and slowly obeyed when told to perform any muscular act. He could protrude his tongue in a spasmodic, jerky manner, and all his movements were performed in a similar way. Course tremor came on whenever voluntary motion was attempted (intention tremor). At other times the muscles were quiescent. The patella's reflex was markedly increased, the leg being violently and repeatedly jerked, the involuntary contractions extending finally to the muscular groups. There was partial paresis of all the extremities. The gait was fairly good, but uncertain and staggering. These symptoms progressively increased in severity, the limbs becoming more and more paretic, the tremor more apparent, and the patient lapsing into a condition of complete dementia. Toward the close of the disease, spastic contraction and occasional clonic convulsions were superadded; bed sores formed, evacuations became involuntary, and swallowing and breathing difficult, owing to a paretic condition of the muscles of the pharynx and chest. Death finally ensued from apnœa.

Necropsy.—Brain and cervical portion of cord alone examined. Dura mater adherent to the surface of the brain to a limited extent near the vertex on the right side. An abnormal quantity of cerebro-spinal fluid was present, brain small, anemic and hard. On section a few large plaques of gray degeneration were found irregularly distributed through the medullary substance of the middle lobes. Great numbers of these plaques of smaller size were also found in the pons and medulla oblongata.

EPILEPSY.

H. B.; aged thirty years; nativity, Delaware; admitted to U. S. Marine Hospital, Wilmington, N. C., February 16, 1887; died July 25.

Necropsy (twelve hours after death).—Body plethoric. Calvarium showed no evidence of injury. There was an increase of fluid in the ventricles of the brain. Brain tissue apparently normal. A full examination of the body was made, but no lesion detected, except in regard to the size of the kidneys. Weights of organs are as follows: Brain, 990 grams; right lung, 440; left lung, 470; heart, 275; liver, 1,130; spleen, 200; right kidney, 65; left kidney, 105.

PERICARDITIS.

G. A. R.; aged thirty-two years; nativity, Virginia; admitted to U. S. Marine Hospital, Portland, Me., June 21, 1887; died July 5, at 10 p. m.

Necropsy (twelve hours after death).—Body well nourished and fairly musular. *Rigor mortis* well marked. Hypostatic congestion, deepening rapidly. Thorax: Pericardium thickened, showing signs of a high grade of recent inflammation, adherent throughout to the surface of the heart. It contained about 60 cubic centimeters of bloody serum. The heart was enlarged, fatty, and somewhat flabby; its surface roughened and covered with plastic lymph. The left ventricle was greatly dilated, and contained large *ante-mortem* clots. The walls broken down, the result of high grade of fatty degeneration. Right ventricle hypertrophied. The muscular structure throughout was markedly degenerated, the valves being apparently normal. Pleura normal. Left lung, inferior lobe somewhat congested, and strongly adherent to the diaphragm, otherwise normal. Right lung normal, except some congestion in lower lobe. Abdomen: Liver, weight, 2,750 grams; apparently normal; gall bladder, normal; right kidney enlarged, mottled, somewhat fatty, and containing pus deposits. Left kidney greatly swollen, firmly adherent to surrounding structures, besides showing signs of disease, similar to those noted in the right kidney.

ENDOCARDITIS.

CASE 1.

M. S.; aged forty-two years; nativity, Germany; admitted to the marine ward, St. Vincent Hospital, Portland, Oreg., June 18, 1887; died August 3.

History.—When admitted patient complained of a sense of uneasiness and some pain in the cardiac region. Temperature for several days was 38.2° C. Stated that he had a chill three days before admission. Upon auscultation no murmur could be heard, but the action of the heart was irregular and tumultuous. About three weeks after admission patient began to suffer with dyspnœa. Some time after this dropsical effusions occurred into the pericardium, pleural and abdominal cavities. He died on the morning of the 3d.

Necropsy (twelve hours after death).—Pericardium, normal; cavity almost filled with serous fluid. Heart, somewhat hypertrophied; in the diastole, aortic, pulmonary, and tricuspid valves seemed normal. Mitral valve: Both segments of this valve were hard and fibrous, with very little elasticity; there were numerous wart-like growths on their margins. There was marked stenosis. The orifice barely admitted the little finger. There were several small calcareous plates on the auricular surface of the auriculo-ventricular opening.

CASE 2.

Myocarditis—Perforation of apex of heart.

A. J. (colored); aged thirty-six years; nativity, Massachusetts; was admitted to the U. S. Marine Hospital, New York, August 9, 1887; died August 25.

History.—On admission, the patient gave the following history: Was first taken sick six months ago, when in Hong-Kong, China. First had pain in the chest and shortness of breath, followed later on by œdema of the feet and legs. On the return voyage he was unable to do any work and was confined to his bed most of the time; on arrival of the ship, he was immediately taken to the hospital; on his admission he was very weak, extremities cold, and greatly swollen; suffered greatly from dyspnœa. Physical examination showed his heart to be greatly hypertrophied, and the apex beat was felt at least 2 inches beyond the mammary line; a regurgelant murmur was heard at the base, and the jugular veins were very much distended, and pulsating synchronous with the systolic of the right ventricle. The urine was found to contain a large amount of albumen and a great number of casts, of the granular variety. Under cardiac stimulants he became comparatively comfortable, but never gained any strength. From August 15 to the 23d his abdomen began to distend, and on the night of the 23d he was suddenly taken with a severe pain in his abdomen, followed by a constant desire to go to stool. This state of affairs continued until the night of the 25th, when he suddenly became worse and died in collapse.

Necropsy (*thirty hours after death*).—*Rigor mortis* slight; great œdema of the lower extremities and abdomen. Lungs œdematous and hypeostatically congested. Pericardium distended; opened, and was found to contain a considerable quantity of sero-purulent fluid. Heart at its apex firmly adherent to the pericardium; greatly enlarged, especially the right side; left ventricle slightly thickened, and the seat of an acute ulcerative endocarditis, involving chiefly the "columnæ carnea," which were soft, friable, and in some places necrotic; more or less inflammation of the whole endocardium was found, valves slightly roughened. This inflammation had also involved the heart muscle to such an extent as to cause the extensive inflammatory adhesion that was noted at the apex. There was a perforation of the heart substance at the apex, and it descended through the pericardium to the diaphragm, where there was also an adhesion. On opening the abdomen, there was found an extensive peritonitis, and there were adhesions to all the contiguous surfaces. The intestines were inflamed and greatly distended with gas. The liver was smaller than normal, and contained some cicatrices on its surface. Kidneys, granular and fatty. The spleen was normal. At a corresponding spot to the adhesion of the pericardium and apex of the heart to the diaphragm there was a circumscribed inflammation, with the same characteristics as noted in the heart. The aorta and blood-vessels were examined; the femoral arteries were found to be completely plugged with emboli, thus causing the œdema of lower extremeties. Brain not examined. The cause of death was primarily from acute ulcerative endocarditis.

VALVULAR DISEASE OF THE HEART.

CASE 1.

Aortic and mitral.

W. McB.; aged twenty-nine years; nativity, New York; admitted to U. S. Marine Hospital, San Francisco, Cal., July 16, 1887; died August 12.

Necropsy (*sixteen hours after death*).—*Rigor mortis* marked; face livid and ecchymosed; general anasarca; abdomen swollen. Chest: There were no pleuritic adhesions, but right pleura was half full of serum; left about one-third full. Both lungs were floated upward and congested, and the lower lobe of right side, where the pleuritic effusion was greatest, were in a semi-collapsed condition. Heart: Pericardium contained some 75 cubic centimeters serum. No indication of pericarditis, except one small patch of membranous fibrin on anterior surface of left ventricle. The heart was very large, weight 880 grams. There was simple hypertrophy of both ventricles, the auricles being merely dilated to a moderate extent; the organ was in diastole, and all the cavities were distended with soft dark clots; the walls were in a state of marked fatty degeneration; all the valves were diseased, except the pulmonary. The mitral and tricuspids were stretched and thinned to the last extreme, but thickened and atheromatous at their edges, yet they seemed sufficient when tested. The most marked lesion was at the aortic valves, which were rough and thickened, rigid and shrunken, so that an orifice nearly 1 centimeter in diameter remained centrally when they were forcibly closed by a stream of water upon them. The aorta for some distance was similarly diseased, the atheroma having reached the stage of calcification in several considerable patches. Abdomen: Distended with intestinal gas and some 2,500 cubic centimeters serum. No peritonitis. A puncture in the peritoneum made by an aspirating needle during the progress of the case, was found plugged with omentum, the omentum having been drawn forcibly into the orifice of the needle by suction of the aspirator, and when the needle was withdrawn, it followed through the peritoneum and tightly plugged the opening; nevertheless, there was no inflammation. Liver: Normal in size, apparently somewhat fatty. Spleen: A little too large; soft, dark, friable. Kidneys: About normal in size, fatty degenerated, with patches of cirrhotic appearance, and in the left organ, several retention cysts of small size. Blood: Dark, clots soft and ill-formed.

CASE 2.

Aortic and mitral—Pneumonia.

P. F.; aged twenty-one years; nativity, Ireland; admitted to the U. S. Marine Hospital, New York, September 29, 1887; died October 7.

Necropsy (thirty-six hours after death).—Rigor mortis slight. Abdomen and posterior portion of the body discolored. General anasarca. Lower lobes of both lungs adherent to costal and diaphragmatic pleuræ. Lungs hypostatically congested, and the left lower lobe the seat of lobular pneumonia. Heart enormously dilated; left ventricle hypertrophied; there were also signs of an old pericarditis at the apex. The mitral and aortic valves were roughened and insufficient. Liver and kidneys cirrhotic. Intestines and spleen normal. Brain not examined.

CASE 3.

Mitral.

G. E. H.; aged fifty-three years; nativity, Sweden; admitted to the U. S. Marine Hospital, New York, October 4, 1887; died October 8.

Necropsy (eighteen hours after death).—Rigor mortis slight; body fairly nourished. General anasarca. Heart: Left ventricle dilated; mitral and aortic valves were both roughened and insufficient. Liver enlarged and fatty. Kidneys enlarged, congested. Other organs mormal.

CASE 4.

Aortic and mitral.

E. T.; aged fifty-five years; nativity, Ireland; admitted to U. S. Marine Hospital, Portland, Me., September 16, 1887; discharged October 31, 1887; readmitted November 14, 1887; died December 12.

History.—This case was one of chronic valve disease, after years of hardship, exposure, and dissipation. When admitted there was marked œdema of the legs and feet, shortness of breath, inability to lie down, and marked anæmia. Under small doses of digitalis, "Basham's Mixture," iodide of potash, and stimulants, with good food, the œdema rapidly disappeared, præcordial dullness abated, the face assumed a healthy color, and the patient improved so rapidly that he was discharged at his own request to go to work. He immediately lapsed into drinking habits, and shortly returned for a "few days more" rest and treatment. The former remedies failing of benefit, small doses of strychnia, with "Basham's Mixture," and iodide of potash, were given. The œdema returned; ascites gave great discomfort, and the urine, which before had about 10 per cent. of albumen, now became scanty, and showed as high as 40 per cent. The abdomen was tapped to relieve the embarrassed respiration, and 6,000 cubic centimeters of almost pure serum removed, with great temporary relief. The kidneys failed to respond more than temporarily to the treatment; urine was almost totally suppressed, and on December 11, 1887, uræmic convulsions supervened, which continued at intervals until his death, at 6.20 a. m., December 12, 1887.

Necropsy (*twenty-eight hours after death*).—Body that of a well-nourished, muscular, middle aged man. *Rigor mortis* well marked. Right pleural cavity obliterated with recent organized exudations, showing a recent high grade of inflammation; lung compressed and filled with purulent fluid. Left lung showing hypostatic congestion, with some purulent fluid. Heart dilated, somewhat fatty, left ventricular walls much hypertrophied, and cavity greatly enlarged, all valves apparently incompetent, and both ventricles filled with *ante-mortem* clots. Liver somewhat softened; gall-bladder distended with 60 cubic centimeters fluid black bile; glands of intestine enlarged throughout; bladder thickened, contracted, and containing 50 cubic centimeters of albuminous urine; pancreas nodular; kidneys contracted; capsule of right showing numerous small transparent cysts, both on section showing decided increase of fibrous tissue, and markedly pale; spleen very friable, and somewhat small. Ileum throughout much thickened. The left testicle was a cyst, with thickened walls. The urethra contained two well-organized strictures.

CASE 5.

Aortic and mitral.

W. T.; aged sixty-three years; nativity, Virginia; admitted to the U. S. Marine Hospital, New York, March 31, 1885; died November 29, 1887.

Necropsy (*ten hours post mortem*).—*Rigor mortis* marked. There were extensive gangrenous sloughs over each trochanter, and over the scrotum and penis. Right lung weighed 1,028 grams; hypostatically congested. Left lung weighed 354 grams. Small portion of lower lobe congested. Heart: Right ventricle small; walls thin; left ventricle greatly hypertrophied and dilated. Mitral and aortic valves thickened; evidences of aortitis; coronary arteries dilated and sclerosed; weight of heart, 450 grams. Spleen very small, weight, 31½ grams. Right kidney small; weight, 81.5 grams; contracted; section shows both interstitial and parenchymatous degeneration; left kidney presented the same features as the right; weight, 103 grams. Other organs normal.

CASE 6.

Mitral.

G. H.; aged thirty-eight years; nativity, Norway; admitted to Marine Hospital, Boston, Mass., July 12, 1887; died December 12.

History.—Valve disease, mitral, with very slow pulse (40 to 60 per minute), dyspnœa, œdema of extremities, general œdema, etc.

Necropsy (twenty-eight hours after death).—*Rigor mortis* present; body very œdematous; pleural cavity filled with a clear serous fluid, forcing up the lungs and misplacing the heart slightly to the right. The lungs were retracted, most marked on the right side. Pericardium filled with serous fluid, clear, amber-colored. Heart greatly hypertrophied and somewhat fatty. The right ventricle contained an *ante-mortem* clot, extending through the auriculoventricular opening into auricle. The tri cuspid opening showed stenosis, the edges being much thickened. A non organized clot, stratified, was found in the left auricular appendix. Extensive lime deposits were present in the cusps and chordæ tendinæ of the mitral valve. The abdominal cavity contained a large amount of clear serous fluid. The liver and spleen were engorged with blood. The kidneys were hypertrophied and markedly congested.

CASE 7.

J. B.; aged thirty-six years; nativity, Germany; admitted to the U. S. Marine Hospital, New York, July 14, 1887; died August 16.

Necropsy (twenty-two hours after death).—Body much emaciated and jaundiced; lungs œdematous and slightly pigmented; pericardium firmly adherent to the heart; left ventricle was hypertrophied and dilated, and there was considerable thickening of the aortic and mitral valves. Heart, muscle soft; cloudy swelling. A few calcareous deposits were found in the arch of the aorta. Liver cirrhotic; kidneys enlarged, due to interstitic nephritis; intestines and spleen normal. Brain not examined.

CASE 8.

Aortic and mitral—Fusiform aneurism arch of aorta.

W. J. W.; aged forty-three years; nativity, Ireland; admitted to U. S. Marine Hospital, San Francisco, Cal., November 29, 1887; died December 15.

Necropsy (seventy-three hours after death).—*Rigor mortis* marked. General anasarca; body fairly well nourished. Considerable pleuritic effusion on both sides and a small pericardial effusion (about 50 cubic centimeters). Anterior surface of visceral pericardium opaque and thickened. Heart: Left ventricle very much hypertrophied; slight thickening of mitral valve; aortic orifice dilated and valves consequently insufficient; they were also thickened and rough. Other valves normal.

A fusiform aneurism was found involving the entire arch of the aorta and the first portion of the descending aorta. The greatest dilatation, about three times its normal diameter, was in the first portion of the arch (ascending portion). There were very marked calcareous changes in the artery, especially in the most dilated portion. Calcareous degeneration also existed in the innominate, carotid, and subclavian arteries. No other organs examined.

CASE 9.

Mitral—aneurism of pulmonary artery.

G. D.; aged forty-one years; nativity, Ireland; admitted to U. S. Marine Hospital, Detroit, Mich., November 18, 1887; died December 16.

History.—When admitted patient complained of pain and a "smothering" sensation in the precordial region, and stated that he had been suffering for two weeks with these symptoms, together with marked shortness of breath upon exertion, and that he was growing worse. He never had rheumatism or syphilis, and there was nothing elicited to throw light on the etiology of the case, except the supposed special liability of sailors to such diseases from the exposure and violent muscular exercise attendant upon that calling—a disputed question. (See article on "The predisposing causes of aneurism," by Surgeon General John B. Hamilton, U. S. Marine Hospital Service, in the American Journal of Medical Sciences for October, 1885.) When first examined he had no fever, his pulse was quick, forcible, and somewhat irregular; a systolic murmur was heard, most distinctly over the apex of the heart, and the area of cardiac dullness was increased. Two grams of potassium bromide favorably affected the heart's action and gave the patient a good night's rest. November 19, a fly blister was applied over the heart and infusion of digitalis administered in moderate doses. November 21 the digitalis was stopped and potassium bromide and ammonium bromide substituted for it. The signs of existing acute endocarditis and pericarditis were at this time evident—the heart's action was irregular and more rapid than before, varying from 100 to 120 pulsations per minute; endocardial murmurs could be heard distinctly, mitral being most prominent; there was nearly constant pain, precordial oppression, throbbing of cervical vessels, slight fever, etc. At no time was his fever high. The mitral murmur was subsequently overshadowed by a murmur at the base of the heart. Later on he had an attack of syncope, but rallied very quickly. He slept poorly at nights; said he felt afraid to lie down, lest he might never wake. November 29, the bromides were discontinued and tincture ferri chloride given, and this, with an occasional laxative and the application of counter-irritants, continued to be the line of treatment until his death, which occurred suddenly on the morning of December 16. Soon after eating a hearty breakfast, he fell back on the bed and expired almost instantly.

Necropsy (nine hours after death).—Body in good condition. *Rigor mortis* well marked; signs of hypostatic congestion; lungs somewhat congested, otherwise normal. Pericardium full of serous fluid, containing fibrinous matter indicating recent inflammation; heart much hypertrophied; weight, 750 grams; cavities dilated considerably. There was thickening of the mitral and tricuspid valves and fibrinous deposits of recent formation upon them. There was also insufficiency of the mitral valves evident on testing with water. An organized clot was found in the aorta and left ventricle. An aneurism, shaped like an acorn, its short diameter being about 2 centimeters, and its long diameter nearly 5 centimeters long, existed in the walls of the pulmonary artery just above the semilunar valve; it had a small opening into the aorta.

NOTE.—This case was reported to the Detroit Academy of Medicine.

Case 10.

Aortic and mitral.

J. C.; aged forty-one years; nativity, Germany; admitted to U. S. Marine Hospital, Port Townsend, Wash., October 5, 1887; died December 20.

Necropsy (fifteen hours after death).—*Rigor mortis* present. Examination of the heart showed the posterior valve of the aortic orifice almost completely ulcerated, and upon the others there were vegetations which, however, had given no sounds of recognition during life. The mitral orifice was, under hydrostatic pressure, found to allow a somewhat free return to the auricle. The free surfaces of the valve showed points of ulceration upon their edges, producing a somewhat fringed appearance. The left ventricle was filled to bulging with a clot, which upon section showed a gray or white center of considerable size and engaging the chordæ. Lungs, normal; death occurred from paralysis of the heart muscle from over distension of its cavities.

Case 11.

Mitral.

F. M.; aged seventeen years; nativity, Maryland; admitted to the U. S. Marine Hospital, Baltimore, Md., September 14, 1887; died January 2, 1888.

History.—The patient on entering hospital gave a history of rheumatic fever having occurred the winter previous. Pain over the heart and shortness of breath had begun within two months. On examination of the heart a ventricular systolic murmur was observed, blowing in character, and with a regurgitating rythm sound, diminishing toward base. Dullness on percussion over upper lobe of left lung. The patient had a cough, with expectoration at times streaked with blood. Pulse soft, irregular, and compressible. There was a tendency to œdema of the lower extremities. The treatment, which consisted of that usually advised, had but palliative effect, the patient dying of asthenia.

Necropsy (twenty four hours after death).—Entire body extremely œdematous, especially face and neck. *Rigor mortis* not well marked. On making the ordinary incision in the abdominal walls about 12,000 cubic centimeters of straw-colored serum escaped. The pleural cavities contained 6,000 cubic centimeters of a similar fluid, which had exerted pressure on the lungs until they were about half the normal size, and œdematous. Pericardium was greatly distended by serum. Heart weighed 720 grams; hypertrophy and dilatation very marked, especially in right ventricle, the walls of which were nearly as thick as those of the left ventricle; both mitral and tricuspid valves allowed regurgitation of fluid as determined by the water test. Liver was very dense in its structure, and the cut surface presented the typical red, blue, and yellow spots of the nutmeg liver. Spleen smaller than usual, hard, and showed the same nutmeg appearance. Kidneys congested and hard, otherwise normal; intestines normal; brain not examined.

Case 12.

Mitral regurgitation—Aneurism of aorta.

T. F.; aged thirty-nine years; nativity, Ireland; admitted to the U. S. Marine Hospital, Chicago, Ill., November 10, 1887; died January 9, 1888.

History.—Three years ago, after exposure to severe cold while engaged in gathering ice, he was taken with a severe chill, followed by high fever, sharp pain over precordial region, accelerated and painful respirations, great weakness and prostration. The patient was admitted to this hospital in April, 1887, suffering from mitral regurgitation, and after about three weeks' treatment was discharged much improved.

November 10, 1887.—Patient re-admitted to the hospital to-day, and states that he has suffered from "chest trouble" ever since the abovementioned attack. Complains of pains over chest, cough, with slight expectoration, general weakness, insomnia, and dyspnœa, which is so aggravated by the recumbent position that he often sits up the entire night.

Treatment.—November 11, ordered the following prescription: ℞: tr. ferri chlor., 8 c. c.; tr. digitalis, 6 c. c.; liq. amm. acet., 50 c. c.; aquæ, q. s., 150 c. c. M. sig: One teaspoonful every two hours.

For the first few weeks after admission the patient was much more comfortable, and his general condition seemed better. This apparent improvement, however, was soon followed by loss of appetite and general digestive disturbances, progressive weakness, emaciation, and œdema of the lower extremities.

December 10.—Tr. strophanthus in ten-drop doses was administered, with occasional doses of bromide of potassium and sulphate of morphia.

December 21.—℞: Pil. strych. sulph: One three times a day.

January 3, 1888.—Dyspnœa severe; oedema of legs and thighs marked; to relieve which local applications of glycerine were made, with fair results.

January 7.—Incisions over each external malleolus and over dorsum of foot were made, and the discharge of serum was quite free.

January 9.—Died at 10.30 p. m.

Necropsy.—Body much emaciated. *Rigor mortis* well marked. Back of body and thighs of livid purplish color. On opening the chest numerous old pleuritic adhesions were found over the surface of both lungs. The lungs were deeply pigmented (the patient was an engineer by occupation) and displaced by the hypertrophied heart. The left lung was pushed upwards and backwards to such an extent that it could not be seen when the chest was opened by the usual incision through the outer extremities of the costal cartilages. Emphysematous patches along lower posterior border. Weight, 420 grams. Lower lobe of right lung in the stage of red hepatization. The upper portion, emphysematous. Weight, 550 grams. The pericardium was much thickened, the two layers being agglutinated throughout. No pericardial sac could be detected. The walls of the heart were slightly thickened. The cavities enormously dilated; this condition of eccentric hypertrophy existing chiefly in the left ventricle and auricle. Mitral valve rendered insufficient by dilatation of left cavities. Aortic valves slightly thickened. The mouths of coronary arteries even dilated to the size of a goose quill. Weight of heart 750 grams. In the front of the ascending aorta about 1 centimeter above upper margin of the aortic valve was found a false sacculated anneurism slightly larger than a hen's egg, having a mouth circular in shape and about 2 centimeters in diameter, its body projecting forward and resting on the intra auricular septum. The sac wall was intact throughout, and showed no thinned spots, indicative of immediate rupture. The cavity of the anneurism contained no deposit of laminated coagulum, and showed no attempt at a spontaneous cure.

Liver normal in size, but appeared fatty. Kidneys normal. Weight of right 160, and of the left 150 grams.

Case 13.

Pneumonia.

J. M. (seaman); aged thirty-two years; nativity, Nova Scotia; admitted to the marine ward Sisters' Hospital, Buffalo, N. Y., January 11, 1888; died February 6, 1888.

History.—When admitted he was anæmic, with a small pulse and marked dyspnœa. Auscultation over heart revealed a murmur most distinct at base, heard during systole, through the interval and up to diastole, if not through it. Sound was reduplicated. In February his dyspnœa became more marked, breathing rapid, and accompanied with much malaise. Deglutition became difficult, only fluids could be swallowed. Skin became hot and dry, and teeth covered with sordes; tongue heavily coated. Chest examination showed consolidation of lower part of left lung. He died on the 6th.

Necropsy (*three hours after death*).—Heart hypertrophied to twice its natural size. All cavities filled with blood, and also coronary arteries. Right auricle filled with venous blood, backing up into vena cava. About 70 cubic centimeters of serum in pericardium. The leaves of the mitral valve were imperfect, the broad base of each leaf only remaining. Aortic valves were the seat of calcareous degeneration. Aorta was normal. Lower lobe of left lung was hepatized. Upper lobe œdematous. Liver enlarged, also spleen, which weighed 900 grams. Both kidneys enlarged to about twice their natural size. Pancreas and peritoneum healthy.

Case 14.

Mitral regurgitation—Chronic Bright's disease.

M. P. D.; aged thirty-five; nativity, Cape Verde Islands; admitted to the U. S. Marine Hospital, Vineyard Haven, Mass., December 21, 1887, suffering from local paralysis, wrist drop, valvular disease of the heart, mitral regurgitation, and chronic Bright's disease; small, contracted kidney. Died January 28, 1888.

Necropsy (*thirty hours after death*).—Emaciation slight. *Rigor mortis* well marked. Pericardium was found to be distended and filled with about 300 cubic centimeters of fluid. Marked myocarditis had existed, the muscular fibers of the heart being changed in color, and pus corpuscles were found between them, especially at the base. The heart was distended, filled with *ante-mortem* clots in both auricles and ventricles, the same being firmly attached to the columnæ carnæ, and even extending for a distance of 6 inches into the aorta. The mitral valves were badly diseased. The aorta gave evidences of recent inflammation, and was slightly dilated at the arch, possibly a beginning aneurism. Lungs: The left lung was slightly congested; otherwise they were normal. Liver: The liver was small, contracted, and capsule adherent. Kidneys: The kidneys were small, contracted, and capsule herent; 6.25 centimeters long and 3.75 centimeters wide; both together only weighed 170 grams; several small cysts were also observed on the posterior surface. The immediate cause of death was paralysis of the heart, occurring during a paroxysm of coughing.

Case 15.

Mitral and aortic.

E. H.; aged thirty-eight years; nativity, Pennsylvania; admitted to the marine ward, Mercy Hospital, Pittsburgh, Pa., January 13, 1888; died January 24.

History.—When admitted complained of pain in the cardiac region, of weakness, anorexia, and an occasional chill. Upon examination a soft murmur was heard with both sounds of the heart, which was thought to originate from the mitral and aortic orifices. The heart's area of dullness on percussion extended to the left nipple. He had on several evenings a high temperature, but nearly or quite normal in the morning. He had one chill after entering the hospital. He was restless and delirious at night.

Necropsy.—An omental hernia existed on the left side, the omentum being elongated, and, by traction, displacing downwards the central part of the transverse colon. The lower third of the ileum was inflamed and the glands of the corresponding parts of the mesentery enlarged. There were no enlarged or ulcerated intestinal glands.

The kidneys, spleen, and liver were normal in appearance. There was hypostatic congestion of the posterior portions of the lungs. There was some enlargement of the heart, due to thickening of the walls of the left ventricle. Each side of the organ contained a fibrinous clot attached to the heart walls. The aortic valves were thickened at their edges and stiff. The inner surface of the first portion of the aorta was covered with calcareous deposit. The mitral valves were slightly thickened.

Case 16.

Mitral, aortic, and tricuspid.

F. R.; aged fifty-nine years; nativity, France; admitted to U. S. Marine Hospital, Detroit, Mich., March 2, 1888; died March 3.

History.—This patient was first admitted to the hospital February 18, 1888, and a diagnosis of Bright's disease was made, many symptoms pointing to that; but repeated examinations later failed to reveal any albumen in the urine and the evidences of valvular disease of the heart became more clearly defined, and March 2 the diagnosis was changed, although the valvular trouble was recognized some time before. He had first noticed difficulty of breathing four months ago on walking, which had increased up to the time of his admission. Two months later œdema of the feet appeared and this extended rapidly, so that, upon admission, his lower extremities and genitals were markedly œdematous. This continued with little change throughout his illness. There was no history of rheumatism or syphilis. Pain was not a very marked feature of this case, but at times he complained of some pain in the chest and back. Moderate doses of infusion of digitalis seemed to benefit him for a time and the œdema was somewhat lessened. Still he continued to grow weaker and died of exhaustion March 3, 1888, at 9 a. m.

Necropsy (seven hours after death).—Body that of a corpulent man, showing much œdema and some signs of hypostatic congestion. *Rigor mortis* very well marked. Abdominal organs generally congested; liver and spleen considerably enlarged. Weight of spleen 320 grams, left kidney 210, right kidney 180 grams. Considerable fluid was found in the péritoneal, pleural, and pericardial sacs, and the latter had some firm adhesions to the heart. The lungs were normal, but congested; heart much hypertrophied, weight 820 grams; *ante-mortem* clots in right ventricle. The aortic semilunar valves were much thickened and the seat of numerous vegetations. One flap of the mitral was adherent to the wall of the ventricle, and the tricuspid valves failed to completely close the right auriculo-ventricular opening. These changes in above-named valves made them incompetent, as appeared on testing with water.

CASE 17.

Mitral—Chronic nephritis.

C. M.; aged forty-nine years; nativity, Portugal; admitted to the Marine Hospital, Mobile, Ala., February 12, 1888; died March 24.

History.—States that he has suffered from heart disease for several years. History of articular rheumatism at various times, also an indefinite syphilitic history. Present condition indicative of serious circulatory disturbance; distressing dyspnœa; livid, anxious countenance. Physical examination revealed marked insufficiency of the mitral cardiac valve, with all its attendant distressing systems. Heart's action rapid and feeble, and impeded by serous effusion into the pericardium. Lungs engorged; copious bubbling rales, and free expectoration of serous sputa. These symptoms disappeared slowly under the influence of appropriate remedies, until the end of the second week, when the pulse became more and more increased in force and the urine (which had before only presented a *trace* of albumen) became scanty and loaded with albumen, in volume 90 per cent. Digitalis and pot. iodid., which had been given, were discontinued. The pulmonary circulation again became engorged, dyspnœa returned; giddiness, flashes of light, and vertigo indicated serious uræmic disturbance. There being no pilocarpine at hand, and there being such marked evidence of capillary spasm, there was now exhibited two-drop doses morning and evening of a 1 per cent. solution of nitro-glycerine, with immediate and happy effect. Under its influence the urine became free from albumen in a short time, more copious, even beyond normal; and there was relief from the uræmic symptoms for some time. Pulse became soft and compressible and more regular. This, however, did not last long, and in spite of all effort he died comatose on the 24th of March.

Necropsy.—Body emaciated. *Rigor* present. Hypostasis of chest walls and loins. Pleuræ and lungs normal, save that the latter were deeply engorged and infiltrated. Pericardium contained 2,000 cubic centimeters of serum. No evidence of inflammation. Heart hypertrophied; weight 875 grams. Muscle of left heart immensely thickened. Left ventricular capacity slightly increased. Right ventricular wall thicker and capacity much increased, showing commencing dilatation. All valves found sufficient save the mitral, the posterior or smaller leaflet of which was bound down, from its attachment throughout two-thirds of its extent, the free edge stiff and unyielding. Kidneys examined microscopically only. Both were contracted, weighing less than normal, 120 grams; capsule adherent, leaving when removed a finely granular surface; the cortex was found atrophied at some points about 2 millimeters in thickness. A few cysts observed in the medullary portions; much fat about the calyces and cut surface of very pale appearance. Chronic inflammation general of these organs. Liver and spleen normal.

CASE 18.

Aortic—tubercle of lungs.

E. A.; aged twenty-two years; nativity, Kentucky; admitted to U. S. Marine Hospital, Cairo, Ill., April 3, 1888; died April 5.

History.—On admission patient was exhausted, very weak, and lower extremities œdematous. Auscultation revealed a rapidly beating heart, with much valvular irregularity, the nature of which could not be discerned. He became quiet, ate, and drank well under digitalis tincture and aromatic spirits of ammonia, and died, while sleeping quietly, of heart failure.

Necropsy (six hours after death).—Body that of a muscular, well nourished, intensely black negro. *Rigor mortis* marked; abdomen much distended with serum. Pericardium and lungs filled with serum and studded with tubercles. Heart dilated, thinned, flabby; left ventricle hypertrophied; aorticvalve almost obliterated; other valves markedly incompetent. Liver contracted, mottled, studded with tubercles throughout; weight, 2,750 grams. Spleen enlarged and a mass of yellow cheesy pus deposit. Kidneys congested; capsules adherent.

CASE 19.

Aortic and mitral—Tubercle of lung.

S. L. (colored); aged forty-one years; nativity, Virginia; admitted to the U. S. Marine Hospital, Saint Louis, Mo., August 26, 1886; died April 15, 1888.

History.—When admitted patient complained of pain in the epigastric region, shortness of breath, swelling of ankles and abdomen, etc. About a month after his admission the diagnosis was changed from acute hepatitis with anasarca to aortic valvular heart disease, the intensity of the symptoms becoming very marked and continuing with varying exacerbations up to the time of death, which occurred very suddenly.

Necropsy (twenty hours after death).—*Rigor mortis* present; body emaciated; abdomen prominent; ankles and feet very much swollen. Lungs, pleuritic adhesions extensive on right side; left side free; right lung very small, contained a few tubercles of a yellowish cheesy nature. Left lung congested, a yellowish frothy material exuding on section. Heart greatly enlarged, coronary vessels turgid; walls of left ventricle very much thickened; cavity of left ventricle increased to about double the usual size; mitral valve incapable of perfect closure; two of the aortic valves shrunken and rigid, with small warty elevations near their edges, causing a valvular insufficiency, the aortic orifice, however, being somewhat constricted. The right side of the heart seemed to be about normal in all regards, even as to size, the great size of the heart depending upon the enlargement of its left side. The aorta and other adjacent vessels were apparently normal. Liver congested and enlarged. The other organs showed nothing perceptibly pathological.

CASE 20.

Mitral—Pneumonia.

J. W. (colored); aged forty-four years; nativity, Tennessee; admitted to the U. S. Marine Hospital, Saint Louis, Mo., April 17, 1888; died within a few hours after admission.

History.—When admitted patient suffered from great precordial distress, cough, dyspnœa, and inability to lie down without signs of suffocation, and there was also decided prostration. The heart's dullness was much increased in area and a coarse murmur was heard most plainly over the apex. Death occurred suddenly, without premonition.

Necropsy (fifteen hours after death).—*Rigor mortis* complete; emaciation moderate; old scars on legs; ankles and feet œdematous; lungs both congested at bases, the left considerably so; heart increased in size; pericardium thickened; pericardial fluid greatly increased in amount; both ventricles hypertrophied, the left one particularly so; both auricles somewhat enlarged; the cavity of the left ventricle very much dilated; that of the right side slightly so; valves all seemingly normal excepting the mitral, one cusp of which was shortened and bound down to the ventricular wall, allowing a perceptible insufficiency; all the heart cavities were distended with dark, clotted blood; the aorta collapsed; the muscular substance of the heart was pale and soft. Liver, spleen, and kidneys all engorged with blood; the kidneys were covered with fat; stomach and intestines distended with gas.

CASE 21.

Tricuspid—Pericarditis.

G. B.; aged forty-seven years; nativity, England; admitted to the U. S. Marine Hospital, Saint Louis, Mo.; January 16, 1888; died April 29.

History.—Dyspnœa; pain about the heart; cough, at times violent, with slight expectoration; occasional vertigo; inability to lie down; legs, face, and abdomen swollen and œdematous; anorexia; scanty urine; albuminuria; heart dullness increased to the left and a subdued murmur, heard plainest over the central part of the heart, were the most prominent symptoms.

Necropsy (sixteen hours after death).—*Rigor mortis* feeble; body emaciated, swollen, and of a purplish color; dark gummy liquid exuding from the mouth. Lungs: Extensive pleuritic adhesions on right side; slight ones on the left. Left lung congested; right lung greatly congested, sections of it sinking when placed in water. Heart: Pericardium completely adherent to heart, requiring force to break it loose; left ventricular walls markedly thickened above the normal; right ventricle about normal in size; mitral, aortic, and pulmonary valves in perfect condition, each holding water as it was poured upon them; right auriculo-ventricular orifice greatly dilated, allowing the introduction of four fingers; the tricuspid valve segments all more or less imperfect, being shortened and knotty; right auricle and vessels emptying into it dilated. Liver, spleen, and other abdominal organs congested; kidneys small; abdominal cavity distended with a clear amber-colored fluid of a strong odor, but unlike urine.

CASE 22.

Mitral insufficiency.

E. E.; aged forty-five years; nativity, United States; admitted to U. S. Marine Hospital, Stapleton, N. Y., February 16, 1888; died May 3.

Necropsy (fifteen hours post mortem).—*Rigor mortis;* great œdema of the lower extremities. The right lung was generally adherent; there was hypostatic congestion; it weighed 640 grams. The left lung was non-adherent and normal; there was hypostatic congestion; it weighed 520 grams. Heart: The left ventricle was hypertrophied, with insufficiency of the mitral valves; there was stenosis of the coronary arteries; it weighed 620 grams. The spleen weighed 153 grams; it was normal. The left kidney weighed 104 grams; it was cystic, containing one or two small cysts; there were two small cheesy foci in the cortical portion; the kidney was granular. The right kidney weighed 99 grams; it was cystic and contained cheesy foci; it was granular. The liver weighed 1,650 grams; the right lobe, near the broad ligament, was attached to the abdominal wall by old adhesions; the gall bladder was full; the liver was normal. The stomach, bladder, and intestines were normal.

CASE 23.

Aortic regurgitant.

J. B. S.; aged twenty-nine years; nativity, Scotland; admitted to Marine Hospital, Port Townsend, Wash., May 6, 1888; died June 4.

Necropsy (eighteen hours after death).—*Rigor mortis* and capillary congestion marked; heart hypertrophied (eccentric) and coronary circulation obstructed; calcareous degeneration about the valves, especially in the aortic, which were retracted and adherent to the adjacent wall. Diagnosis of aortic regurgitation confirmed. Other organs normal.

CASE 24.

Mitral—Pleurisy.

R. B.; aged twenty-four years; nativity, Arkansas; admitted to U. S. Marine Hospital, New Orleans, La., May 28, 1888; died June 5.

History.—Patient stated that he had been for two months in hospital at Shreveport, La., under treatment for consumption. When admitted he complained of cough, severe pain in right chest, and dyspnœa; the latter being at times very severe. Physical examination showed a bulging of the right side of his chest, the intercostal spaces being eliminated; dullness over the lower portion of right lung and over the apex of the left lung, where the expiratory respiration was prolonged, and an absence of all respiratory and vocal sounds (upon auscultation) over the lower anterior portion of the right side of the chest. Above the line of dullness on the right side the vocal fremitus was exaggerated. Change of position had but little effect upon the physical signs. A hypodermic needle was passed into the chest just below the right nipple, and it demonstrated the presence of a serous fluid in the plural sac, probably encapsulated. Heart: First and second sounds were heard, but they were muffled in tone. Area of heart dullness extended, and the chest-walls were lifted with each impulse. The arteries in his neck could be seen pulsating for some distance from the patient's bed. Pulse was 120 and weak; respirations were 50 per minute; feet and ankles were œdematous. He had been a free drinker of alcohol, etc. The trouble with the lungs and pleura was thought to be due to tubercle. There was also undoubted hypertrophy of the heart, and an effusion into the pleural and pericardial sacs.

Necropsy (twelve hours after death).—The body was slightly emaciated. A bloody froth was oozing from mouth and one nostril; there were ulcers on his penis and phimosis, and there was œdema of the feet and ankles; *rigor mortis* was almost entirely absent. The right pleural sac contained about 2,000 cubic centimeters of bloody serous fluid. There were two slight adhesions over posterior and lower portions of right lung. The right lung was very much congested; the left one slightly so, but both of them floated in water, and (with the above exceptions) seemed to be normal. No tubercles were seen. The pericardium was somewhat inflamed, and contained about 50 cubic centimeters of fluid. The heart was so hypertrophied as to have lost its conical form; it weighed 540 grams; its substance was softened; the cavities were filled with *post-mortem* clots, and its blood-vessels (coronary) over the exterior surface were enormously distended and filled with dark clotted blood. Mitral valve was thickened, and one of its cusps was slightly bound down. Left auriculo-ventricular orifice seemed to be narrowed to almost half of its normal size. The right ventricle and left auricle were dilated. Spleen was atrophied, hard, and congested. Kidneys seemed to be normal. Liver was enlarged and pulpy.

HYPERTROPHY AND DILATION OF HEART.

Atheroma of blood-vessels.

T. K. F.; aged thirty years; nativity, Virginia; admitted to the U. S. Marine Hospital at Baltimore, Md., November 19, 1887; died January 27, 1888.

History.—This patient stated he had been sick nearly a year. Had been in hospital at Norfolk, Va., two months. He was short in stature, muscular in appearance, with a large head and deformed face. The thorax was compressed at the side, while the sternum was protruding forward, the result of an accident when a child. Had a sense of fullness and oppression of the chest, much dyspnœa, and at times tinnitus aurium and dizziness; slight œdema of the feet. The patient's face was pale and anæmic; there was a marked tendency to perspire; pulse strong and regular. The absolute and relative area of pericardial dullness extended downward and to the left; there was strong impulse over the seat of dullness. There was also accentuation of the second sound of the heart. The patient was confined to his bed only a few days previous to death, which occurred somewhat suddenly, and apparently from failure of the heart's action.

Necropsy (*seventeen hours after death*).—*Rigor mortis* slight; costal cartilages all firmly ossified. Pericardium contained 40 cubic centimeters clear serum. Heart extremely large, weighing 1,300 grams; ventricles principally affected, being both dilated and hypertrophied; wall of left ventricle was 2.5 centimeters in thickness; auricles of about normal size. Aortic valves were much thickened, irregular, and toward the free edge showed minute perforations. Pulmonary semilunar valves apparently normal. Mitral and tricuspid valves very large and strong, the papillary muscles and tendinous cords being correspondingly hypertrophied. Aorta exhibited patches of atheromatous deposit. Lungs had a few adhesions at surface. Right lung very large and emphysematous, with a small patch of consolidation at the lower margin of the lower lobe. Left lung emphysematous, but contained no solid portion. The vessels of both lungs were calcareous, standing open when cut. Liver considerably enlarged, and showed evidence of chronic congestion in the nutmeg type. Spleen congested; otherwise normal. Kidneys both had small cysts on the surface, containing serum, especially near the lower borders. Left kidney somewhat enlarged; capsule separated easily, and, apart from the congestion found in nearly all the organs, was normal. Stomach small, and large intestines displayed in places the results of prolonged congestion of the blood-vessels. Brain not examined.

ANEURISM OF AORTA.

CASE 1.

Thoracic—Fusiform chronic pneumonic phthisis.

J. S.; aged forty-eight years; nativity, Chili; admitted to U. S. Marine Hospital, San Francisco, Cal., October 21, 1887; died November 18.

Necropsy (*two hours and a half after death*).—Little or no *rigor mortis*. Emaciation great. The lips were stained with blood from the hemorrhage causing death. Thorax: Heart was somewhat fatty, and coronary vessels degenerated apparently, yet the muscular tissue of the organ was little hypertrophied, and almost normally firm to the feel. The valves appeared sufficient, but the aortic segments were thinned and stretched, and their margins rather rough and nodular. The whole aortic arch was dilated to three or four times its normal caliber, except at the transverse portion, where the dilatation was perceptibly less. The inner coat was atheromatous, thickened and roughened, and even calcareous in spots, just above the valves. No clot was found anywhere in the dilated portion, either fibrinous or recent. But at the junction of the transverse and descending portions of the artery, where it lies in close relation with the œsophagus and the origin of left bronchus, the aneurism had eroded the walls of both these structures, and perforation had taken place, simultaneously into both. The ulceration into the bronchus was clearly seen. Into the œsophagus the opening was not fairly demonstrated, but was proved to exist by the great mass of blood found in the stomach. Lungs and pleuræ: The left pleura contained scarcely any adhesions except to pericardium and diaphragm near it, but contained some 500 cubic centimeters serum. The left lung was considerably shrunken in size, a solid mass of pneumonic exudation, slowly breaking down into numerous abscesses of small size. The general color on section was a dark gray. Right pleura contained at the sides and apex, and to some extent in the region of the diaphragm, numerous organized but apparently recent bands of adhesion. The lung completely filled the cavity, being emphysematous throughout, and everywhere congested. Almost in every part, but particularly in lower lobe, numerous small blood-clots were turned out upon section. Probably they were due to the influx of blood when the aortic aneurism burst into the bronchus as described. Stomach contained some 508 cubic centimeters of recent blood-clot, evidently from the ruptured aneurism by way of œsophagus.

CASE 2.

J. C.; aged thirty years; nativity, Massachusetts; admitted to Marine Hospital, Boston, Mass, June 14, 1887; died October 18.

Necropsy (*ten hours after death*).—*Rigor mortis* present. Pleural cavity: A large pleural effusion was found on the right side. This was of long standing. The lung on the right side was compressed. Pleural membrane under the sternum fatty. The pericardium was dilated and containing 150 cubic centimeters of bloody serum. Heart showed several milk-like spots, fatty degeneration, and marked hypertrophy.

A very large sacculated aneurism of the arch (ascending and transverse portion) of aorta was found. The subcutaneous tissue throughout the body was infiltrated with the watery elements of blood.

Case 3.

Neuralgia.

W. A. Mc.; aged fifty-four years; nativity, Nova Scotia; admitted to the U. S. Marine Hospital, Portland, Me., July 14, 1887; died August 2, at 6 a. m.

History.—Unsatisfactory, except great pain shifting from one portion of the trunk to another and occasionally disappearing. Indisposition to exertion; loss of voice at times, and toward the end some vomiting of blood; no special symptoms claimed attention. He became daily weaker, and died quietly of exhaustion.

Necropsy (four hours after death).—Body that of a muscular, middle-aged man, much emaciated. *Rigor mortis* well marked. Thorax: Heart atrophied, and loaded with fat; valves apparently normal. Left lung collapsed; right lung adherent to chest-wall. Transverse arch of aorta greatly dilated, and having the appearance of a large aneurism. The vertebræ and sternum at this point were eroded. The kidneys were anæmic and fatty.

Case 4.

Chronic Bright's disease.

H. B.; aged forty-four years; nativity, New York; admitted to the U. S. Marine Hospital, New York, December 23, 1887; died December 27.

Necropsy (twenty-four hours after death).—*Rigor mortis* marked; slight discoloration of the posterior surface of the body; superficial blood vessels engorged with blood. Heart contracted; all valves normal; weight, 295 grams; left lung, 465; right lung, 625; both lungs engorged with blood. There was a large sacculated aneurism of the arch of the aorta containing fibrinous layers and blood-clots. Both kidneys were cystic and contracted; other organs normal.

Case 5.

Innominate.—Bright's disease.

E. W. P.; aged thirty-seven years; nativity, Wales; admitted to the U. S. Marine Hospital, San Francisco, Cal., January 10, 1888; died March 27.

Necropsy (sixteen hours after death).—*Rigor mortis* pronounced; body fairly well nourished; anasarca of lower limbs. Abdomen: In the peritoneal cavity were some 300 cubic centimeters of sanguinolent serum, and the omentum and small intestines were quite congested, but there was no lymph and no adhesions. Liver was about the normal size; very much congested. Upon scraping a section, it was seen to be light yellowish-gray in color, appeared cirrhosed and at the same time fatty. Spleen blackly congested. Kidneys were both large—one-quarter to one-third larger than usual. Beyond a thinning of the peripheral cortex, which was somewhat pale, there was really no marked evidence of such a diseased state as the urine during life seemed to indicate. Both organs were deeply congested. Thorax: The right pleura contained some 1,500 cubic centimeters serum. The lung was pretty well collapsed from prolonged and repeated compression, but did not appear diseased. At the apex it was bound down by adhesions. The left pleura contained a small amount of serum; no adhesions. The lung was considerably displaced and compressed by the encroachment of the heart and pericardial sac, but was not diseased. Pericardium: The sac was greatly distended, thinned in front, and contained 350 cubic centimeters of serum, and its walls at one part were covered with lymph. The heart was hypertrophied and dilated to nearly twice its natural size, and its cavities were full of bloody and soft fibrinous clots. The aortic appeared sufficient, but the corpora aurantii and attached margins, and to some extent the free edges of the segments of the valve, had undergone a change resembling true bone; still the segments were freely movable and approximated very perfectly. The ascending and transverse aorta was dilated so as to form an egg-shaped cavity, the size of a small orange, full of soft, recent clot. The walls were yellow, thickened, and atheromatous, but fairly smooth. The mouth of the innominate artery seemed stretched to a diameter of 3 centimeters, and this artery and the subclavian as far as the thyroid axis were expanded into an aneurismal sac, the size of a hen's egg, full of partly organized fibrinous clot. The blood supply from the innominate was completely blocked. The tumor, of course, was in close relation to the trachea and bronchi, and the œsophagus, but none of these seemed to have suffered, and no impairment of their functions was noted during life. It had not encroached on the bony environment except behind the upper end of the gladiolus, where pressure was beginning to erode the bone.

CASE 6.

J. G. (colored); aged fifty-six years; nativity, Kentucky; admitted to U. S. Marine Hospital, Saint Louis, Mo., January 16, 1888; died February 7.

History.—Patient stated that he always had good health until about a month prior to his entering the hospital, when he had attacks of shortness of breath, associated with a dry cough, sometimes of a violent nature; he frequently experienced pain in the upper part of the substernal region. These symptoms prevailed to a marked degree at the time of his admission, the paroxysms of coughing and shortness of breath partaking of an asthmatic character, the patient becoming greatly alarmed in his struggles for breath. During these paroxysms he usually stood on his feet, leaning forward with his hands braced against his knees, continuing so until ease was afforded by hypodermatic injections of morphine. Nothing could be learned by physical examination, except that the inspiratory murmur was feeble, and a few mucous râles were detected. These symptoms continued, with varying importance, until about 12 hours before death, when an attack of dyspnœa supervened, which resisted medication and increased in intensity until the patient succumbed apparently from apnœa.

Necropsy (twenty-one hours after death).—Cadaveric rigidity moderate; body fairly well nourished; superficial eschars over the sternum and tibiæ. Thoracic cavity. Both pleuræ adherent at apices, both lungs congested and full of small nodules or tubercles in the apices; heart walls somewhat hypertrophied; valves normal. On removing the lungs, a fusiform, whitish compressible tumor was seen, about 3.75 centimeters in diameter at its thickest part, which proved to be the abnormally enlarged aorta at the transverse portion, and involving the ascending and descending portions, the former but little and the latter for a distance of 2.5 or 5 centimeters. The innominate artery was also much enlarged. The coats of the vessels were much thickened and connected with the surrounding structures; the spinal column notably, which was slightly eroded, and the anterior surface of the lower portion of the trachea; death probably being caused by pressure upon the trachea and the recurrent laryngeal nerve. The other organs were apparently normal.

CASE 7.

Innominate artery.

F. C.; aged thirty years; nativity, England; admitted to U. S. Marine Hospital, Saint Louis, Mo., May 8, 1888; died May 21.

History.—In addition to the usual symptoms of intermittent malarial fever, the patient complained of great trouble in breathing, and in swallowing solid food pain and oppression in the upper part of the chest. A hoarse murmur was heard over the supra-sternal region. Death seemed to occur from asphyxia.

Necropsy (seventeen hours after death).—*Post-mortem* rigidity marked; face discolored and swollen. Pleuræ both slightly adherent at upper part of thorax. Lungs both congested, but contained no noticeable structural changes. Heart about normal in size, soft, dilated, and contained a few yellowish fibrinous clots; valves perfect. A tumor about the size of the heart was seen in the central and uppermost part of the thoracic cavity which proved to be an enlargement of the aorta at the point of the beginning of the innominate artery and extending a couple of inches to either side, and involving the latter vessel to about the same extent. On laying the aorta and innominate artery open, a sac about the size of a walnut was found attached to and communicating with the aorta at the largest part of the aneurysm, and filled with a firm blood-clot; its walls seemed to be formed of the surrounding soft tissues rather than of the aortic tunics. A tough, grayish, stratified clot, about a fourth of an inch thick in places, was detached from the walls of the aneurism. The internal surface of the sternum was eroded at the point where it was contiguous with the aneurysm. The liver, spleen, and kidneys were congested, but normal in structure.

CASE 8.

Subclavian artery.

G. F. (colored); aged forty-eight years; nativity, Virginia; admitted to marine ward, Providence Hospital, Washington, D. C., April 6, 1888; died June 1.

History.—He was first admitted to hospital on February 14, 1888, suffering from severe dyspnœa, coryza, and acute laryngitis. Examination revealed the presence of a subclavian aneurysm and mitral regurgitant disease of the heart. A murmur was also heard at the aortic cartilage but it was partly obscured by the blowing sound of the aneurism. Under appropriate treatment the coryza and laryngitis subsided, while rest in the recumbent posture and the administration of potassium iodide in 20-grain doses three times daily relieved the distressing dyspnœa. He improved until March 2, 1888, when at his own request he was allowed to go to his home. On April 6, 1888, he was readmitted to hospital in great distress and under treatment he again improved, but the dyspnœa recurred at shorter intervals, was more distressing, and his strength was much reduced. The pulsations of the tumor in the neck and the accompanying thrill and bruit were strongly marked. Auscultation revealed a loud murmur over the mitral area transmitted toward the base of the scapula. He grew much worse during the latter part of May and died at 11 p. m. on June 1.

Necropsy (*nine hours after death*).—Body fairly nourished. *Rigor mortis* present. Brain not examined. Lungs emphysematous at the borders and congested throughout. Heart very large and walls of the ventricles showed commencing fatty change (compensating hypertrophy, succeeded by dilatations and fatty degeneration). The ascending and transverse portion of the arch of the aorta were dilated into a large aneurismal tumor, and the right subclavian was also the seat of a large aneurysm, which, having ruptured, could not be removed from the body in its entirety, owing to the numerous and intimate attachments to the surrounding parts. The thymus gland was much enlarged. The tricuspid and pulmonary valves were healthy; the mitral was the seat of atheromatous patches and nodules, and the valve was incompetent. The semilunar valves of the aorta were thick, leathery, and the aortic orifice somewhat narrowed, and numerous deposits of calcareous material on the valves near their margins. The liver was fatty in patches. The kidneys were conjested. The other viscera were healthy.

Case 9.

G. W.; aged sixty-four years; nativity, Georgia; was admitted to the U. S. Marine Hospital at New Orleans, La., October 24, 1887; died October 29.

History.—Had been well save for shortness of breath until about eight weeks ago, when, after heavy lifting, he felt a severe pain in his breast and had difficulty in breathing. Since then he has not been able to work as formerly, although up to last week he was working. Has all the signs and symptoms of aneurysm of the arch. Died rather suddenly, with signs of cardiac failure.

Necropsy (*ten hours after death*).—Large and well-nourished body; adhesions over both lungs, especially the apices; both lungs congested, especially the posterior portions; left lung contains several (seven or eight) calcareous nodules in the apex, measuring 1.5 centimeters in diameter; right lung the same, but none large and not so many as the left lung. Pericardium contains only the normal fluid. Heart somewhat enlarged; mitral valves normal; aortic valves the same, and sufficient to prevent regurgitation; seem to be stiff, however. Aorta contains plaques of atheromatous material. A fusiform aneurysm existed from near the origin of the aorta to the origin of the left carotid, bulging out towards the back at the top of the arch; this was full of old clots; no laminated clots whatever. Liver and kidneys normal.

Case 10.

Femoral artery.

M. W.; aged forty-seven years; nativity, Kentucky; admitted to Marine Hospital, Louisville, Ky., November 28, 1887.

History.—At the time he was thought to be the subject of sarcoma of the thigh. He was in the hospital about six months before, at which time the diagnosis was made. There was, at first admission, a hard, non-pulsatile tumor, about the size of one's fist, on the upper and slightly on the inner aspect of the thigh just above the condyle. There was a history of syphilis dating back several years. In the course of two weeks the tumor doubled in size. Amputation was advised, and the patient deserted. When admitted the last time the thigh was enlarged from the knee to the crural arch; in the largest part the circumference was 77 centimeters. As the patient had been an asthmatic for years, and had an extensive inguinal hernia, and as atheroma was detected in the arteries of the forearm, surgical interference was deemed inadvisable. This opinion, together with the diagnosis, was sustained by Drs. Vance and Leber, both capable and careful surgeons. Two days after admission a small aspirator needle was thrust into the tumor about the middle, half-way between the inner and posterior aspects. Only a few drops of venous blood were obtained. Three days afterwards there was slight oozing from the wound, which was easily stopped. Two days later, December 5, toward 7 p. m., the wound suddenly began bleeding freely. A stream had run from the opening made by the needle, causing death in about two minutes.

Necropsy (*sixteen hours after death*).—Lungs filled with frothy, bronchial exudate; otherwise healthy. Heart rather undersized; hypertrophied concentrically; valves sufficient. There were, however, upon the cusps of the aortic semilunars a number of granular elevations. Ascending and descending portions of aortic arch normal; transverve part aneurismal throughout; about four times normal size, pouching somewhat outward and upward. On account of the long-standing asthma, this condition was not even suspected, the dyspnœa which existed all along having afflicted the patient for years. Nothing special about the other viscera. Upon dissecting the thigh—supposed to be sarcomatous—the outlines of the adductors were destroyed, being merged into a thin muscular sheet, from underneath which was turned out about 6 liters of blood in various stages, from dark semi-purulent clots to wide flakes, bright red in hue, and of almost leathery toughness. From the beginning of the popliteal downward the artery was healthy, and, strange to say, there was no disturbance of the leg or foot circulation. From the popliteal upward to Hunter's canal, the artery was markedly diseased. Its caliber was nearly 3 centimeters, and the coats were quite half that in diameter. Calcified plaques were numerous, and ossific concretions were fastened to the lumen here and there. That part of the artery lying against the femur had been for some time eroded, the blood finding its way upward and outward by degrees, giving neither thrill nor bruit. That an artery, giving way through atheromatous degeneration, should let out its contents by degrees beneath powerful muscles, thereby causing a condition resembling new growth, may be believed; but it is regarded as very unusual that that aneurism of the aorta (thoracic) should have existed without eccentric hypertrophy of the heart, to say nothing of cardiac dilatation.

CASE 11.

Abdominal.

W. L.; aged thirty-eight years; nativity, England; admitted to Marine Hospital, Boston, Mass., September 8, 1887; died September 25.

Necropsy.—(Permission of family for necropsy limited to exploration of the abdomen sufficient to see the liver.) Upon opening the abdominal cavity the liver was removed and found to be healthy and normal in all its lobes. A large puriform aneurysm of the aorta was found extending from the cœliac axis to the bifurcation of the trunk. The folds of the ileum were adherent to this on the anterior surface, and the mesentery was matted down to it in an unrecognizable mass.

ACUTE LARYNGITIS.

R. H.; aged forty-eight years; nativity, Ohio; admitted to U. S. Marine Hospital, Cincinnati, Ohio, October 21, 1887; died October 26.

History.—On admission patient states that he has had similar attacks. Has a harsh, metallic, coarse cough—painful at times; dyspnœa, paroxysmal. Given a mercurial cathartic and spray of morphia and tannin; p. m., breathes much better and coughs less.

October 23 and 24.—Improving; given tonics and "Brown mixture."

October 25.—Cough not so loose; hoarse and brassy.

October 26.—Breathing rapid; cough dry and constant; worse at 1 p. m. Died at 1.30.

Necropsy.—Larynx and pharynx found very much congested. Interior surface of larynx has diffuse and superficial fullness of blood-vessels. Heart and lungs apparently normal. Specimen preserved.

PNEUMONIA—LOBAR.

CASE 1.

L. B.; aged thirty-five years; nativity, United States; admitted to U. S. Marine Hospital, Port Townsend, Wash., September 10, 1887; died September 24.

Necropsy (sixteen hours after death).—*Rigor mortis* present. The upper and middle lobe of the right lung, as also the upper lobe of the left, were completely carnified; immediately sinking when placed in water. At intervals throughout the tissue spots of gray hepatization were present in very considerable numbers. The heart was normal and contained clots, almost of fluid consistency, in both ventricles. Kidneys: Right normal; left slightly cirrhotic, with its capsule more adherent and thicker than normal. Patient died in collapse.

CASE 2.

W. S.; aged twenty-nine years; nativity, Germany; admitted to U. S. Marine Hospital, New York, October 12, 1887; died October 19.

Necropsy (thirty-six hours after death).—Body well nourished. The lungs were in a state of red hepatization, except lower portion of right lung, in which solidification was commencing; other organs normal.

CASE 3.

F. D.; aged thirty-six years; nativity, United States; admitted to U. S. Marine Hospital, Chicago, Ill., November 1, 1887; died November 3.

History.—He was first admitted to hospital on October 26, 1887, with "ulcers of skin of legs." He was quite intoxicated, and being of a peculiar disposition did not speak of any other trouble and none was suspected; at length the sputa was detected in his cup and led to an examination and re-admission.

October 30.—The precussion note was high pitched and dull, almost flat, over the entire lower lobe of right lung; apex resonant. Left lung resonant. Lower lobe of right lung in the stage of hepatization. Temperature 39° C.; pulse 100. Close questioning now elicited the fact that the man had been a hard drinker, and had been greatly exposed just before admission. He was placed on supporting treatment with quinine, flanked by digitalis and am. carb.; whisky badly borne, the stomach rejecting it; blister and poultice applied. There was some nervous prostration, but the breathing was unembarrassed and it was with difficulty that he was kept in bed.

October 31.—Physical examination indicates no change. Quinine poorly borne; temperature, 39.5° C.; pulse, 210. Antipyrine used to lower temperature, and at 6 p. m. the thermometer registered 38° C. Respiration 24 per minute.

November 1.—Entire right lung useless. Temperature, 38.5° C.; pulse, 110; respiration, 25. Left lower lobe now very dull. At 6 p. m. the respiration was labored and 27 to the minute. Temperature, 38.7° C.; pulse, 112.

November 2.—Pulse, 110; temperature, 39° C.; respiration, 28. Heart's action is failing; pulse is quite weak. Medicine used carefully.

November 3.—9 a. m. Pulse, 127; temperature, 38° C.; respiration, 42. Face livid; heart rapidly failing; death at 10.30 a. m.

Necropsy.—Body fairly nourished; *rigor mortis* quite well marked. Entire right pleura adherent. Right lung in stage of red hepatization. Left lower lobe in stage of commencing red hepatization. Heart and other organs normal. Immediate cause of death was failure of right side of heart.

CASE 4.

J. H.; aged thirty-five years; nativity, North Carolina; admitted to U. S. Marine Hospital, Wilmington, N. C., November 23, 1887; died November 26.

Necropsy (*fifteen hours after death.*)—*Rigor mortis.* Body of tall, spare man. No external marks noted. Upper and middle lobes and upper part of lower of right lung in state of red hepatization, rest of lower lobe highly congested. Left lobe normal. No other lesion found. Weight of organs: Right lung, 1,710 grams; left, 495; heart, 392; liver, 2,300; spleen, 250; left kidney, 165; right, 170; middle lobe of right lung abnormally small, fissures between upper and middle lobes incomplete.

CASE 5.

G. L.; aged forty-four years; nativity, Pennsylvania; admitted to U. S. Marine Hospital, San Francisco, Cal., November 26, 1887; died November 30, 1887.

Necropsy (*sixteen hours after death*).—*Rigor mortis* pronounced. Body well nourished; lips blue; face somewhat livid; ecchymotic discoloration of dependent parts of body. Thorax: Right pleura contained about 200 cubic centimeters serum, but no other evidence of inflammation. The right lung was congested and œdematous. Left pleura contained no fluid, but over outer aspect of lower lobe it was inflamed, eroded, and mostly covered with a thin layer of plastic lymph. This was in one place firm enough to constitute adhesions of some strength with the opposing pleura, which was found to be in much the same condition as that of the visceral layer just noted. Left lung, lower lobe, was in a condition of pneumonic consolidation. The stage of resolution had not been reached at any part. The rest of the lung was congested and œdematous. Heart: Pericardium contained about twice the normal amount of fluid. The organ was flabby and its tissue soft and fatty. A fibrinous clot occupied the whole right heart, from the bronchial veins to the division of the pulmonary artery. Another fibrinous clot, commencing just within the left ventricle, passed out into the arch of the aorta some distance. The left heart was empty and flaccid. Liver was one and a half times the natural size and quite fatty. Gall-bladder was quite empty. Spleen twice the natural size—a mere pulp. Kidneys were each enlarged, somewhat lobulated, cortex pale and somewhat atrophied.

CASE 6.

Measles.

M. E.; aged twenty years; nativity, Alaska; admitted to U. S. Marine Hospital, San Francisco, Cal., December 15, 1887, at 4.30 p. m.; died December 17, 1887, at 5.30 p. m.

History.—Owing to his extremely low condition and imperfect understanding of English an accurate history was not obtainable. Said he had been sick three or four weeks with cough and pain in right chest; that the left side was attacked four days before admission and that an eruption had appeared on his face, body, and limbs on the 12th instant. Condition on admission: Very abundant eruption of measles on face, body, and limbs; cough with muco-purulent sputa, with no admixture of blood. Respiration very rapid and shallow. Pulse rapid—120—and feeble. Temperature in axilla 39.6° C. Physical examination: Percussion, dullness over lower half of chest on both sides. Auscultation gave crepitant, subcrepitant, large and moist râles over the same regions, also some friction sounds. A diagnosis of measles, with double pneumonia (with bronchitis and pleurisy) was made. Stimulants: Ammon. carb. and brandy, with 0.33 gm. doses of quinine every four hours and nourishing diet constituted the treatment. The respiration grew more rapid and irregular—50 to 60. The pulse increased in frequency; became soft and feeble. The temperature did not again rise above 39.2° C. In spite of active stimulation the patient failed to rally.

Necropsy (eighteen hours after death).—*Rigor mortis* marked. Considerable emaciation. Ecchymotic patches in dependent portions of skin. Arms, trunk, and thighs covered with eruption of measles. Thorax: Right lung was attached to pleura by numerous adhesions over upper lobe. The lung itself was deeply congested and partially hepatized; in the anterior edge of lower lobe the bronchioles were full of catarrhal exudation. Left pleural walls were adherent everywhere. The bands of adhesion were very numerous and strong. The whole upper lobe and upper third of lower lobe were consolidated, and in section gave the characteristic appearance of gray hepatization. Heart was somewhat fatty in the line of its vessels, and its tissue pale but firm. There was an inconsiderable amount of pericardial fluid. The left heart was nearly empty, but the right side was full of fibrinous clots from the pulmonary and systemic veins, through auricle and ventricle into the branches of the pulmonary artery. Abdomen presented the usual appearance, as concerned the peritoneum and intestines. The liver was a most extraordinary looking object. Its color was a dirty, yellowish white, the surface being spotted with areas of a more pronounced yellowish hue. On section it appeared of a pale, reddish-gray color. The capsule de tached with slight difficulty. The consistency of the organ was rather firm, except in dependent portion of right lobe, where it was somewhat friable. It was somewhat enlarged; there was venous congestion, evidenced by the black blood oozing forth from the cut vessels in making sections. Gall-bladder contained a light, greenish brown bile, quite viscid. Spleen was of usual size and appearance. Kidneys were each nearly twice the normal size, but, singularly enough, appeared normal in every other respect.

NOTE.—Under the microscope the liver was found to have undergone complete fatty degeneration.

CASE 7.

S. C.; aged twenty-seven years; nativity, Nova Scotia; admitted to marine ward German Hospital, Philadelphia, Pa., December 16, 1887; died December 18.

History.—On admission patient was very weak, suffering from marked dyspnœa and hurried respiration. Temperature, 40.1° C.; pulse, 148; respiration, 36. Physical examination showed dullness over entire right thorax, with crepitant and subcrepitant râles. The treatment employed failed to influence his condition, which gradually became more serious till death closed the scene.

Necropsy.—Body fairly well nourished and rigid. Right lung bound to pleura by recent adhesions, and whole surface of organ covered with plastic lymph; substance showed gray hepatization more marked in upper lobes. Left lung apparently healthy. Heart normal in size and weight, but filled with firm clots. Kidneys large, with amyloid degeneration. Liver amyloid and enlarged.

CASE 8.

Pleurisy.

P. B.; aged twenty-three years; nativity, Alaska; admitted to U. S. Marine Hospital, San Francisco, Cal., December 20, 1887; died December 22.

History.—No history could be gotten from the patient, who was very much emaciated and weak. There was cough with profuse expectoration of thick and somewhat nummular purulent matter. Loud bubbling râles over both lungs and diminished resonance. Temperature on evening of admission 38.4° C. Treatment by stimulants: Ammon. carb. and brandy; quinine, and all the nourishment he could take. It was necessary to resort to rectal alimentation on the second day of treatment.

Necropsy (twelve hours after death).—*Rigor mortis* moderate. Both pleural cavities obliterated by very firm adhesions. Left lung completely consolidated and very hard; gray hepatization. Right lung in a state of red hepatization. Heart fatty and flabby. No other organs examined.

CASE 9.

Aneurysm of innominate artery.

J. H.; aged forty years; nativity, America; admitted to U. S. Marine Hospital, Cleveland, Ohio, November 10, 1887; died December 29.

History.—He gave a history of having always been a perfectly well man, never having been sick in his life, and his general appearance bore testimony to this statement, as he looked healthy, strong, and well nourished. This case upon admission presented nothing unusual from an ordinary (not severe) pneumonia, except that the respirations were not simply increased in frequency, but there was a noticeable dyspnœa. In three weeks the patient was able to be out of bed and around the ward, and apparently on the road to a speedy restoration to health. At this point, however, the improvement came to a standstill. The dyspnœa above referred to had disappeared during convalescence, but now gradually returned and became so severe and violent that the last two weeks before his death he presented the appearance of a man in one long, continuous asthmatic attack. On auscultation moist and dry rales were heard over the lungs and loud wheezing sounds over the trachea and bronchia. The patient stated that he had never suffered from dyspnœa previous to this attack of pneumonia.

Necropsy (*nine hours after death*).—All parts of the lungs were thoroughly congested. The middle lobe of the right lung was in a state of gray hepatization. Pieces cut from this lobe sank promptly on being placed in water; pieces cut from other parts of the lungs floated. The heart was enlarged to about once and a half its normal size. The left ventricle and ascending aorta contained very large *ante-mortem* clots. The entire innominate artery was converted into an aneurysm twice the size of a hen's egg, and this aneurism was completely filled with a clotted mass which had a reddish, fleshy appearance and which was rolled out in one mass on laying open the artery. Other organs not examined.

Case 10.

P. C.; aged thirty-six years; nativity, Ireland; admitted to U. S. Marine Hospital, Baltimore, Md., December 29, 1887; died January 8, 1888.

History.—The patient on admission stated that he had been sick on shipboard for two weeks; had, after much exposure, a chill, followed by fever; pain on the right side of thorax, much cough, and dyspnœa. Pulse 100, full and strong; temperature 40° C. Respiration short and hurried. Dullness on percussion extended over the whole of the left lung; respiration bronchial in character. The patient stated that he had taken no medicine, and that his habits were intemperate. Treatment: Mass hydrarg.; pulv. ipecac et opii were ordered every three hours. Hot poultices of mush and mustard kept constantly over the chest. Stokes's mixture given as an expectorant. Eggs, milk, and stimulants given freely. Death due to cardiac failure.

Necropsy.—*Rigor mortis* absent. Bodily conditions fair. On removing sternum two small abscesses were found in the areolar tissue beneath it. Heart slightly larger than usual, but no abnormality found. Right lung entirely consolidated, with exception of the lower border, presenting the abscesses and degenerated tissue of the gray hepatization stage of pneumonia. Left lung contained one spot of consolidation; otherwise fairly normal. Right pleura showed some recent adhesions, which were easily broken down. Walls of gall-bladder very edematous, being 7 millimeters in thickness. Liver and spleen enlarged and congested. Kidneys displayed small points of fatty infiltration, otherwise normal. Intestines normal. Brain not examined.

Case 11.

D. M.; aged twenty-three years; nativity, Canada; admitted to U. S. Marine Hospital, Chicago, Ill., January 17, 1888; died January 21.

History.—Upon admission careful examination evinced the physical signs of lobar pneumonia of the right lung, with extensive inflammation of the right pleura; mild delirium existed throughout the course of the disease. Heart's action very good; pulse full and strong. Nervous depression very marked. Left lung became congested shortly before death.

Treatment.—Tinct. aconite rad. in five drops at a dose. Quinia and morphia, with spts. frumenti in minimum quantity.

Necropsy.—Body well nourished. *Rigor mortis* not well marked; skin mottled with purple spots; lips of a livid blue color. Right pleura found adherent in both its layers; about 1,000 cubic centimeters of serum in sac. Right lung in red and gray hepatization throughout. Sections in water sank rapidly. Left lung and pleura not inflamed, but deeply congested.

CASE 12.

M. D.; aged forty years; nativity, Ireland; admitted to U. S. Marine Hospital, Stapleton, N. Y., January 28, 1888; died February 5.

Necropsy (nineteen hours after death).—Body of a slightly developed adult male. *Rigor mortis.* The right lung was adherent by recently developed fibrinous bands; gray hepatization of upper and lower lobes. The left lung was slightly congested in the upper lobe; hypostatic congestion of lower lobes. Pericardium contained 100 cubic centimeters of serum. Heart was normal. The liver was fatty. Spleen was enlarged; tissue firm. Kidneys normal. Intestines normal.

CASE 13.

W. A. (colored); aged thirty-five years; nativity, Tennessee; admitted to U. S. Marine Hospital, Memphis, Tenn., February 7, 1888.

History.—This patient I first saw at 5 p. m. He was lying on a filthy bed, through which the urine had dropped to the floor. I was told that he had been sick three weeks. He had a chill, followed by a troublesome cough. This was all that those who were with him could tell me. The patient was comatose; pulse was 140 and weak; respirations very rapid, 50 to the minute. He was so near dead that I asked that he be allowed to remain. His friends insisted upon my taking him to the hospital. I had him taken to the hospital. He was admitted at 6 p. m. and died forty-five minutes afterwards.

Necropsy.—All organs healthy, except left lung, which was just passing from red to gray hepatization.

Weight of viscera in grams.—Right kidney, 150; left, 189; pancreas, 98; liver, 1,780; right lung, 325; spleen, 240; heart, 435; left lung, 760. Basal lobe solidified.

CASE 14.

G. C. (colored); aged twenty-seven years; nativity, Kentucky; admitted to U. S. Marine Hospital, Cincinnati, Ohio, February 18, 1888; died February 22.

History.—On admission the patient said he had been sick two days. Has pain in left chest; coughs violently; sputa bloody and sticky; pulse 108; temperature 40.2° C.; respiration, 40 per minute. He grew worse from day to day and died suddenly on the seventh day of sickness.

Necropsy.—*Rigor mortis* very well marked. Body well nourished. Muscular development unusually good. Left lower lobe found completely consolidated with recent adhesions of its pleura; old adhesions of right pleura. Heart full of clots; clots *ante mortem* and *post mortem*. The white clot extended into the left pulmonary artery and branches. Other organs apparently normal.

CASE 15.

W. K. (colored); aged twenty-one years; nativity, Georgia; admitted to Marine Hospital, Memphis, Tenn., February 29, 1888; died March 1.

History.—He had been sick two weeks. He had one severe chill, followed by pain in his chest near the right nipple, with shortness of breath. In addition to this, when admitted there was loss of flesh, strength, and appetite; respiration, 50, shallow; pulse, 140; temperature, 40.8° C. There was dullness over the basal lobes of both lungs and crepitant and subcrepitant rales around the nipple. He died on the following day.

Necropsy.—One lung was in condition of red and one of gray hepatization. Other viscera normal.

CASE 16.

N. F.; aged twenty-five years; nativity, Arkansas; admitted to U. S. Marine Hospital, New Orleans, La., March 15, 1888; died March 24.

History.—Had been sick several days at time of admission. When admitted, respiration 88 per minute; pulse, 108; temperature, 40° C.; grew steadily worse for a few days and then seemed to rally, temperature becoming normal. In twenty-four hours, however, the temperature rose again to $40\frac{2}{5}$°. Stimulants, combined with generous diet, had but little effect. He was more or less delirious all the time. The respirations were very rapid, and vomiting set in. Medicines were given hypodermically; food per rectum. Died on the night of 24th.

Necropsy (thirty-six hours after death).—Body strongly built, muscular, and in good condition. Heart: Pericardial sac contained 250 cubic centimeters fluid. Organ itself normal in appearance. *Ante-mortem* clot, weighing 60 grams, extending into aorta. Valves of heart normal. Pleura adherent throughout to both lungs. A fibrinous exudation organized and formed into membrane covered the whole of the posterior portion of the right lung, like a hood. This membrane was thick, tough, and of a yellow color. Right lung, posterior portion, in state of gray hepatization, breaking down readily; upper lobe, the seat, red hepatization; lung substance tore in removing. Left lung, lower lobe, in state of red hepatization. Spleen hypertrophied and soft. Liver congested. Kidneys, typical pneumonic, "engorged and red." Intestines congested.

Weights of organs.—Heart, 410 grams; fibrinous clot, 60 grams; right lung, 680 grams; left lung, ——; liver, 1,970.

CASE 17.

E. J.; aged forty-five years; nativity, Germany; admitted to U. S. Marine Hospital, Chicago, Ill., March 23, 1888; died March 26.

Necropsy.—*Rigor mortis* well marked; body well nourished; skin of back ecchymotic and mottled from hypostatic congestion. On opening thoracic wall the cavities of both pleuræ were found filled with fluid; evidence of acute pleuritis on the right side; the lower and middle lobes of the right lung were in the stage of gray hepatization; cut sections sunk in water; left lobe reddish brown in color, heavy, and pits on pressure; from its cut surface there was a free discharge of bloody serum, showing the lung to be in a stage of active congestion; heart large and somewhat fatty; valves seemed normal; left cavities comparatively empty, right filled with *ante-mortem* clots.

CASE 18.

Hypertrophy of heart—aortic insufficiency.

C. O.; aged forty-eight years; nativity, Norway; admitted to U. S. Marine Hospital, Cairo, Ill., March 15, 1888; died March 28.

History.—While on way up the Mississippi River, seven days before applying for admission, he fell overboard, and worked for several hours in his wet clothing. A "cold" coming on, he attempted to "work it off" by heroic doses (twelve pills—three daily) of a patent purgative pill ("dose, from one to three on going to bed") for several days. On admission, he complained of weakness, difficulty of breathing; temperature, 40° C.; pulse, 110; respiration, shallow, 42; auscultation showed apparent consolidation of entire right lung. The case improved steadily until the patient became unruly, and refused from time to time to take his medicine or submit to local treatment. His disease assumed the malarial type, rapidly developing typhoid symptoms, terminating in death at 10 p. m. March 28, 1888.

Necropsy (fifteen hours after death).—Body, that of a muscular, middle-aged man, much emaciated; *rigor mortis* well marked; thorax, left pleura showed old adhesions; left lung collapsed; superior lobe congested; right lung hepatized throughout; superior lobe breaking down; heart small; left ventricle hypertrophied; aortic valves incompetent; right heart dilated; walls somewhat thinned; weight, empty, 180 grams; kidneys fatty.

CASE 19.

D. C.; aged thirty-seven years; nativity, Ireland; admitted to U. S. Marine Hospital, Chicago, Ill., April 5, 1888; died April 6.

Necropsy.—*Rigor mortis* well marked. Body well nourished. Thorax opened. Left pleural cavity contained about 2,500 cubic centimeters of serous fluid. Recent plastic lymph effused over whole pleural surface of left side. Upper lobe of left lung in a condition of red hepatization; lower lobe actively congested. Right pleura adherent to lung from old pleuritis. Right lung normal. Normal amount of fluid in pericardial sac. Heart, right auricle and ventricle contained some *post-mortem* clots. One extended some nine centimeters. Left heart entirely empty.

CASE 20.

Pericarditis—Pleurisy.

A. J.; aged thirty-three years; nativity, Finland; admitted to U. S. Marine Hospital at Stapleton, N. Y., April 25, 1888; died May 1.

Necropsy.—*Rigor mortis* and livores present. Right lung weighed 1,270 grams; right pleural cavity contained purulent fluid, and the lung was covered with an easily detachable yellow membrane; on section of lung bronchi found filled with purulent fluid; lung partly hepatized. Left lung weighed 600 grams; there were a few adhesions about apex and base; it was covered with membrane similar to that of the right lung; bronchi in similar condition. The pericardium contained purulent fluid; it was inflamed and roughened. Endocarditis of mitral valves and in the left auricle, probably proceeding from the lung. The heart weighed 270 grams. The spleen weighed 435 grams; it was soft and pultaceous. The left kidney weighed 220 grams; there was parenchymateous nephitis; congestion of blood-vessels of pelvis. The right kidney weighed 200 grams; it was in the same condition as the left. The liver weighed 2,350 grams; it was enlarged and pale; acini of yellow color, increasing in intensity toward center; gall bladder empty. The spleen was congested. The stomach, bladder, and intestines were normal.

CASE 21.

J. M.; aged thirty-eight years; nativity, New York; admitted to U. S. Marine Hospital, Chicago, Ill., May 3, 1888; died May 11.

Necropsy.—Rigor mortis well marked. Body well nourished. Face and chest quite livid. Pericardium contained 60 cubic centimeters of serum. Heart walls flabby. Right auricle and ventricle full of *ante-mortem* clots; left auricle and ventricle full of *post-mortem* clots. Left pleural cavity entirely obliterated by pleuritic adhesions. Left lung adhered to pleura. Right pleural cavity completely obliterated by pleuritic adhesions. Right middle lobe of lung partly hepatized; lower lobe completely hepatized; upper lobe in stage of congestion. Left upper lobe completely hepatized; lower lobe partly hepatized. Other organs normal.

CASE 22.

Gangrene of lung.

E. W.; aged forty years; nativity, Cape Breton Isle; admitted to U. S. Marine Hospital, Boston, Mass., May 6, 1888; died May 12.

History.—Seventeen days previous to admission he fell into the water and was nearly drowned. Next day had a chill, and developed pneumonia, for which he was treated in another hospital. On examination bronchial breathing was heard over both lungs; mucous râles and clicks over both bases. There was considerable dyspnœa and cough, with profuse expectoration of dark-red sputa with an extremely offensive odor. Large ulcers were discovered on both legs and both thighs, and on one arm—the result of application of jugs of hot water. In spite of generous diet and free stimulation the patient gradually sank under the drain on his vitality.

Necropsy (three hours after death).—Body well nourished; *rigor mortis* slight. On opening the left pleural cavity a quantity of disgustingly fetid gas escaped, followed by about 1,000 cubic centimeters of dark-colored fluid with the same odor. Right lung: Weight 620 grams—congested throughout. Left lung: Weight 950 grams; upper lobe congested; lower lobe in a state of red hepatization, with a cavity in the lung tissue about the size of a large orange, opening into the pleural cavity and containing shreds of gangrenous tissue and a little of the offensive liquid before mentioned. Heart weighed 400 grams; a little hypertrophied.

CASE 23.

H. W. (colored); aged forty-nine years; nativity, Missouri; admitted to U. S. Marine Hospital, Saint Louis, Mo., May 19, 1888; died May 25, 1888.

Necropsy (*thirty hours after death*).—Body emaciated; *rigor mortis* marked. Pleuræ adherent, especially on the right side; left lung congested somewhat; right lung had a doughy feel, devoid of elasticity or crepitation; dark brown in color, sections sinking when thrown into water. A dark, frothy fluid escaped from the cut surfaces. The lower lobe when cut into resembled the cut surface of a congested liver. The other organs showed no pathological changes worthy of note.

CASE 24.

Double—Gastro-duodenitis.

F. G.; aged seventeen years; nativity, Norway; admitted to U. S. Marine Hospital, San Francisco, Cal., November 28, 1887; died December 21, 1887.

History.—Had been under treatment for abscess of the cornea for several weeks. On December 16 vomiting and diarrhea appeared without apparent cause, followed next day by jaundice. On the 18th complained of pain in left chest; had slight cough and bloody sputa, and was delirious at times. Examination revealed pneumonia of left lower lobe and congestion of right lung. Pulse and respiration increased in frequency; temperature 39.1° C. There was apparently an increase in the liver dullness, and jaundice became more pronounced. Stools clay, colored, etc. The pneumonia spread rapidly to both lungs, delirium gave place to stupor, and death soon followed.

Necropsy (*seven hours after death*).—*Rigor mortis* moderate; body fairly nourished; a high degree of jaundice, and ecchymotic spots in dependent portions. Chest: Heart, especially the right side, fatty. Pleuræ: A slight amount of fluid in right pleural cavity and recent adhesions on both sides at base. Lungs: Right upper lobe congested and its lower portion was in a state of red hepatization; a small amount of catarrhal exudation was found in the bronchioles of the upper half; lower lobe hepatized in its entirety. Right lung; lower lobes in same state as that of left side; upper lobes congested and somewhat emphysematous. In several spots, from the size of a pea to that of a chestnut, the lung tissue had broken down into a chocolate-colored semi-fluid. These spots were located, one in the left base, anterior surface; two in upper anterior portion of right lower lobe, and one in right upper lobe, near its lower border. Abdomen: Almost entire mucous membrane reddened, an ecchymotic spot about the size of a 10 cent piece on posterior portion, near pylorus. Dodenum—Mucous membrane inflamed. Liver adherent, in part, to diaphram; about one and a half times its normal size, and congested posteriorly; tissue firm. Gall-bladder contained a small amount of bile, which flowed through the common duct with difficulty. Spleen about twice the normal size and tissue soft. Kidneys a little larger than usual, but apparently normal in other respects.

CASE 25.

Double.

H. M.; aged sixty-three years; nativity, Germany; admitted to U. S. Marine Hospital, San Francisco, Cal., October 14, 1887; died October 18, 1887.

Necropsy (*two and one half hours after death*).—*Rigor mortis* already pronounced. Face and neck livid, ecchymotic patches about the lower limbs. Body fairly well nourished. Abdomen distended. Superficial veins about neck and chest engorged and pouring out black blood when cut. Chest: There were recent adhesions in both pleuræ, especially the left; organized bands, but easily torn; they were found especially in front of the upper lobes. Lungs: These were solid, with croupous exudation in both upper lobes. The two lower lobes of right lung were unaffected, scarcely congested, and the same was true of the left lower lobe and lower border of left upper lobe. The stage of resolution had not been reached. Heart: The left ventricle was hypertrophied, the right rather weak. The right auricle was extremely thin. The whole heart was loaded with fat, but the muscular fiber seemed firm. There were no valve lesions and no disease of the great vessels. Right auricle was distended to the point almost of rupture, with a dark semi-fibrinous clot reaching to the ventricle. There the clot became firm and fibrinous, evidently *ante mortem*, and passed out between the pulmonary valves so as to occlude the orifice, mold itself to the upper surface of valves, and occupy nearly the whole caliber of the artery to its second and third divisions. The left heart presented a like appearance, the same in kind, differing only by a less size of clot in auricle and a smaller and softer fibrinous cord reaching into aorta and vessels of arch. Abdomen: Liver was perhaps one-third larger than normal. It was congested in dependent portion, but its texture indicated a chronic hypertrophy and in spots a well marked sclerosis. Spleen was nearly twice too large, dark and pulpy.

CASE 26.

Double.

W. K.; aged forty years; nativity, Finland; admitted to U. S. Marine Hospital, New Orleans, La., October 25, 1887; died November 5, 1887.

History.—Came in apparently moribund, but improved and lived seven days. Had an attack of acute rheumatism just before death, as evidenced by the swelling of his wrists and sheaths of the tendons of the extensors of the same, to which he had been liable for some time.

Necropsy (six hours after death).—Left lung adherent to chest wall all around; tears when separated; is very much broken down; contains four or five abscesses, containing from 5 to 15 grams of pus in the anterior part of lower lobe; right lung like the left. The lower and middle lobes are solidified and broken down in places. Liver enlarged, 2,750 grams; spleen also enlarged. Kidneys congested and soft.

CASE 27.

Double.

J. R.; aged twenty years; nativity, Norway; admitted to U. S. Marine Hospital, Cleveland, Ohio, February 8, 1888; died February 10, 1888.

History.—Patient stated that he had been sick for a week. He was apparently a strong and well-nourished man, but for a year previous he had had a peculiar pallid, waxy complexion. Both lungs were solidified, the lower lobe of each lung being very dull on percussion, and even the upper lobes giving evidence of being affected. Respirations forty-four per minute. The general symptoms were not violent or alarming. The day before he died his strength was good and he sat up in bed, and even had to be cautioned to keep quiet, as he was not suffering, except with the rapid respiration, and death resulted from apnœa following the choking up of such extensive portions of the lungs with exudation.

Necropsy (*six hours after death*).—The lower lobes of both lungs were in a state of red hepatization, the right being more completely hepatized than the left and showing at some points commencing gray hepatization. The upper lobes were extremely congested. The lower lobes sank and the upper lobes floated when placed in water. The liver, kidneys, spleen, and abdominal lymphatic glands were affected with amyloid degeneration.

CASE 28.

Double—Pericarditis.

H. S.; aged thirty-eight years; nativity, Kentucky; admitted to U. S. Marine Hospital, Cairo, Ill., March 3, 1888; died March 6, 1888.

History.—Patient had been on a week's spree, and had slept under a board-walk for two nights. On admission suffered with dyspnœa, weakness, distressing cough, severe pain in chest; temperature, 40° C.; respiration 40, superficial; pulse, 119, thready. On auscultation heart was found much embarrassed and both lungs appeared hepatized. Counter irritation, brisk purgation, and stimulants administered; 250 cubic centimeters of blood taken from right median cephalic vein, and quinia, opium, and pilocarpine, with nourishment; stimulants were pushed. Patient became comatose, and died after twelve hours' stupor.

Necropsy (*nineteen hours after death*).—Body that of a fat, very muscular, middle-aged man. *Rigor mortis* feeble. Chest stained a bright scarlet. Thorax, Pleural cavities obliterated by old and strong adhesions. Heart thickly coated with organized lymph, hypertrophied. Pericardium contained 60 cubic centimeters purulent serum; left ventricle, hypertrophied; aortic valves incompetent; gray hepatization throughout both lungs; right lung breaking down and bathed in pus. Left kidney fatty, right kidney swollen; infundibula filled with pus. Liver mottled, lobus quadratus slightly cirrhosed. Weight, 3,000 grams. Gall bladder moderately full of purulent bile.

CASE 29.

Double—Pericarditis.

P. L.; aged thirty-six years; nativity, Ireland; admitted to U. S. Marine Hospital, Cleveland, Ohio, May 31, 1888; died June 4, 1888.

History.—Patient stated that he had been sick two weeks. Upon admission he was cyanotic; respirations, 30 a minute; temperature, 40.6° C.; dullness over both lower lobes.

Necropsy (*ten hours after death*).—Lower lobes of both lungs were hepatized, the lower left lobe being in a state of gray hepatization, the right lower lobe in a state of red hepatization; in the lower left lobe was a cavity twice the size of a walnut, and filled with pus. The heart itself was normal, but the pericardium was inflamed; the cavity contained pus, and the interior of the pericardium was coated with lymph, presenting what is sometimes termed the "bread and butter" appearance. The abdominal organs were normal. The skull was not opened.

CIRRHOSIS OF THE LUNGS—ASTHMA.

B. C.; aged fifty-eight years; nativity, Virginia; admitted to U. S. Marine Hospital, Baltimore, Md., November 19, 1887; died April 25, 1888.

Necropsy (*fifteen hours after death*).—*Rigor mortis* moderate; body considerably emaciated; heart slightly larger than normal, but valves and tissue appeared normal; right lung was entirely collapsed, forming but a small, dry, solid mass, which lay close up against the spinal column. The entire right pleural cavity was occupied by a series of enormous emphysematous blebs; old adhesions bound those structures to the chest walls at various points. The left lung was in the same condition, but not in as advanced a stage; there seemed scarcely any blood in the lung tissue, and many of the air passages appeared to be occluded. Liver was of the nutmeg variety, evidently resulting from prolonged congestion due to interference with circulation in the lungs. Spleen very dark, congested, and soft. Kidneys hard; capsule slightly adherent, and tissue showed the earlier stages of chronic interstitial nephritis. Intestines and bladder normal. Brain not examined.

ACUTE PNEUMONIC PHTHISIS.

A. A.; aged twenty-two years; nativity, Norway; admitted to marine ward of the German Hospital, Philadelphia, Pa., on January 16; died March 1, 1888.

History.—The only element of interest in this case was the extreme rapidity with which the disease ran its course, resisting and overcoming all measures adopted in the way of treatment.

Necropsy.—Showed large cavities in the upper lobes of both lungs, with smaller ones in the lower lobes. Both organs were firmly bound to parieties by strong bands of adhesions. No other organs were examined.

CHRONIC PNEUMONIC PHTHISIS.

CASE 1.

E. C.; aged thirty-eight years; nativity, Illinois; admitted to U. S. Marine Hospital, Detroit, Mich., January 10, 1887; died September 8, 1887.

History.—Patient was admitted to hospital with lobar pneumonia November 22, 1886, and was discharged January 9, 1887, as improved, and re-admitted the following day under the above diagnosis. He presented the usual symptoms of cough, expectoration, fever, night sweats, emaciation, and chest pains, with physical signs of consolidation most marked over upper lobe of left lung. A marked feature in this case was the hoarseness and almost complete loss of voice from the first. During the last few months his stomach and bowels gave him much trouble, and there was progressive and extreme emaciation.

Necropsy (*nine hours after death*).—*Rigor mortis* fairly well marked; body extremely emaciated. Liver congested; right lobe enlarged; weight 1,550 grams. No tubercle found in mesentery or any of the abdominal viscera. Heart valves normal; *ante-mortem* clot in right ventricle. Right pleura slightly adherent; left firmly so throughout. Tuberculous masses were found in both lungs; most abundant in the upper lobes, in which many cavities were also found, some of those in the left lung being of considerable size.

Case 2.

Epilepsy.

L. P.; aged thirty-six years; nativity, Canada (a half-breed); admitted to the U. S. Marine Hospital, Detroit, Mich., March 29, 1886; died August 18, 1887.

History.—He had been sick about a year when admitted. Sickness began by "taking cold," which seemed to grow worse. When he applied for admission he was much emaciated, but stated that he had been a large man previous to his sickness. He presented the usual symptoms of cough, expectoration, occasional fever, night sweats, chest pains, etc., with physical signs of consolidation in the upper lobes of both lungs. Tubercular deposits were removed from his hand and scrotum at different times during his illness. He also suffered from occasional epileptic fits. During the last few months he had much trouble from indigestion, diarrhea, and irritability of the stomach.

Necropsy (*five hours after death*).—*Rigor mortis* slight; body much emaciated. Heart valves normal; *ante-mortem* clot in right ventricle. Lungs bound to chest walls by pleuritic adhesions, especially firm near the apices of both lungs. Tubercles abundant in both lungs; more in the right than the left and more in the upper than the lower lobes; a small cavity was found in the upper lobe of the right lung, and in the corresponding lobe of the left lung there were several cavities, one of considerable size with ragged edges. The liver was small—weight 907 grams; tissue normal. Other abdominal organs normal.

ACUTE PLEURISY.

Pneumonia.

F. O. (colored); aged forty-seven years; nativity, Michigan; admitted to U. S. Marine Hospital, Detroit, Mich., March 12, 1888; died March 16.

History.—When admitted he stated that he had been sick two weeks; sickness began with chill, followed by fever and pain in the left side, with slight blood-streaked expectoration. When first examined there seemed to be some increase in the area of tubular breathing behind (left lung), but this was obscured by a prominent friction sound over the lower portion of the lower lobe. Respiration at this time was about 30; pulse, 88; temperature, 39° C. The treatment consisted in quinine and Dover's powder, carbonate of ammonia, and sirup of senega, whisky and milk, with hot applications over the affected region. The pain and difficulty in breathing at times seemed much relieved, but on the morning of March 15 he sank into a state bordering on collapse, from which he partially ralied under the influence of large doses of whisky, frequently repeated. At 6 p. m. he was very weak; temperature 39° C.; respiration 60; pulse 120 and weak; tongue covered with whitish coating; expectoration purulent. Death occurred at 1 a. m., March 16, 1888.

Necropsy (*fourteen hours after death*).—*Rigor mortis* marked. Body well nourished. Abdominal organs normal, but somewhat congested. Heart normal; organized clots in left ventricle. Stomach pressed down by left lung, which was much enlarged; weight 1,300 grams; the lower lobe was quite completely hepatized; red fluid exuded on section, and portions of the lung tissue sank in water, contrasting strongly with that of upper lobe and right lung, which were normal and floated in water. Weight of right lung 570 grams. About 600 cubic centimeters of sero-purulent fluid was found in the left pleural cavity.

EMPYEMA—PYÆMIA.

T. W.; aged twenty-two years; nativity, Sweden; admitted to U. S. Marine Hospital, San Francisco, Cal., November 5, 1887; died November 7.

Necropsy (*seven hours after death*).—*Rigor mortis* pronounced. Emaciation marked. Skin, particularly of face and neck, somewhat jaundiced; about the feet and back it was ecchymosed and discolored. There were three abscesses in the connective tissue, whose contents had been evacuated. The largest was some 8 centimeters above right knee, just outside the quadratus muscle. There was a smaller one at the corresponding point on the other limb, and another some 6 centimeters below the knee, inside the leg of the same side. There was a small bed-sore over the sacrum. Thorax: The right pleura was coated with pus, and beneath the visceral layer were several small abscesses somewhat eroding the lung. At the back of the upper lobe a small localized collection of pus had eroded the tissue almost to the bone of the ribs. The right lung was congested and œdematous, but its tissue appeared normal, with the exceptions already noted, and the further exception of a small area of dark softening of the nature of gangrene near the root of the lung. Left pleura presented nearly the appearance of the right cavity, to a degree, however, more marked. In addition, there was to the inner side of the upper lobe a localized empyema containing some 30 cubic centimeters thick pus. This lung was in the same condition as the right, with the exception of a small hepatized area at the apex of its lower lobe. The amount of pus in the pleural cavities was small, and there was no tubercle in the lungs. Heart was rather small, anæmic, coated with fat, but its muscle quite firm. Abdomen was quite distended. Upon opening the peritoneum, the intestines were seen inflated with gas, but there was nowhere evidence of inflammation. Liver somewhat enlarged, yellowish, friable, very fatty. Gall-bladder tolerably full of dark gall. Spleen twice the normal size, almost pulpy, but apparently yellowish, fatty, and not congested. The right kidney was one and a half times the usual size, and contained several small abscesses, and one of larger size which had discharged some 25 cubic centimeters pus into the post-renal connective tissue. The left kidney was also about one and a half times the normal size, somewhat pale, but not remarkably changed, and contained two or three minute abscesses in the peripheral cortical layer. Bladder was somewhat contracted and pale, and contained a small quantity of clear urine and a little purulent sediment.

ACUTE INFLAMMATION OF STOMACH AND ŒSOPHAGUS.

G. G.; aged forty-one years; nativity, Prince Edward Island; admitted to the U. S. Marine Hospital, New York, October 22, 1887; died October 28.

Necropsy (*twenty eight hours after death*).—*Rigor mortis* only slight; body fairly well nourished. The anterior surfaces of both lungs were in close apposition from base to apex, showing extreme distension of air cells, and the posterior portions of the lungs were solidified. Right lung weighed 1,420 grams; a white, fibrinous deposit covered the pleural surfaces of the middle and lower lobes. Left lung weighed 1,075 grams; lower lobe completely solidified, except a narrow strip along the anterior border. Trachea and bronchial tubes, even to the extreme ramification, contained a great number of calcified plaques, and in some places they were so large that it completely constricted the caliber. The mucous membrane of the pharynx, larynx, and trachea was the site of an acute inflammation. The œsophagus contained numerous ulcers of long standing; most numerous about 3 inches above the opening into the stomach. Mucous membrane of the stomach the seat of many hæmorrhagic spots; other organs normal.

CHRONIC INFLAMMATION OF THE STOMACH.

B. M.; aged forty-seven years; nativity, Ireland; admitted to marine ward, German Hospital, Philadelphia, Pa., August 20, 1887, suffering from gastritis; died August 29.

History.—Complained of considerable pain in epigastric region, and to a less degree over entire abdomen. Said he had persistent vomiting for about two weeks. He admitted having been a hard drinker all his life, and said he had been previously in hospitals for treatment for this condition. Examination developed tender abdomen, tympanitic at different places, and extremely dull in others. He said that he suffered from chronic constipation, and his belly indicated accumulated fæces and a circumscribed hard tumor in the right epigastric region. Pulse 100; temperature normal, though free perspiration. Facial expression anxious; respiration hurried and conveying the impression that his condition was more serious than the symptoms positively indicated. Treatment was chiefly directed to the arrest of vomiting and production of catharsis, and bland nutritious almentation, all of which proved ineffective, and the vomiting uncontrollable. His condition varied but slightly until August 28, when his restlessness became more noticeable, and he was removed to a room with barred windows for safety. About 3 p. m. of the same day he was seized with tonic convulsions, causing opisthotonos and extension of ankle-joints, and flexion of elbows, wrists, and fingers. There was also marked congestion of capillaries throughout and difficult respiration, with slow heart action. He died at 4 p. m., August 29, 1887.

Necropsy.—Body well preserved; rigidity well marked and ecchymosis in all dependent parts. General appearance of the body indicated that death occurred in a spasm. The flexor muscles are all in a state of contraction; the knees, ankles, elbows, and wrists strongly flexed. Thorax: Lungs non-adherent, but emphysematous and congested, suggesting a heart spasm, causing mechanical pulmonary congestion shortly before death. Heart, weight 720 grams, normal in muscular development and valves not diseased. So-called "chicken fat" clots were found in both cavities, but were readily removed from the valves, although they seemed intimately interlaced with the leaflets. Abdomen: Omentum was very fatty and dry; in fact the dissection throughout showed general dryness of the tissues. Large and small intestines presented evidence of chronic congestion of the mucous coats. Liver cirrhotic, and weighed 1,300 grams. Left kidney deeply congested and sclerosed; both normal in size. Stomach: There was an indurated mass of tissue surrounding the pylorus, which was removed for microscopical examination. The stomach throughout showed marked evidence of chronic catarrhal inflammation. The pyloric induration removed proved, on investigation, to be a non-specific development of tissue, the result probably of long continued inflammatory action and the muscular effort involved in vomiting. This man had been subject to frequent and prolonged attacks of vomiting, and his life was one of intermittent sprees.

ENTERITIS—PERFORATION OF COLON.

L. S. (colored); aged thirty years; nativity, Mississippi; was admitted to Marine Hospital, Memphis, Tenn., June 14, 1888; died June 20.

History.—Had been sick three weeks when admitted. He complained of very frequent stools, severe pain in his belly, and he had some fever. Under treatment the stools became less frequent. June 18 he became delirious. He was shouting at the top of his voice. He died June 20, 1888.

Necropsy.—The colon was intensely congested on its peritoneal surface, and black and sloughing on the mucous surface. In the right loin there was a small perforation of the colon. The intestines were adherent by recent fibrine.

STRANGULATED HERNIA—INGUINAL.

H. C. was admitted to the Delaware Breakwater Quarantine Hospital March 15, 1888, with the following history:

History.—During the last four years has had a number of attacks of pain following the appearance of a swelling in right groin which was relieved by the disappearance of the swelling. When first seen was suffering intense pains and vomiting a dark fluid with a peculiar odor. On examination a swelling was discovered in the course of right inguinal canal and extending into scrotum which responded to the usual tests for hernia. Failing to effect reduction an incision was made over swelling down to sac and the internal ring divided; it was, however, found necessary to open sac which was found to contain a knuckle of intestines and a portion of omentum, both in a highly congested state; they were returned to the abdominal cavity in the order named, the wound closed antiseptically and a compress applied.

March 16.—Complained of pain in region of wound, which was relieved by lessening pressure.

March 20.—Since operation has complained of some pain in region of wound, and on several occasions taken off dressing and gotten out of bed. To-day a small swelling has appeared at upper portion of wound and is accompanied by some nausea and vomiting. The temperature has been normal.

March 21.—The wound when opened was found to be perfectly healthy, and at the upper angle there was a knuckle of intestine which was adherent and so much softened that it was brought out and sutured to the edges of wound. The vomiting ceased for two days, but returned on the 23d, and death took place on the 27th. There were large fæcal evacuations from the intestines after the 24th.

Necropsy (*twelve hours after death*).—The wound through its whole extent was much swollen, and in the lower portion only partially closed. The intestine was firmly attached to upper portion and was patulous. The abdomen was opened in the median line and the following points noted: The parietal peritoneum was much congested and the intestines glued together in many places, and a small amount of dark fluid found in lower portion of cavity. The ileum was the part attached to wound and through the opening the fæces could be freely pressed. The spleen was somewhat enlarged.

INTESTINAL FISTULA.

C. A. M.; aged thirty years; nativity, New York; admitted to U. S. Marine Hospital, New Orleans, La., December 15, 1887; died January 1, 1888.

History.—For the last two years he had suffered from a fistula in the left iliac region, which apparently communicated with the upper portion of the sigmoid flexure, and through which the fæces constantly were passing. He had also a stricture of the rectum and loss of control over the sphincters, due to a bad case of fistula in ano. His general health was fair, though he suffered occasionally from dyspepsia, constipation, and nausea. The stricture of the rectum was treated by gradual dilatation. The rectum above the stricture, as far as a finger could reach, was patent. Around the fistula there was a large mass of infiltrated cicatricial matter. On December 26, 1887, an exploratory operation was performed with the intention of closing the fistula, if possible, and of resecting a part of the colon. An incision was made through the abdominal walls extending from about 5 centimeters above to 5 centimeters below the fistula, and an examination showed that the entire sigmoid flexure was so matted together with coils of the small intestine that a resection was impracticable. During the operation every antiseptic precaution was used, and the wound was closed carefully. The intestines were not opened.

December 27, 1887.—Patient reacted badly; had no pain, but a great deal of nausea and violent vomiting, which was controlled by ice.

December 28, 1887.—Temperature, 37.8° C.; pulse, 110. No urine was passed during the last twenty-four hours, and hot applications were therefore ordered over the kidneys.

December 29, 1887.—Temperature 36.6° C.; pulse, 86. Small amount of water passed (1,066 cubic centimeters), which contained albumen. Bowels moved during the night and the fæces passed per anum; wound looked well, and the patient had no pain. He was given a hot-air bath.

December 30, 1887.—Temperature, 36.8° C.; pulse, 78; comatose last evening, but brighter this morning; had no pain; passed 320 cubic centimeters of urine during the last twenty-four hours; had two liquid passages per anum during the night; there was oozing at the seat of the operation. The hot-air baths had been repeated, and at 6.30 p. m. he was much better, though he still had nausea and vomiting of a regurgitant character, with but little straining. Passed 292 cubic centimeters of urine since morning; specific gravity, 1014, and albuminous.

December 31, 1887.—Passed 208 cubic centimeters of urine during the night; slept well; temperature, 36.2° C.; pulse, 78.

January 1, 1888.—During the night diarrhea and violent vomiting attacked him, and he sank almost immediately, dying within eight hours after the first spell of violent vomiting. Was comatose at first, but after the second passage from his bowels he became conscious. He complained of no pain, but his abdomen swelled up very rapidly. There was, probably, some fæcal extravasation due to the stitches breaking out.

Necropsy (*January* 2, 1888).—Body: Frame thin and spare. Abdomen was distended with gas, but contained only a little fluid. The peritoneum was clear and smooth, except near the seat of the operation, where everything was glued together by old and recent adhesions. There was no separation of the line of sutures, but in some places it was adherent to the visceral peritoneum. The intestines were distended with gas, and a knot of them was engaged in a kind of pocket, formed by the upper part of the rectum and by a mass of adherent intestines and a band of cicatricial tissue. This pocket was sharply defined, dark red, and adherent generally to its surroundings with soft lymph of recent formation. The rectum was, in the upper part, very much contracted; the distal end of the flexure was dilated to a considerable extent, and the remainder was impervious. There existed a passage for the fæces from the lower portion of the colon (about 10 centimeters from its lower end) down to the ampulla. At the lower end of the sigmoid flexure this passage ran behind, close to the pelvic wall, and from this channel, and not from the gut, the fistula branched. The stitches closing the wound were giving way, and it would probably have opened again. The colon about the false passage was contracted, and its muscular walls were thickened. Kidneys were large and congested, and in several places bloody serum was effused under thin capsules. When cut across the vessels looked as if they had been injected. No evidence of peritonitis was found, except in the left iliac region, and that about the constricted portion of the intestine was very recent, and that at the seat of the operation was partly old and partly new.

DIARRHŒA.

W. N.; aged thirty-two years; nativity, Maryland; admitted to marine ward of the German Hospital, Philadelphia, Pa., May 10, 1888; died June 2.

History.—His family history, as far as known, is good. Always has been healthy until December last, when he began to be troubled with attacks of diarrhœa. Up to last fall he weighed 82.5 kilos; when admitted he weighed 60 kilos. He was very anæmic. His principal trouble at this time was malaria, although attacks of diarrhœa developed on and off since December. Soon after admission diarrhœa developed which resisted all means of treatment. The number of stools from the time he was admitted until the day of his death was never less than three and sometimes as many as twelve daily. During this time he wasted rapidly, yet at times stated that he was getting better. His temperature varied very little from the normal point. He died June 2, at 2 o'clock p. m.

Necropsy (*forty-five hours after death*).—The stomach and whole intestinal tract were extremely congested, and at parts suspicious elevations of mucous membranes were observed. Mesenteric glands were greatly enlarged, and on section no tubercular condition could be noticed. Left kidney was exceedingly congested. Nothing abnormal was found in the other abdominal organs nor in those of the thorax.

PARALYSIS OF INTESTINES.

L. S.; aged thirty-six years; nativity, Sweden; admitted to U. S. Marine Hospital, Stapleton, N. Y., December 24, 1887; died January 1, 1888.

Necropsy (*fifteen hours post mortem*).—*Rigor mortis*; livores. On incising the adominal wall gas escaped; there was fecal matter in abdominal cavity. The colon was enormously distended, pushing up the diaphragm and compressing all the abdominal viscera. The sigmoid flexure, while distended as large as the caliber of the stomach, was filled with liquid fæces and gas. No obstruction existed in the rectum; the mucous membrane was intensely congested. Ileum congested on mucous and serous surfaces; hemorrhage of mucous membrane at a point where ileum was compressed. All glands normal. Heart and lungs normal. A portion of the liver was taken and dissolved in the usual manner, and through the solution, filtered while boiling hot, was passed a stream of sulphureted hydrogen. Then the filtrate was washed and dried. There was a slight yellowish deposit on the paper. This was dissolved in nitric acid and treated with potassium bichromate and potassium iodide, and no precipitate obtained. All the examination was conducted under the microscope and no crystals of iodide or chromate of lead were discovered. The paralysis was due to something else.

ACUTE NEPHITIS.

CASE 1.

J. W. (colored); aged twenty-one years; nativity, Mississippi; was admitted to the Marine Hospital, Memphis, Tenn., March 22, 1888; died April 19.

History.—On December 20, 1887, he was treated in the hospital for acute bronchitis and recovered. January 24, 1888, he was admitted with dysentery and discharged February 14, and March 22 he was again admitted. He said he had taken cold. He complained of dyspnœa, pain in his abdomen, poor appetite, great weakness, and a severe headache. His feet, legs, and belly were swollen. Feet and legs œdematous. He denies that he ever had any venereal disease. The urine contained a large amount of albumen and epithelial and blood casts, with free blood and renal epithelium. Under treatment the œdema of feet and legs disappeared. The ascites was more persistent, as was also the albumen in the urine. His appetite improved. The ascites diminished, as did also the albumen inhis urine. April 19 he became comatose and soon died.

Necropsy.—*Rigor mortis* well marked. No scars in groin. Body emaciated. Mesenteric glands enlarged and caseous. One of the glands weighed 30 grams. The spleen was enlarged, and on section 2 square centimeters of healthy spleen could not be found. There were a large number of bodies which resembled on section caseous mesenteric glands. Similar bodies were found in the lungs and liver. The kidneys were enlarged, flaccid, and in the condition of cloudy swelling.

Weight of viscera in grams.—Spleen, 710; liver, 1,900; right lung, 523; left, 522; pancreas, 150; heart, 260; left kidney, 180; right, 200; weight of man in health, 110 pounds, or 50 kilograms.

CASE 2.

J. B.; aged thirty years; nativity, Norway; admitted to U. S. Marine Hospital at Baltimore, Md., June 13, 1888; died June 17.

Necropsy (*twelve hours after death*).—*Rigor mortis* absent; œdema of face, especially about eyes, very marked. On removing the calvarium a small quantity of clear-colored serum escaped. Vessels of the mem branes much injected. Brain tissue apparently normal. Larynx normal. Pericardium contained 30 cubic centimeters of serum. Heart slightly hypertrophied, otherwise normal. Each pleural cavity contained 200 cubic centimeters of fluid. Lungs were greatly distended, showing emphysema and œdema. Liver softer in structure than normal, probably due to granular degeneration. Spleen twice the natural size and completely pulpified. Kidneys small and imbedded in fat; capsules on separation tore away surfaces of kidneys, leaving rough, granular, dark appearance. On cut section kidneys bore whitish aspect, showing numerous minute red points marking capillary hemorrhages. Stomach and intestines half filled with fluid matter. Structure of these organs appeared normal. Bladder empty.

INFLAMMATION OF THE LIVER.

T. G.; aged twenty-three years; nativity, Florida; was admitted to St. Francis Xavier's Infirmary, Charleston, S. C., October 29, 1887; died November 9.

History.—Patient gave a syphilitic history; had been treated at the City Hospital a year previous for typhoid fever, and lived in a malarial region. Temperature normal; tongued furred; area of liver enlarged; some tenderness over the pit of stomach; bowels constipated, and mental hebetude noticeable. A number of bird-shot were noticed beneath the skin of abdomen. Patient was placed upon an alterative and tonic treatment. Symptoms of a gastro-enteritis developed later, and the temperature was slightly subnormal until death intervened.

Necropsy (*twelve hours after death*).—Heart and lungs were normal. The liver was enlarged and carnified. Mucous membrane of stomach and duodenum presented evidences of a subacute inflammation, the membrane being thickened with whitish-colored spots and here and there covered with a tenacious mucous. The appendix vermiformis was found to be of unusual length and pervious throughout. The other organs were normal.

CIRRHOSIS OF THE LIVER.

CASE 1.

J. F. L.; aged fifty-nine years; nativity, Pennsylvania; admitted to marine ward, Mercy Hospital, Pittsburgh, Pa., July 16, 1887; died August 11.

History.—This man had been treated in the hospital previously for bronchitis, accompanied by asthmatic seizures. When admitted, July 16, he still had a troublesome cough; his appetite was poor; there was emaciation; pallor; the tongue was dry, red, and coated, and there was profuse diarrhea. Soon after this, the abdomen became swollen from ascites, which condition continued until death. Physical examination showed feeble breathing at the apices of the lungs, and there were present all of the signs usually found in ascites. The liver dullness was thought to be somewhat lessened in area. An aspirator was twice used to relieve the discomfort caused by the ascites, the last time being on August 9, when 3,500 cubic centimeters of straw-colored fluid were removed.

Necropsy.—The abdominal cavity contained considerable fluid. The intestines were distended with gas, and their vessels enlarged from venous stasis; the peritoneum was everywhere thickened and granular; the stomach presented several large ecchymotic spots; the liver was smaller than its normal size, weighing 1,500 grams; it was covered with lymph from peritonitis, was very hard to the touch, cut with difficulty, especially at the junction of the right and left lobes; it was not easily penetrated with the finger, and its lobules were not apparent to the naked eye. The kidneys were rounded (pig-backed) on the surface and somewhat lobulated; the capsules were removed with difficulty. The spleen weighed 250 grams; its pulp red and soft, easily breaking down on slight pressure. The heart was somewhat fatty in appearance, otherwise normal. There was evidence of peri-bronchial inflammation in both lungs, principally at the upper halves, and the walls of the bronchial tubes were somewhat calcified.

Case 2.

C. W. M.; aged forty-two years; nativity, Virginia; admitted to U. S. Marine Hospital, Boston, Mass., February 11, 1887; died February 12.

Necropsy.—The lower limbs were œdematous, and serum was found in the abdominal and pleural cavities. Both kidneys were enlarged and congested throughout. The liver presented the so-called "hob-nailed" appearance, and weighed 1,750 grams. The lungs were congested, the left lung being adherent to the chest wall.

Case 3.

E. R. D.; aged seventy years; nativity, America; admitted to U. S. Marine Hospital, Cleveland, Ohio, March 10, 1888; died March 13.

History.—Upon admission there was slight hydro-peritonitis, moderate œdema of the lower extremities below the knees, and of the genitalia; some shortness of breath; absence of appetite, general debility and emaciation, but little or no pain or suffering. Upon the most careful inquiry the patient persistently denied having ever used alcoholic or fermented liquors to excess or habitually, claiming that all through his life he had been particularly temperate in this respect, and that he had led a sober, careful life, with no abuse of his health, except the hardships and exposure incident to his calling as a seaman.

Necropsy (fourteen hours after death).—The liver was contracted to two-thirds the natural size, with a smooth surface, and of a tawny color. Upon section the cut surfaces presented a yellowish, nutmeg appearance. There was moderate enlargement of the spleen. Other organs were normal for a man of his advanced years.

Case 4.

W. B.; aged thirty-eight years; nativity, West Indies; admitted to marine ward of the German Hospital, Philadelphia, Pa., February 23, 1888; died March 29.

History.—He was in the hospital from January 12 to 18, 1888, for treatment of scalded hands; to all appearances he was in perfect health at this time, his hands being the only pathological evidence. There was nothing of note, further than the extreme rapidity with which the injured tissues healed under mild treatment. Readmitted, as stated, in a very jaundiced condition, but complaining only of occasional pains in the epigastric region, and he had, also, a distaste for food, especially meats and "greasy stuff." Examination showed a liver of nearly normal size. Just below free border of ribs, on the left side, a tumor was discovered, about 5 centimeters by 6.25 centimeters, somewhat movable, and apparently connected with the spleen, from its location; its nature was not clearly determined. The evacuations were gray and "clayey" in color. On admission, was given hg. chl. mit., to be followed by sodii phos., 3.9 gms., 4 t. d. Next day, ol. ricini, 3.9 gms. every hour, until free stool occurred. This was continued until March 5, when pot. acetas was substituted for the sodii phosp. in doses of 1.34 gms. t. d. March 11 was given a cold-water enemata, 2.15. On the 17th was given ammon. carb., .324 gms. f. r. m., also, fl. ext. pilocarpine, until sweating was produced. At this time the intellect became clouded and eye-sight imperfect, he being unable to distinguish colors or small objects held up before him. Stools like lumps of clay, not formed, but soft and streaked on the surface with blood, and sometimes small, longish blood clots accompanied the stools; vomiting of bloody fluid, "coffee grounds," tongue not heavily coated, an extremely offensive breath, sweetish in odor. Delirium not at any time active or uncontrollable, but rather of a dull, stuporous character. Pulse averaged about 60, as low at one time as 46; the day before death it was 92.

Necropsy (*March* 31, 4 *p. m.*).—The body was well nourished; skin jaundiced; muscles well developed and the tissues dry. The heart weighed 370 grams; the lungs were normal. Right kidney weighed 150 grams; the left, 200. Liver weighed 1,130 grams, and the spleen 395. Kidneys were deeply congested. All the tissues throughout the body stained with bile. Gall bladder entirely empty and very small. The right lobe of the liver was cirrhotic and about two-thirds normal size. The tumor which had been diagnosed during life was found to be the spleen very much enlarged and hardened at its right extremity, which was firmly attached to the left border of the liver by strong, fibrous adhesions. The indurated portion on section was of almost bony hardness and dirty-white color. It had probably been the seat of an infarction of the vessels, followed by degeneration and caseous change.

CASE 5.

A. L.; aged fifty years; nativity, Portugal; admitted to U. S. Marine Hospital, Baltimore, Md., March 27, 1888; died June 1.

Necropsy (*twenty-one hours after death*).—*Rigor mortis* entirely absent. Body well developed but greatly emaciated. Legs very edematous, and abdomen much distended. On making the ordinary incisions in the abdominal walls about 11,520 cubic centimeters of straw-colored serum escaped; a few flakes and strings of mucus were seen in the fluid. Both lungs were somewhat adherent, much congested, and the left showed a beginning degenerative process. The heart was quite small, the right anterior surface containing a considerable deposit of fat, and one of the aortic valves had a calcareous nodule in its substance. Liver small, rough on the surface, firm in consistence, and showed the cirrhotic structure on section. Gall bladder much distended and filled with thin bile. Spleen small and also cirrhotic. Kidneys not more than half the normal size, with several small blebs on the surface, and other indications of the chronic granular kidney. Stomach about half distended with fluid mass. Intestines apparently normal. Bladder empty. Brain not examined.

ABSCESS OF THE LIVER.

CASE 1.

Pneumonia.

J. M. (colored); aged twenty-seven years; admitted to U. S. Marine Hospital, Cairo, Ill., November 27, 1887, suffering from remittent fever; died December 10.

History.—When admitted he had remittent fever (quotidian in type), slight cough, dullness on percussion and absent respiratory murmur over the base of the right lung, and complained of some pain in the right side and right hypochondriac region. The area of liver dullness on percussion was enlarged. The fever gradually became septic in character; rigors were frequent, but at no time was there much pain in the region of the liver. The lung complication was diagnosed as pneumonic, and the presence of a possible abscess of the liver was not suspected.

Necropsy (*six hours after death*).—*Rigor mortis* marked; body emaciated; extensive pleural adhesion on both sides of chest; right lung the seat of gray hepatization throughout the greater part of it, and the substance is infiltrated with caseous deposit; the inferior lobe is cup-shaped, and the pleura covering it is the seat of recent fibrinous deposit; left lung crepitant. A cretifaction the size of a bean was found near the margin of the inferior lobe. The heart and pericardium were healthy. On opening the abdomen the liver was seen to be very large, and there was marked increase in size of both lateral lobes. A large abscess occupied the greater part of the liver, and pointing toward the upper surface had pushed the diaphragm before it and indented the base of the right lung, producing the cup-shaped appearance before alluded to. The apex of the pointing abscess was surrounded by consolidated lung tissue on every side; it had not ruptured, but, in all probability, would have done so in a few days, discharging its contents into the lung or pleural cavity. The abscess contained about 1,000 cubic centimeters of a very thick inoffensive pus. The omentum was wasted and shrunken. The glands of the mesentery were enlarged in patches, and the mucous membrane of the small intestine was congested in places. The vermiform appendix was provided with a distinct mesentery of its own. The other viscera were healthy.

Weight of the viscera.—Right lung, 1,280 grams; left lung, 480; heart, 415; liver, with abscess, 3,552; liver, without abscess, 2,432; spleen, 320; right kidney, 100; left kidney, 190.

CASE 2.

Empyema.

C. H.; aged forty-six years; nativity, Scotland; admitted to U. S. Marine Hospital, Cairo, Ill., November 10, 1887; died January 31, 1888.

Necropsy (*ten hours after death*).—Body that of a middle-aged, muscular man, much emaciated. *Rigor mortis* absent. Yellow subcutaneous fat over entire body; pigmentary deposit in *recti abdominis* muscles; abdominal viscera in neighborhood of ileo-cæcal valve laden with a fetid, unctuous deposit of a grayish-black color. Peritoneum softened and pus-laden. Abdominal cavity contained about 6,000 cubic centimeters of a light-yellow, flocculent, thin pus. Liver enlarged; weight, 2,500 grams; softened capsule detached; anterior border eroded and blackened; right lobe almost completely excavated by a large abscess. Gall bladder moderately full of grumous, purulent, reddish-brown bile. Kidneys normal in size; congested and infundibula laden with pus. Spleen enlarged, engorged, currant-jelly like, and dropping to pieces on being taken out. Bowels highly conjested; vermiform appendix absent. Diaphragm eroded and perforated. Right lung and pleura completely replaced by pus; no trace of either remaining. Left lung congested and exuding pus on section; left pleural cavity filled with pus. Pericardium loaded with fat and containing 90 cubic centimeters of straw-colored serum. Heart, fatty; small; left ventricle hypertrophied and containing air and some coagulated blood. Right heart valves showing calcareous degeneration.

CASE 3.

J. W. (colored); aged twenty-seven years; nativity, Virginia; was admitted to U. S. Marine Hospital, Cincinnati, Ohio, January 20, 1888; died February 27.

History.—On admission patient said he had been sick for about six months. Now has pain over region of liver, especially posteriorly; also in right shoulder and scapula. Lies most comfortably on right side in twisted manner; feet swollen; has chills occasionally; night sweats; slight cough at times, dry and hacking. He has had considerable diarrhea. Anæmia is very marked. Pulse 92; temperature 38° C. No enlargement of the liver.

January 26.—Pain umbilical. *27th. Epistaxis*, which became more profuse and persistent three weeks later.

February 26.—Died from exhaustion.

Necropsy (*six hours after death*).—*Rigor mortis* well marked. Body very much emaciated. Œdema of feet and legs; 64 cubic centimeters of fluid in pericardial sac; 1,500 cubic centimeters in peritoneal cavity; pleural, none. About 128 cubic centimeters of very thick pus in the liver abscess. Other organs normal.

CASE 4.

Perforation of diaphragm and pleura.

H. S.; aged twenty-eight years; nativity, Germany; admitted to U. S. Marine Hospital, San Francisco, Cal., April 5, 1888; died April 17.

History.—An accumulation of pus had been found in the right thoracic region and an opening made through which a silver tube was introduced and the cavity frequently irrigated. This opening was in the sixth interspace and axillary line.

Necropsy (*twenty hours after death*).—Upon opening the abdominal cavity and pushing aside the intestines a thin yellowish-green fluid came in sight, having been held away from the anterior wall by inflammatory adhesions. The fluid contained an abundance of curdy purulent matter. The intestines were bound together quite extensively by recent inflammatory lymph. When the liver was separated from its attachments it was found to be the seat of a large abscess situated in the outer part of the left lobe into which the opening for drainage had been made. The abscess was 12 centimeters in its vertical diameter and 10 centimeters in its horizontal diameter. The liver was fastened by inflammatory adhesions to the diaphragm, and this in turn to the thoracic wall, the right lung having first been displaced upward a distance of 12 centimeters. An opening from the abscess was also found extending through the diaphragm into another abscess of nearly equal size existing in the lower lobe of the right lung. Two small openings also existed on the lower surface of the liver, allowing the abscess in this organ to communicate with the peritoneal cavity. These abscesses on section presented thick greenish macerated walls, and contained no fluids, their inner surfaces being covered with thick, pulpy débris. The right lung presented a few pleuritic adhesions at its apex, at which part there was some consolidated tissue containing a single caseous mass the size of a filbert, grayish in color but not surrounded, apparently, by tubercular matter. The lung tissue in this locality was red from suffused blood. The left lung was normal in appearance. The heart contained a chicken-fat clot extending from the right ventricle into the pulmonary artery. This organ was otherwise normal.

CASE 5.

C. C.; aged thirty years; nativity, Tennessee; was admitted to the Marine Hospital, Memphis, Tenn., March 19, 1888; died May 1.

History.—He has had several attacks of malaria and occasionally a cold; otherwise he had enjoyed good health. He has been a hard drinker. When admitted he complained of a severe lancinating pain in his right side. The pain was located about 5 centimeters below the free border of the ribs in the mamillary line extended. At this point there was a slight bulging. Percussion showed this to be just above the lower edge of the liver. Aspiration showed pus in the liver. The pus was thick and flocculent and would not flow through the aspirating needle. An incision was made and 250 cubic centimeters of flocculent pus evacuated. The cavity was dressed twice daily and syringed with warm bichloride of mercury solution, 1–10000. The cavity discharged a large quantity of pus. After washing thoroughly the cavity was injected with a mixture of iodoform and linseed oil, 1–20. The patient, could take no solid food; he drank from 2.5 to 3 liters of milk daily. After the incision was made there was no fever, the temperature remaining normal. He died from exhaustion May 1, 1888.

Necropsy.—A large scar was observed in each groin from suppurating bubo; body much emaciated; the liver was much enlarged. Besides the abscess which had been opened there were eight others, varying in size from that of a hickory-nut to a large orange. They were not in any way connected one with another. They were all well defined and lined with a pyogenic membrane. All other viscera normal.

LARDACEOUS LIVER AND SPLEEN.

D. S.; aged twenty-four years; nativity, Austria; admitted to U. S. Marine Hospital, Baltimore, Md., November 12, 1887; died January 10, 1888.

History.—The patient, who had been under treatment four months previous with malarial fever, complained upon admission of loss of appetite, irregular stools, thirst, and pains in the hypochondriac region. His general appearance was jaundiced. Percussion and palpitation showed an enlarged and over-sensitive condition of the liver, with its edges serrated. The abdomen and stomach were distended with flatus. The lower extremities slightly œdematous. The patient gave a history of constitutional syphilis. Further examination during the progress of the disease showed an enlargement of the spleen, the size and shape of which could be distinctly felt. Diarrhœa and collapse terminated the case.

Necropsy (sixteen hours after death).—Rigor mortis well developed. Body much emaciated; skin of an earthy hue. Pericardium contained about 30 cubic centimeters of clear, transparent serum. Heart flabby, but, aside from one very small calcareous patch on aortic valves, normal. Both pleural cavities contained a small amount of serum. The right lung was bound down by firm adhesions. Lung tissue appeared anæmic, but showed no sign of organic disease. Spleen weighed 1,990 grams; its surface was smooth, edges rounded; capsule tense and of normal color; organ felt firm; cut sections showed a brownish-red surface, rather dry and glossy, with here and there a yellowish-white pasty body half as large as a pea; the iodine test revealed these bodies to be amyloid in character, showing the typical sago spleen of enormous dimensions. Liver was about the usual size, but it was firm and rounded. Recent adhesions at the surface indicated peri-hepatitis. Cut surface had slight yellowish cast, which also responded to the test for amyloid degeneration. Kidneys slightly larger than is common, and the same characteristic lardaceous material was also found here. Intestines appeared in their normal condition. Peritoneal cavity contained 250 cubic centimeters of straw-colored serum.

FATTY LIVER AND HEART—ŒDEMA OF LUNGS.

N. G.; aged fifty years; nativity, England; a British seaman; admitted to U. S. Marine Hospital, San Francisco, Cal., January 6, 1888; died January 8.

Necropsy (ten hours after death).—Rigor present. Considerable emaciation and œdema of lower limbs. Lungs very much congested and œdematous, except at apices and front of upper lobes, where there was interlobular emphysema. Heart scarcely more than half the normal size; extremely fatty. Upon the pericardium, over the anterior surface of left ventricle, was seen a small area of old fibrinous exudation. Abdomen: Peritoneal cavity was occupied by a considerable amount of serous fluid. No signs of inflammation of peritoneum or intestines. Spleen was remarkably small and leathery. Liver was somewhat smaller than normal, even for a man so small as the subject. In color it was a pale, dirty yellow, extremely fatty, but somewhat firm to the feel, as there was also a fibroid degeneration of the organ. There was considerable bile in gall-bladder, which was rather pale and fluid. The kidneys were both small, even for a man of the subject's small size. The left organ was somewhat lobulated, but there was no adhesion of the capsule, and upon section nothing was seen to indicate a diseased condition. The intestines were pale and anæmic, and contained considerable gas and watery secretion, but did not appear to be anywhere inflamed, as diarrhœa and pain before death had seemed to indicate.

PERITONITIS—PERFORATION OF INTESTINE.

CASE 1.

G. S.; aged forty-one years; nativity, Sweden; admitted to Marine Hospital, Boston, Mass., September 8, 1887; died September 23.

Necropsy (seven hours after death).—Rigor mortis present. Pleural cavity: No adhesions between pleural surfaces; liquid in pericardial sac slightly increased: Abdominal cavity: Upon opening, about a gallon of purulent secretion was let out. A coating of partially inspissated purulent material coated all the peritoneal surface, and was adherent. A perforation was found from the bowel through into the peritoneal sac.

CASE 2.

Tubercle of lungs and intestines.

A. J.; aged twenty-five years; nativity, Friedland; admitted to U. S. Marine Hospital, New York, May 7, 1887; died August 1.

History.—Patient gave history of being sick for seven months previous to his admission; was first taken with a slight cough, followed later on by night-sweats, etc. On admission his general condition was fair; he did not complain of anything except that his cough troubled him at night. Physical examination revealed a considerable consolidation at both apices of the lungs. The disease made rapid progress, and on the morning of July 29 he was taken with a severe pain in stomach and bowels, followed by collapse. There was complete suppression of urine and slight diarrhœa. Patient died thirty-six hours thereafter.

Necropsy (eighteen hours after death).—*Rigor mortis* marked; body extremely emaciated; lungs found to be generally adherent to all the surrounding structures. Acute tubercular deposits were found throughout the lungs, and in some places cheesy foci. In the apex of the right lung there was a large cavity filled with sero-purulent fluid. Heart small, contracted, and pale; valves normal. On opening the abdomen there was evidence of a general peritonitis involving all the organs; there was a great amount of fibrinous exudate, and in the cavity there was about 1,500 cubic centimeters of thick pus. About 2 inches from the pylorus there were two large, necrotic ulcers, perforating all but the peritoneal coat of the bowels, and from this site was the starting point of the peritonitis. The mesenteric glands were considerably enlarged, and contained a considerable amount of cheesy material. Kidneys enlarged; fatty degeneration throughout. Brain not examined.

RUPTURE OF SPLEEN.

W. K. S.; aged twenty-six years; nativity, Maine; admitted to Marine Hospital, Port Townsend, Wash., April 26, 1888; died June 7.

History.—This patient was transferred from Seattle, Wash., with ulcer of the penis and inflammation of lymph glands, which progressed favorably under proper treatment and prompt incision of glands as suppuration occurred. He appeared, however, to be of a lymphatic temperament, with the tendency to a hemorrhagic diathesis. On May 22 he had a profuse epistaxis, which recurred for several days, necessitating astringent insufflation and plugging of the nares. Later still an acute dermatitis of an erysipelateous character appeared upon the buttocks and hips, which rapidly invaded the abdomen, back, and thighs; purpuric spots appearing upon the forearm and hands, accompanied with a high range of temperature, which condition gradually ameliorated. At an effort at stool he fell into a profound collapse, with a partial rally in the course of forty-eight hours, when this condition recurred and death supervened.

Necropsy (sixteen hours after death).—Body well nourished, but anæmic in appearance. Syphilitic scar upon shin. Considerable fat deposit upon the connective tissue. Lungs crepitant and filled with air. Considerable extra fluid in pericardium. Some old adhesions about left lung, while the right was attached to the diaphragm. The heart was enlarged, with considerable deposit of fat between the muscular fibers. Abdominal cavity was filled with blood, and a large clot was noted in the left hypogastric region, which, upon careful removal, weighed 430 grams. The spleen was found to be ruptured and surrounded by an additional clot, in concentric layers, marking the stages of different hemorrhages. Total weight, 740 grams. Spleen alone, 250 grams. The capsule was almost dissected away by the hemorrhage, and a complete pulpy degeneration of the organ had taken place, obliterating every trace of organized tissue. Other organs normal. Gross speaks of rupture of spleen from blows or efforts at stool, which, however, must be necessarily rare. There was no history of a residence of this patient in a hot climate to account for the degeneration of this organ, and no particular symptoms pointing to its disease.

BRIGHT'S DISEASE.

CASE 1.

E. C.; aged sixty-five years; nativity, Ireland; admitted to marine ward, Sisters' Hospital, Buffalo, N. Y., July 5, 1887; died July 28.

Necropsy (twenty-four hours after death).—Body much emaciated, but considerable œdema of both legs. Thorax opened. Some adhesions between pulmonary and parietal layers of pleura on both sides; both lungs contracted and numerous small scars. Heart hypertrophied on left side, and pericardium contained about 120 cubic centimeters of serum; valves normal; stomach was normal; spleen was atrophied and indurated; liver was contracted and hard, and capsule adherent. Peritoneal cavity contained about 1,000 cubic centimeters of straw-colored serum. Kidneys were of normal size; the left was softened, and the pyramids obliterated, and two distinct pockets contained about 5 cubic centimeters of pus each; the right was softened and pyramids obliterated, but no pus was found. The intestines were congested and even inflamed near the ilio-cœcal junction. No further examination was made.

N. B.—This man was an inmate of the Sailors' Snug Harbor of New York, and was out upon a six months' furlough during the summer season.

CASE 2.

P. F. (colored); aged forty-five years; nativity, South Carolina; admitted to marine ward of St. Francis Xavier's Infirmary, Charleston, S. C., May 24, 1887, suffering with asthma; was re-admitted July 8, 1887, with diagnosis of Bright's disease; died August 2, 1887.

Necropsy (twelve hours after death).—*Rigor mortis* well marked. Cellular tissue of lower limbs, scrotum, and penis well filled with serous fluid. The left kidney was first examined and found somewhat larger than normal. It was pale in appearance and the capsule adherent; with the capsule detached the cortical substance was a dusky red color, granular, and was easily broken. To the knife it was rather resistant and firm; the pelvis of the kidney was normal. The right kidney was much smaller than the left and contracted on its surface by several fissures. The capsule when being detached retained portions of the kidney substance and a section of the organ showed a granular aspect, dark red in color. No microscopical examination was made. The heart was much larger than normal and the hypertrophy of the left side was marked. The mitral and aortic valves were normal. The right ventricle was considerably dilated and its walls thin and dark red. The entire external appearance of heart was dark, veins engorged, and almost black. The lungs were normal in size, and very dark in appearance. There was slight emphysema in both organs. Other viscera not examined.

CASE 3.

J. J.; aged fifty years; nativity, Sweden; admitted to U. S. Marine Hospital, Port Townsend, Wash., September 11, 1887; died September 12.

Necropsy (fourteen hours after death).—Rigor mortis not pronounced. Upon incising the skin the subcutaneous tissues were found infiltrated with albuminous fluid. Heart: Examination showed the heart normal in condition and the ventricles filled with *post mortem* clots. Lungs congested, and pleural cavity contained more fluid than normal (about 75 cubic centimeters) on both sides, though no evidence of pleurisy was discoverable. The kidneys were both smaller than normal, especially the left. The capsules were particularly noticed for their thickness and adherence to the cortical substance. Upon section the fibers of the capsules were easily seen, and both the cortical substance and the pyramidal were pronouncedly cirrhotic. The tubuli, under the microscope, were found filled with epithelium in various stages of disintegration, granular matter, and casts of granular character. The urine found in the bladder measured nearly 16 cubic centimeters, and was highly albuminous and filled with granular and hyaline casts.

CASE 4.

A. B. B.; aged forty-eight years; nativity, New York; admitted to U. S. Marine Hospital, New York, August 27, 1887; died October 13.

Necropsy (twenty hours after death.)—Rigor mortis slight; body emaciated. A large cicatrix was noticed in the right inguinal region, which, on dissection, proved to have been caused for the relief of femoral hernia. Lungs, hypostatically congested. Heart, enlarged; left ventricle hypertrophied. Stomach, mucous membrane along the greater curvature showed signs of catarrhal inflammation. Liver and spleen normal. Kidneys sclerosed, very small, capsules adherent. Brain not examined.

CASE 5.

G. H.; aged twenty-six years; nativity, France; admitted to U. S. Marine Hospital, Baltimore, Md., October 14, 1887; died October 24.

History.—For two months before entering hospital the patient felt fatigue on exertion; had less appetite, and became anemic; complained of pain in the head and lumbar region. Within three days he had an attack of facial paralysis on left side; slight dropsy of lower extremities. Examination of his urine showed it scant in quantity, of high specific gravity, and loaded with albumen..

Treatment.—Light but nutritious diet, potassium acetate, and tincture of digitalis, given four times a day; tincture of chloride of iron and potassium chlorate mixture given after meals; bowels kept well open with compound jalap powders. No improvement was obtained; the case terminated with coma and death.

Necropsy (*thirty six hours after death*).—*Rigor mortis* moderate. Brain: Vessels of membrane filled with dark blood, which escaped when calvarium was removed. No localized accumulation and no clotted blood. No atheromatous patches discovered. Brain normal throughout on section. The heart weighed 625 grams, considerably hypertrophied, and tissue anæmic. No blood clots in cavities. Valves normal. Pulmonary artery congested. Lungs deeply congested, otherwise perfect. Liver normal size, but surface and tissue generally showed cirrhosis. Spleen normal. Kidneys: Weight of right, 532 grams; of left, 627. Kidneys twice normal size; capsule slightly adherent; surface presented gentle elevations and depressions, but smooth to touch; color mottled, white, dark red, and brown. Both cortical and medullary substance increased; tissue firm; pyramids distinct; no congestion about calices. Small intestines showed small dark spots of venous congestion scattered here and there. Large intestines similarly congested.

CASE 6.

Tubercle of lungs.

P. B.; aged fifty-nine years; nativity, France; admitted to U. S Marine Hospital, New Orleans, La., September 28, 1887; died November 10.

History.—Patient had been in the hospital for his present disability several times during the past three years, having been much improved each time and rendered able to work. His history was the usual one in such conditions, dying in uræmic coma.

Necropsy (*twelve hours after death*).—Much emaciated, but somewhat œdematous. Adhesions very dense and general over apex of right lung and on the posterior and lateral portions; left lung the same; also adherent to diaphragm; at the apex, the left lung is torn without separating the adhesions. Opened a small pus cavity in the apex of left lung 4 centimeters across; several small purulent deposits observed and the lung found generally disorganized. The right lung contained several purulent deposits; pericardial fluid normal; heart adherent to pericardium in front near apex; heart hypertrophied, valves normal, but aortic valves seem rather rough. Liver larger than normal, firm, and seems healthy; weighs 4,800 grams. Kidneys small and lobulated, several cysts filled with clear fluid on their surfaces; the cortical portion has almost disappeared, and the cut surface in places is white and glistening; many small cysts observed; left kidney like the right. Spleen large, firm, and congested.

CASE 7.

E. O.; aged twenty-two years; nativity, Jamaica; admitted to U. S. Marine Hospital, San Francisco, Cal., October 27, 1887; died November 11.

Necropsy (*fifteen hours after death*).—*Rigor mortis* not pronounced. Some œdema of face; considerable ascites. Chest: Lungs were congested, somewhat edematous. The congestion was most marked in right lower lobe, and the œdema greatest in left upper lobe. Heart was much enlarged and considerably hypertrophied. The muscular tissue was anæmic, but not flabby. There were no clots, and the ventricles were nearly empty. The mitral valve was insufficient from stretching of the orifice. Abdomen contained a considerable amount of fluid (not measured), but no evidence of inflammation. At the point of puncture where trocar had been used the omentum was drawn in when the trocar was taken out, and was firmly held. Liver was hypertrophied and sclerosed, and one and a half times the normal size. Spleen was greatly hypertrophied and congested and as large as a normal liver. Kidneys were both small and hard, nodular and irregular in outline, but capsule readily tore off. The cortex was almost all gone. The left kidney was perhaps two-thirds the normal size, the right only about one-half.

CASE 8.

C. N.; aged forty-eight years; nativity, Finland; admitted to U. S. Marine Hospital, New Orleans, La., October 28, 1887; died November 11.

History.—Is weak and suffering malarial cachexia; has irregular chills; also shows well-marked symptoms of chronic Bright's disease (large white kidneys), also has stricture of urethra. Had a severe chill October 30, a so-called congestive chill, and almost complete suppression of urine following it; went into a comatose state, and died the second day after in the early morning.

Necropsy (eight hours after death).—No adhesions over either lung; lungs seem healthy, but covered with coal dust; 90 cubic centimeters of clear liquid in pericardium; heart enlarged; valves normal; liver large, firm, and weighs 3,000 grams; spleen large and soft; kidneys large and very much congested; capsules strip easily; several small abscesses as big as peas in both of them; bladder nearly empty; urethra shows two strictures, one which would pass No. 2 E., about 5 centimeters from the meatus, the other 7 E., just anterior to the triangular ligament.

CASE 9.

C. D.; aged thirty-nine years; nativity, Cape de Verde Islands; admitted to U. S. Marine Hospital, San Francisco, Cal., November 2, 1887; died November 18.

Necropsy (nine hours after death).—*Rigor mortis* present; little or no œdema, except of face. A full necropsy was impracticable, and indeed unnecessary, but the kidneys were examined. Kidneys both small, each little more than half the normal size. The cirrhotic and fatty changes were equally marked, and apparently to the same extent in each. Both also were full of small peripheral retention cysts, containing clear urine. In addition, a most remarkable feature was a large retention cyst, the size of a small orange, also containing clear urine, which was situated at the lower end of the left kidney; at its attachment to the organ the substance of the latter was slightly indented. The cyst wall was little more than the distended capsule of the kidney.

CASE 10.

Thrombosis of superior longitudinal sinus.

E. P. (colored); aged twenty-nine years; nativity, Ohio; was admitted to U. S. Marine Hospital, Cincinnati, Ohio, July 2, 1877; died December 12.

Autopsy (eighteen hours after death).—Body poorly nourished. *Rigor mortis* well marked. Superficial veins of body generally full. Lungs normal. Heart: Both ventricles, together with large vessels, filled with *ante-mortem* clots; size about normal; valves in good condition. White clot filling entire length of superior long sinus of dura mater. Very great and general fullness of veins of brain surface. Liver and spleen apparently normal. General congested appearance of intestines consequent upon long-continued diarrhea. Kidneys dark in color and greatly congested; weights, 255 and 275 grams, right and left, respectively. Cortical substance twice the natural thickness. Capsule not adherent.

CASE 11.

Pneumonia.

F. J.; aged fifty years; nativity, Germany; admitted to hospital, Galveston, Tex., December 22, 1887; died January 12, 1888. Diagnosis, Bright's disease.

History.—Patient was admitted with constant complaint of difficulty in breathing. The left side of the heart was appreciably hypertrophied. A few days after admission a pneumonia of the lower part of the left lung was developed, resulting in the death of the patient. Delirium was present during the last two days of his life, with almost complete suppression of urine.

Necropsy.—Pneumonia of the lower lobe of left lung. Heart hypertrophied. Kidneys: Left kidney much diminished in size; capsule intimately adherent; outer surface of the gland roughened and granular. The cortical substance was very much atrophied and contained a cyst about 5 centimeters in diameter, extending into the medullary substance. Scarcely any appreciable change in right kidney.

CASE 12.

Cirrhosis of liver—Stricture of rectum—Fistula in ano.

A. A.; aged forty years; nativity, Norway; admitted to U. S. Marine Hospital, San Francisco, Cal., January 23, 1888; died March 2.

History.—When admitted the patient was very much exhausted by long suppuration, and there was general anasarca, which led to an examination of the urine; it was found to contain about one-third of albumen. He improved considerably under treatment, but a persistent diarrhea set in about February 10, and supporting and stimulant treatment failed to overcome its exhausting effect.

Necropsy (ten hours after death).—Body emaciated and ecchymotic in dependent portions, œdema of feet and legs; *rigor mortis* present; stomach and small intestines healthy; numerous ulcerated spots in colon. One portion of the descending colon (the middle third) was hard like cicatricial tissue, and less than one-half the diameter of the remaining portion of the gut. The mucous surface of this portion was extensively ulcerated. Rectum: Stricture found 4 centimeters from the anus. On each side of the anus (about 5 centimeters) there was a fistula, communicating with the rectum about 7 centimeters from the anus. There was another fistula which entered the rectum lower down. The omentum and mesentery were very fatty. Kidneys about one third larger than normal, the right being a little the smaller of the two; cortical substance almost entirely destroyed, and fatty in portions; considerable fatty deposit in the hilum and pelvis of both. The capsules were also fatty and easily detached; liver was contracted to three-fourths the normal size, and its tissue hard and fibrous; gall bladder contained about 75 cubic centimeters of bile and the surrounding structures were bile-stained. Pancreas and spleen appeared to be normal.

CASE 13.

Dropsy—Diverticulum on ileum.

D. J. D.; aged thirty-nine years; nativity, New York; admitted to U. S. Marine Hospital, San Francisco, Cal., January 7, 1888; died March 21.

Necropsy (seven hours after death).—Body still warm; *rigor* present. Abdomen quite full and prominent; lower limbs, arms, and dependent portion anasarcous. Penis and scrotum edematous. Skin pale. Thorax: Pericardium contained a little more fluid than usual. Heart was very large—a true *cor bovinum*, both ventricles greatly hypertrophied, and auricles much dilated. The right heart and its orifices were full of *ante-mortem* clot. The left ventricle, not fully contracted, contained coagulated blood and a fibrinous clot in the aorta attached to the valves. Pleuræ: Both contained considerable fluid, the right by far the greater quantity; in this were some 1,500 cubic centimeters straw-colored serum. The lungs were compressed but natural. Abdomen: There was a peritoneal dropsy of at least 10,000 cubic centimeters, but no peritonitis past or present could be inferred. The cæcum was much dilated and thinned and likewise a part of transverse colon, from long-continued distension with gas, apparently. Near the cæcum, some 25 centimeters up the ileum, was found a remarkable diverticulum opening into the latter gut, 10 centimeters in length. It was distended, quite thin, and appeared like a membranous sacculation of the peritoneal coat of the gut into which it opened, as shown by the accompanying drawing of the specimen. Liver somewhat enlarged, con-

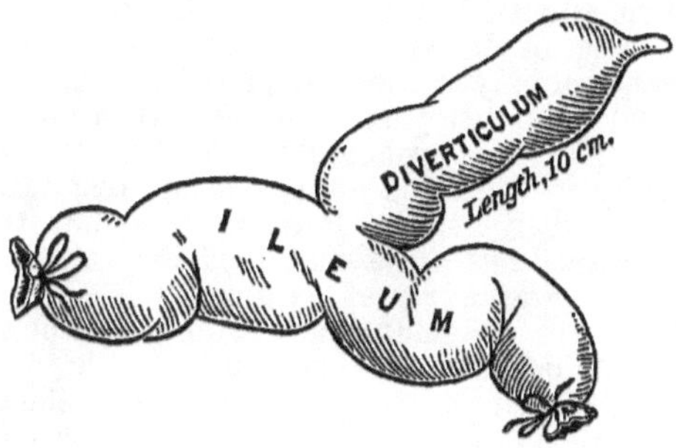

gested, and fatty. Spleen was not remarkable. Kidneys both rather small, granular, full of retention cysts, and quite fatty.

CASE 14.

Kidneys supplied with double sets of blood-vessels.

F. R.; aged thirty-five years; nativity, Norway; admitted to U. S. Marine Hospital, Chicago, Ill., March 6, 1888; died March 30.

Necropsy.—Upper extremities and face emaciated and shrunken; lower extremities œdematous and show several large spots of ecchymosis. Heart small, soft, and flabby; contained fibrinous clots in both ventricles, that in the left extending through the aorta. Cardiac veins dilated and engorged. The kidneys were greatly enlarged, weighing 230 and 250 grams, left and right, respectively; the surfaces of both were smooth and pale, with non-adherent capsules. On section the cortical substance was observed to be greatly thickened and showed a yellowish mottled appearance, while the pyramids were markedly red and well defined. Both organs were supplied with a double set of blood vessels; in the left both sets entered the kidney through the hilum, while in the right the second set pierced the cortical substance about 1 centimeter above the upper margin of the hilum.

Case 15.

Atheroma.

J. L.; aged eighty-one years; nativity, United States; admitted to U. S. Marine Hospital, Stapleton, N. Y., February 29, 1888; died April 10.

Necropsy (eleven hours after death).—Rigor mortis was present. The body contained a large amount of subcutaneous fat. The lungs were found normal, with hypostatic congestion on the posterior surfaces. There was atheroma of the mitral orifice of the heart and of the aortic valves. The left kidney was cystic and cirrhosed; the right kidney the same. The liver was pultaceous and of a dark color. The stomach and intestines were normal. The abdominal aorta was atheromatous and dilated.

Case 16.

Pulmonary emphysema.

R. P.; aged forty-seven years; nativity, Connecticut; admitted to U. S. Marine Hospital, Boston, Mass., April 7, 1888; died April 13.

History.—When admitted patient was suffering from dyspnœa and considerable œdema of lower extremities. The normal respiratory sounds could be heard only at the base of the left lung. Over the entire right lung and the upper portion of the left respiration was high-pitched, noisy, sibilant, and bronchial in character, with marked prolongation of expiration. Owing to the noisy respiration the heart sounds could be scarcely heard. Percussion sounds tympanitic over the entire chest wall. The urine contained a considerable amount of albumen and many granular and hyaline casts. The dyspnœa became progressively worse, amounting to orthopnœa, the sputa sero-sanguinolent, and death occurred suddenly on the 13th.

Necropsy (four hours after death).—Body well nourished and muscular; lower extremities edematous. Both pleural sacs contained a considerable quantity of serum. Right lung: Weight, 1,030 grams; emphysematous, especially at the edges; very edematous, with numerous patches of hepatization. Left lung: Weight, 350 grams; edematous; several tubercular deposits in apex from size of a pea to that of a musket-ball; one of these had undergone softening and another had become calcified; emphysematous at apex. Heart: Weight, 680 grams; left ventricle enormously hypertophied, the walls being 6 centimeters thick and the cavity dilated; mitral valves thickened; aortic valves deformed and extensively calcified. A fusiform aneurism about the size of a small orange involved the ascending and transverse portions of the aorta; this contained an *ante-mortem* clot. Liver: Weight, 1,630 grams; normal. Spleen: Weight, 145 grams, normal. Stomach: Enlarged and distended. Right kidney: Weight, 50 grams; very small and flabby; surface granular; a very thin portion of apparently normal cortical substance was present; remainder of the kidney had undergone extensive fibroid and fatty changes. Left kidney: Weight, 120 grams; surface granular; cortex pale and interspersed with extensive areas of connective tissue. The aggregate amount of normal tissue in the two organs was exceedingly limited. The vermiform appendix contained fecal matter.

Case 17.

J. W.; aged forty-nine years; nativity, Austria; admitted to marine ward, Galveston, Tex., April 17, 1888; died June 20. Diagnosis, Bright's disease.

History.—J. W. was admitted to hospital treatment on April 3, 1888, with diagnosis of remittent fever. Was discharged, recovered from the fever, on April 17, and re admitted on the same day for Bright's disease. Albumen was at no time abundant in his urine, and but few casts of the tubuler could be found with the microscope. His heart pulsated very forcibly, indicating a considerable degree of hypertrophy, but towards the latter part of his life an accumulation of fluid in the pericardium almost entirely prevented one from hearing the cardiac sounds at the apex. Both lungs became very œdematous, and a general œdema came on in spite of active purgation and the use of diuretics. A few days before his death a large phlegmon developed over the right parotid gland.

Necropsy (eighteen hours after death).—General anasarca. Face purple. Large phlegman over right parotid gland. Bed-sore over sacrum. Both kidneys very much atrophied; cortical substances of the right gland almost entirely gone. A few small cysts present in its substance; capsules of both very adherent. Left kidney also showed a thinned cortical substance; its medullary substance was unusually soft and friable. Heart very much enlarged; valves competent. Spleen slightly congested. Lungs œdematous.

ABSCESS OF KIDNEY.

G. R.; aged twenty-one years; nativity, Virginia; admitted to marine ward, Mercy Hospital, Pittsburgh, Pa., September 2, 1886; died November 8, 1887.

History.—Three years before, while living on a farm, he noticed after a hard day's work in the field considerable pain in the right side. This pain continued troublesome about three months, at the end of which time he began to pass blood in the urine. He then noticed some swelling on both sides in the region of the kidneys. The quantity of blood passed was much greater when he attempted to work. After entering the hospital his urine contained a large amount of pus and some blood, and the swelling in the right lumbar region was at times quite apparent, the swelling when most marked extending nearly to the linea alba. With this distension there was considerable pain; so great at night that the use of morphia was required. There was marked hyperaesthesia on the right side, from the lower border of the ribs to the crest of the ileum, and from the spine to the linea alba.

December 22, 1886.—Ether was administered; a long exploring needle was introduced into the kidney at the outer edge of the elector spinæ muscle, and as pus came from the puncture a bistoury was inserted along the groove of the needle, and an opening made sufficiently large to admit the index finger. When this was done the pus flowed rapidly until what was estimated at 1,000 cubic centimeters was obtained. As the finger was passed through the incision the inner surface of the kidney could be distinguished, divided by several thin partitions. A drainage tube was introduced. The patient was much improved after this procedure, the pain disappearing; the urine became clear, except a slight discoloration from blood, and he was for a time more comfortable in every way. After a time, however, the left side became painful and he finally died from gradual exhaustion.

Necropsy.—The omentum contained quite a quantity of fat; intestines healthy. The left kidney was greatly increased in size by extension of the medullary portion, the cortex being quite narrow. At its lower extremity there were three communicating cysts, each about the size of a filbret, and containing a substance which was about the color and consistence of white lead. The kidney substance had a waxy appearance, and gave the characteristic brown color with iodine. The right kidney was considerably smaller than normal; its capsule was intact and there were no signs of suppurative process around the organ. The opening for drainage was still patulous. The medullary portion of the kidney seemed to have disappeared, the inner cut surfaces presenting apertures at the points where pyramids had existed; these apertures communicated with each other and with the pelvis of the kidney; the cortex was quite thin and the external surface lobulated over the pus cavities. The spleen was hard and presented the sago appearance of waxy degeneration. The liver was of normal size and light colored. The walls of the heart were fatty from degeneration. The left lung was universally adherent. Its tissues were congested; the bronchial tubes calcified and a tubercular nodule 2 centimeters in diameter at its apex. The right lung presented some pleuritic adhesions and a similar nodule to that in left, at its apex, but it was of softer consistence.

DISSEMINATED SUPPURATIVE NEPHRITIS.

CASE 1.

Stricture of the urethra.

J. V. (colored); aged thirty-four years; nativity, South Carolina; admitted to marine ward of St. Francis Xavier's Infirmary, Charleston, S. C., July 9, 1887, suffering with stricture of the urethra.

History.—Patient stated that he had suffered with a dribbling of urine for the past year, and had previously noticed that his stream of urine had perceptibly lessened in force and size. He had a gonorrhœa several years ago, and had been treated for six months for irritability of the bladder, when he sought relief at this office. An examination was made, and a stricture found in the membranous urethra. The patient was sent to the hospital, and on the following day was placed on the table for a more thorough examination. Chloroform being administered, I succeeded, after many attempts with smaller instruments, in introducing a conical sound, No. 30, Fr. scale. On account of the weak action of the heart it was decided not to continue the inhalation of the anæsthetic. The patient was then consigned to his bed and on the same evening was seized with a severe chill, the fever rising to 40.5° C. Ten-grain doses of antipyrin were given, and a reduction of temperature followed. On the 14th, a. m., the temperature was 36.1° C., and was 37.2° C., p. m. During the night of the 14th he had another rigor, followed by a temperature of 40°. The temperature still continued to remain above 38.8° until, on the morning of the 18th, he expired. During his illness the pulse was weak, and at times intermittent. Just before death he discharged about a liter of yellowish, frothy fluid, which flowed spontaneously from mouth and nostrils. Two distinct convulsions occurred, and during the entire illness his mental condition was obtuse and gradually deepened into coma.

Necropsy (*twenty-four hours after death*).—*Rigor mortis* slight and decomposition prominent. Abdomen first opened, and intestines found distended with gas. The peritoneal cavity contained about 60 cubic centimeters of dark sanguineous fluid. The spleen was hypertrophied and darkened from malarial congestion. The left kidney was of large size and the capsule perforated by the opening of abscesses in the cortical substance. Diffuse points of suppuration appeared throughout the substance of the cortical portion, and the entire kidney was in an advanced state of disintegration. The pelvis of the kidney was slightly dilated and contained about 3 or 4 cubic centimeters of pus. The right kidney was in a more advanced stage of suppuration, its parenchyma being easily torn and the abscess cavities being larger and more extensive. The pelvis was also distended with about 4 cubic centimeters of pus. The ureters were but slightly enlarged in caliber. The thickening of the inner coat of bladder was quite marked, and ecchymotic spots were distributed over the surface. It contained about 50 cubic centimeters of urine mixed with pus and blood. The urethra was opened, and a dark spot was found in the membranous portion. The stricture was of large caliber. Liver was normal in size, but *post-mortem* hypostatic congestion appeared on its lower surface. Heart normal in size and valves healthy. Slight traces of inflammation of endocardium were seen in left auricle. Lungs and brain not examined.

CASE 2.

Stricture of the urethra—Pyonephrosis—Uremic coma.

M. B. (colored); aged forty-seven years; nativity, Tennessee; admitted to the U. S. Marine Hospital, Cairo, Ill., suffering from stricture of the urethra, extravasation of urine, cystitis, and pyonephosis; died October 30, 1887.

History.—He was first admitted to hospital at Cairo, on May 1, 1887, suffering from a very tight urethral stricture, almost cartilaginous in structure, and which extended through the greater portion of the spongy portion of the urethra. The urine was passed only in drops, and it was necessary to aspirate the bladder several times in order to relieve him. The urethra was opened by continuous dilatation until the urethratome could be introduced, when the stricture was divided and afterwards stretched to the full extent of the divulsor. The urine at that time contained pus, and the frequent calls to urinate indicated contraction of the bladder. A sound was passed from time to time, medicines were administered for the relief of the cystitis, and he left the hospital much improved on August 2, 1887. He was instructed how to use a soft gum instrument, given the proper size, and advised to use it at regular intervals. On October 15, 1887, he again applied for admission. The stricture was a second time divided and dilated, but there were several sinuses in the scrotum and perineum, the calls to urinate were more frequent, attacks of somnolence set in, and the condition of the patient was much worse. The urine was very offensive, contained much pus, and frequent pain was complained of in the back and along the course of the ureters. His condition gradually grew worse and he died in coma on the morning of October 30, 1887.

Necropsy.—Body emaciated. Extensive pleural adhesions on both sides of the chest. Lungs emphysematous at the anterior and upper surface of superior lobes. Heart normal in size; slight beady patches on mitral valve; other valves healthy; atheromatous patches in wall of aorta. Liver fatty. Spleen about normal in size and consistence. Kidneys very small; pelvis filled with pus; secreting structure almost destroyed; ureters filled with pus and dilated to about the size of the forefinger; bladder very small, walls very thick and mucous membrane the seat of chronic cystitis. Stomach and intestines were healthy. Weight of viscera: Right lung, 640 grams; left lung, 1,042; heart, 544; liver, 2,304; spleen, 384; right kidney, 64; left kidney, 128.

CARIES OF SPINE—TUBERCULAR—ABSCESS OF KIDNEY.

A. N.; aged thirty-three years; nativity, Finland; admitted to U. S. Marine Hospital, New Orleans, La., October 27, 1887; died March 18, 1888.

History.—This case was transferred from the Contract Hospital at Galveston, Tex. Patient suffered from Potts's disease of the spine and tubercle of the lungs. Had also acquired the opium habit. Continued to use opium or morphine in small quantities up to time of death.

Necropsy (fourteen hours after death).—Body medium size, emaciated. Antero-posterior curvature of spine. Thorax: Pleura adherent to both lungs. Lungs infiltrated with tubercle; left lung contained a cavity the size of an orange. Pericardial fluid normal. Heart dilated and slightly hypertrophied. Spleen large and soft. Liver amyloid. Kidneys slightly enlarged; left kidney contained an abscess about the size of a hazelnut. Ureters dilated into pouches (hydro-nephrosis) and apparently tubercular to the naked eye. No microscopical examination was made. Caries of eighth and ninth dorsal vertebræ. Brain and cord not examined.

CARIES OF SACRUM—PSOAS ABSCESS.

W. C.; aged twenty-one years; nativity, Maine; admitted to U. S. Marine Hospital, Portland, Me., January 9, 1888; died March 12.

History.—Two years previous to the above date of admission he had fallen from aloft to the deck, a distance of about 20 feet, striking upon his back and spine, particularly the caudal end. It appears from the records of this station that he was admitted to hospital September 20, 1886, and discharged October 11, 1886, "improved." The diagnosis entered was valvular disease of heart and sciatica, and he was treated with cod-liver oil, digitalis, iodide of iron, and repeated blisters on the hip. He applied to the present surgeon in charge for treatment of a "tumor" on the posterior sacral region. Examination of the swelling revealed a pus sac as large as a hen's egg, and upon admission it was opened and explored with Nelaton's probe, which followed along subcutaneously from the posterior opening to a point just back of the great trochanter, where a counter-opening was made and drainage established. About 250 cubic centimeters of flocculent, inspissated pus was evacuated when the tumor was opened. He gradually improved as to this particular lesion, the discharged lessened, the anterior opening was allowed to close, and his discharge from hospital was under consideration at his request about a month after admission when the secretion became more profuse without apparent cause. About the middle of February the patient had an attack of tonsilitis and pharyngitis of a severe and obstinate character, accompanied by a high and persistent febrile movement. Inability to take solid food, and liquid only with great difficulty, reduced his vital powers greatly, and artificial feeding by rectum was resorted to, so rapidly did he begin to show signs of emaciation and septicæmia. This condition was followed by an intense sciatic neuralgia with flexion of the knees on the abdomen. Large doses of alcoholic stimulants with milk and beef tea were continually given, when they could be taken, and morphia in large doses was constantly required. The wound continued to discharge freely a poor, sanious, disorganized pus, sordes appeared on the teeth, a distressing cough and putrid expectoration, in fact all the fatal symptoms of profound septicæmia. The sciatic neuralgia was soon determined to be a developing psoas abscess which shortly discharged through the original opening made to evacuate the sacral abscess. He died from gangrene of the lungs, septicæmiœ, and exhaustion, March 12, sixty-three days after admission.

Necropsy.—The parents of the deceased would only consent to an examination of the seat of the injury and its connecting passages. The sacrum was found carious and necrotic, particularly the second and third spinous processes, and the latero-posterior surface adjoining extending into and involving the sacral foramina, and the anterior surface in contiguous spots. The abscess dependent upon this necrosis had burrowed in every direction under the glutæus, and about the obturator and gemelli muscles. The psoas abscess was followed up through the great sacro-sciatic notch, and almost the entire body of the muscle was gone, leaving only the sac which was full of the characteristic pus. Some caries of the upper lumbar vertibræ was noted. It seems evident from a *post-mortem* view of the case that the original cause of the trouble was the fall, which either fractured the spinous processes of the sacrum, or set up a chronic ostitis ending in necrosis and abscess. This lasting over a year produced a cachectic condition terminating in septicæmia, which excited the formation of the psoas abscess and caries of the lumbar bodies. In a patient whose general health had always been "delicate," as his parents stated, probably having a latent tendency to tuberculosis, the train of symptoms was inevitable from the first.

MUSCULAR ATROPHY—FATTY DEGENERATION.

B. H.; aged thirty-six years; native of Finland; admitted to U. S. Marine Hospital at Boston, Mass., May 8, 1888; died May 16.

History.—Had not been well for a long time, and three months previous to admission he began to suffer with pains of a rheumatic character, and weakness and stiffness in the right arm. These symptoms steadily increased in severity and extended to the other arm, including the muscles of the neck; and also, to a slight extent, those of the lower extremities.

On examination the muscles of the upper extremities, chest, and back were observed to be much emaciated; the scapulæ, especially the right, projected from the back like wings; the muscles between the metacarpal bones of the thumb and first finger of both hands were markedly atrophied. Patient stated that he had lost about 40 pounds in weight within three months. The intercostals and diaphragm also seemed affected, patient being unable to draw a deep breath, and on attempting it the ribs remained motionless; and notwithstanding a strong desire to cough, his greatest efforts resulted in a slight, unsatisfactory grunt; said he "couldn't cough." There was no improvement under the use of electricity and strychnine. On the 14th the dyspnœa became distressing and continued to increase until 12 o'clock on the 16th, when the patient died from apnœa.

Necropsy (two hours after death).—No *rigor mortis;* muscles of chest and upper extremities considerably atrophied. On close inspection of the intercostals they seemed completely transformed into fat, and fatty degeneration could also be detected in the diaphragm, but not to the same extent. Other muscles were examined, but the degeneration in them was not so apparent. Heart: Weight 400 grams and normal. Lungs: Right, weight 680 grams; left, 550 grams; normal in appearance; no pleuritic adhesions. On cutting into them considerable congestion was found at both bases and the bronchial tubes contained a large quantity of mucus. Liver: Weight 2,010 grams and normal. Kidneys: Weight, right, 240 grams; left, 240 grams, both normal. Spleen: Weight, 200 grams; normal. All the viscera were remarkably healthy in appearance. Subsequent microscopical examination of samples of the intercostals and diaphragm confirmed the naked eye appearances, showing almost complete fatty metamorphosis in the intercostal muscular fibers, but to a less extent in the diaphragm.

SUPPURATIVE ARTHRITIS.

Knee-joint.

C. M.; aged forty-five years; nativity, United States; admitted to hospital at Galveston, Tex., July 22, 1887; died August 17, 1887.

Necropsy (eighteen hours after death).—Body well nourished; skin slightly yellowish in color, with large purplish spots on right side of back, and bed-sore 5 centimeters in diameter on the right sacroiliac junction. On opening the thorax, each pleural cavity was found to contain about 150 centimeters of purulent matter, the result of pyæmic suppurative pleurisy. The lungs contained no metastatic abcesses, but were both congested and œdematous, a considerable quantity of bloody serum escaping on section; excised portions of the upper lobe of right lung sank in water. Heart normal; liver and kidneys slightly swollen; other organs normal. On opening the right knee-joint, which, during life, had been the seat of suppurative synovitis (and which had been drained by tubes, passing one through the synovial membrane beneath the patella, and another entering the joint through the popliteal space), the incrusting cartilages of the femur and tibia were found eroded in three separate spots. That of the patella was intact, though lacking its normal luster. The femur posteriorly was denuded of its periosteum for the space of 5 centimeters above the knee-joint. Oh the inner surface of the thigh there was a burrowing of pus along the insertion of the adductoe magnus muscle.

MULTIPLE INJURY.

Fracture of clavicle, first, second, third, and fourth ribs, scapula, and superior and inferior maxillary bones.

J. P. (colored); aged twenty-four years; nativity, Kentucky; admitted to U. S. Marine Hospital, Memphis, Tenn., September 13, 1887; died September 13.

History.—This patient I first saw on the steamer *T. B. Sim.* He was lying on his back in the sun. His face had been cut in two places and a physician had stitched them. The physician said that his lower jaw had been broken. He had been hurt by holding one end of the gang-plank while some negroes ran ashore. The plank caught him and jammed him against a post. On admission his pulse was very rapid and feeble, 150. He gave rational answers to a few questions. The examination was so painful that ether was administered. The left arm was pulseless and dead; *rigor mortis* was already present in it. There were present compound comminuted fractures of the clavicle, first, second, third, and fourth ribs, scapula, superior and inferior maxillary bones. The muscles of the back and left chest were crushed into a semi-fluid mass. The left pleural cavity had been opened. The dead arm was removed and the contused tissues disinfected. There was no reaction, though stimulants internally and hot water externally were used. He failed and died at 8 p. m., in two hours after admission.

Necropsy.—Confirmed the examination. Body that of a man who would weigh 80 kilos. All internal organs healthy.

Weight of organs.—Left kidney, 120 grams; right, 105; heart, 345; liver, 1,381; spleen, 213; left lung, 446; right lung, 575.

SCALD OF BODY (STEAM).

CASE 1.

P. H.; aged thirty-two years; nativity, Ireland; admitted to U. S. Marine Hospital, Stapleton, N. Y., January 22, 1888; died January 23.

Necropsy (twenty eight hours post mortem).—The skin over the entire body was more or less destroyed by the steam, being worse about the neck and back. On opening the thorax the lungs were found congested and the bronchial tubes were inflamed from steam inhaled. Abdominal viscera normal.

CASE 2.

J. C.; aged twenty-six years; nativity, United States; admitted to U. S. Marine Hospital, Stapleton, N. Y., January 22, 1888; died January 24.

Necropsy (twenty-two hours post mortem).—Body of a large, well developed male. *Rigor mortis.* The skin of the body was destroyed in patches of various sizes. The face was swollen. The cornea were destroyed by steam. The trachea and bronchi were congested. The lungs were œdematous. The other viscera were normal.

CASE 3.

Entire body.

M. M.; aged twenty-eight years, nativity, Germany; admitted to Marine Ward Providence Hospital, Washington, D. C., June 11; died June 18, 1888.

History.—He was badly scalded by the giving way of a steam valve on the tug *Hercules*, and as he was exposed to the heated steam for some minutes after the accident it was thought that he necessarily had inhaled some of it. The burns on the exposed parts of the body were dressed with cotton waste and "carron oil" while on the tug, and the patient then conveyed to the hospital. When admitted the clothing was carefully removed, and the burns again dressed with "carron oil." He did not show at this time any symptoms of collapse, but complained of severe pains. The burns were of the first, second, and third degrees, and involved the head, neck, trunk, arms, hands, and lower extremities, in fact nearly the entire surface of the body. Hypodermatic injections of morphia were given for the relief of pain. No elevation of pulse or temperature was noted.

June 12.—No pain in the throat or chest; voice strong; no difficulty in breathing; temperature, normal; pulse, 90 per minute; voids his urine without help, and says that only for the pain in the burns he would feel pretty well. All blisters were punctured to allow the serum to drain away and a dressing of carbolized oil applied. Morphia was still given for the relief of pain, and sufficient nourishment provided.

June 13.—Temperature, normal; pulse, 90 per minute; passed a pretty good night; complains of much pain in his back; burns again dressed with carbolized oil. No throat or lung trouble. Passes urine in good quantities. On the evening of June 13 the temperature was 38.4° C.; pulse 100 per minute; very restless, and has much pain in the back, hands, and arms. He can not lie on either side, and lying on his back so presses on the raw surfaces that a great deal of suffering is caused.

June 15.—Passed a bad night; temperature, 39° C.; pulse, 100; respiration, 22; dressing changed to equal parts of bismuth, subnit. and sodæ bicarb. dusted over the burns. This application was followed by severe pain and the patient asked that it be discontinued. Morphia has been given as required and nourishment has been taken freely. The evening temperature was 39° C.; pulse, 120 per minute; respiration, 25. Complains much of his back. There has been great thirst since the reception of the injury, probably due to the attendant fever and great serus drain from the denuded surface of the skin.

June 16.—Temperature, 39° C; pulse, 120; respiration, 23 per minute; tongue, clean; takes a fair amount of nourishment; complains of great thirst; passes urine and fæces naturally. During the day he became delirious; the delirium was active in character, patient making frequent attempts to get out of bed. Chloral hydrate and pot. bromide were administered during the day, and towards evening he became quieter. Evening temperature, 41° C; pulse, 120; respiration, 25.

June 17.—Passed a very bad night; very delirious, and it required two attendants to keep him in bed; delirium continues, but is low and muttering, and he is evidently sinking; still restless, and there was so much difficulty in taking the temperature that it was abandoned. Pulse, 120; respiration, 26; tongue, dry and brown; 16 cubic centimeters of ol. ricini were given at 6 a. m., and the bowels have moved two or three times. He still passes urine in fair quantities; burns dressed with carbolized oil; dressing difficult, owing to the struggles of the patient; delirium continued during the evening and night, the patient gradually growing weaker, and at 5 a. m., June 18, 1888, he died.

Necropsy (*five hours after death*).—Body that of a well-nourished man. *Rigor mortis* present. Cuticle nearly all destroyed. The abdomen is the only part of the body free from burns. Brain: Venous and arterial congestion noted on removal of calvarium; marked injection of the pia mater over the convexity, sides, and base of the brain, with effusion of lymph over the sulci, near the sylvian fissures. Section of the brain tissue showed numerous puncta vasculosa, and there was decided softening of the corpus callosum, cura cerebri, thalmus opticus, and fornix. The choroid plexes were congested. The larynx was free from œdema;

the vocal chords were clear, free from swelling, and normal in appearance. The lining membrane of the larynx and trachea was free from inflammatory changes. Both lungs were congested, presenting at the lower lobes a condition similar to the stage of engorgement in pneumonia. A few recent pleuritic adhesions existed at the base and posterior surface of the right lung; none were found at the apex or on the left side. Excepting the congestion, the lung tissue was otherwise healthy. The heart was normal in size and valves healthy, with the exception of one of the semi-lunar valves of the pulmonary artery, which was perforated at its junction with the wall of the aorta by a small opening, smooth, polished, and probably congenital. The stomach was much distended with a grumous-looking fluid, and its mucous membrane was congested in patches. The mucous membrane of the duodenum was not congested, and there was no evidence of ulceration in any part of the intestinal tube. The liver was large and healthy in structure. The kidneys were not congested. The other viscera were healthy.

FRACTURE OF SKULL.

Case 1.

Rupture of middle meningeal artery—Compression.

N. B.; aged twenty-eight years; nativity, Ohio; admitted to U. S. Marine Hospital, Memphis, Tenn., October 27, 1887; died October 28.

History.—He was completely unconscious and relaxed. There was no one to give any history. His respiration was irregular and stertorous. At times he would cease to breathe for from five to ten seconds, then take several regular respirations and stop again; respirations shallow; pulse feeble and very irregular—sometimes it would intermit every second beat, then beat very rapidly. Feet cold; pupils fixed and not responsive to light. No reflex could be elicited. There was a contusion of the skin over right frontal eminence. Skin badly contused, but not broken. There was a contused wound of the scalp 5 centimeters from the attachment of the ear to the head and 10 from the external angular process of the frontal bone. The wound was 3 centimeters long and 1½ broad. Hot-water bottles to extremities, digitalis, brandy, and ammonia hypodermically gave no reaction nor any appreciable effect. He died at 1 a. m. of the 28th October, six hours after admission.

Necropsy (nine hours after death).—*Rigor mortis* well marked. Small scars on right knee, and one large scar in right groin. On left side of head, 5 centimeters from the attachment of ear to head and 10 from external angular process of frontal bone, there was a contused wound of scalp, 3 centimeters long by 2 broad, extending to the bone. There was no fracture at the seat of injury. There was a fracture of the left parietal bone at its lower anterior angle. This fracture began 4 centimeters from the anterior inferior angle, and met the coronal suture 5 centimeters from the above angle. The serrations were broken along the coronal suture to a point 4 centimeters beyond the lambdoidal suture. The fracture extended through the great wing of the sphenoid to the anterior lacerated foramen. Within the skull there was a large flattened clot between the dura mater and the skull. The clot inside would correspond in its upper anterior and posterior boundaries to the attachment of the temporal muscle externally. Inferiorly the clot was thinner and extended to within 1½ centimeters of the basilar process of the sphenoid bone. The clot weighed 70 grams, and was formed from blood which had escaped from the middle meningeal artery, which had been torn where it crosses the spheno-parietal suture. Viscera normal. Brain: In the middle temporo-sphenoidal convolution there was a clot which weighed 5 grams; this clot came from a torn branch of the middle meningeal artery. The dura was adherent each side of the longitudinal sinus to the brain.

Weight of viscera.—Right lung, 906; left, 638; liver, 2,437; spleen, 537; right kidney, 171; left, 217.

Case 2.

F. O.; aged twenty-seven years; nativity, Holland; admitted to Grace Hospital, Seattle, Wash., December 10, 1887; died same day.

History.—The patient was injured by falling through the hatchway, a distance of 25 feet, and striking on his head. On examination at the hospital, two hours after the injury, a contusion was found near the center of the vault with much extravasation beneath it. Also a large swelling in front of and above each ear from extravasation beneath the scalp. He was in a completely comatose condition when admitted and died two hours afterwards.

Necropsy (eighteen hours after death).—*Rigor mortis* well marked. On removing the scalp, large clots were found over the location of the anterior fontanelle and at each end of the coronal suture. The force of the blow was received at the junction of the sagittal with the coronal suture, completely disarticulating the coronal suture along its entire length. A small segment was broken off the anterior superior angles of both parietal bones and slightly depressed. From this point on each side a fracture extended backwards and outwards across the parietal bones to the lambdoid suture. Both of the lateral and the superior longitudinal sinuses were ruptured.

Case 3.

Multiple injury.

J. McC.; aged twenty-eight years; nativity, Ireland; admitted to U. S. Marine Hospital, Port Townsend, Wash., July 25, 1887; died July 26.

Necropsy (fourteen hours after death).—*Rigor mortis* present and pronounced. Physical appearance: The entire face was deeply ecchymosed and several bruises were found over its right side and also over the chest wall. Blood was making its exit from both ears, the nostrils, and from the ruptured right eye; the aqueous humor had escaped. Upon examination of the brain substance the right frontal convolution was found inflamed and the meninges upon that side were in a state of high vascularity, with patches of ecchymosis. The parietal bone upon the right side was comminuted near the posterior inferior angle, though the middle meningeal artery was intact. The petrous portion of the left temporal was fractured, probably by *contre coup.* No marks of external violence were visible upon that side. Three ribs, the second, third, and fourth on the right side, were fractured and the lung perforated by fragments of the broken third rib. The patient died in collapse a few hours after admittance.

GUNSHOT WOUND (OLD) OF VERTEBRAL COLUMN.

Aneurysm of ninth intercostal artery.

W. H. (colored); aged twenty-eight years; nativity, Mississippi; admitted to U. S. Marine Hospital, Memphis, Tenn., April 26, 1888; died May 6.

History.—This patient had been in the hospital in August, 1887, for gunshot wound of the abdomen. The bullet entered the body 8 centimeters below the left nipple and 5 centimeters from the median line. The men who came to the hospital with him said he had vomited much blood and had passed considerable by the bowels. He had the hue peculiar to his race when much blood had been lost. There was no evidence that hemorrhage was taking place when he was admitted. It was thought that the bullet had passed through the stomach and become imbedded in the muscles of the back. For the first few days only cracked ice was given by mouth; enemata of milk and beef tea per rectum. He made a good recovery and was discharged after being in the hospital two weeks. He did very well till Christmas, when he went on a spree. He immediately grew worse and was again admitted April 26, 1888. He complained of pain along the course of the lower dorsal and upper lumbar nerves. This pain was paroxysmal, coming on once or twice daily, and was most severe at night. No trace of the bullet could be found. He had lost much flesh and complained of vertigo when standing up. His pain became less and was scarcely felt. Sunday, May 6, he ate his dinner, went to the water-closet, and returned to his bed. In a few minutes he was dead, without sign of pain or distress.

Necropsy.—Body emaciated. Many pigmented scars on legs and thighs. The bullet passed through the chest wall into the abdominal cavity and again into the thoracic cavity. It passed twice through the diaphragm and was found imbedded in the ninth dorsal vertebra. The ball was on the right side of the spine. It had passed close to the aorta and the intercostal artery. Nearly the whole of the body of the ninth and a part of the eighth dorsal vertebræ were eroded. An aneurysmal sac had been formed by suppuration, involving the ninth intercostal artery. The blood at first was retained by the pleuræ, which had become adherent. Then a part of the left lower lobe had become involved. Then this yielded and death came instantaneously. The blood clot in the left pleural cavity weighed 600 grams, and there were 851 grams of fluid besides.

Weight of viscera.—Heart, 270 grams; right lung, 326; left, 317; spleen, 174; right kidney, 220; left, 177; pancreas, 102; liver, 1,699.

GUNSHOT WOUND OF THE CHEST AND ABDOMEN.

L. M. (colored); aged twenty-two years; nativity, Louisiana; admitted to U. S. Marine Hospital, Cairo, Ill., August 10, 1887, suffering from a gunshot wound of the chest and abdomen; died August 15.

History.—He was wounded on August 7, 1887, at a landing on the Tennessee River and was taken on his boat, the *City of Florence*, to Cairo for treatment, arriving at 11 p. m., August 10, 1887. On admission he complained of little pain, but was much depressed and frightened; the pulse was 86, the temperature $38\frac{3}{5}$° C., and the respiration 20; there was slight tenderness over the abdomen, but no tympanitis. The ball had entered the chest almost in the axillary line on the left side, between the sixth and seventh ribs, and was found lying under the skin on the right side anterior to the fifth costal cartilage. The ball was removed from its position; found to be of 38.caliber, conical in shape, and lying beside it was a piece of costal cartilage. During the night the patient was delirious; in the morning the temperature rose a little and there was considerable tenderness over the abdomen. The question of laparotomy was considered, but so long an interval (August 7 to 11) had elapsed between the receipt of the injury and the reception of the patient that it was decided such an operation would be hopeless. He continued in the same condition, the temperature rising on the night of August 12 to 40° C. The delirium continued, but there was not much tenderness over the abdomen. On the afternoon of August 13 he was evidently sinking, and at 4 a. m. on the morning of the 15th he died.

Necropsy (*ten hours after death*).—*Rigor mortis* well marked; body that of a healthy young negro. Brain showed slight cortical congestion; membranes and structure otherwise healthy. Abdomen much swollen, and on section general peritonitis was found. The intestines were matted together in their entirety, and the cavity contained a large quantity of bloody serum. The course of the ball was as follows: Entering between the sixth and seventh ribs on the left side; it carried away a portion of the anterior border of the spleen, passed through the gastro-splenic omentum, wounding a large artery in its course; it then passed through both walls of the stomach, emerging near the lesser curvature; then through the liver (left lobe), emerging to the right of the suspensory ligament; then through the diaphragm, fifth costal cartilage, and lodged under the skin in the position already described. The course of the ball was transversely upward and forward, and the wound was mortal from the beginning. All of the viscera were healthy.

PENETRATING WOUND OF ABDOMEN (STAB).

G. C. L., aged twenty-nine years; admitted to marine ward, German Hospital, Philadelphia, Pa., October 27, 1887.

History.—His previous history, derived from the verbal statements of himself and friends and from the physician who first attended him, presents the following facts: On July 7, 1887, being at the time in good health, and about an hour after eating a full meal, he was stabbed with a dirk knife at a point about 3.75 centimeters to the left of and 2.5 centimeters below the umbilicus. Dr. R. J. White, Chincoteague Island, Va., by request of this office, has submitted the following notes of his connection with the case:

Mr. L. was stabbed on 7th of July, 1887, about dusk. I saw him in five minutes after the cutting took place. He was suffering intense agony. After examination of wound and seeing its serious character, I injected hypodermatically three-quarters grain morph. sulph., which partially relieved him of pain; in half an hour I followed with injection of one-quarter grain more of morph. sulph. I found on examination an extrusion of fecal matter, with a piece of undigested hull of string bean protruding from between the lips of the wound. I could not persuade the patient or his friends to submit to laparotomy. Mr. L. was perfectly conscious all the while. I cleansed the wound after examination (using the finger, with antiseptic precautions) and closed it with silk sutures and iodoform and corros. sub. dressing. There was a considerable quantity of dark fluid blood escaping from the wound for an hour after the dressing, when it ceased. Ice-cold cloths were applied every five or ten minutes; he had several attacks of vomiting. I left him about 2 p. m. the 8th, resting quietly.

July 8, *a. m.*—Temperature 40.5° C.; pulse 140.
July 8, *noon.*—Temperature 38° C.; pulse 120.
July 8, 10 *p. m.*—Temperature 38° C.; pulse 110.

This afternoon Mr. L. professed religion, with all the excitement usually attendant on Methodist revival meetings, there being present somewhere near one hundred friends. This state of things continued until my evening visit. I hardly expected to find him alive many hours after this.

July 9, *a. m.*—Temperature 37.7° C.; pulse 88; respiration 18.

July 9, *p. m.*—Temperature 37.7° C.; pulse 96; respiration 18. He seems much brighter this morning; takes some nourishment—chicken soup—and had a natural-looking stool. Beef tea and whisky enemata were given every three hours. Says he feels sore, but has no acute pain.

July 10, *a. m.*—Temperature, 37.3° C.; pulse, 88; respiration, 22.

July 10, *p. m.*—Temperature, 38° C.; pulse, 86; respiration, 20. His friends to-day request that but one physician be in attendance. I again insisted upon laparotomy, with no better result than on the first day. I was very much disappointed when they positively refused to consent to an operation, as I thought his chances were good. He takes beef soup, beef peptinoids, and milk by the mouth. There is some swelling of abdomen, with pain. An enema of turpentine and mist. assafœtida. About 8 p. m. removed drainage-tube, as all discharge has ceased.

July 12, *a. m.*—Temperature, 37.7° C.; pulse, 86; respiration, 19; p. m., temperature, 37.2° C.; pulse, 80; respiration, 17. Two watery passages from bowels, very bad smelling. Controlled singultus by one drachm of Hoffman's anodyne after all usual remedies had failed; has suffered with singultus last two days; applied fourteen leeches, with relief of all tenderness and no return.

July 13, *a. m.*—Temperature, 37.5° C.; pulse, 80; respiration, 18.

July 13, *p. m.*—Temperature, 37.2° C.; pulse, 80; respiration, 18; more generous diet allowed; nutritious enema stopped; removed stitches, as the wound began suppurating, and supported the part by half-inch strip of Mead's adhesive plaster, and began the use of warm-water dressing and solution of corros. sublim. From this date up to August 2 patient continued to improve, when I noticed a hard swelling in right iliac region, but no indication of pus; applied a bladder of ice; pain ceased and swelling almost entirely disappeared. He also began to complain of pain in the right shoulder.

August 12.—He is allowed to sit up, as the wound appears to be healed, with the exception of a superficial ulcer the size of a dime situated on the left of the stab-wound, the stab-wound being covered with a thin transparent skin.

September 4.—He is now able to walk around the house, and from this time up to October 10 I did not see him regularly, as he was visiting among his friends and relatives. About October 1 he began complaining very much of pain in the shoulders and chest, and the swelling in the right iliac region returned, with some tenderness; for a month he had been troubled with a cough; the wound suppurating and swelling just above the navel. He grew weaker daily and other symptoms grew worse up to October 13, when I concluded positively that there was pus at swelling in right iliac, and I drew about 2 or 3 ounces of pus with cannula. From this time until the patient passed under your care I have no accurate notes, owing to their having been misplaced, which has been the cause of delay in sending you a history of the case.

In addition to the preceding letter from Dr. White, in response to a request from this office, the following extract from a letter from the same writer, published in the September number of the "Medical World," 1520 Chestnut street, Philadelphia, is of interest. Referring to the same case, he says:

There was an escape of fecal matter with several pieces of the undigested hulls of string-beans (I drew a piece of hull about 1¼ inches long from the wound), probably 3 ounces in all. The wound is suppurating. There is a hard and tender spot in the right iliac region, which yields to treatment of typhlitis. One distressing and uncontrollable symptom, singultus, was, thanks to the timely arrival of your Manual of Treatment, promptly relieved by one dose of the remedy, which has never failed you, with no return of the trouble.

In addition, the patient states that he vomited at the time of receipt of wound, but does not remember what. About five hours afterwards he "vomited about a gallon of blood"; also "considerable blood escaped through the wound, with perhaps three ounces of intestinal contents. Wound has never been closed since."

On admission his condition was noted as follows: He was profoundly prostrated after his trip from Chincoteague Island, Va.; very weak and emaciated. Pulse, 120; temperature, 39.4° C.; respiration 30, and very superficial. There was observed a fistulous opening in the abdomen, about $1\frac{1}{2}$ inches to the left of the umbilicus and 1 inch below it, discharging a thin puriform matter, and a somewhat similar ulcer or abscess in the right groin, which, however, was not discharging at the time of admission. The upper portion of the belly was swollen and tympanitic; the lower portion flat and dull; facial expression anxious and indicating suffering. The original wound was not probed at this or any subsequent time. It was determined to attempt to improve his general condition, with a view to the performance of laparotomy at some future period. He was given concentrated nourishment in a form easily assimilated, in small quantities at short intervals, and alcoholic stimulants with morphine to relieve his almost constant pain, digitalis to support his failing heart, and belladonna to stimulate his flagging respiratory power. These efforts were not successful, except temporarily, and he steadily became weaker and more emaciated.

November 4.—Fecal matter, fluid, passed through both abdominal openings, as was supposed at the time, though the result of the autopsy makes it seem probable that the discharge from the upper one may have been carried down to the lower one outside of the abdominal wall by the dressings. The resident physician and the sister in charge are confident, however, that fecal matter did issue from the opening in the right groin.

November 7.—About midnight he complained of severe pain in right side of thorax, which showed dullness on percussion. There was no chill. From this time on he was troubled with cough, continuous pain in the right side of thorax, which grew duller on percussion, and the apex beat of the heart was noticed more and more to the left. Pleuritic abscess was now diagnosed, probably of septicæmic origin. The accumulation was rapid, and in a few days had pushed the liver and stomach well down into the abdominal cavity, and respiration was shallow and labored.

November 21.—Aspiration was performed between sixth and seventh ribs, and 3,320 cubic centimeters of very offensive pus removed.

November 22 and 23.—Respiration was much easier, though unaccompanied by other improvement. There was also fecal discharge from the wounds on these days. After a few days' respite from his dyspnœa and comparative freedom from cough and pain, signs of refilling of the cavity returned, and he rapidly became worse. Stimulants and nourishment were alike repugnant to him, and it was evident that death was near. He died December 13, at 4 a. m., from exhaustion. During his entire treatment he was given enemas every third day, which were followed by normal stools. At no time was it considered safe to attempt an operation requiring the administration of an anæsthetic.

Necropsy (*made* 4 *p. m., December* 13, 1888).—Body extremely emaciated. *Post-mortem* rigidity well marked. An incision was made at the dependent portion of right side of thorax; a glass tube inserted and 3,840 cubic centimeters pus withdrawn. Thorax. An immense pus cavity occupied the right side of the thorax. The right half of the diaphragm was almost destroyed, and its remnants adherent to the liver and contiguous tissues, making it very difficult to determine the exact pathological anatomy. The right lung was almost entirely destroyed, so much so that it could not be isolated and its weight determined. The left lung and heart were comparatively normal in appearance, though displaced towards the left side of the thorax. Abdomen: Stomach pale and flabby and almost destitute of muscular elements. Immediately under the wound made by the knife when stabbed the tissues were inflamed and softened and bathed in pus. There was general and marked peritonitis, with perforation of the peritoneum through which the external wound communicated by means of a fistulous tract, with a perforation of the transverse colon about its middle, and midway between its free and attached borders. The wound in the bowel was small and circular. The colon had been pushed down to the lower portion of the belly. Liver normal in size; not very friable; very pale, as were all the organs and tissues not subjected to inflammatory action. Spleen about one-half normal size. Kidneys both normal in size and appearance. A very careful dissection failed to establish any connection between the abscess in the right groin and the wounded bowel, or any portion of the fistulous tract left by the original wound.

This case has been reported in considerable detail, because of its direct bearing on the propriety of performing laparotomy in wounds of a similar character. The necropsy proves that the wounded gut was easily accessible to an operative procedure which would have given the man a good chance of recovery. When he arrived at the hospital, septicæmia had developed, and there was no time at which it was considered advisable to operate.

FRACTURE OF PELVIS—RUPTURE OF BLADDER.

N. D. H.; aged twenty-eight years; nativity, Maine; admitted to marine ward of the German Hospital, Philadelphia, Pa., March 17, 1888; died March 19.

History.—He was admitted on the above date, giving a history of having fallen from the topsail yard of barkentine *Edwin Cushing*, striking the deck some 60 or 70 feet below. On admission he had a compound fracture of the bones of the left forearm, a scalp wound, which was not serious, and extreme tenderness over anterior lower portion of the abdomen. The pain and tenderness were so marked that it was almost impossible to touch the parts and all movement was necessarily cautious. There was a desire but inability to void the urine, which was drawn off every few hours. The fracture of the forearm was treated in the usual way. There was an ecchymosis over the lower part of the abdomen and thighs and also some œdema. Urine contained small amount of blood. His condition would not warrant a thorough examination under ether, and he never rallied enough for it.

Necropsy (twenty-six hours post mortem).—Body particularly well nourished, with magnificent muscular development. External examination showed fracture of both bones of left forearm, and a scalp wound. The tissues about both of the kidneys were greatly congested, but the organs were normal. The same might be said of the lower colon and sigmoid flexure. There was a complete separation of the pelvic bones at the symphysis pubis. The bladder was ruptured, and the surrounding tissues were infiltrated by urine.

COMPOUND COMMINUTED FRACTURE OF LEG, BOTH BONES.

C. H.; aged forty years; nativity, China; admitted to U. S. Marine Hospital, Baltimore, Md., March 16, 1883; died March 20.

History.—He had a compound comminuted fracture of the tibia and fibula at the lower third, occurring thirty-six hours before being brought to hospital, by having the leg caught in a hawser. Although a severe case, an attempt was made to save the limb. The wound was cleaned, pieces of bone taken out, the parts placed in correct position in a fracture-box, moderate extension used, and hot-water dressing applied. In twenty-four hours gangrene had appeared and extended to the knee. This was thought to be mainly due to the Spanish tourniquet, which had been on his leg from the time of injury to his entering hospital, and which had completely cut off the supply of blood. On the morning of the 19th amputation was performed at lower third of the femur, lateral flaps being made. There was very little loss of blood, the patient recovering from the ether and from the shock of the operation very quickly. With the peculiar characteristics of those of his race when maimed, he became very despondent, stating his desire to die and asking to be given something to kill him. He persistently refused to take nourishment, and while some was forced on him enough could not be given in his exhausted condition to sustain life.

Necropsy (thirty-six hours after death).—*Rigor mortis* not well marked. Body fairly well developed and nourished. Right thigh showed result of recent amputation at lower third made by lateral flaps. Wound contained a drainage-tube, was united by sutures and adhesive plaster, and had not yet begun to unite, but had a healthy appearance. On the inner surface of the left thigh were two small dark spots showing a subcutaneous infiltration of blood, presumably a *post-mortem* change. Brain not examined. All the other organs were flabby and deeply congested, the congestion being especially well marked about the aorta, liver, and pyramids of the kidneys. Small intestines contained seven large lumbricoid worms, otherwise normal condition. Large intestines contained fæces about the sigmoid flexure. The alimentary tract was unusually free from traces of food, containing mostly gas and a little water.

INDEX.

A.

B.

C.

D.

H.

I.

J.

K.

N.

O.

P.

Q.

S.

T.

U.

V.

W.

Y.

O

www.ingramcontent.com/pod-product-compliance
Lightning Source LLC
Chambersburg PA
CBHW030600300426
44111CB00009B/1047
* 9 7 8 3 3 3 7 0 2 1 2 2 1 *